FREEDOM IN THE MODERN WORLD

MODERN WORLD

The 19th & 20th Centuries

Books by Herbert J. Muller

FREEDOM IN THE MODERN WORLD
RELIGION AND FREEDOM IN THE
  MODERN WORLD
FREEDOM IN THE WESTERN WORLD
FREEDOM IN THE ANCIENT WORLD
ISSUES OF FREEDOM
THE LOOM OF HISTORY
THE SPIRIT OF TRAGEDY
THE USES OF THE PAST
THOMAS WOLFE
SCIENCE AND CRITICISM
MODERN FICTION

FREEDOM IN THE
MODERN WORLD

The 19th & 20th Centuries

HERBERT J. MULLER

HARPER COLOPHON BOOKS
HARPER & ROW, PUBLISHERS
NEW YORK, EVANSTON, AND LONDON

To the memory of Josephine Muller

CONTENTS

PREFACE

Like the two preceding volumes in my History of Freedom, this one is designed as a work complete in itself. It takes up the story from about the year 1800, the revolutionary era that culminated in the French Revolution and the Napoleonic wars, and that heralded the continuously revolutionary history of the modern world. It presupposes some general knowledge of previous history, but not of my previous works; to them I refer only in occasional footnotes, which the reader may safely disregard. I need but to repeat briefly the premises I am operating on. By freedom I still mean "the condition of being able to choose and carry out purposes," which includes the primary dictionary meaning of freedom from external constraint, but also the more positive idea of freedom *to* do what one chooses, involving effective ability and available means or actual opportunity; on both counts it means concretely freedoms of various kinds. I am also continuing to study it in relation not only to the state but to society as a whole. In the period I am covering here issues of political freedom moved to the fore, stirring considerably more thought and drama than before, and the extension of political rights led to what is now called the "free society." Yet these issues were also more complicated than ever by radical economic, social, and cultural changes, due most obviously to the Industrial Revolution. One cannot hope to understand the history of freedom in the modern world without going into modern science and technology, the issues forced by an industrial civilization.

So I must at once add that I do not actually "cover" modern history, decade by decade, country by country, war by war, et cetera. I deal only with what seem to me the major developments that have affected our whole civilization. This means that I exclude a vast deal of history of great interest to people in many countries, especially small ones, whose history—as I try to emphasize in passing—may well be more dignified or edifying than that of the great powers on the main stage.

But this still leaves me with an appallingly complex subject: a civilization far more massive, elaborate, and extensive than any before it, now spread over the entire world, which for two centuries has been undergoing continuous revolutionary change, often violent but usually most profound and pervasive when undramatic, and always gathering momentum, no less when the many movements it has generated appear to be headed in every direction, including backwards. Although for purposes of convenience in analysis or narrative one may separate the basic industrial, political, and intellectual revolutions, they of course did not proceed independently, but always kept reacting on one another, to multiple effects. The inveterate tendency to impose order by some single explanatory principle only intensifies the confusion by breeding more controversy, more irresistible theories colliding with immovable thinkers. Except to the most confirmed monists or intellectual militarists (such as doctrinaire Marxists), modern history may suggest the infinite universe of yore, whose center was nowhere and circumference everywhere; or, more precisely, perhaps the continually expanding universe of modern theory, which has the nebulae scattering apart and shooting off into space at an ever-increasing velocity, though still from no definite center and to no known destination.

In attempting to make sense of this history, we have the costly privilege of not only an extraordinary amount of knowledge but as extraordinary a degree of intellectual self-consciousness (and in my repeated use of the term "extraordinary" I mean it quite literally). It has incidentally produced the thousands of treatises on "modern" man and the "modern" mind, and on the sources of the prolonged crisis of our civilization. A historian may feel that all has been said, over and over, and be more oppressed by the task of exposition; for he is likely to bore some readers by musty detail, to confuse others by sketchiness, and to weary all by repetition of such words as revolution, confusion, complexity, and uncertainty. By the same token, he knows that all can never be said, and that much that is being said may be antiquated the day after tomorrow. He is acutely aware that he himself is in history, in society, up to the top of his mind. Through "the sociology of knowledge" he has learned that what once passed for objective thought or pure reason comes down to ideology or rationalization. Even so he can never be sure that he is conscious enough of the usually silent premises of our thought, what too often "goes without saying" in our climate of opinion. Least of all when he deals with modern history can he maintain the pretense of complete objectivity and impartiality.

We are all deeply involved, more or less deeply committed—in particular on issues of freedom.

I may accordingly begin by repeating that my definition of freedom is relatively neutral. The condition of being able to choose and carry out one's own purposes never means that one will naturally make the "right" choices, never assures wisdom, virtue, happiness, or any other good. No more is a free society necessarily healthier than the traditional kind in which most men enjoyed very limited rights. But then I must add that I am far from being neutral on the issues of freedom. If only in fairness to the reader, I have made no effort to conceal my commitment to the values of a free society, substantially to the principles stated by John Stuart Mill in *On Liberty*. Hence the word "liberal," for example, is in this history essentially a good word, denoting attitudes and beliefs that may often be facile or naïve, but that nevertheless activated the struggles for more freedom in the past century. "Conservative," on the other hand, is in my lexicon not necessarily a bad word, since it represents a basically honorable, reasonable disposition, no less essential in a world of revolutionary change; but it is likely to appear in bad company simply because political and religious conservatives provided the main opposition to the cause of a free society. Likewise with the more obviously value-loaded term "social justice." Here it will usually crop up in movements for reform on behalf of workers, the poor, the "underprivileged"—in effect, for more real freedom for the many. While we can never all agree on precisely what is justice, and men of good will can argue for the need of a privileged class or the superiority of the aristocratic over the democratic principle, the historic fact remains that the struggle for freedom has typically been associated with the idea of justice, that in the free societies equal rights to life, liberty, and the pursuit of happiness constitute a basic principle of justice, and that most conservatives now accept the great bulk of the social reforms for which liberals or "radicals" fought over the past hundred years. Again I make no effort to conceal my sympathy with democratic ideals of justice.

Yet my subject remains a fearfully complicated history, with never an occasion for simple hurrahs. I have tried above all to avoid the common tendency to oversimplify its issues. In every chapter I have continued to dwell on not only the risks but the invariable costs of freedom, as essential both for understanding its actual conditions and for appreciating its possible values. My guiding principle remains the principle of ambiguity—another word the reader may weary of, but an indispensable key to a history that has involved a plain growth and spread at once of freedom and of novel forms of compulsion and constraint. And a further reason for stressing it is that I attempt to pay closer attention in this than in my previous volumes to the state of mind of ordinary people, more broadly to the situation of the individual person, which is most ambiguous. We know much more about the thought and feeling of the common people over the last century or so than in the past, first through literature and newspapers, recently through attitude research in the social sciences, public opinion polls, and the like.

Here an immediate trouble is that a lot of learning can be a dangerous thing too. A great deal of popular generalization implies much more precise knowledge than we actually have, and presupposes that the great majority of people all think and feel alike (an assumption especially common in literary talk about the "bourgeois"). So let us ask the critical question: Are Americans freer in this century than they were at the beginning of the preceding one? Today than a generation ago? The usual answer is that they are less free. The obvious answer seems to me Yes and No, in various ways, differing with the various classes and subcultures in a fluid society, and with the countless different individuals, who are by no means so uniform as they appear in the standard generalizations about a standardized mass society. The total picture is not clear or at all simple. But a historian may still hope to make out the major trends, to specify the various ways in which people have been becoming both freer and less free, and to generalize more soundly by keeping an eye on the basic ambiguity—that in the free societies the ordinary person unquestionably enjoys more rights and opportunities than he ever did in the past, while at the same time these societies have been generating massive pressures against the individual, due largely to the very forces of democracy and industrialism that have emancipated him.

Having duly emphasized the exceptional difficulties besetting the modern historian, which might suggest a vain effort to disarm criticism, I should now repeat that he enjoys exceptional advantages. The new perspectives afforded by psychology, sociology, anthropology, and world history illumine as well as complicate his subject. The liberal temper I believe they should induce remains a form of bias—not a freedom from bias—but makes for breadth and openness of mind, readiness to consider new possibilities. The intellectual self-consciousness for which we may pay a heavy price is nevertheless worth the price. One may doubt, indeed, that thinkers in general are so painfully conscious of the social, historical conditions of their thought as they are reputed to be —at least very few seem paralyzed by their self-consciousness; but we surely have more historical, cultural sense than did most thinkers in past ages, and are less likely to assume that provincial, temporal beliefs are universal, immutable truths. We are somewhat less ignorant of our ignorance. We may find it challenging, not merely dismaying.

Hence I should discount some professional assumptions that imply an excessive humility, or perhaps a pseudo humility. From anthropologists we keep hearing that we are all "culture-bound," never more so than when we rejoice in the thought of being "civilized." Though one may sometimes gather that an economic or cultural determinist is an objective scientist—not really culture-bound after all—one may then wonder the more how we can all disagree so radically, many be so hostile to our civilization. At least ours appears to be a remarkably permissive culture, enabling men to subscribe to every imaginable creed. But in fact no one informed about anthropology is absolutely culture-bound. The very value of this study, as of history, is that it makes possible a degree of detachment, a critical perspective on our own culture (and anthropologists themselves tend to be especially critical of its presumptions). Granted that we can no more shed our culture than our skin, we are much more conscious both of its influence and of different possibilities of life; so we are not simply slaves to it, but can and do exercise more freedom of judgment.

Then the trouble is that we violate the scientific taboo against value judgments. In the interests of logical rigor and semantic purity, positivists insist on an absolute divorce between values and cognition, commonly sealing it by declaring that such judgments express "only" emotional responses, or, in the words of A. J. Ayer, are "pure expressions of feeling." This seems to me a pretty careless, imprecise use of language. Although we can never scientifically verify value judgments, thoughtful men manifestly can and do offer some rational justification for them, based on empirical knowledge; they are no more simply "feeling" than simply rattling their cultural chains. Cognition itself not only makes possible more intelligent choices but forces choices for our living purposes. I assume that even the most scrupulous historians cannot in any case avoid value judgments, which enter their habitual assumptions that some men or some works were "great," some societies more "brilliant" than others, some events more "important," and that they may hope to judge more soundly in a full consciousness of what they are up to as well as up against. In this view, a historian of freedom is only dealing more directly with the values and the costs of the powers of mind that distinguish man from all other animals, that have enabled him alone to make history, and that alone make his history worth telling.

No doubt the chief danger remains the habit of judging too freely, the chief need is always the scrupulous effort to be objective and impartial. I am embarrassed by the thought that my values are always showing, even when I dwell on the essential uncertainties of both our knowledge and our prospects. Yet such scruples spring from a commitment to values, in particular to the intellectual freedom and honesty that have been fostered by the rise of science; for they seldom troubled the saints and the sages of the past, any more than the authors of Scripture. And they recall me to the "tragic view" of history I outlined in *The Uses of the Past,* when I first embarked on the study of history: the effort to view it in the spirit of the great tragic poets, at once with irony, with compassion, and with reverence. While it seems to me relatively easy to maintain this approach to the great societies of the past, it has grown ever harder to view our own society in such a spirit. Whether or not one agrees with Croce that "every true history is contemporary history," in that the past answers only to a present interest, anyone trying to understand the history of the past century or so cannot help having in mind the contemporary reality it has led to: an age—or better said a day —when man has embarked on the most extraordinary adventures since he began playing with fire, including projects like landing on the moon that to our fathers would have seemed as fantastic as a cow jumping over the moon; a day that our posterity may look back on as one of the greatest ages in history; and a day that tomorrow might prove the most catastrophic, put an end to all history, or if not, might be ringing up the curtain on a "brave new world" in which men will lose all interest in history.

No thoughtful man can any longer view modern "progress" with simple pride, or the future with simple hope. The reasons for irony are all too plain, and even so need to be dwelt on if only because so many men in high places have too little sense of ambiguity, not to mention compassion or reverence. Many intellectuals, however, are given to too simple an irony, with as little compassion or reverence, often little historical sense. In ridiculing the faith in progress they dwell only on the problems it has created, the folly and the evil of our time. In remarking that man himself is now the main problem, they slight the awesome achievements that have made him so, and they often appear to forget that he has been a sufficient problem to himself for some thousands of years, ever since he became self-conscious. They lament the "death" of values that are still alive in their own thought, and evidently real to their audience. They talk too easily of the "failure" of democracy, of science, of humanism, rationalism, liberalism, and all modern causes, failing to consider the obvious question: What has "succeeded" in history? What has worked "for good," and simply for good? Just because we can never afford to minimize the gravity of our problems, I assume that we cannot afford either to minimize our unprecedented intellectual resources, the extraordinary potentialities we have developed for better as for worse, and the values we have realized in a history that among other things has unquestionably involved a growth in freedom. We are more prone to disillusionment and despair because of the higher expectations created by the despised faith in progress. I write this preface in a sober, even somber mood, as one who does not despair of our future but is not optimistic about it either. Nevertheless, I have written this volume in the pious conviction that modern history still has tragic dignity. Or let me say simply that I am pleased to have lived in this era.

PART I

THE NINETEENTH CENTURY

Chapter One

PRELUDE: THE ROMANTIC MOVEMENT

1. Theme

"What the European peoples want," said Count Metternich at the conclusion of the Napoleonic Wars, "is not liberty but peace." At least peace was all that the people immediately got from the Congress of Vienna in 1815, conducted amid the most elegant entertainments and displays. Metternich's main objective, which was endorsed by the leading statesmen of Europe, was to restore the traditional aristocratic, monarchical order, and at any cost to prevent change. He was abetted by a religious revival, another conservative reaction against the godless French Revolution. On the Continent the Roman Church regained much of its traditional power and privilege, which it exercised to assure obedience among the faithful; in Britain the Anglican Church lined up behind the reactionaries who controlled the government. Politics and religion were united in the Holy Alliance, dreamed up by the pious, misty Czar Alexander of Russia. The sovereigns of Prussia and Austria joined him in declaring their "fixed resolution . . . to take for their sole guide the precepts of that Holy Religion, namely, the precepts of Justice, Christian Charity, and Peace." Having rearranged the map of Europe to suit their dynastic interests, without regard to the wishes of their subjects, the monarchs in fact succeeded in keeping peace among themselves. There were no wars on the Continent for forty years—an uncommonly long time for Europeans to go without one of their favorite historical pastimes.

Yet the stability of the restored order was quite illusory. The era presided over by Metternich was ushered in prophetically by hard times, due to poor harvests and a financial panic; in ten years Europe was swept by three such panics. Worse for the monarchs, many Europeans *did* want liberty. So many had been infected by the ideals proclaimed in the French Revolution, or what Metternich dreaded as "the modern ideas," that he was kept busy in a relentless war on them; but even so popular revolutions were breaking out again by 1830—there was no killing these ideas. The restored Roman Church was likewise breeding violent anticlericalism by its stubborn opposition to the cause of liberty. (It even tried to revive the archaic Inquisition.) The Holy Alliance gave away how little Christian precepts actually guided politics, Metternich privately agreeing that it was a piece of pious nonsense; its chief effect was the increasing hostility it aroused, as more and more Europeans saw in it an unholy alliance to maintain despotism. Another wave of popular revolutions in 1848 made plainer the doom of the traditional order. Although mostly unsuccessful, they finished Metternich himself, while signaling the emergence of a new force—"the masses." Cities in particular were now breeding literal masses: the population of Europe had almost doubled over the past century. By this time, too, the Industrial Revolution was well under way, creating an ever-larger proletariat. The year 1848 also saw the *Communist Manifesto,* another portent of a revolutionary new kind of society that had started growing up without benefit of Marx, king, or clergy.

Change—what Metternich sought above all to arrest—was the very essence of Western history in the nineteenth century. It was not only radical change but much more rapid change than men had ever experienced in the past. As Henry Adams observed, New York in 1800, or still in 1860, was closer to ancient Rome than to the New York of 1900. And his lifelong effort to keep abreast of this change, make historical sense of this dynamic century, recalls us at once to the immense confusions of modernity. Although the conventional periods into which previous history has been decently ordered are artificial enough to provoke endless debate on the significance or reality of any given "age," historians are still generally agreed on the propriety of speaking of the Middle Ages, the Renaissance, the Age of Enlightenment. They are not agreed on an appropriate name for the nineteenth century. How can one label the thought of so diverse a lot as Coleridge, Hegel, Schopenhauer, Comte, Emerson, Marx, Mill, Kierkegaard, Taine, Arnold, Nietzsche, and Spencer? Or the art of Goethe, Wordsworth, Balzac, Hugo, Flaubert, Dickens, Whitman, Wagner, Zola, Dostoyevsky, Tennyson, Ibsen, and Mallarmé? No doubt we are still too close to the century to see it steadily and see it whole, and if our civilization survives it may take on clearer outlines, emerge as another respectable "age"; but that *if*—the radical uncertainty—accentuates the difficulties meanwhile.

The Industrial Revolution alone wrought the profoundest transformation in man's life since the gradual rise of civilization five thousand years ago. It was accompanied by revolutionary developments in thought, such as the theory of evolution, which resulted in as profound changes in the understanding of history. It had more and more to do with the political revolutions of the century, which would culminate in the Russian Revolution. The previous entrance of Russia into Western history marked still another revolutionary complication in a civilization that kept spreading. The identity of Western civilization as a great society with a common tradition became at once more pronounced and more blurred as its offshoots in the Americas grew into independent societies, and as by imperial expansion it dominated other continents, until it brought the whole human race into the scope of its destiny. So it would stage the first world war in history, involving every continent.

This war, however, already looks like the great divide in modern history; and it suggests a possible path through the immense confusion. Until then most Westerners were confident that their history was a progress. Given the tremendous expansion in knowledge and power, they were by no means so foolish in their pride as they may now appear. Their creative achievements included such obvious wonders as the great railways and ocean liners, the invention of the telegraph, telephone, and wireless, the harnessing of electricity, the discovery of X rays—feats the more dazzling because they promised endless wonders to come. By improved technology, medicine, and sanitation they had made an obvious progress in reducing the ageless miseries of famine and plague, want and pain; in the advanced countries men no longer died of starvation by the hundreds of thousands, as they had all through history and still did in the non-Western world. Westerners had made comparable advances in civility too by freer intercourse between nations, the diffusion of knowledge, the reduction of ancient superstition, and the virtual elimination of such ancient evils as slavery. With all this, as both cause and effect, had come a conspicuous growth and spread of freedom—political, economic, intellectual, religious. The future seemed clearly to belong to democracy, which in turn held out the promise of increasing peace and plenty. Common men were enjoying much more opportunity, especially through free public education; they were at last being emancipated from the illiteracy and ignorance that had been their lot throughout history. America above all had flourished as a kingdom of common men, attracting millions of immigrants from the Old World. The soaring aspirations of the New World were symbolized by the first skyscrapers—buildings as typically American as the vivid metaphor of their name.

But these skyscrapers were temples of business, symbols as well of a notorious materialism, which in America made the faith in progress most uncritical and naïve; and the baffled Henry Adams was much more perceptive. He recognized that the tremendous expansion in knowledge and power was not under intelligent control, the "progress" not clearly directed to civilized ends. He was frightened in particular by the seemingly automatic acceleration in power, which he estimated was doubling in every decade; before World War I he ventured the guess that it would reach a momentous climax in about fifty years—just the time, in fact, when men mastered nuclear power and started making hydrogen bombs. Behind Adams loom other prophets who have since taken on stature, notably Dostoyevsky and Nietzsche: writers who from opposite poles proclaimed that the West was headed for catastrophe. All through the nineteenth century, indeed, most of the greater writers were highly critical of the new kind of society that was developing. They ranged from conservatives alarmed by the rise of "the masses" to radicals bent on overthrowing the ruling class that still held the masses down, but they numbered men of all faiths, or of no particular political or religious faith, who were unhappy over the state of bourgeois culture, the main goals of their society. Many of the intelligentsia suffered from alienation, a feeling that has now become almost their badge, but that was much less common in previous societies. By 1900, in a world of ever-increasing plenty, many sons of the prosperous bourgeois were likewise infected by the *fin de siècle* mood.

This widespread malaise might remind us that from its dawn the most dynamic of civilizations had generated endless protest and revolt, often a sense of crisis or impending doom. Immediately, however, it recalls a familiar theme that never seems familiar enough. This is not merely the abuses of power or the corruptions of ideals, but the costs of freedom, the problems inevitably created by every major growth in freedom—the truism that one's real problems begin when one is able to do as one pleases. While Henry Adams dwelt on the blindness of the statesmen and the businessmen who made history in the nineteenth century, he was himself too often blind to the idealism be-

hind the apparent materialism, the positive goods from which the evils
were flowing. Today it is fashionable to look down on this century, no
sophisticate would speak of "progress" except as a theme of derision;
yet it was an exceptionally creative century, in art and thought as well
as technology, and we have to reckon with a history that did involve
considerable progress by commonly accepted standards, including intellectual sophistication.

In this dual view, at any rate, the nineteenth century got under way
appropriately with a movement heralded by Edmund Burke, with whom
I left off in the preceding volume. A conservative in his political thought,
terrified by the revolutionary currents that he sensed were the mighty
tides of the future, Burke had himself anticipated the future in his
youthful essay *A Philosophical Inquiry into the Origin of Our Ideas
of the Sublime and Beautiful.* The sublime, he pointed out, did not
derive from the qualities of simplicity, clarity, order, measure, and
propriety valued by most eighteenth-century writers. It came instead
from the transcendence of conventional good sense and good form, or
mere beauty, and it was marked by a sense of the boundless, something
shadowy, wild, primitive, even terrible, as in the pleasure afforded
by great tragedy. Hence the sublime was to be looked for not in the
specifiable properties of the aesthetic object, but in the subjective
sensations of the reader or beholder, feelings of liberation from the little
self and the daily round of life, feelings of exaltation and awe—such as
Wordsworth would experience in the presence of Nature, and Burke
himself would in the contemplation of the "great primeval contract of eternal society." Or as a historian may experience, on a lower
plane involving more ordinary confusion, when he contemplates the
boundless affair known as the Romantic movement.

Given the many different definitions of "romantic," some of them
flatly contradictory, few if any of them clearly applying to all the writers
and thinkers commonly so labeled, one might wish to drop the term
as a simple nuisance; but as usual we cannot drop it. It refers to real,
stirring, highly significant changes that indisputably came over the art
and thought of western Europe at this time, roughly the years 1780-1830.
The countless definitions at least add up to a commonplace: Romanticism was no school but a many-sided affair, a diffuse movement sprung
from diverse, inconsistent impulses, and moving in different directions
in different countries. Nevertheless it had everywhere some common
basic tendencies. Beginning as a literary revolt against the formal
canons of classicism, and in time branching out into new modes of

philosophy, it involved all along much social criticism; its leading figures were not Romantic in the now popular sense of artists aloof from mundane affairs. (Even the mystical Blake was a friend of Tom Paine and got himself jailed for sedition.) In a history of freedom we may begin to make sense of the movement by viewing it as a response to a revolutionary age. As such it was basically ambivalent, involving at once a revulsion against the ideals of the Age of Enlightenment and a continuation of its major effort at emancipation, in as self-consciously "modern" a spirit.

In their revulsion the Romantics might look like reactionaries, as some indeed turned out to be. In England the early ardor cooled into an ultraconservatism much like Burke's, typified by Wordsworth, Coleridge, and Southey. In Germany, where Romanticism took on the guise of metaphysical idealism, it became a thoroughly counter-revolutionary movement. Everywhere it helped to revive "the spirit of religion" that Burke invoked as the bulwark of the traditional order. Chateaubriand won an immense success with his *Genius of Christianity* (1802), in which he glorified ultramontane Catholicism; the German Romantics, many of whom turned to Rome, defended authoritarianism in both church and state; and Coleridge, more unorthodox in his Protestant theology, indicated as clearly that the spirit of religion still tended to be a conservative spirit in social and political affairs. To this day, writers hostile to the liberal, democratic faith have echoed themes sounded in the Romantic movement.

Yet these same writers (notably T. S. Eliot) have been inclined to condemn the movement itself, for good reasons. Its initial revolt against the reigning classical conventions hardly tended to promote a respect for tradition and authority, the essential principles of conservatism. Outside of Germany the later Romantics mostly remained ardent liberals, devoted to the "modern ideas" that Metternich warred on. As Wordsworth's arteries hardened, Shelley and Byron carried the torch, and Hazlitt set about refuting the political philosophy of Burke. In France the torch was taken up by Lamartine and Victor Hugo; the latter defined Romanticism as simply "liberalism in literature." In eastern Europe this subversive spirit was popularized by its greatest poets, such as the Russian Pushkin, the Czech Mácha, and the Pole Mickiewicz. All over the Continent the Romantic movement remained a major source of inspiration for revolutionaries. It colored almost all the optimistic thought of the century, influencing the thought of Karl Marx himself, and helping to explain why his "scientific" analysis concluded in a vision of a utopian classless society.

Altogether, the movement remained ambiguous through and through, inspiring all kinds of wanderers between the worlds of the past and the future. But first we need to consider its conspicuous "progressive" tendencies, which made it a fitting prelude to an era of immense expansion.

2. *Variations*

The relative merits of so-called classical and romantic art, which are forever debatable, need not be debated in a history of freedom. Here the most pertinent consideration is that the Romantics emphasized the values of freedom and spontaneity in art, and played up as never before the idea that art was "creative"—a term that henceforth became commonplace. They rebelled against the rigid formalism of an aristocratic, authoritarian order, in France ending the dictatorship of the Academy, with its sovereign ideal of correctness. They upheld instead the sovereign powers of Imagination, which as defined by Coleridge was essentially different from mere Fancy and fit to be a sovereign because it was a power of synthesis, involving "a more than usual state of emotion with more than usual order." In this spirit they still admired the classics, if anything more warmly than had the writers of the eighteenth century, because they looked to them for inspiration instead of models and rules. Above all they admired Shakespeare, whose genius was now at last fully appreciated. They were the first really to appreciate medieval art too, and with it Germanic epic and saga, folk art and myth. Whatever their own shortcomings or excesses as artists, they helped to establish a wider, richer tradition than Europe had been aware of.

And so with their more fundamental revulsion against the Enlightenment cult of Reason. The Romantics did not simply repudiate the faith in reason, but at first attacked primarily the narrow rationalism that had played down sentiment, passion, imagination, intuition, faith—both the needs and the powers of the human spirit, essential to full self-realization. Because the fluid, disorderly, incalculable affective life of man is still suspect to scientists, as it has traditionally been to philosophers ever since Plato, we may feel better for being reminded that it is not merely a menace to rational behavior but an obvious necessity for freedom and creativity.[1]

Without wonder and excitement, love and joy, fear and distress, men would have no incentive to choose and carry out any but routine purposes, and surely they would have developed no passion for truth, goodness, or beauty. In any case, the Romantics were still far from belittling the powers of the human mind. As they exalted in particular the claims of Imagination, the soul of Poetry, they became more aware of the deep springs of inspiration or vision, and asserted that the mind had even greater powers than the *philosophes* of the Enlightenment had realized. None made it more godlike than the German Idealists who followed in the wake of Kant's critique of "pure reason." In demonstrating that by such reason man could never know the *ding an sich,* or essential reality of the universe, Kant had also emphasized the active, creative contribution of the mind to empirical knowledge, and by "practical reason" he went on to restore God. His followers carried on by recovering the knowledge of essential reality, which was an ideal spiritual reality required or simply posited by the human spirit; and Hegel wedded it to reason again in his celebrated pronouncement: "The real is the rational and the rational is the real." The whole cosmos was now the philosopher's oyster.

Similarly the Romantics first attacked on humanistic grounds the Newtonian "Nature" deified by the Enlightenment. Its mechanical order, supposedly the key to the "real" world, seemed to them an impoverishment of an infinitely richer reality, false to man's living consciousness and inimical to his living purposes. "May God us keep," exclaimed Blake, "from Single vision and Newton's sleep!" Wordsworth most fully recovered the nature known in immediate experience, the concrete, felt qualities that are most real to men with their eyes open. This recovery was more blessed because Nature remained beneficent: wilder, more rugged and irregular than men would have it in the eighteenth century (they did not care for Alps), but still an essentially harmonious order congenial to the human spirit. German philosophy

---

[1] Among the relatively few scientific studies of it is Silvan E. Tomkins' *Affect Imagery Consciousness* (Vol. I: The Positive Affects: New York, 1962). As positivists, behaviorist psychologists have prided themselves on eschewing such loose terms as "imagination" and "emotion," and other psychologists and social scientists have attended chiefly to the biological "drives" underlying emotion, which they conceive as the basic causes. Tomkins holds that the affective system is primary in motivation, and that the drives operate only when amplified by it.

then lent metaphysical sanctions to such feelings of kinship. Emerson deified Nature again as Over-Soul, enabling men to feel more at home in the natural world than even the Greeks had.

About Man—"the proper study of mankind"—the Romantics were of many minds, or moods. The diversity of view was in itself rather flattering, however, suggesting that he was nothing so simple as a depraved creature or so tame as a "rational animal"; and most writers dwelt on heartening possibilities. In exalting his powers of imagination, the springs of his creativity, they stressed the clearest proof of his actual freedom. Some preserved the natural goodness of man by endorsing Rousseau's celebration of his natural feelings, setting his heart above his head. Chateaubriand gave a religious gloss to such sentiment in his most popular *Genius of Christianity*, which emphasized the poetry or beauty rather than the literal truth of Christianity; he accordingly hoped for a reconciliation of Catholicism with ideals of liberty and progress. In Germany man was dignified as a spirit attuned to the Absolute Spirit, in America he was glorified as a born Transcendentalist. And the diverse conceptions of man were more heartening because they reflected a positive aspiration to diversity as a means to abundance or fullness of life. The boundless Romantic movement went on specifically to celebrate boundlessness. As its poets aspired to the sublime, so it gave a vogue to words like "magical," "ineffable," and especially "infinite." In this aspect it was a revival of the Renaissance Faustian spirit, the insatiable will to know, feel, dare everything imaginable, to which Goethe now gave epical expression, while Fichte gave it philosophical sanction by making Will primary. It heralded an age of gigantic enterprise in art and thought. Hegel, Comte, and Spencer attempted grand syntheses such as had been merely sketched in the Age of Enlightenment, and they were matched by artists—Balzac, Zola, Wagner, Tolstoy—working on a grander scale than any classicists before them.

Associated with this vivid sense of potentiality was a new idea in the air, amplifying the idea of progress come down from the Enlightenment. The Romantics had more feeling for the organic processes of life and growth, in a universe they no longer conceived as a mere mechanism. Goethe was led to speculations about natural evolution, a theory also anticipated by such naturalists as Lamarck and Erasmus Darwin. Hegel proposed his famous dialectic as the key to the development of man, and thus formulated a comprehensive, systematic philosophy of Becoming to supplant the traditional philosophies of immutable Being. He conferred metaphysical dignity upon change, which had been regarded as superficial when not illusory, at best a much less illustrious kind of reality than permanence. History he defined as the history of spirit, under the aegis of the World Spirit, and the essence of spirit he defined as freedom; so he concluded that "the history of the world has been none other than the progress of the consciousness of freedom."

The immense influence of Hegel helped to propagate another major interest that had been stimulated by the Romantic movement—the study of history. This too was at once an outgrowth of the Enlightenment and a revulsion against it, both exemplified in the pioneering work of Herder (1744–1803), the "Copernicus of history." While devoted to the basic ideals of the Enlightenment, especially to the solidarity of mankind, Herder protested against the narrowness of its historical outlook, its scorn of most of the past, or in effect its repudiation of solidarity. Instead of projecting another philosophical outline or merely rational concept of history, he wished to recapture its living essence, which lay in particularity, variety, multiplicity—the uniqueness of all peoples and their cultures. Perceiving much more clearly the organic nature of society or culture, he marveled over such unplanned growths as language and art. Herder's essentially aesthetic interest in history was shared by Romantic poets and novelists, especially Walter Scott, who also pioneered in a concrete, sympathetic, imaginative re-creation of the past. In particular they recovered the Middle Ages, enriching Western culture by appreciation of a period in which the men of the Enlightenment had seen only the reign of ignorance, superstition, and tyranny, dismissing even its glorious art as barbaric—the original connotation of "Gothic."

The Romantic attack on abstract, rationalistic approaches to history then took a different, somewhat anomalous turn in the Prussian Ranke. As he too held that every society and period was unique, "immediate to God," he insisted on a strictly empirical approach and laid the foundations of "scientific" history. In what became a manifesto he defined the proper aim of a historian as to tell "what had actually happened," no more, no less. Accordingly he set about digging into firsthand sources, developing critical methods for sifting and testing the evidence; and by his monumental labors he set an example for historians ever after. In France historians contributed to the ideal, or the illusion, of scientific history as they started fighting the French Revolution over again (a battle that has gone on to this day); they ransacked the archives to support their conflicting interpretations of it. So out of Romanticism came the academic industry of research, which would inspire a great deal of unimaginative, routine fact-finding, but build up a far more impressive body of historical knowledge than any ancestor-worshiping society of the past had ever had. Ranke himself remained true to the spirit of both the Enlightenment and Romanticism by conceiving the close study of particular societies as finally only a means to the history of mankind, the illumination of the "universal relationship" of the basic factors of force and freedom. As a very old man he began writing a world history—a kind that for the first time in history Western civilization was literally making, as it spread all over the world, and that for the first time men had enough knowledge to write.

Meanwhile the "historicism" engendered by the Romantic movement was stirring what Friedrich Meinecke would describe as "the greatest spiritual revolution in the Western world," and what at least looks like a permanent revolution in thought. Europeans were growing more historical-minded than men had ever been in the past. They were beginning to realize the implications of Herder's belief that history—not God, Nature, or Reason—was the key to the understanding of man and society; for it followed that men were products of a particular history, all institutions and beliefs were culturally conditioned, none could be rightly understood without being first placed and dated. It now became clearer, for instance, that styles in art were organically related to a given society, not grounded on universal norms, as classicists had assumed. It was not at first so clear that styles in thought too (including historicism) might be relative and subject to flux, but some thinkers were at least perceiving this in the past, or in the other fellow. Hegel above all spread out the philosophical implications of the new consciousness. He established as major subjects both the philosophy of history and the history of philosophy, which in his view alike taught that any given system of thought could be fully understood only in relation to previous systems, or as a phase in the development of philosophy. If Hegel conceived his own system as a final synthesis, because of some tendency to confuse his reason with the World Spirit, he made it easier for other thinkers to place and date him too.

Other expressions of the Romantics' interest in uniqueness—the particular, the local, the individual—led to possible inconsistencies. Especially in Germany, the Napoleonic Wars stirred up national pride and quickened an interest in the national past. Historians accordingly contributed to the rising nationalism, which ever after would breed narrow, distorted views of both past and present. In the early Romantics, however, local pride was still tempered by the cosmopolitan spirit of the Enlightenment; like Herder, they rejoiced in the uniqueness of all peoples and sympathized with all. Outside of Germany nationalism was commonly associated with the cause of freedom too. Men who believed that freedom was the birthright of mankind naturally felt that it ought to begin at home, among their own people; the nation was the obvious, even indispensable means of giving it a local habitation. This seemed most obvious to such peoples as the Italians, Greeks, and Poles, who were ruled by other peoples, denied freedom in determining their own destiny. The ardent nationalist could therefore be a pure idealist like Mazzini, confident that national self-determination would lead to "the Parliament of Man, the Federation of the World." Byron won universal popularity by dying in the cause of Greek independence—a cause that was enthusiastically supported by liberals everywhere, and that most clearly linked the Romantics with the revolutionary movements in Europe.

Another wayward tendency was the stress on subjectivity that in various forms pervaded the thought and feeling of the Romantics, corresponding to their interest in the unique. In view of their historical consciousness this might have led, logically perhaps should have led, to stress on the limitations of the subjective, or specifically on the individual as a product of his society; but such ideas took some time to spread and really take hold. First the Romantics cultivated more obvious possibilities. In aesthetics they followed the lead of Burke by concentrating on the subjective sensations aroused by the work of art rather than its objective properties. Their own art was highly individualized, employing widely different forms, genres, and styles, no one of which was quintessential (except to critics who have settled on a neat definition of Romanticism). They became absorbed in the inner life, anticipating the rise of psychology; in his Notebooks Coleridge used such terms as "subconsciousness" and "psycho-analytical," which were not yet known to common usage. Since the inner life can be studied only in individuals, they magnified the importance of purely personal feeling or sentiment, and prepared for the vogue of autobiography and the autobiographical novel. In philosophy this self-consciousness culminated in Kierkegaard's existential doctrine of the self, one's own conscious existence as the only reality that really concerned a man, with the corollary that "truth is subjectivity" and "to seek objectivity is to be in error."

But the most apparent reason why the Romantics dwelt on the values of subjectivity was simply that they began as self-conscious rebels. They were claiming and exercising the right to artistic freedom, or to self-expression rather than conformity to the impersonal norms of classicism. They naturally would not dwell on the limitations or the dangers of subjectivity because they were defending the right of the individual to defy convention. Implicitly they were declaring that the individual should *not* be a mere product of his society or culture. On all counts the Romantics spoke the last word in the tradition of individualism stemming from the Renaissance and the Protestant Reformation. Emerson would tell even ordinary Americans that all the virtues were comprised in self-trust, and "Whoso would be a man must be a non-conformist."

In short, the driving impulse was never to play it short. Because of this welter of conflicting tendencies, and behind them the common aspiration to diversity, abundance, or totality, the Romantic movement contained the seeds of almost all the art and thought of the future, including apparent reactions against it. Realism in literature, for instance, was implicit in its interest in the particular and the local. From Stendhal, Balzac, and Flaubert to Ibsen, the severest critics of Romanticism were typically its heirs, who rebelled against it more violently because they knew it so intimately in their own feeling, and never really outgrew it.

Still, it is significant that they felt the need to outgrow it. The immediate reason was the obvious extravagances that survive in popular notions of the "romantic"—the emotionalism and sensationalism, the bombast and melodrama, all the high strut and low fret. But the excesses sprang from more serious modes of irrationality and irresponsibility at the heart of the Romantic movement. These bring us back to its basic ambiguities, the reasons why all along it jeopardized its own cause of emancipating the human spirit.

Most fateful was the revulsion against the rationalism of the Enlightenment. This broadened out into a radical critique of reason that remained a major theme in the thought of the nineteenth century, and led to a much clearer, fuller awareness of the actual limitations of reason, for both philosophical and social purposes—limitations that supporters of a free society can least afford to ignore. Yet for sensible men this awareness only emphasizes the need for constant effort at rationality. Granted the values of the affective life, it manifestly has to be kept under some measure of intelligent guidance and control in order to secure these values, enable men to choose and carry out their dearest purposes. The Romantic appeal to feeling, sentiment, passion, or the claims of the heart menaced the hard-won values that gave the Enlightenment its name. It was the more dangerous for the reason it is always popular—that ordinary thoughtless men may possess abundantly such feeling ways of "knowing" and are likely to believe that they do better with them than trained thinkers do. The Romantics made it harder to maintain public standards of reasonableness, and therefore of civility. They sowed the seeds of the popular anti-intellectualism and the outright revolt against reason that will concern us repeatedly from now on.

Similarly the truths arrived at by imagination or intuition, instead of mere reason, might be considered higher and holier just because they were not demonstrably true. Thus when Coleridge passionately affirmed the primacy of religious faith he tried to buttress it by defining the "Real Sciences" as Morals, Metaphysics, and Theology, reducing the actual sciences to matters of "mere" understanding; but the trouble remained that his "Real Sciences" did not enable men to agree on the crucial question of just what faith, on what grounds. Since believers continued to be hostile to Christians of different belief, united chiefly in their common conflict with science, religion remained a primary source of opposition to the most fundamental freedom of thought, speech, and press, necessary to preserve all other freedoms. Coleridge himself, moreover, was wide open to the mystiques of German metaphysical idealism, which made clearest why such idealism has seldom been conducive to earthly ideals of freedom. Because the sky was no limit to thinkers who made the human mind the key to the cosmos, or remolded reality to suit the heart's desire, they were apt to disdain the practical, critical uses of reason and empirical knowledge. Their Absolute Spirit blessed them with a kind of spiritual or subjective freedom but otherwise consecrated their disposition to absolutism, indifference or hostility to ordinary kinds of freedom. Fichte in particular introduced another fateful theme by his celebration of the primacy of Will. This was in keeping with "the liberation of the unconscious"—one of the honorific definitions of Romanticism; but willful men who trusted to their dream life failed to anticipate that a Hitler might do so, and the dream become nightmare.

Such inclinations were not discouraged by the living "nature" that the Romantics recovered from the abstractions of the Enlightenment. Poets typically idealized nature in much the spirit of Wordsworth, to whom it was a source only of blessed feelings. (As Aldous Huxley observed, he might have been less enchanted had he lived in the jungled tropics instead of the temperate zone.) The possibly facile sentiment that bred the "romantic fallacy" in poetry also appeared in the primitivism that Rousseau had made fashionable, a deal of sentimentality about the "simple, natural life." This not only obscured the perennial issue of just what is the natural life for man but encouraged a dubious mode of freedom, the abandonment to feeling or impulse. The avowed "child of nature" might be Rousseau—or he might be the Marquis de Sade. Men who scorned the norms of mere reason might on principle feel free to indulge neurotic, sadistic, or demonic impulses, and might then be at their mercy, not very free after all. The Romantic movement sowed as well the seeds of the "flowers of evil," the *mal du siècle* to come.

No more was the new interest in history clearly a discipline, still less an emancipation from the tyranny of the past. To begin with, the Romantics were drawn chiefly to a remote past, ideally dotted with picturesque ruins. In redressing the injustice done to the Middle Ages by the Enlightenment, they in turn oversimplified: it now became the Age of Faith, all piety and chivalry, purged of its barbarities and its tyrannies—a view that is still popular in literary circles today. Likewise they celebrated a folkish past, rich in saga, legend, and mythological lore, purged of vulgar reference to the poverty or possible wretchedness of the common folk. Myth now acquired its high repute as a mode of poetic, "timeless" truth.[2] This whole tendency to romanticize the past again betrayed some simple sentimentality, but also some escapism: men were turning to the past out of dissatisfaction with the present rather than for the sake of a better understanding of it. In particular history was serving the interests of conservatives, defenders of the traditional order that Metternich was trying to maintain. Men were idealizing the past in the spirit of Edmund Burke—an avowed "realist" who verged on sublimity, or absurdity, in his portrait of the *ancien régime* as an order of pure gallantry, fidelity, honor, and "exalted freedom," presided over by his adorable Marie Antoinette, with no mention of the millions of unexalted toilers who paid the costs of its elegance. Hence the no less pious Lord Acton lamented that in restoring the treasures of the past the Romantics were "subjecting thereby the will and the conscience of the living to the will and conscience of the dead."

---

2 The issues raised by the rediscovery of the importance of myth are considered in *Freedom in the Ancient World*, pp. 44–45.

A further reason why a historian may no longer simply rejoice in the eminence his subject acquired from the Romantic movement is that professional historians lent considerable support to these dubious tendencies, no less when they aspired to be "scientific." Hegel most explicitly gave history a new glory by asserting its absolute sovereignty as "the world's court of justice." In identifying the real with the rational, he loosely described as "necessary" all historical developments that seemed intelligible, but he was obliged anyway to justify the whole process in which the World Spirit had chosen to manifest itself. Although practicing historians could hardly ring in this Spirit as they dedicated themselves to telling "what had actually happened," both their enthusiasm over their mission and their recognition of organic processes tended to a comparable deification of history. The past could not be altered, it had to be what it was; the historian might then conclude that what had happened was not only necessary but right, it expressed "the spirit of its age"; and his illusion of objectivity might make it easier for him to justify whatever was dear to his own heart, confer a Hegelian blessing upon a selected reality. Thus when Ranke emphasized that rights were historic, not "natural," some of his followers emphasized that whatever rights "history" had granted a people were sufficient, all that the people really needed. As for the revolutionary movements of the day, they tended to agree with both Burke and Hegel that since history was an organic development, not consciously planned by man, it was foolish to believe that men could make revolutions and write new constitutions to suit their own purposes. "History" frowned on all efforts to remake it, approved only the traditionalist who was true to the past.

In Germany history was also pressed into the service of a fanciful nationalism, mingled with racism, that grew popular in central and eastern Europe, especially Russia. The great writers of the German Enlightenment—Lessing, Herder, Schiller, Goethe—had spoken to and for all mankind, while Kant proposed a philosophical theory of history that called for the establishment of a world state, transcending the nation. But Fichte, at first a disciple of Kant, won fame by his *Addresses to the German People* (1807), in which he spoke only to Germans, in what he called their purer, more virile tongue, and told them they were a superior race, assured them the future was theirs. Other Romantics were the more pleased to develop Herder's idea of the peculiar profundity of the German genius because Germany was not yet a nation. They compensated for the political weakness of its disunited states by more grandiose notions of how infinitely deeper, loftier, and richer German culture was than that of other peoples, still infected by the rationalism and empiricism of the Enlightenment. Likewise they supplanted the Enlightenment concept of citizenship by the misty notion of the "folk," which became clearest in its racial connotations. It was to this kind of nationalism that Hegel lent the immense weight of his authority, beginning with the assertion that the Germans were the first people to attain a full consciousness of freedom. According to him, the development of the nation-state was the supreme object of the Spirit in history; with its establishment the dialectical process, rather oddly, appeared to end— he envisaged no "higher synthesis" in a world state, which logically would be better suited to a World Spirit; and he became devoted in particular to the cause of Prussia, the strongest of the German states.

All this bids us pause because when Prussia finally did unite Germany, and under Bismarck made it the greatest power on the Continent, it became apparent that Romanticism had had a deeper, more lasting influence here than in any other country. Down through the world wars it was the spirit of Fichte and Hegel, not of Kant and Goethe, that dominated the nation. And Hegel had sounded another ominous theme in his deification of the state itself. Essentially, to be sure, he conceived it as the indispensable means to cultural development, the "consciousness of freedom," or some higher end; what he apotheosized was a kind of Platonic Idea of the state, like Burke's "great primeval contract of eternal society."[3] At that, he was more sensible than the English Utilitarians in recognizing that men are naturally concerned with public ends, and do not think of the state as merely a means of achieving their private ends. Nevertheless he described the state as "the perfect embodiment of Spirit"—a claim such as no previous thinker had made for it. He declared that "all the worth that the human being possesses—all spiritual reality—he possesses only through the State." He could therefore say that it "exists for its own sake," in effect was an end in itself. The effect was worse because of his loyalty to Prussia, which was humanly un-

---

[3] Since Hegel is going to appear in a generally unfavorable light from now on, I should remark that he has suffered the common fate of philosophers: the worst in their thought is likely to live after them, magnified by their disciples as well as their enemies, while the best becomes taken for granted and may then be forgotten. Even those repelled by the colossal conceit of Hegel may disagree with the philosophical FBI's (such as Karl Popper) who have made him out to be public enemy no. 1.

derstandable but scarcely becoming a spokesman of the World Spirit. Prussia was a pretty crude choice for the Spirit, inasmuch as it was a synthetic state that had been carved out by princes, lacked a rich cultural tradition or any folkish foundations, and had contributed little to the great German Enlightenment. (Herder despised it.) Since its most distinguished tradition was military, Hegel dutifully sanctioned war as a safeguard against the "corruptions" of a lasting peace such as Kant had aspired to: "War has the deep meaning that by it the ethical health of the nations is preserved and their finite aims uprooted." He bolstered the Junker spirit by double-talk about freedom, for which the Germans were supposedly pre-eminent: "positive freedom" lay in "utter obedience" to the state, "complete abnegation of one's own opinions and reasonings." Hegel no more intended than anticipated anything like Hitler's Reich; but the road to it was paved with both his dubious logic and his good intentions.

He prepared for it as well by giving his blessing to the great heroes of history, like Napoleon. Although such men were admittedly selfish, unscrupulous, "morally reprehensible," they were serving as agents of the World Spirit and so should not be subject to the "sentimentalities" of moral reflection. Hero worship, which Carlyle and others proceeded to make into a cult, was of course nothing new in history, but as a conscious cult it was another distinctive product of Romanticism. So was a new kind of egoism nurtured by the related emphasis on subjectivity. In philosophy Fichte linked Ego to the "Eternal and Infinite Will," the creator of nature; as he informed the Infinite, "Thou and I are not divided! Thy voice sounds within me; mine resounds in Thee!" In literature the Romantics were often their own heroes, in transparent if any disguise; they took for granted that their highly personal emotions were the chief source of interest. They developed the cult of genius, the Poet or the Artist as one set apart—a kind of Hegelian hero of culture. Gautier would create God in their image, remarking that he was perhaps "only the first poet of the world." Everywhere the very self-conscious man was naturally inclined to feel superior, or possibly a law unto himself.

Only he might not rejoice in his state, even if he was a lenient lawmaker. As one set apart, he might feel lonely, estranged, lost. The Romantics established the now popular image of the artist, which would have mystified the supremely artistic Greeks: the artist as by nature a nonconformist or rebel, in some sense abnormal, typically "malad-

justed," at best always liable to be misunderstood—in short, "romantic." Most of them were in fact prone to marked idiosyncrasy or aberration. Their temperament might be attributed to the "poetic madness"
known ever since the Greeks, but it was now more insistently eccentric,
often verging on morbidity. It induced a possibly unwholesome consciousness of poetry as a cathartic or an escape, a means of preventing
outright madness—in Byron's words, as "the lava of imagination whose
eruption prevents the earthquake." Byron also epitomized the deep
strain of melancholy that ran through the Romantic movement. As
introduced by Chateaubriand's *René* it was unlike the melancholy of
writers in the past, who generally knew why they were unhappy; in
René it was incurable because indefinable and insatiable—there was
nothing he or anybody else could do about it. Or as Peacock parodied
it in Byron, "You talk like a Rosicrucian, who will love nothing but a
sylph, who does not believe in the existence of a sylph, and who yet quar-
rels with the whole Universe for not containing a sylph." The Byronic
hero made the mysterious sorrow more awful by introducing a demonic
note, brooding over some secret, unmentionable sin or crime in his past
that made him merciless both to himself and to others, fated him to be
forever a wanderer and an exile.

Now, there was no doubt much posturing in this *maladie du siècle,*
much of the not very secret pleasure of narcissism. In setting off waves
of suicides it supported Goethe's charge that Romanticism was novel
chiefly in that it was sickly. Yet the malady went deeper than mere
fashion, it was no transient sickness. It would find religious expression
in Kierkegaard's principle of *Angst,* the "dreadful freedom" that existentialists have made much of. In philosophy it produced the famous
pessimism of Schopenhauer, based squarely on the primacy of Will. It
brings us back to the costs of the willfulness and pride of the Romantics,
and finally to the sources of their ambivalent attitudes of activism and
fatalism, optimism and pessimism—the deep uncertainties of their
revolutionary age. "Dynamic" would remain a good word to our own
day, but many men were painfully aware of the endless flux and struggle that were less agreeable words for it. To them their age felt more
like a crisis than may appear to us children of constant crisis. They
were all inclined to feel like wanderers, "on a darkling plain swept by
confused alarms of struggle and flight."

So we might take another look at the Olympian Hegel, who intimated that the main point of the whole cosmic process since the beginning of time was to produce his system. He was not a lucid thinker,

of course. His grand system was a compound of historical realism, romantic idealism, and metaphysical mysticism, consistent chiefly in the vagueness of its key terms, in which a dialectic resting on a remarkably loose concept of "contradiction" incidentally conferred an ethical necessity upon an authoritarian state with which it had no necessary logical connection, and a vision of a continuous dynamic process of becoming made no provision for further becoming: altogether a Janus-like monument of a century whose deeper thinkers, as Whitehead observed, were likely to be more muddled than any before them. Among the ambiguities of this exalted philosophy of history were its profoundly pessimistic implications. As Hegel read history, not only individuals but whole peoples were continually sacrificed to the progress of the World Spirit, which traveled from country to country, in ways which he neglected ever to explain, at any given stage leaving the great bulk of mankind in a relatively soulless state, and then for reasons as unclear leaving its chosen people behind—as it had left the brilliant Greeks—to drag out their spent life, or die a painful death, like all the others before them. Other German idealists took as dark a view of most of human history, which Schelling called in so many words a "tragic spectacle performed on the mournful stage of this world." As the mouthpiece of the Spirit Hegel was not much given to mourning, but neither did he offer his fellow Germans radiant visions of either indefinite progress or indefinite hegemony. Rather, he at times betrayed a feeling that his own age was coming to an end—as sooner or later it logically had to, given the peripatetic ways of the Spirit. His historical sense was both in theory and in fact a deep sense of mutability, while the kind of "spiritual freedom" he held out was not clearly a freedom to make history to suit men's own purposes. The most certain conclusion to be drawn from his philosophy was that there was no going back, to either the Age of Faith or the *ancien régime* romanticized by Burke and others. One reason for the popularity of nature was that it offered a refuge from history; though some Romantics became more aware of its dread aspects too.

At any rate, the grand Hegelian synthesis broke down. Thinkers after Hegel were less impressed by his intimacy with the Absolute than by his insistence on the relativity and partiality of all philosophical and religious belief. (Long before Nietzsche, he remarked that God was dead.) Students of society would dwell on the nonrational forces that he had called attention to, breaking up his ideal wedding of the real and the rational. Literary men were troubled by more obvious threats to their aspirations to wholeness, or to the power of synthesis that Coleridge celebrated as the essence of Imagination. From the Enlightenment they had inherited basic rifts between reason and faith, thought and feeling, and they began opening a new rift between science and poetry, signaled by Blake and Wordsworth, which would widen into a gulf between the sciences and the humanities. In general, the very sense of rich, diverse, boundless potentiality that distinguished the Romantics may also be described as a deepening confusion over the nature of man and uncertainty over his prospects, because of which they never agreed as substantially as had the apostles of the Enlightenment in their visions of what the future would or should be like.

More significant immediately was a growing tension between writers and society, especially in countries freer than Hegel's World Spirit clearly approved. From Dante on, to be sure, writers had generally been critical of their society. One can make out plenty of discontent, sometimes verging on despair, even in the lusty Renaissance and Elizabethan Age, or the seemingly complacent Age of Louis XIV, and social criticism was the very core of the French Enlightenment. Usually, however, writers had dwelt on the familiar theme of corruption through ambition and greed, or shortcomings by the accepted norms, and when in the Enlightenment criticism became more fundamental, directed at the norms themselves, writers still felt quite at home in their society; excepting Rousseau, they were not frustrated, maladjusted, or alienated types, but reformers or crusaders characteristically confident that they spoke for posterity. Some Romantics continued to sound such confidence despite their personal problems. But others began sounding a different theme, due to be a major theme of the future, in which many of the greater writers would be more hostile to their society, feel less at home in it, than ever before. The keynotes were some words that toward the end of the eighteenth century first came into popular use, or took on significant new meanings that have since become standard: the words "democracy," "industry" as manufactures, "art" as creative or fine art, and "culture" as the high values of civilization.[4]

As has already been noted, the Romantics soon split over the issues of democracy, dramatized by the French Revolution, but almost all

---

4 Raymond Williams pointed out and followed through this lead in *Culture and Society 1780–1950.* He noted other distinctively modern words that entered the language about the same time, such as capitalism, commercialism, socialism, liberalism, egalitarian, humanitarian, ideology, and intellectual; while old words that acquired their modern meaning included business, education, reformer, and revolutionize. One pondering this list may realize why so much that "goes without saying" needs to be said.

were much concerned over these issues and took a definite political stand. A related concern was indicated by another new term, the "middle class," suggesting something more fluid than the old "estate" or "rank"; it was soon followed by "working class" and "upper class," preparing for the "class consciousness" to come. About industry writers had less to say, since the Industrial Revolution was only beginning and was largely confined to England, but they at least anticipated the protests that would resound through the century. Southey was among the first directly to attack the drabness and ugliness that were coming in with industrialism, while Coleridge noted that employers were acquiring the right to buy "the laborer's health, life, and well being"; others attacked the allied spirit of rational calculation, the growing prominence of the economist, and the utilitarianism that Bentham erected into a philosophy; and most were naturally hostile to the materialism of a society increasingly devoted to business, bent on "getting and spending." But in particular literary men were very much concerned about art and culture—values that ever since the Renaissance had generally been taken for granted by all except the sternest Puritans. They began talking about culture so much because evidently it could no longer be trusted to flourish by itself.

An immediate reason was an apparent advantage they enjoyed, the growth of a large reading public. They could now be independent professional writers, no longer needing the support of nobles or any patron except the public, which Oliver Goldsmith had described as "a good and generous master." Byron could win immense popularity by his poetry, Walter Scott make a fortune by his novels; fiction especially would support ever more writers. Hence even conservatives responded by contributing to some democratic tendencies in literature. Wordsworth celebrated the virtues of simple folk, while bringing poetry closer to everyday language; Scott portrayed the folk sympathetically in romances that were more realistic in detail than an aristocratic audience might care for; Germans lifted folk and fairy tale into the realm of art. Less consciously, the Romantics reflected some of the dubious tastes of their middle-class public in their predilection to sentimentality, melodrama, and showiness. A large, palpitating feminine audience swelled the fame of the Byronic hero.

Nevertheless writers were more dependent on this middle-class public, in general acutely aware of its tastes. Literature was another commodity, competing in the market, and there was often a glaring spread between its market value and its literary value. Writers might

therefore disdain "the Public"; Keats wrote that he had "not the slightest feel of humility" toward it, while Wordsworth carefully distinguished it from the People "philosophically characterized." If such
quarreling with the audience was hardly unprecedented, it was growing
more insistent as the reading public grew. The complaints spread from
popular tastes in literature to all the values of the rising middle class,
then to the quality of democratic culture. They force basic issues that
we shall keep returning to in every chapter, for they concern not only
the uses of freedom, the ends of a free society, but the popular attitudes,
sentiments, and desires that affect its political means and all its institutions.

Meanwhile, especially in England, the Romantics further complicated the issues. As self-appointed custodians of culture in a changing
society, they insisted as never before on the high mission of poetry, the
superior kind of imaginative truth it expressed, and its sovereign necessity for the public good; but thereby they were disposed to conflicting
attitudes. On the one hand, they typically asserted that the poet spoke
for Man or the People. Thus Wordsworth described him as the main
"upholder and preserver," who "binds together by passion and knowledge the vast empire of human society"; Shelley called him the un-
acknowledged legislator of the world. On the other hand, their awareness that he was publicly not so acknowledged led them to play up the
rare qualities that made him a special breed of mortal, proud that
he was not speaking to or for them. Soon the artist would appear as an
aesthete—another new word, defining a historically new type.[5]

---

5 This split may be traced to the deeper splits caused by the invention of the printing
press, and the consequent revolution in modes of thought studied by Marshall McLuhan
in *The Gutenberg Galaxy*. In the Middle Ages, as in ancient Greece and other societies,
literature was typically read aloud and regarded as public, not private property; the
habit of silent reading was uncommon. (St. Augustine reported his amazement when
he saw St. Ambrose reading with his eye gliding over the pages, his voice and tongue
at rest.) The printing press not only multiplied but standardized books, creating uniform,
mechanical, repeatable type, and it established the habit of silent, private reading. Although McLuhan exaggerates the revolution due to the rise of "typographical man,"
as might be expected of an author with a novel thesis, I think there is no question that
its effects were wider and deeper than has been generally realized, or than I indicated
in my previous volume. In providing "the first uniformly repeatable commodity, the
first assembly line, and the first mass-production," typography helps to explain such
developments as the obsession with exact measure and quantity that appeared by the
seventeenth century, "the criterion of repeatability in science," the price system, and
the unprecedented isolation of the economy from society. It heralded the "homogeni-
zation" of men and materials, as later of education.

In another aspect, which the Romantics made most conspicuous, typographical man
was a sort of schizophrenic. Print culture began by separating the eye and the ear, and
thought from communal action; it then intensified the growing dissociation of sensibility, sharpened the antitheses between heart and head, body and mind; and it helped

In either case, the lofty idea that the Romantics had of themselves calls attention to their limitations as binders, legislators, or prophets. They failed to make good their promises, often their performance was pretty weak. Matthew Arnold, an admirer, confessed that they did not know enough. Defenders of the Enlightenment might add that they too often undermined the simple sanity needed by any kind of legislator; they heralded a century in which a tremendous growth in power would make wisdom more imperative than ever, and in which not many writers and thinkers were distinguished for wisdom. I should say that no religion of art would have sufficed anyway, least of all when it was so self-conscious, but that it suffered from the same basic defects as the religion of Reason in the Enlightenment. The Romantics had too little sense—imaginative or critical—of ambiguity and complexity.

There remains, however, the epical *Faust*—the greatest single work to come out of the Romantic movement. Labeled by Goethe a tragedy, called by Hegel "absolute philosophical tragedy," it may take us to the heart of the issues raised by this movement as a prelude to the modern world. *Faust* is comparable to the *Divine Comedy* as an effort at universal synthesis. If less obviously sublime, it presents in as vast a theater a more comprehensive image of human experience, including both religious and secular values, embracing all that Western man had gone through since Dante's age. It is still more pertinent because its drama is centered on an aspiration to welcome all further potentialities, keep all horizons open. The unique compact that Goethe's Faust makes with the Devil stipulates not merely that he shall be granted all the goods of this life, but that he shall lose his soul only if he is ever really satisfied and ceases to aspire to still more. He must forever live up to his author's living ideal: "Only he deserves his life and freedom who wins them every day anew."

The trouble with this romantic philosophy, Santayana commented, is that "it is obstinately empirical, and will never learn anything from

---

to create both the "detribalized individual" and the "desacralized cosmos." Thus the Romantics incidentally conceived imagination as chiefly a power of visualization, suited to silent reading. They began to discover the unconscious, the whole realm of mind that readers had grown insensitive to. Now addressing a large public, they grew more directly concerned with the effects and the functions of their art. Above all, they carried farthest the individualism stimulated by the invention of the printing press, which made literature the property of the writer and encouraged him to seek fame. In an age of increasing mechanization and standardization—an outgrowth of print culture that they deplored—they stressed the values of uniqueness and of purely personal experience; but their dilemma remained that they nevertheless wanted to carry on the tradition of literature as a tribal or mythic vision.

experience." But Goethe himself of course knew much more than Faust, and was by no means a simple romantic. He often criticized the Germans who called themselves Romantics, deploring their glorification of the Middle Ages, their conversion to Catholicism, and their otherworldly yearnings as modes of escape from the responsibilities of the here and now. He despised the common license of subjectivity, the self-indulgence and self-pity, the cult of melancholy. He attacked as well the cult of nationalism, the romantic idealization of the German past. For Goethe remained loyal to the rational, civil, cosmopolitan ideals of the Enlightenment, and in literature to the classical Greek ideal. He belonged to the Romantic movement chiefly in that he considered these ideals too narrow and sought to supplement them in a higher synthesis. Cherishing the faith in reason and knowledge, he yet knew that it could not satisfy man's deepest needs nor guarantee wisdom; admiring the measure and control of Greek art, he still wanted more freedom and abundance. In short, he remained true both in theory and in practice to the ideal of wholeness and the aspiration to totality that other Romantics proclaimed, but fell short of because of both their negations and their excesses. He was by all odds the sanest of them.[6]

In *Faust* the clearest sign of Goethe's sanity—or perhaps the means to it—is Mephistopheles. There is much of Goethe in his hero, but as much in his ironic, witty devil. Mephistopheles is antiromantic through and through, mocking all the grand aspirations or grandiose illusions of Faust. He is as merciless in his mockery of the faith of the Enlightenment in reason and science, which in a way begot him. Regarding himself as a superstition, he nevertheless remarks that men have not gained much by dismissing him as a superstition: "They are rid of the Evil One, the evils remain." He suggests, indeed, something evil in his author. Thomas Mann noted a demonic, nihilistic impulse in Goethe, who perhaps relished too much this profane mockery of all human idealism. But primarily Mephistopheles serves to toughen Goethe's idealism. He recalls the many grimly ironic observations strewn through other works, such as this from *Wilhelm Meister*: "The human mob fears nothing more than reason; it ought to fear stupidity if it under-

---

6 As an artist, his one peer was Beethoven, the greatest composer in a century whose music was dominated by Romanticism to the end. Like Goethe a man of naturally strong emotions and some disposition to *Angst*, Beethoven kept them under control, earning the resolution of the Hymn to Joy in the Ninth Symphony before he attained to the sublimities of the last quartets.

stood what is really frightful; but reason is too uncomfortable, it must be brushed aside; whereas stupidity is merely fatal, and that will keep." Throughout *Faust* we are constantly reminded that every article of Goethe's naturalistic, humanistic faith is questionable, no less vulnerable to ironic contemplation than are the conceits of religious faith. Ordinary mortals may continue to wonder how free a man is if he has to win his freedom every day anew.

Whether or not Faust himself learns enough from all his experience, Goethe dramatizes the essential costs of his boundless aspiration, which come down to the tragic knowledge of good-in-evil and evil-out-of-good. He dwells on not merely the paradoxical mixture of spirit and clay in man but the limitations of spirit itself, the fallibility that becomes more marked in its highest reaches, and its liability to apostasy from ordinary, decent human obligations. Margaret, the conspicuous victim, illustrates a deeper tragedy of love, which Goethe considered one of the supreme values slighted by the Enlightenment: even love is never enough, except for a simple Margaret. (And let us remember that the families of Socrates and Jesus were sacrificed to their ideal aspirations.) Faust may accordingly symbolize the basic paradox of Western idealism, which from the beginnings of Europe has been distinctive in inspiring violence, war, even atrocity. So too with the inseparable mixture of pride and humility in both religious and humanistic faith. "Wonder and awe are still the best in man," Goethe says through Faust, in despite of Mephistopheles. In humility he refused to commit himself on the Christian God and immortality, or ever to speak with the finality of Dante, in whom he saw a "gruesome greatness." In pride he committed himself to an unequivocal rejection of the doctrine that to serve God and save his soul man should renounce the world and self—the secular values to which Western men had grown especially devoted. "Children, go back to life," he repeatedly advised; men should go on, always go on; but he denied them any certainty, any assurance of peace in this life or the next, while showing that their earthly journey took them through sufficient hell.

Yet *Faust* is not, finally, a tragedy by either Shakespearean or modern standards. It is the testament of a basically optimistic philosophy. At the outset the Lord announces that he approves of "my servant" Faust and his way of life; as man aspires he is bound to err. At the end Faust is saved, not damned. In between there is little terror or real tension, except in the tragic love episode; the tone of the drama is seldom tragic. Although the hero sins and suffers often enough, Goethe is

quick to forgive him and make him forget, so that he may keep going
on without dismay. Mephistopheles himself backs up Faust's way of
life, for he concedes that he is

> Part of that Power, not understood,
> Which always wills the Bad, and always works the Good.

Hence the mystery about the power above is not really awful, but a
source of other heartening possibilities. Among these is the frequent
hint that Mephistopheles too will finally be pardoned—an idea that
would seem becoming to the Christian God of love and mercy (though
his leading spokesmen have never approved it), but that carries still
further from tragedy. It suggests another remark by Goethe that takes
us to the crux of the matter. He could not write tragedies, he said, because he could not tolerate discords unresolved.

Such discords were due to become more violent, in both the world
of thought and the world of practical affairs. We might therefore draw
inspiration from Goethe's ideal synthesis of thought and sentiment,
knowledge and faith, culture and nature, and be more grateful for
the breadth and wholeness of the last of the universal geniuses of
Europe. At least we should always remember that as a clear-eyed man
of the world he earned his affirmations, his faith that the going might
be the goal. Still, in view of the actual future Goethe is bound to seem
shortsighted, possibly even a little shallow by contrast with the youthful
Christopher Marlowe who conceived a really tragic Dr. Faustus. With
the aristocrat in him who looked down on the "human mob," and remarked casually "rather injustice than disorder," there was also something of a complacent bourgeois, very practical about money matters
and notions of good works. Faust's epic adventure ends in technology:
his last feat is building dikes to reclaim land. Mephistopheles, who had
had a vision of Metropolis with its noisome bourgeois lives and its
"broad squares and streets arterial trying so hard to look imperial,"
now has to serve Faust as an industrial foreman, blowing a whistle. We
may be less impressed by the conscious irony of this episode than by
Goethe's optimism over material progress and his failure to anticipate
the problems that would be created when the Fausts of the future
became masters of tremendous material power.

| Chapter Two | # THE INDUSTRIAL REVOLUTION |

1. The Economic Factor in History

Once upon a time, when history was treated as essentially "past politics," the main outlines of the nineteenth century might have seemed reasonably clear. Britain became mistress of an empire that embraced about a quarter of the world's population. Under Bismarck, Prussia welded the German states into a nation and demonstrated its might by overwhelming France in the war of 1870. Italy too was at last united, entering the concert of major powers. Mongrel Austria-Hungary, an apparent anachronism in an age of rising nationalism, nevertheless managed to hold together and stay in the concert on the strength of dynastic tradition. Russia remained a power in spite of its backwardness by virtue of its sheer size. The United States, still making a point of keeping out of the concert, survived its bloody Civil War and continued its phenomenal growth. Together, Western nations dominated most of the world, imposing their will on the stagnant or decadent civilizations of India, China, and Islam, and in a single generation taking over virtually the entire continent of Africa. At home the major European nations had begun fighting among themselves in the Crimean War, but thereafter they kept their wars limited and remarkably short; warfare among them took up only two or three years all told, as contrasted with at least sixty years in preceding centuries. By shifting alliances, designed to maintain a balance of power, they managed in fact to maintain an apparent stability and to avert a major conflict until the outbreak of the World War, a century after Waterloo. The great powers that started this war were the same powers that had met at the Congress of Vienna under Metternich.

More significant in a history of freedom was the growth of popular government and civil liberties in Europe. Despite the immediate failure of most of the popular revolutions, parliamentary institutions became the rule on the Continent outside of Russia, limiting the power of kings who had formerly ruled as absolute monarchs. Suffrage was gradually extended, and by the end of the century all men had the right to vote in some countries, including even Spain; this right—the most popular symbol of the democratic cause—was strengthened by increasing use of the secret ballot. Serfdom disappeared in all countries. Thought and speech became freer than ever before as censorship of the press was relaxed when not abolished. Religious freedom was established by law in some countries, religious toleration by habit in almost all. Common people were enabled to enjoy more effective freedom by the spread of public education, and by social legislation protecting workers. Everywhere they were freely allowed to emigrate to America, the world symbol of democracy, or to other lands of opportunity.

In view of the World War, however, these simple outlines have blurred and faded. The diplomatic history of the nineteenth century may now seem superficial or academic, and certainly it was not the key to a revolutionary age. Neither, unhappily, does the advance of democracy stand out unmistakably as the most significant development of the century, the main line to the future; it might prove to be only a prelude to the rise of totalitarianism. In any case, another familiar but less edifying theme has come to seem more fundamental—the Industrial Revolution. This is still going on, gathering ever more momentum. All along it had more and more to do with political history, as industrial powers became the leading powers, while it had a profounder impact on society and culture, under whatever form of government. Only it too, of course, is no simple key. The Industrial Revolution is the most apparent source of the abiding confusions and contradictions of modern history—and of added confusions in modern historians.

Among its by-products was the economic interpretation of history, beginning with Karl Marx's theory. The importance of economic factors now seems so obvious that we may overlook one good reason why they were virtually ignored by past historians: they had always been subordinated to noneconomic ends—the serious business of life. Marx's theory of economic determinism would have seemed highly implausible in almost any past society. By now such interpretations have become somewhat less fashionable, at least outside the Communist world; but first we still need to realize why they have seemed so plausible. They make plainer the uniqueness of modern civilization, in which economic interests have in fact become primary.

In all previous civilizations the great bulk of the populace were villagers, engaged in agriculture. The Industrial Revolution created a predominantly urban society, the first great society in which most people made their living in business. For the first time, too, the business class became the ruling class, and success in business a primary means to social prestige.[1] The profit motive, which had been known as greed, was now celebrated as the essential means to social good, the more effective if it were subject to no control but the "law" of supply and demand. Private enterprise, in itself not new, was exalted as never before by a novel gospel of *laissez faire*. Human nature was redefined, Economic Man equipped with an "instinct" to barter and acquire. In America economic freedom was proclaimed the most fundamental, precious freedom, even though the Founding Fathers had neglected to feature it. Conservatives substantially agreed with Marx that economic interests are primary, while popular philosophy embraced the belief that economic motives are the most powerful. "The business of America is business," said Calvin Coolidge—a statement that one can scarcely imagine a national leader making in any past society, and that in the modern world might still seem a little strange for a nominally Christian society; but Americans applauded it.

As the materialism of business leaders supported a materialistic interpretation of history, so their common ignorance of their society and blindness to the history they were making supported certain corollaries of this interpretation. The Industrial Revolution was obviously unplanned, not the work of deliberate revolutionaries. As it gathered momentum it accordingly generated a tendency to dwell on "vast, impersonal forces" and to minimize the conscious purposes in which human freedom consists. Many thinkers assumed that the "real" causes of history are unconscious, or at least quite different from the professed

---

[1] The apparent exceptions in the past were relatively small societies, such as Carthage and Venice. Although merchants also rose to power in ancient Greece, they did not maintain their power and privilege specifically as businessmen. In classical Athens, for example, business was largely handled by foreign residents, who were denied the political rights of citizens; Plato and Aristotle fixed the aristocratic tradition of looking down on trade and the "base mechanic arts," which prevailed in the Roman Empire too. In no civilization did the business class rank at the top of the social scale. In China it ranked at the very bottom, beneath the peasantry.

intentions of the leading actors, and that the "deepest" truths about history are necessarily unedifying, always much less reputable than what men believe to be the truth as they make history with sweat, blood, and tears. They agreed with Marx that ruling ideas and ideals amount to "ideologies," effects rather than causes of historic change. And though this whole way of thinking is naturally displeasing to freedom lovers, they cannot afford to ignore the considerable measure of truth in it, the light it has thrown on the conditions of human freedom. Already, for example, it has outmoded the *Cambridge Modern History* of a generation or so ago, whose fourteen volumes included only three chapters on economics. The significant fact remains that we are still trying to understand and keep abreast of the history that men have somehow been making over the past century, mostly without any real desire for a continuously revolutionary world.

Yet this implies that no economic interpretation of this history is really adequate either. There also remain sound, demonstrable reasons for believing that any such exclusive interpretation not only impoverishes but grossly oversimplifies human history. So far from being purely "realistic," economic determinism has blinded men to some of the fundamental realities of modern life (just as it left Communists completely unprepared for the rise of Hitler). It cannot account adequately even for the Industrial Revolution—the ostensibly economic affair that is our present concern.

To begin with, this was by no means a uniform, automatic kind of process in Europe, but got under way in different countries at different times in different ways. Neither was it a clearly predictable development from the state of the European economy. Adam Smith, the most acute economic analyst of his day, foretold it no more than did any other economist or historian, though machines were already coming into wide use. One excuse for his oversight was that it began without fanfare and long remained a matter of scattered individual enterprise, localized in a few districts in England, especially its North Country—a poor, backward, hitherto insignificant district that no informed man would look to for a revolutionary development, and that was least likely to interest an embryonic Marxist, since it lacked even a substantial bourgeoisie. As men gradually grew aware of the new technological possibilities, their exploitation of them involved more conscious thought and effort on a national scale, and government played an increasingly active role; but this pointed to the importance of such factors as the political system, social structure, and cultural tradition. While the Industrial Revolution

profoundly affected all other major interests, these noneconomic interests had affected its course from the outset. The power of the purse
was both abetted and limited by the powers of the sword and the pen.

In short, we have to deal with multiple causes and effects. We may
concentrate on any one factor, and its effects on other interests, but to
understand its action we have to keep an eye on not only the reaction of
other factors but the interactions of a complex. An agreeable word for
this view of history is "organic." The disagreeable word for it is a
"mess." Either way, we can never hope fully to comprehend all the
interrelations or steadily to maintain a clear view of the society as a
whole; but these remain the given terms of our problem. The assumption that the economic factor is the "ultimate" cause or the "essence"
of the situation leads to as distorted views of history as one would get
of man by assuming that the stomach is the basis or essence of the
human organism. "Spiritual" factors may appear as vital in the Industrial Revolution as the brain in human behavior, particularly if one
remembers that they no more guarantee virtuous or intelligent behavior.

As a specific preliminary warning, before we take up this involved
story, let us consider one of the most momentous of its apparent consequences—the tremendous growth in population. The population of
Europe more than doubled in the nineteenth century, even though
many millions migrated to other continents. Presumably the new
masses of humanity could not in any case have been accommodated
tidily in the old social order, but they were more disruptive because
they were mostly crowded in cities, made up of petty bourgeois and
proletarians—the political "masses" who perpetually alarmed conservatives. Presumably, too, the Industrial Revolution spawned them by its
improved technology, which reduced the ravages of famine and disease;
while medical science saved many lives, a more productive economy was
able to sustain them. Yet this is not the whole story, possibly not even
the main cause. The rapid growth of population began early in the
eighteenth century, some generations before the Industrial Revolution
got well under way, and it continued in countries like Russia that were
not industrialized. Moreover, population grew about as fast over these
two centuries in China, where there was no such revolution or any
apparent economic cause of the immense growth. Conceivably the
technological advance in Europe was as much a consequence as a cause
of the increasing population—a response to a challenge.

In any case, China affords an illuminating perspective. Here the new
hordes of humanity caused no significant changes in the political or

social order, nor was there a continuous Marxist class struggle either, any new alarm over "the masses." The reasons why the Chinese began multiplying so rapidly remain unclear, but the reasons why they continued to put up with an order that left most of them wretchedly poor are more understandable: their whole cultural tradition had inured them to such a state. The plainest clue to both the causes and the consequences of the Industrial Revolution is the radically different cultural tradition of western Europe, a much more open society. This helps to explain as well why no such revolution occurred in any other civilization, even though on the face of their record other societies had the mental capacity and sufficient economic necessity to mother much more invention.

2. Technology and the Machine

In 1851 the Great Exhibition opened in the Crystal Palace of London, a monumental building of iron and glass designed for this grand occasion. It made a tremendous impression as the first international exhibition, dramatizing the wonders that the Industrial Revolution had wrought. "The Queen of the mightiest empire of the globe," noted the *Economist*, "—the empire in which industry is most successfully cultivated, and in which its triumphs have been greatest—was fittingly occupied in consecrating the temple erected to its honour." The *Economist* went on to provide more matter for irony as it explained the deeper significance of the exhibits in this temple: the "devotion to peace" and the promise of a still more peaceful future, the "honour" in which "humble industry" was now held, the "moral improvement" already demonstrated—altogether, the "irresistible assurances that a yet higher destiny awaits our successors even on earth." In recent years historians have been elaborating a further irony in this grand climax of the Industrial Revolution. It was pretty belated for a "revolution" that had supposedly started almost a century before, and they now say really began in the seventeenth century, or even in the sixteenth. At that, England still had more shoemakers than coal miners, more blacksmiths than ironworkers; and few Englishmen were yet speaking of an Industrial Revolution.[2] Now that the name has become standard, many

---

[2] Although the term was coined in the late eighteenth century by some French writer, excited by the political revolution of his day, it did not become current in England until

historians wish to drop it, or at least to get rid of the capital letters. They might not be impressed by one authority who grants that it is misleading but wants to keep on using it anyhow because economic history is an abstract kind, and "a proper name has the virtue that we cannot escape from its emotional associations." Most historians see no virtue in such associations.

Nevertheless I assume that the name is here to stay, and that the most sensible policy is to make the best of it. However uncertain and slow its beginnings, the Industrial Revolution unquestionably did revolutionize society. That it was an undramatic affair, unheeded by most contemporaries, recalls the quiet rise of modern science in the seventeenth century, which as certainly has revolutionized thought. Immediately the ironies may again prepare us for a better understanding of the profound changes, and of the "emotional associations" that we cannot hope to get rid of either. Among the pertinent facts is that thinkers concerned with the economy long remained unaware of the revolutionary possibilities of industrialism, being much more impressed by contemporaries like Malthus and Ricardo who foresaw only an increasingly bitter, futile struggle for the daily bread, due to the pressure of population, and who had no eye for what was going on under their nose. They anticipated the spectacular record of blindness that would be set by hardheaded businessmen and conservative economists down to our time, aggravating the social problems that will concern us later.

One good reason for the conventional assumption that the Industrial Revolution started in late eighteenth-century England was a rising tide of invention, beginning with an abrupt increase in the number of patents granted in the 1760's. While the number was still small—thirty-odd a year—it kept jumping periodically; the new inventions were calling for improvements, stimulating inventive minds in related fields of enterprise. In this process the most striking irony was duly suggested by the head of the U.S. Patent Office, who in 1833 resigned on the grounds that the patents on file had reached the staggering total of twenty to thirty thousand, and the possibilities of invention were virtually exhausted.[3] By the end of the century some 640,000 patents were

---

a hundred years later. It was popularized by Arnold Toynbee (uncle of the present historian of the same name) in his *Lectures on the Industrial Revolution of the Eighteenth Century in England* (1889).

[3] This total may be somewhat misleading because it had been swollen by an early American racket. The Patent Office at that time did not require inventors to prove that their device was original; the only requirement was that it be not clearly harmful to the public. Some enterprising inventors would take this lightly too—especially the makers of patent medicines, fathers of the great drug industry today.

listed in America, a number that would soon soar into the millions, and the most distinctive development had become clear. This was the habit of invention, or in Whitehead's words, "the invention of invention"—a creation of new wonders so systematic and regular that people would cease to wonder at them.

Well before the end of the century people had become proud of their machines, the symbols of the material progress consecrated by the Great Exhibition. They were accustomed, too, to industrial capitalism and the factory system, the social invention that from the beginning had been wedded to technological invention. The machine, however, has remained the popular symbol of the new age, for good enough reasons. In this history a few key inventions may suffice to indicate how one thing led to another, finally to a real revolution in everyday life.

Although James Watt's steam engine (1769) was only an improvement on an engine that had long been used to pump water out of mines, it deserves its textbook fame as both literally and figuratively the initial prime mover of the Machine Age. Watt made it much more efficient for general purposes. It then had an immediate advantage over water power in its independence of geography, season, and weather, introducing the mobility of the new age even before it was used to run boats and trains; any region could now industrialize. Among its earliest customers were pottery manufacturers, such as Josiah Wedgwood, followed by textile manufacturers. Coal mines and ironworks also were quick to adopt it, if without foreseeing the immense effect it would have on their industry: with the wide use of steam power, coal and iron technology became basic. Thereupon it stimulated the invention and development of machine tools, which at first had been little better than those of the Middle Ages; by 1850 most of the machine tools in use today had been invented. Manufacturers were slower in catching on to an innovation by Eli Whitney (inventor of the cotton gin), who before 1800 started mass production in his small arms factory by turning out interchangeable parts, but eventually this "American system" spread in Europe.[4] To meet the demands of all this mechanization, the new profession of engineering arose, replacing the miscellaneous craftsmen whose limited skills had handicapped Watt and the early machine-

---

[4] Interchangeable parts for muskets had actually been introduced by a French gunsmith before the French Revolution. Thomas Jefferson visited his shop when minister to France, characteristically looking into an idea he thought might be useful to America. Whitney apparently had not heard of it, however, but hit on it independently—a common occurrence once the great movement in modern science and technology got under way.

builders. Engineers in turn helped to develop new prime movers, such as the internal combustion engine and the steam turbine. Eventually the dynamo replaced the steam engine as the symbol of the new age.

Another conventional index to the Industrial Revolution that earned its way into textbooks is the textile industry. A series of inventions starting in the 1760's—the water frame, the jenny, the mule—was climaxed by Edmund Cartwright's power loom. That he first drove his invention with a cow did not detract from its historic importance in transforming the etymological meaning of "manufacture": it made the textile industry the first major industry in which the machine replaced handwork. While this helped directly to make Britain "the Queen of the mightiest empire of the globe," its by-products helped to spread the queen's fame by other innovations. As cotton rags became more plentiful, a papermaking machine was perfected by the Fourdrinier brothers, and the cost of paper considerably reduced. By 1830 publishing had been revolutionized and cheap paper was facilitating the spread of literacy.

More decisive for technological purposes was the Railway Age that began about the same time, following upon Stephenson's invention of the locomotive. The building of railroads not only introduced another great industry but stimulated all other industries by speeding up transport and communications; especially in America, France, and Germany it was the chief impetus to industrialization. The railways likewise accelerated the pace of technological advance. In England, for example, the use of power looms had spread so slowly that at the end of the Napoleonic Wars there were only two or three thousand of them, among about a hundred times as many hand looms; twenty years later some hundred thousand power looms were operating. When by mid-century Britain had become "the workshop of the world," as well as its leading shipper and banker, countries awakening to the possibilities could profit by her experience and build up more rapidly. Germany in particular came on with a rush, soon emerging as the greatest industrial power on the Continent. America, spurred by the needs of its Civil War and aided by its wealth of natural resources, started on the spectacular industrial career that as soon made it the greatest power on earth.

In retrospect, this whole development looks quite natural, logical, even inevitable. Authorities now approve the "happy formula" of Sir William Ashley, that it was less a revolution than an "irresistible evolution"—presumably a more scientific word for it (not to say a gentler one in an age grown weary of revolutions). Almost certainly it has at least become irresistible; this side of universal catastrophe, one cannot imagine men putting a stop to invention, much less giving up their machines. The only live issue is the question whether men can master their technology, control the terrific power they have generated. But for this reason it is the more important to recognize that the whole development was man's own doing, not strictly inevitable in the sense of predetermined by any impersonal, external law. To understand the effects it has had on human freedom we must first look into its causes or conditions, always remembering that there was no such revolution or evolution in any other civilization. Today the many leaders in the non-Western world who are trying hard to modernize their countries will testify that for most men industrialism is still not at all "natural."

In general, the pioneers of the Industrial Revolution came out of an old tradition, the genius for technology and business that Western Christendom had displayed from its dawn, or even in the Dark Ages.[5] Their mixed motives may be described as predominantly economic or materialistic, but in any case they accentuate the importance of ideas— greed alone has never made any kind of revolution. With their ingenuity went a readiness for innovation and adventure, which in the past had led to such epoch-making feats as the discovery of the New World, and had then made Europeans more open to change by enlarging their ideas of the world. They were further stimulated by the spreading faith in progress, one of the most novel of Western ideas, owing primarily to the rise of modern science. Science itself may now seem the obvious explanation of the Industrial Revolution, since we think of technology as applied science, but the connection was indirect and again broadly intellectual rather than economic. None of the English inventors who brought on the revolution built directly on the scientific discoveries of the preceding century, as inventors later would on discoveries about electricity. What the pioneers owed science was the pervasiveness of its outlook, the respectability of pragmatic interests, and the wide dissemination of useful knowledge (by contrast with the craft mysteries in ancient technology); they spearheaded a fresh development by combining an interest in business and technics with experimental methods and something of the scientific spirit. And such novel enterprise points to a more specific key. The Industrial Revolution got under steam in

5 For the signs and the possible sources of this practical genius, see *Freedom in the Western World*, pp. 39–40, 45–46, 52–53, 72–75.

England but took a long time to reach the Continent, which knew as much science. (Only little Belgium caught on to it quickly.) It owed most plainly to English tradition.

In the Elizabethan Age England had foreshadowed the revolution by a great expansion of industry, especially the production and use of coal, which made it the leader of European technology. In the eighteenth century it had other economic advantages, including the largest foreign markets and the largest amount of private capital. Most important, however, the English were the freest people in Europe. They had made and finished their political revolution, which enabled them to pursue their other interests relatively undistracted by the political fears that haunted other states. One sign of their freedom was an exceptional degree of mobility, in a society ruled by the aristocracy but comprising a large, fluid, independent middle class; many of the industrial pioneers were sons of ordinary workmen, like as not educated in the new Mechanics' Institutes. Another sign was freedom of association and public discussion, exemplified by the many private societies and an uncommonly free press. Still more pertinent was a tradition of individualism. Stemming from the lusty Elizabethan Age, with its many adventurers, this had been supported on different grounds by Puritanism, or the "Protestant ethic." As Sir William Petty observed in the seventeenth century, "Trade is most vigorously carried on, in every state and government, by the heterodox part of the same; and such as profess opinions different from what are publicly established." Societies formed by the pioneers—notably the Manchester Philosophical Society—included consciously heterodox types like the Quaker John Dalton and the freethinking Joseph Priestley, luminaries in the rising science of chemistry; but all the industrial entrepreneurs were departing from long-established practices, disrupting the traditional order that still prevailed on the Continent.

Granted that the Industrial Revolution was an unplanned affair, or a social evolution, it was nevertheless made by individuals; and it brings up an issue of particular importance in this volume. Western civilization had already made more of the individual, in both theory and practice, than had any other civilization. Wedding Greek ideals of freedom to the Christian ideal of the sanctity of the person, it was beginning to assure him a private realm by bills of rights that protected him against both church and state. From now on it would offer him more economic opportunity and incentive, a wider range of choice in occupation and habitat, and education to implement his choice. But with the Industrial

Revolution it also began to generate powerful new pressures against the individual, of which totalitarianism is only the latest form. Tending immediately to lose his identity in a more impersonal kind of economy, in which his labor was bought and sold like everything else, he was due to become a cog in immense social machinery, while in his private life he was subjected to the pressures of an increasingly standardized mass society. He was then belittled in theory too by the rising social sciences, which cultivated a similar impersonality. He was treated as a mere product of his society or culture; he counted for nothing in view of the "vast, impersonal forces" that governed history; and even his reality was denied—he would be described as a "discredited hypothesis," since he was only a cell in the "social organism," which was the scientific reality. Not to mention his notorious fate of being buried in statistics, or transmuted into the monster known as the "average man," the type that has $2\frac{1}{2}$ children.

Hence I should emphasize the importance of the creative individual in the Industrial Revolution itself. To me it seems obvious that every specific innovation throughout history must have been the work of some individual, just as was every new idea—ideas cannot come out of the head of "society" even if it is called the social organism. The individual remains the most apparent agent of all social, cultural change, the more so because most men are creatures of custom (or as Bertrand Russell said, would sooner die than think—and in fact do so). But now we have more concrete evidence, including sufficient statistics to impress social scientists. I have previously cited Margaret Hodgen's *Change and History*, a thoroughly documented study of technological change in England over a thousand years, covering the records of some 12,000 parishes, which indicates that down to 1900 more than 10,000 of these parishes never once ventured on a technological innovation by taking up a new craft. During the Industrial Revolution itself they remained simple agricultural communities, clinging to their traditional ways, only buying some of the improved tools and new products turned out elsewhere. Hence it was not strictly "England" that started this revolution—it was a number of Englishmen, some of them inventive, more of them bold enough to risk their fortunes on a new kind of business. In particular it was some enterprising individualists in the barren North Country, who had the wit to exploit the mineral resources, water power, and nearby harbors that had always been available there, and the courage to defy venerable tradition, the common hostility of not only the landed aristocracy but the great majority of businessmen still devoted to tried and true methods. Presently some of these frontiersmen turned into such influential crusaders as Robert Owen, Richard Cobden, and John Bright. When the tempo of change quickened and industrialism became an irresistible tide, this is still to say that more individuals were taking to new ways, getting into the habit and then the business of innovation. From first to last the "impersonal" forces gathered strength from the creativity of many persons.

On behalf of the individual, we must then add that the Industrial Revolution was hardly impelled by the ideal of the free, full development and expression of personality. The pioneers were seldom much concerned with the freedom of others. The gospel of individualism that grew popular came down to simple self-seeking, often at the expense of others; the devil might take the foremost as well as the hindmost. The values of individuality might not be realized by the rugged individualists themselves. Although some of the early pioneers were cultivated men of broad, humane interests, like Josiah Wedgwood, their followers included many more men who were exclusively devoted to business and could look like slaves to it, not very free persons by civilized standards. "This amassing of wealth is one of the species of idolatry," observed none other than Andrew Carnegie early in his career, "—no idol more debasing than the worship of money"; yet he admitted that "nothing could be allowed to interfere for a moment with my business career." In society at large the increasing preoccupation with business tended to obscure the values of high culture, the pursuit of truth, goodness, and beauty through which the individual might realize his potentialities more fully, and have more of a mind and a character of his own.

As for industry itself, one consequence might have startled the founders of the Manchester Philosophical Society. An executive of International Business Machines recently remarked that "the most significant change" within industry in the past twenty-five years "has been the discovery that science is important." This might seem to be a remarkably belated discovery—except for the early divorce of business from intellectual interests. The growth of capitalism, which had put the new machines to work, had discouraged such "impractical" interests as philosophy and pure science.

3. *The Rise of Capitalism*

While many men have virtually identified capitalism with democracy, and many others have regarded it as the major enemy of freedom in the modern world, everybody agrees that it has been a mighty force in our revolutionary history, and so especially needs to be understood. And all but the most violent partisans might at least agree on some preliminary observations that make possible a cooler look at it. Capitalism is another distinctively Western development. Although economic historians differ on the extent to which business approached it in antiquity, no other society settled down into this kind of economy, or ever approached the scale of modern business. Accordingly the growth of industrial capitalism was again not due to simple greed, of which all civilized societies have had an ample share. Still less was it due to a lust for political power, any plot to rule the world: while businessmen sought and got enough power to protect their interests, they typically remained preoccupied with private business and left government to others. Essentially it was a spontaneous, organic development, providing the organization required by the new technology. Hence it was inventive—for better or worse—and to this extent a novel institution. But it too was deeply rooted in European tradition.

To recapitulate briefly the history outlined in *Freedom in the Western World,* the seeds of capitalism began sprouting in the very dawn of Western civilization. Medieval merchants early acquired the habit of plowing their profits back into business, accumulating capital instead of hoarding gold or buying landed estates on which to retire and live like gentlemen, as their Roman forebears had been wont to do. They also began forming trading companies, to further their interests in a highly unsettled society still lacking strong central government. By the thirteenth century big banking houses were growing up, firmly establishing financial capitalism. By the sixteenth century some of these houses, notably the Fuggers, were engaged as well in both commercial and industrial capitalism; among other things, the House of Fugger carried on trade in spices, manufactured cloth, and worked mines. Already business was bigger and more highly organized than it had ever been in the Roman Empire. Its growth may be described—quite objectively—as a growth of economic rationality. Mere custom gave way to a more definite system of private enterprise, based on calculated risk, further rationalized by such new institutions as the Bourse and such inventions as double-entry booking; presently it gave birth to the brand-new "science" of economics. The calculating spirit may obviously be a mean one, hostile to spiritual interests, and it repelled many men when it was exalted into the philosophy of Utilitarianism; but in any case it did promote the principle of utility, which is clearly rational and not necessarily ignoble. Now it developed the new technology, the mechanization that may be described as a rationalization of industry.

For such purposes England again had advantages, beyond its considerable capital and abundant resources of coal. Its authorities had ceased resisting the germinal idea that economic progress was both possible and desirable—an idea that now seems perfectly natural, but that never really took hold in ancient Rome, and was quite alien to the medieval guilds. (As late as the seventeenth century decrees prohibited the use of new inventions.) It had given much freer play to private enterprise than had France, for example, where since the reign of Louis XIV the royal government had managed much business. Characteristically, England was the first country to recognize the rights of invention, protected by patents. And behind all such potentialities, once more, was the leaven of the English tradition of individualism. Because the new technology now looks so obviously more efficient and therefore profitable, we may forget that initially it was by no means easy work, bringing in easy money. Lacking political support or any organized backing, the early manufacturer had to be a sturdy individualist, uncommonly enterprising and resourceful.

His factory, the primary symbol of industrialism, was not wholly new either. In France factories had been set up by the government of Louis XIV. Both in England and on the Continent merchant-manufacturers had for several centuries been organizing production by supplying workers in villages with raw materials, sometimes with tools, and then buying the finished cloth at fixed rates. Yet the introduction of machinery in England meant a radical change: instead of bringing work to the home, employers brought workers to a factory. For some time the change proceeded slowly just because it was so radical. Manufacturers had to learn the arts of industrial management; workers had to be trained in not only new techniques but habits of regularity and punctuality—a "new discipline" that was so far from being natural to man that it may still be regarded as soul-killing. (Travelers in "backward" countries may appreciate both the abnormal-ity and the possible blessings of these habits.) Although after 1815 the factory system at last began to expand rapidly, the Industrial Revolution was long complicated by the survival of economic methods it had anti-quated. In mid-century, when England was the world's workshop, many obsolete little textile establishments were still carrying on, and many more weavers were working in their homes for only an eighth of the wages paid workers in large factories.

With the factories grew large companies that were very different from the family-owned House of Fugger. Partnerships or firms were common early in the Industrial Revolution, as men pooled the neces-sary technical and commercial skills, and they grew into stock com-panies as other men learned that it might pay to invest their savings in industry (another idea that most have yet to learn in the under-developed countries). Companies also began learning that it might pay to combine, if sometimes for the possibly nefarious purpose of eliminat-ing competition. From mid-century on the joint-stock company was the standard form of business organization, described honorifically as a means of "democratizing" capital, but flourishing simply for good business reasons, and producing the great bulk of manufactured goods. By the end of the century industrial capitalism had become really big business, represented in America by such giants or monsters as Standard Oil and Andrew Carnegie's steel empire. The latter served as the nucleus of U.S. Steel, the first billion-dollar corporation, formed in 1901. The great corporation climaxed the major trend in capitalism, which was reflected in all other social activities—the drive to organization. The nineteenth century might be called the Age of Organization.

Meanwhile the novel philosophy of capitalism had become so firmly established that businessmen hardly realized that it was a mere theory. Known popularly as *laissez faire* or free private enterprise, based in more technical terms on the principle of the self-regulating market, this too was a contribution of England, specifically of Adam Smith in the dawn of the Industrial Revolution. The physiocrats in eighteenth-century France who coined the term *"laissez faire"* had still substan-tially accepted the traditional system of mercantilism, calling for free trade but otherwise taking for granted government regulation of busi-ness in the national interest, while English businessmen had not clamored for freedom if only because their government had put them under relatively little regulation since the Glorious Revolution. In *The Wealth of Nations* (1776) Smith was the first to formulate clearly and comprehensively the logic of a self-regulating market. Briefly, his argument was that self-interest produced competition, which in turn produced the goods needed by society; in a free market it led to automatic self-regulation by an "unseen hand" because the incompetent were doomed to fail, those prospered who best supplied the needs of society; and so out of constant competition or economic strife came a kind of social harmony. As his follower Ricardo put it, "The pursuit of individual advantage is admirably connected with the universal good of the whole." In other words, Adam Smith argued that *laissez faire* was the rational economic means to the Enlightenment ideal of progress. Although his optimism was for some time obscured by the popularity of the grim Malthusian theory, it fired more thinkers as the Industrial Revolution gathered momentum. The rising capitalists, who at first had no theory but expediency, naturally welcomed this support when their interests collided with those of the landed aristocracy who controlled the government. Well before the middle of the century *laissez faire* became a militant creed, and by the end of the century it was the common sense of conservatives, above all in America.

The actual practice of both business and government was rather different, bringing up anomalies that we must presently consider. But the immediate point remains that industrial capitalism gave business more autonomy than it had ever enjoyed before. While under some state regulation, it had enough political power to have its own way for the most part; for the first time in history the economy was basically a self-directed system. It was a wholly secular system too, by now effectively divorced from religion, operating on principles formulated by economists—a breed of men unknown to any past society.[6] Christian tradition was strong enough to produce the new gospel that capitalism was God's plan for man (even though he had neglected to bless the profit motive in Scripture), but churchgoing businessmen took for granted that on weekdays "business is business," and made their Bible the law of supply and demand (even if they sought to circumvent rather than obey this law). The economy was in effect separated from society except for the assumption that on its freedom and health depended political freedom and social health.

---

[6] Medieval theologians, such as St. Thomas Aquinas, were much concerned about business practice, but of course had no idea of an independent science of economics. They were merely trying to spell out the Christian principles on which businessmen ought to operate, and worried so much over problems like determining the "just price" because they knew that the actual ruling principle of business was simply to buy cheap and sell dear. Today a teacher can easily baffle American students by asking them why this principle might be considered unchristian.

Now, the paradox that unregulated self-interest is the best means to the communal good may have a utopian air to all but businessmen; so first one should note that it made good sense in the relatively simple economy of Adam Smith's day. In another generation it made better sense because of the remarkable achievements of entrepreneurs who were freer than their fellows on the Continent. The plainest justification of the capitalistic system was its immense productivity, granted even by Marxists. It produced an unprecedented abundance of goods: first of all the staples, clothes and household goods; then in time all manner of comforts and conveniences unknown to the wealthiest men of the past. Granted that the capitalists were animated by the profit motive, and that this could be exorbitant, it was neither simply mean nor necessarily antisocial. They could no more be misers than stand-patters as they kept expanding business, manifestly finding the game of making money more exciting and rewarding than the mere possession of it; they were types still rare in the non-Western world, which therefore remained "underdeveloped." Most of them made their fortune by producing consumers' goods, satisfying the wants of their society. One reason why the intelligentsia grew hostile to them was that they gave the public what it wanted, "cheap" goods, instead of what intellectuals thought the public ought to want. Today the rulers of the Soviet are only beginning to catch up with the offerings of the wicked capitalists.

One may then add—still quite objectively—that industrial capitalism nevertheless fell considerably short of its ostensible ideal of a rational, efficient economy. It incidentally rewarded dishonesty as well as ability, encouraging much corruption and fraud; one scandalous example was the patent medicine industry. By its success the system fostered a great deal of unproductive speculation and unearned increment, as in rents; owners of real estate could make millions by merely sitting tight and holding on. Worse, the system repeatedly broke down, and the crashes or panics grew into world-wide depressions. Although men had known hard times all through history, especially scarcity due to drought or natural disaster, these depressions were novel in that they were man-made and due to overproduction, a glut of goods that were still wanted, even needed, but that could not be sold. Eventually economists noted the remarkable regularity of the business cycle, but they proposed nothing helpful to do about it, even insisting that it was quite normal and that recovery must be allowed to come by itself: the experts of a self-directed or undirected system were generally not distinguished for either insight or social common sense. The chief sufferers from the crashes, naturally, were poor workmen. Another distinctive feature of developed capitalism was chronic, widespread unemployment—itself another new term in the modern lexicon, not used by the classical economists of the nineteenth century.

Both the triumphs and the shortcomings of capitalism were most conspicuous in the United States, where businessmen enjoyed the most freedom and opportunity. Here they distinguished themselves by exceptional energy and daring enterprise as they built up a continent, spanned it with railways, and mechanized both agriculture and industry. In one generation after the Civil War they made America the industrial leader of the world. Somewhat less well known is their service as middlemen in opening up the continent, for it was they—not the pioneering homesteaders of popular legend—who directly acquired most of the Western land from the government, and parceled it out. But these not so daring businessmen pointed to one of the main sources of wealth in America, which was pure speculation. They made fortunes by acquiring large tracts of land from the government for a song, doing nothing to improve the land, perhaps never even seeing it. Otherwise their chief contribution to the economy was the panics they helped to bring on, together with big speculators on the markets, by overreaching themselves. They pointed as well to the huge wastefulness of natural resources that distinguished American capitalism, and to the national routines of graft. Corruption and fraud were much more flagrant in America than in Europe, partly because businessmen had bigger sums of money to gamble with, but also because Americans admired "smartness" and deplored only petty theft. As the poet said in "The Latest Decalogue," stealing is "an empty feat when it's so lucrative to cheat." In England businessmen who defrauded the public were subject to severe penalties, one banker (Fauntleroy) even being hanged. In America such punishment for business crimes was unthinkable; its "robber barons" were mostly not punished at all, and exposure of fraud hardly meant public disgrace, still less loss of prestige in the business community. The freedom most cherished by many American capitalists in the nineteenth century was freedom from all social responsibility.

Such youthful excesses bring up the basic anomalies that became more pronounced as capitalism matured. Adam Smith himself had by no means glorified businessmen, instead warning against "the mean rapacity, the monopolizing spirit of the merchants and manufacturers," and emphasizing that they "neither are nor ought to be the rulers of mankind." As for corporate enterprises, he observed that "people of the same trade seldom meet together, even for merriment or diversion, but the conversation ends in a conspiracy against the public, or in some contrivance to raise prices"; and he had as low an opinion of corporations on economic grounds, believing that they would naturally lack a sufficiently enlightened self-interest. He may accordingly look like a poor prophet, the more so because he failed to foresee the Industrial Revolution. But like almost all other prophets he might have complained that his gospel was never tried. The principle of free trade grew popular in England chiefly in matters of grain, and elsewhere it was never cherished; both America and the Continent set about protecting home industries, in keeping with the old tradition of mercantilism. (In a funeral elegy for Alexander Hamilton, a friend praised him for having resisted the "fuzzy philosophy" of Adam Smith.) A primary reason was that businessmen themselves had no passion for entirely free competition, as Smith well knew. While the champions of free private enterprise have to this day celebrated the supreme virtue of competition, capitalists have always sought to reduce or escape it by tariff, trust, monopoly, and cartel.

Another paradox that the champions have failed to appreciate grew out of the indispensable boon of public enterprise. Government did a good deal to promote the rapid development of trade and industry. Besides tariffs, franchises, subsidies, and other gifts (for instance, the huge grants of public lands to railroad companies in America), it built highways and canals, and it provided legal and monetary regulations to facilitate the operations of free markets; what Adam Smith described as "simple and natural liberty" called for extensive planning by the state. The maintenance of state support in turn required a good deal of bureaucratic machinery. The growth of industrialism, and therefore of an increasingly complex, massive society, was bound in any case to result in big government, but free private enterprise helped directly to assure this outcome by its demands as well as its shortcomings. It created its own bugbear, now known as "creeping socialism."

Still more paradoxical were the effects of the great corporation. With its rise the captain of industry—the big, bold entrepreneur—gave way to another historically new type, the professional business executive, who no longer owned the business he managed. Usually a cautious type, described by Veblen as a captain of finance, he called attention to the rise of the great financiers, a kind of reversion to medieval capitalism.

In America, the most awesome power in the land by the end of the century was J. P. Morgan, controller of corporations worth some seventeen billions; an incidental addition to his industrial estate was U.S. Steel, formed after he bought out Andrew Carnegie. But in particular the corporation best exemplified how politically conservative businessmen continued to operate as economic revolutionaries, faithfully performing their Marxist role of revolutionizing the means of production, and in this role working as busily to antiquate their own slogans, above all their gospel of individualism. More than two generations ago John D. Rockefeller himself declared meaningless the chants that still resound today. "The age of combination is here to stay," said the builder of Standard Oil. "Individualism has gone, never to return." His observation needs to be qualified, since big business still provides scope for what he meant by individualism—rugged, aggressive acquisitiveness. (His own most favored industry continues to breed Texas multimillionaires.) Nevertheless he was essentially right. The big corporations had squeezed out many little businessmen, they were due to get ever bigger and control the great bulk of American industry, and they made economic individualism a luxury available chiefly to the few men at the top, not very meaningful to their millions of employees.

Similarly they magnified the obvious social problems raised by capitalism. Many selfish, unprincipled, ruthless men made good in the rising industrialism—but so they had in all past societies. The most serious troubles sprang from the very nature of an autonomous system that was by all odds the most impersonal economy known to history. It was epitomized by the big corporation: nominally owned by its stockholders, actually managed by its board of directors, always sustained by hired workers—all virtually unknown to one another; so a man in a remote office could press a button laying off thousands of other men without ever seeing any of the workers who then suffered hardship, or the stockholders whose interests he was protecting. That the corporation came to be defined legally as a "person," endowed with rights to life, liberty, and the pursuit of happiness, only emphasized the possible abuses of its essential impersonality. It forced the first and last question about the immense power created by the Industrial Revolution. How intelligently, responsibly, justly, was this power being exercised for human, social purposes?

It is fair to say that the capitalists of the nineteenth century were not eminent for a sense of social responsibility, least of all in most enterprising America. The novel system was hardly calculated to promote such a sense. Despite all professions of Christian or democratic idealism, however sincere, the main objective of the system was not freedom, justice, the good life, or any spiritual values—it was only wealth and power, first of all profits for the men on top. If all economies have served chiefly material interests, the important difference remained that for the first time economic interests were considered primary on principle, and state interference with them was condemned as not only unwise but immoral, in America even unchristian. An autonomous system regulated itself in ways less economical and efficient for social purposes because of its impersonality; again the corporation, which separated management from ownership, made it easier for both to disregard any higher responsibility. Altogether, there is no question that an immensely productive economy was not clearly productive of social health.

4. *The Social and Cultural Consequences*

As we now come to our major concern in this history, the effects of the Industrial Revolution on man's freedom, nothing would seem clearer than that they have been profoundly, inextricably mixed; but nothing seems harder to keep clearly, steadily in mind. If anything, writers today tend to oversimplify its issues more violently than they did in the nineteenth century. So let us begin by rehearsing the most obvious, basic ambiguity. The revolution indisputably brought an extraordinary material progress, which has meant a much higher standard of living for most men, more opportunity or effective freedom, a wider range of choice in both material and spiritual goods—solid gains that have been obscured by the ancient convention of regarding wealth as merely demoralizing, and especially by the easy habit of taking our goods for granted. At the same time, no man in his senses will maintain that the revolution has been simply an emancipation, all to the good; it generated not only some universally admitted social evils but new forms of compulsion, massive tendencies to regimentation and dehumanization, a pervasive kind of psychological unfreedom, and in the individual a feeling of impotence intensified by the immense collective power. If almost all thinkers recognize some such duality, many have confused it by attributing the gains to some vague progressive forces while blaming all the evils on capitalism or the machine; whereas the whole industrial system has plainly contributed to both. Our subject is a continuously revolutionary history that should both hearten and dismay all but the blindest reactionaries, the shallowest liberals, and the most doctrinaire Communists.

In a longer historical perspective, however, it is fairly easy to get our main bearings. The ambiguous consequences of the Industrial Revolution hark back to the basic paradox of civilization itself, which from its beginnings meant a great increase in collective wealth and power, and for a great many of its toilers meant more want and less freedom than prehistoric or primitive peoples have generally known. At every point we meet ancient evils in new guises, and new problems aggravated by ancient habits and beliefs. At this point, where I am introducing themes that will be developed in subsequent chapters, one theme is the difficulty of realizing fully at once how old and how novel the drama is.

In this long view we may immediately qualify somewhat the notorious horrors of early industrialism. Shocking as was the condition of most factory workers, especially the many women and children, it was far from novel. In the North Country, the cradle of the revolution, this was no blight on merrie England; one incentive of the early manufacturers here was the unrelieved poverty of the common people. All over Europe, in village as in town, the working people had for centuries toiled long hours, usually for very low wages, and their womenfolk and children had always worked too. Defenders of the traditional aristocratic order were typically like Edmund Burke, as indifferent to their plight as were the "sophisters, economists, and calculators" whose rise he deplored. ("When we affect to pity as poor those who must labor," Burke wrote,"we are trifling with the condition of mankind.") Similarly the drudgery of machine tending has been somewhat exaggerated by the fashion of romanticizing the Middle Ages, the joy of its artisans in their creative kind of work; for their work was hardly spontaneous and most of them managed to keep their joy to themselves, on the record spreading chiefly the belief that labor is the unhappy lot of man. No more have peasants ever been so rhapsodical as literary men over the beauties of nature, the elemental rhythms of life, the joy of growing things, or the blessed simplicities of "Sweet Auburn, loveliest village of the plain." Furthermore, the miseries of the poor were intensified by the recurrence of old problems, such as poor harvests and high food prices, and in England by another wave of land enclosures, which as in the sixteenth century pauperized many villagers. It was landlords, not manufacturers, who instituted the harsh "Speenhamland system" of poor relief, doles to eke out starvation wages that encouraged farmers to keep wages low.

Otherwise there was some excuse for the early evils in that England was quite unprepared for the revolutionary developments that almost no one had anticipated. Governments lacked the machinery, towns the authority, to cope with them. Laws and institutions, like customs and beliefs, were naturally geared to an obsolescent economic and social order. Thinkers were not yet dwelling on the "cultural lag" that has become a commonplace in a revolutionary world (though in our sophistication we have only named the lag, not done away with it). Thus traditionalists who are properly horrified by the evils that came in with industrialism usually overlook the failure of the major churches to do anything about them—a failure that can be condoned only in the light of Christian tradition; for high churchmen took for granted that the poor must always be with us, by the will or the grace of God. It is now hard to realize that well into the Victorian era devout Christians still believed that all natural calamity—for instance the terrible potato famine in Ireland—was intended by the Almighty as a lesson to man.[7] It is as hard to appreciate our blessing in no longer having to worry about famines, for this was the last one of consequence in western Europe.

Yet there is no getting away from the shocking conditions on which early industrialism throve. They need to be recalled because of the many millions who all along—to this day even in wealthy America— enjoyed a very meager share of the benefits of industrial progress, and paid much more than their share of its costs. Women and children were better suited to factory work than men, who, as Richard Arkwright complained, did not readily "conform to the regular celerity of the machine," and they could also be hired for less; so they were soon putting in a twelve- to fourteen-hour day, or working from sunup to sundown, in what Blake called these "dark Satanic mills." The poor-law authorities in England cooperated by delivering batches of fifty or a hundred pauper children to factory owners, requiring them to accept a number of idiots but leaving them free to use the youngsters as they saw fit. Leaders of society shared the sentiment of Alexander

---

[7] This belief was expressly stated by Sir Charles Trevelyan, head of the British Treasury, who was responsible for dealing with the famine. He viewed it with some optimism, assuming that the Roman Catholic priests in Ireland would spell out the divine lesson to their flock.

Hamilton: "Women and children are rendered more useful, and the latter more early useful, by manufacturing establishments than they would otherwise be." An MP pointed out that children enjoyed an added advantage because they were removed from the company of their "miserable and depraved parents," while Dr. Ure immortalized himself by an account of the "lively elves" who found so much sport in being useful in factories, those "magnificent edifices" that were so much more ingenious and profitable than the boasted monuments of ancient despotism. The elves had to keep lively, since they were commonly beaten when they slowed up because of fatigue. They worked harder in mines, though nobody could pretend that these were magnificent establishments; here boys and girls were chained and harnessed to coal trucks like horses, except that they were not indulged with horse collars. On their day of rest they might build up their character in Sunday schools by contributing a penny a week toward their funerals, arranged by burial clubs.

As degrading were the industrial towns to which workers returned at night. Ugly, grimy, filthy, these were soon on their way to becoming the worst blight on the landscape in all history, "making a new Heaven and a new Earth—both black." Lacking sanitation and sometimes enough water, they became ideal breeding centers for consumption, typhus, or whatever plague was handy. Always congested, they lacked as well parks, playgrounds, or any civic amenities except Sunday schools. (As late as 1842 an official reported that in thriving Lancashire there was only one town with a public park and one with public baths.) The obvious contrast with the cities of the ancient "despotic" Roman world—towns less wealthy, but infinitely richer in amenities—brings up a more positive deprivation of the workers. In antiquity workers had enjoyed many days of festival, with ample provision for public amusement, and medieval Europe had continued the tradition of frequent holiday and festivity. Industrial England was no longer merry for both religious and economic reasons: amusement was considered bad for workers, a threat to the "new discipline." Thus a delegation of manufacturers went to London to protest against a bill for the establishment of a licensed theater in Birmingham, informing Parliament that "the Exhibition of Plays have been deemed extremely prejudicial to the Manufactures carried on here, having a Tendency to promote Negligence, create Expense, and corrupt the Morals of the Industrious"; and they were supported by the Bishop of London and the Archbishop of Canterbury, who agreed that a playhouse was indeed a menace in "a great trading manufacturing town." Lacking any other public recreation, workers were more inclined to take to gin; whereupon respectable port drinkers were more convinced of their natural depravity.

At that, industrial workers in England were better off than other victims of the new system, in particular the many handworkers who for over fifty years fought a losing battle against the machine. Labor-saving devices were of course labor-destroying too, and so called out the Luddites, who inspired mobs to smash the hated machines. The spreading protests at first only frightened conservatives, stiffened opposition to efforts at reform. Protestant tradition had by now evolved the conviction that success in business was a sign of godliness, poverty a sign of shiftlessness. The godly went on to prove that God in his wisdom had made poverty not only natural and necessary but beneficial. A decade after *The Wealth of Nations*, William Townsend, who signed himself "a Wellwisher of Mankind," published a dissertation on the Poor Law attacking it as a disruption of "the harmony and beauty, the symmetry and order, of that system which God and nature have established to the world"; efforts to relieve the poor could only create ill will, "whereas hunger is not only peaceable, silent, unremitting pressure, but as the most natural motive to industry and labor, calls forth the most powerful exertions . . . lays lasting and sure foundations for good will and gratitude." At the turn of the century the most influential Malthus (another cleric) most positively condemned the masses to poverty by his iron law of population, which decreed an endless struggle for insufficient food; he accordingly denounced proposed reforms as both absurd and costly, while flatly rejecting "the *right* of the poor to support." Ricardo added his "iron law of wages," which demonstrated that wages would always tend to stabilize at the bare subsistence level. Together they compounded the misfortune that the "dismal science," as economics then became known, developed at a time when its practitioners were still blind to the revolutionary possibilities of industrialism. (A generation later Benjamin Jowett remarked that he always felt a "certain horror" of economists since hearing one of them say that "he feared the famine in Ireland would not kill more than a million people, and that would scarcely be enough to do much good.") The conventional textbooks of the century would give as unrealistic an account of the economy as medieval political thinkers gave of feudal society.

Most fateful for the long run was the growing popularity of Adam Smith's thesis of the self-regulating market. He himself offered this as no gospel but a theory, reasonably qualified, and he conceived his economic "laws" as servants of human interests, not as iron laws that man had to obey willy-nilly. He did not propose, however, that the government step in to protect any class, and his followers vigorously attacked government interference with business as both economically unsound and morally reprehensible. They made a significant exception: government regulation was evil when it protected workers, but legitimate when it aided businessmen. Hence they applauded the Parliamentary Act of 1799 that made illegal all combinations of workingmen, even though trade unionism was a century old. No more did God's ministers help workers when they tried to help themselves; they too now denounced unionism as revolutionary. In general, the celebration of economic freedom confirmed the traditional view that the essence of freedom is the absence of constraints, while it ignored both the evident constraints on workers and the drastically limited opportunities that gave them little real freedom to make anything of themselves. As Anatole France would observe, the poor were after all just as free as the rich to sleep under bridges. And the abiding issues were further confused because the early supporters of *laissez faire* were known as "liberals." They deserved the name inasmuch as they were opposed by the conservatives of their day, and in fact helped to liberate a great deal of energy and enterprise; but with success they became political conservatives, defending the *status quo*, opposing all effort at reform.

In short, the apostles of capitalism seemed bent on proving Marx's charge in the *Communist Manifesto* that it had reduced the worker to a mere "appendage of the machine," reduced all human relations to "naked self-interest and callous cash payment." Their policies might have seemed calculated to make revolutionaries of the workers, and they at least succeeded in stirring up bitter class struggle. Yet this recalls another truth, especially deplorable to Marxists: the class struggle did not lead to revolution in the most industrialized countries, as the *Manifesto* argued it must. By the end of the century workers were generally least disposed to overthrow their government by violence in countries that had the largest proletariat. The plainest reason was that on the whole they were enjoying a distinctly higher standard of living than were the common people in all other countries, or than workers ever had enjoyed in all history. To be sure, they still had ample reason not to feel simply grateful to the industrialists who had made this possible, for they had had to fight for every gain, a great many of them were still very poor, and they all remained liable to hardship because of the recurrent depressions that came with the new economy. When Andrew Carnegie, for example, was making some $20,000,000 a year, on which he paid no income tax whatever, his steelworkers were putting in a twelve-hour day and seven-day week to earn about $500 a year, and they had no social security whatever. But in order to size up the abiding problems we need to review the positive gains resulting from the Industrial Revolution, which until lately were slighted in most studies of it.

As a nation, England obviously prospered. Malthus notwithstanding, it had no real trouble supporting a population that doubled in the first half of the nineteenth century. Industrialism helped by producing mainly cheap consumers' goods, while the land enclosures at least substantially increased agricultural production.[8] If at first most workers remained poor, and many felt worse because of the appearances of greater wealth in the upper middle class, an increasing number became appreciably better off. Economic historians are still disputing whether or to what extent real wages rose early in the century, but there are some pretty clear signs of an improved standard of living, for example, the growth of savings banks, popular newspapers, schools, and educational societies for workmen. Toward the end of the century real wages indisputably went up, in England jumping some 50 per cent in one generation. Common people in the industrialized countries were on their way to their current standard of living, spectacularly higher than that of the technologically backward countries. Whether they were thereby happier it is impossible to say with assurance; but there is no question whatever that most of them possessed more of the material means to happiness—and that other peoples today seem willing to jeopardize their contentment or their possibly more blessed spiritual state for the sake of such means.

As novel in a historical perspective was a related development in the first half of the century. We know of the early horrors of the Industrial Revolution chiefly through a series of reports by Royal Commissions and Committees of Inquiry, recording them in full, specific detail. From these reports Karl Marx got most of his material on industrial capitalism, but without due acknowledgment of their novelty: we know much less about the state of workers before this time because no such

---

[8] Recent researches by economic historians have shown that rural population grew too, in spite of all the supposedly deserted villages, and that many small farmers prospered. One reason was that the unenclosed fields or village commons had been very poorly cultivated.

inquiries had ever been made by government in the past. As Herbert Heaton has observed, what was revolutionary was not the evils but the discovery that they were evils. It was not the ageless misery but the indignation over this misery, and then the positive, concerted efforts to do something about it. Private associations like the Friendly Societies began organizing philanthropy, inaugurating a broad cooperative movement in which such associations would grow much more numerous and active. By the twenties Parliament bestirred itself, repealing the ban on labor unions and getting started on the series of mine and factory acts that provided some protection for women and children, eventually reduced the hours and improved the working conditions for all workers. Towns, granted more authority by the Municipal Corporations Act of 1835, began exercising it to assure better water supply, drainage, and sanitation. Edwin Chadwick launched his long campaign for government action to protect health, which produced the first Public Health Act. Hence when industrialization got started on the Continent it was attended by less misery in the factories and factory towns. Profiting by English experience, government was better prepared to cope with the problems it created and more promptly enacted the social legislation that distinguished the nineteenth century, above all from the *ancien régime*.

The "discovery" of social evils stemmed immediately from the humanitarian movement in the last decades of the eighteenth century, exemplified by the crusades of Elizabeth Fry for prison reform and William Wilberforce for the abolition of the slave trade. Wilberforce was typical of good Christians when he proceeded to join the movement to relieve the poor: he aimed primarily at the "moral uplift" of the poor, and sought only to relieve the symptoms of their plight, not to attack the basic social causes. Nevertheless the growing humanitarian sentiment counted for a good deal. Thus children had long been treated cruelly as apprentices or as workers in mines, not to mention early toil and routine use of the rod. (Even the liberal John Locke had said that they ought to be put to work at the age of three.) Only now did the idea spread that children had a natural right to a childhood of school and play, some measure of freedom from the cares and responsibilities of adulthood—an idea that later produced a characteristic but historically unprecedented Society for the Prevention of Cruelty to Children. Similarly the idea of women's rights now began spreading, after almost two thousand years of Christian history. The victims of the early factories were due to receive a novel protection, and then a more novel kind of opportunity in business, owing to the invention of the type-writer. The Industrial Revolution had much to do with the growing independence of women.

It had plainer connections with the whole effort to promote social welfare, aside from providing a conspicuous need for it. Some of the early manufacturers had been bred in the liberal, humanistic creed of the Enlightenment, as had Adam Smith.[9] Others were disposed by the rationale of capitalism to support such reforms as the abolition of slavery in Europe: Smith pointed out that slave labor was inefficient, actually "the dearest of any." Few employers were enlightened enough to perceive that poorly paid, overworked laborers might also be inefficient, but their self-interest at least enabled them to see the utility of Richard Cobden's crusade against the tariff on corn, the success of which was the most direct boon to the working class in this period. They might likewise come around to the idea that government do more to provide for basic social needs, support a measure of "municipal socialism," inasmuch as private enterprise would also benefit from healthier workers. In this regard an example was set by Joseph Chamberlain, who after quickly making a fortune in the screw business became mayor of Birmingham, and as quickly set about to make it a model city, providing municipal services, clearing out slums, bringing in an art gallery and a university—measures that reduced the death rate 30 per cent.

Most important, perhaps, was simply the livelier sense of possibility. Rooted in the Enlightenment faith in progress, this was now flourishing in an atmosphere of enthusiasm over the practical demonstrations of the power acquired by man. In 1796 Count Rumford (born an American) proposed the establishment of a Royal Institution for aiding the poor by "bringing forward into general use new inventions and improvements," including various "mechanical contrivances by which domestic comfort and economy may be promoted." Another generation and J. A. Etzler was proclaiming "The Paradise within the reach of all men, without labor, by the powers of nature and machinery," explaining how town planning and housing could be revolutionized by artifi-

---

9 Josiah Wedgwood, for example, expressed his sympathy with the cause of the French Revolution even though English politicians were warning that a free French people might become formidable business rivals:

"For my part I should be glad to see so near neighbors partake of the same blessing with ourselves, and indeed should rejoice to see English liberty and security spread over the face of the earth without being over-anxious about the effects they might have upon our manufactures or commerce, for I should be very loath to believe that an event so happy for mankind in general could be so injurious to us in particular."

cial lighting, central heating, and air conditioning. Englishmen would have to wait a long time for this paradise, but meanwhile some were dazzled by promises of one with as revolutionary spiritual improvements too. Both the evils and the potentialities of the Industrial Revolution had inspired the most remarkable of its pioneers—Robert Owen (1771–1858).

An exceptionally enterprising and efficient industrialist by ordinary business standards, Owen was an extraordinarily farsighted one. He not only attacked the social, moral degradation of the new factory system but demonstrated that it was unnecessary, even economically unsound. At New Lanark he provided better food and housing for his workmen, looked to their health, set up a community school, and in general created a decent environment in order to remove the causes of shiftlessness and drunkenness; and thereby he made his mill one of the most profitable in the land. Out of this experience he wrote his *New View of Society* (1813), in which he anticipated the social science of the future by arguing that character was formed in childhood by environment, society was responsible for what would be called juvenile delinquency. Among the first to agitate for factory reform, he also caught public attention by his proposal to set up cooperative village communities, immediately for economic purposes, but ultimately to prove his conviction that in view of "the new powers which men are about to acquire," only ignorance could prevent a society "without crime, without poverty, with health greatly improved, with little, if any misery, and with intelligence and happiness increased a hundred-fold." The failure of the community he himself founded in New Harmony in America only spurred him to broader conceptions of a new socialistic kind of society to be established the world over, in order to assure the breeding of the "new man." He may now look even more absurdly utopian than the dreamers of the Enlightenment, especially because he dismissed the whole past as "insanity" and denounced all religion, offering his program as a "NEW RELIGION, UNCONNECTED WITH FAITH." A dogmatic, intolerant, conceited man—as utopians often are—he grew more obsessed by his vision of a brand-new society, discouraging such vulgar means as a great working-class movement or direct political action.

Nevertheless, Owen dramatized the basic issues of the Industrial Revolution to lasting effect. Out of his profitable mill at New Lanark came fertile ideas that kept germinating, including an idea that businessmen would recognize a century later as "scientific management." If meanwhile his example hardly infected the business community at large, some were impressed by his argument that industrial slavery was even worse than Negro slavery, on both economic and moral grounds, and that social reform made for efficiency too. Immediately he succeeded in getting Parliament to pass the first major Factory Act (1819), which was portentous even though he disowned it because it was watered down. (He had made such radical proposals as that no child be allowed to work before the age of ten, or for more than 10½ hours a day.) His notion of an ideal cooperative community, which helped to inspire the many utopian experiments of the century, survived the failure of all the experiments; it remains alive in modern programs for community centers and garden cities, and was indeed pretty much realized in the *kibbutzim* of Israel.[10] First and last Owen insisted that the most important problems raised by the Industrial Revolution were social and cultural, not merely economic. In England he was the first to see clearly that the "new powers" were bound in any case to transform society, profoundly affect character, and that grave evils would as inevitably result if manufacturers were "left to their natural progress," i.e., to *laissez faire.* Although most businessmen and economists would remain dedicated to "natural progress," more and more thinkers came to agree that the new powers ought to be checked, subordinated to communal needs, and directed to civilized ends.

Owen's socialistic doctrines likewise influenced men who were more concerned than he with political action. The political revolutions are the subject of the next chapter, but here we may note briefly the basic connections between the Industrial Revolution and the growth and spread of popular government. Industrial capitalism was willy-nilly breaking up the traditional order, creating a more open society. Despite its strong oligarchic tendencies, it was a democratic kind of economy in that labor was theoretically free, in fact free enough to stimulate more mobility. It was building up a large urban proletariat, and as Marx would say, was "arming" this proletariat. It was also building up a large middle class, which lent indispensable support to the movement toward democracy. In England businessmen fought for the first Reform Bill

---

10 His own community at New Harmony survived the collapse of his plan for it, and its descendants gave the village considerable distinction down into this century. One member who joined it in Owen's time founded the first American public school open to both boys and girls. Owen's son Robert Dale was elected to the Indiana state legislature, where he battled for free public education and women's rights, and later as a U.S. congressman he introduced the bill creating the Smithsonian Institution. William E. Wilson has narrated the whole history of New Harmony in *The Angel and the Serpent.*

extending suffrage, since the industrial towns were not fairly represented in Parliament, and they took an active part in government,
producing such influential and relatively enlightened statesmen as
Richard Cobden, Sir Robert Peel, and John Bright. From the ranks
of the bourgeois everywhere came most of the social reformers and the
champions of the proletariat (including Marx himself). The calculating, rational spirit that had enabled a once anonymous "middle" class
to come up in the world could be turned against capitalism once it was
enthroned, and breed more discontent because of its vaunted freedom
and individualism. It is no accident that the cause of both intellectual
and political freedom was on the whole farthest advanced in the industrialized countries.

Still, most business leaders were scarcely dedicated to this cause. In
the United States, where capitalism was made the heart of the "American Way," they might be public-spirited or they might say frankly "the
public be damned," but their overriding concern remained economic
freedom for themselves. Elsewhere the rising business class usually remained content to leave government in the hands of the aristocracy,
which could be trusted to protect the interests of wealth. Everywhere
except England it suggested another basic anomaly in the new society.
Businessmen were in a sense the real leaders of this society, responsible
for the tremendous increase in wealth and power, apparently vindicating the faith of Malthus, who in emphasizing how advantageous self-
interest was to society gave added thanks to God for having so amply
endowed men with this motive. As a class they nevertheless revealed a
divine oversight: they were still quite unfitted for either social or political leadership. Despite their growing prestige they did not naturally
inspire reverence, and the greatest of them seldom became anything like
national heroes or got into Halls of Fame; the respect they won was less
for the man than for his money. Novelists and dramatists quite ignored
the captains of industry, except occasionally to ridicule them as social
parvenus. The better artists did not paint their portraits, showing more
interest in the faces of common folk. Their own womenfolk generally
took less interest in their enterprises than wives used to take in the feats
of squires, lords, and warriors. Even in America, where they excited
most awe, they eventually felt obliged to hire public relations men to
make up a suitable "image" of them.

They accordingly suggest the need of some caution as we approach
the cultural consequences of the Industrial Revolution. First of all, I
take it, we still need to emphasize the notorious materialism, the rule

of money and money values to an extent unknown in any great society of the past. It is reflected in many an unconsciously dreadful expression like "What is so-and-so *worth?*"—and the answer so many dollars. The primacy of business may seem no less humiliating when one recognizes that in an industrial civilization business must come first—we are all dependent on it as never before. At best, the growing abundance of material goods, or means to the good life, always tended to obscure the end, the issue of what is the good life for free men. It bred the passion for physical comfort and vulgar pleasure—what de Tocqueville called "the mother of slavery"—that obscured the values of self-realization, or simple self-respect. In America, I have remarked elsewhere, the outcome of our material progress has been the highest standard of low living in history. One must ask how free are men who are conditioned to low purposes, unwilling if not unable to develop their capacities for knowing, feeling, imagining, and aspiring. One may wonder about the many businessmen who seem pleased to say "We're not in business for our health," implying that mental or spiritual health need not be a primary consideration for a man engaged in his lifework; so one may not wonder when they complain that what they are in is a "rat race," but stay in it anyhow.

Yet we still need to realize as well the elementary value of our material progress. Men naturally want first of all to make a decent living, and by this century most in the industrialized countries could count on one. Material abundance may seem vain or spiritually harmful because the traditional wisdom of the ages has always reflected material scarcity and insecurity, emphasizing that true happiness lies in being able to do without; and though this may still be the best wisdom, the surest way to peace of mind or "spiritual freedom," my immediate concern remains the growth of more objective kinds of freedom. What men made out of their novel opportunities or did with all the available goods is another matter we shall keep returning to. Here I should repeat that on the face of the historic record the poverty and illiteracy of the great majority in the past were not conducive to either lofty spirituality or sturdy individuality, that it is quite possible to live the good life in material comfort, with sanitation or even plumbing, and that people who pine for some past age typically assume that they would have been among the few who were educated and well off. (The many lovers of the Middle Ages seldom picture themselves as serfs, not to mention as victims of the Black Death.) Nor is it certain that money values were always the ruling values in the new society. If they were, one might expect the businessmen who made piles of money to have become national idols. As it was, they looked more selfish and grossly materialistic than they often were because they were prouder of their money than were aristocrats born to it, lacked style in spending it, and kept on making it to the end of their life for want of any clear idea what to do with it, or in a Puritan feeling that idleness was sinful. Sired by the "God-fearing businessman," they bred another historically novel type of leader—the "tired businessman."

As ambivalent was the role of the "bourgeois," who with the Industrial Revolution became the dominant class. They in particular forced the pertinent question in an age given to fancying itself as a brave new world: What kind of people in it? By common literary definition they were mediocre, complacent, stodgy, ultraconventional, philistine, literally "petty"—in general, hardly worthy of their Marxist role as oppressors of the proletariat. Especially on the Continent, they were prone to fears of the proletariat that belied their apparent smugness. In England their portrait has been redone, but it remains unflattering. Whereas the Victorian Age was once ridiculed for its complacence and prudishness, the fashion today is to dwell on its underlying doubts and fears, the insecurity betrayed by its very passion for respectability; either way it does not look like an age exhilarated by a new sense of freedom. The Gilded Age in America was more exuberant, but also less dignified, since its aristocracy of wealth lacked the traditional virtues or graces of aristocracy, and as Andrew Carnegie confessed, its gospel of wealth was a slavish gospel. This looked a little strange because it produced so much exhortation to get rich, incessantly urged Americans to cultivate their alleged instinct of acquisitiveness. Nowhere were the lesser bourgeois conspicuous for freedom of mind or spirit.

At the same time, one might still find considerable likeness in the older portrait of the middle class as a sober, industrious, thrifty, responsible class between the extremes of poverty and wealth, neither of which makes for social responsibility. Beneath all the conventionality and the cant lay much simple decency and much moral earnestness, to which the critics of the bourgeois could appeal. By and large they manifested more evident good humor and good will than many of the intellectuals and aesthetes who despised them.[11] Let us contemplate a

---

11 Having dedicated this volume to the memory of Josephine Muller, my aunt, I feel free to add a personal testimony. She was a schoolteacher who would now be described as a middlebrow, or a patron of "midcult"; politically she was an earnest liberal whose

photograph of a Victorian manufacturer driving to church: according to Marxists a ruthless exploiter of his wage slaves, aided by "the opium of the masses"; according to literary people a philistine or a pious hypocrite; but maybe a really devout man, maybe something of a dreamer, engrossed in some project to educate or uplift the workers; or more likely a man of conflicting impulses, a composite of these conventional portraits. The fact remains that the bourgeois provided the leaders in movements toward social reform. Out of their ranks came most of the greater artists, scientists, writers, and thinkers who made the nineteenth century so creative. They were chiefly responsible for all the imagination and high aspiration that also went into the making of this materialistic society, the visions of peace and plenty in freedom, the earnest effort to realize these visions. We might feel humbled as we recall the civil virtues of the Victorians, their habits of reasonable debate and compromise, their freedom from cults of force, violence, and unreason, and from devil theories of history and society—all no doubt supported by too much complacence, too little awareness of the underlying forces that would erupt into the barbarities of our time, but still a reminder that such barbarities were unthinkable to them, and that we may be too much disposed to blame our failures on them, or on the nineteenth century.

Hence we might qualify somewhat a more legitimate complaint, the kind of cities we inherited from this century. In creating a predominantly urban civilization, the Industrial Revolution amplified the historic role of the city, which for all its sins has always been the heart of civilization. It remained the main center of creative activity, as of sophistication and urbanity; it was always a potentially emancipating influence because of its diversity, stir, and restlessness; and the cold, impersonal, artificial way of life that men continued to complain of might still be offset by the privacy and personal freedom it thereby permitted. When the city fathers at length began drawing on the im-

faith was uncomplicated by irony; and as a spinster, always very prim in her ways, she would be suspect to sophisticates who know their Freud. Nevertheless she was not at all pretentious, complacent, shallow, or warped. She was a constant reader, of quite reputable books, and a lover of music; she was a thoroughly conscientious citizen, supporting many a cause; and to her relatives and intimates she was a paragon of devotion, unfailing in thoughtfulness and kindliness. She was too rare a person in her unselfishness and sweetness of disposition to be representative of the middle or any other class, but in her modesty she would have been pleased to think that she only exemplified qualities of simple goodness to be found in a great many people. Deeply indebted to her generosity in my youth, I have lately realized a further debt—a keener awareness of the inhumanity as well as the shallowness of much fashionable generalization about modern society and culture.

proved technology to light, drain, and clean up their cities, the change seemed almost magical. Cardinal Newman—no lover of progress— himself observed how much simple ventilation might do to make men moral and happy. But one sign of improvement was a sharp decrease in crime, which made cities much safer at night than Elizabethan London had been.

Nevertheless the efforts of the city fathers were pretty tardy, usually not very bold in view of the collective wealth and power, and too late to repair most of the damage that had been done. The city was among the conspicuous victims of the rule of business. For some time the growth of almost all but capital cities had been governed by the interests of landlords, and now that they started growing and multiplying faster than ever before, less attention than ever was given to their historic functions as centers of community, civility, and culture, or to any values but those of the self-regulating market. Public parks and playgrounds, schools and museums, were no direct source of profit for private enterprise; businessmen were inclined to view the whole public sphere with indifference, when not with suspicion as a source of taxation and interference. The squalor of the new industrial towns, and of industrial districts in all cities, was a worse blight because it was accepted as a normal by-product, even a necessary condition of business growth, just like the pollution of air and rivers. Henry Adams noted on successive visits to London that "the great city grew smaller as it doubled in size; cheaper as it quadrupled in wealth; less imperial as its empire widened"—illustrating the apparent law of modern history, "the survival of the cheapest." Patrick Geddes summed up the growth of the city more concisely: "Slum, semi-slum, and super-slum."

The worst sufferers were always the millions of poor condemned to the slums, which throve because tenements generally returned handsome profits to landlords (in New York running to 40 per cent a year). The petty bourgeois might be pitied just because they were mostly content with the drabness and monotony of their semi-slums. Neither they nor the very poor were capable of rejoicing in the thought that their betters were taking to super-slums on gridiron streets—Park Avenues lined with unimaginative apartment houses, designed with no eye to sunlight, airiness, or spaciousness. Characteristically the new cities produced no art worth mentioning, and at first neglected to import any. The rising business class failed to spur or to patronize any such great cultural movement as its forebears had done in the Italian Renaissance, but as *nouveau riche* gratified its pride by subsidizing monumental exhibits of tastelessness, which matched about the ugliest fashions in dress and house furnishings in the history of style. Toward the end of the century the wealthy developed a more refined civic pride, doing much more to adorn their cities with museums, galleries, and universities ("cathedrals of learning"), but few bestirred themselves to repair the worst damage. The vast areas of slums could be cleared only at considerable public expense, which was more shocking to the business-minded. The rulers of cities were still dominated by the motives that were making them more congested. A city engineer explained why all the new subways of New York had to lead to Manhattan: "Every transit line that brings people to Manhattan adds to its real estate value." Real estate was the sovereign value.

For the millions of people who were drawn or driven to the cities, however, the crucial point was the radical change from the settled way of life in the village. It was often a painful change, which we can now better realize because of the profound disruptions in the non-Western world. The difficulties of the uprooted were aggravated by the new techniques and habits they had to learn in factories, and especially by the common indifference to the human costs of the material progress. Workers not only lacked social security, any protection against the recurrent spells of unemployment, but were exposed to further psychological insecurity, threats to self-respect. They might suffer from the want of a clear social status or clear sense of social function; as one of their newspapers put it, "The poor man is esteemed only as an instrument of wealth." Their resentments were intensified by feelings of alienation, deeper anxieties that swelled the undercurrents of violence throughout the nineteenth century.

Yet most men evidently welcomed the change, or found sufficient compensations for its costs. The many ambitious ones who flocked to the cities or emigrated to America were replaced by very few fleeing from the trials of city life. At least men obviously grew more flexible and adaptable, accustomed to change. So indeed most must be open to change if society is to remain free and open. In this view the disruption of the traditional order, including the deeply rooted life of the conservative village, was essential to the growth of democracy. We may get a clearer perspective by considering the profound social change that resulted from a single invention—the railroad. In 1835 the editor of *John Bull* declaimed: "Railroads, if they succeed, will give an unnatural impetus to society, destroy all the relations which exist between man and man, overthrow all mercantile regulations, and create, at the peril of life, all sorts of confusion and distress." His alarm may seem more reasonable if we realize that until this time most men never left the region in which they were born, traveling no farther than to the nearest town. Possibly they were more contented so, certainly less liable to confusion. At any rate, the railroad introduced an era in which ordinary people could travel freely, live in a much larger and more varied world, become acquainted with more possibilities of life, acquire a livelier sense of opportunity; and few who have known this kind of freedom would prefer to spend their entire life in a single neighborhood—though this is still a possible choice.

Now that the pace of change has become so much faster, we are more aware of the price we pay in tension, confusion, and disruption. One may doubt that men by and large really want so much change, even though they still applaud the latest wonder, or doubt in particular that most are free and flexible enough to adapt themselves intelligently to it. The uncertainties spring from the plainest ambiguity in the most direct consequence of industrialism—a civilization based on the machine. As Carl Becker summed it up, "Man has more power over things; things have more power over man."

It is a commonplace that in innumerable ways men have become slaves of their machines.[12] Immediately the machine demanded much routine work—trivial, repetitive, unsatisfying, intrinsically meaningless—for which men were not well suited psychologically, and to which they might grow suited only by becoming robots. In praising the division of labor that so greatly increased productivity, Adam Smith himself had deplored its tendency to make idiots of workmen. Similarly the machine demanded that its slaves live in places like Gary, Indiana, described by someone as a city inhabited by four blast furnaces and a hundred thousand people, whose presence there made no human sense except for the furnaces. Hence the Industrial Revolution created masses in a literal sense: no more anonymous or faceless than the peasant masses throughout history, but denser bodies of people, massed both in cities and in factories, more mechanical in their ways, sensing time more as mechanism than as rhythm—something to be watched on a clock, and due to become dependent on machines for their recreation too. The very dynamism of industrial society could seem oddly rigid

---

12 In the following paragraphs I am drawing on passages from published lectures on *The Individual in a Revolutionary World*, but substantially I am repeating the complaints made by hundreds of writers. My excuse remains that this depressingly familiar story is still not familiar enough to too many Americans.

and lifeless because it was so automatic: men *had* to go on making bigger and better machines, and then doing whatever these required, commonly at still more expense of sensuality, spontaneity, and idiosyncrasy. The outcome would be appropriately called "automation," symbolizing the mechanical, inhuman compulsions of industrialism.

More broadly considered, the slave driver was technology—the rationale of modern industry. This meant an idolization of efficiency, in terms of saving time and money, or anything but men. Before it produced the assembly line, it made "function" and "process" other key words of the modern era. While the function of nature was to be exploited with a reckless wastefulness, the function of men became to maintain the efficiency of the industrial process by serving as interchangeable cogs. In mid-century Amiel described the whole development in literary terms: "To crush what is spiritual, moral, human in man by specializing him; to form mere wheels of the great social machine instead of complete individuals; to make society and not conscience the center of life, to enslave the soul to things, to depersonalize man—this is the dominant drift of the age." At the end of the century Frederick Taylor changed the drift into a respectable process by his pioneering work as an efficiency expert. Proposing a "mental revolution" for both management and labor, he declared that they should stop quarreling over their shares of the profits in order to concentrate on the all-important matter, "increasing the size of the surplus," and he demonstrated how they could substitute absolutely standardized, scientific methods for "the old individual judgment" of workman or boss. Taylor ended as a crusader for scientific management, the ideal of completely dehumanizing and depersonalizing industry.

As Marxists saw it, he was only perfecting the capitalistic exploitation of workers. Actually, Taylor was more significant because he was sincerely trying to promote cooperation and abundance, not merely the interests of owners, and illustrated tendencies that might sacrifice the person as much under socialism as capitalism. The increasing rationalization and mechanization of economic activity tended to carry over into other major activities. Human beings remained something of a nuisance to both efficiency experts and systematic thinkers, but their individual differences could at least be ironed out by standardized methods and statistical thinking. In such a climate men came to talk of the "machinery" of the state, or "political machines," and for statesmanship substituted the sovereign ideal of a "businesslike" administration. Thinkers could readily subscribe to theories of mechanistic determinism that denied human freedom, to sociological theories that reduced the individual to a mere product of heredity and environment, or to ideologies that promised technocratic or automatic solutions to all social problems. An efficient rationalism might carry as far from reasonableness and humaneness in thought as in industrialism, and a progressive control of nature lead to a loss of control of the human world.

Yet this account of a technological society is itself highly abstract, and by now more than a little mechanical. The Machine—the Frankenstein of the modern world—is of course no mere inhuman monster; men soon learned that it could be a thing of beauty, and came to fondle and cherish it as they have always been wont to do with their tools. The drudgery of tending it was no worse than much routine toil of the past, but seemed worse because of a new idea it helped to generate— that work ought to be creative and soul-satisfying. The drudgery was partially offset by the increasing opportunities for skilled workers and mechanics, and by the new arts of industrial design. Even the flood of shoddy, ugly goods was not simply a blight, given the many needy who in the past could afford few goods of any kind, but by mid-century manufacturers were getting concerned about good design, beginning to produce more things of beauty (as Josiah Wedgwood had in the early days); and presently men who identified poetry with skylarks, daffodils, stars, and moon began appreciating the poetry of the great bridges, liners, and locomotives. Literary people might have been more grateful for some of the new inventions and other by-products of the Industrial Revolution, for example, the arts of photography and color reproduction, which together with rapid transportation and the museums springing up all over Europe made possible a firsthand knowledge of the world's art. Hence the increasing abundance did not mean merely increasing bondage to things. Things have always had power over man, for that matter, just as stone axes became a "necessity" even though men had got along without them for countless millennia; and it would seem presumptuous to say that the human race is foolish because it has hung on to every useful invention, every technological improvement.

Most mindless is the stereotyped complaint that because of the machine most men now work at what they have to do instead of what they want to do. Granted the ample cause for complaint, the obvious difference remains that the great majority in the past had no real choice. They were born in a fixed status, with a fixed occupation; like it or not, they became peasants or artisans because their fathers were; and they might like it simply because they had little if any serious thought of deciding what they most wanted to do. By contrast, an industrial society not only offered but increasingly forced choices in occupation, habitat, and possible status; more and more of the young in particular were faced with at once the opportunity and the necessity of deciding the kind of life they wanted to lead; and if most men were discontented, the reason was that many felt they had been denied a fair opportunity, many others felt they had made the wrong choice, and all were more keenly aware of the greener grass elsewhere. The cliché that the Industrial Revolution eventuated in a standardized mass society makes it all too easy to forget that in another aspect this is a fantastically heterogeneous society, distinguished by an extraordinary diversity of vocation, skill, interest, and desire, and that never before has it taken so many different kinds of men to make a world.[13] Hence the "masses" created by the Industrial Revolution differed in other important ways from the historic peasant masses. They were less like literal masses in that they were less inert, less prone to fatalistic resignation or passive endurance. With their possibly more acute feeling of insecurity came more hope of improving their lot and more positive effort to do so. Those who attempted to improve themselves by education were aided by another early invention that helped to make a world of difference: the gaslighting that made possible longer working hours in factories also made possible evening classes in schools or halls.

And so, finally, with the drive to organization—the elaborate social machinery required to produce all the machines, and to run a society based on them. By the end of the century another profound change was well under way, since identified as the "organizational revolution": society would be increasingly dominated by big business, big government, big labor unions, big organizations in every sphere of activity. In government, especially in America, such organization would be known and feared as "bureaucracy"; but it created much the same problems in all spheres. It was just as much bureaucracy in business, and had meant as much regimentation, especially for workmen. If they were free to choose their factory, in the factory they were subject to a discipline that discouraged individual enterprise or initiative. The

---

13 In 1841, for instance, the British Census listed some 400 occupations; a century later the U.S. Census listed 25,000. This figure doubtless represents a much finer breakdown; but sophisticates sold on the idea of the uniform "mass-man" might be less depressed if they spent a day walking the streets of any large city (including Gary) and keeping their eyes open.

white-collar underlings in offices, disposed to look down on workers who got their hands dirty, were no more independent, and outside the office were typically less spontaneous in their pleasures or independent in their choices. They had the makings of a type that would become prominent as business grew bigger—the "organization man,"the smooth conformist who by way of individuality could afford little but a super-ficial or synthetic "personality." Corporations not only accentuated the impersonality of the system but most plainly subordinated the interests of the individual to the good of the organization, and in time appropriately identified him by a series of holes in a punch card. Never run democratically, they were not governed either by the principle that in the democracies might affect the political bureaucracy—that the state existed to serve its members, and men should be treated as ends, not merely as means.

Again this whole drive naturally influenced the world of thought. Early in the nineteenth century Saint-Simon, the first philosopher of organization, foresaw the drive and set up a goal for it: "The sole aim of our thoughts and our exertions must be the kind of organization most favorable to industry." Other socialists conceived of different kinds more directly favorable to the common people. Early in our century Lenin made proper organization the key to successful revolu-tion, which in his belief would eventually cause the state to wither away, but which in fact led to totalitarianism—the organization of the whole society. Meanwhile sociologists, beginning with Comte, had contributed ostensibly scientific means and ends, and were in process of setting up a comparable idol—methodology. As specialists in the study of organization have pointed out, it was a "grand device" for enabling men to behave rationally and become greater without having to become any more intelligent, virtuous, or wise as individuals; and just so methodology enabled ordinary minds to do impressive work in social science. The naturally congenial pair would then be wedded in such new professions as "social engineering" or "human engineering," which might legitimatize the research in ways of manipulating people.

Sociologists contributed as much to a parallel theme, at once hearten-ing and depressing, that became another major concern of the century—the effort to reinstate the values of community. Ferdinand Tönnies produced his classic study *Community and Society* (1887), which could have been entitled *Community Versus Society;* he emphasized that rational economic man, specifically the businessman, weakened the traditional bonds that held men together by treating others only as means to his ends. Such studies made plainer the deeper insecurity of industrial workers, who found it hard to feel that they really "belonged" in the system. A corporation was scarcely a genuine community; few men could feel deeply loyal to Standard Oil, no one except maybe Rockefeller would ever die for it. American businessmen themselves tacitly recognized such deprivations by forming Rotary Clubs, becoming Elks and Masons (or members of the Ancient Arabic Order of Nobles of the Mystic Shrine), and joining other such "brotherhoods"; but the fraternal spirit of these social organizations was likely to be rather synthetic, strained or diluted by too much awareness that it was good for business. Likewise the growing interest of management in "human relations" was more professional than humane, calculated chiefly to promote the good of the organization. Social scientists made an interest in personal relations more respectable by calling them "interpersonal," or linking them with a concept of "individuation," but their professional jargon was a poor way of restoring or possibly even restating the values of community. (The specialists who lately recommended the Golden Rule may not have sold laymen by describing it as a useful warning against "suboptimizing in terms of our interpersonal objectives.")

But again there remain the obvious values of organization, for communal as well as business purposes. In a large society it is in fact an essential means to rational social behavior, and to the effectiveness of any ideal social cause. From the beginning of the Industrial Revolution private organizations led the effort to relieve its victims and reduce its evils; the free societies have been distinguished by the growth of such associations to promote or prevent all kinds of possibilities, through which the individual may assert or protect his interests. When organization became systematic and big enough to be called bureaucracy, it still offered plain compensations for its impersonality and apparent soullessness. It not only provided order and stability, and in government a means of checking the abuses of too private enterprise, but everywhere promoted efficiency for some strictly humane purposes, reducing friction and uncertainty. Men who complain of the impersonality of bureaucracy may complain still more when administrators are not impersonal, or play favorites; then they may appreciate the equity of a system that tends to restrict the play of sentiment and emotion, to make authority rational by basing it on proved ability, and so to give employees more personal security. Ideally the big organization may promote personal freedom by still more ambivalent tendencies. Other words for the discipline it demands or the conformism it induces include "cooperation" and "team spirit"; however far from disinterested, the growing attention to "human relations" has at least meant better working conditions and more concern with the contentment of employees. On the other hand, the anonymity of the underlings, and their limited commitment to corporations that are still not real communities, may make them freer to live their own lives.

No more is the whole shift from "community" to "society" simply lamentable. Other ways of describing it are as a shift from status to contract, customary obedience to rational consent, prescribed duty to individual conscience, the closed to the open society—all of which mean more freedom. Tönnies himself described it as a growth from the youth to the adulthood of society. He also regarded his concepts as ideal types, useful for describing change or comparing societies, but not to be taken as literal realities or complete antitheses. Primitive or "folk societies" might approach pure "community," but any growing community has mixed, shifting relationships. (Even the youthful Middle Ages had the Roman Church, whose continued existence suggests that bureaucracy is not necessarily fatal.) Likewise no urban civilization is pure "society," lacking all bonds of community. Traditionalists have as usual violently simplified the issues by picturing the Middle Ages or whatever their favorite age as virtually a perfect community, in which every man knew his place and felt at home, and picturing industrial society as almost purely mechanical, impersonal, and atomistic. To me, two world wars suggest that we do not yet suffer from an excess of rationality or a dearth of tribalism.

They also suggest that the basic question raised by the Industrial Revolution—whether men can control the terrific power they have generated, make intelligent use of it for humane, civilized purposes—remains wide open. On all counts, we may feel more oppressed because we have a more vivid sense of potentiality, for better and for worse. By no count—no simple process of addition and subtraction—can we arrive at the sum of our freedom. At this stage—where, once more, I am chiefly stating themes to be amplified later—I conclude by stressing the implications of these remarks: that the future still is open, that we are still free to debate the means and ends of a better life, and that for this reason we need always to keep in mind the essential ambiguities of an industrial civilization, which entails inescapable tendencies to mechanization and regimentation, while giving people unprecedented opportunities and latitude in choice.

| Chapter Three | # THE POLITICAL REVOLUTIONS |

1. The Dissonant Themes

Despite the growing complexity and confusion of the nineteenth century, it is still easy enough to make out the basic elements of unity underlying the multiple diversities and perpetual conflicts within Western civilization that make it possible, even necessary, to speak of this as a distinct civilization. The major trends led to similar changes everywhere. The Industrial Revolution, which magnified the differences between the "modern" and the "backward" countries, nevertheless affected them all and distinguished the West more sharply from the rest of the world. In political history the common trends were emphasized by the waves of revolution that swept over Europe, as well as by the constant fear of revolution that haunted the scions of Metternich. While some countries became markedly freer than others, all moved in the same direction. World War I, which Americans came to view as a war to make the world safe for democracy, certainly did not break out over any basic ideological differences. Thereafter such differences did split the major powers, but they sprang from the broad movements that introduced "ideology" into the modern lexicon, and they cannot be understood without some knowledge of the revolutionary changes throughout the Western world. This chapter too will cover familiar developments, on the interpretation and judgment of which historians will never agree, but which none would ignore.

The most obviously pertinent theme for my purposes remains the growth and spread of popular government. Although at the end of the century there were still only a few full-fledged democracies, in almost all countries more people had more say in their government, which had become more responsive to public opinion. Almost all had written constitutions that provided for some form of parliamentary or representative government, and permitted the organization of political parties —a seemingly elementary way of conducting public affairs, but in a long view of history an astonishing innovation; at the beginning of the century "party" still had sinister connotations, ranging from "faction" to "conspiracy." Government was doing much more to promote the common welfare, especially through public education; the need of education was universally recognized. The spread of literacy greatly increased the power of public opinion and of the press. Similarly it widened the influence of the intelligentsia, who naturally ranged themselves on all sides of all questions, but included enough liberals and radicals to earn their common reputation as a subversive class. In the early years of our century the trend toward democracy grew so strong that conservatives were reduced to fighting halfhearted delaying actions, and even czarist Russia set up a parliament. The very revulsion against democracy after the World War testified how deep and wide the revolutionary changes had gone. Dictators in Europe paid far more heed to public opinion than monarchs had in their heyday, taking pains to sway or mold it, and when most contemptuous of the common people they were no less concerned to build up their popularity. Communism still proclaims itself "the people's democracy."

A primary source of this whole movement remained the ideals of liberty, equality, and fraternity propagated by the French Revolution. These resounded in the famous revolutions of 1848, popular uprisings so spontaneous and widespread that it is hard to name or count them all. (There were up to fifty of them.) By then the Industrial Revolution had become another major political factor. While expanding the opportunities and the power of the middle class, it bred a more vigorous, assertive working class. Among its by-products was the rise of socialism, which frightened conservatives still more but could not be scotched either. All countries had to deal with their "radicals," another new term in the political lexicon. If the conservative ruling class retained control of the government, it usually did so by making concessions, accepting measures initially branded as radical.

The most extraordinary movement, in view of the whole history of civilization, was the related struggle for equal rights for women. This too was a pan-European affair, whose pioneers included Condorcet in France, Mary Wollstonecraft in England, and von Hippel in Germany. Socialists were among the most ardent supporters, but ordinary liberals also pitched in, notably John Stuart Mill. In the nineteenth century the movement made substantial progress toward legal equality for women, while industrialism offered them much more economic opportunity. Feminists were able to make more converts because of different views that still confuse the status of women, some holding that women were just as good as men in every respect except physical strength, and should therefore have equal opportunity in all occupations except those requiring such strength; others granting that women were essentially different from men, perhaps mostly unsuited for some vocations, and in any case obliged to consider their natural role as housewives and mothers, but holding that they should nevertheless be granted the same civil and political rights. All were agreed on these rights, however, and by the dawn of our century political equality was in sight. Finland led the way in giving women full citizenship, followed by Norway and Denmark. Although the great nations lagged until after the World War, woman suffrage was now only a question of time.

Meanwhile the growth of nationalism, another related development, had likewise deeply affected all Western peoples even as it emphasized and exaggerated their national or racial differences. At first linked with the revolutionary cause of the rights of the people, nationalism remained ostensibly an expression of their primary interests, not merely the interests of their sovereigns, and it flourished because the common people in fact grew much more devoted to their nation or nationality than they had felt in the past. It was itself revolutionary in that patriotism—"my country first"—became the ruling religion of the modern world; God ran a poor second, staying in the running chiefly because he was called on to bless both sides in every war. Most Westerners have long taken for granted the naturalness of this overriding patriotism, but they are beginning to realize its historic novelty because of still another major development it fostered—imperialism. Once the West had dominated almost the entire world, it unwittingly converted non-Western peoples to its religion of nationalism, which has stirred much more fervor than has either of the rival creeds of democracy and communism, while missionary Christianity has run a distant last.

By now the connections between these developments may be less apparent than the disparities or conflicts, the deepening contradictions. Thus while peoples everywhere were growing more nationalistic, insistent on their rights to independence or their own manifest destiny, they were also growing more interdependent, less able to go their own way; in the ever more important economic realm depressions became inter-

national affairs. An expanding civilization was as steadily shrinking the
size of man's world, making more meaningful the concept of "mankind," while also creating the conditions for all-out world war. In
particular we now realize more acutely that none of these political developments simply promoted the growth of freedom, any more than
capitalism or industrialism did. Nationalism often served the interests
of undemocratic states or of statism, even before it assumed the guise
of "national socialism"; socialism, which throve on democratic ideals,
could lend itself to totalitarianism; the increasing service provided by
the state gave it more power, which might become oppressive; freedom
lovers early began complaining of "the tyranny of democracy," especially in America; and so on—to the end of this volume.

Immediately, however, the ambiguities oblige us to consider the
divergences in the political history of the Western nations, their quite
dissimilar responses to similar challenges. Everywhere nationalism took
on different forms, conditioned by the different political traditions and
forms of government. So did socialism, in spite of its common internationalism in theory; as it rose it generated new isms. The idea of freedom, always open to vague and various definition, grew more confused
as it grew more popular and fewer men in the ruling class dared to oppose it openly; in countries that enjoyed little political freedom by
democratic standards the people were told that "real" or "true" freedom
required complete obedience to state, church, or party. Such divergences again bid us to be wary of the stock generalizations about the
bourgeois and the proletariat, or the elite and the masses, which assume
uniform characteristics and invariable tendencies. They should discourage all monistic explanation, as well as the always popular talk
about "the" fountainhead of Western freedom. A civilization with a
common religion and common heritage found in them fountainheads
of tyranny too.

In general, the revolutionary movements in the first half of the nineteenth century sharpened the differences between countries, in some
of which the liberal forces gained strength by partial victories, in others
were crushed and driven underground. To this period we may trace
the basic ideological differences that later split Europe. In particular,
the political history of the century accentuated the differences between
eastern and western Europe even as it brought them closer together.
Russia, which Peter the Great had turned toward the West, continued
to play a major role in its diplomacy or power politics, but out of fear
of revolution the czars mostly did their best to keep out Western in-

fluences; their reactionary policy would be both vindicated and mocked when "Holy Russia" was transformed into the U.S.S.R. by the Western ideology of Marxism. The Balkan peoples were sufficiently fired by the spirit of nationalism to win their independence from Ottoman Turkey, start fighting fiercely among themselves, and set off the conflagration of the World War, but otherwise they remained backward by European standards; their efforts to take to Western ways were impeded by poverty, illiteracy, political inexperience, Russian influence, and a tradition reaching back through the Holy Orthodox Church to Byzantium.[1] Likewise central Europe, excepting little Switzerland, became more sharply distinguished from the Atlantic nations, where the movement toward liberal, democratic government made much more headway. And the political history of England and France, the leading nations in what is now called the Atlantic community, differed in fundamental respects that have come to seem more significant.

There remains the singular history of the United States. Although by the end of the century its immense growth in population and industry had made it a world power, potentially the greatest, European diplomats were still paying it little heed as they worried over their grand alliances and ententes; they were unprepared for the decisive role it was to play in the World War. Americans themselves were no more prepared. Having a continent to themselves, they rejoiced in their aloofness from the nasty politics of the Old World, and except for some lordly gestures and imperial aspirations, befitting God's own country, they ignored their deepening involvement in world affairs. (They even held off for almost twenty years from joining the International Red Cross.) Similarly they slighted their profound indebtedness to Europe, giving themselves almost all the credit for their achievements. Nevertheless, their democracy was basically in fact unique. The most democratic nation at the beginning of the century, and the only one without a titled aristocracy, America was the first to become a full democracy with universal suffrage. It remained a prime symbol of the hopes of common men in the Old World. By the same token its novel history had a deeper significance for Europeans, which Alexis de Tocqueville most fully realized. Less enraptured by America than Condorcet and other men of the En-

---

[1] The difference between the cultural traditions of eastern and western Europe may be sensed vividly in Yugoslavia, which bridges them. A traveler in its eastern regions feels that he is in the "Balkans"; arriving in Zagreb, he at once recognizes a "European" city. Another apparent exception to these generalizations is the Greeks, who in winning their independence were fired as well by the belief that they were inheritors, even blooded descendants of the classical Greeks.

lightenment had been when it declared and won its independence, de Tocqueville sized up much more acutely this radically new kind of society, and the reasons why—like it or not—it represented the tidal wave of the future.

In view of his classic study (*Democracy in America*, 1835 and 1840) an American historian may believe that it is not a sign of national conceit to begin at home a survey of the growth of popular government in modern Western civilization. Always remembering that America owed to Europe its basic beliefs (not to mention most of its technology), we may properly dwell on its importance as a pacesetter. In a New World, blessed with immense resources, it demonstrated most plainly how government resting on the principles of liberty and equality, the will of the people, and majority rule might promote the common welfare; and as the purest democracy it also made plainest the inherent problems of such a society, including its tendencies to menace personal liberty. Remembering the national conceit, we might note that pacesetters do not always win the race.

2.   *Democracy in America*

America is the oldest country in the world, Gertrude Stein explained to her French friends, because it was the first to enter the twentieth century. Lately the oldest of the democracies, and the greatest of industrial powers, has been showing its years: it has become a world symbol of conservatism. Its people have grown most fearful of revolutionaries, vindicating de Tocqueville's prophecy that revolution would become ever more unlikely in America. Its historians have been reflecting its conservative temper by treating its whole national history as a conservative affair. Some have discounted the famous American Revolution as not really a revolution, only a War of Independence, while others emphasize that in any case it implanted in this country no such revolutionary tradition as Europe has known. Certainly the "American Way" that emerged was by no means a radical way. "Radical" was a worse word in America than in Europe, and Americans who were so labeled were usually pretty tame by Continental standards.

But Gertrude Stein of course intended her remark as a paradox. America has always been known as a youthful nation, for much more obvious reasons. "We are the pioneers of the world," wrote Herman

Melville; "the advance guard sent on through the wilderness of untried
things, to break a new path in the New World that is ours. In our
youth is our strength; in our inexperience our wisdom." In the nineteenth century all writers dwelt on such qualities, which Americans
typically described as energy, vigor, bounce, confidence, and unspoiled
innocence, while foreign visitors were likely to use such adjectives as
callow, uncouth, noisy, and spoiled. In this century, when Van Wyck
Brooks wrote of America's "Coming-of-Age," Herbert Croly was still expounding the "promise" of American life, editing a new magazine called
the *New Republic*. Come of age, many Americans grew more painfully self-conscious than older peoples are wont to feel. They began
to realize that in an era of ideology their country had no ideology
but America itself; so they worried over the problem of defining Americanism, or discovering who they were. The growing pains of an old-
new country then magnified the familiar paradoxes or contradictions
of American life. Plain to all but the simplest patriots, these have
stirred endless disagreement over the "essence" of Americanism. Nevertheless the disagreement indicates as plainly that this essence is not
simple or pure, and it suggests the usual lead through the principle of
ambiguity or the naturalness of paradox. For the most part it comes
down to the old story of swings in fashion, specifically to differences
in emphasis on conflicting tendencies that all historians recognize.
Beneath these differences one may find a wide agreement on the sources
of contradiction.

Thus there is little question that de Tocqueville singled out a primary source in the principle of equality. America soon became known
as pre-eminently the land of equality, which both friends and foes
of democracy recognize as one of its distinctive, essential principles.
It took hold more quickly in the New World (outside of Latin America)
because the colonial aristocracy lacked not only titles but the support of a state church, in Europe a pillar of the *ancien régime*. The
idea of equal political rights grew out of a rare feeling of social equality, expressed in an aversion to pretensions of rank. As the supercilious Englishman Thomas Grattan observed, even Americans who
aspired to be aristocrats were "altogether unaware that the pride of
birth is the fundamental basis of an aristocracy."[2] The main question
is whether Americans had such an overriding passion for equality at

---

[2] Since he added that another absolute essential was "large landed possessions, with a
train of dependent serfs or tenants," it should be noted that many Southerners did come
up to his requirements. Grattan's firsthand observations were confined to the North.

any cost as de Tocqueville believed, and in particular whether it was
so dangerous a menace to freedom as he concluded. He himself recognized that the idea or feeling worked ambiguously, fostering self-
respect and independence of spirit as well as the tyranny of public
opinion. He also perceived that another reason for the strength of
egalitarian sentiment was that it was not an aspiration to uniform
equality, least of all in the possession of goods; he knew of no country,
he remarked, "where a profounder contempt is expressed for the
theory of the permanent equality of property." The living American
ideal was something like equal opportunity for all men to make good;
so it was all the better if a poor boy made a lot of money. The materialism for which America became known was rooted in its very idealism,
and it flourished because poor boys in fact had exceptional opportunities to make a better living.

In other words, America soon became pre-eminently the land of the
common man. Once democracy was established, the "common people"
was no longer a term of condescension or disparagement. Abraham
Lincoln expressed the national sentiment when he said that God must
approve of common men, since he had created so many of them. American writers did not call their farmers "peasants," they spoke much less
of "the masses" than Europeans did, and typically they shied away from
such expressions as the "working class" or the "proletariat"; to their
mind the many poor Americans were not a permanent lower class.
Differences centered on who this sovereign common man was, just what
he was like. At first he was usually an independent farmer, still better
a frontiersman; later he became a Horatio Alger type, a little businessman on the make. But always he was a free man, ideally self-reliant,
enterprising, individualistic, freedom-loving; so Emerson, Whitman,
and others were unhappier when he appeared to be actually the materialist and the conformist described by de Tocqueville, "common" in
the worst sense of the word. The many harsh critics of him in recent
times speak out of this long dual tradition. Even those who hanker for
an aristocratic society (like the Old South) rarely say in so many words
that he ought to be deprived of his equal rights and his opportunities.

At any rate, his rise was unquestionably a major theme of the nation's
history through the age of Jackson. The authors of the Constitution had
mostly feared the common man, designing their system of checks and
balances to keep him in his place. The Federalists continued to fear
him and oppose his demands for political equality; they adhered to
the venerable tradition going back to Plato that democracy meant mob

rule, and was bound to end in civil war or anarchy. When Thomas Jefferson defeated them in the election of 1800, he accordingly described his victory as another "revolution," and conservatives wholeheartedly agreed—some showering him with abuse so violent that it might have suggested the scurrility of the rabble. For another generation they went on sounding the conventional objections to democracy, though perforce with a bourgeois accent: lacking a nobility, they had to make property the necessary qualification for wisdom and virtue, or for privilege and power. As Daniel Webster said, "Power *naturally* and *necessarily* follows property," and from this Marxist premise he deduced that government ought to rest on property. Behind all such possibly selfish interest lay the deeply engrained belief that men without property were naturally irresponsible, at best incapable of judging the national interest.

Jefferson's expressed faith in the common people was indeed a novel political faith, shared by very few European thinkers even in the Enlightenment. It was especially bold in the America of 1800—still a poor, backward, thinly settled country. Everything depended on the people, and they were ill-educated, far behind Europe in cultural resources. They had little art, science, or any but political thought; their few little colleges were graduating only a hundred or so students a year; and they were as backward in technology, in 1803 having only five steam engines. Their self-confidence was based most obviously on ignorance, typified by their naïve boasts of their "enlightenment." Yet ordinary Americans also had qualities that might justify Jefferson's improbable bet on them. Unlike many of their betters, who in a revolutionary era were echoing European fears of "innovation," they were open to change, often eager for experiment and adventure. They appeared to be on the average more intelligent or mentally alert than the common people of Europe. And they had the positive advantage of a social and political system that made much thriftier use of its human resources, providing more opportunity and scope for talent and industry, and giving its conservatives much less entrenched power.

Although as President, preoccupied with foreign affairs, Jefferson did little directly on behalf of the popular cause, he helped to assure its triumph by making the Louisiana Purchase on his own, further stimulating the rapid growth of the nation. This doomed both his dream of a simple agricultural republic and the cause of the traditionalists. By the 1820's the population of the United States had more than tripled, almost half the people were on the move, and a dozen frontier states had been admitted. Egalitarian sentiment was especially strong in the raw new states, which took to universal suffrage from the beginning. The East too was stirred by the ferment of a wide-open society, and immediately by popular agitation; outside the South, states began dropping their property qualifications for the vote. Public education spread in response to popular demand. National issues were confused because all candidates, including the inheritors of the discredited Federalist party, took the Jeffersonian name of Republican; but in 1828 the popular movement culminated in the election of Andrew Jackson. His presidency remains a historic landmark because it ended all questions of whether the common man was to enjoy equal suffrage, and raised the more difficult questions that were to haunt American democracy to this day.

We must therefore qualify at once the popular simplicities inspired by Jackson's victory. This was not simply a victory of the frontiersmen, nor a clear proof of Frederick Turner's famous thesis that the Western frontier was the cradle of American democracy and the national character. The frontier did indeed strengthen democratic tendencies, cradle progressive movements, and it had as much symbolic importance, forming the national image of the American as a daring, rugged individualist with a passion for freedom—an image that influenced thought and behavior no less if it is called a myth. But these tendencies had already developed in the East too, which provided many of the pioneers (and incidentally helps to explain why democracy did not flourish on the moving frontier in Latin America or Siberia). The East, in particular the city, was most important in the Industrial Revolution that was beginning to transform America, and to create problems that would be confused or obscured by the romantic legends of the frontier. Jackson drew much popular support in the East, especially from city workers. And "the hero of New Orleans" could appeal more readily to all kinds of Americans because no one had or could have a clear idea of just what he proposed to do: he offered no positive program in what came down to a typical American campaign, determined more by personalities and political ambitions than by clear-cut issues.

Immediately, however, such uncertainty about "the will of the people" underscores the main theme—the rise of the common man. One reason why the large majority voted for Jackson was that his party followers called themselves "Democratic Republicans." (Before long they would be known simply as Democrats.) His victory alarmed aristocrats of property interests, for what soon turned out to be good reason.

In his first year he began his attack on the National Bank, which was government chartered and supported but privately controlled. In exercising its great power over the money market it was not accountable to government or the people, as its director Nicholas Biddle made a point of emphasizing; and in the bitter struggle that followed, Jackson defined the issue in as emphatic democratic terms. "The humble members of society," he wrote in a veto message, had a right to complain of their government when laws granted special favors that made "the rich richer and the potent more powerful." On behalf of business interests Daniel Webster then sounded the perennial theme of conservatives thereafter: by seeking "to influence the poor against the rich," the President was "wantonly" stirring up class war. Chancellor Kent, a survivor of the Federalists, reproduced the style of their attacks on Jefferson by calling Jackson "a detestable, ignorant, reckless, vain and malignant tyrant." Hence the battle lines were more clearly drawn when Jackson ran for re-election against Henry Clay, who supported the bank and was backed by the great bulk of the wealthy class. Clay's party, formerly known as National Republicans, now called itself Whig to indicate that it was carrying on the heroic tradition of resistance to tyranny. Even so the common people were not impressed, returning Jackson to office by an overwhelming majority.

He gave some substance to the charges of the Whigs in that he was indisputably a strong President, unafraid to use his powers of veto, firm in asserting his full authority as Chief Magistrate. Although he had shown little promise, he earned his reputation as one of the greater Presidents by rising to his responsibilities, growing surer of his purposes, and demonstrating that power may not only corrupt but bring out the best in a leader; whatever his mistakes, President Jackson was surely a man of much more stature than the glamorous hero of New Orleans. Most important, he made the Presidency a great office, and essentially a democratic one. The first President to be elected by the people instead of state legislatures—another democratic innovation of the period—he accordingly confounded the wisdom of the Founding Fathers, who had designed the office to fit George Washington: the President was to be a dignified chief of state above all politics or "faction," further insurance against mob rule, while the main business of government was to be carried on by Congress. Jackson announced that as President he was "the direct representative of the American people" and that it was his "especial duty to protect the liberties and rights of the people against the Senate, or the House of Representatives, or both together"; it had long been apparent that Congress was likely to be more responsive to special interests than to public opinion, as "both together" now made plainer by supporting Nicholas Biddle and his National Bank. Jackson grew more confident and resolute if only because he knew he had the people behind him. Although the Presidents after him were more often than not mediocre or weak, the greater ones could and did exercise great power, act boldly as national leaders, especially in times of national crisis. Like Jefferson and Jackson, Abraham Lincoln and Franklin D. Roosevelt also would be charged with "tyranny" by outraged conservatives, arousing much more virulent hatred than the Coolidges would; but all the strong Presidents remained accountable to the people, none was in fact a dictator or tried to become one.

Much of the credit for the dignity of the American Presidency belongs to the common people. The cumbersome system of checks and balances could hardly have worked, indeed, had they been so rapacious and unruly as the Founding Fathers assumed, but under Jackson they started refuting more positively the charge that democracy meant mob rule and must lead to anarchy or ruin. However lawless on the frontier, they respected the basic laws of the land, the more so because they now had more say about them; democracy created the popular reverence for the Constitution, which had been designed to prevent it. The poor refuted another ancient charge by not setting about to fleece the rich or cry for their blood; ordinary Americans had ample respect for property, which many owned and almost all hoped to acquire. Nor did universal suffrage produce the tyranny of the majority so much feared by both de Tocqueville and the Federalists. Such tyranny appeared chiefly in the social pressures of public opinion, to be considered in a later chapter; de Tocqueville himself offered little evidence of political tyranny in Jackson's America. Jackson and his hand-picked successor Martin Van Buren put through no measures more radical or tyrannical than a law doing away with imprisonment for debt.

Jacksonian democracy was vindicated immediately even by its defeat, in a pendulum swing normal to a party system. The Whigs came into power by campaigning on its slogans, having passed over both Henry Clay and Daniel Webster for William Henry Harrison, a "democratic" man of the people whom they equipped with a log cabin birthplace. (He was born a Virginia aristocrat.) Henceforth no candidate would dare to speak superciliously of the common people or ever to challenge the principle of political equality. By the same token, however, the Jacksonians were unhappier in their defeat. The Whigs had won a sweeping victory by unearthing another military hero, manufacturing phony issues and slogans ("Tippecanoe and Tyler too!"), supplementing the blah-blah of stump oratory by torchlight parades and hard cider.[3] Evidently they had not insulted the intelligence of the American people. They recall the unflattering popular word for such smashing victories at the polls—a "stampede" of the voters. They bring up the dubious elements in Jackson's legacy, and the abiding issues of majority rule, supposedly representing the will of the people.

The spoils system introduced by Jackson was more ominous because he saw it as no mere expedient for financing his party, but a reform. In explaining that training and experience in government were not essential for high office, were in fact dangerous, since long tenure led men to forget that they were only servants of the people, he added that ordinary intelligence was sufficient for good government, reflecting the popular assumption that little government was needed anyway. He reflected as well the popular faith in the untutored wisdom of the common man, a wisdom more of the heart than the head. In minimizing the gullibility of voters, this heightened its dangers—and the dismay of his followers when their heart led the common people to elect the hero of Tippecanoe. Andrew Jackson signaled, to a considerable extent sanctioned, the most obvious shortcomings of American democracy.

Thus voters would habitually elect men of quite ordinary abilities, who if they lacked the supreme qualification of birth in a log cabin made more of a point of running for office as plain folk, no different from other common men, and in office might make it plainer that they were not in fact superior. Campaigns would ordinarily be conducted on a low enough intellectual level to discourage men of superior abilities from entering political life. Thereafter, to the end of the century, America produced few statesmen, proportionately many fewer leaders of distinction than it had in its revolutionary period, when out of little Virginia alone came—in one generation—Washington, Jefferson, Mason, Madison, and Marshall. Jackson's spoils system helped to lower still more the moral tone of political life. It facilitated the rise of the political boss, a type peculiar to popular government, but not one of its glories. It led to the notorious venality of American politics, and the

---

[3] Nicholas Biddle contributed this sage advice on Harrison's campaign: "Let him say not one single word about his principles, or his creed—let him say nothing—promise nothing. Let no committee, no convention—no town meeting ever extract from him a single word, about what he thinks now, or what he will do hereafter. Let the use of pen and ink be wholly forbidden as if he were a mad poet in Bedlam." Some of Senator Goldwater's supporters would thrust similar advice on their candidate.

popular acceptance of any unscrupulous deals short of blatant corruption as normal politics. As the double standard of private and public morality became engrained, Americans did not expect simple integrity of their representatives, but had little respect for most of them either, except in the excitement of campaigns. The very success of Jacksonian democracy made them more heedless. Proud of their novel rights and free ways, men could indulge the luxury of ridiculing their representatives—much as medieval men revered the sacred office of the Papacy and mostly hated the Popes.

The main source of political corruption soon became business, which made politics too a business. The Railroad Age got under way in Jackson's time, and one reason why it moved faster in America than in Europe was that railroad companies bribed legislators lavishly to get free grants of land and other favors. (In Wisconsin, for example, the La Crosse and Milwaukee Railroad paid out almost a million dollars to win an award of a million acres; items listed in its accounts included "One governor—$50,000" and "Thirteen head of Senators—$175,000.") Although Jackson fought business when its power seemed excessive, he otherwise lent support to the emerging gospel of the American Way. As a frontiersman, he naturally approved the ideal of the "self-made" man (a phrase coined by Henry Clay) and was inclined to favor *laissez faire.* He and his followers had none of Jefferson's fear of either industrialism or "the mobs of great cities," but began adapting Jeffersonian democracy to the needs of an industrial urban society. This effort was of course sensible, absolutely necessary. Only it revealed the basic limitations and confusions of their thought.

Neither Jackson nor any of his followers thought through the fundamental issues of democracy, or the further problems raised by the changes coming over America. Like ordinary Americans, they were too concerned with immediate "practical" interests to think hard about either the theory they were operating on or any long-term policies; the future—now obviously on America's side—could be trusted to take care of all its problems. Their main goal was simply popular sovereignty. This perforce entailed a concern for the rights of the common people, but they were little troubled by the critical question of to what extent, in a representative government in which the majority literally never rules, its often vague, confused, and conflicting wishes are, can be, and should be heeded by its representatives. They were no more troubled by such problems as the rights of minorities, which would be an everlasting headache for the thoughtful minority concerned about civil liberties. In general, they did not face up to the possible folly of the majority or the actual mediocrity of popular culture; sure that America would keep progressing and become ever greater, they begged the questions of progress toward what, greatness by what standards— the ends of national wealth and power. In particular, they were inconsistent about the role of government. While Jackson had vigorously asserted its authority over private interests and strengthened the powers of the Presidency, his followers retained the characteristically American suspicion of authority and the traditional belief that the best government was the least government.

Hence they made easier the triumph of the Whig interpretation of the American Way. This defended the interests of business and property by dropping all appeal to aristocratic principles. There were really no classes in America; all Americans were free and equal; all common men could become self-made men. If poor, they had the advantage of more incentive to make their fortune, as would be endlessly demonstrated by Horatio Alger. Radicals who called for reform on behalf of workers were not merely unsound but un-American, insulting "the manliness and independence of the laboring men." The only threat to liberty was the government, when it went beyond its proper function of protecting the rights of property and aiding business. And so on. The discarded Federalist principles had had at bottom the dignity of a candid, honestly reasoned, comprehensive theory of state and society; the liberal Lord Acton was especially impressed by John Adams and other American conservatives because he believed that unlike European conservatives they were defending universal principles, not the selfish or merely customary interests of monarchy, an established church, a professional army, a hereditary aristocracy. By contrast the new gospel was wholly unphilosophical. The Whig party that sponsored it was neither genuinely liberal nor genuinely conservative, having no moral end in view, no real concern—aristocratic or democratic—for human dignity. Its platform was patently not conducive to good government, nor even sound business, because it was essentially unrealistic and irresponsible when not intellectually dishonest. Yet this gospel was to dominate American government to the end of the century.

Now, the reasons for its success were not simply discreditable. If many leading Whigs were hypocritical or cynical, others could be sincere enough because of the rapid growth of the nation, the ample evidence of the value of free private enterprise. More to the point, the gospel expressed the feeling of most common men. Since so many owned their own land and home, they could appreciate the actual importance of property as a means to personal independence, and they were inclined to accept the unrestricted rights of private property because their experience confirmed the doctrine that these were rights to the fruits of one's own labor. Although they complained when they were gouged by businessmen, they believed implicitly in *laissez faire* as they kept hoping to come up in the world by their own enterprise; their favorite story remained the success story, their popular heroes the frontiersman and the barefoot boy who made good. For such reasons the heirs of Jefferson accepted much of the gospel, as Andrew Jackson had. They attacked chiefly the monopolistic practices that limited the opportunity of little entrepreneurs or barred the rise of barefoot boys, while they continued to fear the power of government as possible tyranny, which it had so often been throughout history. In short, the American Way was by no means pure fiction or fraud. Purified of its grosser materialism, supplemented by ideas of social responsibility and human rights, it was essentially the liberal tradition come down from John Locke. It manifestly had much to do with not only the material progress of America but the early growth of democracy.

Political scientists have therefore been discounting the conflicts emphasized by most American historians, especially by the liberals who have pictured a long struggle to assure the effective freedom of the common man. The latest emphasis is on the solidarity of America, the consensus beneath the surface conflicts. Thus Louis Hartz emphasizes that de Tocqueville was right from the beginning in discerning the principle of equality as the key to American democracy; never having known a feudal *ancien régime*, Americans were indeed "born equal." In this view the Federalists never had a real chance, the Whigs had the wit to exploit the actual consensus, and the later liberals or Progressives were deluded, failing to realize that they too were committed to basically the same American Way. Richard Hofstader has spelled out at length the implications that the liberals were shallow and naïve, brothers under the skin of Herbert Hoover. One who believes that as usual the new fashion has swung too far should acknowledge that it illumines essential differences between America and Europe, beginning with the lack of a real revolutionary tradition in this country, thence the long lag in social welfare legislation, the minor role of the Socialist party, the commonly insignificant differences between the major parties, the persistent inconsistency in political thought—all explaining why Americans find it especially hard to understand and cope with the revolutions all over the world in recent years. Marxists in turn might brood over the power of the Horatio Alger fable: an ultrabourgeois fable that helped to prevent the growth of a suitably intense class consciousness and violent class struggle, and that never became so popular on the Continent.

Yet there has obviously been plenty of serious conflict in America. It has repeatedly involved differences as fundamental as those between Andrew Jackson and Nicholas Biddle—differences that the Whigs merely cloaked. De Tocqueville was prophetic on this score too when he observed that the rise of manufacturers was creating an aristocracy of wealth, the most serious threat to the principle of equality, and predicted that it would be the harshest aristocracy known to history because of its callousness rather than simple brutality. His worries over the tyranny of the majority nevertheless led him to slight the possible tyranny of minorities, which all history might lead one to expect. Madison was in this respect more acute, foreseeing the danger that a minority might succeed in dominating government by exploiting popular passions, precisely as the Whigs did. Such tendencies were plain enough even in Jackson's America to make absurd de Tocqueville's assumption of "the absolute sovereignty of the majority"; the common man was far from having it all his own way. The new fashion in political history obscures the still plainer trend thereafter, the growing gap between the ideals and the realities of American democracy—contradictions so glaring that they too made it unique, in that no other people were so prone to an uncritical acceptance of a conventional image of democracy. However shallow or unsophisticated the liberal democrats, they were seeking to realize ideals of liberty and equality that were not in fact cherished by most of the controllers of economic and political power, who were still operating substantially on the assumption of the Federalist John Jay: "Those who own the country ought to govern it." As I see it, the issues raised by the liberals need to be complicated, not minimized.

The problems of the future began emerging in the decades after the triumph of the Whigs in 1840. The growth of manufactures now created a permanent new class of factory workers, who still put in a twelve- to fourteen-hour day and had a harder time because they did not clearly resemble the popular image of the common man. They were not actually independent, able freely to go West as the long popular "safety-valve" theory of the frontier assumed; the great majority of them remained factory hands. Their early strikes and efforts to form unions had been condemned by the courts, which charged them with criminal conspiracy, and though in the last years of Jackson's administration the union movement made considerable progress, it was soon crushed by the panic of 1837 and the long depression that followed. Economic inequality grew more pronounced with the emergence of a new class of millionaires (another American word), described by a leading journalist as "the brightest examples of prosperity in this *touch-stone* land"; the most radiant Commodore Vanderbilt piled up a fortune of over $100,000,000 (in the course reducing the wages of his traction workers). Another new problem arose from the increasing horde of immigrants, many of whom—especially the illiterate—settled in the mill towns and cities. Here they looked like "masses," justifying the fears of Jefferson; they eased the rise of political bosses and the reign of graft. By no choice of their own they contributed as much to the growth of slums, dismal examples of poverty in this touchstone land. Since they helped to keep wages low they aroused hostility among native-born workers, which would keep the melting pot seething with prejudices against racial minorities. Parties like the Know-Nothings showed up. Denied both social and economic equality, the immigrants served to intensify the illiberal tendencies of Populist movements, which bore along much popular prejudice. Fear or hatred of Catholics, Jews, city people, and assorted "aliens," together with businessmen's fear of "radicals," "foreign agitators," and the like, would always complicate and confuse the American consensus.

At the time these problems were overshadowed by the bitter conflict over slavery, which broke up the Whig party and split the Democrats before convulsing the whole nation. In predicting that revolutions would become rarer in democracies, de Tocqueville had noted that America might be an exception because of the issue of slavery; and the New World now outdid the Old in a great civil war, by far the bloodiest war of the century. It obliges a digression from our main theme, the intrinsic issues of democracy. Inexhaustibly fascinating to Americans, the Civil War has produced a wealth of song and legend, a gallery of national heroes, and some hundred thousand books—almost all tending to make Americans forget that it was not only a parochial affair but essentially a national disgrace.

The onset of the Civil War exposed the weaknesses of the peculiar American political system. The Buchanan administration was paralyzed by a feeble President and a divided Congress, both unable to formulate a clear policy or to take decisive action. The new Republican party elected a minority President in a typical campaign in which it evaded the main issues, playing up instead such popular issues as homesteads and railroads, and inventing the legend of the Rail Splitter to go with the log cabin; Lincoln himself made no speeches and showed no awareness of impending crisis. The press, which had already done its worst by sensationalizing every provocative incident, remained mostly irresponsible. The violent partisans on both sides indulged their emotions more freely because of the complacent assumption that if war did break out it would be short, easy, and romantic. Indiscipline and irresponsibility then helped to prolong it. Some brilliant generalship, more old-fashioned chivalry and gallantry, and a possibly attractive amateurishness were offset by a vast deal of inefficiency, waste, blunder, and corruption. Only rough estimates can be made of the casualties, in part because of the countless desertions on both sides.

As for the deeper causes of the war, the diverse explanations are ultimately alike unflattering to America. The early histories that prolonged the hostilities by making the South the villain of the drama were succeeded by more impartial studies indicating that both sides were at fault; sympathy with the South throve on the still-popular assumption that the Negro was hopelessly inferior to the white man. Then came the versions of an "irrepressible conflict" between two irreconcilably different cultures or societies, including Charles Beard's theory that the "real" cause of the war was not slavery but an inevitable economic conflict; these all implied that a free people were simply incapable of settling their differences by rational, civil means, or of controlling their history. They therefore called out the various "revisionists," who diagnosed the war as needless, emphasized its irrationality, blamed the fanatics on both sides, and suggested that Americans went berserk. Since World War II they in turn have come under attack, especially for their view of the war as only a dreadful mistake; their critics at least partially justify it by insisting that it was fought over a fundamental moral issue, the evil of slavery. Only this brings up the embarrassing fact that the United States had lagged behind the rest of Christendom, for slavery had been abolished in Europe and even "backward" Latin America. The recent spate of books commemorating the centennial of the Civil War may be more depressing, at a time of world crisis, as a reminder of the common provinciality of American historians.

Both in fairness and in humility one may note that the South built a good American case for its now unpopular cause. It had plain eco-

nomic grievances, such as tariffs that favored Northern business interests. Fearful of domination by the North, it raised the always difficult
problem of the rights of minorities. Southerners could argue in all
sincerity that they were loyal to the Constitution, especially to the
principle of states' rights upheld by Jefferson, and could appeal to the
right of revolution proclaimed in the Declaration of Independence,
reaffirmed by Lincoln as well as Jefferson. They could also consider
themselves good Christians, since the Bible clearly legalized slavery.
They could maintain that they treated their slaves better than supposedly free factory workers were treated in the North, where employers
recognized no responsibility toward them, simply discharging them
when they became sick, got crippled, or grew old. At that they were
supported by some Northern business interests, which accepted slavery
because it was profitable. (As James Gordon Bennett exclaimed in the
New York *Herald,* protesting against an antislavery meeting, "What
business have all the religious lunatics of the free states to gather in
this commercial city for purposes which, if carried into effect, would
ruin and destroy its prosperity?") There was plenty of prejudice against
the Negro throughout the North too, and ample hypocrisy. Lincoln
himself played politics with the issue in his debates with Stephen
Douglas, ringing out his famous house-divided principle, but also re-
assuring the voters "I am not, nor ever have been, in favor of bringing
about in any way the social and political equality of the white and
black races."

Yet in a history of freedom the main point remains that the South
was fiercely defending chattel slavery, and that it had itself been enslaved by this institution. It had brought on its economic grievances
by its exclusive devotion to King Cotton, growing ever more dependent on the North for shipping, banking, and even food. The profits
of slavery went mostly to a small minority, while the many poor whites
were worse off because the South was backward in education too. Alien
to American democracy as an aristocratic society, resembling the feudal
Old World, it fell short of aristocratic distinction in its culture. The
leisure that enabled wealthy slaveowners to lead a rich life of chivalrous
fantasy and conceit fostered little creativity in art or thought. The
South produced one acute political thinker in John Calhoun (who with
Burke and John Adams has lately become a god of the "new conservatives" in America), but his thought was always clouded when not
vitiated by its ruling motive, to defend slavery; with his penetrating
criticisms of egalitarianism and majority rule went much nonsense

about how slavery had been a "great blessing" to both races, "the great stay of the Union and our free institutions." Thereby he made clearer the logical connections between the ideals of liberty and equality, indeed the necessity of a principle of equality for the maintenance of human rights, or the democratic ideal of freedom for all. As it was, the South refused to compromise on its "peculiar institution." Its many moderates were voted or shouted down by the many zealots who insisted on the blessing of slavery; hopes of a solution by gradual emancipation were doomed by laws prohibiting emancipation, while criticism of slavery was virtually prohibited; and in the Deep South, which was deepest in illiteracy and popular ignorance, hysteria verged on a reign of terror.

Democrats may therefore believe that some good came out of the Civil War. The Union was preserved, and with it the power and prestige of America that would almost certainly have been weakened had the South won. The Emancipation Proclamation, which Lincoln issued on his own, was followed by the Constitutional Amendments prohibiting slavery or involuntary servitude, forbidding the states to abridge the equal rights of citizens. In Lincoln the nation acquired the most beloved of its heroes (outside the South). Another President of little initial promise rose to greatness under the stress of awful responsibility; and having touched sublimity in his Gettysburg Address, he became a Christlike martyr by virtue of his assassination. He merited his apotheosis as in truth a man of sorrows, with a Christlike magnanimity of spirit. Granted that legend has glossed over his shortcomings and magnified his qualities as a man of the common folk, Abraham Lincoln remains an ideal symbol of the democratic faith.

His assassination, however, destroyed whatever chance there may have been of avoiding the disgraceful aftermath of the war. The defeated South again had plain grievances under the rule of carpetbaggers and scalawags, but again had immediately flaunted its intransigence: the Confederate states adopted "Black Codes" that drastically limited the rights of ex-slaves. When these were declared illegal, the Ku Klux Klan set about preserving the Southern way of life by violence and terror. After the Amnesty Act of 1872 the states soon managed to nullify the new Constitutional Amendments and restore complete white supremacy; Jim Crow laws condemned the Negro to social inferiority. Denied the blessing of slavery, plantation owners developed the sharecrop system, which was as uneconomical and more callous, assuring the degradation of poor whites too. These compensated by developing intenser prejudice against the Negro. The upshot was that the South continued to lag far behind the rest of the nation, economically, politically, and culturally. Its aristocracy did little but cultivate more sedulously the legend of its chivalry, illustrating what Ellen Glasgow wrote of Southern women, that they were "capable of dying for an idea, but not of conceiving one." Many of its poor remained illiterate for want of public schools, and helped to make it a happy hunting ground for demagogues. All suffered from the incubus of a social system that with the establishment of the United Nations would become a serious embarrassment to the whole nation.[4]

In the North the Civil War was followed by the scandalous corruption of the Grant administration, the worst in American history until President Harding came along. As Henry Adams commented, the good General Grant was in the presidency a Neanderthal type, and the "progress" from Washington to him might alone refute the theory of evolution. He accordingly brings us back to our main theme, the basic issues of democracy. Although his administration may be condoned as a natural letdown after the long tension of the war, it was portentous as the prelude to an era of rule by business, unabashed materialism, and mediocrity or worse in political life.

"Labor is prior to and independent of capital," Lincoln said in his first annual message. "Labor is the superior of capital and deserves much the higher consideration." His Republican party, however, had shown more solicitude for capital in its platform, for instance by promises of tariffs and easy admission of cheap immigrant laborers. With the help of tariffs, Northern industry expanded immensely in meeting the needs of the war, and was as immensely profitable; a newspaper reported that wartime New York alone boasted of several hundred millionaires, whereas twenty years earlier there had been only a couple of dozen in the whole country. Much of the profit was made at some expense of patriotism.[5] Nevertheless taxes were promptly repealed at the end of the war, while the high wartime tariffs were left in. Businessmen were now

---

4 American diplomats might wish that there were some decent way of allowing Mississippi to secede.

5 In 1863 Thomas Mellon noted that "such opportunities for making money had never existed before in all my former experience," and advised his son not to be such a goose as to enlist, "be seduced from his duty" of becoming "a smart, intelligent businessman"; and the young man did not disappoint the founder of the aluminum fortune. Among other famous fortunes that were hatched at this time—Armour, Morris, Pillsbury, Rockefeller—was that of young Pierpont Morgan, who for $3.50 each bought 5,000 condemned carbines from the government in the East, and smartly sold them to troops on the Mississippi for $22.

in the saddle. As an untraditional society, America was to be the preeminent example of how unregulated private enterprise works out, given substantial aid by government.

Again the boasts about the American Way were backed up by sufficiently awesome achievements. Granted that industrialists had the advantage of vast natural resources, they displayed remarkable enterprise in taking advantage of their opportunities, rapidly building up America into the greatest of industrial powers, giving it more steel and oil, more telephones and telegraph wires—more of almost everything than any other nation produced. Animated more by a love of money-making than a love of money, they were more daring and imaginative in making it than were most European businessmen. Typically they were more liberal with their money too. Andrew Carnegie would set forth the principle of moral trusteeship, arguing that in return for the opportunities their society had given them, the wealthy were obliged to assist it, exercise their proved abilities in large-scale philanthropy; and he proved his sincerity by not only giving away millions—anticipating the singular historic phenomenon of Rockefellers unto the third and the fourth generation busy in giving away the fortune of John D.—but endorsing the radical idea of steep inheritance taxes, as a proper penalty on those who failed to discharge their moral obligation to society. Trustees or no, businessmen were directly responsible for the wealth and power that enabled America to become a leader of the democracies. Allan Nevins has therefore deplored the "feminine idealism" that has been apologetic about all our dollars, leading other historians to do lamentable injustice to "the heroes of our material growth."

A masculine realist must acknowledge, however, that American business was often grossly inefficient as well as hugely wasteful. Thus the largest railway system in the world was built at exorbitant cost, paid by the public, and much of it was very poorly built. Certainly the heroes were rewarded lavishly enough, no less when they milked instead of built railways and other industries; by the end of the century millionaires were counted by the thousands and billionaires were in sight. Many made fortunes by fraudulent manipulation of "other people's money," most had got rich too quickly to have Carnegie's sense of social responsibility. Conscience was stilled by the "social Darwinism" of Herbert Spencer, who in America won a popularity such as no philosopher had ever enjoyed before. Spencer gave what passed for scientific authority to the theory that free competition was the essential means to progress, assuring "the survival of the fittest"; so millionaires were *ipso facto* the fittest, and if ruthless were only obeying the law of evolution, which only a feminine idealist could deplore.[6] It also followed that any state interference or effort at social reform was a violation of cosmic law that could only impede progress. The extraordinary vogue of Spencer obscured the main drive of free competition, which was to lessen or do away with competition by industry-wide associations and secret agreements on prices—efforts that were at first ineffective because businessmen found it hard to trust one another, but that eventually culminated in the well-organized trusts, including the "Money Trust" that monopolized big credits and became the greatest power in the economy.

But our main concern here is how the common people fared, and how independent they remained now that most of them were no longer self-employed as they had been in Jackson's America. By and large they obviously prospered; their standard of living rose as the nation achieved the highest per capita income in the world. They at least retained more feeling of independence, and a livelier sense of opportunity, than common men in Europe. Still, there were always a great many who were poorly off. We cannot say precisely how many and how poorly, since little study of them was made in a society that resisted the idea that it had a poor class (except maybe the foreign immigrants), but the American Way was unquestionably hard on millions of little men. Farmers, who were about the most truly competitive class in America, had many a bad year and never an easy time holding their own against the stronger organized interests they had to deal with, such as railroads, grain dealers, elevator operators, and bankers. Most maintained a precarious independence by heavily mortgaging their land; more and more lost the vaunted independence of property owners, by 1900 about a third of them being tenants. Industrial workers, whose number increased tenfold in the second half of the century, were mostly not property owners, and they were liable to insecurity because of frequent layoffs and prolonged unemployment

---

6 A pretty example was a Sunday-school talk by John D. Rockefeller. "The growth of a large business is merely a survival of the fittest," he explained. "The American Beauty rose can be produced in the splendor and fragrance which bring cheer to its beholder only by sacrificing the early buds which grow up around it. This is not an evil tendency in business. It is merely the working-out of a law of nature and a law of God." As one who detects here the fragrance of oil too, I might add that I am living testimony to the vogue of Spencer. God help me, I was named after him.

in depressions. They had to put up as well with poor working conditions, including the highest rate of accident in the world; most employers neglected to install safety devices since they were not held liable for accident. Efforts of workers to organize for self-protection were constantly fought by employers and menaced by depressions. As the panic of 1837 wrecked the early labor union movement, so the panic of 1873 wrecked a later one. In the period from then to 1898, known as the "Great Depression" and climaxed by the worse crash of 1893, conflict grew violent as workers fought slashes in wages by strikes, which were broken by force. (In one steel strike Carnegie's hired gunmen muted his principle of moral trusteeship by killing ten workers while he went off grouse hunting.) At the end of the period only some half a million of the 17,000,000 factory workers were organized.

They made less headway in securing legislation to protect them. Workmen's compensation, limitation of working hours, protection of women, and other such regulations common in Europe were effectively denounced as socialistic and un-American. When the states began passing such laws, the courts struck them down, holding that they were violations of property rights or freedom of contract. The Supreme Court, made up largely of former corporation lawyers, emerged as the supreme guardian of *laissez faire*. Conservatives continued to maintain that government was the main threat to liberty and human rights, even though business had dominated it ever since the Civil War. The Republican party, which provided all but Grover Cleveland's administrations, was consistently on the side of business, but Democrats were hardly distinguishable; their platforms reflected no basic difference in philosophy and gave as little idea of the real problems of the period. There were a few bright pages in the dreary political record, such as civil service reform. There was also some confusion due to conflict of interest between big and little business, and to the flourishing business of politics; politicians devoted much private enterprise to promoting their own interests, extorting remarkably fancy sums from companies seeking favors. Now and then businessmen joined in the revolts against the most scandalous or arrogant of the city bosses, like Tweed, who were giving America notoriously the worst municipal government in the Western world. But in Washington the corporations usually retained firm control.

One change of some consequence was that American businessmen at last began following the example of the British by entering government. The powerful Senator Aldrich typified the "Millionaires' Club" that controlled Congress in the last decades of the century, during which Mark Hanna finally organized the Republican party on a sound business basis. When popular indignation over monopolies forced such concessions as the Interstate Commerce Act regulating railroads, it was carefully drawn up so as to give them no serious trouble; Aldrich described it as "a delusion and a sham . . . made to answer the clamor of the ignorant and the unreasoning." The Sherman Antitrust Act was similarly provided with the necessary loopholes, becoming known as the "mother of trusts." The Supreme Court could be depended upon to spot all the loopholes. In the severe depression following the panic of 1893 the Court distinguished itself by declaring unconstitutional an income tax, which every other sovereign nation was free to impose. Most of the wealthy did not yet subscribe to Carnegie's principle of moral trusteeship. The prevailing attitude was summed up by Frederick Townsend in *The Passing of the Idle Rich* (1911):

> The class I represent care nothing for politics. . . . [But] touch the question of the tariff, touch the issue of the income tax, touch the problem of railroad regulation, or touch the most vital of all business matters, the question of general federal regulation of industrial corporations, and the people amongst whom I live my life become immediately rabid partisans. . . . We are not politicians or public thinkers; we are the rich; we own America; we got it, God knows how, but we intend to keep it if we can by throwing all the tremendous weight of our support, our influence, our money, our political connection, our purchased senators, our hungry congressmen, our public-speaking demagogues, into the scale against any legislature, any political platform, any Presidential campaign that threatens the integrity of our estate.

This dreary history had an implication especially dismaying for liberals. In the 1880's, when the Rhode Island legislature sent Aldrich to the Senate and someone remarked that Standard Oil had done everything with the Pennsylvania legislature except refine it, the people kept re-electing such legislatures, returning Aldrich to the Senate for four more terms. Likewise they voted in the mediocre Presidents, to the tune of wholesale bribery and fraud. Immigrants got the blame for the corruption, which in cities they obviously made easier, but born Americans did the corrupting and its beneficiaries got ample support all over the country. Businessmen had more power and prestige in democratic America than in Europe for the reason observed by de Tocqueville: the principle of equality naturally tended to generate a consuming passion for material well-being, and with it a particular respect for success in material pursuits. The common man's fear of big business was stirred chiefly when his own material interests were menaced, and it could therefore be allayed by promises of a full dinner pail.

Yet this is not the whole story. The common man hardly made a worse record as a voter than the wealthy, educated classes, who consistently supported the business philosophy and the politicians who ran under its colors, however mediocre or unscrupulous. (Among the disciples of Spencer's crude gospel of social Darwinism were Presidents Charles Eliot of Harvard and Nicholas Murray Butler of Columbia.) He at least remained independent enough to assert himself and his rights, sensible enough not to be fooled all the time. Continuous popular agitation during this period bred an astonishing assortment of reformers and third-party movements, from Greenbackers to socialists and even anarchists. It made best sellers of such "radical" works as Henry George's *Progress and Poverty* and Edward Bellamy's *Looking Backward*. By the end of the century "the heroes of our material growth" were under mounting attack, more on the defensive than were businessmen in Europe. It was not surprising that the majority of the people responded to the Progressive movement, which finally organized resistance to the long reign of business and marked another turning point in American history.

The Progressives exemplified the American genius for private associations that de Tocqueville had noted as another by-product of the principle of equality. Committees, leagues, and societies of all kinds sprang up everywhere and cooperated or federated to battle for reforms. Among their earliest successes was the regulation of child labor, a reform no less notable because it was shockingly belated; within a few years almost all the states passed laws limiting the working hours of children and setting minimum ages for leaving school. Agitation to regulate the working hours of women had tardier but similar success, as in 1908 the Supreme Court at last upheld a ten-hour act. All workers were aided by laws providing for accident compensation, tenement and factory regulation, and public health standards, and the union movement picked up again. Meanwhile the "muckrakers" attracted hundreds of thousands of readers by exposing the inner workings of big business, and the connections between business and both "the treason of the Senate" and the corruption of municipal government. All states made the bribing of voters more difficult by introducing the Australian secret ballot (first adopted by Massachusetts in 1888). In Washington the Progressives won the support of Theodore Roosevelt, the first President since the Jacksonian era to attack "the malefactors of great wealth." Although he blustered more than he used the big stick, he did much to popularize their cause, while helping to put through such reforms as the first Pure Food and Drug Act. Under the Taft administration much more Progressive legislation was pushed through Congress, in particular the Constitutional Amendments legalizing the income tax and providing for direct election of the Senate. The drive for woman suffrage made such progress that its victory was practically assured, a dozen states having granted them the vote. The whole movement was consummated by the administration of Woodrow Wilson, whose promise of a "New Freedom" was carried out by the most extensive legislation in American history before the "New Deal" to come.

The subsequent decline of Progressivism was not due merely to the distraction of the World War. Businessmen too had organized to combat its program, with considerable success. Much of the reform legislation had the usual loopholes, which could be widened into breaches with the aid of the courts and compliant administrators; labor unions were still branded as radical and un-American, so effectively that only about a tenth of industrial workers were organized when the war came; and all the old slogans would resound as brassily as ever when the Republicans took charge again in the Harding-Coolidge-Hoover era. The return to "normalcy" also called attention to the characteristic limitations of the Progressives. They were typically better at moral indignation than at understanding the economy and the new society, and counted too heavily on reducing the power of money by simple remedies like trust busting and the direct primary. In keeping with Populist tradition many were provincial, the more fearful of both big business and the big city because nostalgic for the vanishing simplicities of rural America; as Theodore Roosevelt observed, they were at bottom not really progressive but retrogressive. Many were suspicious of labor unions too, and some veered to the right out of fear of alien socialism, even though the Socialist party led by Eugene Debs was strictly nonrevolutionary. Others ended in dubious battle, such as William Jennings Bryan's defense of the old-time religion against the heathenish theory of evolution. Most characteristic was their tendency to isolationism—the cause of preserving the purity and innocence of America from the insidious corruptions of the Old World.

Yet the Progressive movement was far from being a superficial or transient disturbance. It is easier to criticize now because it bequeathed solid, enduring reforms, "new freedoms" that have long been taken for granted. The Progressives at least managed to bring American democracy into the twentieth century, and to begin adopting its avowed ideals to the facts of modern industrial life. They awakened Americans to the necessity of government regulation to secure real freedom for the common man, and the possible value of more rather than less government in promoting the common welfare, thus preparing the way for Roosevelt's New Deal when "normalcy" collapsed in the worst of its normal depressions. They brought out the ideal quality of American materialism: the simple belief that the common people ought to enjoy the decent living they naturally want and need first of all, the simple hopes that the apostles of *laissez faire* constantly promised to fulfill but so often let down. They enlivened another traditional expression of the principle of equality, which from Jefferson on had stressed the dignity and worth of all men, and the right of all to a fair chance to realize their potentialities. The battle for women's rights in particular emphasized again the logical necessity of a principle of equality for the sake of freedom and justice. (Its leaders soon discovered—as the Abolitionists had—that their opponents had Scripture on their side.) Altogether, the Progressives were fervent and successful enough to justify the concept of an American liberal tradition beyond *laissez faire* and the popular rhetoric about Americanism.

Inasmuch as most conservatives came around to accepting the bulk of the reforms, one may say that the Progressive movement maintained the American consensus. It did much more for free private enterprise too than its champions appreciated by protecting it against its excesses and abuses, helping American business to become more enlightened and responsible, and more efficient too, through the tardy discovery of what Robert Owen had demonstrated a century before, that humane management might pay. Hence Progressivism forestalled any possible rise of revolutionary Marxism, whose disciples point out quite truly that it was a bourgeois, not a proletarian movement. It may accordingly remind us that the "ideology" of America remains a very modest, ramshackle affair. The consensus on broad simplicities or vague generalities that has kept the nation united has likewise kept most of its public debate uncommonly shallow or irrelevant. Thus when the Progressives managed to have their way with the federal government, business and propertied interests began making a fetish of "states' rights," since they found it easier to influence when not to bribe state government; the argument still goes that the services provided by state government are more efficient, enlightened, and incorrupt, less injurious to the character and less menacing to the freedom of the people, than are services provided by the federal government, because state government is much "closer" to the people. (Readers might ask themselves how close they feel to their state government, or whether they vote more regularly in state than in national elections.) At the same time, the consensus could have the virtues of its defects. The absence of clear-cut, fundamental philosophical differences between the major parties that exasperates orderly thinkers, clouds debate, and befuddles voters has also toned down political conflict, prevented differences from becoming so irreconcilable as they did before the Civil War, and facilitated the compromise necessary to the maintenance of a free society. (And readers might ask themselves whether they would prefer the major parties to take clearly opposed stands on such burning issues as civil rights for Negroes or peaceful coexistence with the Soviet.)

In this light we may reconsider, lastly, the democratic principle of "the will of the people," which in effect is always the will of the majority. On many if not most specific issues this will is confused and uncertain, as it is bound to be in pluralistic America with its uncommon diversity of regional, racial, religious, and subcultural interests—a society rather different, once more, from the standardized mass society that strikes the literary eye. When the opinion of the majority is fairly clear it may still be disregarded by the government, for a variety of reasons. Congressmen are likely to give more heed to organized minorities or pressure groups; the federal government—the reputed leviathan that is swallowing up states' rights—is in fact often at the mercy of local interests, sometimes of the chairman of a Congressional committee; and bureaucrats too, supposedly rising to "monocratic control," have to play politics every day. (The Department of Agriculture, for example, has reported an average of 159 requests a day from congressmen.) On both counts there has been little apparent danger of the tyranny of the majority, much less of mob rule, except during periods of patriotic hysteria whipped up by McCarthys. Yet American history from Jefferson to Wilson indicates clearly enough that "the will of the people" is not a meaningless concept, nor in practice a mere fake. It bears out the argument that democracy best assures that government will carry out the popular will. Those in power may or may not respect this will, but they are disposed to heed it simply because they want to get re-elected, while the party out of power is always in search of a majority. What counts is not my vote, or even any assurance that the majority will vote, but the awareness of political leaders that many people will do so.

The chief question, I should say, remains whether the popular will can be trusted to be sufficiently intelligent and enlightened, or "government by salesmanship" sufficiently responsible. But it remains open because the common people in the democracies have made a considerably better showing than traditionalists thought possible.

3. *Democracy in Britain*

"Very nearly everything in history," said some Englishman, "very nearly did not happen." This flippant observation, so grating to those who wish to see logic in history or just to make decent sense of it, might nevertheless seem to apply to the political development of Britain in a century of far-reaching change. Its history gives little immediate impression of either inexorable logic or the wisdom of farsighted leaders. Speaking of Sir Robert Peel, Trevelyan observed that the greatest English statesman of the period characteristically could never see four years ahead, and to do justice to the achievements of Peel he cited the wisdom of Oliver Cromwell: "None goes so far as he who knows not whither he is going." The country kept going toward democracy by fits and starts, through muddled compromises, in ways displeasing to both idealists and historical materialists. While periodic spells of hard times evoked agitation, an otherwise exceptional prosperity made it possible to carry through extensive changes, but the prosperity might as logically have discouraged efforts at reform; in any case Marxists had little to do with the whole process, which mostly violated the iron laws of Marx. Among its chief agents were the "Philosophical Radicals," fathered by Jeremy Bentham: bourgeois types, scarcely radical by Continental standards, unlike all other radicals before and after them in their stress on prudential values, their appeal to utility instead of flaming ideals or revolutionary hopes. So far from making liberty or equality a sovereign ideal, Bentham had attacked as rhetorical nonsense the abstractions of natural law and natural rights incorporated in the American Declaration of Independence and the French Declaration of the Rights of Man and Citizen.

Yet the political history of England was more orderly than that of

either America or France, so much so that one might as truly say that
nearly every important change was almost bound to come in some such
manner as it did. The whole development makes quite good sense in
the light of English tradition, which had evolved parliamentary government in ways unpremeditated, firmly established the rights of Englishmen in an unwritten Constitution, and secured these rights by a
Glorious Revolution in which almost nobody got killed or had a chance
to win glory. With all the inconsistency or illogic went a good deal
of much more uncommon good sense and good will, a moderation that
could give the muddle the fairer name of reasonable compromise. Social
and political change was impelled immediately by the Industrial Revolution, but it was made easier by the engrained habits of free public discussion, open criticism of rulers, coupled with a respect for authority
and with that rare wonder of political history—the institutionalized
idea of a "loyal opposition." The Philosophical Radicals, whose democratic objectives were indeed radical enough for their time, remained
true to tradition in seeking to achieve these objectives by civil, constitutional means, seeing no need of revolution. Now known as liberals
because of their ultimate success, they established the theory and
practice of liberal democracy to which John Stuart Mill gave classic
expression. While helping to maintain the stablest government in
Europe, this also preserved the fullest respect for civil liberties. Today
one can scarcely imagine either a Communist revolution in Britain or
a Committee on Un-British Activities.

The violent reaction against the French Revolution, heralded by
Edmund Burke, may then serve to emphasize the sober truth that liberal
democracy in Britain was nevertheless a hard-won achievement. From
first to last a primary source of conflict was the principle of inequality
that was also deeply engrained in an aristocratic society, and constituted a fundamental difference between Britain and America. Fears
of the "laboring poor" made matters worse for the early victims of the
Industrial Revolution, inspiring repressive measures like the banning
of unions. Public discussion of parliamentary reform was prohibited,
and champions of the common people were persecuted, jailed, even
tried for high treason. As the Tories took over the government for a
generation, they enlisted religious fervor in their crusade against "the
infidel philosophy of Tom Paine" and other reformers. The defenders
of the "happy constitution in Church and State" managed to couple
Jacobinism and Popery, exploiting the traditional dread of the Roman
Church, though no church was more hostile to Jacobinism or to demo-

cratic principles. Similarly they combated such further menaces to the "national liberties" as public education. While the Archbishop of Canterbury helped to defeat a bill providing for elementary schools throughout the land, none other than the president of the Royal Society for the advancement of science thundered that educating the laboring classes would only corrupt their morals by enabling them to read "vicious books," and "instead of teaching them subordination, it would render them fractious and refractory . . . insolent to their superiors." A few years after Waterloo, when one out of seven Englishmen was a pauper, came "Peterloo": an orderly but huge gathering of working people on St. Peter's Fields in Manchester, met to demand parliamentary reform, so frightened the magistrates that they set the military on them, killing a dozen and wounding hundreds more. The Tory ministry promptly approved the shooting without bothering to inquire into it.

Still, this most infamous aftermath of Waterloo was a petty disturbance by contrast with the bloodbaths that awaited French workers; and even so most Englishmen were appalled by it. The indignation in all ranks put an end to any possibility of a reign of conservative terror. Shortly after Peterloo the government began making concessions to the "laboring poor," repealing the ban on labor unions. By this time, too, Canning was liberalizing foreign policy. In supporting the Metternich regime Britain had at least refused to join the Holy Alliance, and it now opposed Metternich's war on all popular movements toward constitutional government and national independence; Canning let it be known that "while England was no friend to revolution, she did emphatically insist on the right of nations to set up for themselves whatever form of government they thought best, and to be left free to manage their own affairs." He therefore supported the Greek War of Independence, which was frowned on by the Duke of Wellington, the hero of Waterloo. He did much more for Americans than most of them ever appreciated by supporting as well the Monroe Doctrine: the power of the British fleet discouraged the intentions of the Holy Alliance to help the Spanish monarchy recover its colonies in Latin America.

The most apparent reason why high Tories like Wellington lost control was the power of public opinion. Thus in jailing the publisher of Tom Paine's *The Rights of Man* the authorities were rightly alarmed: it was immensely popular, selling more than 200,000 copies in two years. After the reaction marking the ascendancy of his rival Burke, Paine again became popular, especially with the working class. The new democratic movement then found as forceful a native spokesman in

William Cobbett. A strident journalist, often coarse in his indignation over the oppression of the poor, Cobbett gave more trouble to the authorities because he was nevertheless no Jacobin but an English kind of radical, calling on Parliament to act and demanding that workers be given the vote. And all along the influence of Jeremy Bentham was spreading. To Karl Marx, Bentham was "a genius in the way of bourgeois stupidity," who thereby became the "oracle of the common-place bourgeois intelligence of the nineteenth century"; but this was to say that he was a very considerable power. Perhaps a fairer way of saying it is that his school of Utilitarianism or Philosophical Radicalism best epitomized the distinctive logic and/or illogic of English political development.

Now, most obvious today are the limitations and extravagances of Bentham. While severely criticizing on empirical grounds the abstractions popularized by the Enlightenment, he was himself an old-fashioned rationalist, more pedantic than most, and more ludicrous in his faith in schematic logic, illustrated by his effort to devise a precise calculus of pleasure and pain. In applying his criterion of utility, the greatest happiness of the greatest number, he took an incredibly limited view of feelings, sentiments, desires, motives, or the sources of happiness. No ostensibly empirical thinker ever exhibited less experience or elementary understanding of human nature, the "Springs of Action" he carefully tabulated; in his tables man was a creature of appetite who lacked not only such springs as conscience, self-respect, aesthetic sense, and love of order but even a thirst for action and power. Bentham had as little historical sense, especially of the transparent power of customs and institutions he thought useless. For a "philosophical" radical he was most conspicuously deficient in a philosophy of history or society. He never questioned his naïve assumption that calculated self-interest necessarily led to both individual happiness and social good.

His immediate followers were generally as uncritical of his premises, all too loyal to his spirit. As for pleasure, Bertrand Russell observed, "one feels that they had read of it in books, and supposed it must be a good thing, but that in their lives they knew nothing of it." Otherwise they accentuated the bourgeois tendencies of the master's thought—the narrow concept of utility, the distrust of sentiment, the neglect of spiritual interests, the faith in the calculating spirit, the reduction of morality to the shrewd egoistic virtues, or to what seemed good to a society of shopkeepers. They differed chiefly in making more of the doctrine of *laissez faire* that Bentham had adopted from Adam Smith.

With this they assumed more or less unconsciously that some kind of "natural law" did after all govern society, assuring that harmony and order would come out of the pursuit of self-interest, and they asserted more explicitly an essentially negative conception of government as mere arbiter or policeman. They seemed as unconscious that the useful social services they urged on it, such as provision for public health and education, would naturally result in more government or state "interference."

Nevertheless, the Philosophical Radicals were remarkably effective for the long run. Virtually all the major reforms of the century—legal, political, social—may be traced to them. The easy criticism of the principle of utility too often implies that it is simply mean or vulgar, whereas Edmund Burke himself had appealed to it, as had almost all the greater political thinkers of England. The difference was that despite his narrowness Bentham was much more realistic, consistent, and thoroughgoing than his predecessors, as well as more optimistic about the possibilities of improvement. As John Stuart Mill observed, he was too often blind to the value of established institutions and beliefs, but no thinker had ever had so keen an eye for the practical abuses they obscured, all the crusted falsehood, inhumanity, and downright absurdity they sanctioned. He got started as a student of law, with its venerable maze of legal fictions. While conservatives kept talking about the "true liberties" of Englishmen, and lawyers declaimed that "the judicial forms are the shields of liberty," Bentham forced the pertinent question that nobody had asked: "What judicial forms? What liberty? Whose liberty?" He then had no trouble showing that the forms often served chiefly as shields of corruption and degradation, "liberty in rulers to oppress subjects." So he proceeded to analyze other customs and institutions—religion, war, imperialism, aristocracy, monarchy— always asking relentlessly: "What is the use of it? What or whom is it good for?" Among the misfortunes of nineteenth-century America was that it had no critic so acute as Bentham.

It was his awareness in particular of the practical abuses of authority that finally led Bentham to advocate democracy. Although he was long hostile to the principles of the American and French revolutions, and always concerned primarily with good government rather than ideals of liberty, equality, and fraternity, the principle of equal rights was implicit in his criterion of the happiness of the greatest number, and his assumptions that all men had a more or less equal capacity for happiness, the happiness of every man should count. He could not help perceiving that the aristocratic state of Britain was administered mainly in the interests of the privileged few, with customary indifference to the happiness or the misery of the greatest number; and when the government ignored the reforms he proposed, he concluded that a government not in fact representative of the people could not be held accountable to them either. He then went all the way to democracy—a fuller democracy than the America of his day. To assure that the good of all would be considered by rulers, he called for universal suffrage with a secret ballot, even votes for women. As logically he called for not only full freedom of public discussion but public education for all, as a prerequisite for both enlightened self-interest and intelligent suffrage. Still another democratic principle implicit in his thought was a natural, if possibly unphilosophical tendency to individualism. His crude psychology of self-interest, his stress on the egoistic virtues, and his endorsement of *laissez faire* all focused attention on the individual, who might put in a stronger claim for rights because he was supposed to be prudent and calculating, and more useful to society when self-assertive.

At worst, the fallacies of Utilitarianism were less dangerous than most philosophical fallacies because they did not invite rhetoric or double-talk, and were more readily corrigible; all its propositions did invite empirical analysis. Call it bourgeois, pedestrian, earthbound, Bentham's philosophy may still appear to advantage by contrast with German metaphysical idealism, and with the political thought of its Romantic or religious critics. At least its prosaic common sense made much better sense for the purposes of a free society. Always it focused attention on practical evils and concrete freedoms, instead of justice and freedom in the abstract. It drove home the commonplace but at the time radical idea that poverty and misery are not conducive to social health, or simply that "all pain is an evil"—a remark of Bentham's that upset respectable people. Even his naïve ideas about "a sum of pleasures," in which push-pin counted for as much as poetry, could be put to good use. As restated by John Plamenatz, his logical imperative was essentially "Act so as to ensure, so far as you can, that people get what they want, according to their own preferences." We may then drop the question of whether a society so governed is necessarily "happier" than traditional societies. We are left with other troublesome questions that did not trouble Bentham enough—for instance, whether people are generally good enough judges of their own interests, not to mention the national interest, and to what extent good government (which he tacitly assumed would be run by superior men like himself) should look ahead of their immediate, usually shortsighted wants. But we are left, too, with a liberal principle: a willingness to take people as they are, respect their wants, consider first their preferences instead of what we think they need or ought to want—the possible conceit behind the inveterate impulse to coerce. This principle helps to explain why most Utilitarians were in fact liberals devoted to the cause of personal freedom, even though it is not certain that free men are happier.

Or call them bourgeois, and it calls attention to the major role played by their class in the movement toward democracy, particularly in their first decisive political success—the Reform Bill of 1832. The support the Philosophical Radicals won from the growing middle class was characteristically not disinterested: this class was mostly not represented in Parliament, which was controlled by the landed aristocracy with the aid of the many "rotten boroughs." The outcome of the long battle for parliamentary reform now looks like as characteristic a tame compromise, and may make the popular enthusiasm over it seem ludicrously British. By enfranchising only householders who paid a yearly rent of at least ten pounds, the Reform Bill left half the middle class and the whole working class without a vote, and so made the quickly disillusioned workmen only more class-conscious. The moderation of the English, Mill remarked, was due to caution more than insight; they were too pleased with any medium just because it was a medium. Nevertheless the measure was something like a revolution by the standards of Burke, and was so viewed by many Tories and high churchmen. While doing away with the rotten boroughs once and for all, it ended the aristocratic monopoly on government; the Whig aristocrats who now came into power could hope to maintain it only by the support of the middle class. Plain radicals like Cobbett had supported the bill as about the most that public opinion was ready for, since many workers were still uneducated, neither clearly prepared for suffrage nor uniformly bent on having it. The reform Parliament then proved itself by promptly enacting further reforms, some revolutionary enough by contemporary American standards, notably the abolition of slavery throughout the British Empire (the slave trade had previously been abolished), and a Factory Act that assured effective regulation of child labor by providing for government inspectors.

A few key men and events may suffice to body out the main themes in British political history thereafter. The repeal of the Corn Laws (1846), another notable victory for public opinion, was immediately another for "bourgeois" interests. Richard Cobden, the leading crusader for free trade, was a cotton manufacturer quite aware that it was good for English businessmen. He could therefore sound unctuous when he maintained that it was also "agreeable to the highest behests of Christianity—to buy in the cheapest market and sell in the dearest"; while he defended the complete freedom of manufacturers to run their business as they pleased. John Bright, the "radical cotton-spinner," agreed that manufacturers should not be oppressed by regulation of working conditions. They were also alike, however, in their sincere devotion to such causes as international peace. Cobden crusaded so fervently—all over Europe—because he saw in free trade the means to world peace. Others joined him in attacking the Corn Laws out of a humanitarian desire to aid the poor. In general, English businessmen who entered government were more philosophical and responsible than American business leaders, and won a larger political following because they had a clearer concern for the national interest. Spencer's social Darwinism never had any such vogue in Britain as it did in the United States, nor was liberty so completely identified with *laissez faire* in a "British Way." When untaxed American millionaires were preening themselves on their fitness, Joseph Chamberlain, another "radical" manufacturer, was demanding a graduated income tax to pay for more social reforms.

The repeal of the Corn Laws was also portentous in that it was put through by a Tory ministry, under Sir Robert Peel. Here again it is possible to detect low motives, since Tory landowners were beginning to learn the political wisdom of playing up the grievances of factory workers in order to hold their own against the business class (who worked up a comparable solicitude over the grievances of rural laborers). Yet it was no less significant that a government made up largely of landowners had been willing to sacrifice their economic interests. The English aristocracy was proving much less stubborn and shortsighted than the French aristocracy was before and after the French Revolution. One may find a utilitarian moral in the political history of Britain: its conservatives—both aristocratic and bourgeois—learned to accept change more readily and gracefully than did their compeers on the Continent.

Their severest test was the great Chartist movement that got under way in 1838, one of the years of depression. Rapidly sweeping the country and attracting more than a million signatures, this inspired enough rioting by class-conscious workers to suggest an incipient revolution. What caused all the uproar was the demand for a new charter of liberties, a Magna Carta for workingmen, with the famous Six Points suggested by American democracy: universal male suffrage, a secret ballot, equal electoral districts, annual parliaments, removal of property qualifications of MPs, and payment of members. The upper classes came through the test in their usual manner, inglorious, bowed, and unbloodied. The Six Points were immediately denounced as revolutionary, though all but annual parliaments would in time become law. Macaulay expressed the typical Whig attitude, declaring that while a little more parliamentary reform might be a good thing, universal suffrage would ruin the nation. The government met the peril by jailing or transporting the principal leaders of the Chartists. Already, however, the movement had begun petering out on its own, because of confusion and dissension within its ranks; and it collapsed entirely in 1848—the very year when revolutions broke out all over Europe. Yet another reason for its collapse was that it had not simply failed. Alarm over the violent disposition of the aroused workmen had expressed itself more sensibly by the support of more reforms. These included the radical Ten-Hours Bill, the battle for which was led by no proletarian radical but by Lord Shaftesbury and the manufacturer Fielden. Hence the bitter class struggle did not come to a head in open class war, and Britain was spared the revolutionary contagion of 1848.

When the campaign to enfranchise the workers was renewed, it was no longer primarily a proletarian movement. Its leaders were John Bright and Gladstone, who harked back to the Philosophical Radicals; it was supported by the petty bourgeois, who also lacked the vote; and the Reform Bill of 1867 that finally extended suffrage to many in the lower classes was put through by the Conservative ministry of Disraeli. While men of the old school resigned themselves to the ruin of the nation, the new voters made a respectable start by promptly putting Gladstone into power. Under the "Grand Old Man" the old Whig party, representing chiefly the upper classes, was transformed into the Liberal party, with a broad mass appeal. England at last caught up with Bentham by establishing universal public education (1870). Among other approaches to the ideal of equality was an order opening the civil service to all classes by competitive examinations. Social reform became a normal democratic process instead of a lordly or grudging concession by the ruling class. Disraeli made a point of naturalizing reform in a new Conservatism, which competed for the vote of workmen by enacting legislation in their interest. Gladstone finished his work as a Liberal statesman by a Reform Bill (1884) that gave almost all men the vote.

Even apart from his specific accomplishments, Gladstone stands out as the leading political figure in this movement to liberal democracy. "I was brought up to distrust and dislike liberty," wrote the godliest of British statesmen, "I learned to believe in it. That is the key to all my changes."[7] The unabashed, unsophisticated moral earnestness that may now appear ultra-Victorian was at the time a godsend for the democratic cause. Backed by great energy, and informed by a utilitarian concern for the business of good government, it did much to make this cause thoroughly respectable. Above all, it led Gladstone habitually to address the new electorate of common men on a high plane, treating them as rational and responsible beings—a tribute not commonly paid Americans by their politicians. In his constant appeal to public opinion he might edify by exposing his limitations in intellectual acuteness and depth, but he set a truly lofty example by discussing serious issues in as serious a tone, appealing to intelligence and the sense of justice instead of vulgar emotion and self-interest.

Another key figure in the transition was John Stuart Mill, the "saint of Victorian rationalism," who by a somewhat agonizing reappraisal made over Philosophical Radicalism into an explicitly liberal philosophy. While his thought was still grounded in theory on the principle of utility, his concerns were much broader than Bentham's, involving more the moral ends than the efficient means of a free society. He took up the problems raised by the oncoming democracy, not anticipated by Bentham, in particular the possible tyranny of the majority, the practical abuses of authority backed by public opinion. He was also more concerned with the interests and needs of the working class than of the business class, which by now was taking good enough care of itself. Perceiving that unregulated competition restricted the actual freedom of workers, he gave up his early *laissez faire* liberalism, accepted the need of state interference, and gradually veered toward socialism. In his *Principles of Political Economy* he argued for economic freedom in a profounder sense, maintaining that all economic and political institutions were man-made and therefore changeable, and that the main

---

[7] Debunkers may note that he was no friend of the North in the American Civil War. Among the unhappy lessons in the education of Henry Adams was the discovery in later years that it had been Gladstone—not the unscrupulous, cynical Lord Palmerston —who urged taking a strong line against the North that might have brought Britain into the war, with incalculable consequences for the future of American democracy. But traditionalists might be reminded that it was the upper classes who favored the slave-holding South. British workers supported the North even though they suffered most directly from the loss of Southern cotton, by which the textile industry was hard hit.

consideration should be social needs rather than alleged economic laws. The principle that actually governed his political thought was not mere utility but respect for human dignity, the intrinsic goods of humanity and civility, and more especially the intrinsic worth of individuality or personality. One might argue, for example, that the totalitarian state provides more efficient government, or even that the happiness of the greatest number in Hitler's Germany was increased by the persecution of Jews; but one may be certain that in any case Mill would absolutely condemn any form of tyranny or persecution.

He remained a professed Utilitarian, however, making it too easy for Nietzsche and others to condemn him as only another teacher of shop-keeping ethics, while his insistent moralistic tone has also laid him open to the fashion of deriding Victorian saints; and his basic inconsistency points to further difficulties for those who subscribe (as I do) to his liberal ideals. In going beyond the hedonistic calculus of Bentham to a more civilized concept of human happiness, Mill made his celebrated statement that it was better to be a man dissatisfied than a pig satisfied, a Socrates dissatisfied than a fool satisfied; but what, then, becomes of public happiness as the criterion of ethical good and the object of the state? What to do about the democratic majority who are content with material well-being, have no desire to take to the ways of a Socrates? Mill worried enough over the tastes and opinions of this majority, but he had no clear answer to such questions. He was as uncertain at the critical points of his argument when he took up the issues of personal freedom in his essay *On Liberty*. The only liberty worth the name, he said unequivocally, was that of pursuing one's own good in one's own way, so long as one did not intrude on the liberty of others; society had no right to constrain the individual for his own good except when he was clearly harming or likely to harm others. The obvious objection remains that almost anything one says or does may influence others in ways possibly harmful, the obvious difficulty is where to draw the line. Always high-minded himself, Mill tended to slight the problem of the responsibilities of freedom and the necessity of compulsion even for liberal purposes, to assure healthy conditions for freedom. Likewise in stressing the values of individuality he slighted the values of community, and for the individual himself the need of psychological security, the feeling of "belonging." While in his fear of tyranny he always implied and often stated considerable pessimism over the natural proclivities of man, his argument for liberty rested on what now seems too optimistic a view of human nature. Habitually he talked of man's interests as a "rational being," a "progressive being." Though much more aware than Bentham of the power of custom or simple inertia, he had little more idea of the power of the irrational, which among other things makes it harder to take men as they are and to deny the need of protecting them against themselves.

Yet Mill by no means preached an easy faith, or anything like a guaranteed progress. He most clearly refutes the invariable charge—by both conservatives and Marxists, and now also by neo-orthodox theologians, devotees of *Angst,* and all manner of "realists"—that liberalism rests on a shallow optimism, a naïve faith in reason and man. Like John Locke, Mill made quite modest claims for the powers of reason; as an empiricist he never pretended to possession of the ultimate truths known to the orthodox, the certainties typically claimed by political conservatives, nor the pseudo-scientific certainties of the Marxists. He had as modest hopes for the future, always hedged by fears, never exalted by the utopian dreams that sustained most radicals and revolutionaries; his contentment with "mere" reforms reflected a limited faith in human nature. Like Bentham, he was much more keenly aware than conservatives of the common abuses of authority, and he preferred democracy because he knew that political power was always liable to dangerous abuse, not at all because of any simple faith in the wisdom of the majority; he would never have been taken in by the naïve faith in a dictatorship of the proletariat. His concern for personal freedom made him as acutely aware of not only the political but the growing social pressures against the individual. For all such reasons Mill was able to draw up his classic case for personal freedom, which was a distinctively modern ideal. As Benjamin Constant pointed out, freedom for Greeks and Romans had meant the right to participate actively in public affairs, not a right to privacy or full enjoyment of an independent personal life; their kind of freedom in fact required considerable sacrifice of such independence. The personal freedom cherished by Mill was a more difficult kind to maintain, and the faith it required a more difficult faith to defend. So far from evading the difficulties, he went out of his way to spot and try to meet them.

Mill's inconsistencies and uncertainties are understandable in view of his sustained effort to adapt his principles to an era of radical change, but they are easier to discount and supplement because of his frank admission of ultimate uncertainty, and especially because of the breadth and liberality of his thought. While praising Bentham for his persistence in questioning all established beliefs, he did as full justice to the conservatism of Coleridge (and by implication of Burke), another great seminal thinker, who had made it his business to recover the essential meaning and value of established institutions, thus "rescuing from oblivion truths which Tories have forgotten, and which the prevailing schools of Liberalism never knew." One of his major arguments for the fullest possible freedom of speech was the need of equal representation of the partial truths in the everlasting polarities of practical life and thought—the principles of conservatism and progressivism, aristocracy and democracy, sociality and individuality, cooperation and competition, discipline and freedom. He maintained more emphatically than liberals before him that variety of opinion and endless disagreement were not merely the price one had to pay for this freedom but a positive good, a necessary condition for hopes of improvement. As for the practical difficulties in applying his principles, it is impossible anyhow to draw hard and fast lines in all questions of personal freedom and social obligation, as Mill knew; and since lines must nevertheless be drawn somehow, I should say that there is no better guide than his honest, liberal, humane spirit. If he gave too little heed to the deeper needs of community, all history before and since bears out his belief that the greater danger is not too much freedom and individuality but the impulses to coerce and to conform. And if his theoretical utilitarianism confused his actual concern with spiritual values, they were united in his belief that a free society fostered the development of more and better *persons,* who could contribute more to the possible improvement of society. Hence he was so bold as to argue that women too should be treated as full-fledged persons.

Needless to add, England fell considerably short of Mill's ideals. In their contentment with any old medium, so long as it preserved the comfortable prejudices of old forms (as in their state church), the English were always likely to lose much of the benefit of both new ideas and old ones. Nevertheless they continued to move toward liberal democracy, in part because of Mill's considerable influence.[8] His *Principles of Political Economy,* which had a sweeping success in his bourgeois society despite his criticism of its business philosophy, may

---

[8] It is pleasant to remember that Mill was elected to Parliament as a Liberal even though he consented to be a candidate only after stipulating that he not be required to campaign, to support the party program, or in any way to sacrifice his personal independence. His trust in ordinary human nature was at least partially vindicated by a meeting of workmen he consented to address. When some brought in a placard reading "The lower classes, though mostly habitual liars, are ashamed of lying" and asked whether he had written this statement, he hesitated for a moment and then said firmly that he had; whereupon he was roundly applauded. The leaders of the workmen assured him that they wanted honesty, not flattery, from their representatives.

remind us of the despair of Marx in England. Like other exiled revolutionaries there, he could make out no real prospects of revolution. "Prolonged prosperity has demoralized the workers," Marx wrote, adding that "they totally lack the mettle of the old Chartists." He complained as bitterly of their trade-union leaders, who were content to work for immediate gains—gains they could rightly expect to make by peaceable means. He was unhappier in the very freedom he enjoyed, since it was granted in complacence and indifference. While Mill won many readers, few intellectuals or workers paid any heed to the revolutionaries in their midst, and the authorities added insult by ignoring them; so they could only battle among themselves. In the most advanced capitalistic country, which should have been getting rotten-ripe for revolution, the lonely Marx had the least success in arousing the proletariat or frightening the bourgeois. He would not have rejoiced either in his most positive influence, in instigating the formation of the Labour party; for when it entered the lists (after his death) it failed to dedicate itself to class war.

No more revolutionary were the influential Fabians, who carried further the socialistic tendencies of Mill. Bourgeois intellectuals, they were practical men in the utilitarian tradition, not much concerned with theory, still content to work for piecemeal reforms by democratic processes, through the existing parties. (They named themselves after the Roman general who by his prudent tactics had done most to drive Hannibal out of Italy.) The working class also continued to vote for Liberals or Conservatives instead of its own Labour party, which at the end of the century had only two representatives in Parliament. When the Conservatives then managed to alienate workers by supporting a reactionary legal decision that jeopardized their right to strike, they turned to the Liberals. In the ten years before the World War the last Liberal ministry killed all hopes of revolution by a flood of social welfare legislation—workmen's compensation, an eight-hour day for miners, a sweated industries act, old-age pensions, unemployment and health insurance, etc. English socialism would remain democratic.

All in all, the tardier achievement of democracy in Britain gave it some clear advantages over American democracy. As the aristocracy learned to accommodate itself to change, it could keep on contributing its experience in leadership, at best the aristocratic virtues. Business never acquired such political power as in America, nor became so ruthless and corrupt. (Not until 1856, incidentally, was the first businessman raised to the peerage by a reluctant Queen Victoria, and the next one so honored came thirty years later.) Politics remained a profession, not a business; the typically British term "public servant" retained quite different connotations from the American equivalent, "politician." The common people were generally more sober voters, less likely to honor either mediocrity or demagoguery; candidates could "stand" instead of "run" for office, and stand with more dignity. The national consensus centered more on a traditional organic concept of society than on *laissez faire,* and involved more respect for civil liberties and individuality than for rugged individualism. Serious thinkers had more apparent influence on both political leaders and public opinion, and had to contend with much less anti-intellectualism. British men of affairs were mostly more cultured and assured, less inclined to hostility to the intelligentsia, than were self-made businessmen, while the common people retained more of the traditional respect for learning, or for intellectual as well as political authority.

Other differences stemming from the aristocratic tradition of England are more debatable. Its political history indicates that the ideals of liberty and equality are not actually one and indivisible, since Englishmen cherished their long tradition of liberty while having, until recent years, much less sentiment of equality than Americans; and they accordingly seemed less fearful of being thought eccentric or queer. Yet their history indicates as clearly the intimate connections between these ideals. Workmen realized it in their long struggle for suffrage or equal political rights, to protect their interests and enjoy more freedom of opportunity; an unchallenged aristocracy would hardly have extended to them the rights and opportunities they eventually won. Even so, there remained a wide gulf between the upper and lower classes, a pronounced social inequality as well as an extreme economic inequality. Higher education was a privilege reserved almost exclusively for the upper class, very few sons of workmen being admitted to Oxford and Cambridge. A largely self-perpetuating elite put much stock in blood and rank, which entailed the usual artificialities. In a traditional society governed by unquestioned custom, inequalities based solely on birth instead of ability may make common men more content with their status, give them the security of a caste system; but with the rise of democracy the artificialities became much more conspicuous and possibly objectionable. The playing fields of Eton bred many gentlemen of no particular intellectual or moral superiority, and as many simple snobs. Aristocratic complacence smiled on much haughty incompetence in high places, even to the egregious stupidity and callousness that ordered the charge of the Light Brigade.

"Theirs not to reason why"; and possibly the common people were better off because still habituated to their lowly status and limited range of choice. The fact remains that there was much less equality of opportunity than in America, which meant that many men were less free to realize their abilities. Those seemingly content with their status seemed more servile too, especially the petty bourgeois; they dearly loved the lord for his title alone, looked up to the young gentleman because of his rank regardless of his abilities. At the same time, the many shabby-genteel among them were more conscious of their poverty than were all but the poorest workingmen, and so were likely to be more disdainful of the dirty "common" people; George Orwell described their characteristic attitude toward the lower working class as "sniggering superiority punctuated by bursts of vicious hatred." Workers in turn were prone to class hatred. Although most were evidently not bitter enough to feel as "alienated" as Marx would have them, slum dwellers often made plain their hostility toward their well-dressed betters. Generally the working class was disposed to be more class-conscious than American workers, at least mistrustful of the upper class that was so sharply separated from it, and of the law that was on the other side. The solidarity promoted by the limited opportunity of workingmen helped to preserve their self-respect, but also bred a kind of conformism that limited their independence. Richard Hoggart observed that as powerful as the American pressure to keep up with the Joneses was the pressure to keep down with the Atkinses.

The last word, I judge, belongs to the distinction of the British in achieving democracy with a minimum of violence and residue of bitterness. Since the rise of the Labour party their political development has led, quite logically, toward more economic and social equality. But their lordly tradition has also produced a crop of angry young men, and only in recent years, with the growing resentment of unearned privilege, has Britain been facing the problems of social democracy.

4. *Revolutions on the Continent*

For reasons quite conventional, a survey of the growth of political freedom on the Continent must still be focused on France. It not only became the most democratic of the major powers there but remained the "father" of revolution, a primary inspiration to fighters for freedom in all other countries. Successful uprisings in Paris set off the wave of revolutions in 1830, and again the greater wave in 1848, which in Atlantic countries won lasting gains for the popular cause. In central Europe, where they were crushed, they provoked a reaction that fixed the divergent political course of the German peoples. The Franco-Prussian War, followed by another revolution in Paris, then accentuated the usual complications, or somewhat less conventional notions. France lost ground in the nineteenth century. It remained a prime symbol of the cause of liberty, but its history was not a radiant example for freedom lovers, still less for devotees of revolution.

First it calls for apologies to the lesser democracies, which I am dismissing briefly here for the usual reason that they had little influence on the main stage. Their history was generally more dignified than that of the great powers. Thus the Switzerland of today was virtually assured in 1848, by a constitution modeled after the American; within a generation it proceeded without further revolution to introduce universal suffrage. By formally declaring its policy of absolute neutrality it became an island of peace in Europe, while serving like England as an asylum for political refugees. Belgium, which the Congress of Vienna had artificially joined to Holland, rebelled in 1830 and won its independence, but both nations thereafter had a comparably peaceful history; their early revolutions won constitutional government, together with freedom of speech, press, and association. Although their electorate was restricted to a very small minority until near the end of the century, Belgium then went all the way to universal suffrage, and eventually the Dutch followed suit, also without violence. Likewise the Scandinavian countries gradually evolved into democratic states from the beginnings of limited monarchy, won in Denmark in 1848, and the assurance of civil liberties. All these countries prospered under more popular government, which as in England proved to be more stable too.

By contrast, once mighty Spain continued to lag behind the rest of the Atlantic community both economically and politically, suffering from generally atrocious government under monarchs supported by a reactionary Church. A successful revolution in 1868 followed the new mode in western Europe with a constitution providing for parliamentary government, civil liberties, and religious toleration, but this was too advanced for the country, leading to some years of anarchy. Spain then settled down under a more mildly liberal constitution. Its republicans were a minority, however, in a predominantly agricultural society with a small middle class. A poor, largely illiterate peasantry carried on its tradition of superstitious piety, hatred of *novedad,* or at best quixotic idealism. The Catholic Church remained powerful and hostile to liberal principles; it too was loyal to tradition when it gave its blessing to General Franco. Otherwise Spain was important chiefly because of its legacy to Latin America. Although some of its colonies grew more vigorous upon winning their independence, most had little success in learning the art of self-government after centuries of rule by Crown and Church. Big landowners, military dictators, and a powerful clergy collaborated in arresting the growth of a strong democratic tradition, and in preserving an extreme inequality that made freedom nominal for most people. As in Spain, a small middle class has only begun to contend with the great wealth of a very few and the wretched poverty of the great many.

Italy too may be passed over briefly here, even though it grew into one of the greater powers, because it was preoccupied chiefly with its struggle for independence and unity against Austria and the Papacy. This cause was indeed linked with the broader cause of republicanism by Mazzini, Garibaldi, and other leaders; the Kingdom of Sardinia that in 1871 finally made Rome the capital of a united Italy had been made a constitutional monarchy by the revolution of 1848. But the struggle inspired no new political thought or institutions, and the *risorgimento* that properly excited Italians was little more original; none of its writers won an international reputation. Once independent, moreover, the new nation was not actually united. Besides old regional animosities, it was distracted by the continued hostility of the Pope, now "the prisoner of the Vatican," who ordered the faithful not to vote in national elections; its liberals had to keep struggling with the Church over such further issues as the control of education. Its government also had to contend with the heritage of centuries of foreign and ecclesiastical rule: inexperience in self-government, backward industry and education, widespread poverty and illiteracy, and a large conservative peasantry far behind the fervent minority who had led the *risorgimento*. At the end of the century the humiliating defeat by the Ethiopians in the battle of Adowa exposed how weak Italy still was. In this view one may appreciate the achievements of the government in the early years of the twentieth century as it set about modernizing the nation, building railways and highways, schools and hospitals, etc. One may also better understand why Italy succumbed to Mussolini, and why millions of its still poor people have voted Communist in spite of papal threats of excommunication.

Over the same period Germany was far more successful in making itself over into a great modern nation. It had a head start in an earlier *risorgimento* that had produced much more original, influential thought, and it then had a plainer advantage in greater mineral resources; but its brilliant success was due as well to much more efficient government, backed by a more disciplined people. Unhappily for liberals, however, it was not due to democratic government or a liberal tradition. Rather, it emphasized that the most influential German thought was hostile to this tradition. Germany complicated the issues of freedom long before it went Nazi and directly, violently imperiled the democratic cause that had seemed to be sweeping the world; for it had outstripped France too, once the greatest power on the Continent. It emphasized the need of closer attention to the democratic example set by France.

Given the celebrated passion of the French for classical order, measure, lucidity, and logic, one must begin by remarking that their political history in the nineteenth century was full of romantic excess, marked by violent rhythm but little apparent rhyme or reason, and looks much murkier and less logical than that of the muddling English. While France was the recognized cultural leader of Europe, the second homeland of all civilized men, its revolutionary struggles were the most savage, and they were all fought to bloody death in Paris, the capital of the civilized world. Behind the physical violence lay much intellectual violence, symptomatic of further spiritual contradictions. In one aspect more individualistic than the English, never so obedient to either party discipline or the state, the French were in another aspect more inclined to authoritarianism, political or philosophical systems that subordinated the individual. They also looked more bourgeois, and in the countryside more peasantlike, while their complacent belief in their cultural superiority over all other peoples made them in a way more provincial. Their thinkers magnified their internal differences and aggravated their local problems because they assumed that they were thinking for all mankind. Before Marx, Frenchmen did most to popularize the words "socialism" and "communism," ideas that were scarcely lucid to most of the workers they inflamed, or the petty bourgeois and the peasants they frightened, but that intensified class feeling and helped to start the open class war that according to Marx should have broken out in more industrial Britain.

Nevertheless one may make clear enough sense of French political history too by beginning with the French Revolution, the immediate source of confusion and conflict. Out of it came both the democratic

ideals and the bitter opposition to these ideals that have kept French
intellectuals fighting the revolution ever since. Through it came the
liberal tradition of the Enlightenment, which maintained ideals of personal freedom together with the intellectual freedom for which France
was noted; long before Mill, Benjamin Constant defined the rights of
the individual against the state and majorities in much the same terms.
Through it came as well the tendencies to authoritarianism and absolutism, reflected in the political ideals of Rousseau and the practice of the
Jacobins, which aided reactionaries in preventing the liberal tradition
from gaining so wide an acceptance as it did in Britain and America;
thus radicals would often stigmatize both civil liberties and property
rights as mere bourgeois prejudices. Another by-product of the Revolution was the cult of Napoleon, a national idol revered by many republicans too, which dimmed the universal ideals of the Enlightenment
by a blazing celebration of the *gloire* of France. But the basic trouble
remained the profound disruption lamented by de Tocqueville. The
Revolution had shattered the old aristocratic order but failed to replace
it with a viable order; it had popularized an ideal of equality that could
not be killed, but that was neither embodied in government nor engrained in manners, customs, and habits of thought; it had taught the
common people to despise instead of reverence authority, but had not
lessened their fear of it, only stirred more hatred of those in power;
and it had permanently split the intelligentsia, bred a violent partisanship that flourished on mutual excess.

Indeed, the famed lucidity and logic were at the root of the political
confusion and disorder. Following in the wake of the *philosophes* of the
Enlightenment, the French intelligentsia had more evident influence
than their fellows elsewhere, and typically they were much more concerned about logical theory than practical results. Whereas the English
had developed a tradition of concrete liberties, embodied in institutions
and supported by empiricism, French intellectuals translated ideals of
liberty into rational, abstract, universal terms. They could appear to
advantage in their devotion to lofty principle, their clearer awareness
of the gap between ideal and reality, and their refusal to put up with
convenient prejudices or flabby compromises. They could also look more
foolish, hopelessly unrealistic, basically unreasonable. They were in
any case more given to ideology or ism, and always torn by conflicting
ideologies. They deepened the split between the Right and the Left,
which was more conspicuous in France than in any other country. They
further weakened the national consensus by their tendency to splinter

on principle; the lucid French would not stand for such blurred generalities and loose compromises as held together the major political parties in America, and so kept breaking off and forming the many parties that have cluttered up their political stage, made "the will of the people" a still fuzzier concept. Otherwise they were akin in a saving tendency to skepticism that also sprang from their lucidity, and helped them to keep their heads; only it exposed them to a disillusionment that might carry to an extreme again. Having perceived before Marx that the state was an instrument of class rule, many were inclined to agree with him that democracy was a mere sham.

For the same reasons, however, the French intelligentsia could and did speak for all Europeans, if not for mankind; so they gave more point to the political drama that began in the Restoration period after Waterloo. The royalists and aristocrats who took charge at once demonstrated that they had learned nothing from the Revolution, were only more intransigent in their resolve to stifle all opposition to their rule. The Catholic clergy likewise declared its abhorrence of republican principles, taking the stand that it would maintain throughout the century. Its most vigorous spokesman, Joseph de Maistre, was a frank reactionary who pined for both the Inquisition and absolute monarchy, and foreshadowed the violence to come by glorifying war as a "divine" institution. Nevertheless he was an exceptionally acute, original thinker, more prophetic because of the radical skepticism on which he based his absolutism. He announced a major theme of the century by launching a philosophical offensive against the whole liberal creed and the faith of the Enlightenment on which it rested, demonstrating with inexhaustible zeal and acumen the limitations of reason, and the natural capacities of man for irrational belief and behavior. Meanwhile a radically different theme was being sounded by Saint-Simon, pioneer of socialism. Although he may seem as futile as de Maistre because he proposed a utopian Christian socialism, neither revolutionary nor democratic, and expected it to be instituted by the rising bourgeois, he too was influential and prophetic. Saint-Simon was one of the first thinkers to foresee the consequences of the Industrial Revolution, including the drive to organization, and to start trying to realize its exciting possibilities for making men free. Nor was his faith in the bourgeois simply foolish. He could see the best qualities in the class that had largely made and won the French Revolution, and was now again in the vanguard, thereby inclined—as Marx too perceived—to identify its cause with ideals of justice or the cause of humanity.

At least the bourgeois realized the fears of de Maistre as early as 1830, when a revolution that took only a few days and very little fighting overthrew the autocratic Charles X and replaced him with Louis Philippe, a "citizen-king" who promised constitutional government. Based on the maxims of 1789, this revolution was a more purely bourgeois affair; and it marked their lasting triumph over the old aristocracy. Unfortunately, it failed to bring out their best qualities. The ministry of Guizot that symbolized the new regime introduced one notably progressive measure—a program of public education requiring every commune to have at least one primary school. Otherwise Guizot and his party displayed chiefly the narrow, shortsighted self-interest that gave the bourgeois their bad name. They laid no firm foundations for a new order because they had no program, no policy except to conserve government of and by the propertied class. Except for some regulation of child labor they ignored the problems rising out of the Industrial Revolution, the growing discontent of city workers, who had been worse off than the peasants ever since the French Revolution and were steadily getting poorer. They managed to stay in power chiefly by bribing candidates for office, which was made easier by property qualifications that restricted the vote to a small minority. Guizot's answer to demands for some measure of political equality was simple or cynical: "Get rich!"

Indirectly, however, his government did much to propagate the revolutionary ideals it flouted by not only generating but tolerating outspoken criticism. Paris was soon stirred by an extraordinary ferment. Known since the Enlightenment for its intellectual hospitality, it now became the Mecca of the European intelligentsia. With artists and writers, all manner of liberals, radicals, and revolutionaries flocked or fled to it from all over the Continent, especially the lands of oppression. Among them was Karl Marx, who learned to disagree with almost all the rest, but like them conceived of freedom as an international cause, and for his different reasons was as optimistic about its prospects. (His later expulsion from France was due to a formal request by the Prussian government.) Frenchmen contributed their full share to the intellectual excitement, and to his education. Proudhon published *What Is Property?*, with its celebrated answer: property was theft. Louis Blanc called for state socialism, Barbès and Blanqui for violent revolution. Off the presses of Paris came a flood of works attacking the evils of capitalism, while popular journals as boldly exposed the corruption of the government.

This grew so thoroughly unpopular that the revolution of 1848 again took only a few days and a little blood to finish off Guizot, then send Louis Philippe packing. The victors set up a republic, in which the working class was at last represented. The poet Lamartine, a leader in the new government, lent a lofty rhetoric to its republican ideals. More to the point, universal suffrage was really tried for the first time in Europe. Conservatives might have been heartened by the initial democratic election, for the vast majority of the deputies voted in by the people were not wild-eyed rabble-rousers, but men of the respectable upper class.

Less happily, the election exposed deep splits in the ranks of the republicans. They had no clear goal in common beyond the traditional maxims of liberty, equality, and fraternity, which to most middle-class people were comfortable only when they remained abstract. The Paris workers had more radical, socialistic ideas, such as "the right to work" popularized by Louis Blanc, and thanks to all the ferment of the preceding decade they also had more vigorous leadership than did workers anywhere else on the Continent. Within a few months differences hardened into the now familiar division of Left and Right, more specifically of workers against the bourgeois and peasantry; and both sides forgot about fraternity in a growing fear and hatred. When the government announced the closing of the national workshops that had been hastily set up to assure the right to work, the Paris workers started their own revolution, the "June Days." Once more it lasted only a few days, but this time it was fought fiercely to the death, which came to uncounted thousands. The desperation of the workers, hopelessly outnumbered and outpowered, was matched by the mercilessness of the government troops.

Inasmuch as we have learned a good deal about revolutions since the time of Burke, and many are inclined to agree with him on their folly, we need to consider first the question he virtually ignored—*why* men now indulged in such violent folly. The Paris workers, still very poor, had plain grievances. Men aroused by the revolutionary stir of the age could no longer be told that the common people had put up with such grievances all through history, by the will of God. The popular ideas about the Rights of Man that Burke denounced as "abstract" and "metaphysical" were scarcely more so than the "prescriptive" rights and the "prejudices" that he cherished as essential to social health, and certainly "the right to work" would seem as concrete as any. Least of all could the bourgeois tell workers that revolution was simply futile,

for they had won solid, enduring gains from both the revolutions of
1789 and 1830. Yet the Paris workers were not simply heroic martyrs
to a lofty cause. They were rebelling against a democratically elected
government, whose policies expressed the will of the great majority.
The country still lacked the material means of assuring every man a
job and decent income, and it was clearly not yet ready for socialism
or any radical change. Neither were the workers themselves. Mostly
uneducated, they had only vague, confused ideas about what could
or should be done about their grievances. Their leaders were hopelessly
split, some harking back to the Jacobins and Babeuf, others to Saint-
Simon and Fourier, and none except possibly Louis Blanc had worked
out a definite, feasible program. Doomed to defeat, the workers were
as obviously doomed to disappointment had they won their revolution.

However understandable such confusion under the circumstances,
it underlines the historic significance of the terrible June Days. The
first conscious rebellion of the proletariat was more the cause than
the result of the class war now proclaimed by Marx. In France it left
a legacy of hatred that assured the indefinite continuance of class war,
and the cult of revolution. It fostered the growth of a radical rather
than liberal working-class movement, which would make democratic
compromise more difficult. It vindicated the prophecy of de Tocqueville, a member of the National Assembly. "Before long," he had
written, "the political struggle will be restricted to those who have
and those who have not: property will form the great field of battle";
and he remained among the few who refused to commit themselves
to either Right or Left because both were illiberal.

Immediately "those who had" proved his judgment by forming the
Party of Order, dedicated to the "Defense of Property, Religion, and
the Family," which grew popular especially with the clergy and the
peasantry even though—or because—the socialists were not attacking
religion and the family. When radicals began winning by-elections,
the defenders of moral order put through an electoral law that largely
disfranchised the unpropertied. Less consciously, they helped to destroy
the new Republic. The presidential election after the June Days had
exposed the vulnerability of democracy by giving a huge majority to
Louis Napoleon, who exploited the popular confusion and dissension
by appealing to both Right and Left, and cashing in on the glory of
his uncle Bonaparte. Having campaigned on a pledge to leave "liberty
untouched," he now posed as its defender against the reactionary Assembly, proposing that universal suffrage be restored. When the Assem-

bly refused, he staged a *coup d'état* like that of the great Napoleon, dissolved the Assembly, and took over the government. In 1852 a popular plebiscite confirmed the end of the Republic by another huge majority, making him Emperor Napoleon III. He boasted that he was the man "to end the era of revolutions."

In the course of restoring the Empire, Louis forgot about his devotion to liberty. He kept the press under tight censorship, socialists and republicans under close watch by the police, and once emperor he backed up his boast by arresting and exiling many thousands of them. There is little question, however, that he had most of the people behind him; and herein lies his historic significance. Louis Napoleon was the first ruler in Europe to master the art of leading or misleading the common people, now become a force to be reckoned with. Given his obvious vanity and strut as a Napoleon, historians are still debating the sincerity of his devotion to the public welfare, but at least he clearly took a larger, more enlightened view of it than Guizot had. There was more in him too than appeared in the shrewd analysis of Marx, who in the *Eighteenth Brumaire* explained his success by his appeal to the petty bourgeois. While granting more economic freedom to businessmen in order to build up French industry, which was still far behind the British, Louis earned the title he fancied as "emperor of the workmen" by letting them vote, instituting programs of public works, recognizing labor unions, and introducing social welfare legislation. Whatever his motives, he foreshadowed the rise of fascism— unforeseen by Marx and his followers because it was not simply a class movement. Although never so brutal or despotic as the Fascist dictators, Louis Napoleon was like them in that he appealed to all classes, while exploiting the sentiments of nationalism and imperialism.

Meanwhile Bismarck had learned from him that concessions to workers might strengthen autocratic rule and the power of the state; but he repaid his mentor by putting an end to him and his dreams of imperial glory. Louis had been steadily losing his popularity as his grandiose diplomacy produced little but fiascos. He had never impressed many of the intelligentsia, who kept smuggling in the works of Victor Hugo and other ardent exiles, and opposition grew stronger when he began liberalizing his rule, permitting more freedom of press and assembly. Louis Adolphe Thiers became famous by demanding the "five fundamental freedoms," civil liberties assuring government in accordance with majority opinion as expressed in free elections. "Official candidates" had an ever harder time maintaining the government's majority despite all the influence and money behind them. Hence the inglorious war of 1870 only clinched the failure of the man who thought he was destined to end the era of revolutions. When Napoleon surrendered to the Prussians, another revolution in Paris promptly restored the Republic.

This began in what Anglo-Americans might consider the best democratic tradition. The proclamation of a new government met no opposition from the supporters of the Emperor; peaceful elections set up a new National Assembly; the Assembly chose as executive the moderate Thiers. But then established revolutionary form led to another civil war, much like that of 1848, only still bloodier. The workers' representatives soon grew suspicious of the conservative majority of the Assembly, who were bristling in their fears of the radicals in their midst. These now numbered some Marxists, but workers were again confused and divided by various programs, including anarchism, or by leaders without definite program except more revolution. Marx, who later celebrated their heroism in what he saw as the first great battle of the proletariat, at the time thought that the armed Commune they set up in Paris was a blunder. At any rate, Thiers was backed by the great majority of the bourgeois and peasantry when he ordered the army to besiege Paris; the Communards alienated many sympathizers, including Louis Blanc, by starting a reign of terror; and they then went down in another desperate, hopeless struggle, much fiercer than any battle in the Franco-Prussian War, as neither side gave quarter. At least 20,000 were killed, many of them simply massacred.

As the Third Republic settled down, it was accordingly saddled with the customary legacy of fear and hatred that made it harder for France to become a model democracy. Most members of the National Assembly wanted to restore a king, and most likely would have succeeded had not France now had two Pretenders, both stubborn. In 1875 a new constitution was framed to accommodate both republicans and monarchists; its uncharacteristic compromises, designed as temporary expedients, effectively discouraged any enthusiasm or popular reverence for it. Under a government that was rarely bold or enterprising the nation remained relatively backward in industry, public education, and social legislation. One reason was that it soon developed its many political parties, no one of which could ever achieve a clear or lasting majority; hence it ran through many cabinets, usually lasting less than a year. Another reason was that the Republic always had to contend with powerful, ultraconservative monarchists, and as powerful, hostile a clergy; education suffered because church and state continued to battle over its control. At the end of the century the deep animosities that split France came to a boil in the notorious Dreyfus affair, when dispute over a Jewish officer who had been framed was intensified by being broadened into a fundamental "philosophical" controversy over the national interest, republicanism, liberalism, rationalism, and the values of modern civilization. Monarchists and churchmen again united in battling to maintain the guilt of Dreyfus, a cause which they made out to be essential to the preservation of France and Christendom, though Jesuits in particular made it uglier by exploiting anti-Semitism, the poison now spreading over Europe again.[9]

Still, the defenders of Dreyfus won. The reactionaries were thoroughly discredited as his innocence was proved beyond question and the perfidy of his accusers exposed, but there remained more significant reasons for their defeat. They had been fighting a losing battle ever since the establishment of the Third Republic, which had made France the first European country to have effective universal suffrage, no longer government dominated or manipulated. Unimaginative, unadventurous, unexciting, this republic nevertheless made it a liberal democracy, in much the same way that England moved toward democracy, and suggesting much the same kind of prudential or pragmatic moral, if one still not to the liking of many French intellectuals. The moderate Thiers provided competent leadership, in a few years managing to pay off the huge indemnity of billions of francs that Bismarck had imposed. His moderation was unquestionably wise, since France was still largely rural and strongly Catholic, not yet ready for the more radical programs of Léon Gambetta and others. It presaged an era of stable government, under a constitution that nobody revered but that would last down to our time. Within a decade the monarchist majority melted away, republicans won firm control of the government. The revolutionary slogans "Liberty, Equality, Fraternity" were again inscribed on all public buildings, and Bastille Day was made the national festival. New laws guaranteed the rights of the individual, the basic freedoms of speech, press, and assembly. Workers were conciliated by the right to organize labor unions. Thereafter the many political parties at least helped to hold in check the extremists on both the Right and the Left. Following the Dreyfus fiasco, which resulted in the legal separa-

---

9 It should be noted that some distinguished Americans too were anti-Semites—for example, Henry Adams and Henry James. Adams supported the aristocratic opposition to Dreyfus.

tion of church and state, the many embittered Catholics were gradually offset by others who began reconciling themselves to republican principles, as Catholics long since had in the United States, while monarchists dwindled into a small, if noisy minority. French socialists were led by Jean Jaurès, a liberal, democrat, and pacifist.

His assassination on the eve of the World War may then recall the persistent threats to a democracy not yet firmly rooted in habit, sentiment, or national pride, and the basic anomalies of a society famed for its sophistication, rationality, and disciplined intellect. Ideals of liberty were clouded by an extreme social and economic inequality. A very wealthy few had great power, controlling the Bank of France and much of the press, and with the help of bribes generally managed to have their way in the national legislature, so that they still paid no income tax. Although French capitalists showed less enterprise in developing industry, which remained backward, the government often aided them by suppressing with armed force the strikes that workers increasingly resorted to after 1900. The workers still got little sympathy from the peasants, who were mostly as conservative in politics as backward in agriculture. The French bureaucracy, which carried on independently of politics, accentuated the generally conservative practice of the people that contrasted strangely with all the revolutionary theory. For all such reasons the intelligentsia—the custodians of the culture that was the nation's pride—were still prone to radical discontent with their society. While Maurice Barrès and Charles Maurras maintained the extremism of the Right, Georges Sorel carried on for the Left by his program of "heroic socialism," in which he denounced the "democratic superstition" and any gradual reform, declaring that only by violence could workers realize the "high ethical values" of socialism and save the degenerate modern world.

All in all, French tradition makes understandable the Vichy regime to come, and the subsequent rise of one of the strongest Communist parties in Europe—alike almost unthinkable in Britain. Nevertheless the most important point in a history of freedom remains the immense influence of France on Europe as a primary source and symbol of ideals of freedom. The democratic world was properly shocked by its ignominious collapse in World War II. For both its intellectual and its political tradition contrasted sharply with German tradition, out of which came Hitler—not inevitably, to be sure, but not illogically either.

The political history of modern Germany too may be traced to the French Revolution. Early enthusiasm over its ideals, together with the influence of the Enlightenment come down through Lessing, Kant, Schiller, and Goethe, created the core of a liberal tradition, but the enthusiasm soon gave way to the counterrevolutionary movement of the German Romantics. In national pride these associated liberal ideals with alien influences, or the enemy. Out of their reaction came the major political themes of nationalism, racism, statism, authoritarianism, and militarism, all linked to the drive to national unity that had been spurred by the Napoleonic Wars. Fichte's *Addresses to the German Nation* became its gospel. From his romantic concept of the primacy of will Fichte deduced that education must "completely destroy freedom of will," make it utterly reliable by making its decisions conform to "strict necessity." This discipline was especially important for Germans because they were "called upon to begin the new era as pioneers and models for the rest of mankind." In view of their mission the state had "a higher object than the usual one of maintaining internal peace, property, personal freedom, and the life and well-being of all"; it was this object that called for a military establishment. Other Romantics took to glorifying the state and completely subordinating the individual to it because a strong state was needed to achieve the national unity befitting the cultural, spiritual superiority of the Germans. Rude foreigners might note that Goethe and Schiller wrote stirring dramas celebrating struggles for freedom by the Dutch and the Swiss, but no German ever wrote a great drama about such a struggle by the Germans.

First, however, we must note that their tradition was as ambivalent as any other. Goethe, Kant, and other spokesmen of the German Enlightenment were always revered. In their spirit Grillparzer warned against the trend he perceived in mid-century: "Humanity—Nationality—Bestiality." At that, German militarism was still far from bestial. In 1814 Boyen, a disciple of Kant, had proposed universal military service in Prussia for the sake of lifting both service in war and the life of the nation to a higher moral plane. Prussian discipline was in this aspect much more than a means to efficiency: it meant devotion to an ideal of duty, selfless, almost ascetic, which might look more honorable by contrast with the selfish individualism and shameless materialism to which so many free men in France, Britain, and especially America were becoming addicted. For similar reasons German thinkers might honor the Prussian state. They owed much to its founders just because it was a deliberate, artificial creation; and they felt no urgent need of a defense against the state, if only because Germans had had no political revolution to implant the idea of the rights of citizens, but also because they believed, like Burke, that duties should always come before rights. German political history would demonstrate as clearly as the French Enlightenment and Revolution the power of spiritual factors in history, if also the reasons why the spiritual is not to be equated with the purely ideal. And certainly the Germans had good reason for pride in their culture since the brilliant flowering of their own Enlightenment, then of Romanticism. The very backwardness of their business class at the time was in this respect a boon, for while the English and Americans were much more enterprising in pursuing their material interests, the German burghers were more devoted to cultural interests. They acquired their reputation as dreamy types, sentimental and romantic.

The ambiguity of German idealism was most pronounced in the thought of Hegel, who gave the full sanction of *Geist* to nationalism and statism. His grand synthesis was not only a highly imaginative, original, impressive feat, but one that might impress liberals too. Offered in the name of reason, it retained the universalism of the Enlightenment in its concept of world history. In including the popular idea of progress, defined as a growth of freedom, Hegel offered a considerably richer, more mature conception of it than had Condorcet or any other thinker before him. He pictured the historic development of man more truly, not as a progress in virtue and happiness, but as a process of growing up, becoming more fully conscious, realizing the distinctive potentialities of humanity. His dialectic emphasized a cardinal principle of tension and conflict that was likewise realistic, and especially pertinent for a revolutionary era. It might hearten as well as sober liberals, for it could readily be turned against political conservatism, as in fact it soon was turned against religious orthodoxy, a bulwark of such conservatism. Hegel permitted criticism of all reigning authority, and himself ventured some even of his idealized Prussian state. Freedom as he conceived it could be realized only in and through the state, but not by unthinking obedience to its laws; it required a conscious, strictly conscientious acceptance of the state as a rational, moral order.

Yet the main tendency of Hegel's thought, and his actual influence, were unmistakably hostile to the liberal tradition. Despite his intimacy with the World Spirit, he was obviously provincial in his arbitrary selection of the Germans as the special agents of the Spirit. His whole system was essentially less rational than mystical, being supported by a contempt of science and the ordinary empirical uses of reason. He had an arrogant way with historical facts, simply ignoring recalcitrant ones; or in Friedrich Meinecke's words, his thought was not besmirched by "the filth of reality." A Prussian respect for power made it still easier for him to give the blessing of Spirit to the Prussian state, and specifically to the principle of *raison d'état*, on which Bismarck would operate as ruthlessly as had Frederick the Great, one of his world-heroes; in his own unbesmirched words, "Philosophy transfigures the element of actual reality which seems to be unjust." Most specifically illiberal was Hegel's political thought. In deifying the state as the source of all rationality, morality, and freedom, he did not insist that government be responsible to its citizens. While his theory of history demanded rebels to assure continuous progress, he plainly preferred obedient men now that the Prussian state had realized almost perfect "freedom"; he distracted Germans from disagreeable realities by emptying the idea of freedom of ordinary political meaning, declaring that its "highest" form was complete obedience to the state. Similarly he soothed them by denouncing the principle of rights as "atomistic" or "abstract," whereas any concern for the individual has to be atomistic, and on the face of it personal rights would seem more concrete than his state. As flatly he condemned democracy, like Burke arguing that it was a menace to freedom, but neglecting even to consider the argument that it may be a necessary condition of freedom. His ideal government was monarchy, though again he neglected to demonstrate its superiority.

In Hegel's own day the monarchs of the German states were sufficiently devoted to the "highest" form of freedom, if still with little sense of high mission. Following Waterloo they imposed a strict censorship and increased the powers of the police in order to keep their subjects uncontaminated by cruder notions of freedom. They succeeded in keeping most of Germany economically as well as politically backward by maintaining the medieval privileges of the landed nobility, which included restrictions that discouraged industry. A few exceptions, such as the free merchant city of Hamburg, were more than offset by the dominance of Prussia. Here Frederick William III was most sedulous in his loyalty to the policies of Metternich and the Holy Alliance, lacking only the sophistication of Metternich. The feudal Junker caste, unparalleled in western Europe, monopolized the high posts in government and army even though it was not highly educated or cultivated. The burghers were docile, content to ape the nobility; they were so little accustomed to freedom or power that when the government decided that a measure of *laissez faire* would help in catching up with France, it had to use pressure to install this foreign idea. The next

Frederick William, who ascended the throne in 1840, still believed that he ruled by divine right, suggesting that Prussians had not yet come out of the Middle Ages the Romantics were celebrating. "No power on earth," he announced, "shall ever persuade me to exchange the natural relation between prince and people for a contractual and constitutional relation; or to countenance the insertion, between our Lord in Heaven and this country, of a piece of written paper, like a second providence, to rule by its paragraphs and to take the place of ancient sacred loyalty."

Immediately he was proved wrong. In spite of the censorship and the police, many Germans were infected by ideals of freedom, especially in the universities, which had developed an anomalous tradition of academic freedom. In 1848 the news from Paris touched off revolutions all over the land, known together as "the revolution of the intellectuals" because they were led by students and professors. In Berlin the king was so scared that he caved in after only a few hundred had been killed, and later was persuaded to accept a constitution inserted between him or God and Prussia. In other German states princes likewise gave in quickly. Everywhere liberal constitutions were adopted, guaranteeing civil liberties; they were no less novel for being unoriginal, only imitations of the French. Elections were held for the first time in Germany, and its one and only parliament was set up. A National Assembly met in Frankfort amid great popular enthusiasm.

But the revolutions everywhere ended in debacle—the most complete failure of the popular cause on the Continent. Despite much individual idealism and heroism, they demonstrated chiefly the political immaturity of the Germans, verging on the ludicrous in their futility. The best excuse for their failure, economic troubles that sent prices soaring, brought out the worst in the bourgeois. In Berlin, fearful of the workers, the weak middle class turned to the king, whose troops promptly crushed the remaining rebels. The Junker-led army emerged as the greatest power in the country, with an authority such as the military had nowhere else in Europe. Although the new Prussian constitution curtailed feudal privileges and rewarded the bourgeois by other concessions, it was basically an aristocratic document. A parliament with limited powers, subject to the absolute veto of the monarch, was elected by property owners, of whom the Junkers were by far the most influential. Thereafter the growing middle class disappointed both democratic and Marxist theorists by failing to achieve the power of its fellows in England and France; Prussia remained dominated by its nobility, military, and bureaucracy, all loyal to the monarch. Its constitution lasted to the end of the World War.

Elsewhere in Germany the revolutions took on the air of a comic opera, but with ominous undertones. Revolutionary fervor was diverted from political and social reform to the cause of national unity. After some painful deliberation, the National Assembly in Frankfort offered the Prussian king the crown as emperor, only to be turned down; the crown was worth nothing coming from such a body, wrote Frederick William, since it did not "bear the stamp 'by the grace of God.'" Another distraction was the Poles, who years before had won the sympathy of liberals everywhere by an unsuccessful uprising to recover their partitioned country. Although the assembled democrats had first announced the "sacred duty" of restoring Poland, east Germany unfortunately contained a large Polish province that wanted independence; and the National Assembly now made history by reversing its sacred duty, deciding that this province was rightly German. In a ringing speech one Wilhelm Jordan (a Berlin democrat) proclaimed the need of awakening "a healthy national egotism," and asserted bluntly, "Our right is that of the stronger, the right of conquest." The awakened majority rose to his conclusion: "Freedom for all, but the power of the Fatherland and its weal above all!" While they would have to wait some time for their united Fatherland, it soon became clear that this was to be their only satisfaction. Further riots and revolts by unregenerate democrats were put down; the princes preserved their expensive little thrones and courts without cost of social or political reform; rigid censorship was restored; all liberal parties were killed. The ideals that started the revolution were not killed, to be sure, since too many Germans had been stirred up by a revolution of their own, but they caused no more serious uprisings. Their complete failure in 1848 was a lasting curse on the democratic cause.[10]

Otto von Bismarck accordingly fulfilled the prediction of Hegel that the unification of Germany would be achieved by policies unlike those of liberal England and France. Upon becoming minister in 1862, the

---

10 America perhaps gained most from the German revolutions of 1848 through the many refugees who settled in it, such as Carl Schurz—immigrants more independent and talented than most. Other exiles, however, may remind us of the confusions of German tradition. Thus Heine, one of the earliest, is famous as an ardent lover of freedom, a radical, and an intimate friend of Marx; so it is usually forgotten (as Marx wished it to be) that he was a violent reactionary in 1848. He hated mobs, revolutions, and democracies, while he was as infatuated as any German Romantic with an idealized medieval past.

dedicated creator of modern Germany proceeded at once on his mission
of creating it in a Prussian manner: it was to be no mere federation, or
United German States, but a nation formed and dominated by Prussia.
He began by building up the army, introducing compulsory military
service for all able-bodied males—a drastic restriction on personal freedom that is now taken for granted, but that Prussia was the first country
to impose. To a balky parliament he gave his celebrated warning: "The
great questions of the day will not be decided by speeches and the
resolutions of majorities—that was the blunder of 1848 and 1849—but
by blood and iron." When the lower chamber refused to vote the
necessary appropriations, he ruled without a parliament for some years,
arbitrarily levying taxes; his government was responsible only to the
monarch, who consented to his defiance of the constitution. Within two
years he tried out his military machine in Denmark, adding Schleswig-
Holstein to the Prussian domain. Two more years and he crushed
Austria, the rival claimant for leadership of the Germans. He was then
free to provoke the Franco-Prussian War, the most awesome demonstration of the military might of Prussia and apparent vindication of his
blood-and-iron policy. With this he achieved his supreme goal: the
king of Prussia became Kaiser Wilhelm of the German Empire—an
empire that in 1871 was solemnly proclaimed in Versailles, the palace of
the "Sun King" Louis XIV.

By similar methods Bismarck made Germany a great industrial power
too. While encouraging businessmen by protective tariffs, he was the
first major statesman deliberately to break away from the policy of
laissez faire; the government guided the industrial expansion and itself
took over the ownership and management of the railways—a "socialist"
measure that would have horrified contemporary America. He made
rapid progress with the aid of the Prussian tradition of discipline,
which made it the duty of businessmen to serve national instead of
merely private interests. At the same time Bismarck had the wit to give
up Prussian methods of treating workers. A thoroughgoing conservative
politically, always fearful of radicals and socialists, he abandoned his
early policy of simply suppressing them, instead stealing their thunder
by putting through much social welfare legislation, such as a system of
insurance that protected workers against accident, sickness, and old age.
His government likewise made education free and subsidized it liberally.
Since the German common people were both better educated and
better disciplined than the French, Bismarck's Germany soon got far
ahead of France industrially, and provided a higher standard of living

for a rapidly increasing population, now much greater than that of once more populous France. In all respects it became the first great modern power on the Continent.

Bismarck's evil reputation outside Germany makes it too easy to disparage his extraordinary achievements. The most successful statesman of the century, and one of the most farsighted, he was a Machiavellian in the best sense of the word, rational and realistic, never power-mad or fond of blood and iron for their own sake. His end always controlled his means, and it was a limited end—to create and maintain a strong Germany, not to dominate all Europe. Having crushed Austria, he did not seek to finish it as a major power.[11] The much harsher terms he imposed on France, after a war its rulers had been as eager to fight, were still not designed to finish it either; and he was then content to stop. Bismarck was too sensible anyway to entertain Napoleon's imperial dream, but as a good conservative he wished to preserve the traditional order and so prevent popular revolutions. As he later told the czar, it was now more than ever before in the interests of great monarchies to avoid war. In the same spirit he preserved the interests of his Junker class by concessions to the common people. Like the wisest English conservatives, he was far more subtle and enlightened than his predecessors, realizing clearly the need of coming to terms with the popular forces of the modern world. Thus he introduced universal suffrage for elections to the Reichstag, foreseeing—as German liberals feared— that it might be a means of strengthening his ministry. For prudential reasons he likewise permitted freedom of the press. Add his legislation on behalf of workers, which anticipated Roosevelt's New Deal by fifty years, and ordinary Germans became freer under his autocratic rule than they had ever been except for a brief spell in 1848.

Yet Bismarck's very shrewdness brings up the evident limits of his foresight and his wisdom, and finally the heavy costs of his success. His seizure of Alsace-Lorraine—perhaps his chief blunder—assured the permanent hostility of France, realizing the prophecy of Marx that it would lead France to seek an alliance with Russia and bring on a world war. It emphasized that his first and last concern, which he pursued

---

11 It should be added that its defeat was hardly a setback to the cause of German freedom. After initial success in dispatching Metternich, the revolution of 1848 had failed as miserably in Austria. The one major reform to come out of it, an Act of Emancipation that tardily abolished the relics of serfdom, then assured an otherwise reactionary government the support of the peasantry. The Austrians were so docile that a dozen men could handle the job of censorship, even though all printed matter had to be approved by the government.

ruthlessly on principle, was the power of Germany, or more precisely of the Prussian state—it was not peace, freedom, justice, or any moral end such as concerned the English Utilitarians, whom Germans looked down on as soulless and vulgar. Given this power, and no other clear purpose, Bismarck's inheritors might employ it to support a less rational, realistic nationalism and militarism, especially because the Prussian state as he left it lacked effective checks against ambitious or foolish rulers. His legacy was more dangerous for the same reason that his achievement was so impressive: this was quite literally his own doing, done from on top, a credit to his genius rather than any political genius of the German people. It was therefore not simply ironical when, in 1890, the vain young Kaiser Wilhelm II dismissed the "Iron Chancellor," for Bismarck had held himself accountable only to the monarch, not to the people. In his heyday Nietzsche had written a bitter verdict on his success: it had meant "the extirpation of the German soul for the benefit of the German empire." After the catastrophe of the World War—a war that Bismarck himself would have done his best to avert, but that was nevertheless a logical outcome of his blood-and-iron policy—Max Weber wrote more soberly on his failure to give the people political training. Under his paternalistic rule "the nation lost the habit of that positive and decisive cooperation in its own political destiny by means of elected representatives, which alone can educate political judgment."

To outsiders a just verdict would seem more complex, for Germans did not actually lose this habit—they had not yet acquired it. Bismarck at least permitted them to begin learning, even gave them some help. The Reichstag always retained enough power to cause him trouble. Universal suffrage did not merely strengthen his administration but produced more independent voters than he had bargained for, especially social democrats; prewar Germany had the largest, most disciplined socialist party in Europe. The press also remained independent enough to educate political judgment, and carry on the liberal tradition that survived the debacle of 1848. On the other hand, Bismarck himself had maintained the Prussian tradition of an authoritarian state, with a ruling Junker class devoted to no ideal beyond a powerful, disciplined nation; and the crucial point remains that all the worst in him lived after him. As chancellor he had not been responsible to any mere majority in the Reichstag, whose limited powers included no effective control over the army and its budget, or now over the imperial ambitions of Wilhelm II. The Junkers were disposed to support these ambitions, some for cynical reasons of expediency; they distracted the nation from internal discords, particularly those created by the growing strength of the socialists. Militarists exploited the nationalism that had been the heart of Bismarck's policy, and become more blatant in his own day. His devoted follower Treitschke (later to be canonized by the Nazis) won his popularity as a historian by a lifelong effort to intensify national pride, a mission he coupled with a glorification of the state as "the most supremely real person," and of war as the sublime test of both the national character and the state. The Kaiser then brought Bismarck and Treitschke up to date by befriending the big industrialists and financiers who were helping to establish German might. Some fifty men, an Austrian consul reported in 1906, absolutely ruled the German economy—carrying on the tradition of exclusive rule from the top.

The continued strength of this tradition weakened opposition from below. The Social Democratic party kept on proclaiming the ritual revolutionary purposes of socialism, but in other ways remained loyal to the spirit of its founder, Ferdinand Lassalle—a dictatorial type who had negotiated with Bismarck, the more easily because he too was a patriot devoted to the ideal of a strong state; somewhat too disciplined, the party discouraged independence within its ranks and was generally much less devoted to the cause of democracy than was the French Socialist party. The influence of liberals and freethinkers, to whom the Kaiser was not at all friendly, as generally remained academic, and within the universities was offset by many conservative professors.[12] Always there remained the powerful officer class, unlike that of other countries: more arrogant, unconditionally devoted to the military profession, trained to put military efficiency above all other considerations, and more dangerous because the army was not under civilian control, while Germans were brought up to regard it as the soul of the nation. It aggravated the misfortune that as a nation Germany failed to develop any idea that could win other nations to its side.

Especially characteristic was the unique Free Youth movement that grew up in the generation before the World War, attracted a large middle-class following, and included most of the political and intellectual leaders of the future. This reflected a discontent with modern

---

[12] As an academic, I am not proud to add that professors in nineteenth-century Germany had not only high prestige but wide influence—more than professors had in any other country. They helped conspicuously to mold the popular image Germans had of themselves, their past, and their manifest destiny. They might therefore stir some misgivings about the high-minded American educators who want schoolteachers to do more about molding character as well as mind, teaching moral and spiritual values, and rescuing the youth from confusion and doubt.

industrial society suggesting alienation, anticipating the angry young men of recent times. It was unique in that it was of and by the youth, not organized for them like the Boy Scout and other such movements elsewhere. The German youth, however, were not very angry or really rebellious. Their *Bunds* sounded no call for individual freedom, had no political program beyond loyalty to the *Reich*. Devotees of *Geist*, they expressed their protest against the reigning materialism by *Wandervogel*, a return to nature, the simple life, and a German past featuring the usual medieval ideals and "the folk." Essentially their movement was a revival of Romanticism, illustrating its deep, lasting influence on German thought and feeling. Like their forebears they were nationalists and racists, given to a sentimental folkishness that involved no real concern for working people and their problems; they yearned for a hero, for themselves a Wagnerian death; they tended to be antirational, anti-intellectual; and they were fundamentally illiberal, after the war explicitly contemptuous of the liberalism of the new republic. Naturally they failed to rejuvenate their society. They were too vague, soft, and bourgeois to be labeled young Nazis (Hitler despised them); but their mentality made fertile soil for nazism, which in rising to power made use of their *Bunds* and their typical fondness for uniforms.

So the prophecy of Jacob Burckhardt in the nineteenth century was realized. "I have a presentiment that may now seem completely mad but yet will not leave me," he wrote as a lover of the Germany of the Enlightenment. "The military state must become a large-scale industrialist. . . . The development of a crafty and enduring tyranny is still in its infancy: it is in Germany that it will probably first grow to maturity." We may now add that the tyranny did not long endure, another German republic has kindled the ashes of 1848; but it still has to contend with the older tradition that triumphed in that fateful year, and with the ghost of Otto von Bismarck. In the past decade its historians have been contributing to what Francis Löwenheim calls "a great Bismarck renaissance."

5.   *The Rise of Socialism*

"A spectre is wandering over Europe today," began the *Communist Manifesto*, "—the spectre of communism. All the forces of Europe have united to exorcise it." Written by an obscure German journalist in

England, on behalf of a tiny party, the eloquent *Manifesto* created no sensation whatever when it was published, early in 1848, nor was it waved about in the revolutions that erupted shortly afterward. Although the rulers of Europe were properly alarmed by all popular movements, they were not in fact haunted by fears of Marx's communism, which as yet was hardly lusty enough to produce a specter. Outside of Prussia, he had won what little fame he had chiefly by attacks on socialists who were better known. Immediately his boast brings up the confusions of the whole socialist movement, which was indeed beginning to arouse the "insane fear of socialism" deplored by de Tocqueville.

It embraced a broad spectrum of diverse theory, ranging from the idealistic or "utopian" varieties of Robert Owen, Saint-Simon, Fourier, Proudhon, and others to the ostensibly scientific socialism of Marx, but mostly not corresponding to the popular notions about it. The early socialists were not revolutionaries, bent on overthrowing the government by force, but were committed to peaceful methods; most were not atheists either, nor hostile to religion; and most were bourgeois, with a following that was not purely or even predominantly proletarian, any more than the labor union movement was predominantly socialistic. Some, however, did justify the popular alarm. Owen and Proudhon attacked religion point-blank, others were at least hostile to the established churches, and Blanqui preached the necessity of violence. As socialism spread, both its objectives and its methods varied in the different countries, and were further confused by association with other isms, which might cloud even its collectivist ideals. Proudhon, for example, was at heart a sturdy agrarian individualist; he modified his early belief that private property was theft, decided that every man ought to have enough property to assure his personal independence, then attacked competition as the root evil, and concluded by denouncing not only all coercion and violence but all government. Hence his political credo: "No more parties, no more authority, absolute liberty of man and citizen." Out of Proudhon's thought, which was popular enough to earn a savage attack by Marx, came the nonpolitical movement of syndicalism, which grew most powerful in France, Italy, and Spain, countries with a strong agrarian tradition, and took to the general strike as its chief weapon. With it was associated the anarchism of Bakunin, a leader of the first Workers' International, who like Proudhon condemned all forms of the state, but differed in despising gradualism and glorifying the method of violence, finally of pure terrorism.

Marx's success in getting Bakunin expelled from the International helped to break up the organization, which had grown rapidly since its impromptu beginning in 1864. It expired as early as 1876 (in Philadelphia, of all places).

Nevertheless the International had emphasized the underlying unity of the socialist movement, which remained clear enough to warrant the introduction of a new term in the political lexicon, and to give dictionary makers no more trouble than other basic terms. Described by a Frenchman as "grandchildren of Rousseau," the early socialists inherited his belief that man had been degraded by society and could become free only in a community of equals. They differed in being much more optimistic about the possibility of establishing such a community, and eager to provide the common people with an abundance of material goods instead of holding up an ideal of primitive simplicity. They reflected the major developments since Rousseau's time—the French Revolution and the Industrial Revolution. More specifically, the diverse socialists were united by their opposition to *laissez-faire* capitalism and their call for some kind of socialization of the economy. Although at first not strictly revolutionaries, they nevertheless represented another essentially revolutionary movement, which went far beyond the ageless, nameless discontents of the poor and resentments of the rich; for they offered programs, distinct means to achieving a radically new kind of society—what had been only a dream of some simple Christians, or a delusion of millenarians.

In Marx's view, all the early socialists were utopians not because of their visions of the ideal society but because of their belief that these could be realized by peaceful persuasion instead of revolutionary violence. To us children of violence, they look utopian for more obvious reason. All had much too simple a faith. None was a profound thinker, almost none except Saint-Simon had a philosophy of history or anything like an adequate understanding of history. Their shallowness was dangerous because they tended to use freely such terms as "immutable" and "inevitable," betraying a self-righteousness and implying a determinism that could alike become harsh. Similarly their common hostility to the state not only accentuated the shallowness of their political thought but encouraged other possibly despotic tendencies. Short of the violent anarchism of Bakunin, some projected a supposedly spontaneous, nonpolitical, "organic" kind of collectivism that might demand as much sacrifice of the individual; his "humble function" (as Sidney Webb would say) was set by the "social organism." Others, in particular

Saint-Simon, substituted for the art of politics the business of administration, or rule by experts, which called for a rejection of political
equality. The ideal positivistic state of Comte, likewise dedicated to
efficiency, called for drastic restrictions of freedom too.

On the whole, however, the socialist movement was both in theory
and in effect clearly a movement of emancipation for the common
people, at least down to the World War. Its leaders were devoted to the
interests of the poor, the novel idea that widespread poverty was in
the modern world not merely an evil but a social crime. They gave
more concrete meaning to the formal ideals of the French Revolution
by working for more equality and actual freedom for workers, in
general more economic as well as political democracy, while most
except Marxists remained committed to democratic means. The socialist parties demonstrated that the pioneers were by no means simply
impractical men either, but at bottom more realistic than most conservatives in assessing the needs and the potentialities of an industrial
society. Although they won no country before the war, they had become
a real force in most, and had achieved some of their specific objectives
through their influence on liberals and even some conservatives, such
as Bismarck. Shortly after the war they achieved much more through
the first labor governments, beginning in Sweden. Socialism generated
more confusion, indeed, by its very success. While socialists continued
to attack capitalism, the advanced industrial countries developed mixed
economies, with increasing government enterprise and regulation of
private enterprise, which would make their ritual descriptions of capitalism almost as unrealistic as the slogans of its champions. And among
the major casualties was the powerful analysis of Marx. By the time he
became famous, the system that he had argued was by its nature doomed
to self-destruction, had strictly ceased to exist.

But even so we still have to reckon above all with the immense influence of Marx. Little read until near the end of his life (1818–1883),
he had gained a more devoted following than any other socialist, and
he soon became universally recognized as the leading thinker of the
movement, eclipsing all of the many other thinkers he had attacked. The
Communist Manifesto won its notoriety as a revolutionary classic, read
by millions; it made good Marx's boast, as from now on rulers everywhere were perpetually haunted by his specter. The inaugural address
he composed for the first Workers' International laid out a political
program that survived its collapse, beginning with his declaration that
the emancipation of the working class must be won by this class itself;

while intellectuals like himself continued to provide the necessary
leadership, socialism in Europe was henceforth stamped indelibly as
a proletarian movement. *Das Kapital* (1867) justified the fifteen years he
sacrificed to it, in the belief that it would be his major contribution to
humanity: it became the Bible of communism, from which no follower
could depart without incurring charges of heresy. No less important
was Marx's influence on countless thinkers and leaders whom he failed
to convert. He remains by all odds the most influential social and political philosopher of modern times, if not of all times. No student of
history or society today can write as if Marx had not lived. Few would
maintain that the course of Western history, and lately of world history,
would have been just the same.

Now, taken separately, his basic ideas were not original or new. Marx
was deeply indebted to Hegel, of course, no less because he stood the
famous dialectic on its head. With the Hegelian vocabulary he took over
the concept of history as a continuous process, not consciously made
by men, and of society as an organism, not an aggregate of atomic
individuals, nor a deliberate creation. A very bookish man, he was also
indebted to many French and English as well as German thinkers for
his emancipation from Hegel. Hence one may find all the elements of
his revolutionary system in older writers, mostly respectable ones: the
labor theory of value in Locke, Adam Smith, and Ricardo; the inevitable
recurrence of depressions, due to excessive plenty, in the Swiss economist Sismondi; the power of property and class interests in the American
Federalists; the increasing degradation and misery of the proletariat
in Robert Owen, with the wealth of documentation provided by the
Royal Commissioners; the theory of history as class struggle in Saint-
Simon; the dictatorship of the proletariat in Babeuf and Blanqui; the
classless society in Rousseau and early socialists; and so forth. More
broadly, Marx owed immeasurably to Western tradition, from the
Prophetic indignation over social injustice to the rise of science, the
secular rationalism of the Enlightenment, the faith in progress, and
the revolt of the Romantics. He was very much a European thinker,
as much a man of his age—not to mention an alienated German intellectual who suffered from poverty and carbuncles.[13]

Yet his system as a whole was unquestionably original. Its borrowed
elements were welded into a massive, comprehensive synthesis, made

---

[13] He suffered little if any, however, from his Jewish origins. He never mentioned that
he was a Jew and of course was not one by religion. His sensitiveness about his origins
appears chiefly in the animus he usually expressed against the Jews.

more formidable by a new method of analysis, which enabled Marx to formulate new questions, give new answers to old questions, and become the most acute student and critic of his society in his day. For political purposes it offered a new program, with a new strategy for achieving it, that transformed political struggles by making them more purely class struggles. If Marx tended to overlook his indebtedness to his predecessors, the much sharper, firmer statement he gave to their ideas justified his own comment on the *Communist Manifesto*: "What I did that was new was to prove 1) that the *existence of classes* is only bound up with *particular, historic phases in the development of production*; 2) that the class struggle necessarily leads to the *dictatorship of the proletariat*; 3) that this dictatorship itself only constitutes the transition to the *abolition of all classes* and to a *classless society*." And if to all but Communists his system is as vulnerable as formidable, alike because of basic inconsistencies that make it impossible to speak of "true Marxism" or "true socialism," these too sprang from essential differences between Marx and almost all the radicals and revolutionaries before him.

Needless to say, he was no liberal, humanitarian reformer. But he set himself further apart from other socialists and revolutionaries by fiercely rejecting, at least in theory, all appeal to conscience and good will, ideals of justice, notions of natural rights, sentiments of liberty, equality, and fraternity, or in general the moral principles they assumed were universal and ultimate. Marx attacked them so savagely because he believed that such moralism was both futile and false, mere bourgeois sentimentality; it could only perpetuate the ignorance, self-deception, and hypocrisy from which men had suffered throughout history. No individualist either, he rejected as well both the immediate claims of the individual and any dependence upon the idealism or the heroism of individuals. He was resolved to appeal instead solely to the facts, to reason, specifically to the logic of the historical process. This determined good and evil, it had produced the bourgeois, it now demanded uncompromising class war. Moral indignation over the poor and oppressed would do no more good than it ever had done; one had to know and obey the historical laws that had created the proletariat and would assure its triumph. In all this one may see some self-deception, since Marx certainly saw much evil in capitalism and often expressed indignation over it; but as certainly he had much more historical sense than the socialists before and around him.

The intellectual appeal of Marxism, at any rate, owed largely to his theory of history, his claims of scientific validity for it, and his resolute efforts to maintain the attitude or the appearance of objective analysis. To his followers he gave a conviction of certainty that could rescue them from the confusions of the modern world, secure them against the common fate of alienation, demoralization, anxiety, or despair. His theory was more heartening because it was not a crude determinism, implying any automatic, predetermined operation of forces external to man. The "social forces" described by Marx were purely human forces, not governed either by anything like Hegel's Spirit; however unconsciously, men alone made history and gave it meaning. Hence the proletariat had to *will* its freedom, and it was predestined to triumph only because Marxists could be confident that once it had grown class-conscious and enlightened it would so will.

To thinkers at large Marx offered new insights and a mode of analysis that could yield further insights. It should no longer be necessary to remark how much he illumined by his economic interpretation of history, especially modern history. No thinkers before him had ever presented so incisive, thoroughgoing an analysis of their society as Marx did of his. No contemporary thinker—least of all the classical economists—contributed so much to an understanding of the new capitalistic economy: the constant revolutionizing of the means of production, the tendencies to both expansion and centralization that would produce giant organizations, the basic contradictions, and the steady erosion of its own foundations; and with all this the radical transformation of values, the revolutionary effects on the whole society. Similarly Marx contributed to a much clearer, fuller awareness of ideology, immediately the power of class interests in thought, more broadly the general acceptance of ideas that serve primarily not to explain the world but to maintain the social order. He may be called the founder of "the sociology of knowledge." It is hard to do justice to him simply because so much of his thought has been generally accepted, become the commonplace even of his violent opponents, and seeped down even into what passes for thought in routine political oratory.[14]

As a political program, however, Marxism gained force more obviously from its moral appeal. Most of its followers had none of Marx's

[14] An instructive, if possibly not very fruitful, exercise might be to spot the "Marxist" ideas in the rhetoric of conservative congressmen. One might begin by rereading the list of revolutionary proposals at the end of the *Communist Manifesto*—such subversive proposals as universal suffrage, free public education, a graduated income tax, suppression of child labor, and the reclamation of waste lands.

squeamishness about ringing in all the old sentiments, appealing to ideals of justice. Ordinary workers, to whom *Das Kapital* was mostly incomprehensible, could at least get the idea that they were being exploited; men would hardly fight and die on the barricades on behalf of a labor theory of value, or even of historical necessity, which had dutifully evolved capitalism. The fervor that made Marxism a crusade was due immediately to its war on social injustice, a high cause fortified by the vision of a classless society—a purely democratic, essentially Christian kind of society. Long before socialism attracted such religious thinkers as Paul Tillich, Marx's officially atheistic version had a religious quality exemplified by the many martyrs it produced, and the many fanatics. And again a great many of the unconverted could agree that workers were in fact being exploited, the state was often an instrument of oppression. Intellectuals in particular were impressed by his concept of alienation. This was confused by his statements that man himself was alienated by capitalistic society, which implied some nonhistorical norm that his system logically cannot provide, since all past societies were afflicted by class struggle; but at least Marx called attention to the psychological effects of exploitation, and to the broader consequences of work that provided very limited opportunity for self-fulfillment.[15] Altogether, Marx's analysis of a self-regulating economy made possible efforts at more intelligent, humane control in the public interest. By both his attacks on now admitted evils and his contributions to a better understanding of capitalism, he did more than any other thinker to invalidate his own thesis of the increasing misery of the proletariat that would inevitably bring on the revolution.

So we are brought to the basic inconsistencies in his thought. Despite his apparent single-mindedness and wholeheartedness, there are a number of quite different Marxes—not so many as there are Platos, or enough to give every man his own Marx, but enough to keep his fol-

---

[15] I should confess that this now most popular concept of alienation is often not clear to me. It applies clearly enough to many people, especially among the intelligentsia, but I am uncertain when social psychologists say that ordinary Americans—forever accused of being too complacent and conformist—are also alienated. Presumably they have in mind some norm of mental health or maturity, but this too may be vague, and in any case psychologists and sociologists do not agree upon such norms, still less any absolute norm. The concept is more dubious because one usually gathers that many more men suffer from alienation today than ever before—an assumption that suggests the usual forgetfulness of the brute anxieties to which the masses were exposed throughout history. Or perhaps alienation is a luxury that can be afforded only by men who no longer have to worry about starving to death.

lowers forever split, and on almost every basic issue to provide an ambiguous one.[16] Thus the angry Hebraic prophet and the neutral scientific analyst in him naturally did not see eye to eye. Although they might unite in his fierce attacks on misguided socialists, the one denounced the evils of the bourgeois, whom the other declared were products of history, not properly to be blamed, in a sense rather to be applauded for their creation of the proletariat, since they were doomed anyhow. At that, the indignant judge was the more consistent —he detested the bourgeois to the end of his days. It was the systematic analyst who was cloudy or ambiguous at critical points, even though as a political leader Marx sought at every point to equip his followers with rigorous, definite, unequivocal doctrine.

Most obviously pertinent for this history is his doctrine of "historical necessity." For both his philosophical and his political purposes Marx insisted on "tendencies working with iron necessity towards inevitable results," so as to give his theory the authority of scientific law, discredit the utopian varieties of socialism, and guarantee his own seemingly utopian vision of a classless society. He accordingly declared that the doom of capitalism and the dictatorship of the proletariat were alike strictly inevitable. When he added that this was no automatic process, but due to man's own work and will, he still gave men no real choice in futures: "We only show the world what it is that it *must* acquire even against its will." Those who want some choice may be as dissatisfied with Engels' well-known definition of freedom as "the recognition of necessity," since it states only one of the conditions of freedom, and one that does not necessarily assure it. (I for one do not expect to be freer if or when I recognize that I have an incurable disease—any more than were the clear-eyed victims of Stalin's purges.) Nevertheless, Marx always insisted on the necessity of constant struggle by the workers, implying that they had a power of responsible, effective choice that he denied the doomed bourgeois. Like the believers in predestination before him—St. Paul, Mohammed, Luther, Calvin—he was

---

[16] Shortly after starting this chapter, in Yugoslavia, I sat in on a symposium on "Man Today," concentrated on issues of freedom, which was attended chiefly by philosophers from the Communist countries but included a few from the Western democracies. Disagreement was quite civil and amicable—until the Marxists started fighting among themselves. The Russian delegates became furious with the Yugoslavs, whose Marx was humanistic, open-minded, somewhat liberal, and much concerned about the individual. All agreed, however, that true Marxism meant true freedom, and that bourgeois society could not provide real freedom. As a bourgeois liberal, I felt confirmed in a certain complacence, mingled with some skepticism, against which the reader should be warned.

himself a man of terrific determination, and the new idea of progress made his gospel the most extreme example of Western activism. In the *Communist Manifesto* he went far beyond any mere recognition of necessity, for he proclaimed that whereas in bourgeois and all previous societies the past had determined the present, in Communist society the future would determine the present—presumably in ways somehow necessary, but due wholly to the will of the emancipated proletariat.

Somewhat cloudier and more confused were his related doctrines that the forces of production were the "basic" determinants of society and history, and that ideas and beliefs—moral, political, religious, philosophical, etc.—were only "superstructure" or "ideology," reflecting the underlying material reality but amounting to a "false consciousness." By "basic" he almost always meant not merely the necessary conditions of social life but the essential causes of all social change, and he was the more pleased to concentrate on economic forces because he believed that these could be determined with the precision of science—an illusion that revealed the bourgeois positivist in him, and that kept Marxist historians as happy. Marx was too sensible, however, to deny completely the independent power of ideas and beliefs, and at times granted them some incalculable influence, for example, in the golden ages of art. After his death Engels hedged still more, declaring that the forces of production were only "ultimately decisive" or determined change "in the last analysis" (a convenient phrase that can mean as little or as much as a writer wants, or can conceal the truth that he has no clear meaning in mind); he endowed the superstructure "with a movement of its own" that might modify the economic basis "within certain limits," though unspecified. Most difficult was the problem of locating science, which manifestly had had an immense influence on society. In the Marxist scheme it should logically belong with the basic forces of production, which it was in fact profoundly changing through modern technology; yet it was unmistakably a form of ideology, and in Marx's view by no means a "false consciousness." He accordingly evaded the difficulty by declaring emphatically that science had been pressed into "the service of capital," but otherwise usually treating it as an independent force.

About his own thought he was not seriously troubled: he obviously considered it a true representation of the social reality, unlike all other ideologies. He failed to consider, however, some obvious questions this raised about his loose concept of ideology; for the superstructure of his society included a great many diverse, conflicting beliefs, some of

them did not at all clearly serve class interests, and even those that
did might well have elements of objective truth, especially since his
bourgeois society had somehow produced and grown to respect pure
science—a development he neglected to explain. His devout followers
resolved his apparent inconsistency quite simply. They decided in
effect that there were two kinds of ideology, one true and one false.
Since they took for granted the absolute, exclusive truth of Marxism,
they exempted it from the analysis and criticism to which they subjected
all other social theories. They failed as well to ponder the implications
of the great importance of Marx himself, whose influence was about
the plainest demonstration in political history of the independent power
of ideas.

Another subject they neglected was the philosophy of man, on
which Marx was more profoundly ambiguous. Explicitly he conceived
man as a creature of history whose consciousness was determined by
the material conditions of his society. So considered, man did not look
much like a potentially perfectible animal, or in social life a rational
one; Marx's attacks on appeals to humanitarian sentiment and moral
principle emphasized what a poor, ignorant, deluded, hypocritical creature he had been throughout history, how brutalized by class struggle,
and how limited in his capacities for idealism. Thus he scorned the
early socialists primarily because they assumed a sense of justice and
reasonableness in the bourgeois, whom he saw as mere slaves of their
cash economy. Yet running all through his works is a quite different
concept of man. It appears that when not "alienated" he is naturally
rational, imaginative, creative, cooperative, potentially virtuous—altogether quite fit for the ideal classless society. This concept, which was
scarcely accounted for by historical materialism, obviously derived from
the Enlightenment and the Romantic movement. It was the humanist
in Marx (now being recovered in the satellite countries) who determined the otherwise surprising outcome of a historical process governed by economic forces rather than spirit: a society in which men
would at last be free, fully realize their humanity, fulfill themselves in
spontaneous creative activity, and all (as Trotsky would add) become
capable of achievement hitherto reserved for a few geniuses. In so
doing they would fully realize their individuality too. Meanwhile,
unfortunately, Marx's neglect of the claims of the individual helped
to justify the brutal indifference to his rights when the first Communist
states were established.

Still another basic ambiguity appears in the critical question whether his system is an open or a closed one. As a follower of Hegel, Marx was an avowed relativist; since all ideas were the reflections of a particular society and age, it followed that none had absolute validity, no moral principles were universal and ultimate. It also followed from his dialectic that Marxism should be open to constant revision; as Engels wrote, in this view of history "the demand for final solutions and eternal truths ceases once for all." Marx sometimes criticized the rigid doctrinaires in his camp, indeed, declaring that he was not a "Marxist," and he could be flexible in both practice and theory. The program for immediate action that he laid out in the *Communist Manifesto* revealed some apparent opportunism since it consisted mostly of mere reforms, including some that the bourgeois Utilitarians had long been working for. In an address to a congress of the International he even qualified his basic doctrine of the necessity of revolution, saying that the different traditions of countries must be considered, and that in some countries, such as Britain and America, workers might obtain their objectives by peaceful means. But again there was another Marx, dogmatic and absolutist. An inverted Hegel who offered his theory as no mere hypothesis but absolute truth, and went on to promise a final universal solution, he in effect declared his system closed to any basic revision. In his own camp he tolerated no dissent or serious deviation from his teachings; he provided ample texts to support the inflexible attitude that would make "revisionism" a form of treason. In this sense too he made Marxism a religion, of the Roman Catholic sort. And again his devout followers, above all Lenin, only magnified the inconsistency they seemed blind to. Lenin made atonement to Hegel by standing Marx on his head, making politics instead of economics primary; but in as good faith he remained a doctrinaire, fiercely intolerant of others who took liberties with the gospel.

And so he recalls us to the actual consequences of a revolutionary creed in which he saw nothing ambiguous. The ruling tendency in Marx's thought, and still more plainly in the thought of his Communist followers, was the tendency to absolutism or intellectual dictatorship. The ruling ideas remained the familiar ones announced in the *Communist Manifesto*: democracy was nothing but a sham, government was completely controlled by the bourgeois, they were bound by the nature of capitalism simply to exploit the proletariat, their rule could be ended only by revolution, this would inevitably result in the dictatorship of the proletariat, etc. Given the historic outcome, one has to rehearse the elementary objections to Marx's system.

It was not scientific, of course, in any strict sense.[17] His theory of history breaks down most obviously when applied to other civilizations, illustrating again that Marx was very much a European thinker of his own time. On Western history, where it was most illuminating, his insights were vitiated by his scientific pretensions, or strictly unscientific spirit. Never content with mere hypotheses, he claimed certainty for historical "laws" that he could not possibly verify. He had no scientific warrant in any case for his positive predictions of inevitable outcomes, but in fact Marx made a notably poor record as a prophet. If his influence had much to do with the profound political changes in the Western world, he nevertheless failed to foresee these changes. His most apparent success, the Communist nations established in his name, only demonstrated that his theory provides no basis for predicting what a new society will be like. His followers overlooked the plainest implication of his dialectic, that it too would breed contradictions; so no one was more dismayed by the tyranny of the Soviet than were disillusioned Marxists.

Here the utopian in Marx was to blame. His promise of a classless industrial society in which the state would wither away was as fantastic as any of the visions of the early socialists, seeming less absurd only because he was much vaguer and never bothered to give as serious, detailed an account of it. But much more dangerously absurd were his no less vague notions about the dictatorship of the proletariat that he set up as the immediate goal. To begin with, there was no good reason to believe that the workers would faithfully carry out to the end the heroic, martyr's role as redeemer that he assigned them. Their "ideology" was basically no different from that of most of the bourgeois; they worshiped the same gods, had the same personal goals, wanted the same material goods; and only the most desperate or most idealistic could be expected to devote their lives to a distant revolution, believe that their "true" interests were class interests that would be realized after their death. There was every reason to believe that they might be easily distracted or misled, and that their cause would continue to provoke as much disagreement among socialists and revolutionaries as it

---

17 One may safely disregard the epistemology and dialectical materialism on which his social theory was supposedly based. Marx himself neglected to expound this philosophy, leaving only some scattered passages, and though Communists always refer to it reverently, they have done very little with it either, for the good reason that it provides no scientific basis. Non-Communists may find a further excuse for irreverence in Trotsky's statement that "the will to revolutionary activity is indispensable to understanding the Marxian dialectic." This suggests something rather different from the scientific spirit, resembling the ancient religious doctrine that faith is necessary for understanding, not vice versa.

did in Marx's lifetime. Come the revolution and the dictatorship of the proletariat, which alike required strong leadership, there was as good reason to expect the emergence of a new elite, a class who would do the dictating for the workers, or more likely to them. None of the "utopian" socialists were blinder than Marx to the elementary problem of political power, and the obvious dangers of its abuse in a socialistic as in any other kind of state.

Behind the utopian was a bourgeois intellectual, very bookish, who had little direct association with workers, little understanding of their mentality, and who was as poor a psychologist as Jeremy Bentham. But the primary reason for Marx's failure as a prophet was his basic doctrine of economic determinism. While making possible his many insights, this blinded him to the importance of all the other social factors that he lumped together as ideology or mere superstructure. Thus his argument in the *Communist Manifesto* for the inevitable revolution—the increasing misery of the proletariat and its increasing mass as the petty bourgeois were forced down into its ranks—rested on the assumption of the entirely free play of economic forces; but no European country in fact permitted such complete *laissez faire*. The unmistakable improvement in the living standards of the proletariat testified, among other things, that government was not entirely controlled by the bourgeois and democracy not a mere sham. It also emphasized how violently Marx simplified capitalistic society by reducing it to but two classes and insisting by definition that their interests were irreconcilable, their only true relation was conflict; he ignored the plain measure of cooperation between them, all the interests, sentiments, and moral beliefs they had in common, without which no society could ever endure, and no class either. He slighted as well the independent power of knowledge and understanding, ideas and ideals—what enabled men to choose their ideology or be in different ways as reactionary, conservative, liberal, or radical as they pleased. Hence he learned very little from all the changes in Europe during his lifetime, which led Engels to confess later that they had greatly underestimated the capacity of capitalism for internal development. Despite occasional second thoughts, and worries over the effects of prosperity on English workers, Marx adhered to the outdated thesis of the *Manifesto*. His legacy to his disciples included an engrained inability to size up capitalism realistically and keep abreast of the times, fortified by a conviction that they alone were realists, far ahead of the times, and that name-calling was an exercise of independent thought.

All their shortcomings were more grievous because of the basic illiberality of Marx. He degraded politics by reducing it to class war, branding compromise as cowardice or treachery, insisting that finally its issues could be settled only by force. Thereby he not merely portrayed but evoked the worst in the bourgeois, intensifying class hatred on both sides. For men of good will he made reasonable, civil debate difficult if not impossible by both his theoretical dogmatism and his personal manners, exemplified by his ferocious attacks on fellow socialists. Typically he was not content to refute the arguments of his opponents but impugned their motives, denied their good faith; so it was not surprising that the purge became the realistic way of settling differences. At best he undermined the independence of the intelligentsia, the main source of their value to society, by giving them no alternative but communism; one had to be all for it or against it—there was no middle ground between thesis and antithesis; so it came down to a crude choice between good and evil, black and white. Marx cheapened it by declaring that existing rights and liberties, so hardly won, were merely formal, or what his Communist followers would call "petty bourgeois categories." Most fateful was his deliberate appeal to the method of violence, the cult of revolution—the "veritable panegyric" on revolution that Lenin was pleased to find in the more humane Engels too. Marx was again wildly utopian in his faith that out of bloody revolution would come universal peace and brotherhood, the salvation of mankind.

What actually came out of it is the subject of a later chapter. Here it should be repeated that before the World War the great majority of socialists agreed that their objective was not only a social organization of the economy but a democratic organization of society; and though most of them admired Marx, they did not believe in the inevitability, the practical necessity, or the ideal value of a violent revolution. Yet for several decades now Marx had been the best-known, best-hated of revolutionaries, "the Red Terrorist Doctor"; and even at this stage thoughtful men could discern deeper reasons for alarm. While his devastating analysis in *Das Kapital* was more remarkable in that he worked it out in England during a period of prosperity, when capitalism was booming, revolutionary Marxism was symptomatic of serious ailments beneath the complacent surface, beneath even those he diagnosed. It reflected a deep uncertainty and anxiety, appealing to many intellectuals as well as workers by its promise of a total solution, absolutely guaranteed—what might be called a reactionary gospel. It signaled the growing disposition to violence, irrationality, and fanaticism, sprung from the deep unrest, in a society headed for the catastrophe of a world war.

The outbreak of this war exposed another serious oversight of Marx's. One popular charge against socialists—that they were internationalists and pacifists, hence unpatriotic—had been substantiated by many a lofty speech and pious resolution in the congresses of the Second International. The International had not passed, however, one possibly effective resolution—a pledge to call a general strike if there was a threat of war. By this time socialists had become almost respectable in Europe; most of them breathed fire perfunctorily, if at all; and they were quite loyal to their country. When the war broke out, it was hardly surprising that all socialist parties voted overwhelmingly to support their own country. In his scorn of appeals to sentiment, Marx had greatly underestimated the power of sentiment, in particular what had long been the most powerful sentiment in the Western world—nationalism. He was quite wrong when he declared that "the workers have no fatherland." The specter wandering over Europe was not class but national war, and it was more awful because the forces of Europe had not united to exorcise it.

6. *The Growth of Nationalism*

As we have seen, the "simple" sentiment of patriotism sprang from another novel, revolutionary development, as complicated and paradoxical as any other in the modern world. At the Congress of Vienna the hardheaded Metternich and his associates had paid no heed to this sentiment; they restored the map of Europe without regard to peoples and nationalities, considering only the traditional interests of royal dynasties. Nationalism accordingly throve as a liberal cause, associated with ideals of freedom, fostered by sympathy with subject peoples who sought independence. Then its less agreeable potentialities were exposed in 1848, when supranational popular revolutions turned out to be chiefly nationalistic movements and began clashing with one another. Thereafter it became more exclusive, especially in central and eastern Europe, where it was supported by ultraconservatives too. It also became more confused, as everywhere it spread through all ranks of society and was identified with diverse aspirations; it brought economic and cultural as well as political changes, among other things spurring the drive to industrialize and modernize. As it both promoted and threatened the independence of peoples collectively, so it was linked with all the major forces that were both promoting and threatening personal freedom. Most obviously, however, it generated a vast deal of feeling: mainly unreasoned, often violent and ugly, always dangerous, but more dangerous because it was by no means simply irrational or evil; feeling that almost all of us share, and that makes it both harder and more necessary to keep one's head as one reviews the growth of nationalism.

Now, its roots are indeed simple, and as old as human society. It is an outgrowth of primeval tribalism, the loyalty men have always felt to their group. The reason why it is only a few centuries old is as simple: throughout history there were no large, unified nations, only kingdoms or empires in which the great bulk of the illiterate populace could have no live sense of community or common destiny because they knew virtually nothing about history, geography, affairs of state, or any other frame for such large ideas as "China" and "America." In this respect medieval peasants were much like peasants in all previous societies, except that there was not even a strong state over most of them. Otherwise, however, Europe had ample seeds for the growth to come. Its heritage included the Hebrew idea of a chosen people with special destiny, the Greek and Roman tradition of civic patriotism, the related tradition of popular sovereignty, and the wider loyalties inspired by the Roman Church. At the same time it embraced different peoples with different languages and cultural traditions, and these embryonic national communities provided the basis for the nation-states that began emerging in western Europe in the late Renaissance.[18] However Christian, their monarchs made quite plain the supremacy of the national interest as they saw it, and the abler or more dashing ones aroused considerable patriotic fervor, in peoples growing more conscious of themselves as Spaniards, Englishmen, Frenchmen. But this fervor was still far from being so widespread and habitual as modern nationalism, again for an obvious reason: the national interest was determined by the king and a small ruling class. The common people, still largely ignorant of history, geography, and affairs of state, were strictly subjects with little if any voice in their government; so they were likely to have as little idea of living or dying for their country.

---

18 On the emergence of this new kind of state, see *Freedom in the Western World,* pp. 199–206.

It was therefore no accident that England was the first country in which the sentiment of nationalism became widely, deeply engrained. Sowed by the heroics of the Elizabethan Age and nurtured by a popular theater, this matured when the revolutions of the seventeeth century secured the "true and ancient rights" of Englishmen. Thereafter it flourished on the growing wealth and power of England, but it was associated more with pride in these rights than with military glory. "Rule Britannia," the first popular national anthem (1740), boasted that England was "great and free," whereas all other nations not so blessed "must in their turn to tyrants fall." The sentiment was all the stronger because it was seldom fervent or intense, usually matter of course when not complacent; it was rooted in a truly national life, in which public opinion was a real force and ordinary men could feel that England was indeed *their* country. Such honorable meanings of nationalism were inherited by Americans, who in declaring their independence linked them with universal rights. Although their patriotism became more blatant, it was always associated with pride in "the land of the free," and from Jefferson on the greater national leaders and writers repeatedly declared that the American cause was the cause of all mankind.

In Europe this ideal kind of nationalism was proclaimed most resonantly in the French Revolution. Its early leaders likewise linked the cause of France with the universal cause of liberty, equality, and fraternity; they had behind them the cosmopolitanism of the Enlightenment, which had given the old word "humanity" its modern meaning of "mankind." When Napoleon set out on his wars he at least posed as a liberator, and was at first accepted as one by many liberals in other countries. Meanwhile patriotism at home had swept the land as never before in European history. All over France altars to the fatherland were set up with the inscription "The citizen is born, lives, and dies for the fatherland"—a claim that the "Sun King" Louis XIV could never have made or made good in his most vainglorious moods. The people's armies that defended France proved the power of this sentiment by fighting much better than the professional armies of the kings of Europe.

With the beginnings of the Romantic movement, another ideal theme was introduced by Herder. An ardent cultural rather than political nationalist, not at all bent on furthering the interests of the nation-state, or in particular of the Prussia he despised, he dwelt instead on the claims of language, which he saw as the main agent of nationality or cultural community; he spurred the belated interest in living languages and vernacular literatures that was among the by-products of nationalism.[19] Although he had a particular admiration for German, he respected all languages and cultures, and so far from holding that the Germans were the chosen people of the future, he expressed a higher opinion of the potentialities of the Slavic peoples for peaceful, civilized purposes—an idea that later stimulated Slavic intellectuals. Still a man of the Enlightenment, Herder loved all nationalities the more because he believed that a realization of their true values would promote the good of mankind, even the cause of peace. Similarly his interest in "the folk" and their lore and song, hitherto virtually ignored, was not merely literary but democratic, reflecting a belief in human equality. Herder best illustrates a value of nationalism that we are now likely to overlook—that it made possible the growth of internationalism, and may even be considered an indispensable preliminary. Only an awakened, self-conscious people is capable of wider interests and sympathies, conscious activity on an international scene.

On the whole, early nationalism was clearly a movement of liberation. While it served a fundamental need, now that there was much less natural reverence for kings (even the Sun King had done poorly as a father symbol), it was more rational than the traditional loyalty to the monarch, and stimulated more public spirit and public enterprise. Its growth meant that peoples were consciously entering history, acquiring a more vivid sense of both their past and a possibly better future, and with this more sense of dignity. If their expressed aspirations were typically grandiose, they were none the less a stimulus to many men, especially the young. Thus when the Greeks started their war of independence, their National Assembly proclaimed that they were "descendants of the wise and noble peoples of Hellas," and that they were fighting a holy war "to reconquer the rights of individual liberty, property, and honor—rights which the civilized people of Europe, our neighbors, enjoy today." Among the many liberals everywhere who felt that "the children of Solon" were again carrying the torch was the ardent young Mazzini. For Italy, which Metternich had dismissed as a mere "geographical expression," he conceived a "sacred" mission as a new Rome—a Rome of the People—to lead the way to a United States

---

19 In the seventeenth century, when French became the universal language of Europe, it was not even taught in French lycées or used in the higher instruction of the universities, where Latin was still the only dignified tongue. Nor was there a chair of French literature until toward the end of the eighteenth century.

of Europe; and the Young Italy movement he founded in exile not only aroused the enthusiasm that enabled Garibaldi to succeed but inspired similar movements, which kept sprouting and spreading down to our century, breeding Young Turks, Young Arabs, and Young China. In the course of these national awakenings, moreover, many men discovered the values that Herder had popularized, beginning with the resources of their own language, literature, and folklore. The aroused nationalities—Russians, Czechs, Poles, Finns, Hungarians, Norwegians, Irish—now began contributing more to the art and thought of the West, greatly enriching its common heritage.

From the beginning, however, patriotism was a refuge for possibly more dangerous types than scoundrels, in particular the kind of zealot who had bloodied European history since its dawn. In the French Revolution citizens suspected of any hesitancy about living and dying for the fatherland were soon having a hard time. Danton pronounced the death penalty for everyone "who directly or indirectly opposes the measures taken for public safety"; and presently he was rewarded with this penalty by Robespierre, the purest patriot of them all. No personal rights were secure when one's whole duty was to serve the fatherland. Abroad the zealous people's armies soon forgot that they were fighting for universal liberty and peace, or anything but France; they grew as indifferent to the rights of other peoples. Vicariously they shared in the glory of Napoleon, whose ambitions included another passion as old as recorded history that nationalism would serve—the passion for power. Other peoples ceased to welcome liberation by Napoleon. The most lasting effect of his conquests was the nationalistic spirit he awakened, especially in Germany and Russia.

The German Romantics then laid the intellectual foundations of the exclusive kind of nationalism, quite different from Herder's, that grew popular in central Europe. This still had an ideal quality, beyond the willing self-sacrifice that all patriotism inspired, since the Romantics were convinced of the superiority of German culture; in this respect they were less crude than many American patriots. But more plainly they foreshadowed the outcome of German nationalism: in the land of Bismarck *Geist* was linked with *Macht*—not freedom.[20] With militarism it stimulated a chauvinism that went well beyond simple devo-

---

[20] In distinguishing these dual traditions of nationalism, I am substantially following Hans Kohn's account of its rise in his many works on the subject. Although he writes as an avowed liberal, and perhaps a somewhat too optimistic one, his account seems to me in general balanced and just.

tion to one's country, and bred more hatred of other peoples. Much more reactionary by all European standards was Russian nationalism, which went back to the "Great Patriotic War" of 1812 and was nourished by German Romanticism. Its Slavophil spokesmen were mostly supporters of the autocratic czar, still the father symbol of "Holy Russia," and the most powerful supporter of the Metternich regime. Their abiding influence will concern us when we come to the Soviet, but we might note here Karl Marx's opinion that Slavs were always disposed to despotism and none of their countries was fit for revolution.

He might well have excepted the Czechs. They had been made self-conscious by František Palacký, the "Father of the Nation," who under the influence of Herder had written a history of the Czechs in which he emphasized a liberal tradition going back to Jan Hus, their great martyr in the struggle for freedom. Another patriot, Havlíček, warned them against the idea of Pan-Slavism that the Russians were spreading, with an eye to their designs on Ottoman Turkey. As he pointed out, there was no real unity among the Slavic peoples, and Czechs had no reason to support either Russians or Poles—peoples who had been enemies for more than two centuries, alike chiefly in their common oppression of the Slavic Ukrainians. The Poles (who now declared that the Russians were really of Mongol descent, not Slavs, and by Russian scholars were themselves rechristened as "Sarmatians") enlisted more sympathy from European liberals than any other oppressed people, but for somewhat mistaken reasons. Their great poet Mickiewicz had dreamed up the loftiest imaginable national ideal for them in *The Books of the Polish Nation from the Beginning of the World to the Martyrdom of the Polish Nation* (1832), the thesis of which was that the country had been crucified because of its devotion to liberty and the brotherhood of all peoples, and that with its resurrection "wars shall cease in all Christendom." Nevertheless the German democrats at Frankfort were able to find a good excuse for changing their minds about them, alleging a solicitude for the Polish peasantry: the many Polish exiles clamoring for the restoration of their nation were mainly from the aristocracy and gentry, who had maintained serfdom all through its independent history. Havlíček lost his initial sympathy for their cause when he discovered their continued oppression of their peasantry in Austrian territory. Down through the world wars the exceptionally independent spirit of the Poles would remain primarily nationalistic, not a democratic or brotherly spirit.

Slavic nationalism in southern Europe only added to the confusion, with eventually more fateful consequences. Immediately it collided with Hungarian nationalism, which in 1848 had inspired a successful revolution against Austria. Under the flamboyant Louis Kossuth the Hungarians issued a Declaration of Independence on the American model, initiating his fame as a great republican; but they were a minority in their own land, whose peasants were mostly Slavs—Serbs, Croats, Slovenes, etc.—and were not invited by Kossuth to enter the government. (There were also many Romanians, a mixed people known as "Vlachs" who had used a Slavic script until the eighteenth century, when their teachers introduced a Latin one; whereupon they learned that their language was Roman in origin, and felt superior to both Hungarians and Slavs.) The claims of language, so cherished by Herder, then led to civil war. Although Hungarians had only in recent years begun using their own language instead of German or Latin in their Diet, they now made its use obligatory in school and government, and thereby angered the Croats, who had lately grown proud of their "Illyrian" tongue. The upshot of some confused fighting and indiscriminate pillage was the restoration of Austrian sovereignty. Austria managed to continue ruling its many diverse subject peoples, in part because they distrusted or hated one another more than they did the Austrians; when it accepted Hungary as an equal partner (1867), the Slavs turned to Russia, the "Big Brother," in the hope of realizing their national aspirations; and out of Young Bosnia—an offshoot of the movement that Mazzini had initiated—came the high-minded student who touched off World War I by assassinating the Austrian Archduke Ferdinand.

Meanwhile the Industrial Revolution had introduced further complications. Indirectly it helped to propagate and intensify the sentiment of nationalism by speeding up communications, breaking the cake of custom, inducing men to look to the future instead of the past, and in particular by swelling the population of cities. Nationalism on the Continent was primarily an urban movement; it was a means to feelings of community in the city masses, many of them recently uprooted and needing some substitute for the forsaken pieties of the village, very few of them capable of such larger loyalties as "mankind" or even "the workers of the world." Directly industrialism stimulated economic nationalism. A generation before Bismarck, Friedrich List returned to Germany from fast-progressing America to tell his former countrymen that "true economics" was literally political economy, its proper basis was not free trade but "NATIONALITY," and only equally advanced nations could afford free competition. Nations ambitious to industrialize soon did follow the example of America, protecting their infant industries by tariffs. Hence the Industrial Revolution created the all too familiar paradox, that nationalism grew ever stronger precisely when international communication and trade were making nations ever more interdependent. Likewise it forced the all-important question of the ends of nationalism, the uses being made of the growing national power and pride. On all counts it accentuated the ambiguous effects on political and personal freedom.

The subject peoples of central and eastern Europe were handicapped because the spirit of nationalism was fathered by a few intellectuals, at first largely confined to a small literate minority in scattered cities. When it spread to the still uneducated peasantry, the great majority could naturally envisage little beyond the hopes of freedom from foreign rule. Hence it was not merely Jan Hus or Palacký that made Czech nationalism more liberal and cosmopolitan than that of the southern Slavs: Czechs had the advantages of their ancient capital of Prague, a larger middle class, more industry, and proximity to western Europe. In the independent countries that were building up industry, nationalism was most closely tied to the cause of progress. Here the awakened common people could acquire more confidence in their own prospects. They were better able to participate in their government and their culture, they could and did take to demanding more freedom and opportunity. As their standard of living rose, industrial workers grew more patriotic in spite of Marx and all the congresses of their International, if only because their government was doing them more direct, concrete good.

On the other hand, nationalism manifestly could and did serve as a distraction from the cause of reform or the advancement of the common welfare, even when it was not deliberately exploited by rulers. It menaced the individual by most explicitly subordinating his good to the national good, spreading the idea that there was no greater good than dying for one's country. A man's supreme duty was always to his country, right or wrong; it muffled the claims of God, humanity, civilization, personal conscience, simple decency, or life itself. Since the nation was commonly identified with the state, nationalism could serve to increase the powers of the state at more expense of individual liberty. All such tendencies were more dangerous because the greatness of a nation was as commonly identified with its power. They came to a head in 1870— another major turning point in European history.

Within Germany popular opposition to Bismarck had faded as he went on winning his wars; his success confirmed the illiberal tendencies of German nationalism. Then all Europe suffered from his crowning success in the Franco-Prussian War. Hitherto there had been no arms races, but now military strength became a primary objective of the leading nations; all built up their armaments, which modern weapons made a still heavier burden. On the Continent all followed the Prussian example and introduced compulsory military service, requiring their able-bodied young men to give at least three years to their country. The military, which operated under its own laws, had considerably more say about the determination of national policy. The common people who paid the costs of the military machines had little real say about them, or about the diplomacy that made them necessary. In all countries foreign affairs were in the hands chiefly of aristocrats, who conducted them chiefly behind closed doors; it would take later historians to make public the doings of diplomats. Most people knew little about foreign policy, having only some indiscriminate fear or hatred of "Germany" or "Russia"—cloudy abstractions that obscured all the other simple people like themselves.

Because of such feelings most people accepted the new restrictions on personal freedom, which might therefore be considered no real loss of freedom. Compulsory military service came to be regarded as a natural constraint, the kind of duty that men had always owed to the tribe or the state, and that was now compensated for by pride in the nation. So in patriotic ardor Frenchmen had been the first to submit to conscription during their Revolution, as Americans in turn did in their Civil War. Yet there remained the obvious reasons for questioning the sacrifices people were making to nationalism, even apart from the many persons who felt that the new compulsions were unwarranted constraints on their freedom. Losers in war of course got nothing for their sacrifices, and felt more humiliated in so far as they were patriotic. Dead soldiers were no longer free men even if on the winning side, while their families and friends had to suffer, and most people might get little if any positive benefit out of the national victory. Above all, the question remains whether the sacrifices people were making to the new god were reasoned choices—really their own, really free. And again the Franco-Prussian War signaled the plainest reasons for doubt.

Upon the onset of the war, France was swept by an ardent patriotism recalling the days of the Revolution. So was Germany, under the very coolheaded Bismarck. By this time the spread of literacy and the growth of the press made it easy to whip up feeling all over a country. Rulers who appealed to the nation's pride and honor were not necessarily guileful, still less cynical; the people were now sufficiently nationalistic on their own, and the popular press was likely to be still more so—it would give increasing trouble to statesmen inclined to be prudent or peaceful. At any rate, patriotic fervor now welled up in waves, swept the whole country, approached mass hysteria. Under these conditions the choices made by most men, involving life or death for many, hardly look like free, reasoned, responsible choices.

Such emotionality, seemingly a sign of national confidence and love of country, might well up from frustration or insecurity too.[21] In any case, it exacted a toll in all countries. In America patriotic fever had brought on the Civil War, a struggle much more murderous than either side anticipated. In relatively staid England jingoism grew strong enough to kill the hopes of those like Cobden that free trade would lead to world peace. (Cobden lost his seat in Parliament because of his opposition to the inglorious Crimean War.) National pride stiffened opposition to the demands of the Irish for Home Rule, despite the best efforts of Gladstone, and saddled the country with a long, bitter controversy, the more stupid because the subjection of Ireland brought no concrete benefits whatever to the common people of England. In France the cult of Napoleon that inspired the vain ambitions of the Emperor Louis Napoleon helped to bring on the disaster of the Franco-Prussian War. Later the Dreyfusards exploited nationalism to the hilt in the violent controversy that convulsed the country.

This was aggravated by an uglier related sentiment that had grown popular—racism. When Count Gobineau published his *Essay on the Inequality of the Human Race* (1853–1855) introducing the theory of the supreme importance of blood and the need of keeping it pure, his friend de Tocqueville protested: "Don't you see how inherent in your doctrine are all the evils produced by permanent inequality: pride,

---

21 Lucien Febvre has lamented that we have no history of human emotionality, the feelings of fear, love, hatred, joy, pity, etc. Such a psychological history might throw much light on the conditions, values, and costs of freedom. It would be very difficult to write, however, even apart from the uncertain, conflicting evidence of the feelings of the common people in past societies, because feelings are so often ambivalent or unlike what appears on the surface, yet not necessarily so unlike as sophisticates now tend to assume. One might be tempted to "explain" the rabid nationalism of the Germans, for example, by an underlying feeling of inferiority, a compensation for freedoms denied them, or some sort of neurosis easy to make out in many Romantics; but under Bismarck and his successors it looks to me like a compound of genuine confidence, loyalty, obedience, arrogance, and conceit. Only after the defeat in World War I, with the rise of Hitler, does it look clearly neurotic.

violence, the scorn of one's fellow men, tyranny and abjection in every one of their forms?" Gobineau's theory was not at first popular in France, since he asserted the superiority of Teutonic or German blood, but it helped to support anti-Semitism. Englishmen were attracted by it out of pride in being Anglo-Saxons—a race, as Ruskin observed, "mingled of the best northern blood." Many Americans also grew prouder of their Anglo-Saxon blood, especially when they looked down on the new immigrants from southern and eastern Europe, and many more welcomed racism as a confirmation of the natural, permanent inferiority of the Negro. But it was Germany, as de Tocqueville predicted, that took most enthusiastically to the idea of innate racial superiority—"Nordic," "Aryan," or simply German. Here too its popular association with anti-Semitism was most firmly cemented, with the aid of Wagner, Treitschke, and other prophets. This in turn was most explicitly linked to attacks on the liberal, democratic creed; the Jew was by definition not only an alien but a liberal and an internationalist. All such prejudices were incorporated in the influential Pan-German League that was organized by prominent men at the end of the century, and that advocated a ruthless militarism to realize the Nordic mission of creating a great empire and ruling the world. Anti-Slavic too, it was matched by Pan-Slavism, a looser movement but similarly dedicated to an imperial mission.

It is unnecessary to point out that racism menaced the freedom of many millions of men long before Hitler came into power. We must ask, however, why it grew so popular, and in the form of anti-Semitism so virulent, at a time when Europe was at the zenith of its power and prestige, had the least reason to fear other races, and prided itself on its superior civilization. Nationalism was the most apparent reason, no less because all nations included peoples of different stock. The racial theory offered a good excuse for countries denying self-determination to other peoples (as the Germans did to the Poles in their midst), or hankering for aggression on other countries. Among intellectuals it fell in with various tendencies, such as social Darwinism, elitism, Hegelianism, and determinism; it was a new mode of "historical necessity." For people at large it was an easy way of feeling more self-important. Yet racism also belied the apparent complacence and conceit, especially in the nasty form of anti-Semitism. People really sure of themselves, confident of their national destiny, would not find it necessary to flaunt so fake a proof of their superiority. It is significant that Gobineau was profoundly pessimistic about the prospects of modern civilization, and

was reproached by de Tocqueville for his "fatalism" too. Jews in particular—everywhere a small minority—were obviously serving as
scapegoats. Racism fed on frustration and insecurity, the nameless
resentments and anxieties of men not very free in spirit. It was another
symptom of the growing irrationality that culminated in Hitlerism.

It was likewise another anomaly in a civilization distinctive for its
cultivation of science, since historians and social scientists have repeatedly pointed out that racial theorists lack the scientific authority they
claim.[22] As an international enterprise, science recalls the basic anomaly, that nationalism became the dominant religion in an era that was
becoming more international in both fact and outlook. International
societies of all kinds were multiplying in Europe, international congresses meeting every year. Nations were forming the Universal Telegraph Union and Universal Postal Union, getting together to set up
uniform patent laws and uniform copyright laws. Passports disappeared
everywhere except Russia and Ottoman Turkey. Men were more conscious of themselves as Europeans than ever before, aware that Europe
was leading the world, as "Christendom" had once dreamed of doing.
They considered peace—not war—the normal state. And despite their
alleged devotion to the fatherland, many millions of them were migrat-
ing to other lands. America alone might have refuted racism, for while
the melting pot always seethed with animosities, many different peoples
were nevertheless helping to make it a world power, and were becoming
Americans.

All this international enterprise may also remind us that the growth
of nationalism was neither simply anomalous nor simply evil. Nations
were more willing to recognize fully the equal existence of other nations than they had been in past centuries, down to the partition of
Poland; in diplomacy and war they still sought limited objectives, as
Bismarck had, without thought of destroying their rivals or denying
their equal rights to sovereignty. In western Europe and America
nationalism continued to be associated with the cause of individual

---

[22] I should add that their honorable revulsion against racism has perhaps led them
too far in denying any significance to race as a factor in history. Physical anthropologists
point out that there unmistakably are racial differences, and that one might reasonably
expect them to count for something, especially when geneticists declare that men inherit
some temperamental predispositions as well as physical characteristics and mental capacities.
But the main point is still that all civilized peoples today are peoples of mixed blood,
there is no pure race, and no evidence that pure blood is better than mixed. One comes
closest to purity in the surviving primitive peoples. The Germans were most ludicrous
in fancying themselves as "Aryans," a people who vanished ages ago, and at that comprised different peoples by the time they entered history.

liberty, the rights of self-determination by other nationalists, the hopes
of peaceful progress and plenty for all. These ideals stirred constant
protest against its exclusive tendencies, among many others by Mill,
Renan, Lord Acton, William James, and Jean Jaurès; and in Germany
too there were always spiritual descendants of Kant, Herder, and
Goethe. Politically, moreover, nationalism worked to unite as well as
divide men. Austria at least approached unity by learning to treat its
subject peoples more liberally, eventually granting them full suffrage.
In Scandinavia national self-consciousness promoted both aspirations
to freedom and feelings of solidarity, leading to the peaceful separation
of Norway from Sweden (1905), and to a pan-Scandinavian movement
that sought unity without nonsense about a Nordic mission.

Yet the course of events on the main stage, dominated by the great
powers, brought out chiefly the worst in nationalism. The World War
only made plainer that liberalism had failed to capture and control
the most powerful sentiment in the modern world, which it had helped
to generate. The democracies too got ever more involved in pure power
politics, in which they made paramount their own national interests
and conceived these interests primarily in terms of national power
rather than their avowed ideals. They were therefore deeply implicated
as well in another portentous development—"the age of imperialism,"
also dating from about 1870.

7. *The New Imperialism*

Although the word "imperialism" was coined in the middle of the
nineteenth century, the phenomenon was of course a very ancient one,
almost as old as civilization. Europeans had begun to get the idea in
their Crusades and had fully caught on to it several centuries before,
when the Atlantic nations created their colonial empires.[23] Britain had
continued to build up its empire, if in a casual, haphazard fashion.
During the Napoleonic Wars it appropriated Malta, some islands in
the West Indies, and the Dutch colonies of South Africa and Ceylon,
and shortly afterwards it made British possessions of the Indian territories that had been administered for trading purposes by the East
India Company. Yet the British had little imperial ambition, and could

---

[23] See *Freedom in the Western World*, pp. 176–186.

go about the business casually because after Napoleon the major Continental powers were no more interested in it. Most statesmen had come to agree with Adam Smith and Bentham that colonies were not really profitable possessions. In 1852 Disraeli made his famous statement about "these wretched colonies" that were "millstones around our necks," but in a few years, thank God, would all be independent. At about the same time the German fleet was sold at auction. It was indeed a "new" imperialism that set in after 1870, quite suddenly.

Disraeli himself signaled the change by committing his party to an imperialistic policy, buying shares in the Suez Canal, and a little later proudly bestowing on Queen Victoria the title "Empress of India." By this time all the leading powers were embroiled in a wild scramble for colonies. Within a generation they divided up virtually the whole continent of Africa. In the Far East Britain added Burma, Malaya, and Borneo to its dominions, France took over Indo-China, and Germany joined them in taking bites out of China, picking up a Pacific island here and there. Britain got the lion's share everywhere, inspiring the boast that the sun never set on the British Empire, and the rejoinder that God wouldn't let it because he couldn't trust Englishmen in the dark. At the end of the century the United States entered the free-for-all. Americans had been content to confine their manifest destiny to their continent, annexing Texas and forcing Mexico to cede the Southwest after a war that was not one of the brightest pages in the nation's annals, but for their more disgraceful war with Spain they rewarded themselves with some Spanish colonies. They introduced a new note by launching their imperialism at the expense of a European country instead of non-Westerners. Another new note was added by Japan, an Asiatic power that by this time was sufficiently Westernized to entertain imperial ambitions, and to begin exercising them on Korea and China.

By now the age of imperialism looks like an unmistakable disaster for the Western world, and above all for the democracies. They have suffered most from the resurgence of the colonial peoples, whom they everywhere treated as inferiors. This resurgence suggests, however, that the new imperialism was not simply a disaster for the rest of the world. Everywhere it resulted in a partial Westernization, a process that involved some acquaintance with the values that had enabled Europe to become not only more powerful but freer than the societies of the non-Western world. Eventually the colonial peoples began clamoring for rights and opportunities they had never enjoyed before they came under European rule. The contemporary uproar that has made so plain the evils of imperialism has also obscured other plain truths about it.

To begin with, the new imperialism was not clearly due first of all to industrial capitalism, or specifically a drive for raw materials, new markets, and new sources of investment for surplus capital. True, business interests were almost always involved. British merchants, with American aid, brought on the vicious "Opium War" that began the long humiliation of China, forcing it to admit their lucrative trade in the drug; and some later business adventurers played a more prominent part, notably Cecil Rhodes. Everywhere, too, there was ample exploitation to make plausible the Marxist thesis. The United States offered a naked example when it took to "dollar diplomacy," sending out Marines to protect American investments. Nevertheless, capitalism did not instigate much of the imperialistic enterprise. Italy and Russia joined in even though they had neither surplus manufactures nor surplus capital. France conquered Algeria, Tunisia, and Morocco without any marked urge by businessmen, and its government then had a hard time getting them to follow the flag there. The advanced industrial countries actually got little of their raw materials from their colonies, their capital flowed chiefly to other European or American countries, and their industry depended on colonialism little more than it has in recent years, when capitalism has been flourishing without such aid. As for the great business adventurers, the earliest was King Leopold II of Belgium, who in the Congo built up by and for himself a colonial empire eighty times as big as Belgium, and made an immense fortune by managing it as a kind of private socialistic state.

Except for Leopold, the plainest reason for the new imperialism was again nationalism. The governments had economic motives because nationalism had become economic—they were afraid that their rivals might set up tariff walls around their colonies; but their primary concern was power. Thus Italy took to imperialism as soon as the country was united: this was the way to build up national power and prestige. Similarly fear of war was both cause and effect of the rage for colonies: the powers wanted naval bases, since big navies were becoming fashionable even before they were needed to protect colonies. One reason why Americans started the Spanish-American War was that by 1898 they had the third largest navy in the world, though in the preceding decade they had been content with a little one smaller even than Chile's. And in all countries imperialism flourished for the political reasons known to Disraeli: in committing the Conservative party to the new policy, he shrewdly judged that it would be popular with the voters. The middle class rose to it as at once a new mode of complacence and a source of excitement. So far from being a product of the class struggle, or a further means of exploiting workers at home, it was no less popular with workers. More anomalous support came from missionaries, now active all over the world. In their zeal for spreading Christianity into all corners, they had more evident success in converting pious Westerners to imperialism than natives to Christianity.

They accordingly bring up the illusions that inspired the new imperialism, to the point of fatuousness. It soon became a compulsive business; once the scramble for colonies started, all the powers had to join in willy-nilly—colonies were status symbols. They would be costlier for future generations because of the national pride in them, which would be affronted by their demands for independence. Meanwhile they were in fact mostly millstones, no more profitable for the nation as a whole than they had been in Adam Smith's day. Though they made fortunes for some businessmen, they paid no tribute to the government and brought no relief to taxpayers, only heavier burdens for the upkeep of the military needed to protect them. By the time of the World War Germany, for example, had spent about half a billion dollars on its colonies, which accounted for less than one per cent of its foreign trade. The powers were still blinder to the long-range possibilities of their aggressions on the great majority of the human race. "There lies a sleeping giant," Napoleon had said of China. "Let him sleep, for when he wakes he will move the world." Stirrings like the Boxer Rebellion, coupled with the rise of Japan, created some popular alarm over the "yellow peril," but this only fortified the conceit of Europeans and Americans, who took for granted that they would indefinitely rule the world, and rightly so. Despite their cultivation of history and supposed historical sense, they were mostly as blind to the profound disruption they were causing in ancient civilizations. Conservatives and lovers of the traditional order worried no more than Burke had over what was happening to the venerable order of India— a question Burke never asked when he attacked the corruption of Warren Hastings. Liberals simply rejoiced in the introduction of Western ideals and Western science, with little if any thought about the cultural costs to men bred on radically different ways of thought and feeling, unable to become Westerners by any simple effort of will. Marxists had no more real concern for the "backward" countries except as exhibits of capitalist imperialism, since they lacked a proletariat suitable for revolutionary purposes. Missionaries working with primitive peoples typically had little respect for their culture, more concern over their indifference to pants and corsets.

Yet they also bring up the genuine idealism that helped to popularize the new imperialism. All the cant about the "white man's burden" was more unfortunate because it obscured much moral earnestness and unselfish endeavor, however self-righteous or misguided. Disraeli explicitly subordinated financial profit to "those moral and political considerations which make nations great," a pride of empire that involved no thought of world domination but boasted of the sympathy of the colonies for the mother country. Joseph Chamberlain, another ardent imperialist, had more thought of trade and profit but still an honorable vision: "To organise an Empire . . . greater and more potent for peace and the civilization of the world than any that history has yet known— that is a dream if you like, but a dream of which no man need be ashamed." Cecil Rhodes himself had such a dream. While his tremendous energy was devoted chiefly to making a fortune in diamonds and gold, it was stimulated if not informed by the purpose of furthering the mission of the Anglo-Saxons, chosen by God to spread the blessings of freedom, justice, and peace. (Among the by-products of this purpose were the Rhodes Scholarships.) And many colonial administrators had a high sense of responsibility, worked earnestly to improve the living conditions of peoples who were in fact backward, in some respects "inferior" by almost any civilized standard.

India is the clearest case in point. Karl Marx, who wrote much about British rule here, himself paid tribute to it. After duly remarking the wooden ways, the low motives, and all the crimes of Britain, he pointed out that it was at least creating the material conditions for the necessary social revolution; and after granting that this meant a grievous disruption of the traditional industrious, peaceful ways of thousands of villages, he added: "We must not forget that these idyllic village communities . . . always provided a firm basis to oriental despotism, confining the human intelligence within the narrowest limits, making of it the obedient traditional instrument of superstition, stunting its growth, robbing it . . . of all capacity of historical activity." India was in this respect representative of all Asia, in which the only equality was an equality in poverty and ignorance, and the enlightened had made no effort to emancipate the masses. The pride of the great Asian societies had long since degenerated into arrogance, fortified by ignorance and obscurantism.[24] In India, the spirituality on which Hindus

---

[24] The celebrated example is the Chinese emperor who, at the end of the eighteenth century, dismissed a British mission that was seeking to establish diplomatic relations

prided themselves authorized gross idolatry and indecency, pilgrimages to Juggernaut, ritual murder, infanticide and child sacrifice, and the burning of widows. English officials were understandably appalled by such practices, and might be forgiven their violation of venerable tradition when they tried to suppress them. Likewise their increasingly snobbish aloofness from the natives was given some excuse by the caste system, since they had to be a separate caste, and by holy Brahmans might be treated as virtually untouchable.

Hence the English not only brought law and order to a chaotic country but awakened a society that had long been stagnant. While building railways and introducing modern technology, they introduced as well Western science, philosophy, and literature in the higher education they provided for. They gave India both the material means and the spiritual stimulus for efforts at a unity it had never known. It was an Englishman, indeed, who suggested the founding of the Indian National Congress (1885), the first free assembly of the kind in the history of Asia, which dedicated itself to the task of making India fit for representative institutions. When leaders of the Congress later grew hostile to the English, for sufficient reasons of exploitation and oppression, they were still indebted to them for the standards by which they condemned the kind of practices their ancestors had accepted as normal. Some Hindus learned as well to deplore social evils that had never troubled their Brahmans, in particular the caste system that condemned millions to live as Untouchables. English rule made possible the blend of Western and Hindu idealism best typified by Gandhi.

Elsewhere colonialism brought at least a degree of modernization. If this was a mixed blessing, it included some material goods that the whole non-Western world learned to cherish as real goods. Even those who insist that we have no right to regard so-called primitive cultures as inferior to civilized ones may grant that people were better off when their ills were treated by modern medicine instead of magic or witchcraft. Likewise the rulers provided at least some education for some of their subjects, who then saw no virtue or bliss in ignorance either, and might appreciate some spiritual goods of the West too. In all the

---

and improve trade with China: "As your ambassador can see for himself, we possess all things. I set no value on objects strange or ingenious, and have no use for your country's manufactures. . . . It behooves you, O King, to respect my sentiments and to display even greater devotion and loyalty in future, so that, by perpetual submission to our Throne, you may secure peace and prosperity for your country hereafter." The emperor graciously condoned the ignorance of the envoy in view of "the lonely remoteness" of his island.

societies that had been civilized before Europeans broke in, many of the intelligentsia came to realize that European domination was due not merely to superior technology but to the stagnation of their own society, basic faults in their tradition. And their protests against their rulers were seconded by many Western intellectuals. The new imperialism was novel as well in the volume of criticism it stirred at home, and the indignation over its abuses. It was missionaries who called attention to the shocking exploitation of the Negroes in the Congo, which Leopold had done his best to keep quiet; whereupon public indignation forced the royal slave driver to introduce some reforms and surrender his immense private estate, which was put under the control of the Belgian parliament.

Still, the crucial issue was the fact of exploitation. It was only most shocking in the Congo, where the brutal toil reduced the population from some twenty to ten million or less. As an American missionary wrote, "This rubber traffic is steeped in blood, and if the natives were to rise and sweep every white person on the Upper Congo into eternity there would still be left a fearful balance to their credit." When the Belgian parliament took charge, it mopped up the worst of the blood but made little effort to educate the Negroes, none at all to fit them for self-government. It typified the prevailing policy of the European powers, which was to administer their colonies with an eye primarily to their own interests, not the interests of the natives. However just or unjust their rule, it certainly involved no major effort to spread the blessings of liberty or equality. Britain, which by and large had the best record, was in this respect like all the other European powers. When it set a rare example in empire by granting self-government to dominions covering more than half its territory, these all comprised people chiefly of English or European stock; territories in which non-Westerners predominated remained Crown Colonies, whose people were ruled as subjects, not citizens, and had only powerless representative assemblies if any. None of these was so grateful for British rule as to reject the dream of self-rule.

The increasing resentment of the colonial peoples created no serious problem for Europe until after the World War. The resurgence of the whole non-Western world, which bids fair to be the most momentous drama of our time, is matter for a later chapter. We may then consider more closely, too, not only the impact of the West on ancient societies but the resources and the limitations of their own tradition, the possible lessons they have for Westerners, and in particular the light they throw on the conditions, the values, and the costs of freedom. In this context the earlier rise of Japan becomes more suggestive. Meanwhile our concern is the effects of the new imperialism on the triumphant West itself.

Its costs were pretty steep even in the prewar period. The popular delusion that the acquisition of more territory automatically increased the power or the greatness of the nation had to be paid for in armaments to match. German military expenditures, which grew tenfold in the two decades following 1870, went up still more when the imperial government decided it had to have a big navy too. Englishmen had to maintain the largest navy in the world, now considered absolutely essential to the preservation of the Empire. The arms race emphasized that the major powers were losing control of their foreign policy, or their actual power of self-determination. They were stuck with navalism. More broadly, they were obsessed with power—the need of which was the main lesson the non-Western peoples learned from Europe, to its own detriment.

The irrationality of imperialism was no less apparent in the United States despite its relatively piddling adventures. It had had good practical reasons for wresting territory from Mexico, but it had no need whatever of Puerto Rico and the Philippines. Subduing the Philippines after its annexation cost more men and money than had the war with Spain, and it then brought profit only to some private interests, at some cost to taxpayers. Theodore Roosevelt, who as Assistant Secretary of the Navy had privately seen to it that Admiral Dewey's fleet was ready to sail against the Philippines the moment war was declared, as President spelled out the imperial implications of its annexation: the United States now had to be "the dominant power on the shores of the Pacific Ocean." A great navy then swelled the nation's pride at considerably more cost to taxpayers, without yet serving any imperious need of self-defense. Dollar diplomacy again benefited only some business interests, while building up a vast, enduring fund of resentment and ill will in Latin America. And the jingoism that went with the new imperialism played up an internal menace to democracy—the rise of the yellow press. Pulitzer and Hearst followed the promising example of North-cliffe in England, who exploited imperialism as a profitable form of sensationalism; they helped to bring on the war with Spain by a circulation battle, vying in lurid accounts of Spanish barbarism. Later the yellow press might be as violently isolationist, but it could always be trusted to substitute flag-waving for reasonable debate, and to make wise, courageous statesmanship more difficult.

Similarly it exploited another by-product of the new imperialism, an intensified racial prejudice. Racism was the most convenient justification of imperialism. Since almost all the colonial peoples were black, brown, or yellow, it followed that the white race was congenitally superior, whether or not it shouldered its "burden." Feelings about color grew stronger, especially in the Anglo-Saxon world. The British in India treated the natives as social inferiors too, no matter how cultivated they were. Americans, long inured to prejudice against Negroes, widened their antipathies; the yellow press played up the "yellow peril." Both racists and imperialists were susceptible to whatever other prejudices were popular or handy. The Rev. Josiah Strong, one of the earliest popular preachers of America's imperial destiny, was typically hostile to Catholics and immigrants.[25]

Needless to say, all the talk and feeling about color intensified the bitterness of the colonial peoples, who could never hope to be treated as equals. But again the West itself suffered meanwhile from the conceit of its inherent superiority, the popular assumption that it alone represented the "civilized" world. Its idealism was corrupted by self-righteousness when not smothered by self-interest. In America Theodore Roosevelt had a shrewd eye for the realities of international power politics, but he typically dressed up in high moral terms his program for strengthening the nation's military power, appealing to the cause of civilization and international justice, which meanwhile required the policing of all the "semibarbarous" non-European peoples "for the sake of the welfare of mankind"; he thereby compounded self-interest with an idealism that may well have been quite sincere, behind even the seeming hypocrisy of dollar diplomacy, but that helped to assure the fatal confusion and blunder of American foreign policy over the coming generation. In Europe the new imperialism was symptomatic of the vanities and hypocrisies, delusions and obsessions, which would plunge it into a most terrible, pointless World War. It emphasized that the Western culture that had invaded ancient societies and was molding their education was itself profoundly confused, scarcely likely to steady them or simply uplift them, much more likely to stir an ardent nationalism, and an aggressiveness that would shock the Western aggressors.

---

25 The quality of his Christian faith appeared in his demonstration that the Anglo-Saxon race, especially in America, was destined to dominate the world. Among its advantages was its "peculiarly aggressive traits," and Americans were pre-eminent for another "most striking feature" of the Anglo-Saxon—"his money-making power." The Rev. Mr. Strong was secretary of a missionary society.

| *REVOLUTIONS IN*
THOUGHT AND CULTURE

1. The Role of the Intelligentsia

Although the nineteenth century popularized the concept of "the spirit of the age," its own spirit remains harder to define than that of any previous age. In all fields of thought and art it amplified the conflicting tendencies generated by Romanticism, often carrying them to extremes, and it produced various other movements that never merged into one great movement. The immediate sign of confusion is the many new isms it created—utilitarianism, positivism, transcendentalism, individualism, capitalism, socialism, naturalism, impressionism, symbolism, etc. It might therefore be called the age of "isms" —another word it coined—since its self-consciousness about them and evident fondness for them suggest a distinctive enough spirit. Only this accentuates the confusion, the failure to resolve them in any positive, characteristic creed or style, comparable to those of the Middle Ages, the Renaissance, or the Enlightenment. It also brings up another of the many anomalies running through the age. The self-consciousness was heightened by the labors of research men, mostly plodding, old-fashioned types, who kept breeding ever more of their academic kind and accumulating an immense body of knowledge. Knowing so much more, thinkers grew warier of conventional schemes of understanding —including efforts to define the spirit of any age.

These efforts can never be wholly successful, of course, and if taken literally are bound to simplify much too much. Yet a cultural historian can hardly avoid something of the kind as he tries to define the fundamental differences between societies and ages, now in a fuller awareness of organic interrelations that anthropologists call configurations or patterns of culture. Given all the radical change that most plainly distinguished this age from all previous ones, I take it that we have to begin once more with the tiresome word "revolutionary" (still another of its coinages). Overworked though it is, and overloaded with emotional connotation, it nevertheless does strictly apply to much of the cultural activity of the age. More thinkers than ever before sought deliberately to revolutionize thought, in more different ways. New styles in literature and painting were sometimes as radical as the many blueprints for a new social order, involving differences in not only modes but premises. It was conspicuously an age of revolts, much more extensive than earlier ones against church or monarchy. The spirit of revolt pervaded the entire culture, leading to attacks on every major tradition, and then often to counterrevolts, which included attacks on modern civilization root and branch. Popular culture, always essentially conventional, was itself a radically new development because of the great importance it assumed and the endless criticism it called out. Again even the many research workers who were not in the least bent on revolution were generating one of sorts, inasmuch as the eventual upshot of their academic labors was the "knowledge explosion." And some cloistered men, like Einstein and Planck, were quietly effecting the most profound revolution in thought, exploding the foundations of physics—ever since Newton the very model of a science, the principal guarantor of certainty in knowledge of a lawful universe.

The most apparent reason for the far-reaching changes remains the impact of the political and industrial revolutions. Most writers and thinkers responded directly to these revolutions, all were affected by them; if only for this reason they grew much more concerned with the temporal than the eternal, in a culture grown as notoriously secular. Yet their response was a creative one, no mere ideological reflection of material changes, and it had in turn a positive impact on society, as Marxism itself illustrated. In every field of culture activity was to some extent independent, carrying on from its own traditions and achievements, maintaining the autonomy of all major interests in an increasingly pluralistic society. The cultural and intellectual history of the age is therefore harder to plot than its political and economic history. While the nations moved toward more popular government and more industrialism, writers and thinkers charged off in every direction. The major interests they represented likewise took different courses. Science advanced most independently by its own methods and most directly influenced all other interests, but philosophy, religion, history, literature, and the fine arts all went their own ways, sometimes roughly parallel, sometimes divergent, while also influencing one another. Higher education moved most slowly, many of the older institutions hardly budging; Henry Adams complained that universities typically prepared students for life in the eighteenth century. Others might describe their conservatism as dignified, suited to their role as custodians of high culture, or of traditional values needed more than ever in an age of technology and business.

At any rate, the increasing use of "academic" as a bad word brings up the much more active, distinctive role of the intelligentsia, the self-conscious intellectual leaders of the age. It was a typically ambiguous role. Although writers and thinkers in the past had often been critical of their society, since they judged it by rational or idealistic norms, in this age of progress they grew much more persistently critical, often profoundly hostile. Their animus was due in part to the nagging thought that they were not really leading their society. Given the primacy of business interests, which were giving the age its terrific drive, they were remote from the main centers of power and had less apparent prestige than they thought their fellows had had in the aristocratic past. Radicals generally remained optimistic, confident that the future was theirs, and many others were buoyed up by the faith in progress; yet all were liable to a sense of alienation, which in Russia had given birth to the term "intelligentsia." They might often feel simply ineffectual as they forever criticized, to no avail. Toward the end of the century some turned their backs on society, taking to ivory towers or schools of art for art's sake—deliberate modes of "escapism" now familiar, but except for holy men historically rare. By this time all had more cause for dismay in the commercialization of popular culture, which had become another big business, manufacturing tons of trash; the yellow press alone had more evident power over public opinion than did the intelligentsia. More and more thinkers were explicitly minimizing the power of reason in governing society and controlling history, declaring in effect that the intelligentsia were bound to be ineffectual. Marxists were insisting that all but their own kind were only reflecting class interests. Freudians would soon assert that all creative writers were only compensating for their frustrations by fantasy or substitute gratifications, and that seemingly objective thought, including Marxism, was mostly rationalization or wishful thinking.

Still, these thinkers were themselves obviously influential. The intelligentsia as a class were in fact exerting a wider, more direct influence than in any past age, with the possible exception of the Enlightenment.

They had grown into a substantial class, much more numerous than ever before, and because of the growth of a large reading public they had a much more substantial audience too, especially among the bourgeois they so often berated; they were popular enough so that it usually took no great courage to express unpopular opinions. If they had little immediate effect on public opinion, they were transforming the whole climate of opinion. They were spearheading the advance of science, which no one would deny has profoundly affected the modern world; they publicized the new theories, brought out their implications for thought in other fields, extended science into social studies. As political thinkers, social critics, and reformers they were demonstrating that ideas may be more powerful than vested interests, which themselves owed much to once novel ideas, such as the theory of *laissez faire* that had become the common sense of businessmen. It was the intelligentsia —not the proletariat—who made the revolutions in our century. Even literary men, whose social influence is harder to gauge and therefore easy to minimize, at least pointed up a basic anomaly of the age. In Europe they were especially inclined to attack their society, usually describing it as mediocre, sometimes as decadent, doing most to give the nineteenth century its bad reputation; and their own works were further evidence of its unflagging energy and creativity, the ceaseless ferment out of which came the many novel commonplaces of our century.

As contradictory were the plainest influences of the intelligentsia, beginning with their contribution to both the growing unity and the growing disunity of Western civilization. A cosmopolitan class by tradition, they were brought closer to their fellows in other lands by rapid communication and transport; most of the greater writers and thinkers soon won an international reputation, new movements spread all over Europe, and everywhere intellectuals waved the banner of humanity. The uncommon diversity of style in art and thought itself represented a widening of common interests, marked incidentally by the welcome of such newcomers on the European scene as American poets and Russian novelists. At the same time, the intelligentsia were producing influential spokesmen for nationalism, which on the Continent they were largely responsible for, and many others were provincial in effect because proud of their national culture, with which their own prestige was associated. When the World War broke out, the great majority of intellectuals were as fervently patriotic as were the common people.

Meanwhile national differences had further confused their role. In

Germany and France they had considerable prestige because of a common respect for the values of the mind, but worked to quite different effect. German intellectuals served chiefly as pillars of their society; the radicals among them, like Marx, were long subject to exile. French intellectuals were typically more independent, often revolutionaries of various kinds, and were given to jaundiced views of their society, which to their fellows in other lands looked like a very heaven. England took its intellectuals less seriously, and thereby perhaps helped them to be more effective: they could go on working calmly and sensibly, without the fanfare of either public adulation or public hostility. American intellectuals had the oddest lot. Although independent enough and often critical of their democracy, they were rarely hostile to it, mostly proud of it, and disposed to share the national optimism; but even so anti-intellectualism was most pronounced in the United States. By the time of the World War, moreover, America was beginning to specialize in the development of professional types that made it harder to speak of the intelligentsia as a class. These included technicians, economists, behavioral scientists, assorted experts—brainworkers who might not have wide or pure intellectual interests, nor be devoted to the contemplative, appreciative uses of mind, but who nonetheless exemplified its critical and creative uses. However categorized, they were clearly gaining influence, getting closer to the centers of economic and political power.

Here, like the purest intellectuals, they might or might not advance the cause of freedom. The intelligentsia everywhere were still to be found in all camps, from the most reactionary to the most revolutionary, for reasons quite easy to understand: by their very nature they were disposed to both liberal and illiberal attitudes. On the whole, I judge, their influence definitely furthered the growth and spread of freedom, as it had in the Age of the Enlightenment. But because of this belief (not to mention a predisposition of historians to favor the intelligentsia, with whom they naturally identify themselves) I should first emphasize that on every issue they were no more pre-eminently liberal than wise.

As intellectuals, they were liable to "the unmeasured anger against human stupidity" that can be, John Morley observed, "one of the most provoking forms of that stupidity." As a self-conscious elite, they were liable more specifically to supercilious attitudes toward the common people. Literary men in particular often indulged a somewhat vulgar scorn of vulgarity, and a contempt for the bourgeois tinged with bourgeois complacence. They gave "culture" its priggish connotations by a too-easy disparagement of utilitarian interests and the simple material goods valued by ordinary men; they tended to depreciate the material achievements of the century long before most men were enjoying the full benefits of these achievements. Both liberals and radicals who attacked the bourgeois on behalf of "the people" were likely to go sour when they tardily realized that most people wanted nothing more than to become good bourgeois, and failed to realize that the ordinary conventional life—the routine life that the overwhelming majority of men have lived throughout history when they had enough to eat—is not necessarily indecent or inhuman. Others lent weight to Marx's charges against them by much social criticism that appealed to lofty moral principles or spiritual truths, but displayed little sense of the realities of class structure or serious concern for fundamental reform.

Marx himself illustrated more serious dangers besetting intellectuals. Because of their common feeling of frustration or alienation they were prone to humorless, inflexible attitudes, which cluttered their social criticism with the stereotypes they deplored in popular thought. They tended at once to overlook the simplicities and to oversimplify the complexities. On the Continent especially they were addicted to total ideology, "the opium of the intellectuals"; only it seldom relaxed them, instead usually tensed them. In short, the nineteenth-century intelligentsia were not conspicuous for sanity or wholeness. The greatest of them were generally less reasonable than their forebears in the Enlightenment, and seemed least capable of an easy look at life, or the simple good humor suited to a democratic way of life.

Yet as a class the intelligentsia provided ample correctives for all such illiberal tendencies. However inclined to dogmatism, they were inclined as well to be more flexible, open to new ideas, and tolerant of differences of opinion than ordinary men who lived unthinkingly by custom and convention. Whatever their ideology, they helped to free thought from the tyranny of unconscious ideology, or blind faith, and willy-nilly promoted an open society by the many isms they created. They maintained the liberal tradition that their forebears had developed if only because they were naturally independent, thinking for themselves, and had become a free, open, fluid class, no longer bound by ecclesiastical authority or any need for aristocratic credentials. As naturally they were disposed to support the freedom of speech and press necessary for them to be and express themselves. Since most were not aristocrats by birth nor wealthy bourgeois by either inheritance or aspiration, they were likely to favor the cause of the common people. It is not surprising that in western Europe and America the intelligentsia generally led the movement toward democracy, and that in central Europe they did most to keep alive its ideals, despite the failure of the revolutions they led in 1848.

Likewise their insistent social criticism mostly furthered the interests of a free society. If business and the bourgeois were too easy game, they were nonetheless fair game by democratic or any civilized standards. Much of the criticism was concentrated on social injustice, with evident effectiveness. From all camps came legitimate complaints about the quality of bourgeois or democratic culture, the uses being made of increasing freedom and prosperity. On the face of it this all too familiar criticism was much less effective, but by the same token it was always pertinent; however supercilious, it at least maintained the necessary standards of excellence, helped to educate many sons of the rising bourgeois. No less pertinent was much criticism of the liberal faith itself, including some that came from the far Right. If the radical skepticism of Joseph de Maistre, for instance, made ludicrous his insistence on the absolute authority of the Roman Church, many liberals might have profited from it much more than they did, and learned earlier the dangers of a tender-minded optimism. So too with the root-and-branch attacks on modern civilization by such writers as Kierkegaard, Dostoyevsky, and Nietzsche. Little heeded in their own day, they went deeper than the revolutionary critique of Marx in ways that men have learned to respect since the experience of world wars.

Or perhaps have tended to overrate, in humiliation rather than humility. The revolutions in thought force more troublesome issues, which also go deeper than the immediate issues raised by Marxism. Like the other grand efforts at synthesis, from Hegel to Spencer, Marx's system has not stood up well, surviving mainly as a political program; and it perhaps best explains why none of the isms or ideologies won the day. It had given thinkers more awareness of ideology, which could be turned against the claims of any one brand. It was also typical of an age of acute, relentless analysis, a spirit as fatal to any grand system. The profound critique of reason that began with Hume and Kant was carried on by almost all the leading thinkers of the century, in different ways but to the same general effect. Supplemented by the growing historical-mindedness and oncoming sociology of knowledge, it culminated in an intellectual self-consciousness unparalleled in the history of thought. At the end of the century, when Durkheim, Weber, Pareto,

Mosca, and others were revolutionizing social thought, Freud was beginning to revolutionize the concept of mind itself.

The most apparent effect of this whole growth of self-consciousness was drastically to limit the range and the power of conscious choice. In the name of scientific determinism some thinkers explicitly denied that man was a free agent, or had any real choice. Others who stopped short of a thoroughgoing determinism concentrated on the impersonal, involuntary, unconscious forces governing social change, and represented man as not the creator but the creature of his history. At the end of the century the "deepest" truths about man and society centered on nonrational or irrational behavior. This preoccupation could easily glide into a celebration of the irrational, a contempt for humane values, as it did in Sorel and the leaders of fascism. It could support authoritarianism and a contempt for democracy, as it did in Pareto and in de Maistre before him. It could undermine any or all faith, and justify the popular scorn of intellectuals themselves. The most influential thinkers were seemingly committing what Julien Benda would call *"la trahison des clercs"*—betraying the intellectuals, as well as the cause of human dignity and human freedom. We are reminded that from de Maistre on the intelligentsia had provided leaders for anti-intellectualism.

Nevertheless, the radical critiques of reason were to a large extent clearly valid, and together with the revolutionary social thought offered many valuable insights. They constitute a remarkable advance in our understanding of man, society, and history. They could accordingly serve the purpose of liberals too, illuminating the difficult conditions on which a free society has to operate. By their attacks on convention or tradition they might widen our range of actual choice, increase our power of effective choice. And again the intelligentsia provided antidotes for their excesses by their very existence as a class. They still had to have a basic confidence in the power of intellect, their chief claim to authority, and in the value of knowledge, their chief stock in trade. Hence most of the leaders in this whole movement were not simply attacking reason or seeking to discredit it, any more than Hume and Kant had. At the end of the century most—like Durkheim, Max Weber, William James, Freud, and Croce—were still basically rationalists, who in confining the powers of reason were trying to strengthen its legitimate claims. They were still loyal, too, to the essential values of the Enlightenment, and to the broad cause of freedom. Almost all of us who cherish this cause likewise hold to the essential faith of the Enlightenment, I think, and logically must hold to it, first of all to a faith in a sufficient power of reason, a sufficient capacity of men for reasonable behavior; and if so, we might as well admit it.

As it is, many men seem apologetic, painfully self-conscious, fearful of appearing quaint or naïve. The obvious dangers and the actual abuses of the revolutionary new thought will be among the recurrent themes in the rest of this long chapter. At this point they bring up the fundamental ambiguity in the modern history of freedom. The intelligentsia stand for the actual power and the actual freedom of the human mind, which has profoundly transformed our world, given us immense power that is no less due to intellect if driving motives are described as economic. They distinguished themselves by exceptional independence and boldness in inquiry, criticism, and innovation. While leading movements that were giving ordinary men unprecedented rights and opportunities, they spread the idea that the future was going to be ever better, nothing was impossible. And they above all were paying the costs of this extraordinary intellectual progress. If most were still sustained by feelings of emancipation and hopes of progress, many were suffering from the basic confusion and uncertainties due to the undermining of the traditional faiths—in God, in reason, in man, or in any absolute. A swelling undercurrent of pessimism carried premonitions of the *Angst* to come. Some, like Henry Adams, were recoiling from the boundless future, fearing that man could not control the tremendous power generated by intellect, and that his wondrous doings would be his undoing. Others who clung to the traditional absolutes worried over the skepticism of their fellows, the presumed demoralization of the free society.

As we approach, finally, the major developments in the various fields of culture, we are faced with a deeper disunity. The autonomy achieved in every field, with the growth of a secular, pluralistic society, has manifestly served to liberate thought and art. While the resultant diversity of interest and belief always troubles thinkers devoted to intellectual law and order, it is more conducive to freedom than is uniformity of belief, a culture dominated by religion or a single ideology, not to mention a totalitarian state. Yet the value of such independence can be fully realized only in a basic community of interests, through an education that inculcates a respect for all major interests, ideally a decent understanding of all. As it is, modern culture is rent by notorious conflicts between major interests, often bitter hostilities. Still more troublesome is the sharp separation of these interests, for the sake of economy, efficiency, or purity. In the world of thought, as in the industrial world, we are confronted with a dazzling wealth and a depressing waste of resources.

In particular the nineteenth-century intelligentsia deepened a major split. To the radical dualisms of Western tradition—body and soul, matter and mind, natural and supernatural, etc.—they added another between science and the humanities, the "two cultures." Literary men and philosophers as well as religious thinkers grew more hostile to science, resentful of its increasing prestige, which overshadowed their own interests or belittled their claims. Positivistic champions of science retaliated by a balder insistence that it was the only significant way of knowing and dealing with reality, giving it a virtual monopoly on truth. Scientists themselves seldom bothered to enter the hostilities, but they widened the gulf by their single-mindedness and their steady advance. As specialists they often had too narrow interests to look like intellectuals, and in any case they continued to move further away from the cultural homeland, out of the ken of other intellectuals, even of fellow scientists in other fields. By the end of the century there were some ten thousand scientific journals, read by very few but specialists. Scholars in the humanities worked to much the same effect as they pursued their researches and spawned technical journals of their own, accumulating a mass of knowledge that obliged ever more specialization or narrowing of interests, and that swelled the novel complaint that we had much too much knowledge. Because of their devotion to fact it may be said that our whole culture is basically "scientific." Nevertheless they did not bridge the gulf or put a truce to the hostilities—they only aggravated the basic problem. Western culture was not merely split but fragmented.

There is no putting it all together again. I take for granted that we cannot hope to order all this knowledge, incorporate it in another grand system. No more can we do away with specialization, which has become absolutely indispensable. We may hope, however, to find some common concepts or underlying principles of unity in the common enterprise of seeking truth. We must hope to transcend the narrow, jealous, exclusive attitudes that not only waste so much of our intellectual wealth but impede the immediate effort to understand the cultural history of the past century. And at least there is no impassable barrier between the "two cultures." It is clearly possible to respect both science and the humanities, as men did in the Enlightenment and many still do. It is clearly necessary if education is to be truly liberal, free men are to live and think as whole men, and a free society is to deal intelligently with its problems. Science as such cannot answer authoritatively the all-important questions about the good life and the good society, or tell us immediately the proper uses to be made of the power and the freedom it gives us; there is no true science of wisdom, virtue, or happiness—for all men the most vital concern; and social scientists are most emphatic in declaring that value judgments are none of their business. Disciples of the humanities nevertheless cannot afford to ignore the relevance of scientific knowledge about the universe, man, and society, still less the value of the scientific spirit, in judgments about how men ought to manage their lives and their government; for neither can poets, philosophers, or theologians speak with absolute authority about these vital matters. Among my primary concerns in the long survey that follows is the elementary need of more simple wisdom.

2. *Science*

The triumphant progress of physics in the nineteenth century overshadowed the feat of a Russian mathematician named Lobachevsky, a much quieter but possibly greater revolutionist than Lenin. Early in the century he defied an axiom of Euclid's by assuming that through a given point *more* than one parallel can be drawn to a given line; and on this seemingly nonsensical postulate he built up a complete geometry. Other mathematicians proceeded to construct non-Euclidean geometries to suit themselves—for instance, by assuming that *no* such parallel could be drawn. Together they heralded the triumph of the postulate over the axiom or the self-evident truth—one key to the revolution in twentieth-century physics.

Meanwhile, however, physicists sensibly continued to operate on the basis of Newton's "celestial mechanics," the grand scheme that had climaxed the rise of modern science, most triumphantly demonstrated the new powers of thought that made its rise the most fundamental, permanent revolution of the modern world. They held to the axiomatic concepts of matter existing in time and space, mass acted upon by forces that caused motion. They concentrated with particular success on the study of energy, the cause or consequence of mass in motion— a study appropriate to a dynamic age of industrialism exploiting new sources of power. The concept of energy became basic with the discovery that sound, heat, light, electricity, and magnetism were only different forms of it. As Clerk Maxwell observed, this made possible a "more complete unification of knowledge"; among its major by-products were the laws of thermodynamics and his own brilliant electro-magnetic theory of light. Investigations of electricity proved especially fruitful for industrial purposes, leading to the key invention of the dynamo and the growth of the great electrical industry. Henceforth science and technology were intimately connected by more prompt, systematic application of new discoveries. And by this time science had become thoroughly popular, taught in all schools, featured in the popular press, recognized by common men as the basic source of modern "progress."

Nevertheless, the advances in physics were somewhat embarrassing to scientists. Physicists were discovering that such phenomena as light and electricity could not be explained satisfactorily in mechanical terms. Their experimental findings increasingly failed to jibe with Newton's laws, as well as common-sense ideas of "matter." Even so they were hardly prepared for the startling turn their science took in the early years of our century. Einstein dropped Newton's axiomatic concepts of absolute time and space as independent realities, denied the self-evident truth that events can happen in different places at the same time; and with the help of non-Euclidean geometry he worked out his theory of relativity. Planck introduced quantum theory, based on the preposterous idea that in the atomic world energy and motion are not continuous, like speed and distance, but occur in little jumps— like an automobile, say, that can go twenty or thirty miles an hour but not twenty-five, or that shows up at every milepost but not in the country between. "Matter" became still mistier when it appeared that the recently discovered electron was not a solid little lump but only an electric charge—whatever that was. The upshot was the revolution in modern physics. The most extraordinary adventure in the history of thought, this has radically transformed our conceptions of not only the physical universe, but the meaning and aim of science.

Only it is not yet really "ours": it has not in fact transformed the ideas of most men about the nature of science. The revolution has enormously widened the gap between advanced scientific thought and general knowledge, the common thought of educated men, while popu-lar science is even more remote from it than popular religion is from the teachings of Jesus. Except for some notion that the universe has grown much queerer, its profound significance is not widely realized; what most men still applaud or attack as science is a cluster of dubious assumptions centered on a kind of mechanomorphism, derived from classical Newtonian physics. This served as the model for all other sciences, even though they dealt with quite different matters. It also inspired the various modes of materialism, determinism, and positivism that still pervade the intellectual climate, and in the guise of "realism" generate much crude scientism. Such tendencies provided ammunition for the attacks on science by churchmen, literary men, and philosophers. They supported the common idea that science was at best only a form of materialism, which should be confined to a sort of intellectual red-light district so as to prevent it from contaminating "spiritual" values.

Now, science may always look like the villain in the modern intellectual drama because it has been the primary disruptive force. It has continually caused obvious trouble by proposing theories that conflicted with traditional beliefs, and deeper trouble by revolutionizing habits of thought while not transforming habits of feeling. Nevertheless it remains the basic source of our extraordinary intellectual resources. Like it or not, science is an irreversible force, at least as long as civilization endures; for no educated man can ever think as if it had not been, and there is no chance whatever of calling a halt to it, any more than of junking all the knowledge it has given us about the universe and man. The sensible policy would seem to be an effort to feel more at home with it, immediately for the sake of historical understanding, ultimately for the sake of maintaining our freedom. I am assuming, at any rate, that as far as it goes science gives us our most positive, reliable knowledge; so I wish to go as far as it will take us, in every field of thought. But for just this reason it is important to get as clear an idea as possible of how far it goes or can go, what are the current and the essential limits to the positive knowledge it gives. Much of the contradiction we have to deal with comes down to simple confusion over these matters, or to a failure to realize that they are not at all simple matters. It has accentuated the basic paradox: that the triumphant advance of science—always the plainest demonstration of the freedom and the power of human reason—did not by any means simply advance the cause of freedom and reasonableness, but created new threats to it, even apart from the common abuses of the material power it gave society.

First of all, it is not clearly possible to define precisely the limits of science, determine just what it can and cannot tell us. What we have to deal with is not "science" but a big, not always happy family of sciences, headed by physics, whose practitioners seldom bother their heads over this philosophical question and at best can speak with authority only about their own field. Philosophers of science, the presumed authorities, are still debating the implications of the revolution in modern physics, while in all quarters there is much sharper disagreement over the scope and authenticity of psychology and the social sciences. But for our present purposes it may suffice to spot the main sources of confusion.[1] Long before Einstein it should have been clear that science gives us only a partial, hypothetical description of "reality," never a complete explanation, never the final truth or the whole truth, never "all that matters." The deplorable consequences of its advance were due primarily to much sweeping conclusion that claimed its authority without legitimate right, and to as much elementary fallacy.

Let us consider, for example, this recipe: 10 gallons of water, enough fat to make 7 bars of soap, enough carbon to make 9,000 lead pencils, enough phosphorus to make 2,200 matchheads, enough iron to make one medium-sized nail, enough lime to whitewash a chicken coop, and small quantities of magnesium and sulphur. It is a recipe, of course, for a human body. And however thoroughly you stir, you of course do not get a human being. You have only the chemical ingredients: a useful kind of knowledge (especially for one interested in using bodies as fertilizer) but hopelessly inadequate for a scientific or any other kind of understanding of human beings. No sensible person would deny this. Nevertheless it has often been said that man is "really" or "only" a collection of chemicals. Behind such careless statements lay the serious belief that the physical basis of life is the essential truth about it, the key to the "real" causes of all being and behavior. It led to the famous statement by Taine that what we call virtue and vice are chemical products like sugar and vitriol. In psychology it came out in the behaviorist dogma that there is no such thing as "consciousness" —there are only movements in the brain. It seeped down into everyday thought as the vulgar materialism that declares only tangible things are real, or money is all that matters.

From this belief it logically followed that human behavior was no

[1] In this brief space I am perforce riding roughshod over most intricate, abstruse problems of epistemology. For a fuller treatment the reader may consult Chaps. 3 and 4 of my *Science and Criticism*. Needless to add, I cannot here do anything like justice either to all the developments in science since 1800, but am singling out a few that bear most directly on issues of freedom. The reader should know that by now we have several hundred journals of abstracts from the many thousands of scientific journals, and that at last report we had not yet started abstracting the abstracts. Derek Price adds that at the rate scientists are multiplying, in a hundred years we would have two of them for every man, woman, and child.

more free, purposeful, and responsible than the behavior of chemicals, but determined by physical laws. Scientists have a natural bent for determinism because of their search for regularities and uniformities, invariable relations or necessary connections, and over the past century they discovered a great deal about actual determinants—physical, biological, psychological, social. This was again very useful knowledge, making possible more intelligent behavior. But again some thinkers mistook these partial accounts for complete explanations, or the conditions of behavior for its "essential" cause, and so insisted on an absolute determinism, usually mechanical. Short of such complete denial of man's freedom, science encouraged the tendencies to regard people as merely products of heredity and environment, to concentrate on mechanical, involuntary, or conditioned behavior, and to minimize the power of conscious purpose and rational effort. Science had the curious effect of belittling man, its author.

All such tendencies were abetted by the spread of positivism. When Comte asserted that "observation of fact is the only solid basis for human knowledge," he was trying to uphold the very important distinction between verifiable knowledge and beliefs (as about God) that cannot possibly be verified. He went further, however, asserting that any proposition that cannot be reduced to a simple statement of fact makes no sense at all—an assertion that could be as fatal to the claims of poetry as of metaphysics and religious experience. Positivists after him held to a naïve realism that discredited man's inner world as "merely" subjective when not illusory, since it cannot be observed. In keeping with Comte's rejection of such concepts as "natural rights" and "the sovereignty of the people," the idea spread that all belief lacking scientific credentials was simply groundless. Positivists developed the habit of loosely calling "meaningless" statements that strictly were only unverifiable.[2] In general, they tended to discredit a

---

2 I write with some feeling as an erstwhile literary critic who once had to review a book by a convert to logical positivism. Its thesis was that if a critic wrote that a book bore the name of Zane Grey, had 320 pages, cost $2.75, and weighed a pound, he was making meaningful statements; but if he added that this novel was inferior to the novels of Dostoyevsky he was lapsing into a meaningless statement—it was impossible to prove. So it went on for a hundred tedious pages or so, systematically doing literary critics out of their job: possibly a good thing, but a rather inhumane operation, and certainly an outrage upon literature. Among the elementary facts overlooked by the author was that virtually all men who know anything about literature can and do agree that Dostoyevsky is a greater novelist than Zane Grey, and that any reputable critic can give very good reasons for this belief.

In my present concerns I run into more such embarrassments. T. D. Weldon, for example, asserts that it is "pointless" to talk of the foundations of democracy, or to argue

serious concern with values, a concern that is more necessary just
because value judgments cannot be scientifically verified. They most
effectively divorced science from the humanities.

We may then add that for practical purposes few men really believed
all this sort of thing, and that none behaved as if they believed it. All
kept living like human beings, feeling unlike a collection of chemicals.
All kept praising and blaming their fellows, and sometimes preening
themselves, as if they were free, responsible agents. Out-and-out determinists published their views, trying to change the minds of other men,
appealing to intellectual honesty, implying a moral duty to accept the
disagreeable truth—exemplifying the unverifiable faith of science
itself, that men *ought* to seek the truth, which again implied that men
have a real choice. Positivists likewise continued to exemplify the
empirical reality of "freedom," as behaviorists did of "consciousness,"
no less because it was semantically disreputable and metaphysically
mysterious, and outside their working hours they usually displayed
sufficient concern for interests and values lurking behind "meaningless"
statements. Yet the trouble remained that in the name of science,
in the avowed interest of clarity and precision, a great deal of confusion
was created. The inconsistency between declared beliefs and living
beliefs deepened the confusions of the modern world. Many other men
who rejected these ostensibly scientific doctrines became more liable
to the futility of spurning science itself, or proclaiming its "bankruptcy," for the sake of some superior kind of truth that was never
demonstrably true. In their turn they confirmed the popular misunderstanding of science as a merely utilitarian affair, irrelevant to spiritual
values. On all counts it became harder to make intelligent use of the
important findings about the determinants or necessities of man's
life, to maintain the necessary distinction between valid knowledge
and unverifiable belief, and at the same time to maintain faiths,
such as that in a free society, in an awareness that no living faith is
strictly verifiable.

This whole effort will never be easy. Twentieth-century physics has
not cleared up the confusion and gives no promise of resolving the
difficulties; by the time relativity and quantum theory become engrained in common knowledge there is no telling where theoretical
physicists will be, except that their new frontiers will be as distant from

their superiority over the foundations of totalitarianism, because "no such foundations
exist." Like the free society, I am presumably up in the air.

such knowledge. But meanwhile this uncertainty indicates why the revolution in physics has at least removed the major obstacle to harmonious relations between science and the humanities. It has made plainer that science offers a partial, approximate, hypothetical account of the natural world, not the unvarnished truth and nothing but the truth, and that the premises of the materialistic, mechanistic philosophy which saddled scientific thought were metaphysical assumptions, not physical facts. "Matter" as now conceived is remarkably intricate and elusive, no longer the solid stuff of familiar experience, but the main point is that physicists do not pretend to know, or need to know, what it really *is*. They are content to regard it as a symbol or formula useful for their main purpose, which is only to tell how this mysterious something behaves. They accordingly make up theoretical constructs, tentative models for selected aspects of its behavior, with an eye to their own convenience as well as the goings-on in the physical world. When Einstein remarked that "space" has the physical property of transmitting electromagnetic waves, he added that we "should not bother too much about the meaning of this statement"; instead he often paused to admire the subtle realities "invented" or "created" by modern physics, which would include electrons described as "wavicles" or "waves of probability"—fictions apparently meaningless by the standards of naïve positivism, since the wavicles cannot be observed or even pictured. As for the "cause" of their outlandish behavior, this remains so uncertain that some physicists believe they do not really need the concept of causation, which they can never prove anyhow; but all are agreed that the concept of mechanical causation is at most convenient only for some kinds of physical behavior, quite inadequate for others. In the atomic world they know of no strict rules governing every particle but only probabilities, statistical laws, such as emerge from the rolling of billions of dice.

In thus undermining the main argument for absolute determinism, modern physics by no means proves the reality of human freedom.[3]

_____

3 Since there is still much loose talk about Heisenberg's Principle of Indeterminacy, it seems necessary to repeat that this applies only to our knowledge of the behavior of electrons, not to the behavior itself. It states that we cannot possibly know both the position and the velocity of an electron, and so cannot determine precisely its future behavior; it does not state that its behavior is necessarily haphazard. Similarly the substitution in quantum theory of statistical for mechanical laws still allows for a very high degree of probability, which enables scientists to lay their bets with confidence, and in physical objects that we can get our hands on amounts to regularity. However uncertain the destination of any given electron, we can be quite sure that in the mass they will continue to obey the known laws, and no crowd of them will ever desert a bar

For disciples of the humanities it should be enough that as far as our
most exact science goes, there is no logical necessity for denying this
freedom. Similarly the revolution in physics has undermined the naïve
realism that regarded valid knowledge as wholly objective, reality as
purely external, and that degraded the inner life of man—the realm of
values—as wholly subjective, real only in some low sense of the word.
It has emphasized the "human standpoint" in all knowledge, even apart
from its hypothetical basis; for in the atomic world, at the very "heart"
of reality, the scientist now knows that he cannot simply observe it,
and realizes, in Heisenberg's words, that ultimately man "confronts
himself alone." Others may view more calmly the obvious human
element in history and the sciences of man. They may realize the deep
connections between science, philosophy, and literature as alike imaginative constructs, making comparable use of symbols, giving significant
form to facts that never speak for themselves. The differences between
these approaches to the external world remain most important, and
will surely generate further controversy; but the controversy may be
more fruitful now that modern physics has made it clearer that all alike
are approaches, to a "reality" that cannot be surely, completely, absolutely known.

Since many thinkers still claim absolute truth for their opinions, or
believe that only such truth can do for man, it should also be noted that
the basic uncertainty resulting from the scrapping of Newtonian axioms
by no means implies complete uncertainty or the lack of any solid
foundations. Apart from the fact that most of the everyday laws remain
valid when subsumed under new theories (just as Newton's formulas
still hold for the measurement of earthly time and space), the recognition that truth is up to a point man-made, not merely "given," may be
considered a sign of man's mastery of his world; but in any case it meant
an emancipation of thought. The stupendous imaginative adventures
of thought that began with Einstein and Planck made possible as stupendous advances in positive knowledge and powers of control, for
instance, of nuclear energy. They accordingly bring us back to the rare
values of science that were obscured by all the confusions and conflict.
Beyond the steady advance in knowledge that it inaugurated, these were
the intellectual, moral, spiritual values of the scientific spirit: the ideal
of a disinterested pursuit of truth maintained, without coercion and

---

of metal to join a bird. In recognizing the necessary approximateness and measure of
uncertainty in our knowledge, we should rejoice that we can still count on regularities
and necessities; else we could never enjoy any real freedom.

without parade, by a growing community that united individual independence and international cooperation, gave its members complete freedom to inquire and to follow wherever the quest might lead, but a freedom always disciplined by a respect for fact and a demand for utter truthfulness that were hardly maintained in religious communities, not to mention business and politics. Often disagreeable and now dangerous as is the knowledge that science has given us, most of us are still committed to its faith that men ought to keep seeking the truth; and the scientific spirit is among the necessary means of cutting the costs of this knowledge, checking its abuses.

In this perspective we may size up better the most influential idea that came out of nineteenth-century science—the theory of evolution. Although it was an old idea, going back to the Greeks, and had been in the air for a century before Darwin, he earned his fame by transforming speculation into a scientific theory, backing it by substantial evidence, and equipping it with a plausible explanation by his theory of natural selection. It entailed a radical break with scientific as well as traditional thought about the world; for like Newton, most thinkers still took for granted fixed species, in a static, immutable, finished world, and agreed with Hegel that "in nature there happens 'nothing new under the sun.'" The idea of evolution then proceeded to travel all over the world of thought. Everywhere it stimulated an interest in genesis and development, siring treatises on the evolution of religion, morals, the family, private property—everything under the sun. As it pervaded the whole climate of opinion it affected all serious thought and seeped into popular thought as well, in ways typically diverse and contradictory.

So we might note at once that by the standards of physics the theory of evolution is not a really first-rate theory. It cannot be formulated in mathematical terms or conclusively verified by experiment, it does not enable biologists to predict, and it does not state a universal law, applying only to a particular historical development on this earth. It also involves enough uncertainties in detail so that religious Fundamentalists periodically announce that the theory has been disproved. In fact, however, it is universally accepted by biologists, for sound reasons. All the evidence accumulated since Darwin supports the idea that life and man have evolved, in much the way he stated. Geneticists have made the process of natural selection clearer by their discoveries of genes and mutations, the variations it works on. The theory of evolution might therefore serve to dispel some popular misconceptions of science and "the" scientific method, as if there were only one. Sociologists and historians in search of laws might realize that a good scientific theory does not have to assure prediction, such as Marx and others too freely indulged in. As for universal law, there might well have been a similar evolutionary process on other planets, since it is now believed that some form of life may exist on millions of them; but it might be as salutary to realize that all we know for sure is a local process on a relatively young minor planet, which gives little ground for conclusion about the point of the universe or the purposes of a Creator.

On earth Darwin's theory nevertheless aroused much cosmic speculation, leading to opposite conclusions. Many men were depressed by its implication that man had not been specially created but was only a cousin of the ape, a latecomer in an endless struggle for survival that seemed as bloody, brutal, and pointless as Schopenhauer had made out. Darwinism was one of the main sources of the growing pessimism that haunted an age of progress; it would be said that life itself might be only a disease that afflicted matter in its old age. Many other men, however, were cheered by the apparent confirmation of the idea of progress, which now looked like a law of nature. Darwin himself suggested the consoling reflection that in the war of nature "the vigorous, the healthy, and the happy survive and multiply," and later he added that since "natural selection works solely by and for the good of each being," its tendency was "to progress towards perfection." The most popular Herbert Spencer was much more emphatic. "Progress is not an accident but a necessity," he proclaimed. "What we call evil and immorality must disappear. It is certain that man must become perfect. . . . Always towards perfection is the mighty movement."

Hence we are brought back to the endless confusion generated by the advance of science. Natural selection does not in fact work solely for the good of all creatures (not to mention Darwin's Victorian notion of the "happy" animals prospering), nor does it make progress a law of nature. Although biologists usually regard the increasingly complex, elaborate forms of life that evolved as in some sense "higher," they have no positive criterion of biological progress, still less of perfection, and they know that the fate of most of the higher forms has been extinction; whereas the unadvanced oyster has survived for some two hundred million years, the much more rudimentary amoeba seems almost immortal, and at that it cannot hope to compete with the everlasting rocks—no form of life can be so "successful" as what nature had produced before life got started.[4] As for the human race, evolution offers no guarantee whatever of its indefinite progress or even its survival. The brainpower evolved in man's biologically short history may save him, but has obviously made it possible for him to destroy himself, and should remind us that just because he has a power of choice, no other animal is so stupid as a human fool. For the kind of optimism spread by Spencer was not wholesome for a free society. Granted that the liberal faith grew up on hopes of progress, and requires a measure of optimism about human potentialities, belief in an automatic progress could assure only immaturity, possibly irresponsibility. It blinded men to the risks of freedom, the costs of progress. It led Spencer himself to attack all efforts at social reform by government as an interference with the "mighty movement" and a violation of natural law. Evolution likewise comforted conservatives by decreeing that change must be very, very gradual—except in business and technology.

The most plainly unfortunate consequence of the theory was the "social Darwinism" Spencer popularized by his phrase "the survival of the fittest," which Darwin took over from him. The phrase was constantly rung in by the partisans of rugged individualism, racism, militarism, and imperialism. They erected the law of the jungle into the basic law of human life, declaring tacitly and sometimes explicitly that might makes right. Most of the fittest were too ill-read to know that Karl Marx also had welcomed Darwin's theory, as a scientific warrant for his theory of the class struggle in history and the violent revolution that was bound to destroy them; but again none of them had any such warrant. Apart from the uncertain criterion of biological fitness, the slogan only obscured the real issue, the at once elementary and very difficult question of what is fittest for civilized men, no longer living in the jungle. And when Thomas Huxley attacked this "gladiatorial theory of existence," which Darwin also deplored, he still confused the issue. "Social progress," he declared, "means a checking of the cosmic process at every step and the substitution for it of another,

---

4 Natural selection has also produced many odd developments, such as the love life of the praying mantis, in which the female has the habit of devouring the male after intercourse. One may suppose that the male is no longer needed (and nature is notoriously spendthrift), but even so this habit would not seem to aid the species in its struggle for survival. If it suggests the superior fitness of the female, nature has not encouraged a Strindbergian war between the sexes in other species. In some it has instead produced sexual display characteristics, like the train of the peacock and the antlers of deer; though these would appear to be a more positive nuisance in any struggle with other species.

which may be called the ethical process"; man had succeeded by creating an "artificial" world of his own, whose ideal end was the survival of the ethically best. Nevertheless it remained unclear how a child of nature *could* defy the cosmic process, succeed by such apparently unnatural behavior—except by the power of an immortal soul, which Huxley did not believe in. Behind his thought lay another questionable phrase, suggested by Malthus, which Darwin and early evolutionists constantly stressed—"the struggle for existence."

While struggle is obvious enough in the natural world, especially among the many "higher" animals that prey on others, it is not a precise word for vegetable life and much animal behavior. (The long-lived oyster, for example, appears to be one of the most passive of creatures.) A competitive society was slow to recognize that another basic factor in evolution was cooperation: a less dramatic kind of behavior, most marvelously organized in the insect societies, that extends far down into the animal world, through the many flocks, herds, and packs, to the kind of unconscious mutual aid in schools of fish (or possibly the oyster bed), and that among the "higher" animals is most conspicuous in man. Although he has always struggled with other species and with his fellows, and no doubt always will struggle with both, he rose in the natural world primarily as a social animal, who by cooperation managed to develop culture, transmit it through the marvelous agency of language, master more and more arts and skills, and finally become civilized.[5] For a social animal with distinctive powers of mind the "ethical process" was not an artificial but a quite natural process; the "fittest" societies always had to depend on the cooperative as well as the competitive virtues, even for their aggressive purposes. Today free societies have the more need of conscious cooperation, with the attendant habits of fair play, reasonableness, and willingness to compromise peaceably, because they have given freer play to the competitive impulses of individuals.

To this whole development Darwinian theory called attention by stimulating studies of cultural evolution. These were at first oversimplified by the common assumption of a linear progress from savagery to civilization, which swelled the conceit of modern man. They then tended to humiliate him by the "genetic fallacy," the assumption that the origin of an institution or belief is still the key to its "essence." This scholarly kind of conceit, which flourished even though—or be-

---

5 On his long evolution in prehistory, see *Freedom in the Ancient World*, pp. 1–28.

cause—we do not and cannot certainly know prehistoric origins, menaced not only religion but all spiritual values, since their origin was necessarily "primitive"; science itself might be described as merely a developed form of magic (though let us add that for many a man on the street this is pretty much what it amounts to). But in time scientific study induced a more modest or mature kind of pride. Anthropologists and archaeologists illuminated the extraordinary wealth of the human heritage, at once our immense indebtedness to the prehistoric "savages" and the immense changes that have occurred in the past ten thousand years, during which biological evolution produced only slight changes. They made possible both a deeper sense of our common humanity and a fuller awareness of cultural diversity, with its implications of human plasticity. There is little question, I think, that the study of cultural evolution has on the whole been fruitful for civilized purposes.

There is considerably more question about the impact of evolutionism on philosophy. Some thinkers, notably Bergson, responded with theories of "creative" evolution, based on the assumption of a cosmic or divine purposefulness, and apparently becoming to a mighty process that had produced the human spirit. Although these won a considerable vogue, impressing even such worldings as Bernard Shaw, they had a shaky scientific basis, if any, and under analysis may look less edifying. Most biologists see no evidence of purposefulness or creative forethought in a process of natural selection that works on random mutations, almost all of which we now know are harmful to the creature, and that produces only temporary successes, adaptations like as not leading to eventual extinction, while it is always exorbitantly wasteful of life. As for man, the untold generations that toiled and suffered in darkness led the deeply religious Berdyaev to conclude that the idea of evolutionary progress was the best reason for doubting the existence of Providence.

Bergson also dwelt, however, on some plainer implications of evolution for man's own purposes, which have had a wider, more lasting influence. He emphasized the profound shift, heralded by Hegel, from philosophies of Being to philosophies of Becoming, based on the knowledge that in nature there *have* been new things under the sun. He conceived mind as primarily an instrument of adaptation—the pragmatic concept that was at the heart of the philosophy of William James, and that was worked out most thoroughly by John Dewey (who like Bergson was born in 1859, the year *The Origin of Species* was published). For Dewey in particular growth was the fundamental fact of man's long history. He therefore attacked all fixed, immutable, absolute standards of goodness or rightness, as not only invalid but ethically bad: they impeded further growth, discouraging efforts to develop human potentialities, extend and enrich consciousness, and make life ever more worthwhile. Similarly the business of philosophy in his view was not the discovery or contemplation of absolute truth, but always a necessarily unfinished business, a continuous effort to adapt thought to new knowledge and changing conditions of social life, or to deal with specific instead of ultimate problems. Its one fixed principle was adherence to the method of intelligence, so far as possible to scientific method. Dewey's experimentalism was explicitly adapted to the interests of a democratic society, which he maintained could best promote human growth and best realize the values of science, itself democratic in method.

To most thinkers Dewey now seems much too optimistic. He minimized not only the costs of both biological and cultural evolution but the hazards of social experiment, including the manifest possibility of employing the method of intelligence for evil purposes. In any case he forced the basic issue of relativism, a spreading doctrine that had come out of both historical study and evolutionary theory. Up to a point his attack on fixed, absolute standards clearly supported the interests of a free society by fostering tolerance, broad-mindedness, liberality of spirit—the disposition to live and let live that was more necessary because men were now less able than ever before to agree on any absolute truths about God and the good life. In the nineteenth century the most fervent defenders of such truths were typically political and religious conservatives, hostile to democracy. At the same time, democracy had grown up on the proclamation of "self-evident" truths about "inalienable rights," and it clearly involves something like fixed standards of justice, because of which Dewey himself could never tolerate the bold experiment of totalitarianism. Since most men evidently still need to believe in the absolute truth of their moral principles, they might be demoralized by relativism. It has unquestionably bred some moral confusion and moral slackness, especially because many people were already given to a sloppy kind of cultural relativism ("Every man to his own tastes") that amounted to an indifference to any standards of excellence. But whatever the sum of its consequences, the most apparent confusion, I should say, sprang from cultural lag.

In the prewar period, avowed relativists were a small minority, hardly popular, made up chiefly of thoughtful people who were apt to be

intellectually and morally more responsible than conventional believers. Most men remained sure enough of the absolute rightness of
their ways, if only out of tribal or individual conceit; defenders of
absolute standards virtually monopolized the public platforms and
pulpits, and could always count on a better press; leaders of both Right
and Left went on affirming and denouncing in ringing terms. (And let
us remember that neither Fascists nor Communists are relativists.)
While the study of history and society made always plainer the actual
relativity of values, and forced the problem of how then to maintain
that ideals of freedom, justice, and human rights were not merely local
prejudices, most men simply reasserted that their beliefs were grounded
on eternal verities. While the idea of evolution spread all over and
some writers spelled out the fundamental changes in behavior during
man's relatively brief history, most continued to recite the proverb
that human nature is always and everywhere the same, you can never
change human nature. Common sense only amplified the contradictions. Simple men who rejected the absurd, heathenish idea that they
were descended from apes nevertheless liked to think that they were
"progressive," were scornful of such types as "old fossils," and took
for granted that the historically rare attitudes expressed in this evolutionary language were simply human nature; while those who made
good in business knew that the ruling motive of man is the profit motive, "fitness" consists primarily in an aptitude for making money—
beliefs that would have seemed strange in almost all past societies.
By contrast the philosophy of Dewey was likely to unsettle and distress men for the same reason that it heartened and exhilarated some,
since its openness and adventurousness sprang from a principle of
necessary uncertainty, and it could never promise security; but his
experimentalism was at least suited to a revolutionary world of actual
uncertainty and insecurity, in which there was no safety in sitting
tight.

Biologists themselves were long distracted by a comparable lag, the
controversy between mechanists and vitalists: the one dutifully trying
to apply the concepts of classical physics and explain everything by the
laws of mechanics, the other pointing out that these laws could not
explain the elementary facts of life and growth, but substituting vague
concepts of *élan vital* or Aristotelian entelechy that were useful only for
baptismal purposes. Not until our century did they begin to settle on
the basic concept of organism, centered on the fact that a living cell—
the foundation of life discovered early in the nineteenth century—is

no mere aggregate of matter but an organization of it, or a whole different from the sum of its parts. Unlike a machine, an organism is continually renewing itself, "dying and becoming"; its spontaneous internal activity is as essential as its response to external stimuli. This concept would accordingly enable biologists to deal more freely with purposeful behavior ("purpose" had been a problem for mechanists, most easily disposed of by tabooing the word), and to regard man in good conscience as a self-determining organism, which he always feels he is. Appropriately, if ironically, the concept of organism also brought biology closer to modern physics. Physicists were conceiving the atom as likewise an organization of energy, concentrating on events or behavior instead of "matter," and on such related concepts as electromagnetic "fields"; the continuities facilitated the development of biochemistry and biophysics, today among the most exciting frontiers in science. As appropriately, biology was linked with other sciences by similar concepts—the social organism, "patterns" of culture, the "configuration" or Gestalten of mental life.

Meanwhile laboratory workers in the life sciences continued by ordinary scientific methods to make valuable discoveries for which men might be more grateful than they were for the grand theories. It is easy now to forget how much the "materialistic" nineteenth century contributed to human welfare by its rapid advances in medicine and hygiene—vaccination, public sanitation, pasteurization, antiseptic surgery, or the simple blessing of anesthesia. To do justice to these advances would take another volume, but at least let it be said here that among the great liberators in history was Pasteur. If some literary men might be distressed by a public opinion poll in France that ranked Pasteur as the greatest Frenchman who ever lived, they too might rejoice that he was ranked far ahead of Napoleon.

Somewhat more mixed were the blessings that came with the rise of psychology as a life science, instead of a branch of philosophy. Although its wide and deep influence on modern thought was only beginning to appear before the World War, it had developed sufficiently to spot the main difficulties it raises. Its pioneers—among others Wundt, Brentano, James, Pavlov, von Ehrenfels, McDougall, and Freud—pretty well established its present status, which is not strictly a science of psychology but an assortment of psychologies: schools differing in their methods and basic concepts, first of all in their concept of "mind," their distinctive subject. (In a poll some years ago psychologists generally agreed that a definition of their profession had to be historical and social—or in other words, psychologists are people known as psychologists.) Their disagreements tended to become acrimonious just because they could never design controlled experiments to resolve them, and their theories were not in good scientific fighting trim. Their own findings about the principles of interest, habit, need, function, etc., only emphasized that they could not hope to be as detached as physicists. In an intellectual and cultural history the major difficulties remain that "psychology" is much less pure or exact a science than the natural sciences, that it has nevertheless deeply influenced thought, that its influence owes to both its exaggerated claims and its important findings, and that to appreciate its value calls for considerably more tact than many psychologists have exhibited.

Auguste Comte had set the basic challenge by excluding psychology from the family of sciences on positivistic grounds. There could be "nothing like scientific observation of mental phenomena," he declared; introspection would never do, if only because the mind had to pause from activity in trying to observe this activity. The behaviorists then got around this difficulty by confining psychology to behavior that could be observed, ruling out psyche. Without fanfare Pavlov set out on his great pioneering work, by experiments on dogs discovering and exploring the very important phenomenon of the conditioned reflex. American behaviorists proceeded to demonstrate by experiments on babies that human beings too could be conditioned. Thereby they illuminated a process that determines much habitual thought and behavior. Many responses that may appear to be reasoned, spontaneous, or "free" come down to reflexes, which are only most apparent in the emotion touched off by the sounding of slogans that is commonly mistaken for thinking; the response of 100 per cent Americans to cries of "Red" is as automatic as the flow of saliva in Pavlov's dogs.[6] From this insight, now a commonplace of thought, behaviorists went on to fruitful inquiries into all manner of conditioned behavior. Even their effort to get rid of "consciousness" sprang from an understandable, if mechanical impulse: in reducing states of mind to bodily movements, they were trying to maintain the principle of continuity in the natural world that scientists find congenial.

---

6 More reputable thought may still suggest the parable of the pike. Separated by a sheet of glass from minnows in a tank, the pike goes on banging its head into the glass as it tries to get at the minnows, but eventually it stops, proving that even fish can learn; only it still leaves the minnows alone when the glass is removed—it has learned its lesson so well that it would starve before touching them. Both ultraconservatives and old-line Marxists may seem as inflexibly adjusted to a state of affairs that no longer exists.

Yet this effort only accentuated the limitations of their science. Apart from the misfortune that behaviorists took their stand on mechanistic concepts that physicists themselves had already found inadequate, this not only debarred them from dealing with obviously significant mental phenomena, but reduced them to the futility of denying such significance merely because they were unable to deal with it. They were led into as elementary a fallacy by their insistence that bodily movements were the only reality; for granted the common assumption that states of mind are somehow caused by such movements, these states are manifestly not the same thing. Their very self-conscious negation of consciousness was the more absurd because it was quite unnecessary: all their findings about behavior were no less valid if one assumed the reality of psyche, not to say more valuable because of the conscious use that could be made of them. For a historian their vaunted objectivity only called attention to the cultural influences on science. Bertrand Russell once remarked how different animal psychology was made by Thorndike and Koehler: "Animals studied by Americans rush about frantically, with an incredible display of hustle and pep, and at last achieve the desired result by chance. Animals observed by Germans sit still and think, and at last evolve the solution out of their inner consciousness." Pavlov was content with modest claims; but in America the national swagger and the national itch for quick, sure results came out in John B. Watson's announcement that if he were given a baby at birth, and complete control over its conditioning, he could make the child anything he wanted, from a clod to an artistic genius— incidentally providing therewith a curious demonstration of his dogma that all behavior is mechanical, unless one assumes that his own conditioning had given him delusions of grandeur. (He ended up in advertising.) And though behaviorists in time outgrew such extravagance, they set the basic fashion that would prevail for a generation. American psychologists continued to reduce mind to something easier to study or to concentrate on immediately practical researches, long neglecting such unique human endowments as personality, thinking, imagination, and capacity for creativity. (Lately a specialist in personality wrote that among the most noteworthy of current tendencies was the rediscovery of the self, which by 1900 had "perished as a psychological entity.")

Hence many neglected as well the pioneering work of William James, whose *Principles of Psychology* (1890) was once most popular. James might be considered typically American in another respect—his willingness to sacrifice logical rigor and precision for the sake of abundance and concreteness, and ideally of human dignity. While "scientific" enough to anticipate behaviorism, he was concerned primarily with the immediate, concrete reality of mental life, phenomena that might not be strictly observable but could be reported, and that he had a genius for reporting sensitively and vividly. Creative writers found especially congenial his account of "the stream of consciousness," the continuous flow of sensations, feelings, thoughts, fancies that meant ever-changing "states of mind," with shades and fringes, suggestions of the inarticulate goings-on in the back of the mind—an account that was obviously realistic, but still quite different from the simple sensations and definite "ideas" assumed by the traditional atomistic psychology. At the same time James emphasized the active functions of the mind as a selective agent that "gave" attention, concentrated on its chosen interests, and pursued its own purposes instead of merely receiving and associating sensations, mechanically reacting to stimuli. In analyzing its various activities—perceiving, attending, reasoning, imagining, willing, etc.—he likewise kept an eye on the mind as an organic whole, which in the stream of consciousness appeared in the unity and continuity of selfhood. Altogether, his psychology did not add up to a system, the basis of a school, but it contained the germinal ideas of almost all the schools to come. Its lack of system was compensated for by a rare spirit of openness to new possibilities, which was perhaps more becoming to an unfledged science. As a dying man James heard Freud lecture, and told him: "The future of psychology belongs to your work."

By this time (1909) some men were beginning to realize that Freud was one of the great pioneers in the history of thought. Although the idea of an unconscious mind was at least a century old, he made it a revolutionary idea by working out the new techniques of psychoanalysis and systematically constructing a formidable theory of mind, a depth psychology that has had by all odds the profoundest influence on modern thought. He belongs, as he said, with those who have "disturbed the world's sleep." However questionable his theory, its influence is almost certainly permanent; in our world consciousness will never recover its innocence, thought never put away the disturbing knowledge of the dark powers of the unconscious. And though the prewar world was still sleeping soundly, or was unaware of the significance of its uneasy dreams, we must pause here to consider the main bearings of Freud's thought. It was not only a monumental exhibit of the new science of psychology, and of the basic problems it raises, but a distinctive product of nineteenth-century science, a culmination of the major intellectual developments of the century, and perhaps the most striking example of their ambivalent consequences for human freedom.

From classical physics Freud took over his essentially mechanistic vocabulary, as in his concepts of "resistance" and "repression," or of the unconscious as a kind of mental space into which forces were turned back and dammed up. He assumed a complete determinism in mental life, insisting that nothing—no dream, fancy, impulse, slip of the tongue —was accidental or lawless. In these terms he handled the old-fashioned theory of instincts he got from biology, conceiving them as invariable necessities of universal human nature. At the same time he took to evolutionary theory, finding his keys in genesis and early development, specifically in the murder of the primal father, the source of the Oedipus complex; to the end he represented this as an actual historical event. Although now and then he warned that his whole account of the mind should not be taken too literally, at bottom he remained committed to a rather naïve positivism; he regarded his theory as the fundamental, essential truth about the mind, not a partial, hypothetical account, often buttressing it by such terms as "incontestable" and the "only possible explanation." He was most clearly in the line of modern intellectual history in his insistence on the primacy of the unconscious, which he described as the "true psychic reality." Ego or reason had to carry on an incessant struggle with the irrational id, now in the knowledge that the odds were always on id; and in time Freud made the struggle still harder by introducing the superego, which saddled ego with a sense of guilt, another constant threat of neurotic anxiety. On all counts he stressed the inexorable necessities that governed mind, not its possible freedom or actual creativity. More than Engels he insisted that freedom was possible only by the recognition of necessity, and he allowed men a much more limited, precarious measure of it. Since the necessities he dwelt on were ineradicable instincts, blind monsters of the unconscious that could never be tamed or civilized, together with a cruel superego that was an inevitable consequence of civilization, he made little provision for growth, or for the heartening possibilities suggested by man's evolution. As he saw it, the driving instincts were bent on regression, not development or growth.

Now, it should be obvious that psychoanalysis is far from being an exact science. All of Freud's key terms are vague, metaphorical rather than scientific, and their correspondence to psychic "reality" is never certain. All his interpretations are impossible to verify, none is the "only possible explanation." The therapeutic successes of psychoanalysis no more prove its truth than the common successes of witch doctors prove the truth of magic; for often its methods fail to work, different analysts get results by different theories, and they go on battling over their differences because again they are unable to perform a critical experiment to settle them. The early followers of Freud made the scientific status of his theory still more questionable by erecting it into a gospel, excommunicating dissenters as heretics, while the early deviationists—Adler, Jung, and others—were typically as dogmatic about their own theories. All exemplified the more serious dangers of the vocabulary of psychoanalysis, which made it too easy to stigmatize disagreement as "resistance" or wishful thinking, and to question the intellectual integrity of almost any thinker. Few had the wisdom of a nineteenth-century mental doctor who said "Better no classification than a false one"; for they would continue revising and quarreling over their classification, but also continue freely slapping on their patients labels, like schizophrenia, that might imperil their chances of recovery. One consequence is the utter confusion of law today, when psychiatrists will line up for both sides on the issue of the sanity of a defendant, or the practical question whether he is "sick" or "bad."

By now no less obvious are the cultural influences on Freud's thought, to which he generally remained blind, and which made it among other things a symptom of his age. Fundamentally, he mistook Western mentality for universal human nature, Western proclivities for fixed instincts. His famous Oedipus complex, for example, is not in fact clearly universal or fundamental, since anthropologists report finding little if any sign of it in some cultures. More broadly, his radical dualism of conscious and unconscious reflected the dualism of Christian tradition, his radical pessimism over the id the doctrine of Original Sin, his ruthless superego the Christian sense of guilt. He reflected as well the ruthless competitiveness of his society in his view that the deepest, strongest instinct was aggressiveness, the "natural" relation of man to man was hostility, and impulses to sociality were weak and secondary. As Malinowski remarked, he endowed his primeval horde "with all the bias, maladjustments and ill-tempers of a middle-class European family." In Freud himself there was a Puritanical kind of bourgeois that magnified the harsh necessities of life, making "reality" necessarily painful as an antithesis of the "pleasure principle." Habitually he treated work as simply an onerous necessity, sex as simply a problem, art as merely fantasy, play in adults as merely escape; he had little to say about the natural goods of life, the normal pleasures in doing and making, resting and playing, loving and sharing, learning and communicating, aspiring and creating. Similarly he slighted the values of civilization by dwelling primarily on its discontents, the "instinctual sacrifices" it necessarily imposed, "the fatal inevitableness of the sense of guilt." His disposition to a gloomy fatalism may be viewed as a wholesome revulsion against the naïve faith of his contemporaries in progress and reform, or as a deep sense of impending crisis; but this is to repeat that Freud was very much a man of his age, not the detached, impartial analyst he aspired to be and usually thought he was.

Yet this also brings us back to the very great importance of Freud's work, which may be more fully appreciated in a clear awareness of its limitations and excesses. His many acute insights are at least half-truths. Thus his interpretations of dreams are often farfetched, the more so because of his assumption that all dreams must have a hidden significance and mental life is never what it seems; but that dreams often do have such significance is now generally accepted. (Plato had hinted as much: "In all of us, even in good men, there is a latent wild beast which peers out in sleep.") So is the idea, long ridiculed by positivistic doctors, that organic diseases may be caused by states of mind. Many of Freud's original concepts have become commonplaces, from his basic concept of a divided personality—unaware of its deeper motives and desires, unwilling or unable to admit them, struggling with itself, seeking devious satisfactions—to the derivative ideas of repression, sublimation, fixation, regression, compensation, and defense mechanisms. The main point is still that he opened up the whole world of the unconscious. If he obscured the truth that conscious motives play a larger part in modern society than in almost any past society, he revealed the unconscious drives that may be more powerful just because of the increasing rationality of modern organization, and more dangerous because their characteristic goal is all or nothing, now or never. The many depth psychologists after him would keep on revising his interpretations—as Freud himself conscientiously did—and in particular they began recognizing the cultural causes of neurosis that he attributed to biological instincts, perceiving that the "reality" they were trying to adjust men to is a temporal social reality; so it remains unclear just what is "normal" for man, or whether there is a "basic" personality beneath all the diverse cultures. Nevertheless these very questions throw light on our own norms, deepen Freud's revolutionary contributions to the understanding of our own behavior.

Viewing him as a man of his age, we may likewise see more clearly the ambivalence of Freud's stand, sometimes the basic inconsistency. Despite his emphasis on the primacy of the unconscious, he never glorified the id or supported the many thinkers who attacked the claims of reason. At bottom he was an old-fashioned rationalist, still loyal to the faith of the Enlightenment in reason and science. At times he even echoed its faith in progress, indulging the hope that the human race would finally grow up. "Where Id was, there shall Ego be," he wrote; and he concluded *The Future of an Illusion* with a sober testament:

> We may insist as much as we like that human intellect is weak in comparison with human instincts, and be right in doing so. But nevertheless there is something peculiar about this weakness. The voice of the intellect is a soft one, but it does not rest until it has gained a hearing. Ultimately, after endlessly repeated rebuffs, it succeeds. This is one of the few points in which one may be optimistic about the future of mankind, but in itself it signifies not a little.

The power of intellect also signified a principle of freedom obscured by Freud's habitual insistence on necessity and "fatal inevitableness." As Otto Rank observed, his old-fashioned mechanistic determinism was inconsistent with his therapy, which was based on the assumption of the freedom, power, and responsibility of the human will. And because it is chiefly his pessimism that now endears him to many writers and religious thinkers in an age of anxiety, it is important to remember that Freud entered modern thought as a liberator, for just this reason meeting widespread hostility.

Directly he helped to succor the millions of mentally ill, whose sufferings had been intensified by the ignorance of doctors and the common feeling that their illness was shameful. His influence seconded the pioneering efforts of Dorothea Dix, Clifford Beers, and other crusaders against the barbarous treatment of the severely ill or the insane in institutions—another of the many movements that are barely mentioned if not ignored in most histories, but that have contributed more to the welfare or the effective freedom of millions of people than have most "historic" events. Freud helped as well to free more millions, especially women, from the tyranny of rigid Puritanical convention, the feeling that sex itself was shameful. He made possible more humane as well as realistic judgment by breaking down the sharp distinction between normal and abnormal, while discrediting the devil theories of sin and youthful delinquency.[7] Above all, Freud's thought embodied the first principle of wisdom—"Know thyself." Judging by modern experience, he was more realistic than Jung and others who have stressed different possibilities of the unconscious, finding in it sources of deep wisdom or transcendent truth; but at his gloomiest he remains a potential liberator. In giving men a clearer awareness of the powers of the unconscious, the actual menaces to human freedom and dignity, he left them less at the mercy of these powers.

Also linked with evolutionary theory, lastly, was the rise of the social sciences—a less revolutionary but still novel, distinctive consequence of the spread of the scientific spirit. Although there had been much rational speculation about society before the nineteenth century, only now did it become an empirical study and thinkers settle down to look for evidence, eventually go out and create evidence. Evolution emphasized that human society was the outcome of natural processes. Another stimulus was the rapid pace of change, which made men more aware that they did not really know much about society—the matrix of their life and their thought. The development of social science was complicated by its intermediary position between the humanities and the natural sciences, but by the end of the century it was recognized as an independent domain. Sociology was firmly established, anthropology was going its separate way, and students of government were calling themselves political scientists.

Because so much important thought has come out of the social sciences, we must again note at once that they are not, and can never hope to be, on a par with the natural sciences in precision, certainty, and warranted prediction. Social scientists are perforce up to their neck in their subject matter, or more precisely over their head in it, and cannot detach themselves from it. Neither can they lay hands on it, put it under a microscope, peer into its structure, isolate its elements, perform controlled experiments on it, or verify any comprehensive

---

7 In this spirit, I think it is now high time to put in a word on behalf of parents. While psychiatrists have long shown infinite tolerance for their patients, they have shown very little for parents, tending to blame all mental ills on faulty upbringing. In the conventional analyses, conspicuously affectionate, devoted parents have been as suspect as harsh ones—they can't win. But at least we no longer hear so much about the prime importance of toilet training in the formation of character.

theories about it. It is not only immensely complex but never still;
"society" is a vast conglomeration of different societies, all fluid, whose
evanescent present is still harder to comprehend because of uncertain
knowledge of their past. Hence the very progress of social science has
revealed more clearly its basic limitations as a science. Its great pioneers
—Comte, Marx, Spencer—were confident system builders who alike
talked freely of universal laws, and ended with utopian predictions.
They were followed by monists who found the key to the whole social
process in some simple principle, such as imitation, conflict, or the herd
instinct. The revulsion against all these premature systems then led to
a concentration on fact-finding that produced much useful knowledge,
but mostly of limited significance. Especially in America it would also
entail much slamming of doors against theory, more elaboration of
methodology with less attention to the theory implicit in decisions
about what facts to look for and why; it flourished on a kind of scientific
innocence, including the covert illusion that once a great enough mass
of facts had been accumulated, laws would somehow emerge all by
themselves. A French mathematician accordingly described sociology
as the science with the most methods and the least results. By now the
vast accumulation of data, with almost as vast a terminology or jargon
and as overpowering a battery of methods, may only emphasize that
social scientists have not yet come up with any comprehensive, universally accepted theory comparable to evolution, not to mention any
great laws.

As for their specialized subjects, economics was the most placid in
the nineteenth century since it was already established as an independent discipline. The leading economists did not worry much over
its scientific status, and until toward the end of the century were little
affected by the revolutionary developments in science, philosophy, history, and the economy itself, or by such mavericks as Marx. Most of
them adhered to classical economics, which was scarcely a liberating
influence now that *laissez faire* had become established policy. The
study of government also continued without aspiration to scientific
status; the political classics of the century, such as the works of de
Tocqueville, Mill, Bryce, and Bagehot, still belonged to the humanities. Specialists in political affairs began behaving or looking like
scientists only in our century. The traditional study of political forms
was then buttressed by empirical research that led to the current
emphasis on political behavior, with the familiar result of more useful

knowledge and more controversy over basic concepts and principles.[8] Among the first major works in the new mode was *Political Parties* by Robert Michels, whose "iron law of oligarchy" demonstrated how all parties tended to become self-perpetuating oligarchies; but Michels was a sociologist. So far the most original, seminal thought in the social sciences had come out of sociology.

In view of the current disrepute of the early system builders, it is well to recall the sound reasons for the fame they won. Comte, who coined the term "sociology," got the new science off to a good start by stressing its continuity with the natural sciences, yet refusing to reduce it to physics or biology. One of the first to study the distinctive "industrial society" that was emerging, he dwelt on the supreme importance of labor, not gold, and the promise of liberation for the working class; in regarding industrialism rather than capitalism as the essence of this new society, he minimized the class conflict that was doubtless more important in his day, but his analysis may now seem sounder than Marx's. Of the originality of Marx nothing more need be said here except that he went much deeper than the classical economists if only because he studied the economy in relation to the whole society. Herbert Spencer took a still wider and longer view of society, but in particular a more organic one; he most fully developed the basic concept of society as an organism, which would prevail over the mechanistic, atomistic concepts that still governed the other sciences. All had broad humanistic interests that were preserved by Emile Durkheim, usually considered the founder of "modern" sociology, and his contemporary Max Weber.

Durkheim's work on suicide (1897) was a model as an objective, empirical study of a problem involving complex spiritual factors. He maintained a comparable balance in his study of aboriginal religion; though himself an unbeliever, he concluded that religion had been the primary means to the sense of solidarity that made a society. Both studies led to the concept of *anomie* that he gave social thought—the sense of drift resulting from the disintegration of value systems, which was especially pertinent for modern society. Still, other scientists might ask embarrassing questions of Durkheim. Could he claim anything like

---

8 An extensive report on "The Present State of American Political Science," prepared a few years ago by Charles Hyneman, concluded that it was a parlous state of utter confusion, complete disagreement over proper subject matter and aim. A historian or a student of the humanities, long inured to such a state, may view it with less alarm, if also with some doubts about the claims of this "science."

scientific validity for his conclusion about religion? In assigning it so much importance, might he not be leaning over backwards, obliquely reflecting the bias of his society? Did he in any case have a scientific right to pass these seeming value judgments? Such questions deeply troubled Max Weber, another key figure in the development of the new science.

The main problem as Weber saw it was to devise a rigorous methodology that would keep clear of the opposite dangers of conventional moral judgment and a naïve positivism that precluded a concern with values or implied moral indifference. Rejecting the positivist dream of a universal scientific method, he spent years working out a scheme of hypothetical analysis that involved the idea of postulates lacking in the system builders, and more specifically the construction of "ideal types," anticipating the "models" that social scientists are now busy setting up. Thus Weber pointed out that Marx's socioeconomic theory could be a most useful construct, but was pernicious when it was regarded as essential and literally true. His famous study *The Protestant Ethic and the Spirit of Capitalism* might have caused less controversy had critics heeded his plain statement that he was not treating Protestantism as the "cause" or essential explanation of capitalism, but merely inquiring into the possible extent of its influence, which helped to explain why capitalism did not develop in other civilizations. Among other fruitful inquiries were his studies of bureaucracy and charisma, a term he made standard in contemporary thought. These were quite different sources of power that alike menaced freedom, one of his most cherished values. Charismatic leaders introduced an irrational, unpredictable element into history, displeasing to scientists, but their power could not be ignored. When most successful, however, they had an ironic fate: the church or the empire established, the revolution won, there set in the "routinization of charisma"—including bureaucracy. Weber worried especially over the growth of bureaucracy, which he considered the deepest tendency of the modern world, bound to prevail under either democracy or socialism. "All economic weathercocks," he wrote, "point in the direction of increasing servitude." The rule of bureaucracy was more troublesome because it was essentially rational, linked with the broader development of rationality in science that he was disposed to approve of.

But Weber too might still be embarrassed by more fundamental questions. Social scientists could complain that his study of the Protestant ethic was more historical than sociological, at best of limited significance; it yielded no generalizations about any necessary connections between religion and the economy. In particular those devoted to his own humane values could complain of his final decision about the problem of values. Weber declared that sociologists must refrain from judgments about social good or evil, because as scientists they could claim no certainty for them and their business was to stick to verifiable evidence. His position was quite honest, reasonable, very possibly necessary; it still left sociologists free to analyze value systems, or make comparative studies; and in view of the long tradition of groundless claims to certainty it could be regarded as a declaration of intellectual independence, a liberation for seekers and lovers of the truth. Yet it meant another radical dualism. Weber was asserting that the science he revered could say nothing about the ideals he lived by, which had to be accepted on faith and came down to a personal preference. He too was in effect divorcing science and the humanities. He himself felt this as a crisis of Western culture, since never before had they been so sharply separated. The divorce might seem too absolute for a science that could not anyhow claim certainty for any comprehensive generalizations; and it might serve, as it did, to nourish illusions of objectivity and realism in social scientists less acute or less humane than he.

Of other such possibly ambiguous liberating influences a few examples must do. At the turn of the century Pareto published his acute critique of Marxism, stressing the power of nonrational sentiments, together with related concepts that he eventually worked up into another elaborate system. This has gone the way of the earlier systems, after a vogue reflecting the popularity of the kind of realism that discredited faith in reason, but he offered more insight than any thinker before him into the multiple factors and complex interrelations of the social process, and analyzed more thoroughly the actual power of the nonrational. Veblen, nominally an economist, came closer to sociology in his classic *The Theory of the Leisure Class,* in which he dwelt on consumption rather than production and emphasized that the driving motive of men was not so much economic gain as social status; he gave social thought the now familiar ideas of "conspicuous consumption" and "conspicuous waste," most apparent in the American way of life. Sumner's *Folkways* helped to make as familiar the idea of the all-pervading influence of mores. It was in line with the development of anthropology, which had contributed the fundamental concept of culture in the new sense defined by E. B. Tylor in his *Primitive Culture*

(1871): not belles-lettres or sweetness and light, but "that complex whole which includes knowledge, belief, art, law, morals, custom, and any other capabilities and habits acquired by man as a member of society." In the prewar period the great importance of this concept was not yet widely recognized (the Oxford Dictionary did not admit the new definition until 1933); but under Franz Boas and others anthropology had made enough progress to assure its future as scientifically perhaps the most respectable of the social sciences, and for students of the humanities the most suggestive.

After the early simplified outlines of the evolution of culture, and then miscellaneous museum collections of exhibits of primitive culture, which out of context seemed more bizarre or barbarous, Boas led the way to a systematic study of cultures as a whole, exploiting the advantages anthropologists had in small, relatively simple societies and more detachment from their subject matter. They were less likely to be tempted by techniques of measurement that might give the illusion of mathematical exactitude. In their small societies they could more easily make out organic principles congenial to humanists: "patterns" of culture, which gave sense to beliefs and customs that by themselves seemed fantastic; matters of form and order instead of quantity and mechanical cause and effect; "styles" in ways of life as well as the arts. In time anthropologists would recognize the fundamental importance of symbols: as a culture-building animal, man was essentially a symbol-using one. But the most broadly significant implications of their study remained the plainest ones—the power of culture and the diversity of cultures. These were also the most ambiguous. One might be dismayed by the fuller realization of men's slavery to custom, their common acceptance of whatever way of life they are born into, their submission to seemingly arbitrary restrictions on their personal freedom—all the more irrational because of the conspicuous relativity of values. Or one might be heartened by the freedom and creativity of the race exemplified in the extraordinary range of values, and by the anthropologists' powers of sympathetic understanding, their own insistence on the values of breadth and tolerance—the measure of liberation from slavery to one's own culture. In either case there remained the valuable awareness summed up in the saying, not yet familiar enough, that the most important thing to know about a society is what it takes for granted.

Long before this, however, a quite different development had been signaled by Adolphe Quételet, a Belgian mathematician who devoted himself to gathering and analyzing social statistics, and attempting to derive laws from them. He published his findings in a book *On Man* (1835), subtitled "An Essay on Social Physics," that Comte denounced as an abuse of his new science. Quételet also helped indirectly in the founding of the Statistical Society of London, which announced that it would take pains to exclude "all opinions" and confine its attention rigorously to "fact," so far as possible to figures. Toward the end of the century Charles Booth (a wealthy manufacturer) spent years accumulating at first hand an immense amount of data about poverty and misery, published in his monumental *Life and Labour of the People in London*. This not only revealed the appalling extent of poverty but exploded the still popular idea that the mass misery was due to shiftlessness and indiscriminate charity. It directly inspired similar studies in America.

Here the rise of sociology was stimulated in particular by an interest in social reform, or more broadly the interests of democracy, which would remain a persistent concern to this day. But Americans soon began developing quite different interests as in effect they backed Quételet against Comte. They would cultivate social science much more extensively than Europeans, under the name of "behavioral science" make it most conspicuously a fact-finding industry, pride themselves on its practical value, pride themselves as well on excluding value judgments, and simply drop the whole question of the validity of their science because they were getting "scientific results," proved by a wealth of statistics. Their work spelled what one authority was recently pleased to call a "revolutionary change": the whole field of behavioral science became "technical and quantitative, segmentalized and particularized, specialized and institutionalized, 'modernized' and 'groupized'—in short, Americanized." It became characteristically American as well in its willing service of business. By now most social research is attitude research, and most of its financial support comes from industry; its business sponsors are interested only in such practical matters as motivation, consumer attitudes, evaluation of advertising campaigns— knowledge useful for selling goods, or cashing in on gullibility. Hence many outsiders no longer regard social science as a possible liberation, but fear it as a means of manipulating people, an aid to exploiting instead of controlling the powers of the irrational.

This "revolution" takes us well ahead of our story, since it dates from World War II. But it focuses more sharply the issue that is our immediate concern—the claims, the achievements, and the shortcomings of the social sciences, and their bearings on the issues of a free society. Even before the efficient bureaucratization of social science in America, its progress was deepening the ambiguities and paradoxes that Max Weber brooded over. It was preserving the unfortunate legacy of a naïve positivism, uncritical or unconscious of its promises. It was illustrating the dangers of the autonomy claimed by social science, which were more serious because it was not actually so autonomous as its specialists believed, but powerfully influenced by other social developments that they were too often unaware of.

Always, of course, the fact-finders were adding to a stock of valuable knowledge. Much of it was useful for practical purposes; government would draw on it increasingly in decisions about policy and means of carrying out policy. More of it was broadly useful for insights into contemporary society, as in the Lynds' pioneering study *Middletown*. For strictly scientific purposes the factual research was indispensable as a groundwork for theory, a means of checking up on earlier theory, and an antidote to the inveterate tendency to easy, sweeping generalization, for example about the state of religion, morals, or the family. The chief value of all the positive knowledge now at our disposal, I should say, is the clearer awareness it may give of how much we do not know, or how much less than is implied by popular generalizations. Similarly its obvious utility might make clearer how limited and uncertain this utility is, and how much less has been contributed to an understanding of fundamental social problems, not to say any solution of these problems.

But this leads to the obvious limitations of the fact-finders, their common illusion that by sticking to the facts or the figures they were being wholly objective, purely scientific. From the outset their methods and aims were seldom determined by the question what are the fundamental problems, what in human society is most essential, significant, or desirable to know more about. They were determined rather by simple convenience, what was easiest to find out. In America this possibly sensible policy would be too often vitiated by an artificial antithesis of facts versus theory, and a rage for quantitative results, which encouraged much fragmentary, superficial, often trivial research that obscured the fundamental problems. Nor were the new breed of social scientists humbler than the much bolder thinkers before them. While playing it safe, they were inclined to be quite confident, sometimes brash in their assertions of the importance of their work and the promise it held for society. As specialists in social behavior, they might seem more naïve because they typically neglected to look into the implications of their own behavior. Add that such superficiality is common enough in any branch of inquiry, including the humanities, and that still more common is the narrowness due to specialization and academic bureaucracy, it only calls attention to their neglect of this larger problem too.

The immediate trouble was not mere specialization but special*ism*, the tendencies to pedantry and arrogance in all fields. Long ago Arthur Balfour protested against "the pernicious doctrine that superficial knowledge is worse than no knowledge at all," for such knowledge is all a man can hope to have and enjoy about most subjects. With this came the more dangerous notion that no opinion is worth much unless it is based on thorough research—only the expert is qualified to speak. It was most insidious in the social sciences because these deal with matters about which thoughtful men in the past always assumed they were entitled to have opinions, and today still must have opinions, finally trust their own judgment. If most laymen are still too sure of their opinions, experts are as plainly liable to arrogance, and the pertinent questions remain: Are social scientists in general noted for their wisdom? Is their judgment on social and political problems eminently trustworthy? One reason for doubt, apart from their endless disagreement, is that in America they were carrying furthest the tendencies fostered by the advance of science and its alliance with technology. As specialists they grew devoted to technical "efficiency," in both their own labors and their social ideals, at some expense of humane interests. They talked most freely of the "functions" of men as servants of social purposes, "role-players," or anything but human beings trying to enjoy their lives. They illustrated the increasing functional rationality in the organization of modern life that troubled Max Weber: a rationality that could be unreasonable because it lost sight of broad human purposes, the ends of civilized life. In our own time the spectacle of physicists devising hydrogen bombs, and then experts coolly calculating whether the casualties of a nuclear war might be cut down to a hundred million and thereby make the war feasible after all, has demonstrated luridly how an increasing control through knowledge and efficient organization might end in a complete loss of control for human purposes.

Within social science, the division of labor led to a further neglect of fundamental problems. Whereas the pioneers had been much concerned with historical development, Durkheim ruled out any consideration of it; the "social fact" as he defined it was present, external, and observable, so as to distinguish sociology from history. Thereafter most sociologists settled down to studies of contemporary society regarded as static, like the stable nature studied by physicists, and so overlooked both the problems created by traditions and the plain fact of continuous change. Dynamic analysis would naturally be much more difficult, or they might question the possibility of a science of social change (which some are now attempting); but in any case their approach sharply limited their view of the revolutionary society that bred them. Until lately they paid as little attention to culture, either popular or intellectual, presumably because culture had become the province of anthropology, or perhaps because it was uncomfortably close to the humanities and the realm of values; since anthropologists concerned themselves chiefly with primitive societies, the most distinctive developments in modern culture also went largely unheeded. Anthropologists in turn ignored change, for the better reasons that their primitive societies were relatively static and lacked historic records, but their studies of "man" were limited by another oversight. In dwelling on the uniqueness of their societies and the remarkable diversity in ways of life, they long neglected the universals of culture, the underlying similarities that make it possible to speak of our common humanity, or the common understandings that enabled them to speak with primitive peoples. Relativism ran wild, some now confess; and it might not have done so had scientists remembered a commonplace of the humanistic tradition, that what unites men is at least as important as what separates them.[9]

The taboo on value judgments more sharply limited the possible wisdom of social scientists. It led many to insist that we have no right whatever to pass such judgments on different cultures, which amounted to a denial of the claims of knowledge and understanding, put reasoned beliefs on the same footing with blind prejudices, and in effect declared that ideals of intellectual or any other kind of freedom were merely cultural or personal prejudices, again confusing thought by implying that unverifiable judgments were simply groundless. Within social science the taboo led specialists to shy away from any study of values, and so tended to obscure the most elementary realities of social life, that as a social animal man always is and must be a moral animal, and moral relations are more primary than economic or any other kind. As

9 A. L. Kroeber, late dean of American anthropologists, commented wryly on a similar neglect in the new science of linguistics. He expressed a professional awe of its rigor and elegance, due to its concentration on the structure of language, but added that linguists were ignoring the problems or meaning; while they acknowledged that language had meaning, they appeared to regard it as "a kind of impurity," a little of which unfortunately had to be admitted. Kroeber lamented that the purists could not spare the time to make studies of meaning, which would be most helpful to earthy anthropologists.

a culture-building animal he is as necessarily a creator of values; the organization or pattern of a culture can be fully understood only in terms of its values. And the common requirements of social life and culture are again the clearest basis for the long-neglected universals, which are not necessarily the "highest" values, but do provide some basis for value judgments.

Meanwhile social scientists themselves were nevertheless committed to values, of course, even apart from the intellectual values of science itself, or their assumption that their opinions on social problems were better than the opinions of laymen. Their professional bias disposed them to favor not only the functional values of organization but the deeper, apparently inconsistent values of community. Most sociologists and anthropologists have been highly critical of modern society, in America usually by democratic standards, in Europe sometimes by aristocratic or authoritarian standards, but everywhere because of a characteristic professional ideal that has further confused the issues of a free society. The ideal is a completely organic society, stable, well integrated, well adjusted to its environment: an ideal actually realized only in ant and bee societies, but most nearly approached by primitive societies. Tacitly when not explicitly, many have subscribed to Plato's belief that a sound society requires uniformity of belief, or in modern terms, must be unified by a common ideology. In general, what the thoughtful have seen most clearly is the threats to integration or the symptoms of disintegration—the atomic individualism in theory and rugged individualism in practice, the breakdown of parental authority, the tendencies to *anomie* and alienation, the rising rate of suicide, etc. Needless to add, these are very important developments, and we are indebted to social scientists for much light on them. But we still need to add that in their professional capacity they have generally not taken kindly to a pluralistic, open society, which is also much harder to analyze, and that because of their neglect of history and change they have tended to slight the relative stability of the Western democracies in a revolutionary world.

In particular they have tended to minimize the claims of the individual. Always something of a nuisance to men seeking uniformities and regularities, the individual was most likely to be belittled in studies of the social environment. Durkheim (himself a political liberal) declared that his proper role was performance of his social function, and stressed the need of subordinating individual conscience to the "collective conscience." Others proceeded more directly to deny his importance by conceiving the scientific reality as the "social organism," implying that he was only a cell like those in his own organism; hence he would be described as a "fiction." Such abstractions seemed more plausible because of the usual neglect of change, since scientists treating society as if it were static could overlook the apparent importance of the individual in initiating change. He was therefore most thoroughly discredited by anthropologists. He served only to transmit the culture they studied, which was ready-made, intact, complete; they explicitly denied him any measure of independence, or of genuine individuality, by declaring that he was wholly a product of his culture. Even genius, according to Leslie White, is one "in whose neuro-sensory-glandular-etc. system an important synthesis of cultural events has taken place"; culture somehow did all the work by itself (as one supposes it wrote the book to which White carelessly signed his own name). Anthropologists long ignored elemental realities that were most conspicuous in their own society but apparent enough even in the simpler, better-integrated societies they studied: that there are always some conflicting aims, as well as differences over how to achieve common aims, and always some accepted variants, without whom there could be no novelty or change, or in the long run even survival for the society, just as evolution itself was possible only because of individual variations.

I should therefore repeat emphatically the assumptions on which this history is based: that society is not in fact a biological organism, least of all when it becomes so highly organized as civilized societies are; that the individual is never a mere cell but has some independent existence, behaving or misbehaving in some ways of his own choosing; that as a product of his society or culture he is still strictly an individual, unlike all the other products; that the creative individual is the most apparent agent of social and cultural change; and that whatever value the social sciences have in promoting understanding and social well-being can be realized only in the lives of individuals. If most social scientists would now readily grant all this in theory, they still tend to ignore and obscure it in practice, mainly because their chief concern is properly the social environment, but partly too because it is always much easier to study routine behavior, the determinants of such behavior, and the limits on personal or collective freedom than it is to study independent, creative activity, relatively free behavior. Until lately, social scientists made very little study of the conditions of creativity, of the intelligentsia as a creative class, of the importance of exceptional individuals in setting models for group behavior, and of the response of ordinary men to such influences. As David Riesman has said, "We are only beginning to understand the power of individuals to shape their own character by their selection among models and experiences."

Riesman recalls us to the abiding value of the scientific spirit, the endless self-criticism it encourages. All the limitations and the excesses I have noted have been amply recognized by leading social scientists. But the last word at this stage might still be spoken by Max Weber, who near the end of his life gave an address to students on "Science as a Vocation" (1918). Having stated that "nothing is worthy of man as man unless he can pursue it with passionate devotion," he spelled out all the costs of his own lifelong devotion to science. It demanded strict specialization, "the capacity to put on blinders" that outsiders could always ridicule; at that the scientist knows that his work will in time be antiquated—this fate "is the very *meaning* of scientific work," which "*asks* to be 'surpassed' and outdated," as a great work of art never is; he must know, too, that science not only can never answer the all-important question: What shall we do and how shall we live?, but can never prove his own living faith that scientific knowledge is "worth being known"; and when he looks around him he should realize that the "increasing intellectualization" to which science has contributed most has *not* increased the general knowledge of the conditions under which men live, but rather has made men much less knowing than the savage, and so has carried on the long "process of disenchantment" that began with civilization:

> Abraham, or some peasant of the past, died "old and satiated with life" because he stood in the organic cycle of life; because his life, in terms of its meaning and on the eve of his days, had given to him what life had to offer; because for him there remained no puzzles he might wish to solve; and therefore he could have had "enough" of life. Whereas civilized man, placed in the midst of the continuous enrichment of culture by ideas, knowledge, and problems, may become "tired of life" but not "satiated with life." He catches only the most minute part of what the life of the spirit brings forth ever anew, and what he seizes is always something provisional and not definitive, and therefore death for him is a meaningless occurrence. And because death is meaningless, civilized life as such is meaningless; by its very "progressiveness" it gives death the imprint of meaninglessness.

Weber's own "disenchantment" owed something to the defeat of Germany in the World War: he had been patriotically devoted to the German cause too. That his country was more obviously devoted to power than to the cause of freedom may suggest the unfortunate consequences of his scrupulous exclusion of science from the realm of values and ideals. If the social scientist has no right to say anything about these matters, beyond expressing a personal preference, he cannot logically be blamed if he prefers to accept the prevailing ideal of national power; so in America he could feel as free to sell his services to advertisers—their values were none of his business either. Yet Weber was always acutely aware of these contradictions, never complacent in his faith, never brash. Those who cherish the humanities and the arts should be pleased to note that his work has not been antiquated, and is unlikely to be, in part because sociology is not so rigorously scientific as he hoped to make it, but also because of his deep concern with fundamental problems that will never be completely solved, with values that will endure as long as science and civilization endure, and with the elemental realities that Abraham knew better than most social scientists.

3. *History*

History, wrote Augustin Thierry in 1834, "would be the hallmark of the nineteenth century," and would give it its name. Although this still nameless century was a great age of science, it was indeed more distinctively an age of history. Much more historical research was carried on than had been in all the previous centuries of Europe put together. The range of inquiry was widened, tools were sharpened and methods systematized. Historians drew on such related disciplines as mythology, philology, and archaeology, which also grew up in this period. While most continued to focus on history conceived as "past politics," they gave more attention to the economy, culture, and the whole social context of affairs of state. Their interests invaded all fields of thought, producing histories of law, art, literature, philosophy, religion, etc. Together with their fellows in other fields they began studying the great Eastern societies, laying the groundwork for the world histories of our century. Above all, thinkers in general grew more historical-minded. Marx and Engels went so far as to say that history was the only science, since it embraced the evolution of both nature and man; others saw it at least as the essential key to an understanding of man and society, agreeing that no institution or belief could be properly understood without a knowledge of it. For such reasons the philosopher Collingwood ventured to say that "we might very well be standing on the threshold of an age in which history would be as important for the world as natural science had been between 1600 and 1900." James Harvey Robinson would declare more confidently that our knowledge of history was our greatest single aid in preserving us from the fate of past societies.

Since this proud introduction may suggest only the conceit of a historian, I should repeat at once—as always—that the progress in the study of history was by no means a pure triumph or emancipation from ignorance. It produced much dubious interpretation of the past, which can be much more dangerous than simple ignorance of it; historians lent support to racism, militarism, imperialism, and all the other illiberal causes of the century. At best the real gains in understanding led to a clearer awareness of the limits of possible understanding. One reason why many thinkers still seem not very historical-minded in their actual practice is that historians failed to achieve anything like the sovereign authority some claimed and more dreamed of. We are still a long way from that threshold beheld by Collingwood, and I see no prospects of our ever getting closer to it. Meanwhile we have to deal with another major development that was ambiguous through and through.

It began with the German movement heralded by Herder, now known as "historicism," that Friedrich Meinecke described as "the greatest spiritual revolution of the Western world."[10] While still conceiving history as the naturalistic, humanistic, autonomous study the men of the Enlightenment had made it, Herder objected to their narrowly rationalistic, "mole's eye" view of the past. Philosophers were properly concerned with abstract concepts and natural scientists with the search for uniformities, but the historian's distinctive task was to portray the infinite variety and copiousness of concrete reality, the uniqueness of every culture, and a process of continuous change. To Herder the prospect was intoxicating: "What work there is to be done on the human race! the human mind! the culture of the earth! all spheres! times! peoples! forces! . . . Universal history of world culture!"

---

10 The reader should know that "historicism" is neither a precise term nor one habitually used by historians, and that it has taken on different meanings. What Karl Popper has attacked under this name, for example, is not at all the concept of Meinecke. I am using the term as merely a convenient label for the sea change that came over the writing of history.

In his view this grand enterprise precluded any systematic approach, calling rather for an effort of sympathetic imagination, or as he was the first to say, a historian had to "feel" his way into past ages or different cultures; but since his view remained essentially empirical, it could be reconciled with the next phase of historicism, Ranke's teaching that history was properly a science. A scientific historian still had to deal with the basic facts of particularity, variety, uniqueness; in Ranke's famous (if unscientific) phrase, all societies were "immediate to God." The difference was that historians now developed a systematic approach, rigorous methods for collecting and sifting their data, judging the authenticity of both their documentary sources and the works of their fellows, and so approaching his goal of telling "what actually happened." The Prussian Historical School became the major training center for students everywhere. And to the end of the century most of the greater historians—Mommsen, Taine, Fustel de Coulanges, Lord Acton, Bury—continued to believe that history was or could be truly scientific.

Meanwhile a quite different but related development was making the century an age of grand theory, or philosophy of history. Hegel's philosophy struck Ranke as "scholastic," since again it reduced the wealth of historical experience to the poverty of abstractions, and Herder might have been appalled by his ruthless disregard of unique cultures, since in any given era he pictured some one people as carrying the torch, ignored all the many other peoples. (Indeed, he rarely if ever used the term "culture," preferring his cloudy *Geist*.) Yet Hegel more than any other thinker spread the idea of the supreme importance of history, its absolute necessity for philosophy or any understanding of man, and he nourished the highest hopes of it as an emancipation, the means by which man could at last become fully self-conscious and free. Despite his World Spirit, moreover, he maintained its autonomy as a secular study, locating all the significant meanings and purposes of the human drama in a process on this earth, not in a life to come. Though his own philosophy of history soon went out of fashion, it was followed by other influential theories, notably those of Comte, Marx, Taine, Buckle, and Spencer. The very aspiration to scientific history that discredited Hegelian metaphysics encouraged a search for universal laws. Henry Adams observed that four out of five historians worth their salt had surely felt "that they stood on the brink of a great generalization that would reduce all history under a law as clear as the laws which govern the material world," and he himself ventured his "dynamic theory of history," based on concepts of energy suggested by physics.

By now historians are rather different: it appears that four out of five today would never dream of venturing such a great generalization. Their wariness of brinkmanship may be regarded as the maturity of historicism, a sober judgment on all the grandiose philosophy that departed from the wisdom of Herder and Ranke. None of the universal theories of history have won universal assent, for the sufficient reason that none are clearly valid, all tend most obviously to oversimplify, distort, or falsify history. Unfortunately, however, the circumspection of contemporary historians does not always suggest the wisdom of maturity. More often it suggests timidity, pedantry, or provinciality, a fear of philosophizing coupled with an innocence of the philosophy implicit in every written history. It belies Croce's statement that "the philosophy of history has disappeared because historical knowledge has become philosophical." It gives reason for some melancholy reflections on the grand enterprise that began with Herder.

His encyclopedic ideal ceased to be a shining inspiration when infinite particularity and copiousness were bodied out in countless monographs, and history became swamped by facts. With the rise of the Prussian Historical School, and then everywhere the academic industry of research, the new methodology encouraged an ever-narrower specialization and dignified much "mole's eye" research; it would fully exhibit the defect of its value, that it required no high order of intelligence or imagination. At the same time, historicism itself amounted to a philosophy of history, involving some questionable assumptions, no less when it entered its "scientific" phase. The Prussian Historical School also produced considerable high and wide generalization, not always handsome, which might be more dangerous because its professors believed they were now being scientific. While scorning the "vague generalities" that had satisfied former generations, Ranke himself talked freely of "the spirit manifesting itself in this world," sometimes describing it specifically as the spirit of God; and though he somehow knew it was not the World Spirit described by Hegel, he was likewise inclined to believe that it had ordained the absolute sovereignty of the state and blessed *raison d'état*. After another generation of disciplined research Treitschke was still able to announce that history was "the objectively revealed Will of God, as unfolded in the life of the State" —and most divinely in the Prussian state.

We are accordingly brought back to the disagreeable consequences of the rise of history, in particular for the interests of a free society. Such nationalism would no doubt have developed anyhow, but it was encouraged by the emphasis in early historicism on the uniqueness of every nation, and it soon got powerful support from historians. Germans were only the most notorious offenders. French historians fathered the cult of Napoleon, while the democratic Michelet wrote as fervently patriotic history, with considerable animus against the English; Englishmen bolstered the national complacence by their Whig interpretations of history, the most popular Macaulay assuring his countrymen that they were "the greatest and most highly civilized people that ever the world saw"; Americans were as proud of their special destiny, tending to grow more provincial as the department of American history was separated academically from European history; and school textbooks everywhere featured national history, usually presented in a narrowly nationalistic spirit.[11] Paul Valéry accordingly described history as the most dangerous product ever concocted by the chemistry of the brain:

> It causes dreams, inebriates the nations, saddles them with false memories, exaggerates their reflexes, keeps their old sores running, torments them when they are at rest, and induces in them megalomania and the mania of persecution. It makes them bitter, arrogant, unbearable, and full of vanity.

Although the statism supported by the Prussian School had no logical connection with historicism beyond its affinities with German nationalism, it illustrated a more general tendency to make history a means of strengthening the tyranny of the past rather than emancipating men from it. Historical consciousness was always liable to antiquarianism, and then to an evasion of the responsibilities of the present by doting on the past. In the most influential Ranke it confirmed a temperamental devotion to the traditional order; as a scholarly conservative he characteristically showed little understanding of the revolutionary political and economic developments of his own age. His pupils were in general more explicitly hostile to popular causes, disposed to believe that among their academic duties was the prevention of revolution, and so to convert historicism into a revolt against modern history, or an effort to stem it. Similarly the Germans tended to make a fetish of "the

---

11 When America entered World War I, I remember having to memorize in high school a list of the "causes" of the war, which even then struck me as pretty crude. I assume that the authors of the list were school superintendents, not eminent historians, but historians on both sides distinguished themselves by the ardor rather than the judiciousness of their patriotism. God and history were lined up behind every nation.

spirit" of an age, regarding as proper and necessary everything that was in accord with it; and the spirit of past ages was typically authoritarian. (They made an exception with the Age of Enlightenment —its spirit was shallow and crude.) Hence they supported the opposition to ideas of natural rights, on the grounds that all rights were purely historical; and again most past societies had denied political rights to most men. A new school of historical jurisprudence founded by Savigny, a friend of Ranke, emphasized that law was not founded on universal principles but simply grew out of local customs. As Treitschke added, "history" knew nothing of inalienable rights or of government instituted to secure such rights.

The exaltation of history and its works likewise encouraged an emphasis on determinism rather than human freedom, or than the singular powers of creativity indicated by all the unique cultures that stirred the enthusiasm of Herder. While Hegel described universal history grandly as a progress toward freedom, he insisted above all on historical "necessity" as he saw it, and grew increasingly hostile to conscious efforts to make history in ways he disapproved. Marx of course insisted still more on such necessity; freedom defined as consciousness of it permitted no toleration of men who defied his iron laws. But it was especially the aspiration to scientific history that led away from ideas of freedom and creativity, or inspired historians to explain them away. Thus Taine laid it down that "nature and history are only the unrolling of universal necessity," and set an example by looking for appropriately uniform causes, determinants as invariable if not automatic as the determinants in nature. These could be found most readily in the material conditions of social life, in race and milieu, in impersonal, involuntary processes—anywhere except the conscious determination of men. Similarly the revulsion against the romantic hero-theory of history carried to the opposite extreme of denying great men any independent force in history: they were merely agents of impersonal forces, or as geniuses in culture merely expressions of "the age." Other implications of scientific determinism were insinuated by the habitual talk about "forces" and "movements," for historians might forget that the forces they dealt with were strictly immaterial and immeasurable, the movements were only changes in societies that did not move.[12] In trying to work out his "dynamic" theory Henry

---

12 The seductiveness of physics may help to explain why "power" became the most fashionable concept in political science. Political scientists seemed to consider it not only more realistic but more precise than such old-fashioned concepts as freedom and justice.

Adams was made gloomier by these fallacious analogies, which suggested to him that as a force reason "must obey the laws of force," or as a form of "vital energy" it must obey the second law of thermodynamics about the dissipation of energy, "submit to the final and fundamental necessity of Degradation."

Potentially more troublesome for historians were the plain implications of relativism in the early stress on unique societies, all "immediate to God." This led Wilhelm Dilthey to the exhilarating conclusion that historical consciousness had shattered the last chains that philosophy and natural science could not break, liberating thought from dogmatic absolutism by its revelation of creative freedom and manifold potentiality: "Man has now achieved freedom." It led others to a healthy skepticism that not only encouraged a sympathetic interest in different creeds and cultures but could ease the painful doubt of believers who discovered tardily that the universal pretensions of their creed were in fact only pretensions. But it could also lead, as in time it did, to a radical distrust of the powers of mind, the possibilities of rational judgment. In any case it raised embarrassing questions for historicism. Was not this itself only another cultural fashion? Could a historian really be objective and scientific? Could historical consciousness provide a valid philosophy of man and society? Could it demonstrate any essential truth about history except that all was relative, transient, contingent?

Although Ranke and his early followers were not embarrassed by such doubts, they were bound to crop up with the growth of historical knowledge and self-consciousness. Jacob Burckhardt soon observed that history was actually "the most unscientific discipline." Dilthey tried to rescue it by distinguishing between natural and cultural or humane sciences, making "explanation" the object of the former, "understanding" of the latter, and equipping each with an appropriate logic and method; but his critique of historical reason left its logic imprecise, uncertain, and inconclusive. By the end of the century historians were growing inclined to agree with Burckhardt. Just because they had dug up such a wealth of data some were recognizing the evident reasons why history was far from being so exact, reliable a science as the natural sciences. Assume an "ideal" historian, quite impartial, with access to all the documents, in possession of all the pertinent data, he still could "understand" a given history only by interpreting it, singling out the important events, determining the main causes, sizing up the main consequences, or in other words finding meanings that were not simply given, not all there independent of the observer; and he could never strictly verify his interpretation by appeal to observed fact, controlled experiment, or any other scientific method. Take all the actual, fallible historians and they were never able to resolve their different interpretations, agree on the ranking of the many causes they made out or the many meanings they came up with, still less on any universal "laws" of history. They were therefore free to go on rewriting history indefinitely, could always be sure of a job; but they might not rejoice in advantages that deprived them of the illusion that they could tell, once and for all, "what actually happened." Meinecke, who in hailing the "greatest spiritual revolution" of historicism had made a demigod of Ranke, ended by going over to Burckhardt.

Now, most English and American historians still did not worry much over the limitations of their "science," for what seem to me good sensible reasons. Meinecke aggravated the problem by not only his too exalted idea of historicism but his heritage of German idealism, the assumption that German thought was naturally much deeper and richer than the empiricism of the English. His spiritual mentors had not been content to seek a decent balance of culture and nature, or in historical practice to occupy a modest middle ground between rigorous fact-finding and grand metaphysical theories, without the illusion of acquaintance with God's will. Hans Meyerhoff indicated another needless worry when he noted "the somber and paradoxical reflections" of Burckhardt, who in declaring that history was most unscientific had added, "yet it contains much worth noting": for this is a paradox only if one assumes that the methods of the natural sciences alone give valuable knowledge. Add that historians employ such means as "insight" and "imagination," vague terms corresponding to rather mysterious faculties for which there is no clear room in positivistic logic or behavioristic psychology, and no sensible man should be either surprised or dismayed; in everyday experience we all know that there are such ways of perceiving and understanding, and that they are indispensable. Otherwise the problems of history were aggravated by the familiar simplicities of either-or thinking. As Dilthey distinguished too sharply between the natural and cultural sciences, or explanation and understanding, so other men asked: Is history a science, or is it an art? The simple answer is that all good modern history is both.

The most important point, I should say, remains the most obvious one—that we have indeed learned a great deal worth knowing, through an impressive progress in the study of history over the past century.

If modern historicism no longer looks like a great spiritual revolution, one reason is that we now take for granted its novel achievement in establishing the ideals of impartiality and objectivity, making standard what has come to seem the most natural kind of history, but a kind seldom attempted in the past, hardly dreamed of in most societies, least of all such "spiritual" ones as ancient Israel and medieval Europe. The progress was due immediately to the use of roughly scientific methods in digging up and verifying data, which have given us a substantial body of positive knowledge about "what actually happened," no less reliable because of the diverse interpretations. It was due more broadly to the scientific spirit, the ideal of a disinterested pursuit of truth, or in simpler human terms, the ideal stated by Lord Acton: "History demands sympathy with those we do not love, and detachment from those we do." This ideal of impartiality became at once more necessary and more possible with the growing awareness of the inescapable limitations of history as a science—perhaps the most valuable discovery of the century. The progress was accordingly not a steady advance toward final, absolute truth but a growth in understanding, a more comprehensive view and a deeper insight into the multiple factors of history; and again a major gain was a fuller awareness of complexity, or the difficulties of understanding. The "great generalizations" contributed both more and less than their authors intended by offering new perspectives, opening up new dimensions, raising new questions, provoking new controversies; like Marx's economic determinism, they could be more useful when discounted, regarded as sights or leads instead of laws. Always the deficiencies of every individual historian were offset by an increasingly critical professional community, inured to the publicity of the scientific method, which could be trusted to check up on his work, expose his fallibility, and suggest his liability to personal, class, national, religious, and philosophical or ideological prejudice.

Hence the community provided correctives for all the dubious tendencies of historicism, beginning with nationalism. Most of the greater historians were good Europeans, as was Ranke. If as a Western community it was still liable to cultural prejudice, or to unconscious philosophical assumptions, it began growing aware of these too as Western civilization spread over the world and modern history became global history. The long view afforded by evolutionary theory was filled out with perspectives from sociology, psychology, anthropology, comparative religion, world history, and the history *of* history. We are accordingly left with many different theories of history, which may be regarded as a mere confusion or sign of failure, but also as a wealth of perspectives. Although they cannot be pieced together or fitted into a grand synthesis, they have enabled us to see much more, understand more; and one need not be simply distressed or confused by the shifting perspectives, any more than is a traveler who views a city successively from a distant mountaintop, different hilltops in its vicinity, its suburbs, and its main thoroughfares, and then explores its side streets and back alleys.

So viewed, history since Herder has been more of a revolution than Meinecke made out in early historicism. Potentially, and to a considerable extent actually, it has been a radical emancipation, freeing thought from much tyrannical illusion about a simplified past. To the same extent historical consciousness has been a more philosophical consciousness, especially as the illusion of scientific history faded. Many liberals have rediscovered what their ancestors knew in the Enlightenment, that their creed assumes a philosophy of history as well as a political theory. They may therefore welcome the fuller knowledge history has given of actual historical necessities, actual determinants of both thought and behavior: a knowledge, once more, that is especially important for the maintenance of a free society, in a technological age of massive, irreversible forces. It is still to the good to realize how precarious is the life of freedom, how strong and constant the tendency to evade collective and individual responsibility. In this humility we may then add that history comes down to a history of human freedom, and historians, as Ranke said, are always dealing with the scenes of this freedom. However deterministic their theory, in practice they always imply human responsibility when they deal with major conflict and change, and typically they take sides; their routine adjectives—such as wise, just, or brutal for men, brilliant, corrupt, or decadent for societies or ages—imply their judgment that the good cause won or lost, the change was for better or worse.[13] And if historical consciousness in the free societies has killed the hope of arriving at the absolute, ultimate truth about history, it has done no worse than modern physics about the natural world, while it has

---

13 William Dray has pointed out that no effort at fairness or increase in knowledge can resolve the conflicting explanations of the American Civil War, for example, because these come down to different standards of value, and concepts of value cannot be kept out of theories of historical causation, except by a rigorous determinism maintaining that the war was absolutely inevitable. Assumptions of human responsibility necessarily raise moral issues, in this case such judgments as whether war is a greater evil than the toleration of slavery.

suggested more clearly why we may be better off for not believing that we know this truth. Henry Adams remarked that historians themselves were fortunate in not having discovered the great law that four out of five dreamed of, for if they did they could be sure of getting into serious trouble with the vested interests and authorities of society. The rest of us might rejoice in their failure because it leaves history open, like the free society itself. We may count on the prospect of more predictions of inevitable outcomes, but also on the actual uncertainty that is a condition of human freedom.

Finally, however, there remains a less agreeable way of viewing this whole development. The major philosophers of history in the nineteenth century carried on the tradition of the Enlightenment by giving earthly history a "meaning" that made seemingly unnecessary the traditional faith in a transcendent City of God. Man was advancing toward freedom and self-consciousness, or the triumph of reason and science, or a classless society—toward some much better state that would redeem the long bloody record of suffering and failure. Most ordinary historians who stuck to their local lasts still believed that history was a progress— the most novel of the "great generalizations." At the end of the century Lord Acton, as editor of the prospective *Cambridge Modern History,* wrote that history itself was "a progressive science," and that "we are bound to assume, as the scientific hypothesis on which history is to be written, a progress in human affairs." By now the progress in historical understanding has made Acton's hypothesis appear incredibly naïve to most thinkers outside the Communist world. Many declare that the very question of the "meaning" of history is meaningless, because quite unanswerable as far as positive knowledge goes. Many more men simply feel that man's history is meaningless. There is hardly a historian or philosopher to defend the faith in progress.

We may therefore be more impressed today by the pessimistic undertones in the historical thought of the past century. The generally optimistic Herder had taken a cyclical view of *Volk* cultures that could be pretty depressing, since their time at the peak was typically brief, the period of decline much longer; most of history then appeared to be as uninspiring as it was in the view of Hegel, who condemned most peoples to a barren, repetitive, pointless existence. In mid-century Ernst von Lasaulx revived the ancient theory of cycles, arguing that Europe was on the decline. Burckhardt criticized his theory on the grounds that we have no clear standards for determining peaks or declines, but even so he believed that Europe was degenerating, and on the same grounds he rejected the theory of progress. Nietzsche, who was as historically conscious as any thinker of the century, returned to the idea of endlessly recurring cycles while insisting more emphatically on the degeneracy of the modern age. Even Herbert Spencer speculated on a possible kind of cosmic cycle in the alternation of Evolution and Dissolution, and pointed out that in any case Dissolution was an actual complement of the evolutionary process, the eventual fate of all life on earth. Brooks Adams worked out the "law of civilization and decay," incorporated by Henry Adams in his dynamic theory of history, which likewise foreboded only ill for modern civilization. The stage was set for Spengler.

All these gloomy theories were no more "scientific" than the hypothesis of Lord Acton, and might serve as further proof that the question of the "meaning" of history is strictly meaningless. Yet this remains a natural, significant question, no more pointless than the question individuals ask about the meaning and purpose of their own lives. It may make much academic historical research seem more piddling, superficial, parochial, remote from the living purposes and the social needs that history presumably should serve. It brings up the deepest issues of the modern world: the common hollowness or emptiness of life amid unprecedented material progress, the common lack of clear, civilized purpose in the ceaseless display of terrific energy, the common unconcern over the ends of freedom (another "meaningless" question), which have facilitated the notorious abuses of freedom in a civilization that no thoughtful man can any longer assume is bound to keep on progressing, or to be saved by its knowledge of history. We may answer bravely that history, like the life of the individual, has no certain meaning because men are still free to give it diverse meanings. If so, we must add that they cannot give it—cannot get away with—any meaning they have a mind to. They are clearly free only within the sharper limits set by our fuller understanding of history, and without the positive assurances once offered by most historians and philosophers of history. The uninitiated might better begin by reading not Lord Acton but Burckhardt, Nietzsche, and Henry Adams.

Then they might go on to realize the therapeutic value of history in freeing men from the tyranny of a false or fixated past, the vanity of petty concerns, and the delusions of manifest destiny, while possibly compensating for lost assurances by a heightened awareness of the wealth of meanings and values that men have created in defiance of mortality, and that have survived all the historic failures. These might still excite the wonder felt by Herder. They at least support his belief that man's history has been a development, which has now culminated in a deeper, fuller sense of "mankind": a development that is not necessarily a progress but certainly not mere endless recurrence either, that has involved continuity as well as cataclysm, and that may still give some sense of direction, point, and purpose.

4. Philosophy

"By reason of this attainment of self-consciousness by the will for truth," wrote Nietzsche, "morality from henceforward—there is no doubt about it—goes *to pieces*: this is that great hundred-act play that is reserved for the next two centuries of Europe, the most terrible, the most mysterious, and perhaps also the most hopeful of all plays." We have already noted the role of philosophy in this drama, which may seem no less terrible because it no longer seems mysterious. The self-consciousness was attained by the acute, sustained, often devastating critique of reason that was the basic philosophical enterprise of the nineteenth century, signifying that revolution had reached the very heart of philosophy. It not only attacked the faith of the Enlightenment but undermined all claims to the certitude philosophers had always sought, corroding the intellectual security almost all had felt even when rejecting traditional beliefs. One of its romantic modes was the insistence on subjectivity as the source of truth, the world as literally "my idea," which left no basis for possible agreement. One of its "realistic" modes, the insistence that philosophy was only an ideological reflection of class interest, as effectively denied the other fellow's claims to objective truth and the possibility of basic agreement. While all first principles were called into question, no new consensus of belief emerged. Thought, like morality, went "to pieces." The popular prefix in surveys of modern thought is "dis"—dissociation, discontinuity, disintegration, disorder, discord.

The play is still going on, nobody knows how many acts are to come. Yet it is still a highly purposeful drama, which has not clearly brought us closer to intellectual anarchy or chaos since Nietzsche wrote; and if it is no more clearly the "most hopeful" of plays, we need as usual to discount somewhat the popular accounts of an intellectual "crisis" that has been going on for over a century. In *Philosophy and the Modern World*, for instance, Albert Levi declares: "The faith in a real future

has been destroyed." Actually this faith is still very much alive: surely
in the Communist world, and at least as a hope in many thinkers in the
democracies. Levi exaggerates our plight by the familiar practice of
contrasting it with an idealized account of the unity and security of
Periclean Athens and medieval Europe. He forgets the saying of his
mentor Whitehead that "it is the business of the future to be dangerous"—a job, let us add, that it has never fallen down on, as the Greeks
in particular were always aware; their thinkers had little faith in a "real
future." He is also led into exaggeration by pure logic, asserting that
the multitude of intellectual alternatives today creates "a paralysis of the
faculty of intellectual choice"—as perhaps it ought to do, but certainly
has not done; "paralysis" is not the word for the many men at typewriters busy on another volume on the crisis of our civilization and what
we must do about it. Levi's own book is an excellent account of the
unusually vigorous intellectual activity in the modern world. This has
been the more vigorous because it lacked consensus and was not dominated by any one authority or school—any more than philosophy had
been in ancient Greece.

Throughout the nineteenth century philosophy was never simply
negative, and the continuous critique of reason by no means a confession
of bankruptcy or surrender to confusion and uncertainty. It was again a
positive, creative response to a changing world, often very bold, involving as continuous an effort at reconstruction. It was suited to a dynamic
age by the characteristic stress on principles of Becoming instead of
Being. Its increasing attention to evolution and history opened it to
other influences from natural science, psychology, and sociology, which
offset the tendencies to division by efforts at inclusiveness. Thus the
Synthetic Philosophy of Spencer was an astonishing attempt to organize
all the scientific knowledge of his day, and apply it to all fields of
thought. His grand system failed to stand up, like the others before
him, and so recalls the failure of any school to maintain the allegiance of
more than a minority, provide a new center of authority; the multitude
of alternatives that amplified the freedom of men to choose their own
philosophy of life, as their own religion, meant as well a fragmentation
of thought and lasting uncertainty about all first and last questions.
But if one laments the loss of intellectual security one should add that
too many critics of reason were too certain of their conclusions, not
skeptical enough. The early response of Comte was typical: sensing a
moral, spiritual crisis due to the weakening of traditional authority,
he proposed a completely authoritarian solution in his ideal positivistic

state. The openness of nineteenth-century philosophy to new possibilities was still hedged by the old hankering for closed systems of thought.

In short, the developments in philosophy too were profoundly ambiguous. Always critical of traditional rationalism, sometimes tending to the futility of despising the power of intellect that as philosophers they were themselves exercising and demonstrating, most of the important thinkers were not simply antirational; together they complicated rather than repudiated the cause of reason. Similarly they complicated the cause of freedom, in different ways promoting, obstructing, and confusing it, while displaying an exceptional degree of intellectual freedom, and usually upholding some mode of "true" freedom. All of them have been roundly condemned, as they themselves were wont to condemn their predecessors; but in this history they call for hung verdicts.

Thus what is now most apparent in Hegel is the rape he committed on both reason and ideals of freedom, in the name of Spirit, with the aid of an insufferably ponderous, obscure vocabulary that he made the trademark of German philosophy. Few freedom lovers deplore the revulsion against his pretentious system by most of the leading thinkers after him. Nevertheless the continual attacks on him were a tribute to not only his originality but his lasting influence as the first major philosopher to take history into full account, and to comprehend the development of philosophy in terms of just such reactions. All except Marxists might now agree that he illuminated the history of philosophy and culture more than Marx did, made it easier to date and discount both dialectical materialism and his own metaphysical idealism. Since his insights have entered the common sense of philosophy, in terms more civil, it might seem inhuman to oblige students to struggle through the morass of his verbiage, compensating for their pains only by slaying the dead monsters of his metaphysics or exposing the transparent fictions of his logic; but one should remember the reasons why John Dewey as a student found in Hegel's synthesis "an immense release, a liberation." It liberated him from an oppressive sense of divisions, the sharp separations of nature and culture and of self and the world, thereby spurring his own effort at synthesis on empirical grounds.

Even so it is possible to experience as much release in turning to Schopenhauer, the great pessimist and "irrationalist," and one of the most savage critics of Hegel. He attacked the abuses of philosophy by personal, political, national, or material interests, as exemplified in Hegel's seemingly Olympian thought. Such abuses illustrated Schopenhauer's cardinal doctrine of the primacy of will, the blind energy that he conceived as the ultimate reality of the cosmos. He demonstrated its actual primacy in man, whose basic drives—beginning with the will to live—are manifestly prior to thought, not dictated by reason. In his acute analysis of the subrational, often unconscious will he anticipated Freud's discoveries, just as he anticipated Darwin by his idea of the evolution of will from physical energy through the rising forms of life to the conscious life of man. His insights were more useful for rational purposes because he never glorified will, as Fichte had and his disciple Wagner would. For Schopenhauer was not actually an "irrationalist." So far from expressing contempt for intellect, he put his whole trust in its power, calling upon men to suppress their will, put an end to the blind striving that caused endless strife and misery throughout the natural world, and in mankind appeared as the "primary and ineradicable egoism" that was the source of all wickedness too. How man could do this was not too clear if will was in fact the essential reality of life; but at any rate he preached a saintly ethic of pity, humility, altruism, chastity, and asceticism, in the evident conviction that at least some men could eradicate the ineradicable egoism. He even held out the sublime, if rather preposterous hope that would man utterly renounce will and commit race suicide, the will itself and therefore the whole evil world would somehow come to an end.

Most men, however, are still not heartened or edified by this possibility, which Schopenhauer himself hardly banked on; and the most pertinent issue remains his famous pessimism. Though he refrained from any romantic display of self-pity and did not invoke "the spirit of the age" either, his thought was symptomatic of the melancholy and world-weariness running through the Romantic movement, and prophetic of the pessimism that would thereafter cloud an age of apparent progress, darken many a page of the deeper writers and thinkers. It was prophetic as well of the ennui that would settle on many men, sated with restless desire or endless activity lacking any high purpose; Schopenhauer was the first philosopher to do justice to the real evil of boredom. However neurotic himself, he built a strong logical case for his pessimism. It had a clear value for a too optimistic society as a sober reminder of all the suffering and misery throughout man's history, which Hegel took much too lightly as a spokesman of Absolute Reason, and a more sobering awareness of the terrible powers of the irrational, which no other philosopher had so fully recognized. As a possible compensation it offered the freedom of contemplative being rather than doing—freedom from the necessities that always bind doing.

Yet it meant a complete rejection of faith in a free society—faith in any actual or potential improvement through freedom, reason, knowledge, and cooperative effort.[14] Discount his personal misanthropy, it harked back explicitly to the pessimism about man's earthly condition that runs through most of the world's religions, and that inspired the common injunction to renounce the world, the common hopes only of a life to come. As explicitly Schopenhauer held up the ideals of passivity embodied in Eastern religion and philosophy, especially Hindu mysticism, with which Europeans had lately become acquainted. This is indeed a perennial mode of wisdom as of holiness and "spiritual freedom"; but the fact remains that logically it does not, and historically did not, encourage active efforts to combat the evils of poverty, promote social reform, or extend earthly freedoms.

The clearest, most emphatic statement of an alternative wisdom was offered by John Stuart Mill. He explicitly declared that the case for ideals of freedom and democratic government finally rested on the assumption that the active type of man is preferable to the passive type. While recognizing the dangers of the "striving, go-ahead character," especially when energy was devoted chiefly to money-making, he steadily maintained that it was better for both society and the individual if all men were given the fullest possible freedom, opportunity, and encouragement to strive for self-betterment, develop their capacities, and take an active part in their government. One may now repeat that Mill's view of man as a potentially rational, progressive being has come to seem too optimistic; he might well have taken Schopenhauer more to heart. He was not so original a thinker either, or in any sense a revolutionary one; his critique of rationalism went no further than a "philosophy of experience" in line with the English empirical tradition and the inductive logic of science, his treatise on which also seems too simple today. Always he sought primarily to maintain public standards of reason against any form of obscurantism, irrationalism, transcendentalism, apriorism, or absolutism that menaced freedom of thought and speech. Immediately he is important as a witness that the basic faith of the Enlightenment was far from dead, and nineteenth-century philosophy not simply adrift. One major line of continuity came down through

---

14 Schopenhauer was apparently illogical in demanding "voluntary and complete" chastity, poverty, etc., since if men had the power to go to such extremes it would seem reasonable to believe that they might be able to make some decent improvements in their condition. In declaring that "unrest is the mark of human existence" he likewise overlooked the plain truth that it is the source of the joys of aspiration and creativity as well as of suffering and boredom. At any rate, he held out no hope of social improvement for a being he conceived as essentially an anarchic egoist, not a social animal.

Mill to Bertrand Russell and John Dewey. *On Liberty* remains a classic.

Still, it became one because it was not merely a conventional defense of liberty, but stated some novel principles suited to a revolutionary age. In the long view, even Mill's premise of the superiority of the active type of man and life was novel; for most of the moral and religious teachers through the ages had held up the passive ideal, with its virtues of humility, patience, and obedience, and its wisdom of limiting rather than expanding desire and range of choice. As uncommon was his insistence that variety of opinion is a positive good. While consistently holding to such premises of the liberal faith, he saw clearly the necessity of adapting this faith to a changing world, in particular to the growth of democracy, technology, and science, which he recognized were threatening as well as fostering the cause of freedom. Despite his high regard for science, he had no such simple faith in it as did Comte, Marx, and Spencer. In an age of ideology or noisy ism Mill's creed was novel because it was not a doctrinaire liberalism, but remained open on principle, flexible and resourceful, dogmatic only in its opposition to orthodoxies old or new, any closed ideology. His unexciting contribution to the critique of reason may seem remarkable simply because he remained consistently loyal to a principle of reasonableness.

Such reasonableness was scarcely the hallmark of the much more brilliant Nietzsche, perhaps the greatest prophet of the century, and certainly one of the major protagonists in the hundred-act morality play he prophesied. Neglected during his lifetime, he soon began to enjoy the "excessive fame" he predicted to his publisher shortly before he went mad. His wide influence was singularly mixed; in the large company of his admirers—among others Freud, Adler, Thomas Mann, Gide, Malraux, Berdyaev, Sorel, Mussolini, H. L. Mencken, and Sartre—nobody can say who were his "true" disciples. He founded no school because he formulated no clear system or method of thought, was as much poet and prophet as philosopher, and in no role offered any assured program of salvation. His thought was extraordinary in its penetration, complexity, and conscious ambiguity, and also in its constant tendency to extravagance, which gave it an air of violent simplicity. Always insisting on the need of thinking and living dangerously, Nietzsche more than any other philosopher laid himself open to easy, dangerous abuse. He despised the utilitarian "pig philosophy" of Mill; but only in Mill's spirit of reasonableness can one fully appreciate the value of his thought in the cause of individuality—full, free self-realization—to which they were both devoted.

The most apparent difference between them was that Nietzsche came by this devotion as a post-Romantic, another great "irrationalist." He was an apostle of will, celebrating specifically the will to power condemned by Schopenhauer; he scorned the faith in reason and science as the essential means to wisdom and truth, scorned the fear of passion that went with it; he gloried in the new freedom from "the fear of reason," the courage to be "absurd"; and like Kierkegaard he gloried as well in a frank subjectivity, freedom from the pretense of impersonality. He amazed Freud by his insights into the willful, passional depths of the mind, and into the rationalizations of unconscious motive or irrational behavior—insights that made him a better prophet than Marx on the convulsions and catastrophes to come. Yet no more than Schopenhauer was he simply a Romantic or an irrationalist. While attacking both the inadequacies and the excesses of traditional rationalism, and of the new religion of science, he attacked as well the anti-intellectual, obscurantist tendencies of Romanticism; no philosopher had a keener sense of both how precious and how precarious is the life of the mind, how hard it is to be clear-eyed and intellectually honest. In this spirit he despised, too, the tendencies of romantic subjectivity to narcissism, self-pity, sickliness. Since he ended in madness he may be regarded as a victim of his age, a prime exhibit of the deep maladies of alienation and anxiety; but he never whined, paraded his woes, or made a cult of *Angst*. According to Ernest Jones, Freud remarked that Nietzsche "had a more penetrating knowledge of himself than any other man who ever lived or was ever likely to live."

In particular he had more historical sense than any philosopher before him. Unlike Hegel and Marx, Nietzsche retained a saving awareness that his own thought was historically conditioned, and never claimed the authority of either Absolute Reason or science; acutely conscious of the relativity of values, he realized the inescapable ambiguity of any positive philosophical stand. Nevertheless he took a very positive stand, far removed from simple relativism. He attacked historicism because it encouraged an evasion of the responsibility of value judgment, or else an easy acceptance of traditional values. In his view history could never be understood by a detached spectator, but only through a deep sense of human involvement and commitment, the absolute necessity of declaring a choice. Although he was pleased to call himself the "first immoralist" and place himself "beyond good and evil," he was much like Mill in his intense moral earnestness, insisting still more that morality must come first. A more precise term for the upshot of his philosophy of perspectivism was "the transvaluation of values." He seemed like an immoralist only because he stood the Christian ethic on its head, declaring that what it called evil was good, and vice versa. To its "slave morality," sprung from a fear of life and designed for the cowardly mob, he opposed his "master morality," a "religion of the freest, gayest, and noblest souls." Its essential virtues were the historic virtues of aristocracy: a lofty sense of personal honor, backed by "faith in oneself, pride in oneself," the courage to express fully the essential will to power, and dedication to the ideal of the "superman"—not merely "Know thyself" but "Surpass thyself." In these terms the modern world was degenerate, headed for catastrophe, because it was dominated by the contemptible slave morality, "the will to nothingness."

One may therefore wonder how the weak and cowardly had become so powerful, why Nietzsche had to spring to the defense of supermen, why he had forever to exhort men to express the will to power that he declared was the basic drive in man. But first one must note that his savage criticism of modern society was much to the point for democratic purposes too, as may be seen more clearly by considering Emerson's comparable gospel of self-reliance. He despised the rule of mediocrity, the slavish conformism, and the as slavish devotion to material values, all in the interest of a paltry "happiness," and the more contemptible because in the name of Christ. He was as contemptuous of the supermen in business, whose will to power came down to a mean passion to make money, and who had no lofty sense of honor, no style, no taste for the aristocratic values that made life worth living—"virtue, art, music, dancing, reason, spirituality." Similarly he decried the nationalism endorsed by Hegel, in which he recognized another menace to personal freedom and self-respect; he was prophetic as well in foreseeing the dangers of this vulgar religion, which would enable plutocrats, demagogues, and dictators to exploit the hopes and fears of the masses.[15] And it was for the sake of freedom—true independence of spirit—that he attacked the whole faith in progress, all promises of happy outcomes (like a classless society), all hopes of saviors human or divine.

Most distinctive in Nietzsche was another quality that he rather questionably assigned to his born aristocrats—a "radical irony." He knew

---

15 In view of his reputation as a proto-Fascist, one might ponder this credo: "First of all, I believe in personal relationships. I hate the idea of dying for a Cause, and if I had to choose between betraying my country and betraying my friend, I hope I should have the guts to betray my country." Except for the "hope," this might have been written by Nietzsche. Actually it was written by E. M. Forster, as one of the main articles of his liberal creed.

that healthy aristocracies never questioned their values, but he also knew that these values were finite, unsanctioned by any absolute authority, unrewarded by any certainty beyond their own reward. While he proclaimed that the future belonged to his superman, and that society would be restored to health after some terrific crisis, he did not believe that it would stay healthy; for he knew that historic aristocracies had always degenerated, he saw in history only a cycle of growth and decay. His radical irony, which was as foreign to Emerson as to Hegel and Marx, was rooted in an unflinching pessimism. Nietzsche had a deeper tragic sense of life than any other philosopher of the century, including Schopenhauer. But it was deepened as well by his reverence for the human spirit, which on these hard terms could assert and maintain its own values, as the Homeric heroes had. Hence he railed at the Christian tradition, reflected by Schopenhauer, that made "this world" a term of reproach, encouraged a fear or hatred of life, and cried out for a Savior. He denounced everything that made for weakness, weariness, exhaustion, or negation of this life. Knowing the worst, he rang out his lusty Yea to life. In view of the catastrophes he predicted, he can be the most bracing philosopher of the century.

This Nietzsche, however, hardly won the future, or yet bids fair to win it. So far the catastrophes have underscored chiefly the irrational, illiberal, inhumane tendencies of his thought. "Politics on a grand scale will date from me," he boasted; but the grandest of his political disciples have been such supermen as Mussolini and Hitler. Although he almost certainly would have despised them, especially Hitler, they and their followers could draw on much of his doctrine, and as much loose or wild talk. In celebrating the will to power he specifically celebrated "strong and dangerous instincts," including egoism, foolhardiness, revengefulness, and rapacity, and he laid it down that "exploitation" was the law of life; as a gloss he suggested that "a good war halloweth any cause." He also celebrated "the will to illusion," remarking that it was "nothing but a moral prejudice that regards truth as of more value than illusion"; his scorn of the cowardly "slave morality" could readily embrace those who might prefer a respect for truth to the illusions and moral prejudices of a Hitler. Above all, Nietzsche attacked democratic principles point-blank, lumping them with Christian principles as only another form of slave morality. He could never stomach the "illusion" of equality; his pages are lurid with his contempt of the common people, his hatred of "the herd" (not to mention his fierce antifeminism—the emancipated woman was too much for the superman). His own moral prejudice supported the myth of the elite that would be popularized by Mosca, Pareto, and others: the presumption that the few who dominated the great majority throughout history, or who now wished to dominate it, were necessarily superior, entitled to great power and privilege, even though men have never been able to agree on uniform standards of superiority, and the historic record bore out Nietzsche's admission that the supermen had always grown degentrate, now needed special protection against the herd.

It is impossible to assay the total influence of Nietzsche, determine which of his heady teachings chiefly affected thought. But since with our hydrogen bombs we simply can no longer afford rule by his supermen, any free play of the "dangerous instincts," even a "good war," I assume that the last word should be a sober reflection on his irrationalism. In his tirades he anathematized such indispensable qualities as public spirit, temperance, modesty, sympathy, kindliness, altruism, and brotherly love. Except for the respect his aristocrats accorded those like themselves, he degraded the basic virtues of sociality by labeling them all "herd instinct." The issue here is not merely his contempt for Christian and democratic idealism, but his basic conception of man. In asserting that the will to power was the distinctive essence of man, he spoke out of a cultural tradition going back to Hobbes, characteristic of a highly competitive society, in his day supported by social Darwinism, and due to get further support from psychoanalysis; Alfred Adler would make this will the key to human behavior. Nevertheless, by Nietzsche's own account it did not actually appear to be the primary drive, since he was forever railing at the masses of men who were slaves instead to the herd instinct, and his concept was no less questionable if one adds that what he really meant was that the will to power was the source of the best in man. His own ideal superman looked more like a Renaissance artist than a warrior, and he obviously despised most of his contemporaries who were most freely indulging this will, in business, politics, and nationalistic diplomacy; but he provided no rational criteria for making these necessary distinctions. He could not because he had made the essence of man a nonrational instinct, more akin to the aggressive instincts of other animals than to the distinctive nature of a social animal with powers of mind. Mill's basic concept of man as a potentially rational being was at least as valid, and his ideal of reasonableness more clearly suited to the needs of a civilized society. All we have learned about the powers of the irrational has only made it clearer that we cannot afford to sneer, as Nietzsche did, at "the party of humanity."

Similar issues were forced by the intuitionism of the more humane

Bergson, who was once much more popular too. To begin with, he exalted intuition as a complement rather than an enemy of intellect, and the means to a more genuinely empirical philosophy than positivistic science was inspiring. He conceived it as instinct that had evolved into a kind of "intellectual sympathy," suited to the pragmatic, creative uses of mind, which "glimmers wherever a vital interest is at stake," and now and then throws a piercing light into the darkness that intellect cannot penetrate. Always it represented the claims of immediacy, concrete experience of flow and quality, as a mode of valid knowledge. For restoring these claims William James hailed Bergson as the "Copernicus" of modern philosophy. Others called him the first modern philosopher to "take time seriously": not only the evolutionary process but "pure inner duration" as the essence of man's life, the key to the unity of the self; time as "incarnate," the whole past remaining present in the depths of the unconscious self; or simply time as felt and lived, not measured by the clock. Literary men found his intuitionism especially congenial because it rescued art as well as philosophy from the negations of positivism, asserting that art was not only a significant way of knowing reality but a means to deeper insights, fuller consciousness, and real understanding instead of mere explanation. Bergson further dignified the powers of intuition by making it the clearest proof of human freedom: it explained why men may suddenly break away from habit and convention, and especially at moments of crisis make up or change their mind "without any reason, and perhaps even against every reason," which may sometimes be "the best of reasons." He himself was led toward religion, specifically Roman Catholicism; but throughout the troubled political times in which he lived, from the Dreyfus affair to Vichy France, he remained a liberal and a democrat.[16]

Most of his French disciples, however, ended as political reactionaries. Although Bergson remarked that any beginner would always find it easy to criticize his intuitive philosophy, the obvious trouble remained that his followers could as easily use it to justify any old belief, especially absolutisms weak in rational claims to validity. At best it had no further philosophical use for purposes of either knowledge or social action, for it could explain nothing beyond the strictly ineffable truth it asserted—explanation, like analysis, was the business of mere intellect or science. Its most apparent use was to resist the claims of reason and

---

16 In his last testament Bergson stated that he would have formally joined the Church except for his fear of discomfiting his fellow Jews, then being persecuted by the Nazis. Meanwhile the Church had put his works on the Index.

science. Bergson himself tended to support such hostilities by insisting that intellect limited man's vision, distorted or to some extent falsified reality, and that only intuition could give real understanding, grasp the essential truth. Like Nietzsche, he provided no rational basis for criticizing its claims—dealing with all the different things, including some patent absurdities, that men have "known" by intuition. On his grounds almost anything might go, and as usual the irrational went most smoothly. Sorel, who came under his influence as well as Nietzsche's, may illustrate why most thinkers who share Bergson's belief in liberal democracy do not lament the sharp decline in his popularity and prestige that set in well before his death.

To my mind, the values of his thought were much clearer in the pragmatism of his admirer William James. True, James also remains easy enough for beginners to criticize. In locating the truth of an idea in its practical consequences, or "cash value" in experience, he plainly tended to slight the claims of logic, minimize the crucial problem of determining the consequences of beliefs, and cash in too quickly on congenial beliefs. Thus in arguing that when evidence is insufficient we must consult our "passional nature," whose needs give us a right to believe, he said, "God means that you can dismiss certain kinds of fear"; but so does a belief in good fairies or black magic, God means too that you may catch other kinds of fear, and only God knows what belief in him has meant or may mean altogether. Like Bergson, James opened the door to anti-intellectualism for the many men who are all too eager to trust their intuitions or their passional natures. Yet his pragmatism stipulated much more discipline. While recognizing the limitations of intellect, he never disparaged its claims or handed philosophy over to any "higher" faculty; he recognized as clearly its absolute necessity for knowing and dealing intelligently with concrete problems. Himself trained as a scientist, he fully respected the scientific spirit and always kept an eye on the "irreducible and stubborn facts." If his pragmatism was not rigorous enough to deserve the name of "method" he gave it, it nevertheless meant constant checking of intuitions or passional interests against all available evidence. In particular, it meant a rejection of all pretensions to ultimate certainty, absolute knowledge, or Bergson's intuitive intimacy with ineffable reality. It denied any claims to truth that would block further inquiry.

All in all, James suitably capped the philosophical enterprise of the nineteenth century by aspiring to totality instead of unity. Unity was no doubt the more obvious need, but as obviously philosophers were still inclined to impose it by mandate, sometimes in the name of science, sometimes in defiance of science, in either case accentuating the actual disunity, making it harder to realize the pragmatic aim of philosophy stated by Santayana—"to unite a trustworthy conception of the conditions under which man lives with an adequate conception of his interests." Meanwhile James realized the possible advantages of our philosophical predicament, the wealth of new knowledge and new thought that precluded certainty and created confusion. He remained hospitable to new potentialities, eager to hang on to all real goods, impatient only of the needless negations that wasted our wealth and caused more confusion. For a free society, now able to provide the means for the life abundant, he could be a better philosophical guide because he was content to put up with a really open world of becoming, in which no issue was closed, and with a "wild world," of variety, novelty, contingency, uncertainty. He belonged with the empiricists he called "tough-minded," willing to pay the costs of his way of free speculation and adventure. As for its possible excesses, he remarked that without too much we cannot have enough, of anything; and at that he could confess as an old man that for the purposes of a mere lifetime reality isn't so damned plastic after all. But at least he had proved the real possibility of maintaining firm conviction while admitting uncertainty and insecurity, even insisting that our faiths must be "hypotheses" and must never put on "authoritarian pretensions."

No more were philosophers in general all at sea at the end of the century. Bradley, Royce, Croce, and others were carrying on the tradition of philosophical idealism, typically in a much more liberal spirit than the Germans before them. Santayana was defending "the life of reason," paying tribute to the critique beginning with Hume and Kant that had destroyed our epistemological innocence, made us aware that we are men thinking, but adding sanely that we need not be obsessed by this awareness, and that by thinking we had gone on learning much more about the natural world. Vaihinger, Pearson, Poincaré, Mach, and others were establishing the philosophy of science, refining the naïve positivism come down from Comte, making scientists more aware that they had been operating on a philosophy all along. Russell and Whitehead were embarking on the studies that would produce their elegant *Principia Mathematica,* the foundation of modern symbolic logic. Dewey was beginning to develop the pragmatism of James into his more systematic philosophy of instrumentalism, with more attention to social and political problems. In Spain, roused by the humiliation of

the Spanish-American War, Unamuno was following independently in
the wake of Nietzsche, attacking both rationalism and obscurantism in
a tragic sense of life that led back to God. Free men who wanted to know
all the answers might feel all at sea; but at least there were plenty of
life rafts and beacons about, and for the adventurous all the horizons
were open as never before. The growing awareness of the great hundred-
act morality play at least signified that men were not simply drifting
or sailing blind.

5. *Literature*

In an age dominated by business, technology, and science, one might
expect imaginative literature to be a negligible factor. So in fact have
concluded many practical men, notably scientific students of society;
sociologists gave literature little if any attention as a significant index
to sentiments, attitudes, motives, and beliefs, still less as a positive influence on thought and behavior. Yet the rulers of society—presumably
quite practical men—continued to act as if it did have an appreciable
influence. They kept it under surveillance when not censorship, while
conservatives habitually expressed alarm over subversive or immoral
books. There were plain reasons, indeed, for taking literature more
seriously than ever. With the growth of a large reading public it became
more intimately connected with the communal life than it had been
since ancient Greece, and it was still more widely discussed, much more
so than philosophy and science. In the nineteenth century, when the
novel emerged as the major literary form, it came closer to the interests
of the common reader; with the rise of realism more serious attention
was given to everyday experience and ordinary people, who in the past
had entered literature chiefly for comic purposes. Writers began dealing
directly with the social and political problems of the day in sociological
fiction and drama, creating a new genre. In all forms of literature social
criticism grew much more explicit and insistent than in any past age.
And wholly practical men like yellow journalists and advertisers—the
experts in popular psychology—began testifying to the power of art
by exploiting its crudest effects to sell their wares.

However incalculable the social influences of literature, at any rate,
I am assuming that a historian must reckon with them. Imaginative
writers have always been significant at least as spokesmen of their so-

ciety, among the primary sources for inquiries into the values of a society. In an age of wide publicity, constant ferment, and wholesale
revaluation they surely affected sentiments and attitudes as much as
literature may, especially because they were so often bent on ferment-
ing.[17] I also assume that even apart from popular literature, to be
considered later, their influence was not necessarily wholesome or liberating. Like the intelligentsia as a class, the major writers ran the whole
gamut from reactionary to revolutionary. Because so many felt impelled
to set up as critics or judges of society, we must first look into their
credentials for this role—the basic reasons why their insistent criticism
should be heeded, and why discounted.

Now, creative writers as such were not especially qualified for an
understanding of history, government, the economy, science, or the
underlying causes of revolutionary change. Given the long aristocratic
tradition of high culture, we might expect many to be overly hostile
to their new kind of society and the new audience they were dependent
on. While naturally tending to resent the reign of business and material
interests, they might be too jealous of all competitors for their traditional prestige, and too disdainful of the material goods their readers
rejoiced in. At the same time, they ran some risks because of their emancipation from tradition, the breakup of the ready-made aesthetic and
philosophical premises on which the great writers of the past had usually operated. As realists they might only record the surface appearances,
the forms of confusion, the loose sequences of one damn thing after
another. When seeking to get down to fundamentals or deal with the
"big" questions, they might suffer from strain, lacking powers of
thought not required of artists in more settled societies. Because they
were more sensitive and imaginative than most men, they might succumb to idiosyncrasy or freakishness; and they were always liable to
emotional excesses, all the fever symptoms of their society.

By the same token, however, we might expect to find many on the
growing edge of society. They were more sensitive than most practical
men to both the good and the evil potentialities of all the material
progress for broad human purposes. But creative writers also had special

---

[17] To give these statements a proper objective or scientific air, I cite a contemporary
sociologist who has discovered the relevance of literature for his professional purposes:
"The literary creator has the ability to identify with wide ranges of experience, and he
has the trained capacity to articulate through his fantasy the existential problems of
his contemporaries." Further evidence of the power and prestige of literature, incidentally,
is that in the nineteenth century scientists, like statesmen and all public figures, were
still expected to write a civilized prose.

qualifications as social critics simply because of the dominant forces in the modern world, which made their say not less but more important. Their natural subject matter was the qualities of immediate experience, the particular, the concrete, the personal—all that was left out of the quantitative abstractions of industry and science, often sacrificed to the drive to technical efficiency. In particular they were concerned with the individual, the person who ranked so high in democratic theory, but who was being belittled in thought by the growing preoccupation with impersonal forces, menaced in daily life by the growing pressures of mechanized industrialism and a mass society. Always they were concerned with values, or the ends of freedom, which practical men tended to slight, social scientists were learning to ignore on principle, and logical positivists would declare were none of the proper business of philosophy either. Since they dealt with the all-important realities of love and hatred, joy and sorrow, hope and fear, and the all-encompassing fate of mortality, the very advance of science and technology heightened the possible value of literature as a means of translating the revolutionary new ideas and conditions of life into the terms of these abiding sentiments and common understandings. Ideally, writers might naturalize and humanize the new meanings, make men feel more at home in their revolutionary world; but in any case this was the need they addressed, most of the greater ones quite consciously, no less when they resented or rejected the terms of modern life.

So let us consider the dictum of Lionel Trilling: "Literature is the human activity that takes the fullest and most precise account of variousness, possibility, complexity, and difficulty." I should say that most modern literature falls short of this standard, but that it nevertheless compares favorably with most social science and political philosophy (not to mention political oratory and popular sermons). In any case, this seems to me a useful standard by which to judge writers in so far as they offer a criticism of life. It is especially pertinent for liberals, who typically have had a live sense of possibility, a somewhat restricted sense of variousness, and often too little sense of complexity and difficulty, but it may expose as clearly the limitations of supposedly more realistic conservatives. It prepares us for the usual ambiguities as we survey some of the major trends in a literature marked by much more diversity, conflict, and confusion than usual.

The realistic novel, the first distinctively "modern" genre, was essentially a quite natural, understandable development. With Balzac, Stendhal, and Flaubert realism began as not only a revulsion against the extravagances of the Romantic movement but an appropriate effort to portray the new society that was emerging. The *Human Comedy* was especially suited to the age as a monumental secular work in prose, never so lofty as Dante's *Divine Comedy*, yet an even bolder enterprise, vaster in scope than any work before it. As a self-styled "doctor of the social sciences" or "zoologist" of his society, Balzac also pointed to the scientific impulse that stimulated the growth of realism, corresponding to the effort of historians to tell "what actually happened." Another appropriate stimulus was a kind of democratic impulse. While Balzac chose his protagonists from the middle class, Stendhal introduced a plebeian hero in *The Red and the Black*, and later realists conferred the dignity of serious artistic treatment on humble peasants and proletarians. Such diverse writers as Dickens, Zola, Hardy, Hauptmann, and Tolstoy alike declared in effect, and sometimes in so many words, that before art as before the law all men were equal. Hardy went so far as to say that the tragedy of his obscure Wessex folk could attain a majesty and grandeur "truly Sophoclean."

By now we all know that realism may cramp imagination, and that it has inspired a great deal of dreary, superficial, mechanical fiction, lacking any suggestion of majesty or grandeur. Hence we may forget that it can also be a mode of emancipation, and that first it let in much light and air. Flaubert created a sensation with *Madame Bovary*; the lawsuit against it as an "immoral" work was a landmark in the struggle for literary freedom. Likewise the furor stirred up by Zola, and in drama by Ibsen, helped to establish the right of authors to deal freely and frankly with subjects that respectable people preferred to ignore or hush up. Youthful readers in particular can testify how liberating or even exhilarating honest, unsparing realism may be—and today still is in lands, such as Turkey and Latin America, that are only beginning to develop a genuinely native literature.

But from the outset realistic fiction was shot through with deeper ambiguities. Balzac, Stendhal, and Flaubert, all still romanticists at heart, were not really fond of homely reality or humble folk, and much less fond of the bourgeois. The *Human Comedy* was a devastating analysis of a society now ruled by bourgeois money values, *Madame Bovary* a more mordant expression of a loathing of them. While announcing what was to remain a major literary theme ever after, Balzac and Flaubert were also typical, however, in that they were themselves bourgeois, and knew the bourgeois so intimately because they had something of their mentality. Balzac especially not only pleased them by his addiction to loud colors, shrill tones, and melodrama, but was awed by their success, shared their fear of the masses, and indeed was politically less liberal, more devoted to monarchy and the Catholic Church; he often seemed frightened by the implications of his radical analysis of society, which would attract Karl Marx, since it suggested little real variousness or any but evil possibility. He brings up a common difficulty in assaying the influences of literature, that writers are generally much profounder as artists than as social thinkers, and that revolutionary artists or unconscious rebels may be avowed political reactionaries. Balzac's chief social influence may have been on Marx and others who saw in the future only one possibility—the doom of the bourgeois.

Beyond the obvious but always difficult question of how truly the realist portrayed his society, or plumbed its depths, lay a further complication: to whom and for whom was the writer speaking? In the past the greater writers had usually assumed that they were speaking for their society as a whole, if not to it, or when most aristocratic they were addressing those who counted, the rulers of society. Given a much larger reading public, the answer was less clear except for those (like Walter Scott) who were content to be popular entertainers. The many writers hostile to the bourgeois were attacking what was on its way to becoming the ruling class, while generally they were not addressing the aristocracy that might still dominate the government and high society. Most no doubt still assumed that they were writing on behalf of Man, even apart from those who would specifically take up the cause of the common people. But some were writing more consciously on behalf of an elite that was not in power; so they were likely to feel both proud and unhappy. "What's the good of all this?" wrote Flaubert to a literary friend. "Is our chatter the answer to any need? Between the crowd and ourselves no bond exists. Alas for the crowd; alas for us, especially." Alas indeed for such self-conscious literati, for still other reasons. The most gifted of them were by no means so ineffectual as they sometimes felt, being due to have a substantial audience, mostly drawn from the bourgeois, and a wide, lasting influence; but they were also more limited than they realized, more at fault for their woes.

This theme was foreshadowed by a fundamental difference between Balzac and his fellow rebel Stendhal. The individual, wrote Balzac, "exists only in relation to society"; and in the sociological novel he fathered the individual would often be reduced to a mere specimen, typically quite unheroic. By contrast, Stendhal's plebeian hero was an archindividualist. While as an acute psychological study *The Red and the Black* anticipated the preoccupation with the inner, private world, it introduced the major theme of the individual versus society. Emphasis would naturally fall on the uniqueness of the individual, the actual freedom he exemplified and the further freedom he aspired to; the sympathies of writers would generally be with the rebels against convention. Stendhal both complicated and confused the issues, however, by his romantic kind of individualism, making his hero a self-conscious immoralist, and implying that the individual could be himself only by realizing what distinguished him from his fellows, disregarding what united him to them, or all that he owed to his society. He himself subscribed to the romantic cult of the hero, and of the artist as by nature a rebel in advance of his time. (He seemed pleased by the idea that he would not be understood until 1900.) This very self-consciously superior individual was in for trouble, perhaps more than he was worth. While likely to be undemocratic, contemptuous of the "common herd," he was liable to loneliness, estrangement, alienation, and so might become a neurotic specimen—not really freer after all than the guinea pigs in some sociological novels. In *Letters from the Underground* Dostoyevsky would present a more acute analysis of a man who gloried in his individuality, and who was wretched in it, deliberately did evil because he could think of nothing better to do with it, and thereby only intensified the purposelessness of his life.

In Flaubert such romantic individualism took another paradoxical form of some consequence. His famous doctrine of impersonality, requiring that the novelist keep out of his story and let it speak for itself, might suggest an ideal of objectivity in keeping with the scientific impulse of realism; but for him it was rather a matter of artistic purity, in keeping with his dream of an ideal literature without subject matter— a doctrine of art for art's sake that anticipated the complete repudiation of both realism and bourgeois society. Artistry alone could compensate for the mean materials of *Madame Bovary* and *The Sentimental Education*; having deliberately chosen romantic nonentities for hero and heroine, the artist was the great individual in these novels. Flaubert's apparent obsession with such materials then raises a further question. His much admired portrait of Emma Bovary (which incidentally strikes me as somewhat overdrawn, not very subtle) was scarcely representative enough to warrant the popular conclusion that "Bovaryisme" or self-deception was the key to the whole century. One may suspect some self-deception in Flaubert himself, or at least a blindness to the more significant possibilities—for better and worse—of a society much more various, complex, and dynamic than his novels intimate. His disgust with it drove him to write historical novels, seek escape into the past, but *Salammbô* was as wanting in compassion and love; it made plainer that he stood for no clear ideal of human dignity, no positive cause other than art. Hence one may have some reservations about the incessant criticism of the bourgeois, as the natural enemy of the artist, that Flaubert helped to make the mode. I judge that it was on the whole a healthy influence, calling attention to the very real threats to personal freedom, integrity, and dignity. Nevertheless it could be a mechanical attitude, suggesting a deficient sense of "possibility, variousness, complexity, and difficulty."

In this regard the not at all "fine" art of Zola was considerably more complex and profound. His "naturalism" marked the entrance of the proletariat into literature as the protagonist, and with it of all the ugly, sordid, brutish detail that made him known as the "Slimy Giant." His theory that a novel should be a thoroughly impersonal, objective laboratory experiment was also the clearest illustration of the possibly deplorable influence of scientific thought on literature; his gigantic *Rougon-Macquart* cycle (twenty volumes) was intended as a complete demonstration of the workings of heredity and environment, the determinism proclaimed by Taine. But Zola too was a much better novelist than thinker. Despite his elaborate appearance of impersonality, his sympathies were unmistakably with the downtrodden, and he was not actually a thoroughgoing determinist either, concluding instead that with the aid of science social conditions could and should be greatly improved; so the Slimy Giant ended, ironically, in the warm mist of utopian socialism. First, however, he had presented the fullest, most precise account to date of the complex issues of industrial society. His *Germinal* is not only a terrifically powerful but an admirably balanced, comprehensive rendering of a class struggle, more penetrating than any study to be found in classical economics, and more just and humane than the Marxist version. The bourgeois who appear here are diverse types and are also treated with some sympathy.

By comparison the social novel in England was a pretty tame affair. Mrs. Gaskell, Kingsley, Dickens, and others wrote vividly and sympathetically of the industrial poor but with limited understanding, clouded by fear of radicalism and possible violence, or of any political program for emancipating the poor. The most to be said for their novels as social studies is that they represented an important innovation, were suited to the English temperament and political tradition, and possibly enlisted more effective sympathy for the cause of social reform than more militant, radical works would have done. The mid-Victorian novel in general was likewise sharply limited in its realism, and more a reflection than a searching criticism of its society. We who have been "born to the superior condition," wrote Trollope, look with "awe and horror at the misery of many of our brethren"; but he concluded this digression with a reminder that "this inequality is the work of God," and that the idea of equality was naturally offensive, suggesting communism and "insane democracy." When Thackeray entered a long public debate over whether it was a writer's duty to show "the whole truth" or only its agreeable, edifying aspects, he defended the popular conclusion: writers should aspire to purity, they had no right to introduce the sordid. (In *Vanity Fair* he suggested some ironic reserve: "We shall only hint at the existence of vice and wickedness, in such a light, easy, agreeable manner that nobody's fine feelings will be offended.") Except perhaps for George Eliot and Meredith, who gave fiction more intellectual content, the major novelists presumably had little effect on basic attitudes, sentiments, and beliefs beyond dignifying them, at best refining them; certainly they conveyed no deep sense of complexity or difficulty. No more did the most popular Tennyson in poetry. In *In Memoriam* he expressed the gnawing doubts of his age, which were actually undermining the foundations of its faith, but he gratified his readers by resolving all doubts, giving a lofty moral tone to the general incapacity to follow through a line of thought to a disagreeable conclusion.[18]

Literary intellectuals, however, were much more critical of their society, especially its culture. From Carlyle on, they were as deeply concerned in their way as Balzac was over the new society, now in full bloom. The way of Carlyle became notoriously illiberal, authoritarian, proto-Fascist, in the worst tradition of Romanticism; he introduced the theme of utter contempt for "the masses" to which writers would remain susceptible. But his chief influence on later critics derived from his initial attack on "Industrialism" (a word he coined) and the new

---

[18] Lest all this seem simply disparaging, let us remember that many a masterpiece— the *Divine Comedy, Hamlet, Phaedra,* and *Paradise Lost,* to name a few—has had negligible influence on its age, and has been less significant as a portent of either literary or social movements than have some lesser works. If greatness may make more difference in the long run, its influence is usually less obvious. *Vanity Fair* seems to me one of the great novels whether or not it stirred up its readers. As for the obtrusive wholesomeness of the Victorians, one might note a morbid strain in the modern temper: the greater Victorians became interesting only when it was realized that many were not really placid, but were torn by doubt and disquiet, premonitions of the fashionable *Angst* to come.

"Mechanical Age," with its faith in machinery, its worship of Power (to which he himself succumbed), its principle of "Cash Payment as the sole nexus" between men, its spiritual poverty, and so on. This was the heart of Matthew Arnold's criticism of a "mechanical and external" civilization, infested with "philistines" who declared the greatness of England in terms of its wealth and power. To it he opposed his ideal of culture, "sweetness and light," or somewhat more specifically, "the harmonious expansion of all the powers which make for the beauty and worth of human nature."

Celebrated though this ideal is, Arnold was apparently quite ineffectual, since all the tendencies he deplored have grown still stronger. Today he may seem more ineffectual because of his typically Victorian limitations. Apart from his priggishness, he had something of the mentality of the middle class he was always attacking, in particular its basic complacence, disturbed chiefly by fears of the common people; he worried over the menace of "Jacobinism" or "Americanized" hordes. He had little understanding of the economy, as of culture in the broad anthropological sense of the word. Although he defined culture as right knowing and right doing, he had little to say about the necessities of doing, proposing no basic reform in social or political institutions. He bore out F. W. Bateson's observation on the Victorians, that the evils they denounced were always individual, the cure was always an appeal to the "heart" or the conscience. The evils remained, a constant source of the gnawing fears; so ordinary Victorians reassured themselves by still more stress on respectability, including the ludicrous taboos imposed on literature as on genteel conversation. (Thus no lady was ever pregnant—only "in an interesting condition," which would interest no gentleman.) Arnold met the menace by invoking the powers of right thinking, putting in a more urgent call for Culture as the main bulwark against Anarchy. One may feel that he left culture high and dry, the more so because he believed that poetry could take the place of religion too.

Yet what Arnold was saying was always important, and the more necessary because—as he knew—the forces against him were gaining strength. His ideal of culture was basically as liberal as Mill's; it was not the cultivation of belles-lettres for an elite, but a general expansion of the powers of all members of society, or an improvement of the public taste. If his failure to back his ideal with a political program exposed his limitations as a social thinker, he had some excuse in an age that put too much trust in programs or mechanical solutions. Once society had grown more democratic there remained no way of achieving Arnold's ends except the way of education, to which he had devoted his life, and which can never bring sure or quick results. His essential values became clearer when William Morris, the young Bernard Shaw, and others broadened the education he offered and supplemented it by a socialistic program. "It is the province of art," Morris now wrote, "to set the true ideal of a full and reasonable life" before the working class, a life in which "the perception and creation of beauty" would be felt as a vital need. His own efforts as an artist were somewhat anomalous, involving such creations as Morris chairs that only the prosperous could afford; but in the spirit of Arnold he deplored the popular emphasis on the "machinery" of socialism, apart from its moral and cultural ends. Their basic criticism is still to the point, having been echoed by countless writers and educators ever since; which is to say that it has not been wholly ineffectual after all.

Meanwhile the "American Renaissance" had brought America into the mainstream of European literature, and spread somewhat different influences. Emerson, Thoreau, and Whitman impressed many an ardent student abroad as individualists and spokesmen of the democratic faith, of which America was still a world symbol. At home they contributed to the national idealism by more than their affirmations. They too were highly critical of their society, by cultural standards like Arnold's, but also by earthy democratic standards.[19] But thereby they bring up a more troublesome issue. Emerson and Whitman were never long or deeply troubled, always reaffirming an optimistic faith in the cloudy terms predicted by de Tocqueville, terms uncomplicated, as Yeats remarked, by "the Vision of Evil"; and they set the liberal, democratic tradition in American letters. To this day writers devoted to this tradition have typically expressed similar visions of American life: always critical and always finally optimistic, only superficially ironic, often immature, not so much ambiguous as vague, absent-minded, or unconsciously inconsistent—in general, visions of variousness and possibility with too little

---

19 Whitman's comment on Arnold illustrates the basic difference: "Arnold always gives you the notion that he hates to touch the dirt—the dirt is so dirty! But everything comes out of the dirt—everything: everything comes out of the people, the everyday people, the people as you find them and leave them: not university people, not F.F.V. people: people, people, just people!" Arnold in turn was repelled by the yawps of Whitman, saying that to a good European his conspicuous originality was precisely his demerit. Nevertheless in *Democratic Vistas* Whitman judged American democracy by essentially Arnold's standards, denouncing its materialism and its "all-devouring" business, asserting that so far it was "an almost complete failure in its social aspects, and in really grand religious, moral, literary, and aesthetic results."

sense of complexity and difficulty. Looking back to the American Renaissance, we may be more impressed by the pessimism of Hawthorne, and especially by the rare tragic sense of Melville. Of all American novels *Moby Dick* most clearly measures up to Trilling's standard; but it was long neglected in America, its greatness was not generally recognized until after the World War. It suggests a still more troublesome thought for supporters of a free society: that of the modern writers who by general consent stand out as the writers of genius—beginning with Balzac, Stendhal, and Flaubert, and coming down to Yeats, Proust, Joyce, Rilke, Kafka, Lawrence, and Eliot—few have been liberals or democrats, and almost all have been hostile to modern civilization, expressing a dismal view of its possibilities.

And so with the great Russian literature of the nineteenth century, the most impressive addition to the Western heritage. It included such liberal, tolerant, humane writers as Turgenev and Chekhov, the latter particularly welcome because of the freshness of his art in short story and drama. But the giants were Dostoyevsky and Tolstoy. Fundamentally different in their art and thought, they were nevertheless much alike—seemingly democratic in spirit, actually ambivalent, and ultimately antiliberal.

Both preached directly a gospel of simple brotherhood and love. They never expressed disdain for the masses or the common life, instead revolting against such genteel ideals of culture as Arnold's. "Down with culture!" cried Dostoyevsky: "the thirst for culture is an aristocratic thirst"; and Tolstoy expounded his famous thesis that no art is great or good unless it is comprehensible to common men. In the name of solidarity both attacked what Dostoyevsky called the "terrible individualism" of the modern world, which estranged men from society and gave only an illusion of freedom; real human freedom could be achieved only in and through community. Alike thoroughly realistic as novelists, both proclaimed as thoroughly utopian ideals that might suggest the modern faith in progress. Dostoyevsky affirmed that "beyond all doubt" the destiny of Russia was a universal mission, to reunite all mankind in peace and love. Tolstoy became famous the world over for his pure Christian pacifism and anarchism.

Yet both attacked the whole Western way of life—not only its materialism and hypocrisy but its basic faith in progress through freedom, reason, and knowledge. Anti-intellectual and antirational, they exalted the type of the simple fool, even the apparent idiot, whose wisdom was wholly of the heart; and characteristically they denied that there was any other wisdom. Dostoyevsky was an outright political reactionary. As a novelist distinguished by his extraordinary insight into the complex depths of the human mind, he took time off to preach asinine simplicities about Holy Russia, trumpet a crude, ugly nationalism; while impressing the Western world by his revolutionary psychology, he was most popular at home as a jingo. Tolstoy's imperious "sense of reality," his forte as a novelist, engendered a kind of determinism that undermined the apparent freedom, spontaneity, and responsibility he exalted in simple folk. In *War and Peace* he furiously attacked the idea that great men made history, and went on to demolish the belief that men could ever consciously plan or control their history; he rejected all liberal optimism, all faith that by rational methods men could improve their society. As Isaiah Berlin points out, Tolstoy's skeptical realism carried him to substantially the same position as Joseph de Maistre's dogmatic authoritarianism. And at home both Dostoyevsky and Tolstoy were cast as prophets in a more profoundly ironic drama. By their common scorn of mere reform, gradualism, liberalism, and the Western way of compromise, their utopian passion for the total solution—their typically Russian all-or-nothing spirit—they helped to prepare for the triumph of communism, a heathen creed that both would have repudiated, but that proclaimed anew the universal mission of Holy Russia.

In the meantime the intense social consciousness of all the great Russian writers set off strikingly a contemporary movement in France that seemed bent on proving that Western society was as hollow and decadent as Dostoyevsky in particular made out. Mallarmé was perfecting symbolism: a "pure poetry" of image and metaphor, without logical content or ordinary significance, that aspired to convey an indefinable, mystical kind of meaning by "the alchemy of the word." This harked back to Flaubert's dream of a purely formal literature, with the least possible subject matter, ideally about Nothing. It was in line with a broader movement of art for art's sake stemming from Romanticism, which also came through Flaubert. Aestheticism assumed diverse forms in such writers as Baudelaire, Verlaine, Rimbaud, Huysmans, and the Goncourts, but all its disciples were highly self-conscious and antisocial. Its influences spread to England, where Pater and Oscar Wilde most explicitly made it a doctrine of life for art's sake. German converts to the new idolatry included Stefan George.

This whole movement may be viewed as a struggle for artistic freedom. It was a protest against both the didacticism of middle-class literature and the mechanical techniques of naturalism, which alike confused art with life and restricted imaginative freedom and spontaneity. It aspired to give literature the autonomy enjoyed by science, and with it as complete authority, by exploiting purely literary effects. Against the prevailing materialism and positivism in the world of thought it asserted the claims of not only creative imagination but sensibility and subjectivity, the knowings of immediate experience, the unique sensations and emotions of the individual. Through the modes of impressionism and symbolism it opened up new possibilities of suggestiveness and expressiveness, a more direct, intense, at best precise communication, from which almost all the greater writers of our century profited. But first and last it was a revulsion against bourgeois society: immediately against the philistinism that demanded utility of literature as of all other activity, and found it useful only for entertainment or for moral edification; more profoundly against the hollowness of life, the degradation of spirit for the sake of material progress—a dehumanization that evoked premonitions of disaster. "Need I describe," wrote Baudelaire prophetically in his private journal, "how the last vestiges of statesmanship will struggle painfully in the last clutches of a universal bestiality, how the Governors will be forced—in maintaining themselves and erecting a phantom of order—to resort to measures which would make our men of today shudder?" If aestheticism accordingly looks like a mode of escapism, this may still be a sensible way of dealing with an intolerably stuffy or decadent society, maintaining personal independence and integrity, or in time possibly making good Wilde's boast that "Life imitates Art more than Art imitates Life." At least the Ivory Tower was not simply a disreputable establishment, since in it had worked the likes of Spinoza, Newton, Kant, and Darwin—seeking truth for truth's sake.

Yet the aesthetes were deliberately turning their backs on society, disclaiming any responsibility to it, as these thinkers had not. Neither had any school of artists before them: the great ages of literature, from ancient Greece on, had never proclaimed the ideal of art for art's sake. It was unmistakably a sympathy of *malaise*. Nietzsche described it as the croaking of despairing frogs in their stagnating swamps. Gentler critics might say that the aesthetes were seeking in art a salvation that science could never offer and religion no longer had the power to assure, but that this was no go for the long run. They were themselves haunted by the fear of sterility, a prominent theme in the poetry of Mallarmé. Having defined poetry as "the language of a state of crisis," he offered only style as a response to crisis; behind the handful of poems he spent his life polishing there was little original thought. Others suffered more plainly from ennui, recalling that among the sources of the movement was Schopenhauer's exaltation of art as a mode of emancipation from will and passion. They got some satisfaction from their will to *epatér le bourgeois,* or simply to confound them by deliberately making their art difficult, and they could be as complacent as the bourgeois in their very feeling that their culture was decadent, reveling in it instead of lamenting it. "I am the empire at the end of the decadence," wrote Verlaine, who like Baudelaire before him admired the Silver Age of the declining Roman Empire. But a more suggestive epitaph on the whole movement was offered by Rimbaud: a genius who wrote his masterpieces in his teens, gave up poetry before he was twenty, spent the rest of his short life in hell, and when hearing in Africa of his fame said simply, *"merde pour la poésie."*

For the purposes of a free society, at any rate, it was hardly desirable that Life imitate this kind of pure Art, which at best was reserved for an ultraexclusive elite. As de L'Isle-Adam's hero Axel said, "Life? Our servants see to that for us." The art-for-art-sakers might have been more dismayed, indeed, by their apparent kinship with the popular literature they despised, for this too served chiefly to provide entertainment and escape. As it was, they remained unembarrassed because they were also akin in that typically they had neither a comic nor a tragic sense of life. They ignored all but artistic possibility, artistic difficulty. Since except for literary technique they represented a retreat, they were pretty much in line with Bourget, Barrès, Brunetière, and other reactionaries who were largely dominating the French world of letters toward the end of the century. Barrès indicated another possible community for the romantic individualist: having won his fame by *Le Culte du moi,* he betook his precious self to the cult of nationalism, a Fascist kind exalted by both anti-Semitism and contempt of the masses.

That the whole movement proved by no means merely sterile was due in part to the vitality of the realistic impulse. Among its offshoots was impressionism in fiction, exemplified by Conrad, Virginia Woolf, and above all Proust: a finer realism achieved by a rendering of immediate sensory impressions, and the "luminous halo" enveloping them, instead of a literal reproduction or inventory of appearances. So Proust, a follower of Mallarmé and another romantic "escapist," shut himself up with his asthma in a cork-lined room and set about recovering his whole past experience, in the course presenting a remorseless analysis of his own neurosis, and a devastating exposure of the corruption and vulgarity of his fashionable society, Another offshoot was the *Ulysses* of James Joyce, who among many other things united the techniques of symbolism and naturalism. But no less important was the predictable revulsion against aestheticism and neo-Romanticism, in a society far from stagnant. One notable consequence was the birth of modern drama—the realistic prose drama of Ibsen. Having begun with poetic, romantic plays about the "heroic" past of Norway, Ibsen went abroad in Europe, where he began to recognize and despise the aesthete in himself; the fashionable kind of "isolated aestheticism," he wrote home, "seems to me now as great a curse to poetry as theology is to religion." He proceeded to take out his disgust with sentimental romanticism in *Peer Gynt,* and then settled down to the social-problem plays that so scandalized and stirred all Europe.

These bring up another cluster of major questions about modern literature and life. Here we need not worry so much as literary critics over the problem of topical or "timely" drama—its inescapable fate of becoming dated, losing some of its power. Granted that we can no longer be so thrilled as our grandparents were when Nora slams the door on her husband at the end of *A Doll's House,* declaring her right as a woman to a life of her own, the main point for a historian remains that she did thrill or shock our grandparents, that Ibsen accordingly helped to win for women rights now taken for granted, and that by his boldness he also helped to give writers more freedom, the right to dramatize unconventional issues.[20] Similarly *Ghosts,* which no longer strikes us as a revolutionary play, was in its day rightly hailed as "the beginning of a new literary era." But as a realistic bourgeois tragedy it raises issues of lasting concern in a history of freedom.

Most obviously it represented a drastic reduction in tragic drama. Whereas the scene in Greek and Shakespearean tragedy had been a

---

[20] As an erstwhile literary critic I might repeat, however, that a responsible artist need not worry over his interest to posterity, that he can be respected even if he speaks powerfully only to his own age, that timeliness is not necessarily fatal to enduring interest, and that even the "timeless" classics all contain some dead wood—topical references that cannot have for any but scholars the live meaning that they had for the audience they were addressed to. It seems remarkably easy for literary scholars to forget that the great Athenian dramatists, for example, were in fact Athenians and were not writing simply for and about Man, but were dealing with political, moral, and religious problems of particular interest to their fellow Athenians, in terms not always of such vital significance to readers today. For that matter, we can never be altogether certain just what any classic meant in its day, except that it could not possibly have all the meaning that generations of critics and scholars have read into it.

In my discussion of Ibsen I am adhering to the main ideas I expressed in *The Spirit of Tragedy.*

palace or a public place, it was now a bourgeois parlor. Oedipus and Hamlet had dwindled into Oswald, a helpless, unheroic victim of syphilis inherited from a dissolute father. The spectator was no longer stirred to broodings over the first and last questions of the meaning and purpose of man's life, but was left with some ideas about the falsity of conventional bourgeois marriage, and the once unmentionable "social diseases." Instead of splendid poetry he listened to everyday prose. And these restrictions were a quite deliberate choice by a mature artist (Ibsen was over fifty at the time): he had concluded that modern life did not permit grandeur. Certainly there was little grandeur or splendor in most of the realistic or naturalistic plays that flooded the theater thereafter. Generally they were true to commonplace life, often they spotlighted its drab, mean, ignoble, or sordid aspects; their protagonists had little stature or force, and when not commonplace were likely to be either base or neurotic. They might excite pity, sometimes indignation, but scarcely awe. By and large realistic tragedy, or tragicomedy, was not designed to lift the spirit, heighten the capacities of free men to ponder deeply, feel greatly, or aspire loftily.

Yet Ibsen had good artistic reasons for his choice, which was not simply a restriction. In concentrating on contemporary social problems he was first of all widening the scope of drama. The artist could hope to illumine the distinctive conditions of modern life, deepen and intensify awareness of them, convey the poignance, the terror, and the wonder of the familiar—as some of the greater realists have done. *Ghosts* itself was not actually so prosaic and so limited in import as may at first appear. One source of its power is its "timeless" theme of remorseless, fated doom—the tragic logic of the inescapable consequences of evil, here the ancient idea of the sins of the fathers. Its bourgeois parlor is haunted by the larger meaning suggested by its symbolic title and made explicit by Oswald's mother: the ghosts of all sorts of "old dead beliefs," which are especially troublesome in the modern world, but have haunted the living in all periods of marked change. The parlor looks out on mountain peaks that at the end are lit by a rising sun, suggesting the radiant life she had aspired to, and recalling another ageless theme she had stated: "We are so miserably afraid of the light, all of us." *Ghosts,* like all the social plays of Ibsen, was an effort immediately to emancipate men from bourgeois conventionality, ultimately to free them from such fear of the light—to help them to discover their real selves, or their true human condition.

More disturbing, accordingly, is the stark pessimism of the tragedy.

"I cannot bear it!" shrieks Oswald's mother, and as the curtain falls she stares at her doomed son in "speechless horror." There is no apparent reconciliation or acceptance here, but only shock, then a numb despair. Hence it is repeatedly said that modern writers are quite incapable of writing genuine tragedy. Greek and Shakespearean tragedy had been in some sense an affair with the gods, in a universe ruled by some kind of divine or moral order, however mysterious; but there is no such order in Ibsen. Like Conrad and others, he senses only an "immense indifference," the utter insignificance of man in a soulless universe; no flights of angels sing the modern hero to his rest. Worse, we are told, writers can no longer see a tragic dignity in man's fate because they cannot respect the human spirit, much less create heroes with the splendor and stature of the tragic heroes of yore. They know that like the wretched Oswald, men are victims of heredity and environment. They have since learned that man is a creature of glands and hormones, reflexes and complexes, never really master of his soul. What was once an affair with the gods has therefore come down to an affair with the bourgeois neighbors or bosses, a mean environment, or with as mean a self, enslaved by ignoble or neurotic impulse. And this is a matter of vital concern for a free society. It might get along without tragic drama, as throughout history most societies managed to do; but it can hardly hope to flourish without a belief in the dignity and worth of man.

Again, however, the realistic tragedy heralded by Ibsen was not in fact simply bleak and mean, nor an invitation to mere despair. *Ghosts* bears out his own statement of his pessimism, that he did not believe "in the everlastingness of human ideals," but did firmly believe in man's capacity for idealism; for he was implying here that men were fit for a better life, they need not be so afraid of the light, the evil was to some extent remediable. At the same time he was facing up to the actual complexity and difficulty of the human condition today. Modern tragedy, in both novel and drama, may be regarded as a proper development of the basic realism of Greek and Shakespearean tragedy, in terms of modern knowledge and experience; for the immense universe known to us is not clearly governed by a divine or moral order, we have learned much about the hereditary and environmental forces that do largely determine the fate of most men, and we know more precisely why the human condition may often be actually helpless and hopeless. "If way to the Better there be," the realist may say with Thomas Hardy, "it exacts a full look at the Worst." Nevertheless, he may still respect the human spirit. Writers have often stressed the dignity of obscure, humble people, like

Hardy's Wessex folk, Hauptmann's Drayman Henschel, Chekhov's three sisters, and Dreiser's Jennie Gerhardt—all of them greater than their fate. The most pessimistic Conrad most nearly recovered the splendor of high tragedy. Altogether, modern tragedy lacks the magnitude and resonance of Greek and Shakespearean tragedy, and may not give so exalted a pleasure; but at its best it may still provide an experience comparable in kind, and has at least retained the essential faith in the dignity and worth of the human spirit.

As for Ibsen himself, finally, what fired so many of his followers was his scorn of mean convention and his passion for personal independence, as the supreme value of life. This stemmed from the tradition of romantic individualism, and as Marxists pointed out, it was backed by no social or political program. (Political radicals joined conservatives in denouncing *Ghosts*.) In reply Ibsen observed that they wanted only liberties, not liberty. But his most effective reply was a vision much more complex and ironic than theirs. He had already demonstrated in *Peer Gynt* that romantic individualism could be mere egoism. In *The Wild Duck* he turned on himself, mocking the ardor for social reform that had made him famous, pointing out that this too could be a mode of egoism; and his spokesman insists out of compassion that most men would only suffer from the liberty and light he always called for—they could live happily only on illusion. In his last plays, in which his protagonists are heroic personalities much like Nietzsche's superman, he dramatized the abuses as well as the costs of his gospel of individualism; by their will to grandeur or power his heroes wreck both their own lives and the lives of others. Ibsen's last hero was the artist himself, the heir of the romantic cult of genius: another egoistic idealist, but grown aware of "the fundamental duplicity of all ideal endeavor," which tends to weaken the bonds with one's fellow men, destroy "the love that belongs to the life of earth"—to obscure the elemental fact of our common humanity and common fate of mortality. In this spirit one may add that Ibsen was never conspicuous for compassion and charity, but that these qualities do dignify much modern tragedy, and that they are among other natural consequences of the realism, skepticism, and pessimism of the modern temper.

As in his later works Ibsen moved from realistic to symbolic drama, he also recalls us to the bewildering variety of modern literature. Strindberg too moved from naturalism to symbolism and expressionism, while further emphasizing that Scandinavian writers had now entered the European scene and were enriching the common Western heritage. So were Irish writers, who began cultivating their native resources instead of writing like Englishmen. National pride found less attractive expression in the chauvinism of Kipling and the flamboyant proto-fascism of D'Annunzio. Zola's naturalism, apparently dead in France, went abroad, reaching England in the early novels of Gissing and George Moore, America in the novels of Norris, Crane, and Dreiser. At the same time Henry James was refining the technique of fiction by his exquisite artistry, which incidentally supported the popular literary idea that conservatives were naturally the prime defenders of all civilized values, democrats or leftists were as naturally more or less loutish. The very urbane Anatole France nevertheless carried on the tradition of the Enlightenment, as had Renan and others before him. Bernard Shaw, the greatest disciple of Ibsen, also indicated that the liberal cause could still enlist reputable writers—not to mention the many honorable second-rate writers, indispensable to the support of any social or literary cause. Thomas Mann at last honored the much reviled bourgeois by a prose epic, *Buddenbrooks,* which like Galsworthy's *Forsyte Saga* portrayed the decline of a family over generations, showed how they were cursed by the want of beauty and love, yet treated them with dignity and also showed how in decline they produced a more sensitive generation. And so on. As the World War approached, other outstanding figures of our century were emerging—Rilke, Gide, Yeats, Joyce, Eliot, D. H. Lawrence—but there was still no great movement or clear direction in literature, only premonitions of more conflicting tendencies.

What all this adds up to by way of influence on modern society no one can say. For a judicious reader, to be sure, the total effect of literature since Balzac is an ample account of "variousness, possibility, complexity, and difficulty." It could develop a tough-mindedness too often lacking in the liberal temper, especially because writers so often dwelt on the worst in the modern world. The bewildering variety was itself to the good in a free, open society, as a sign of much independent, vigorous, bold response. On the face of it, the age was by no means so sterile or decadent as some writers made out, and was far from the stagnation that settled on Rome, Islam, and other civilizations in decline. The exceptional variety in literature was also an involuntary tribute to bourgeois society, which provided writers with not only a more substantial audience than aristocracy had in the past but a more eager one, and possibly more stimulating because it was less uniform in its tastes, less set in its ways. Writers who were little appreciated in their lifetime—Melville, Kierkegaard, Nietzsche, Rimbaud, Henry James—were for that reason more extravagantly honored later on. No previous society was ever so eager to recover and revere neglected genius. Only the shades of the great writers of all time can appreciate the spectacle that has come to seem natural: living writers—like Joyce and Eliot—being honored by whole volumes of critical appraisal.

On the other hand, the obvious trouble remains that most writers offered a partial, one-sided criticism of modern life, and most of their following were not clearly judicious readers. We are confronted by a welter of conflicting influences that mostly tended to generate or confirm too simple, narrow a view of either possibility or difficulty. The endless experimentation may look feverish when not faddish. And uncertainty about the dominant influences might be heightened by the growth of a kind of inconclusiveness in literature itself, due to the breakup of traditional forms and modes that had reflected a common-sense view of life. Dostoyevsky led the way in dissolving conventional patterns of character and motive, emphasizing incongruous or seemingly inexplicable impulses; symbolists and impressionists rejected the familiar orderly kind of description, analysis, and narration; others were giving up the traditional plots with a definite beginning, middle, and end, in favor of slices of life, streams of consciousness, dream plays, and all manner of wavering, discontinuous actions. Again this whole tendency may be considered another sign of the vitality of modern literature, a recognition that the "reality" of immediate experience is much more complex, mysterious, and elusive than it seemed to earlier realists; or it may be considered another reflection of the immense confusion and uncertainty of modern life.

At any rate, it had deep correspondences that suggest a significant enough conclusion for my present purposes. It was anticipated by impressionism in painting, paralleled by the development of nonrepresentational art and by the broken rhythms and dissonances of modern music. Historians too were realizing that there is no such thing as plain, unvarnished fact. Sociologists were exploring nonlogical behavior, undermining the common sense of traditional social thought. William James pointed out that conventional analysis obscured or falsified both the inchoate, incoherent elements of consciousness and its vital unity. Freud was opening up the world of the unconscious, revealing that the reality of mental life was quite unlike its appearances. Physicists were giving up the materialistic, positivistic concepts of scientific common sense, and were demonstrating that physical reality was fantastically different from appearances. Creative writers were not directly influenced by all these developments, but as sensitive men they caught the pervasive awareness that the traditional modes of apprehending or representing reality were inadequate. Ideally, they were helping to reorient their readers to the new perspectives on man, society, and the natural world.

6. *Religion*

Although the tardy consideration of religion in this chapter may seem irreverent, the excuse for it is simple: the nineteenth century was surely not a great age of religion. Christianity was far from being a major inspiration in its political, industrial, and intellectual revolutions. Rather, it suffered from all of them, since all fostered the growth of the most secular culture known to history. Long before Nietzsche announced "God is dead," Kierkegaard, now recognized as the most original Christian thinker of the age, wrote that for Martin Luther's 95 theses he substituted just one—"Christianity does not exist." Actually, of course, it was always a real force; the current religious revival is only the latest in a series of revivals; and even the many godless men owed much to the traditional faith for their new gods. Nevertheless, the devout are the first to emphasize the decay of religious faith. Otherwise religion was an important factor chiefly because of one unflattering reason for this decay, that the leading churches opposed rather than led the movements toward democracy, social justice, and intellectual freedom. Toward the end of the century they began changing their policies, suiting them to the changes that had taken place in the sentiment and belief of many of their followers; but this was strictly a tardy response, not a spontaneous, independent spiritual movement. One can fully appreciate the significance of these changes—the support now given by most of the churches to the cause of democracy—only by reviewing the tedious story of their prolonged hostility to this cause.[21] Or to cite Paul Tillich, "The first word to be spoken by religion to the people of our time must be a word spoken against religion."

---

[21] In what follows I am substantially recapitulating my *Religion and Freedom in the Modern World*. I should add that in condensing so much I may give more offense to the devout, since I cannot fully qualify all my generalizations and bald statements of fact, and in particular I cannot do full justice to the imponderable influences of Christian spirituality. All readers should keep in mind that I am treating here chiefly the activities of organized religion—what is always plainest in the historic record. Established churches are naturally conservative institutions, and as I have indicated, they lagged behind the advanced thought and the idealism of many of their members.

The story again begins with the French Revolution, though on a seemingly anomalous note. This provoked a widespread religious revival, from which the Roman Church especially profited; the Papacy recovered much of its political power and prestige in Europe. It appeared that Christianity had risen successfully to the challenge of the Enlightenment and the Revolution. As the Papacy proceeded to reassert its authority and tighten its control, however, it made no concessions to the popular ideals of liberty, equality, and fraternity. The revolutions of 1830 and 1848 only stiffened its opposition to demands for more popular government and civil liberties. During the pontificate of Pius IX—the longest in history (1846–1878)—the Church put up its most stubborn, uncompromising resistance to the trend of the age. On the whole it succeeded in maintaining its authority, and at least the nominal obedience of most Catholics, but at considerable cost. Anticlericalism grew most bitter in the Catholic world, especially France and Italy, the leading Catholic countries; in France the Church alienated moderate republicans as well as democrats, while in Italy the unification of the country that Pope Pius did his best to prevent left him a "prisoner of the Vatican." In the non-Catholic world the Roman Church consolidated its reputation as the major enemy of freedom.

Protestantism typically made a much more confusing record, since its many diverse sects included some that were democratically inclined, and its basic principle of individualism continued to breed rebels against the authority of both state and church. Excepting France, the cause of democracy made most progress in Protestant countries. Yet it did so without the aid of the leading churches, and against the opposition of state churches in particular. The Church of England remained politically conservative, supporting the Tory reaction to the French Revolution; its clergy provided the most solid opposition to the Reform Bill of 1832 and then to the Chartist movement. At best it only accommodated itself more gracefully than Rome to the political changes it was unable to prevent. On the Continent the Lutheran churches, the most influential of the Protestant churches, differed chiefly in their relative aloofness from political life, or placid acquiescence in the *status quo*. In Germany they remained loyal to Luther's policy of supporting monarchy, giving Bismarck and the Kaiser no serious trouble. They would give Hitler none either until he began dictating to them too.

Similarly the major Protestant churches were not in the vanguard of the related struggle for social reform, any more than was the Roman Church. Here Christian sentiment unquestionably was a powerful stimulus, most obviously in the humanitarian movement that had produced the crusade against slavery led by the Evangelical Wilberforce, and had then inspired efforts to relieve the poor. Church leaders, however, were mostly indifferent to the movements for reform when not actively opposed to them. A sufficient witness is Kenneth Latourette, author of the most optimistic history of Protestantism in the nineteenth century: after dwelling enthusiastically on the "Christian spirit" of the social re- formers, he acknowledges that they were laymen, and that they en- countered more hostility than support from high churchmen. Reformers were also distracted by the Protestant addiction to crusades against drinking and vice, the effects rather than the causes of poverty, and to popular religious revivals, which like Methodism reminded the poor that their real enemy was the Devil. Another distraction was the "Prot- estant ethic," the gospel of individualism: Protestantism was more dis- posed than Catholicism to stigmatize poverty as a failure due to indolence and shiftlessness.

Still another source of confusion was revolutionary socialism. Since most of its leaders were openly hostile to religion, all the churches tended to condemn all forms of socialism as inherently godless, and more broadly to oppose the whole labor movement. As a result they perman- ently alienated a large segment of the working class, especially on the Continent, and strengthened the appeal of revolutionary socialism. Many other workers who kept baptizing their children out of habit drifted away from the churches, whose spiritual message had little con- nection with their vital interests, much more apparent connection with the well-being of pewholders. (An American minister who in 1900 con- ducted a nationwide questionnaire to find out why workers were not going to church got an almost invariable response: the Protestant church was run by and for the rich, and went out of its way to damn labor unions and strikers.) Since prosperous businessmen felt little need of their message, the churches held their own chiefly among the petty bourgeois and the peasantry, above all in the more backward countries.

In the world of thought the story was much the same. The Roman Church opposed on principle freedom of speech and press, which Pope Gregory XVI had denounced as a "deadly and execrable liberty," and coupled with "the absurd and erroneous maxim, or rather insanity" of freedom of conscience. As naturally the Church opposed all historical, philosophical, and scientific thought that menaced its dogmas and its claims to infallibility in matters of faith and morals, which is to say that it was hostile to most of the significant thought of the century. Pius IX made a clean sweep of the distinctive faiths of the modern world in his *Syllabus of Errors,* in which he damned some eighty heresies, including not only all the basic freedoms but the faith in independent reason, in science, in progress, and so forth. The most eminent Catholic spokesmen of the time, such as Cardinal Newman, agreed with him that the liberal creed was the root evil of Western civilization. A few years later Pius rounded out his arduous career as a medievalist by putting through the dogma of papal infallibility (1870). Although this crowning affront to the rest of Christendom worried some Catholic rulers and more laymen (notably Lord Acton), it got the necessary backing from the Catholic hierarchy.

Protestantism again pursued a more confused, irresolute course. Its churches were obliged when not disposed to tolerate more freedom of thought by its initial rejection of the absolute claims of any human authority. By the same token, however, it was more dependent on the authority of the Bible, conceived as the word of God. It therefore got more conspicuously involved in the notorious conflict between religion and science, especially over the theory of evolution. As in the time of Galileo, churchmen were the aggressors in this conflict. Once more they insisted on the literal truth of Christian dogma and creation myth, implying a positive knowledge of the natural world that religion could not actually offer and had no positive need to claim. They likewise spurned a growing mass of historical evidence that the Bible was a human document, whose many authors were as fallible and inconsistent as inspired. By this defiance of new knowledge they committed the Christian faith to a humiliating war that it was bound to lose, and lose without honor. They of course failed completely to halt the advance of science, which suffered only incidental embarrassments from the conflict. Religion suffered much more from a growing doubt and disbelief.

For a free society the consequences were as much more complicated. Although science can say nothing about the question whether there is or is not a God, it plainly tended to weaken Christian faith by not only its heretical theories but its demand for evidence, its refusal to accept any belief merely on authority. The scientific spirit led to the critical, historical studies of the Bible, the foundation of Christian faith; whereas the orthodox had been pleased to believe that their religion alone was historical, all others were mythical, scholars now demonstrated that much of its dogma had no sounder historical basis. Belief in its uniqueness and purity was likewise weakened by the new study of comparative religion, or what Max Müller called the "science of religions." Well-disposed scientists, such as Durkheim and William James, proposed "explanations" of religion that might seem reasonable or flattering, but were still likely to trouble men who had taken for granted the absolute truth of their own faith. At the same time, however, these scientists made it plainer that science could never take the place of religion, except for the few for whom it was a calling. They sufficiently discredited the naïve Marxist doctrine that religion was merely class ideology. Though too many ministers were doing their best to make the doctrine plausible, religion remained among the conspicuous bonds that held society together. In the modern world there was indeed much less feeling than ever before of the "sacred" as a real power, the "Other" as a living presence; Mircea Eliade has observed that "the completely profane world, the wholly desacralized cosmos, is a recent discovery in the history of the human spirit." But most men were not yet really at home in such a cosmos, they still felt the need of religion to give their life meaning and purpose, and they might feel it even in a heavenly class society.

Hence a great many people obviously suffered when their faith was shaken. They were prey to the spreading pessimism, the feeling of the utter insignificance of man in a universe quite indifferent to him and his aspirations. They had weaker defenses against all the familiar spiritual ills of the modern world, the threats of insecurity, anxiety, and neurosis. The once unthinkable barbarities of modern warfare suggest how all feeling of the sanctity of the person may shrivel in a world in which nothing is sacred. One need not believe that the Christian faith was the historic fountainhead of the free society, or that it is essential to the preservation of such a society, to agree that it did foster some essential ideals, and that its decay has entailed some threat to the vitality of these ideals. In view of its plainly ambiguous role we can never be sure of its total effects in the past, and today we still know very little about the crucial question, to what extent it actually influences social behavior; but I assume that only a shallow materialist will maintain that its influence has been negligible, only a narrow rationalist that it has been simply an incubus, and only a naïve sophisticate that psychiatry is an adequate substitute for it.

Nevertheless, the embattled churchmen themselves may be held largely responsible for the decline of Christianity. They bore out the warning of the deeply religious Coleridge: "He who begins by loving Christianity better than truth, will proceed by loving his own sect or church better than Christianity, and end in loving himself better than all." More specifically, Coleridge warned that belief in the absolute, literal truth of the Bible was a superstition in which "there is a heart of unbelief." As it was, churchmen alienated many men of good will by their obscurantism and bigotry in defending their dogma. They damned honest doubt as a moral offense, a sin against our Lord. While they were seldom able to impose strict censorship, they exerted public pressures that could be effective because of popular ignorance and prejudice, and that amounted to a kind of terrorism, in particular against educators. Their measure of success was accordingly a doubtful boon to Christianity, but their failure a much plainer boon to a free society; for their opponents were defending not only certain theories but the principles of intellectual freedom and honesty. For such reasons the loss of faith was not always a painful experience, or simply demoralizing in its social effects. To many men (like the young Somerset Maugham) it brought a feeling of emancipation. They felt freer because of the incessant wrangling of the churches over their dogmas, the fears and hatreds stirred by mere differences in denomination, which made religion a socially disruptive force too. It is now easy to forget that in the nineteenth century the great majority of Christians still believed that a man's salvation depended on his denomination—and no less because most would have been quite unable to define and defend the essential differences between their sect and others.

Churchmen also bedeviled the issues of religion by equating it with spirituality, in effect giving it a monopoly on spiritual values, which we may all agree are essential to social health; wherefore it is essential to realize that the spirit in man that seeks beauty, truth, and goodness need not be a specifically religious spirit, as a vast deal of the world's great art and thought makes clear. The scientific spirit in particular has been more disinterested, strictly less "materialistic," than the conventional religious spirit, which has always propitiated the heavenly powers in fear or in hope of assured rewards. Likewise in insisting on the necessity of faith churchmen assumed that "true" faith was necessarily religious, and only so could really do for man; whereas democracy rose with the growth of secular, humanistic faiths, including the heretical faith in science and progress, and it is now threatened by the strictly godless faith of communism, which God knows has been fervent enough. One could argue that our supposedly faithless age suffers from too much faith. In any case religious thinkers persistently confused this issue too, for they habitually demonstrated the inadequacy of secular ideals by contrasting them with ideal Christianity, dwelling on their shortcomings in practice while ignoring the flagrant shortcomings of historic Christianity and the abiding vulgarities of popular religion. They confirmed what Whitehead in piety called the "dangerous delusion" that religion is necessarily a good thing. In particular the clergy harped on the idea that morality depended on religion, only religion could make men behave. It is very hard, once more, to size up the actual state of either morals or religion in any given society; but the historical evidence chiefly supports the conclusion one might draw from the countless sermons over the centuries on the sinful behavior of Christians, that there is no clear, uniform correlation between them. The emphasis of churchmen on the practical need or the utility of religion was a vulgar giveaway of the actual decay of Christian faith.

The plainest truth remains that throughout most of the nineteenth century the leading churches failed to provide a high order of spiritual leadership, much less of intellectual leadership. So far from being on the forefront of the age, they lagged far behind the advances in knowledge and thought, as well as social and political developments. While alienating many people, the clergy bored many more by the common irrelevance of their preaching. They seldom came to grips with the actual problem of doubt and disbelief, which was not a perverse refusal to believe but a simple inability any longer to do so; they insisted on the absolute necessity of faith by arguments that made it seem only more arbitrary or unreasonable, like the schoolboy's definition of faith as believing what you know ain't so. Similarly they failed to meet the challenge of relativism, merely reaffirming the absolute truth of the Christian gospel, a revelation that had been granted to a small minority of mankind, while they continued to disagree violently over its interpretation and its application to social, moral issues. Above all, they long evaded the primary challenge of their age, the most obvious reason why Christian faith was losing its vitality—the primacy of business and its money values. Popular thought was not seriously contaminated by the scientific spirit, after all, and public opinion always accorded Christianity a conventional respect, at least much more than it did to "freethinkers" (who in America today are still considered subversive types and kept off the airwaves); but the living faith of the ruling class was invested in a profit system that was basically inconsistent with the Christian gospel. Churchmen who attacked science were typically political conservatives, much friendlier to business interests. Protestant churchmen did most to sanctify *laissez faire,* the profit motive, and all the private property so acquired. In America Bishop William Lawrence proclaimed that "Godliness is in league with riches"—a statement hardly to be matched in

the history of any other of the "higher" religions, except possibly Mohammedanism in its most corrupt era under the Caliphs of Baghdad.

In view of this record, the eventual effort of the long-established
churches to adapt themselves to their revolutionary age may appear almost revolutionary. Under the pontificate of Leo XIII, the much more
liberal successor of Pius IX, the Roman Church began to reverse its
traditional policy of opposition to popular government. Leo issued his
encyclical *Libertas* (1888), in which he declared that liberty was a noble
gift of God befitting the dignity of man as a rational animal, and prepared the faithful for his belief that the Church could get along as well
with democracy as with absolute monarchy. He accordingly advised
French Catholics to cease warring on their Republic. In another famous
encyclical, *Rerum Novarum,* he then made clear that Catholicism had
never really approved of *laissez faire.* While opposing socialism by invoking the "natural rights" of private property (borrowing, rather oddly,
a doctrine popularized in the French Revolution), he called on Catholics
to support legislation protecting factory workers and themselves to form
labor unions. The Roman Church did not thereupon recapture the allegiance of the proletariat, still less become a stronghold of democracy;
but at least Leo made it easier for Catholics to accommodate themselves
to the modern "errors" condemned in the *Syllabus* of Pius IX, which in
democratic America most of them had not really believed were errors.
The Catholic Church in America, which was prospering mightily, had
already indicated that democracy was not a deadly heresy.

The shift in Protestantism was less pronounced because it had always
been more susceptible to the modern errors. Many of its followers had
actively supported democratic and reform movements, and more had
been taking to the faith in progress. But toward the end of the century
the clergy too grew more active. In America the "social gospel" took
hold, many a minister advocating economic reforms, some (like Walter
Rauschenbusch) even attacking capitalism itself, and all spreading the
idea that sin or evil was not merely theological but sociological. William
T. Stead had a sensational success with his book *If Christ Came to
Chicago,* and the Rev. Charles M. Sheldon a still greater one with
In His Steps, which sold more than twenty million copies; he dramatized
the idea of approaching all social problems by simply asking "What
would Jesus do?"—a question that might not yield an automatic or adequate solution, but could make Americans aware that Jesus had not
preached their gospel of wealth. In England the belated discovery of
slums helped to inspire the founding of the Christian Social Union,

which before long induced ecclesiastical congresses to take up social issues; the Lambeth Conference agreed that the Anglican Communion should join the democratic campaign for social justice. On the Continent German Lutheranism remained conservative, but there were stirrings that would eventuate in efforts to revive Christian socialism. Although Protestantism too failed to win back the working class, and would continue lining up on all sides of all issues, its leaders henceforth included proportionately many more liberals.

It also took the lead in the movement known as Modernism, an indispensable effort to come to terms with science and modern knowledge, which helped to preserve the faith of most educated Christians. This was anticipated by some liberal sects, notably the Unitarians (whose influence in America was far out of proportion to their number because of their appeal to the intelligentsia), but the most notable work was done in the shade of Lutheranism. Under the influence of the German historical schools, religious scholars embarked on the extensive researches into early Christianity that led to the "higher criticism" of the Bible as a human, historical document; while outraging the orthodox, this facilitated an accommodation with science by removing the major obstacle, belief in the literal truth of Christian mythology. Christians could then accept the Bible as divinely inspired only in a general sense. The outcome was a still wider variety of belief, confused by the always troublesome question of where to draw the line, how to decide just what teachings were divinely inspired or absolutely true. Modernism no doubt earned the reproaches of the devout by producing much vague faith, often pretty cool, far short of a deep, wholehearted commitment.[22] Many of the intelligentsia looked uneasy because they wished to preserve the poetry of Christianity at the lowest possible theological cost, and found it hard to say in so many words that the faith was *true*. Nevertheless Modernism invigorated Christianity by the attention it forced on issues that could not be evaded indefinitely, and it was hardly more confusing than the spectacle of endless clash between countless different sects all claiming the infallible authority of Scripture. It enabled educated Christians to be more wholehearted at least in that they could respect both science and religion, no longer had to keep their faith in a separate compartment from their intellectual interests, or to worry over every major advance in knowledge as simply a threat to it.

---

[22] Acceptance of the theory of evolution, for example, was eased by its popularity in the business world. Henry Ward Beecher, converted by Herbert Spencer, explained that "design by wholesale is grander than design by retail."

At any rate, Modernism was clearly beneficial for the purposes of free societies, which were already pluralistic anyway. It naturally induced a more liberal, tolerant faith. If the growth of tolerance owed a good deal to mere religious slackness or indifference, it was with many Christians a matter of firm conviction, a positive ideal. It reinforced democratic movements, since ministers liberal in theology were usually liberal in politics too. Similarly the growth of religious freedom in the nineteenth century, which was doubtless due to considerable indifference or a pre-occupation with business, was due as well to the active efforts of liberal Christians. Gladstone, for example, was instrumental in doing away with the religious tests for admission to Oxford and Cambridge; the venerable strongholds of Anglican conservatism or inertia were thrown open to Nonconformists and even to Catholics. (Lord Acton was pathetically happy when he was offered a chair at Cambridge, which as a young student he had been unable to enter.) Altogether, the values of Modernism were accentuated by the revulsion against it early in our century. The Fundamentalists who held out for the old-time Biblical religion were typically given to the old-time bigotry and prejudice, as in rural America and especially the South. Their authoritarianism tended to be more neurotic than that of Catholics, as is so apparent in the South today. They most plainly belied the popular thesis that Christianity was the cradle of our liberties, or is now their chief bulwark, by their continued efforts to censor and coerce, and their conspicuous indifference when not hostility to civil liberties.

Today liberal Christianity is more vulnerable to the charge of shallow optimism, since it characteristically took a hopeful view of human nature and adopted the faith in progress; so we may be more impressed by another of the dark prophets of the nineteenth century—Kierkegaard. Little known or heeded in his own day (1813-1855), he did not come into his own until after the World War, but meanwhile he had demonstrated that the once revolutionary religion of Christianity was still capable of producing a revolutionary thinker suited to the modern world. Kierkegaard embraced all the Protestant churches in an outraged scorn of the easy, comfortable, respectable kind of faith they were preaching to their bourgeois society, declaring that no greater injustice had been done to Christ than by naming their religion after him. He was as scornful of all efforts to make Christianity purely reasonable. Its very essence was paradox, "the absurd" in which all faith had to begin—perfectly symbolized by the faith of Abraham, who at the Lord's bidding prepared to slaughter his beloved son Isaac. More specifically, the absurd was centered in the condition of the individual or the self, the "subjective" reality that was the essential truth, the existential reality that alone should really concern a man. One had to "venture wholly to be oneself" as an individual, "alone before the face of God," aware that one was free to choose but absolutely responsible to God, never free to shift this responsibility to church, state, mankind, or any other intermediary. The last word in Emerson's gospel of self-reliance, it led Kierkegaard to his quite different, now most popular concept of *Angst*. A man could become conscious of his being only through "fear and trembling," he had to learn that "to exist as the individual is the most terrible thing of all," he had always to struggle against despair, the natural condition of man. And so on, through all the famed intricacy, elusiveness, and ambiguity of Kierkegaard's thought that we need not go into here.

We must note, however, that despite his apparent subtlety and his extreme individualism, born of Romanticism, Kierkegaard was at bottom a rigid, ultraconservative authoritarian, in the long antirational tradition of Christianity. He permitted no freedom to doubt or even to question the "incomprehensible" truth revealed in the Bible, his sole source of authority. He was as illiberal in his social and political thought, directly attacking the movement toward popular government as another sign of the dangerous "insubordination" of his fellows. As an archindividualist preoccupied with the solitary individual, he was as remote from the spirit of Jesus as were the bourgeois preachers of his day, and much further from any social gospel, offering only a way of salvation that was hardly available to common men. And though he anticipated the modern "theology of crisis" by his stress on *Angst,* he did not foresee the crisis of European civilization; unlike the godless Nietzsche, he had no historical sense to speak of. Neither did Dostoyevsky, another rebel against European civilization who now ranks with him as a major religious prophet of the century. Dostoyevsky seems more truly prophetic because of his vision of the horrors in store for the materialistic West, the universal confusion and "cannibalism" that would result from its faith in reason and science; but he coupled this with his ludicrous vision of the salvation that would come from Holy Russia, its Orthodox Church, and its peasants, with their craving for "perpetual and unquenchable suffering." It has been remarked that his famed Christian compassion embraced chiefly prostitutes, gamblers, drunkards, and such—it did not extend to ordinary, decent, hard-working people, much less to Turks, Western liberals, or any enemies of Holy Russia. Kierkegaard and Dostoyevsky are no less vulnerable to ironic contemplation than are the optimistic Christian liberals of the century.

They accordingly suggest some further incongruities, first in the notorious decay of religious faith. All along Christianity plainly had considerable influence on public opinion, conventional attitudes that might not govern actual behavior but at least affected public policy, public education, and popular culture. Protestantism in particular grew more vigorous and expansive during the nineteenth century, with many a revival; its worldly success was more remarkable because it was centered in industrialized countries, where rootless, profane cities were growing at the expense of the staid, pious countryside. Although church attendance fell off, at the end of the century the churches were generally more popular than they had been in the eighteenth century, in part perhaps for just this reason: men who no longer felt obliged to listen to routine sermons or go through the weekly motions might find it easier to retain the conventional respect for religion. If God had suffered, his ministry prospered. Nor was God really "dead," as Nietzsche thought. The broader cause of religious spirituality profited from the study of comparative religion, a growing respect for the great Eastern religions and then for primitive religion too; studies of the latter were giving men a more vivid sense of the universal idea of the "sacred" than the men of the Enlightenment had had. Christianity itself was always in the background of Western culture, pervading the thought and feeling of the intelligentsia too. Its influence appeared in not only the many religious writers and thinkers but in the opposition it generated, and the efforts to find secular substitutes for its "superstitions"; one can scarcely imagine such types as Comte, Marx, and Nietzsche in the great Eastern societies. By his furious attacks on its "slave morality" Nietzsche also recalled a truism easy to forget: almost all men, including unbelievers, still subscribed formally to Christian ethics, which we may assume counted for something despite the rather different ethics of the business world and the nation-states.

Still, the vitality of Christian tradition remained a mixed blessing. It dignified the invariable coarseness of popular religion, now a brotherhood in not only superstition but gross materialism and complacence —especially in America, where the churches were becoming perhaps most popular. Otherwise the ideal of the brotherhood of man was a less conspicuous influence than the exclusive, divisive tendencies of the churches. Religious prejudice continued to breed animosity, against Protestants in Catholic countries, Catholics in Protestant countries,

Jews in all countries. The liberal pontificate of Leo XIII did not prevent the French church from engaging in the disastrous Dreyfus affair, with the support of the Catholic press in all other countries. His successor, Pius X, officially stamped out Modernism in the Catholic Church. Most educated Protestants remained Modernists of sorts, if not under that name, but Fundamentalists were more vociferous. They dominated the popular religious revivals, led by such vulgarians as Billy Sunday.

These tendencies make more understandable the very limited success of the great missionary movement of the nineteenth century, in which all the major sects gave further proof of the vitality of Christianity. It converted only a tiny fraction of the non-Western world, made negligible inroads on the major Eastern religions. While some primitive peoples were induced to put pants on, civilized peoples were likely to be repelled by the exclusiveness of Christianity, a kind of arrogant conceit that linked it with Western imperialism. And if in most missionaries this conceit was innocent, sprung from a provincial ignorance of other religions and civilizations, it recalls that the Christian churches were not yet capable of providing enlightened spiritual leadership for a civilization that was creating One World. They were only beginning to come to terms with a revolutionary world, and showed little sense of the deepening crisis that would erupt in the World War. When this broke out, they promptly put God on the side of their country. It would take two world wars really to awaken them to the challenge of world crisis, and to stir belated efforts first of all to achieve unity in Christendom itself.

7. *The Fine Arts*

Although the abundant, original activity in the fine arts does not appear to have been so positive an influence on social and intellectual history as it was in the Renaissance, I remain disposed to believe that like literature, it too may have affected modern society more than one gathers from most historians and sociologists in our age. The arts drew not only an increasing audience in the nineteenth century but an increasingly representative one; most works were publicly displayed or performed, not confined to palace or aristocratic salon. Many were self-consciously experimental or rebellious, helping to establish the now popular idea that the artist is a born rebel and naturally ahead of his time. If such works were at first usually condemned or else simply ignored, in time they found an audience that for the same reason was more enthusiastic about them, disposed to feel emancipated by them. Whether real or imaginary, the liberating influences of art were confirmed by the spread of the Romantic concept of it as above all "creative." By now the extraordinary vogue of this term—popular in business and advertising circles too—may obscure the values of art; today any work is creative that is "different," however superficial or valueless the difference, and people forget that anybody can "create" a nuisance. But at least the vogue emphasizes that artists created much that was quite new, and that made some real difference. It suggests as well that a historian of the century may proceed without pretending to know just how much difference the fine arts made in social history. They were certainly significant at least as another index to modern society: sometimes an expression of its ruling interests and values, sometimes a revolt against them, in either case a reflection of major social and cultural developments. Whatever independent influence they had was related to these developments.

By general consent, the least impressive achievements of the century were in architecture, the most public of the arts, and so most significant for a social historian. Remembering the churches of Christopher Wren, one should begin by noting that its notorious eclecticism was not necessarily bad per se. Even those who insist on a functional or "organic" concept of art might describe the mixture of neoclassical, Romanesque, Gothic, baroque, and other styles as a variety suited to a free, pluralistic society, or to an age that was moving away from fixed canons and absolute standards. By the same token architects were by no means simply imitative either. They designed not only some buildings of recognized distinction but a few quite original ones, such as the Crystal Palace in London; they began exploring new structural possibilities by introducing the use of iron and steel; with this they developed the concept of functionalism and drew on the new profession of engineering; and at length the alliance with technology evolved a distinctive modern style, creating the skyscraper while producing such superb monuments as Brooklyn Bridge.

Yet until then the enterprise of architects had generally been far less bold and imaginative than the enterprise being displayed in both the world of thought and the world of business. They had failed to rise to the challenge of the Industrial Revolution in designing the many new buildings that were called for—factories and railroad stations, opera houses and museums, etc. In public buildings and monuments they had mostly distinguished themselves by the extravagantly poor taste for which the Victorian era, the Second Empire in France, and especially the Gilded Age in America are now famous, reaching such peaks of pure ugliness as the old State Department in Washington. While for millionaires they built spurious Rhine castles, Tudor mansions, and Swiss or French châteaux, for ordinary prosperous Americans they designed many a gingerbread house that seemed more grotesque by contrast with the comeliness and dignity of colonial architecture. At best these residences went well with the cast-iron stags and Indians on the lawn, the stuffed birds, bric-a-brac, and whatnots in the parlor, all the confectionery and upholstery, and the costumes of the ladies of the house—about the least attractive dress in all history.

Hence architects had some excuse in the limited freedom they enjoyed as servants of the public. They naturally had to cater to the tastes of their patrons, the values of a rising bourgeois who mistook gaudiness and pretentiousness for elegance and distinction; if too willingly, they gave the *nouveau riche* pretty much what they wanted, or deserved. Even such an original creation as the Crystal Palace was portentous in both senses of the word: itself a big new thing, it was designed to display the new abundance of things turned out by industry, and it presaged an era of thinginess in which quality would count for less than quantity and size, material means would become ends in themselves, and economic power would be largely separated from traditional culture. Meanwhile architects were further handicapped because little attention was yet being given to town or city planning. Capitals like Paris might be fitted out with imperial avenues and squares, compensating for the destruction of some fine old quarters, but industrial cities were not inclined to waste time and money on such public enterprise. Congested centers were more profitable, as were tenements and slums. Housing for the common people anticipated Le Corbusier's description of a home as "a machine to live in." Homes were as uniform and interchangeable as machines, though not so well designed or built —people were less demanding or less valuable than efficient machines.

Perhaps the best thing to be said about nineteenth-century architecture is that the worst about it was said in its own day, in particular by John Ruskin. In developing the still relatively novel idea of an organic relation between art and society, Ruskin inquired into the "political economy" of art and stressed that the bad taste in architecture was symptomatic of a sick society, specifically a mechanical, *laissez-faire* society governed by business values. As a typical Victorian he took a high moral line in demanding wholeness, "spiritual goodness," even nobility of the artist, and he defined the norms of a "healthy" society by as typically romantic an idealization of the Middle Ages; yet he rightly maintained that art was an index to the quality of a civilization, and that architecture especially was a public concern of vital importance. When lecturing on a suitable style for a new Exchange, to an audience that wanted the most for their money, he remarked that they did not really care about architecture, they would be happy with "the newest and sweetest thing in pinnacles"; and for a building dedicated to their "great Goddess of 'Getting-on' " he could suggest only "decorating its frieze with pendent purses," making the base of its pillars broad enough for the sticking of bills.[23] As an unabashed moralist, Ruskin went on to force most eloquently an issue of real consequence for a free society.

This was not merely the common spectacle of ugliness, in an industrial society that was creating more of it than any previous society—it was the mentality of nominally free men who accepted it as natural and normal. It was not only the millions condemned to slums, disgraceful though these were, but the millions of others brought up on drab streets, in box houses, amid furnishings lacking clean design or honest craftsmanship, with hardly a suggestion of natural or man-made beauty in the vicinity. The "basic drives" listed in our textbooks—hunger, sex, etc.—are generally visceral, and the "basic needs" feature security. Much less has been written about natural curiosity, the sense of beauty, the creative impulse, and the delight in the world about that are so apparent in children, at least before they go to school, and that suggest other vital needs. The common neglect of such needs surely tended to impede the realization of individuality, obscure both the means and the ends of personal freedom. "The great crime which the moneyed classes and promoters of industry committed in the palmy

---

[23] Because Ruskin now seems old-fashioned, it is worth recalling that he was often very bold. He told an audience of manufacturers, for example, that they had spent their entire lives encouraging public extravagance and corrupting public taste:

"Every preference you have won by gaudiness must have been based on the purchaser's vanity; every demand you have created by novelty has fostered in the consumer a habit of discontent; and when you retire into inactive life, you may, as a subject of consolation for your declining years, reflect that precisely according to the extent of your past operations, your life has been successful in retarding the arts, tarnishing the virtues, and confusing the manners of your country."

One might hope that American industrialists would ponder Ruskin's words, now that their advertisers have firmly established the idea that the primary function of an American outside his working hours is to be a consumer.

Victorian days," concluded D. H. Lawrence, "was the condemning of
the workers to ugliness, ugliness, ugliness . . . formless and ugly sur-
roundings, ugly ideals, ugly religion, ugly hope, ugly love, ugly clothes,
ugly furniture, ugly houses, ugly relationship between workers and
employers." As for political life, all history indicates that a sensitivity
to beauty is no guarantee of sweetness and light in rulers; but it can
help to induce civility. Especially in prosperous America it might have
given a higher tone to both political and social life.

Music in the nineteenth century raises more complicated issues. It
flourished as never before, calling out at least four times as many
composers as had served the eighteenth century, and still more popular
performers. The achievements of composers were in general much more
distinguished than those of architects, beginning with the towering
genius of Beethoven. The many who prefer Bach and Mozart may still
respect Beethoven and his greater followers, and applaud in particular
their development of the symphony. One of the grandest and most distinctive creations of Western civilization, the symphony helped to make
music the most cosmopolitan of the arts; all the greater composers were
performed in all countries. But most eminent were the German masters,
from Bach to Wagner. German intellectuals now popularized the idea
that the peculiar genius of the German people was musical—again supplementing the rationalism of western Europe.

We may accordingly be reminded that music has more evident effect
on people than do the other nonverbal arts, and also that its effects are
not only incalculable but variable, possibly impure, sometimes dubious.
Thus the symphony may be regarded as a supreme demonstration of
at once freedom and control in the attainment of a kind of ideal synthesis; the triumphant resolution in which it usually ends, imposing
order on the emotion it has aroused, best illustrates why both Confucius
and Plato believed that music was fundamental in education as a means
to a harmonious soul—a particular need of modern man. Nevertheless
one may suspect that many listeners experience too easy, superficial a
purge, or are too fond of the bang at the end. In the nineteenth century
music remained predominantly romantic, much more so than literature
and painting, and it built up a taste for obvious effects, involving considerable expense of form, structure, or "pure" music—what entranced
Schopenhauer, Flaubert, Poe, Nietzsche, and other refugees from the
world of logic and common sense. It developed such looser forms as
program music, "colorist" music, tone poems, and rhapsodies. Virtuosos
now won a sensational popularity, indicating that the public was more

impressed by a mastery of technical difficulties than a mastery of musical form or emotion. Another popular form was operetta, a classy mode of musical entertainment. Most popular was "grand" opera, in which musical genius was too often lavished on melodramatic librettos, magnificent voices cried out the banal sentiments of pasteboard characters, and the dying gasps that shook the rafters might justify Voltaire's remark that when a thing is too silly to be said, one sings it. Opera could be really grand, as in the best works of Wagner, Verdi, and Moussorgsky; but it got its name more obviously from the ostentation of spectacles held in baroque opera houses, and the glitter of jewels in the boxes.

Most significant for the purposes of this history was the monumental enterprise of Richard Wagner. He aspired to make opera the supreme expression of "the spirit of a free humanity" in the modern world, as Greek tragedy had been in Athens, by a comparable union of music and poetry, or more specifically of Beethoven and Shakespeare. To Wagner this was a strictly revolutionary enterprise, for whereas the Greek theater had been unaffectedly communal, he had to contend with a bourgeois audience that regarded opera as mere entertainment and had no clear or common goal except the pursuit of wealth and pleasure. He accordingly chose his themes from the old Germanic myths, which he thought expressed the underlying spirit of the folk and like all myth revealed "what is eternally human," fit for the "universal language" of music. Immediately he won the enthusiastic support of the youthful Nietzsche, whose *Birth of Tragedy* among other things provided a historical and philosophical basis for Wagner's somewhat cloudy intentions. Nietzsche was most ardent about the master's major project, the Bayreuth Festival: the locus of a ritual, communal drama that was to purify society. "It will be a universal *soul-bath*," he noted in his journal, "and a new realm of untold blessing will be revealed there."

The clearest revelation was the *Ring of the Nibelungs,* which in 1876 inaugurated the Festival to the applause of an audience drawn from all over Europe—the greatest triumph to date in the history of music. The theme of Wagner's epic cycle was explicitly purification. By her defiant self-sacrifice Brünnhilde assures the death of the old gods and ends the curse of the lust for wealth and power symbolized by the ring; her immolation heralds a new era of free humanity. Still unclear, however, is humanity's verdict on the greatness of this epic. To my mind, Wagner succeeded in achieving a primeval kind of grandeur, creating a powerful impression of the end of a world; others find it only grandiose. But one may venture a few fairly objective comments. Even Wagner's admirers may grant that as a poet he was no Shakespeare, even his detractors may admit his originality and power as a composer. Both might agree with Thomas Mann that his art was "magnificently equivocal."

In any case, there is no question that Wagner failed to establish a great new tradition, or clearly to purify his society. Nietzsche was bitterly disillusioned by the Bayreuth Festival, which as a fashionable, costly affair attracted chiefly "the leisure rabble of Europe," types hardly up to soul-baths. He grew as disgusted with the equivocal art of the master, especially his addiction to "idealistic lies." The ostensible "naturalism" of Wagner only cloaked his heritage from the Romantic movement, beginning with the cult of genius that nourished his colossal egoism. He was prone to the neurotic excesses of romanticism, such as the yearning for darkness and death that runs through *Tristan and Isolde.* The spirit of the Folk that he invoked was a romantic myth, remote from the realities of modern life; his mindless hero Siegfried may suggest an adolescent superman. He succumbed as well to the nationalistic myths of the German Romantics, betraying his ideal of a "free humanity soaring above all barriers" by a vulgar chauvinism, not to mention his anti-Semitism; he was pleased to see in Bismarck the statesman of the glorious new era heralded by his Siegfried and Brünnhilde. And even before he gratified his bourgeois audience by his equivocally "Christian" opera *Parsifal,* which Nietzsche saw as a complete surrender to the age, Wagner had revealed plainly enough that he was at heart an unpurified bourgeois himself. By his ostentation of grandeur, luxuriance of emotion, and resounding volubility, to the accompaniment of much obvious theatrical effect, he had always given his society essentially what it wanted. The realistic drama of Ibsen was better calculated to purify it.

In fairness to an operatic achievement that remains impressive, and a Festival that continued to give pleasure to many music lovers, I should add that had the undeniable genius of Wagner been healthier, and his thought profounder, he still could not have realized his dream. Although Wagnerian societies enlisted many eminent subscribers (such as Mallarmé, Verlaine, Shaw, and Valéry), he had no creative followers in his grand enterprise, for the sufficient reason that a ritual, truly communal drama is no longer possible in the modern world, at least so long as it remains free. Medieval men had such a drama in their Passion plays, since Christendom was still relatively united by a com-

mon faith; conceivably Nazi Germany might have developed something
of the kind, though a vulgar kind, had it won the war and all its people
been sold on Hitler's racial and national myths; and conceivably Communist countries might still develop a communal drama, though most
likely it would not be a great tragic drama, and the chances of anything
like it grow slighter as writers are granted more freedom, or "socialist
realism" is allowed to become at all realistic. Free, pluralistic societies
have no real chance. They may hope for something better than the
commercialized theater of Broadway, but they cannot hope to produce
epical works expressing the spirit of their people, or to make of any
modern capital another Athens. No more can they hope to recover a
unified culture, governed by uniform religious, national, or any other
communal ideals. Instead of pining for a lost unity, their intelligentsia
might better make a more earnest effort simply to keep communications
open between the major domains of science, philosophy, religion, literature, and the arts, while also appreciating the values of diversity
and abundance that come with freedom and pluralism.[24]

Wagner brought up another now familiar theme by his highly original style, which at first struck many music lovers as barbarous, cold,
or incomprehensible. As Beethoven grew older and deafer, he had
grown more indifferent to the tastes of his public, and to the topical
interests expressed in his opera *Fidelio* and his "Heroic" symphony;
his last quartets suggest a sublime indifference, recalling his remark,
"I must despise the world which does not know that music is a higher
revelation than wisdom and philosophy." Composers after him were
freer in innovation but usually comprehensible enough to the public.
By the end of the century, however, they were beginning to rebel
against the prevailing romanticism, to seek new modes of freedom or
purity, and so to create the so-called "crisis of tonality," sprung from
dissatisfaction with the harmonic system employed by Western music
for centuries. Debussy, Stravinsky, Schönberg, Hindemith, and other
moderns would give increasing trouble to the public. And to the composer as well. No longer content with traditional forms, he had now to

---

[24] Once upon a time, we may be reminded sadly, the dance was a communal affair with
sacred meaning, carried on in some place where everyone could dance and make music.
Now it is an art form performed in concert halls for the few, and for the many a
form of relaxation in the evening. As Gerardus van der Leeuw wrote, "When we dance
we do not pray; when we pray we do not dance. And when we work, we can neither dance
nor pray." But in perforce living such compartmentalized lives we might remember that
the dance as an art form may provide a considerably richer experience than the typically
monotonous tribal dance; just as religion may gain in loftiness or depth what it has
lost in breadth or intimate association with dance, work, and community life.

decide what kind of music to compose, and to spend more effort in developing a new style. On the face of it, he enjoyed his freedom as a pioneer, the hope of educating the public to new possibilities of musical experience; but he might also suffer from the strain, not to mention the hostility of a still uneducated public, the apparently incorrigible desire to read familiar drama and emotion into music. He might forget what Schönberg himself said, that plenty of good music can still be written in the key of C major. The jagged rhythms and the discords of much modern music were plainly suited to modern experience; but as understandable was the growing popularity of Mozart.

Still more revolutionary in the meantime had been the developments in painting, appropriately centered in France. In the second half of the nineteenth century this emerged as the leading art, so dominant that in popular usage "art" became virtually synonymous with painting. It was distinguished by much more fundamental diversity in style than Renaissance painting, or that of any other society past or present. Its many isms differed radically from the various styles in architecture in that they were mostly not revivals or modes of eclecticism but original styles, accompanied by a consciously new aesthetic program or philosophy. They reflected a profound change, which was made more conspicuous by the museum—a unique institution that no other civilization had ever had, and that presently began to house the art of the whole world. (An exposition of Japanese prints in Paris helped the Impressionists to find themselves.) In all past societies artists had typically been employed by the community, or specifically by its rulers, and among the primary purposes they served was religion. Now the painter was on his own. No longer subject to the wishes of priest, king, or noble, he was quite free to choose his subject matter and his style, express his personal vision of the world. Social scientists might therefore have learned from him that the individual is indeed real and unique, a creator as well as a creature of his society, while materialists and positivists might have learned that his completed picture—a material object—was essentially no more "real" than the "subjective" idea or fancy that gave birth to it. But the painter's freedom entailed the usual costs. Its ambiguous consequences may be indicated by the proliferation of diverse attitudes toward nature, society, man, and art—toward everything but God, whom painters might believe in but as painters mostly ignored.

Landscape was long a primary subject. It was rendered in somewhat novel ways by Constable, Turner, Corot, and Millet, and more revolu-

tionary ways by the Impressionists. The latter were especially fond of
bright landscapes, or scenes of people enjoying themselves in the outdoors; it was at this time that painters went outdoors with their easels.
These suggestions of city people's pleasure in nature for holiday purposes were offset, however, by the appearance of a new theme, suggestions instead of the awful aspects of nature, its immense indifference
to man when not its apparent hostility to his purposes. As Rilke observed of the Worpswede school of painters, "We may as well admit
that landscapes are something alien to us, that we are terribly alone
among trees that blossom and torrents that flow by . . . . Thus we become
convinced that in the background we shall find nature the most cruel
and most alien of all." Still another approach was suggested by Cézanne,
who observed that all forms in nature could be reduced to the sphere,
the cone, and the cylinder: a seemingly cool, mathematical view appropriate to an age of science. The Cubists would carry further this
suggestion of "exploitation" for purely artistic purposes. Early in the
twentieth century painters began turning away from landscape, leaving
it largely to popular or amateur painters, or to the business of calendar
art.

By the same token they were turning away from society too, ignoring
the interests of their public. Early Romantics, like Delacroix, had produced some riots of color on huge canvases that were likely to impress
wealthy bourgeois, and academic painters continued to solicit attention
by the mere size of their canvases. The revulsion against romanticism
then led to naturalism, a style that has likewise gone out of fashion, but
in its day served more democratic purposes. Courbet, a self-proclaimed
democrat and champion of the proletariat, exposed the vulgarity and
hypocrisy of the middle class that was bent on holding them down;
Daumier most directly and persistently satirized the bourgeois rulers
of society; and Millet introduced another new theme by dignifying the
life of the peasantry.[25] The later realistic school in America did much
the same for the common people as Dreiser and others were doing in
fiction. But meanwhile the Impressionists had paid the most direct—
and paradoxical—tribute to modern society. They painted joyously
its characteristic scenes, indoors and out: bourgeois parlors and bou-
doirs, cafés and gardens, boulevards and parks, music halls and race

---

25 Ironically, Millet furthered their cause in a way quite contrary to his intentions. His
peasants were viewed as downtrodden types, "stunned" by their hard lot; they inspired
Markham's most popular poem "The Man with the Hoe." Millet thought he was rendering their elemental strength and fortitude.

courses. They ignored its drab, grimy, ugly scenes. At a time when writers were harping on the sins of the bourgeois, they sounded no note of social protest.

The immediate paradox is that the Impressionists were not at all popular—their very name was given them by a journalist in a spirit of derision. Nevertheless it was not strange that their society failed to appreciate their tribute. They were quite unconventional artists, indifferent to history, the nation, or any "big" subject, devoted to painting as an autonomous art, who were absorbed in the expression of a revolutionary kind of artistic truth. By their experiments in light and color they sought to recover "the innocence of the eye": to forget that grass is green and shadows are black, and to render what the eye actually sees before its perceptions are dulled by habit. Their experiments were in line with studies being made in physics—a connection that some grew aware of. Like the adventurers in natural science, philosophy, and psychology, they were departing from not only tradition but the realism of common sense; they too were asserting that things were not as they appeared to the conventional eye, "reality" was more subtle, complex, and elusive than the realists in art and thought had made out. Despite their joy in the scenes of modern life, they were also affronting the aspirations of the respectable to solidity, stability, and security; for they painted the glimmer and shimmer of the fleeting moment, a world —both natural and human—in constant flux.

In winning autonomy for painters, the Impressionists accordingly anticipated the price they might have to pay for it. Some were condemned to extreme poverty, all were exposed to public scorn or the worse trial of public indifference; they caught just enough attention to create the popular image of the artist as a naturally queer type. Cézanne proceeded to work in utter solitude. Others felt alienated; the primitivism introduced by Gauguin signified a revulsion against modern civilization. All tended to make a religion of art, no less because their art remained secular or "profane" and their vision of the world was growing more private. As André Malraux observed of the moderns, "Rarely have so many artists sacrificed so lavishly to an unknown god." While their dedication exalted them, it made them more liable to estrangement and excess, on lower levels to the compulsive kind of unconventionality of the bohemians, or at their most intense to the tragic fate of Van Gogh and Gauguin. No freedom is more ambiguous than that of gifted men obsessed.

The successors of the Impressionists were more clearly on the fore-

front of an expanding or exploding culture, and their more revolutionary art was as much more ambivalent. Cézanne, the prophet of modern
painting, welcomed the discoveries of the Impressionists about light
and color but repudiated their realistic intention. His aim, he wrote,
was not "to reproduce nature" but "to express the sensations aroused
by nature"; and though in his pictures the familiar appearances of the
world were still recognizable, he felt free to distort them in order to
render some inner vision. He signaled the open revolt against "literary"
painting, which was pleasing most obviously for its beautiful, dramatic,
or anecdotal subject. As photography was emphasizing that the criterion
of great painting is not mere fidelity of representation—the camera
could always be more accurate—Cézanne led the way to a concentration
on its distinctive medium, the formal principles of composition and
color. In other words, he led a return to fundamentals, or to "pure"
art. With the turn of the century painters began moving steadily toward
nonrepresentational or abstract art, renouncing all effort to convey the
familiar illusion of reality. Their credo would be summed up in the
famous statement of Clive Bell: "The representative element in a work
of art may or may not be harmful, but it is always irrelevant. For to
appreciate a work of art, we must bring with us nothing from life, no
knowledge of its affairs and ideas, no familiarity with its emotions."

   Immediately nonrepresentational art represented a kind of emancipation, even apart from the obvious freedom it gave painters. It asserted
the supremacy of man over nature, or of the observer over the observed;
it declared that man was free to transform nature to suit his spiritual
needs, and so was master of his own meanings, creator of his reality.
Painters responded enthusiastically to the new opportunities. Whereas
they had been prone to the malaise of the *fin de siècle,* they now felt
that they belonged to an elite vanguard that was extending the range
of experience, enriching the possibilities of expressiveness, reasserting
the power of the human spirit against all the tendencies to mechanization and regimentation. The revolution in art corresponded roughly
to the revolution in physics, which was liberating thought from materialistic, mechanistic concepts; Kandinsky, Delaunay, Klee, and other
painters reported their excitement upon finding their intuitive feelings
or personal vision confirmed by modern science. And though they
still met hostile incomprehension from the great public, they were
beginning to create a stir and impress some wealthy buyers. Under
their aegis painting would become more widely popular than it had
ever been since the Renaissance. They were on their way to earning the

most impressive tribute to the social power of their art, which was paid by the modern dictators: Hitler and Stalin both considered modern painting not only a subversive influence but one dangerous enough to require suppression.

Still, this emancipation had questionable aspects, which might support the charge that it was a form of "bourgeois decadence." One may doubt the possibility of bringing "nothing from life" to a painting, as demanded by Clive Bell, but his demand implied a divorce of art from life that might make it strictly irrelevant to all other major interests, perhaps somewhat inhuman. Abstract art may look like another form of dehumanization, in a society already dominated by the abstractions of science and business. The art of portraiture, still cultivated by Cézanne and Van Gogh, suffered when it was turned over to academic or society painters. The dignity of man was not clearly enhanced either by the distortion of the human figure in the paintings of the Cubists, Picasso, and many others, and presently in sculpture too—once devoted to the glorification of the human form. Similarly the "inner" meanings the painters found in nature might be less rich, warm, or gratifying than the familiar meanings of tradition, derived from common experience in the natural world. Some visions were too suggestive of bare geometry, others of a kind of violation of nature; in shying away from obvious pictorial beauty, painters were liable to an aggressive scorn of pleasing appearances, a strained deformation. A further reason for stress on the grotesque or apparently ugly was that the emancipation of art meant among other things an emancipation of the unconscious, which would be celebrated in the surrealism and Dadaism to come. An early premonition was the rage for archaic, primitive, and naïve art, including children's drawings. This betrayed some understandable longing for the lost world of magic, when man felt more akin to nature; but it could raise some doubts about the intellectual and imaginative powers of the heirs of Raphael, Rembrandt, and Cézanne himself.

All such possible excesses were nourished by the essential subjectivity of nonrepresentational art, in the Romantic tradition. If people found unintelligible most modern painting (like much modern poetry), the fault was no doubt most likely to be their insensitiveness or inexperience, but it might be a primary failure of the artist in conception or communication. Thus advanced painters would typically bristle if asked to state the "meaning" of their picture, but would bristle too if it were accepted as merely decorative, like a Persian rug; evidently it did have some meaning after all, presumably a profound one; only it might be a private meaning. There was no clear standard of reference by which to determine its import or value, distinguish the profound from the vague or pretentious. The insistent subjectivity of painters also made them liable to social irresponsibility, which would appear in the fashion of "disengagement": the true artist must never commit himself to any social cause. Most obviously, the emancipation of art produced a babel of isms, inevitably involving a deal of extravagant fashion or mere fad. One prewar example was Futurism: an ultra-aggressive art dedicated to the glorification of modern technology, and of chauvinism and war, trumpeted by the usual manifestoes—a movement that flourished on some talent and more bombast, and was as short-lived as noisy.

Since I cannot help bringing something of life to painting, am unsure of my taste, and do not know enough about it to know why I like what I do, I should not venture to pronounce a summary verdict on the revolution in art. Possibly it is another feverish sign of the breakdown of civilization that Toynbee makes out, symptomatic of loss of control, "schism in the soul," barbarization, and the "archaism" suggested by the rage for primitive art. Possibly it may turn out to be the beginning of another great tradition, richer because of the sophisticated respect for primitive art. But at least it certainly represents another creative response, intelligible as an effort to develop an art suited to our radically different way of life. Whatever one's judgment of the achievement and the promise of modern art, it has maintained the Western tradition of bold, unflagging creativity.

8. *Education*

Out of all the cultural confusion and conflict of the nineteenth century emerged one commonplace but most remarkable agreement—the necessity of public education. The ruling class had naturally resisted agitation for free public schools, as a menace to the established order, while churchmen feared secular education as a menace to the true faith. Hence prosperous England was not shocked when a survey in the 1830's revealed that of children who did go to school most spent only two years there, and many were not even taught to read and write. Yet in the last decades of the century almost all European countries made education not only free but compulsory. By another generation most (outside of eastern Europe) had built up an adequate school system, even though it required large, unwonted expenditures by government. For the first time in history, all people in theory, and most in practice, enjoyed the opportunity to become literate. There is no more extraordinary development in the history of freedom.

From the beginning this had been a consciously democratic cause. In England the Benthamites, in France supporters of the Revolution, and in Prussia liberals like Stein and Humboldt had alike championed a system of education in which all children would be given an equal opportunity. They were abetted by the humanitarian movement and Romanticism, which nurtured a tender interest in the budding mind of the young. From Switzerland spread the influence of Pestalozzi, who was introducing a more liberal curriculum designed to develop all the capacities of children—intellectual, artistic, practical, moral—without the physical beatings traditionally considered necessary to mold character and mind. But a major stimulus to public education was the growth of industrialism. Even political conservatives could see that an industrial society required more literate workers than did an agricultural society, and that education could then build up the national power. Hence Germany took the lead. The reactionary Frederick William III, who put a stop to Humboldt's nonsense about democratic ideals in schools, had at least perceived that proper education might keep his subjects more contented and obedient; his successors realized the usefulness of vocational schools in particular; and under Bismarck Germany led all Europe in technical and scientific education, thereby succeeding in getting ahead of England in modern industry.

We are accordingly brought to the usual ambiguities. Public education was revolutionary too as a mode of group regimentation of children, subjecting them all to a uniform discipline, preparing them for the similar discipline that most would meet in factory and office. When education was made not only free but compulsory, many common people were still aware of this apparent incongruity that now seems natural; stupid children were more obviously handicapped, and poor parents might resent the loss of their children as wage earners. By this time, too, young men had become subject to military discipline through conscription. For the most part they submitted willingly enough to all this standardized conditioning, even too willingly to become fully developed individuals with minds of their own; but many must have suffered from the strains of adaptation and the new possibilities of frustration. The more rebellious among them might realize that education was designed to serve the needs of the nation more than the needs of the individual. In most countries, especially France and Germany, the school system was kept under centralized state control; when Kaiser Wilhelm II ascended the throne he formally instructed teachers that their primary duty was to combat the subversive doctrines of socialism. In other countries teachers knew without being told that schools were no place for critical inquiries into the possible defects of the economic, social, and political system. The cause of free, disinterested inquiry was not helped much either by the struggles in most countries between church and state over the control of education, since both sides were bent on indoctrination. Any education beyond technical training must involve some indoctrination, to be sure, since liberal education itself implies a philosophy, and the social value of free inquiry and free criticism is a debatable faith. The point remains that the schools of Europe commonly neglected to indoctrinate students with this faith.

A further reason for their neglect was that almost everywhere the school system remained fundamentally aristocratic. In England as well as France and Germany the lower classes, or the great majority of people, got only a primary education; a secondary education was a privilege reserved almost exclusively for the upper classes. Primary schools could not go far beyond the three R's, and such other subjects as they taught were usually learned by rote. Germany perhaps did best for its common people by way of curriculum, which under the early influence of Pestalozzi had come to include such subjects as nature study, drawing, and music, but its pedagogical methods remained conspicuously Prussian, emphasizing unquestioning obedience to the authority of the teachers and the prescribed texts; if the youngsters indulged in any free thinking it was on their own, under a cloud. Secondary schools everywhere were typically no less conservative in both curriculum and method because of their aristocratic purpose. The young gentlemen received a primarily classical education, supplemented by some mathematics and perhaps philosophy, and glossed by traditional piety. The efforts of liberal educators to introduce such "modern" subjects as science and the modern languages had only a very gradual success. They made least impression on the great "public" schools of England—Eton, Rugby, Harrow, etc.—that set the standards for other secondary schools. Thomas Arnold, the father of Matthew, helped to secure their devotion to the classical curriculum of the Renaissance, aided by one of its practical consequences: the overwhelming majority of available teachers were able to teach nothing else.

In the universities of Europe the story was much the same, with the notable exception of Germany. Prince Albert, consort of Queen Victoria, realized that Britain's industrial leadership was threatened by the promotion of science and technology in German universities, but he died before he could do anything about it. "How vastly different the course of British history might have been," observed the editor of *Nature* in 1928, "had the Prince Consort lived, say, another twenty-five years." As it was, Oxford and Cambridge kept their form until too late, dropping only their venerable religious requirements. By now one may be more inclined to honor their resistance to the trend to professionalism and utilitarianism, and their enduring contributions to urbanity as well as humanistic learning, all that has kept them among the great universities of the world; but in any case they long resisted the notion of Huxley, Spencer, and others that a knowledge of science was essential for a liberal education in the modern world. As they continued to dominate the national life, their prestige far outweighed the example of London University, which since its Radical origin had been hospitable to professional training; so the emerging provincial universities were slow in following this example. Young Englishmen with the best names, if not always the best brains, continued to move from the playing fields of Eton to the colleges of their ancestors.

By contrast, Humboldt had at least succeeded in establishing at Berlin the freedom of both professors and students to pursue their own interests instead of teaching or studying a prescribed curriculum. Early in the century German universities began supplementing their classical and philosophical studies by increasing attention to not only philosophy and history but mathematics and natural science, and by mid-century these had become the dominant studies. Germany was recognized everywhere as the great center of specialized research, both pure and applied; its universities most nearly approached the now common ideal of an institution where seekers of all kinds of higher learning could be satisfied. Among the countless scholars they attracted from other countries in the nineteenth century were up to ten thousand Americans. And among their attractions was a related principle that the Germans, rather surprisingly, were the first to name and uphold—academic freedom.

Although professors and students in the medieval universities enjoyed considerable such freedom in practice, they were of course not granted it on principle, or ever allowed to question the basic doctrines of Christianity; and thereafter universities were always subject to royal or ecclesiastical interference. Academics who suffered because of their unorthodox views included such eminent examples as Peter Abelard and Galileo. In England the protracted torpor of Oxford and Cambridge—especially during the Age of Enlightenment—owed something to their exclusion of Catholics and dissenters. In Germany too academic freedom remained limited, not extending to political issues. After the Revolution of 1848, when professors were carefully screened by state authorities, those who might have had liberal or democratic proclivities usually kept their views to themselves; like other civil servants, they were not privileged to criticize the government, and few dared to do so. (Among the exceptions was the historian Mommsen, who openly criticized Bismarck.) Yet the Germans had proclaimed the principles of *Lehrfreiheit* and *Lernfreiheit*—freedom of teaching and learning. Within their universities professors did enjoy such freedom, which they could maintain more readily because they elected their own deans and rectors, while the government helped at least by protecting them against sectarian pressures and public opinion. Early in the century Harvard scholars were amazed to hear a state-appointed professor of theology express doubts about divine revelation; George Ticknor informed Thomas Jefferson about this remarkable freedom of inquiry. Toward the end of the century the term "academic freedom" finally entered the American language. In all the democracies it took its place among the essential freedoms—another remarkable development, in view of the universal, age-old tradition of teaching the youth only proper ideas, or indoctrinating them with the wisdom of the ancestors.

Meanwhile public education in the United States had had a rather different history, becoming to a more democratic society; and this we need to consider more closely because it most fully illustrated the basic issues raised by the whole extraordinary effort of modern societies to educate all their members. The battle for free schools for all children got under way in the Jacksonian era, against the same kind of opposition it met in Europe. Businessmen and the upper class in general fought the idea because it meant that the wealthy would be taxed to provide education for the poor, an inequity they considered the more grievous because the wealthy were *ipso facto* intelligent, the poor were mostly unfit for education; or if fit, they should prove it by paying for their schooling as respectable people did. Religious groups joined the opposition on the grounds that "godless" schools would undermine the moral foundations of society, as well as the financial support of their own schools. All saw in free public education un-American tendencies that would eventually be called "creeping socialism." Hence the hostilities continued long after the school system was established. In the great depression following the panic of 1893, when businessmen demanded a reduction in all government expenditures that did not directly aid business, they attacked in particular the extension of high schools, which might make workers dissatisfied with low wages.

Nevertheless, America moved considerably faster and further toward a democratic system of education than did the great European nations. In the seventeenth century Puritans in New England had set the precedent by establishing free primary schools for the whole community— a Magna Carta in the history of education. Congress set another precedent by federal aid (today still a bugaboo of conservatives) in the Land Ordinance Act of 1785, apportioning a section in each township for educational purposes. The democratic sentiment of equality, always an impetus, was seconded by the uncommon ambition of common men, especially in the West. Another native stimulus was the need of assimilating the growing horde of immigrants, which in 1852 led Massachussetts again to set a precedent by making attendance at school compulsory. On all counts public education became a basic article in the national faith, in time replacing religion as the primary assurance of the greatness of America. Most distinctive was the growth of the American high school. Designed to meet the demands for opportunities that the private academies provided for the upper class, this was always a democratic, not an aristocratic institution. It was opened to girls too, who by the end of the century outnumbered the boys. Outside the South, the whole public school system was geared up for the immense expansion to come in our century.[26] Now proud of "the little red schoolhouse," most Americans forgot that it was providing what amounted to "socialized" education.

Colleges had grown as rapidly, far outnumbering the universities in

---

26 In the South Calhoun had sounded the conservative keynote during the early struggle for free schools. "The poor and uneducated are increasing," he wrote; "there is no power in a republican government to repress them; the number and disorderly tempers will make them the efficient enemies and the ruin of property." He might have seen in education a possible means of forestalling this dreadful prospect, but he concluded instead: "Education will do nothing for them." After 1876, when the Southern upper class regained the power to assure government in its own interests, states at once began repealing laws that provided for public education. At the end of the century no Southern state required attendance at school, fewer than half the children went to school, and only a very small minority reached the eighth grade. The "ruin of property" had been prevented. Unfortunately, the owners and tenant farmers of the impoverished land were still at a disadvantage vis-à-vis the much more prosperous North, where property had somehow managed to hold its own despite public education.

any European country. The couple of hundred founded before the Civil War included twenty state universities, and the Morrill Act passed during the war made it certain that these would flourish all over the country by granting every state 30,000 acres of public land for each member of Congress to help support them. (Public education came out with a domain about the size of Belgium.) Private colleges, which were long hostile to them, more than held their own, especially when millionaires acquired the habit of endowing them with fortunes. The state universities led the way to the characteristically American stress on technical training, or "practical" education, since the Morrill land grant called for the establishment of agricultural and mechanical colleges to supplement the liberal arts. As characteristic was the spread of the free elective system, championed by President Eliot of Harvard. Well before the World War the prescribed classical curriculum was on its way out. Of the traditional discipline there remained only such vestiges as compulsory chapel and the supervision of social life on the campus, to justify the popular expression of college "boys." And "girls": women had had their own seminaries since early in the century, and many more had flocked to the state universities. Americans were also forgetting the traditional view that "education renders females less contented with the lot assigned them by God and by the customs of society," and so makes them "less useful."

During this rapid growth Americans contributed little to any philosophical theory of education beyond their broad democratic ideal. Leaders in the profession, who concentrated on such practical matters as method and organization, had the typically ambivalent attitude of Americans toward Europe: proud of the progressiveness of their New World, but awed by the venerable institutions of the Old World and the fame of its universities.[27] In the 1890's, however, Americans began working out their own theories. William James applied the generous principles of his psychology to educational problems in *Talks to Teachers,* long the most popular work among teachers. Above all, John Dewey published his works on "progressive" education. Destined to

---

[27] Awe of the German universities in particular led to the importation of the German Ph.D., acquired by "scientific" research, which dominated the humanities too. Until recent years, for example, the preferred type of doctoral dissertation in literature was a piece of biographical or historical research, into literature at least a hundred years old, which required little critical ability and made as little if any contribution to aesthetic appreciation beyond the tracking down of "influences." The style of such dissertations was appropriately neutral or stale; liveliness or imaginativeness was suspect as unscholarly. The graduate student is still not one of the freest types in America.

become by far the most influential theory, this was American through and through in its pragmatic stress on education for democracy. While seeking better adaptation of the individual to society, Dewey departed from the long tradition going back to Plato by aiming at the development of individuality, stressing "the infinite diversity of active tendencies and combinations of tendencies of which an individual is capable."

He became a leader as well in the movement for academic freedom, a principle that American educators had been slow to recognize and defend. The broader principle of civil liberties had first to be established, since the authors of the First Amendment had scarcely intended as much freedom of speech and the press as the courts now permit; like almost all thinkers of the time, they took for granted the traditional right of states to suppress "seditious libel" or "licentious" statements, which could still cover any harsh criticism of the government or any radical ideas. Thomas Jefferson, who sinned more than once against his stated principles, himself tried to proscribe the teaching of Federalist doctrines at the University of Virginia which he had so proudly founded and dedicated to "the illimitable freedom of the human mind." In the private colleges there was little idea of such freedom because almost all were denominational, with presidents and many of the faculty drawn from the clergy. Religious interests sought control over the state universities too, with some embarrassing success. (President Tappan of Michigan, for example, lost his job because he served wine at dinner.) They were supported by public opinion, which in the democratic West tended to be more intolerant than in the more sophisticated East. Protestant educators seeking funds promoted another idea the respectable found congenial; as one theological salesman put it, "Like the pillars of Hercules, Education and Religion define and defend the path of trade." Hence new pressures against faculties rose after the Civil War, when *laissez-faire* capitalism became recognized as God's primary plan for America. Boards of trustees, increasingly made up of big businessmen, then accentuated an apparent anomaly: American colleges and state universities were run much less democratically than European or especially German universities. Faculties did not choose their presidents and seldom had an assured voice in the administration; trustees and presidents exercised the right to hire and fire as they pleased. In the not-so-gay nineties a number of liberal professors were dismissed, on such charges as having stated publicly that the railroads during the bloody Pullman strike were as lawless as the workers.

By this time, however, the dismissals touched off something of an uproar. Controversy over Darwin's theory had led to protests against the long accepted restrictions on the religious liberty of professors; in the name of science some now claimed an ethical right to teach freely. German influence spread the idea that academic freedom was the very essence of a true university. One president (Chadbourne of Williams) boldly espoused the alien notion that professors were not the hired help of a college—"They *are* the college." If most presidents played along with the trustees who appointed them, some defended their faculty against the pressures of business interests. Professors themselves, long inert if only because they were mostly conservative themselves, banded together to put up increasing resistance, and then were further emboldened by the success of the Progressive movement. In 1915 the American Association of University Professors made academic history by a formal, comprehensive declaration of the principles of academic freedom and tenure, including the right of professors to speak out as citizens too, or to enjoy a freedom outside the university that few Germans had dared to exercise. Henceforth these principles were widely accepted in theory, outside the denominational colleges, and were defended in practice by the AAUP.

Yet it has always been kept busy. It had at once to contend with the hysteria of the World War, which stirred up attacks on professors all over the land. (President Nicholas Murray Butler of Columbia distinguished himself as a patriot, or a butler of his trustees, by formally withdrawing the right to academic freedom for the duration, while the trustees instituted the first loyalty investigation.) The hysteria was more ominous as a portent, for teachers in America would remain more exposed to the vagaries of public opinion than are teachers in the European democracies; for most Americans the issue of academic freedom is strictly academic except when they get alarmed over "radicals" in the colleges. Similarly Dewey's theory of education grew most popular in a perverted form, the subordination of intellectual discipline to the sovereign aim of "life adjustment": Americans were all too eager to become well adjusted at any cost, excepting hard study, and to believe that the most important things one learned in school were not learned from books. Just because their school system was the most democratic, it best exemplified the inescapable difficulties of the singular modern effort to educate everybody, and finally the anomalies of this enterprise, the unexpected costs of the gains in freedom for the common people.

To begin with, public schools remained largely under the control of local communities. This assured the people a more direct voice in education, encouraging them to take an active interest in it, but it also assured routine, mediocre education in most of the little red school-houses. As in Europe, schools emphasized learning by rote, the acquisition of information rather than training in thinking; memory—in particular correct spelling—was prized the more highly because it was easy to test, and to display to fond parents. Other than such "practical" results, taxpayers were interested chiefly in economy. The pay of teachers was notoriously low; by the end of the century they were earning somewhat more than common laborers, but less than skilled ones. Enterprising teachers were further discouraged because they were exposed to local prejudices, and especially in rural America enjoyed less freedom in their private lives than any other profession except the ministry. (In the current alarm over the pressures to conformism, writers forget that Main Street was no citadel of personal freedom or culture.) Everywhere teachers had at best an uncertain academic freedom.

Also as in Europe, education was dominated by conservative influences, again most conspicuously in the West. Textbooks were typified by the extremely popular McGuffey's *Readers,* which sold well over a hundred million copies. While providing some solid literary fare—more than most American schools do today—these were designed to inculcate patriotism, sound morality, and the qualities essential to success in business. The whole curriculum in both grade and high schools was no more calculated to stimulate a spirit of independent inquiry or criticism, or to foster individuality. Literature was drawn chiefly from the genteel tradition, while art and music remained frills; history was always patriotic and simple, complicated only by regional pride and prejudice; civics was as utterly conventional, not to say un-utterably dull; economics, if taught at all, carefully evaded controversial issues or ideas likely to upset businessmen (as it still does in American high schools); natural science shied away from fundamental ideas, like the theory of evolution, disturbing to conventional piety. Only exceptional teachers encouraged independence in judgment, which on questionnaires most still rank low in the qualities they prize in students—they prefer obedience and politeness. Since youngsters who asked basic questions upset the class routines, all but the boldest or rudest learned to stop asking them.

Hence those who went on to college typically remained conventional in their thinking. After the World War, the cry would go up that the colleges were hotbeds of socialism, godless professors were corrupting the youth; but in fact radicals were always a small, unpopular minority, much less numerous and vocal than in most European universities. American students were disposed to the attitudes that have since grown more pronounced, prizing a college education less for its intellectual content than its economic and status values. Since they generally identified their interests with the upper class to which they either belonged or aspired, a solid majority of college graduates would unfailingly vote Republican in every presidential election. Prewar America was heading toward the current state of higher education, in which the problem is not to protect students from dangerous ideas, but to get them excited about any fundamental ideas.

A particular reason for the growth of intellectual apathy and political illiteracy was that more and more students were going to technical colleges—engineering, agriculture, business administration, home economics, etc. The emphasis on technical, vocational training that began with the Morrill Act was of course indispensable, above all in America. Not only did an industrial society require all kinds of technicians, but many more college students here than in Europe came from the middling ranks of society and had to think first of earning their living; berths were not waiting for them in government, army, or family estate. As sensible was the earlier welcome given the sciences by American than all but German universities, in particular because the traditional classical education had become routine, poor even of its kind; few of its products ever turned to the classics for pleasure or profit once they had finished their course. But by the time of the war the pendulum had started swinging to the opposite extreme. While departments of classics were attracting a dwindling fraction of the students, both the liberal arts and the pure sciences were losing ground to vocational studies and applied science. Alleged "institutions of higher learning" were beginning to offer more and more instruction that was neither high nor learned, such as courses in advertising and hotel administration. The very meaning of a "liberal" education was fading: it had once been distinguished from merely practical training as an education of the mind suitable for "free" men. And already the American obsession with the practical had got profoundly impractical results.

Henry Adams, class orator of the Harvard class of 1858, later complained that his four years in college had been a complete waste of time. He had never heard of such key thinkers of the age as Comte and Marx, nor had he been given the tools he needed for further education, a mastery of any modern language, or of the universal languages of mathematics and science. In another generation American universities would offer such opportunities, but they were still not up to the essential task of education as Adams defined it: "running order through chaos, direction through space, discipline through freedom, unity through multiplicity." They were turning out few "men of the world," equipped to understand their revolutionary society. The many students concentrating on technical studies could graduate without any such understanding, the rudiments of intelligent citizenship. Although popular theory had it that their scientific training automatically carried over into thinking about other subjects, what carried over most obviously was not the disinterested scientific spirit but the emphasis on efficiency and know-how, habits of thought that accentuated the mechanical tendencies in modern life. Students of the humanities, on the other hand, commonly had only a smattering of some science and its laboratory technique, and seldom got a grasp of the fundamentals of science—its language, its logic, its philosophy. The elective system was becoming a shambles; many students shopped around and came out with a miscellany of courses, often elected primarily because they were offered at an hour that fitted conveniently into the student's schedule. Like Henry Adams, many if not most remained quite ignorant of the revolutionary thought of their day, as of the economy, and might graduate without even a clear realization that they were living in a revolutionary world. From now on, H. G. Wells would say after World War I, history is a race between education and catastrophe; but one reason why catastrophe had won the first heat, and would win the next one, was that formal education was hardly aware of any race. Nominally the most educated people in the Western world, Americans were about the least prepared for the world wars and the world depression in which they would play a major role.

In fairness to educators, one may then note the extraordinary difficulties they faced. There is of course no clear, sure way to an adequate understanding of our world—Adams himself spent a lifetime trying to understand it. The difficulties were steadily magnified by the immense expansion of knowledge. Ideally, university students should be well grounded in the traditional basic subjects, the humanities and natural science, but they should also be acquainted with such important new subjects as economics, psychology, sociology, and anthropology; and all efforts at comprehensiveness are bound to look superficial. Ideally, too, education should give students a live sense of Western tradition and its values, our common heritage, yet make them aware of the common dangers of traditionalism and cultural lag, much inherited belief

that is no longer clearly suited to modern knowledge and social conditions; and any effort to train them in flexibility and openness of mind
involves the always delicate task of helping them to unlearn much of
what they have been taught, which is bound to antagonize most parents
and taxpayers. This task has been further complicated by the ever-
accelerating pace of change. A well-educated graduate of 1900 would
be seriously uneducated in 1930 if he had learned nothing in the in-
terim. As it was (and still is), most Americans assumed that once they
got their diploma their education was finished; they were too busy to
keep on learning; and they might well be less intelligent and responsible as voters than many who never went to college.

There remains the most obvious problem of mass education. Inevitably it entailed some sacrifice of quality, and of the individual. It was
perforce geared to the needs and interests of average students; backward, bright, or creative students were always likely to suffer. In so far
as the school system approached the ideal of equality of opportunity, it
became more difficult to show anything like equal concern for the
person, Dewey's individual capable of "infinite diversity." In America
the decentralized administration of the schools made possible an exceptional variety and constant experiment in education, but it assured a
conspicuous inequality in standards; nor was quality guaranteed when
educationists began turning out hordes of teachers crammed with
methodology and jargon to match, but commonly not matched by a
command of the subject they were preparing to teach. And though
before the war America still fell far short of the ideal of equal opportunity, since only a small minority of young people could afford to
finish high school, the main issue of mass education had long since
become obtrusive.

Outside the South, almost all Americans could read and write. In
a land where public education had become a religion, the question
remained: *What* did they read and write? Their interests were being
served by a great publishing industry, mass production of newspapers,
magazines, popular books, means to self-education; and on what kind
of fare were they feeding their minds? Freed from bondage to ignorance,
what were they doing with their freedom? Matthew Arnold was among
the many who had been pressing such questions. "Consider these
people, then," he wrote of his compatriots in *Culture and Anarchy*,
"their way of life, their habits, their manners, the very tones of their
voice; look at them attentively; observe the literature they read, the
things which give them pleasure, the words which come forth out of

their mouths, the thoughts which make the furniture of their minds."

One look was enough for dismay. The extraordinary public enterprise of modern society was producing the type of the half-educated man: one who in America especially was likely to be less respectful of learning than is the illiterate man, more complacent about his vulgar tastes and opinions, brash and noisy. Schools were turning out hordes of customers for the yellow press—a new power in the land. Readers were gorging themselves on garbage. All in all, public education had generated another strictly revolutionary development—mass culture. Popular culture was indeed as old as civilization, since everywhere the peasantry retained their arts, rites, and lore while literacy and learning became the possession of a few; but the educated had generally ignored this substratum of high culture, or if it was forced on their attention, had dismissed it with cursory disdain. In the modern world popular culture is fundamentally different in that it is massive, ubiquitous, blatant, impossible to ignore or to dismiss lightly. It has counted for a vast deal more by molding the mentality of the great majority who now, for the first time in history, had a voice in determining national policy, setting social goals, ultimately deciding the fate of the free society. I should add at once that popular culture is as complex a phenomenon as all the other revolutionary developments of our age, and that its issues have therefore, as usual, been commonly oversimplified; but on both counts it calls for a close look, in a historical perspective.

9. *Popular Culture*

When the Romantic movement aroused more interest in "the folk," some writers and composers drew themes from them, but critics (such as Arnold) still paid little heed to their culture. Only in our time has it been systematically explored by students of folklore. And one reason for this belated interest is that it is vanishing. It had been rooted in the countryside, which men kept leaving for the industrial towns or the big cities. In these they began acquiring a quite different kind of culture, their children were brought up in the ways of city workers, and their grandchildren might possess few if any relics of the quaint lore of the village. The popular culture of the cities then began invading the village, where schoolchildren could learn to appropriate it;

Grandpa, wise in the ancient ways, would become more of an antique or entertainer than an oracle or counselor. Everywhere those who could read took to the new, up-to-date cultural fare.

This whole story accordingly begins with the invention of the printing press. While the habit of silent reading developed a rare power of detachment that helped men to become more disinterested in their thinking, it could also help them simply to evade the effort of responsible thought, strengthen the habit of escape into a world of fantasy. Pascal was alarmed by the growing passion for entertainment, a distraction from the serious business of salvation. In the eighteenth century, when a sizable middle-class reading public emerged, writers deliberately set about providing entertainment, especially by novels. Serious writers now began speaking disparagingly of "popular writers" and worrying over popular taste. Since they too were writing for the market, they usually expressed mixed feelings, chiefly dismay over the crude tastes of the public, but tempered by some hope of a gradual spread of cultivated taste. The rise of the Romantic concept of literature as a great liberating force inspired more optimistic hopes in some generous writers. Schiller, for example, looked forward to a new "joyous realm" of creative art, state-wide, in which the fundamental law would be "to grant freedom by means of freedom."[28]

In the nineteenth century the reading public grew large enough to be called a mass audience. When French newspapers hit on the idea of printing novels in serial form, the popular demand was so great that only an industry of hack writing could meet it. (The very prolific Alexandre Dumas employed more than seventy collaborators.) In England publishers were most industrious and catholic, flooding the land with penny serials, sensational newspapers, "family" journals, and the like. In America the dime novel was an instantaneous, huge success, which would keep redskins biting the dust ever after. The new era of the mass media had dawned. And long before the motion picture heralded the high noon of TV, popular culture had been radically transformed. In the past it had been essentially an indigenous, spontaneous growth, nurtured by many anonymous men who tinkered with the traditional tales and songs, now and then started a new one; however limited or coarse in its understandings, it had been at least a genuine expression of the thought and feeling of simple people. Now it was manufactured by professionals. It was a synthetic mass culture

---

28 For a detailed review of this early history, see Leo Lowenthal's *Literature, Popular Culture, and Society*, a pioneering sociological study, and an uncommonly sensible one.

produced for consumption by the common people, not nurtured by them. Most of its producers might share the low tastes they catered to, not be so cynical as in time many became, but in any case they were professionals apart from the people, employed by businessmen. In giving the people what they evidently wanted, writers and publishers were nevertheless exploiting vulgar desire, cashing in on the immaturity of the new reading public; and to some extent they were surely creating desire. Many were quite conscious of their power to influence people, and as deliberate in the exercise of this power. The degree of "mass indoctrination" was only most apparent in the sensational press, which in ostensibly informing public opinion created the new industry of publicity or propaganda.

In short, the blessing of literacy appeared to be bringing out chiefly the worst in people. From the beginning the great bulk of popular literature was trash. It was so bad that even publishers running out of cheap materials would not think of reissuing any of it when its copyright had expired. Always destined to perish without a trace, it never perished quickly enough, and it always left some trace on the minds of the people who gorged themselves on it. English writers were the first to become seriously concerned about it as not merely an aesthetic but a social, moral, intellectual problem. Americans, generally more optimistic about education as a cure-all, were thereby due to become most troubled. Although we can never be certain how much people were actually affected by all the print they devoured over the past century, their reading tastes were at least a significant index to the quality of their thought and feeling, the level of their sense and sensibility—the kind of mind they brought to bear on clearly vital issues. In the darkness of our TV high noon, I assume that a historian must say emphatically the worst about popular culture, especially in Britain and America, the most advanced democracies.[29]

Granted that the mediocre works of past ages usually perished with little trace, we may still be confident that they were not so bad as the huge quantity of trash manufacured for free men. This was not merely mediocre art—it was not art at all. It tended to unfit its avid readers for

---

29 I should add that I am confining my attention to these countries for the further reason that I cannot pretend to be well informed about popular culture in all European countries. But trash is obviously no Anglo-American monopoly. The vulgarity for which America in particular is notorious among the intelligentsia all over the world is evidently much less offensive to the common people of the world; Hollywood grade-B films (like chewing gum and Coca-Cola) seem to be popular everywhere. I assume that as other countries grow more affluent they will be faced with much the same cultural problems.

an appreciation of any genuine art. The constant sensationalism that seemingly stimulated people could in time only dull their sensibility. While the professionals continued to ring changes on such indispensable sentiments as loyalty and love, their tone constantly falsified them, made it harder for simple people to be honest, responsible, and wise in their own fashion. They debased not only literary taste but the common language, emptying many a word of fine meaning or any real meaning. At best they evoked only stock responses, engrained immature attitudes, blunted or stunted the powers of independent judgment most needed in a free society. One may therefore doubt that the flood of trash made people happier either—the only rational justification of the mass-entertainment industry. The tawdry world of fantasy it provided was a poor substitute for reality, which people might have found or made more interesting and satisfying by their own efforts, individual and communal, and which in any case they had to cope with.

But say the worst about popular culture in the democracies, it becomes more necessary to dwell on the complexity of the issues it raises. Literary men too often equate culture with fastidiousness, overlook the legitimate claims of mere entertainment, and now tend to romanticize the folk culture of the past that their forebears ignored or despised. This had scarcely bred any more passion for truth, beauty, goodness, or holiness than the mass culture that displaced it. Men who felt stirrings of such a passion were least likely to feel that illiteracy was a blessing, more apt to realize that the "genuineness" of their folk culture owed considerable to genuine ignorance. The spread of literacy at least meant a rise in the general level of knowledge and awareness: a public somewhat better informed, somewhat less provincial, whose deficiencies were more glaring because ignorance was no longer considered the natural or proper state of the common people. If most half-educated people were conspicuously gullible, their forebears had been more uniformly gullible, prey in particular to egregious superstition. Mass indoctrination was less certain in its efforts than the tyranny of custom and tradition in the past.

Above all, popular culture was by no means so uniform as popular generalizations about it imply. "The masses" who frightened political conservatives and now alarmed literary critics remain a crude category, created by the intelligentsia as well as industrialism. Break them down into upper-lower, lower-middle, and other such classes, we may specify their interests somewhat more precisely, but we are still generalizing roughly about a society that was growing more fluid and heterogeneous than any before it. Popular culture embraced a much wider range of interest, taste, and aspiration than had folk culture. It was also less sharply separated from high culture, including some popular master-pieces, such as *Don Quixote*. Likewise it embraced a considerable body of reputable, second-rate work by the many minor writers who are always begotten by great literature, always important in helping to keep literature substantial and vital. Critics who worry because popular writers are invariably overrated tend to forget that youthful readers normally develop an interest in literature by starting with such writers. And however unhappy serious writers were over popular taste, on the face of the record literature did not suffer from it. The greater writers went on doing their work to suit themselves. The literary market supported much more variety, vigor, and boldness than had the patronage of Italian princes in the Renaissance, or the court of Louis XIV at Versailles.

Among its distinctive products were the works of Mark Twain and Dickens. Mark Twain set out most deliberately to become a popular author and was always businesslike in his methods of writing, aiming at pleasing all the people all the time; once established, he did not dare to publish openly the bitter, pessimistic views of his later years. At the same time he was very much a man of the people, who normally made little concession to their interests and tastes because he had basically much the same attitudes. Dickens made as little sacrifice of artistic integrity in becoming the most popular of the greater novelists; in this respect he differed from Mark Twain chiefly in that he was less democratic, given to a petty-bourgeois fear of "the rabble." Both accordingly had obvious limitations as artists and as critics of their society. Yet as obviously both were great writers, neither was a mere entertainer. Their works embodied considerable social criticism that might make their readers think. And both owed their opportunity and their reputation to the new reading public, not to literary critics or the learned class.

Before generalizing, let us consider the range of popular literature in the much ridiculed Gilded Age, to which Mark Twain gave its name. At the bottom were countless millions of dime novels, which we must look into presently. Not far above them were the romantic novels of Mrs. E. D. E. N. Southworth, the most popular of what Hawthorne called that "d——d mob of scribbling women"; they specialized in senti-mental, moralistic, religious novels that were sure-fire sells. But there was also a substantial audience for the greater English novelists, apart from Dickens, and for the classics. Road companies toured the land with repertories that usually included Shakespeare; English travelers reported that Shakespeare was performed more often in America than in England. Between the classics and the dime novels lay a wide variety of work, mostly perishable, which nevertheless refuted the charge that popular culture was simply commercialized or standardized. Folk humorists like Josh Billings, Petroleum V. Nasby, and Bill Nye carried on in the spirit of Mark Twain, with much broad satire of the Gilded Age. Bret Harte helped to create the enduring vogue of the short story, *Ben Hur* the rage for historical fiction. The *Memoirs* of Ulysses Grant enabled Andrew Carnegie to boast of the superiority of American culture, proved by the fact that he was paid a quarter of a million dollars for them, whereas John Milton got only ten pounds for *Paradise Lost.* The shrewd Mr. Dooley of Finley Peter Dunne put Carnegie in his place, together with other boastful or pompous Americans. Schoolchildren were brought up on the innocuous poetry of Longfellow and Whittier. As adults they read the immensely popular "Man with the Hoe," symbolizing "humanity betrayed, plundered, profaned and disinherited." Similar sentiment made best sellers of Henry George's *Progress and Poverty* and Bellamy's *Looking Backward,* and prepared for the great success of the muckrakers. Continental imports ranged from Jules Verne to Victor Hugo and de Maupassant.

And so it went in other realms of popular culture. Hundreds of lecturers (including fastidious Englishmen) roamed the land as they did nowhere in Europe, in response to a hunger for self-education or self-improvement. In small towns Americans crowded the tents of Chautauqua to be both entertained and edified. Women were depressingly earnest about cultural uplift, sponsoring lyceum courses and forming literary societies, like as not pretentious, but helpful in civilizing the West. Both men and women were enthralled by popular preachers, from the highly commercial revivalist Dwight Moody to the "atheist" Robert Ingersoll. Come back to earth, they attended minstrel shows, jubilees, and the circus of P. T. Barnum, builder of an entertainment empire; they got decently sentimental over the songs of Stephen Foster and barbershop ballads; they got a fantastic amount of pleasure and boredom out of after-dinner oratory; they flocked to the comic operas of Gilbert and Sullivan; they bought the prints of Currier and Ives, now collectors' items; they began visiting the art galleries and museums that all the big cities were establishing; they were developing an eager interest in popular science; etc., etc. In general, Americans amply demonstrated that they were parvenus in culture, but not simply ignorant or depraved. If few appreciated the most distinguished writers and thinkers who came out of the Gilded Age—Henry Adams, Josiah Gibbs, Charles Pierce, Henry James, William James—some fortune-makers were preparing a potential audience for them too by endowing public libraries and colleges. Henry Adams was most critical of his society; but in 1919 his *Education* would head the list of best sellers in nonfiction.

In England the persistent strain of earnestness in popular culture was still more marked. A swelling tide of works popularizing knowledge and culture lapped into even the cheapest periodicals. Their authors were almost invariably superficial, often ignorant, fond of such crude devices as "comic" grammars and histories; their publishers anticipated the great American industry of making everything easy and agreeable, or your money back. Nevertheless they testified to the characteristic aspiration to self-improvement stimulated by democracy. Workingmen formed groups to help educate themselves, listened to such lecturers as Thomas Huxley, and read Ruskin, Morris, and Henry George. They marked off another important mid-region of mass culture, which from the time of Tom Paine had nurtured efforts at social and political reform. In popular fiction this developed the type of the propaganda novel, from now on a social force to be reckoned with. Lovers of literature must consider the possibility that *Uncle Tom's Cabin* had more effect on history than have had the works of Shakespeare.

Workmen who read or tried to read serious books were indeed a small minority. Most were content with the unadulterated trash that was produced for them, and that in fiction was wholly escapist. They accordingly force the main issue—the effect of all this trash on popular mentality. Literary critics have always assumed that it was a very bad effect. So I suppose all of us who value literature must assume. But just because the problem is so serious a one for the democracies, I think we again need first to discount somewhat the conventional alarm.

To begin with, this is a fairly old story, and not simply a matter of class. In the eighteenth century the middle-class public was amply gratified by the kind of thing now charged to "the masses": true and love story magazines, gossip journals, sensational titles ("Adultery Atomized"), fiction exploiting sex, violence, horror, and sadism. Some distressed literary men recalled that Elizabethan drama had also been full of crude horrors, and often ended in a bloodbath. Alexander Pope concluded the *Dunciad* with a prophecy:

Art after Art goes out, and all is Night. Thy hand, great Anarch!
Lets the curtain fall; And universal Darkness buries all.

More than two centuries later, however, the curtain has not yet fallen.
Contemplating the appalling flood of escapist fiction in the past century,
we might remember in humanity that millions of poor devils needed
some escape from the industrial slums in which they lived, and that
most genteel people were more concerned about their abominable
tastes than about the wretched living conditions that formed these
tastes. We may doubt, moreover, that they were seriously harmed by
this fiction—as much as sophisticates may have been harmed by the
escapism of art for art's sake. Richard Hoggart has pointed out in his
admirably balanced study of the uses of literacy that the English working class commonly regarded literature as mere entertainment, never
so important as it seems to literary critics, and did not confuse it with
real life, which they knew all too well was quite different. It might
even have helped them somewhat to escape their predicted fate of becoming a deadened *lumpen-proletariat*. At least the record does not
suggest that they were corrupted, degraded, or brutalized by all the
penny serials, for drunkenness and crime fell off in the second half of
the century.

No doubt the chief aid was the gradual improvement in their standard
of living, such benefits as better sanitation and ventilation, or even such
simplicities as the zoo and the panorama to replace the village maypole.
Yet their culture also helped to maintain their self-respect and simple
decency. Matthew Arnold himself noted the "generous instincts" that
always ran through popular literature. Their fiction echoed the sentiments expressed as well in their "family" journals, popular songs,
Christmas cards, and calendar art: sentiments always trite, but still
genuine. They were pleased to believe that what mattered was not
money but homeliness, friendliness, and cheerfulness, a good family
life, solidarity with one's fellows, and a power of stoical endurance,
fortified by the right and the ability to say, "At least I've got my
self-respect." Always, as Hoggart stresses, their values were expressed
in concrete, sensory, personal, intensely human terms. They insisted on
keeping life humanly interesting and significant in spite of all drabness
and meanness; and at that they were still content with heroines who
kept their bosoms to themselves. In this spirit they maintained a firm
sense of right and wrong. Written all over their culture were the bold
words "good" and "evil," "sin" and "guilt"—again with naïve or

garish meanings, but again taken quite seriously, disclaiming any disposition to "escape" from the moral responsibilities of real life. They
were neither so neurotic nor so self-indulgent as many of their cultivated
betters.

Probably middle-class readers were more affected by all the escapist
literature they fed on. More conventional and snobbish, they were likely
to take more seriously the dream world of their fiction, featuring the
life of the gentleman—the beau ideal of a grouse-shooting, fox-hunting,
port-drinking leisure class—but also the values of conformism, the
rewards of their own smug virtues, the rainbow at the end. Even on
upper levels most Victorian novel readers were inclined to agree with
Darwin that there ought to be a law against unhappy endings. From
these levels, where Tennyson's *Enoch Arden* won its great popularity,
down to *The Rosary* and *East Lynne,* middle-class culture was shot
through with a sentimentality that was more insidious because readers
tended to consider it an ideal version of real life, or essentially true to
life. Perhaps worse than the vulgar trash was all this gush, which
easily turned into the cant for which Victorian England became notorious.

Only here again some reservations are called for, as always with the
despised bourgeois. One reason why the middle class could indulge in
so much easy sentiment was its basic moral earnestness, in the light of
which its complacence could look like firm conviction. This lent some
dignity to its snobbish pretensions and its deference to the gentleman,
for in a supposedly materialistic society it was still deferring to birth,
breeding, and manners—not to money. Despite the increasing secularism, moreover, and the weakening of religious sanctions, it was insisting
on the supreme importance of virtue. However conventional and narrow
its conception of virtue, its basic sentiments and values too were essentially genuine. Thus its sentimentality over romantic love and the
supreme virtue of chastity in women—the most popular themes in the
fiction it lapped up—reflected its living devotion to the family and
family life, considered the essential breeding ground of character.
Similarly the middle class maintained the ideal of service and discipline,
or the pre-eminence of duty over rights. Here the quality of its virtue
was not unstrained by self-interest, since it tended to confuse the public
weal with its own welfare, and its devotion to law and order was a means
of keeping the lower class in its place; but at least it helped to keep
public life on a distinctly higher plane than it had been in the aristocratic eighteenth century, when politics was flagrantly corrupt. Vic-

torian England was neither corrupted nor enervated by its material prosperity.

The blend of moral earnestness, stuffiness, and high selfishness that distinguished its middle-class culture was for practical purposes best expressed in *Self-Help,* by Samuel Smiles. Published within a year after Mill's *On Liberty,* this immediately became much more popular. "The solid foundations of liberty," preached Smiles, "must rest upon individual character; which is also the only sure guaranty for social security and national progress." The function of government was merely negative, being primarily the "protection of life, liberty, and property." While he added that the glory of free Englishmen was their uniform subjection to "the national code of Duty," he did not dwell on any national obligation to the many unpropertied workers, or on their very limited economic liberty and security. Law could never make shiftless people sober, industrious, and provident—traits which every Englishman could acquire by "his own free powers of action and self-denial." If it appeared, somewhat strangely, that the poor were the ones who chiefly had to learn self-denial, individual character remained all, and it was always enough in a land of free enterprise.

Self-Help was a best seller in America too, as were other typical works of Smiles—*Character, Thrift,* and *Duty.* Much more popular here, however, was Horatio Alger, whose hundred-odd novels had a tremendous sale continuing into our century, totaling many millions of copies. (Scholarly estimates run as high as a hundred million.) Alger's works not only were easier to read but added some native ingredients to the recipe for success. He blessed his heroes with luck as well as pluck, and he often set off his endless variations on the story of how a poor boy got rich with a subplot about how an idle rich boy got poor. But his main advantage was that the success story had long been the favorite of ordinary Americans, who felt less bound to their class than did Englishmen. He was always expressing truly popular beliefs, never serving as a mere lackey of the business class.[30] As a millionaire Andrew Carnegie likewise made a big hit with his article "The Gospel of Wealth." Chautauqua lecturers never wearied of expounding the social benefits of competition, private property, and the trusteeship of men who made fortunes.

---

[30] I write humbly as one who read at least a dozen of Alger's novels in my boyhood, even though I soon grew aware of a certain monotony in their plots. I recall, too, that among the choice possessions of my elders was a copy of Elbert Hubbard's most popular *A Message to Garcia,* a limp-leather edition befitting his classier version of the Alger ethic.

Still more distinctively American were the dime novels that Erastus Beadle started publishing in 1860. These featured Western heroes out of the tradition of Cooper's Leatherstocking, crack-shot hunters and trappers whose favorite avocation was rescuing beautiful maidens from the Indians; and within a few years they were selling by the million as a gifted editor (Orville J. Victor) devised formulas that facilitated mass production by a staff of writers. When business competition forced some variation to give the illusion of novelty, the market was enlivened by the appearance of such related types as Deadwood Dick and the most famous Buffalo Bill: self-made men who in the Wild West invested the Horatio Alger hero with a more glamorous virility and daring. (Buffalo Bill was made, or made up, by a press agent out of a quite ordinary, obscure scout.) Finally the Cowboy emerged: in real life a disreputable type, associated with desperadoes, but now transformed into the hero who was to dominate Western fiction to our day, and in movies to become popular all over the world. He remained squarely in the tradition because he was kept too busy fighting Indians and outlaws, and rescuing heroines, to waste his talents on tending cows.

Now, the dime westerns at first flourished on authentic sentiment. This harked back to the primitivism of Rousseau, the celebration of the simple, wholesome life close to nature, which America best exemplified. It drew more heavily on the democratic agrarian idealism of Jefferson and his followers, the belief that the independent farmer was the model of natural dignity and integrity, free from the corruptions of city life, and therefore the main hope of American democracy. Above all, the Western hero represented the most distinctive type of national hero, the ideal of the daring, resourceful pioneer and frontiersman—anticipating the famous thesis of Turner that the advancing frontier was the main key to the growth of American democracy. Yet the partial truth of his thesis was scarcely validated by all the popular sentiment about the Wild West. This only obscured the harsh realities of the life of Western farmers, a great many of whom were hard up, not really independent, because at the mercy of merchants, speculators, bankers, and railroad men—rugged types much more popular with the national government. In particular it obscured the plainest, most significant fact, that America was becoming a great urban, industrial, capitalistic nation. The sentiment nourished illusion even as the frontier was passing out of history, postponing the shock of the realization that it was gone for good, but thereby leaving Americans more confused, uncertain of their destiny or their responsibilities, disposed to blame all social evils

on the corrupt city, indisposed to respond boldly to calls for "new frontiers." And meanwhile the dime novels kept flourishing on a popular
mentality that was considerably beneath the possible dignity of nostalgia. Folklore had become pure "fake-lore."

This fiction had never, of course, given an authentic account of the
Wild West, which was unknown to some of the hacks on the assembly
line. Buffalo Bill, speaking through ghost-writers, was a phony through
and through; and he entered the pantheon of national heroes of a
people who prided themselves on their shrewd practical sense, their
hardheaded realism, their contempt for suckers. (He himself was
eventually taken in by the legend his press agent concocted, as an old
man telling all comers how in his youth he had been an epical pioneer
standing "between savagery and civilization.") Lacking any real ethical
or social meaning, Henry Nash Smith observes, the Western novel could
develop only by straining and exaggerating its formulas. Orville Victor
had found it easy to meet the early competition, telling his writers to
kill a few more Indians; in time the routine slaughter built up the
cult of violence that would entertain youngsters as much as it did their
nominally adult parents. The heroine too was suitably coarsened. Beginning as an ultragenteel type who in the most desperate circumstances
always talked and behaved like a perfect lady, she became Calamity
Jane, an Amazon able to hold her own in any hard-drinking, gun-toting
company of man-killers. And the growing sensationalism had a more
ominous aspect. In the early alarm over popular literature, well-disposed
critics had made some allowances: it would naturally take time to educate the new reading public, improve their taste. By the end of the
century, however, well-wishers had more reason for alarm. So far from
improving in quality, popular literature seemed to be getting steadily
worse, more positively degrading. In widening the gap between serious
and vulgar literature, making adult readers of either more incapable of
enjoying the other, it was destroying the possibilities of a common
culture.

A similar change for the worse had come over newspapers, which
had been bad enough. In America as in England publishers had early
made the crucial decision, whether to concentrate on informing or
entertaining the public: they plumped for entertainment. Although
the newspaper had been a civilizing influence in rural and frontier
America, giving at least some news of the larger world, the great burst
of papers all over the land meant that Americans consumed an immense
amount of periodical trash, and the latest gossip became the chief read-

ing matter of many who had formerly pored over their few books. (Among the casualties was the Bible—once widely read and a conspicuous influence on American culture.) Political news was seldom reported fully or impartially; the papers served chiefly as media for the calumny and invective of rabid partisanship. They gave little attention to the world of art and thought, or any important issues beyond those simplified or obfuscated by popular preachers. De Tocqueville noted their most distinctive feature: three quarters of the paper was filled with commercial advertisements. Eventually business took charge. By the end of the century personal journalism, which had produced some famous editors, was giving way to syndicated newspapers. Some of the big papers settled down to more responsible reporting of national and world news, but most featured a more lavish provision of what was to remain the daily fare of Americans—crime, scandal, gossip, sports, comics, etc. The sensational press made plainer the only kind of freedom of the press that really concerned most publishers: the freedom to be irresponsible. What determined the news that was fit to print was what paid.

As the independent country editor was doomed, so the folk element was disappearing from popular culture, and with it much individuality. Big popular magazines were replacing books on the living-room table, minstrel shows and road companies were losing ground to theatrical syndicates, and Hollywood was in the offing. While the major purveyors of popular culture were accentuating its synthetic quality, they were more obviously molding public opinion, and in ways more uniform. Newspapers and journals, owned or controlled by men of wealth, typically supported conservative interests; most would give up such radical ventures as muckraking. If the sensational press might attract renegades like Hearst, its mass appeal raised issues more depressing to well-wishers of democracy. It made more glaring the insensitiveness of the public to the elementary distinction between sense and nonsense. Much political oratory of the time—as all through the Gilded Age, and still today—was so blatantly hollow and insincere that one might wonder how any adult could have been impressed by it; yet the blah-blah was applauded, the politicians were re-elected.

In the applause, let us add, joined many respectable people who looked down on dime novels. One may then take a more jaundiced view of middle-class tastes in fiction, gratified by such celebrities as Elinor Glyn, Gene Stratton Porter, and Harold Bell Wright. Although much of this best-selling fiction was concocted and swallowed as mere entertainment, and may therefore be considered harmless, much was read as literature; and the more wholesome it was thought to be, the more unwholesome were its likely effects. It was not only remote from the realities of modern American life but shallow and crude in its representation of any human reality. Its popularity was due to its wholesale appeal to ready-made attitudes, carried out stylistically by salting the tail of every trite meaning. It guaranteed freedom from complexity, or from any hard thought or deep feeling. Its happy ending was always easy, arrived at by heroes who had only to circumvent villains, hurdle paper obstacles set up to create the illusion of suspense, and carefully evade any difficult moral issue. When it brought in the popular theme of religion, it confirmed the sloppy thought and feeling that passed for devoutness in a land pleased to worship both God and mammon. In seeming good for people, it only forced the question of what Americans were good for. Readers habituated to easy optimism and easy idealism were not apt to deal intelligently or responsibly with the growing complexities or compulsions of modern life, not to mention such personal problems as getting along decently with a husband or a wife rather different from the romantic heroes and heroines who lived happily ever after an ending that for adults is only a beginning.

Such popular literature may in any case be considered more pernicious than the worst of the trash. The trash was at least completely divorced from high culture, but the fiction mistaken for serious literature competed with high culture. Its readers were likely to be more self-satisfied. Criticism of their taste stirred up the democratic disposition to be hostile to standards of excellence, and to proclaim the inalienable rights of mediocrity and vulgarity. Hence popular writers joined businessmen, politicians, and Fundamentalist preachers in maintaining the tradition of anti-intellectualism in America. This raises questions about even the best of these writers. Dickens and Mark Twain, who alike fortified the complacence of their readers by their own hostility to intellectuals or highbrows, did not clearly win their popularity by their qualities of greatness. *Innocents Abroad,* with its mechanical, provincial satire, long sold much better than *Huckleberry Finn,* Mark Twain's masterpiece. Still more divergent were the levels of understanding and appreciation among readers of "good" books, apart from the many who bought them only to display on the living-room table.

But these complications recall the difficulties of sizing up the consequences of popular culture. The total picture in prewar America was not at all clear, despite the unmistakable trend toward "mass culture." This was growing more heterogeneous as well as more standardized, in keeping with the increasing variety and abundance of material goods. The wider range of choice it offered still included some genuine folk art, notably jazz, which would grow popular with many of the intelligentsia too. Similarly the "lively arts" were producing some performers of universal appeal, such as Charlie Chaplin. Otherwise the spreading gap between mass and high culture was being occupied by a larger, more amorphous cultural class drawn from all social ranks. Now known as "middlebrows," these readers were essentially a by-product of the new popular culture, by definition not highly cultivated in their tastes or drawn to the "best" books, and so liable to the current charge of creating a more insidious menace to high culture. To literary critics they looked ultrabourgeois, always addicted to the incipient book-of-the-month, often to the pretentious; served by slicker writers, with popular reviewers to endorse their conventional tastes, they were likely to be more hostile than pure lowbrows to the most original or unsettling art and thought. Yet they cannot be dismissed as mere "massmen." To a historian, more important than their cultural limitations were the earnest efforts of some millions of people to raise their sights and improve their minds.

At least the middlebrows helped to offset the increasing sensationalism on the lower levels of mass culture by some rise in the general level of sophistication. They were responding to the stirrings that would shortly produce the "second American renaissance," including the first American drama of distinction. They were heeding their critics too, making best sellers of works like *Main Street* that attacked conventionality or conformism. Meanwhile many women among them had joined the many national clubs that were studying social problems, educating voters, supporting settlement work in the slums, and pressing for reforms. Women in particular complicated the popular tendencies to self-indulgence and irresponsibility by a puritanical disposition to believe that recreation ought to be edifying, leisure time ought to be improved —driving their children to read dime novels on the sly, saddling them with the idea that reading "good" books was a chore and culture was never really fun, perhaps inducing allergies to match their own anxieties; yet also giving them some awareness of a wide range of choice in cultural fare suited to every taste and capacity, and making it possible for them to explore more freely, become emancipated from an invincible preference for dime novels. They might remind us that the great majority of Americans at least paid lip service to the importance of culture, clung to the vague idea that there are "finer things of life," and that a great many of them confused the issues by their clichés, saying that they knew nothing about art or culture but knew what they liked, while they were at once too sure and not really sure of their tastes, whether commonplace or "genteel," and often felt uneasy because uncertain what they ought to like, or unable to appreciate what the Joneses liked.

Altogether, prewar America most clearly foreshadowed the increasing contrariness of the great consuming public: a land that was due to be swamped by tabloids, comics, soap operas, sadistic thrillers, all manner of exploitations of sex, while at the same time symphony orchestras, little theaters, and art shows would spring up everywhere, and always millions kept on satisfying their creative impulse by puttering and repairing, growing and making things, cultivating new hobbies. The uncertainties of our knowledge about the actual effects of popular culture as a whole, what it has done to the minds of people, were also due to be accentuated as a free people would indulge in patriotic hysteria during World War I and its aftermath of a Red scare, elect such monumental nonentities as Harding and Coolidge, enjoy the spree of a big hollow boom that ended in a terrific crash and depression, cling to the comfortable illusion of isolationism until Pearl Harbor, take out their pains and the frustrations of the aftermath in the hysteria of McCarthyism; yet somehow manage to preserve their free institutions under all these stresses and strains, maintain the record of the established democracies as the stablest governments over the past century, assume unprecedented responsibilities, and keep on providing a substantial audience for their many critics, making best sellers of books about the insidious menaces to the freedom they are supposed to value less than security and conformity.

PART II

THE TWENTIETH CENTURY

Chapter Five | *W O R L D   W A R   I*

1. *The Coming of the War*

On June 28, 1914, a young Serbian nationalist in Sarajevo fired the shot
that killed the Austrian Archduke Franz Ferdinand—a shot that was
immediately heard round the world, because of the wonders of modern
communication, and in a month brought on the conflict that was the
major turning point of modern history, marking the end of the old
world. The date was well chosen: it was St. Vitus' Day. Europe proceeded to go out of its senses, teetering, stumbling, floundering into a
civil war even more stupid than the American one, but like it in that
it was far longer and bloodier than almost any leaders foresaw, and
than any country was prepared to fight. The reasons for its outbreak
were as foolish as the reasons offered by some religious sects that had
long prophesied that the world would end in 1914. Although both
sides soon began announcing lofty war aims, they were engaged in a
pure power struggle in which their actual aim was simply victory. At
stake was no cause of freedom, justice, international order, or any other
clear ideal above patriotism. As a boy at the time, I responded in an
arbitrary way that now seems fairly sensible. My playmates and I decided that we ought to choose sides to cheer for, each of us at once
picked his side, and at first I had little reason to regret that out of the
hat I picked Germany—it kept winning all the battles.

Yet our cheering also made sense because of the fervent patriotism
on both sides. It has become much too easy to condemn the folly of
our fathers, in a self-righteous spirit more offensive because of our
own addiction to folly. It is important to realize that the patriotism
involved a genuine idealism, an exaltation of loyalty, comradeship, love,

and readiness for self-sacrifice, with at first relatively little hatred. The motives of most supporters of the war were by no means so selfish, materialistic, or ignoble as were implied by the explanations of it that became popular in the postwar disillusionment, and that bred other dangerous illusions. It was something that the combatants felt the need of stating their aims in moral terms, formally justifying themselves before the court of world opinion, and that most men of good will came to believe that ideals of freedom, justice, and peace were at stake; else there would be no hope for this cause, or for humanity. And whatever our hopes, we can fully comprehend the folly and the horror of the greatest war in history to that time only in a recognition of this idealism. It helped to keep men fighting to the bitter end, which turned out to be as far from the original aims of the combatants as from their later avowed aims. It was the most catastrophic example of the most terrible paradox of Western civilization, that ever since the Crusades its uncommonly deep-rooted addiction to violence has been as deeply connected with its idealism.

At first glance, the outbreak of the war was more obviously paradoxical. Europe had long grown accustomed to not only brief, limited wars but the good reasons for the spreading belief that war itself would soon be a thing of the past. Among them were the many signs of the "concert of Europe": the international congresses that set up regulations for telegraph, postal service, patents, copyrights, etc.; the international conferences of scientists, economists, and other scholars; the multiplication of international societies of all kinds, swelling to over a thousand the congresses held during the century. A number of successful efforts at international arbitration had been climaxed by the establishment of the Hague Court for such purposes. Pacificism was steadily on the rise; by 1914 there were well over a hundred peace societies, which had been meeting in Universal Peace Congresses. A few years before, Norman Angell had won wide fame by *The Great Illusion,* in which he demonstrated that large-scale war was impossible because simply foolish: economic interdependence made it certain that victors would suffer as much as losers. Many of the intelligentsia were amplifying such arguments, pointing out that workers obviously had nothing to gain from war, but that it was bad for business too, especially for the many capitalists engaged in foreign commerce and investment. And almost everywhere the visions of increasing peace and order had a substantial base and fabric in the increasing plenty, the phenomenal spread of popular government, public education, and institutions promoting the public welfare. True, for some time fears had been growing that war was imminent, possibly inevitable, but even so it seemed unthinkable. Most thoughtful men agreed with Bergson: "War is probable but impossible." No enlightened man could believe that Europe, the leader of the civilized world, was on the verge of anarchy.

Strictly speaking, indeed, it was not. The kind of international anarchy suggested by the World War was made possible by something more dangerous than anarchy—the immense organization of power, economic, political, and military. This enabled both sides to carry on in spite of the terrific losses in men and materials. So did the major developments that had inspired hopes of lasting peace. The interdependence that stimulated the growth of internationalism also made it likely that more nations would be drawn into the hostilities; a European civil war soon became a world war. Popular government helped to make and keep it popular, literally a people's war. On the home front everybody could contribute to the immense war effort—technicians, workers, journalists, teachers. Women too could now do their bit, in office and factory as well as school and hospital. In retrospect, the war still does not look like an inevitable outcome of the history of the nineteenth century, but it was at least a natural outcome. The long preoccupation with its causes, due both to guilty conscience and the scale of the catastrophe, may make it seem more perplexing than it was. Like most senseless human behavior, it is not really hard to understand; and its lessons are all too obvious.

The most apparent reason for the war remains the growth of nationalism and militarism. The collaboration and arbitration between nations always stopped short of what each considered its vital interests, in particular the size of the armaments now required to protect them. The emergence of Germany as a mighty power, which had frightened other powers into building up great war machines, in turn made Germany more fearful of encirclement by enemies. Hence the "concert of Europe," never a real harmony, was permanently rent by rival alliances. The alliances were designed to maintain a balance of power, or if possible to achieve imbalance—superior strength; they were held together chiefly by ambition and fear, which could only perpetuate uneasiness and assure that any war would become a general war. Italy joined Germany and Austria-Hungary because they made it a better offer than France did or could; otherwise Italians hated the Austrians, their erstwhile masters, who had no more love for them. Britain and France were akin as democratic societies, but over the centuries they had chiefly fought each other, and they were not drawn together now by deep sympathies or popular demand; diplomats arranged their alliance in a common fear of Germany. The inclusion of czarist Russia in their Entente made no ideological sense whatever, being inspired only by awe of its vast potential strength, and considerable illusion about its actual strength. In a more reasonable world Russia would have hooked up with the Central Powers, for it had never fought Prussia, it shared Austria-Hungary's fear of internal revolution, and it was ideologically akin to both in its conservative, autocratic tradition. The war was hardly a showdown struggle between democracy and despotism.

So considered, it was fitting that the catastrophe was touched off by an assassination in Sarajevo. Bismarck had predicted, in his wisdom, that "some damned foolish thing in the Balkans" would start the next war. The newly independent Balkan countries had already fought furiously among themselves, but their foolishness was compounded by the clashing interests of the great powers, especially Russia and Austria-Hungary. Russia had nurtured its paternal solicitude for its Slavic brethren because of its "historic mission" to wrest Constantinople from the Turks—a mission long thwarted by Britain, but now opposed by Germany too because of its own ambitions in the Near East. Austria-Hungary had not only imperial interests in its neighbors but Balkan peoples within its fantastic borders.[1] These restless peoples induced it to take a militant line after the assassination, if only because its leaders felt that its position had been weakening, and a current economic depression made them more fearful of revolution. Otherwise there was hardly a "crisis"; the Austrian government waited almost a month before delivering its formidable ultimatum on Serbia, giving it only two days in which to accept impossible terms. Its leaders were by this time resolved on war, having got an unreserved promise of support from the German government; so they rejected the conciliatory reply to their ultimatum and promptly declared war. When Russia began mobilizing in support of the Serbs, Germany sent it an ultimatum, sent France

[1] To recall the strange, forgotten map of prewar Europe, what is now Yugoslavia then included the independent kingdoms of Serbia and Montenegro, the isolated Austrian province of Dalmatia, the nominally autonomous kingdom of Croatia under Hungarian rule, and the province of Bosnia-Herzegovina under joint Austro-Hungarian rule. The Austrians might have agreed to an independent confederation of these Slavic peoples (excluding those living along their own seacoast on the Adriatic), but the Hungarians—or more precisely the Magyars, who ruled the mongrel kingdom called Hungary—firmly opposed any such diminution of their sovereignty or encouragement to their subject peoples. Their intransigence accordingly helped to bring on the fatal foolishness that occurred at Sarajevo, capital of Bosnia-Herzegovina.

another, and within a few days declared war on both. Austria, which had forced the issue, may look more foolish because it had no stomach for fighting Russia, waiting several days before declaring war on it— a duty it was recalled to by sharp words from Germany.

Inasmuch as the Central Powers had formally started the war, they laid themselves open to the charge of guilt they were saddled with at its conclusion. By now historians are generally agreed that all the leading powers shared in the responsibility for the disaster, which the Germans at least had not deliberately provoked. All had been implicated in the secret diplomacy and the open armament race that built up tensions, created the war fever. In every country diplomats who wavered or worried over the appalling possibilities of a general war were kept under pressure by the military, all set to go with their war plans and timetables. Yet historians are also mostly agreed that Germany had more than an even share in the guilt, for reasons of particular concern in this history.

If it had good cause for its fears of being encircled by enemies, Germany had intensified the fear and the hostility by its own consistent aggressiveness. Dedicated to the militant nationalism built up by Bismarck, but no longer tempered by his prudence, it was a conspicuous exception to the spread of pacifist sentiment. While people elsewhere were impressed by Angell's *The Great Illusion,* Germans read more avidly a book published a year later (1911), General von Bernhardi's *Germany and the Next War,* which argued that it was not only their right but their duty to make this war, and in particular to crush France—France "must be annihilated once and for all as a great power." Their militarism was more naked and dangerous because the German army had much more power at home than did the military in other countries, and was not under civilian control. It was ardently supported by Kaiser Wilhelm II, who was fond of telling the world about his "mailed fist" and "shining armor." He was all the vainer and more arrogant because he was cowardly; he was so erratic, irresponsible, incredibly tactless, and often frenzied that his intimates (such as Chancellor von Bülow) doubted his sanity; and under the German political system he was about the most powerful man in Europe. Although at the last moment he got nervous, admitting that the Serbian reply to the Austrian ultimatum "dissipates every reason for war," he did not withdraw the promised support of Austria. His army went ahead with its long-prepared secret plans, which called for the immediate invasion of Belgium to get at France. This strategy, in violation of the neutrality that Germany had bound itself by treaty to observe, quickly proved to be a fatal diplomatic blunder. As the Kaiser had long done his eccentric best to earn the reputation he would win as the primary villain of the war, so Chancellor von Bethmann-Hollweg assured the guilt of Germany in the popular mind by his complaint to the departing British ambassador about all this fuss "just for a word —'neutrality'—just for a scrap of paper."

In this light France and Britain appeared to much better advantage. They had urged Austria to give Serbia more time, urged Serbia to make all honorable concessions short of sacrificing its independence. The French government was concerned primarily with self-defense, and it carefully refrained from overt aggression if only because it was uncertain of British support, which it desperately needed. Britain ran true to form, muddled and honorable. Like Parliament and public opinion, its Liberal Cabinet was split; Lloyd George himself was undecided, while others were definitely against entering the war. What settled the issue, for both the government and the great majority of the people, was the German invasion of Belgium. Even so, the decision to fight was made with more sorrow than the leaders of Germany displayed, or the Kaiser could understand. On the eve Sir Edward Grey made his prophetic remark: "The lamps are going out all over Europe; we shall not see them lit again in our lifetime."

Nevertheless, the issue of guilt remained confused because the clearest aims of the Allies were not clearly lofty. France had scarcely built up a reputation as either a peace-loving nation or a champion of oppressed peoples. Its most apparent motive was revenge for 1870, recovery of Alsace-Lorraine; its military had plans for a grand offensive, fired by dreams of Napoleonic *gloire*. Britain too had a war party (including the ardent young Winston Churchill), fired by its primary concern—the German threat to its naval supremacy, which it could justify only as a necessity for protecting its vast empire. Its military had its own secret plans and agreements, in particular a naval agreement with France unknown to its people. Its foreign policy had been determined by a Foreign Office under little more effective popular control than that of Germany; Sir Edward Grey might or might not have thought about the lamps of Europe when, in 1907, he arranged the Entente with benighted Russia. As for Russia, it helped to ignite the conflagration by its immediate mobilization on behalf of the Serbs. Czar Nicholas may have meant it when he told the world, in the first week of the war, "We also fight for our Slavic brothers, our companions in faith, our blood relations." In any case, he was a man of limited intelligence and education, often swayed by his foolish wife, otherwise torpid enough to justify the comment of the Kaiser (his cousin) that he was fit only "to grow turnips"; and he was another of the most powerful rulers in Europe. Upon ascending the throne he had announced, "I want everyone to know that I will devote all my strength to maintain, for the good of the whole nation, the principle of absolute autocracy." Count Witte, the ablest of his ministers, summed up the good he brought to the nation: "this insane regime; this tangle of cowardice, blindness, craftiness, and stupidity."

Even so, Russia brings up the deeper, more complex issues of the war. In speaking of it, as of "France" or "Germany," we must remember that we are referring to the actions of governments, not of the millions of people under them. The World War was due directly to the failures of diplomacy, and almost all the diplomats of Europe were still aristocrats, not elected by the people or directly responsible to them. Often they paid more heed to the royal cousins—Wilhelm, Nicholas, and George of England—whose casual notes and talks gave the oncoming catastrophe a more trivial than tragic air. At the same time, they by no means foisted the war on the common people. Everywhere, including Russia, it was enthusiastically supported by the great majority; the Russian peasant-soldiers were especially loyal as they fell by the millions. The pressure of public opinion gave European diplomats some excuse, in fact, for the superficial or transient successes that masked their failures. Primarily the opinion of the city masses, this was enflamed by the sensational, superpatriotic press exploiting the tribal nationalism that compensated them for the loss of village or regional loyalties.

By the same token, the war was not plotted by "capitalists" or munitions makers, who were doing a very profitable business as it was because of the armament race. As aristocrats, the diplomats gave little more attention to the interests of businessmen than of workers in playing their professional game; their dispatches rarely mentioned economic conditions. Lloyd George reported that when the British Cabinet debated whether to enter the war, bankers were "aghast" at the threat to the whole credit system in London. Hence the war was not directly due either to economic imperialism—the favorite explanation of Marxists. By this time the imperial frontier had gone the way of the American frontier: all the available lands had been grabbed and staked out. The leading powers were no longer disputing over the possession of colonial territory; a few years earlier, Morocco had provided the last important dispute of this kind. Although Germans still yearned for a colonial empire, or resented the British Empire, their motives were primarily nationalistic or militaristic, not economic. Their imperial dreams emphasized the prevailing atavism—the universal lag of political thinking behind the advance of modern technology.

This was the major economic factor. Capitalists indeed exercised great power, directly in their own interests, but chiefly because they served the national interest as conceived by government, and in particular by war offices. The old balance-of-power politics that diplomats continued to play grew steadily more dangerous because of the immense power behind them, which subjected them to heavy pressures from the military and made it impossible any longer to calculate nicely on local, limited wars. Bismarck himself might have been unable to control the mighty war machine he had done so much to build. Technology now enabled the German military to draw up elaborate war plans for setting a million or so men in rapid motion, completely equipped, while army officers sat on the boards of cartels and banks, had their hands on both government and industrial controls; the army amounted to an independent hierarchical society within the state. And the German people fondly regarded it as the embodiment of the spirit of the nation. Just so the French regarded their army, the British their navy. An extraordinary rationality in organization and technique was at the service of antique, irrational purposes.

We are accordingly brought back to the basic anomalies of prewar Europe. It was basking in its unparalleled affluence, its mastery of nature, its identity as the "civilized world," its conviction of supremacy over the entire world; and then came the most sudden, terrific disaster in history, entirely from within and through its own fault. The disaster struck a society more historically minded than any before it, more keenly aware of change, yet unmindful of the plainest consequences of the novel history it had made, the imperious necessity of simple common sense because of the tremendous power at its disposal. One of the very few statesmen who clearly foresaw the chaos to come was the socialist Jean Jaurès, who warned Frenchmen that just because of "the instruments of terrifying destruction created by modern science" the war would not be a short one; and for his wisdom he was promptly assassinated. (His patriotic murderer was not tried during the war.) By the same token, there were ample premonitions of disaster. The universal shock over the sinking of the *Titanic* was symbolic: the greatest

ship ever built by man, supposedly unsinkable and foolproof, had gone
down on its maiden voyage, signifying that the master of nature was
no match for a mere iceberg. The complacence of the "civilized world"
was belied more plainly by the crudity of its conflicts, as of the nationalism, racism, and militarism that aggravated them. These sentiments
flourished on not only popular ignorance but anxiety and fear. Europe
was feverish—much more so than its "sick man" Turkey. Its social and
cultural ills, apparent enough on the surface, were symptomatic of an
underlying spiritual crisis that could blow up the affair at Sarajevo—
no graver than a long series of international crises—into an excuse for
a world war.

The sensational press that throve on the city masses exploited not
only their craving for excitement but a more ominous disposition to
violence. This cropped up in many industrial strikes, the spread of
terrorism, an unprecedented series of political assassinations, and the
popular resort to lawlessness. Even in staid Britain suffragettes took
to defying the police, smashing windows, cutting telegraphic wires,
slashing paintings in galleries—behavior unseemly enough for men,
but shocking in ladies. Germans too were not so stolid as they appeared;
their workers were restless enough to keep the Junkers worried, and
their bourgeois were susceptible to the malaise reflected in the Youth
Movement. Patriotism was the panacea for sufferers from discontent
or an emotional void. Everywhere the common people could easily be
worked up into a war fever, no matter how strange their national allies
might be—Britishers and Russians, Germans and Turks—nor how
arbitrary and exorbitant the requirements for maintaining the national
honor.

The intelligentsia were prey to more acute and varied ills. For a century some had been uttering prophecies of disaster, more had been
sounding variations on the theme stated simply by Frederic Harrison:
"The *status quo* is impossible." Then they might give up their society
as hopeless, as some poets and painters did; or they might take to ideological violence, as many thinkers did; or they might indulge a kind
of secret passion for destruction that one may detect in most of the
gloomy prophets. (Of Henry Adams, Saint-Gaudens remarked that if
the world blew up, he would probably yell "in delight and derision
as he sailed into the air.") All were liable to the confusions and anxieties
resulting from the breakdowns of the traditional faiths—in God, in
absolute standards, in the power of reason, then in science too. As the
war approached, there were also signs of what someone called "the un-

conscious boredom of peace." The youth were attracted to such creeds as the Futurism of Marinetti: "We want to glorify war, the world's only hygiene—militarism, deed, destroyer of anarchisms, the beautiful ideas that are death-bringing, and the contempt of woman." The outbreak of the war signified a failure of mind, a corruption of mind; yet the intelligentsia were not simply shocked, numbed, or saddened by it. Like the common people, the great majority of them at once rallied around their flag.

Although a harsh critic might now call their patriotism a treason to their cause as intellectuals, it sprang from a natural loyalty to their particular cultural tradition, the immediate source of their idealism. Many a young writer felt the positive exaltation expressed by Kipling: "In the Gates of Death rejoice!" In Germany Thomas Mann hailed the war as "a purification, a liberation, an enormous hope"; he foresaw the prospective victory of Germany as one of "soul over numbers" and over the "civil corruption" of peace. Even Max Weber, who had long warned of the coming disaster, now felt that the war was "great and wonderful." Others who were distressed by it remained hopeful, like Bergson: he foresaw the rejuvenation of France and the moral regeneration of all Europe, though at the cost of terrible sacrifices. Very few anticipated the actual outcome of the war and its aftermath, the end of the old order. Their failure as prophets was pardonable, since the extraordinary achievements of Europe—both material and intellectual—had made it impossible for anybody to predict or calculate the future with the degree of assurance that Bismarck had. Yet their failure was due as well to some feeling of relief over the coming of the war, which might resolve the impossible *status quo*. Europe had it coming in a deeper, Freudian sense. For various reasons, sometimes expressed, more often inarticulate or unconscious, most of its people really wanted war. They were not so free in mind or spirit as they liked to think they were.

2.   The Conduct of the War

Another compelling reason for the disaster in Europe was that its statesmen and generals at once overestimated and underestimated their national power, substantially agreeing with Norman Angell that a prolonged war would be economically impossible. All the general staffs

had planned on a short, decisive war; no country had made military
or economic preparations for a long one. Otherwise Austria and Russia
would hardly have squared off over Serbia, for ever since the days
of Metternich their statesmen had been haunted by the fear—known
to Bismarck too—that war might stir up more popular revolutions.
Only a good quick victory could avert this dreadful possibility, serve
to distract their people from the political problems at home.

As it was, Germany nearly vindicated the statesmen. In the first month
of the war its armies carried out splendidly the plan drawn up by
Schlieffen years before: they rolled through Belgium, then rolled as
steadily through western France, with the objective of encircling and
destroying the French army. They did even better than expected on
their eastern front, where the Schlieffen plan called only for a holding action, if necessary some sacrifice of Prussian territory, until France
had been crushed; they virtually ended the Russian threat by the
smashing victory at Tannenberg that made von Hindenburg famous.
There remained, however, a striking anomaly—the inaction of the
German navy. The Kaiser, inspired by Admiral Mahan's book on the
supreme importance of seapower, had insisted on building a great fleet
to challenge British supremacy, and thereby had assured the enmity
of Britain; yet Admiral von Tirpitz had been unable to find out how
his navy fitted into the war plan. Now he learned the reason: there was
no plan for it. The Germans, who made the best military record in the
war, nevertheless illustrated a peculiar problem of the modern world:
the military cost nations much more than ever before, and had as
much more power, both material and political, but could never be
trusted to employ it intelligently even for their own purposes.

Thus the French had eased the German success by sticking to their
own plan, which characteristically called for a grand offensive straight
to the Rhine.[2] For the sake of this offensive, which never got really under way, their commander Joffre obstinately ignored the German advances on his left until too late. His soldiers were further handicapped
by the nation's pride, which had led the army to reject indignantly
a minister's proposal that grayish trousers be substituted for the traditional red ones; so they marched into battle in the loudest of colors,
still easier targets for the efficient Germans. Meanwhile the small Brit-

---

[2] The whole story of the first month of the war is very well told in Barbara
Tuchman's *The Guns of August,* a thoroughly scholarly as well as popular book. Its
success is incidentally another sign that "middlebrow" tastes are not necessarily a menace
to culture.

ish expeditionary force, which was as eager to distinguish itself, was frustrated by its jittery commander, Sir John French; he soon lost his nerve and refused to stop retreating. (A brief stand at Mons inspired the fond national legend that the British bore the brunt in these bad days and saved France, but in fact they never engaged more than a small fraction of the German army.) As might have been expected, the awesome Russian hosts failed to perform like the steam roller they were supposed to be. The native incompetence of their minister of war was fortified by contempt for the newfangled talk about "modern war," or the possible insufficiency of bayonets. Nevertheless the poorly armed Russian rank and file made do with courage, carrying on for a long time in spite of huge losses that their leaders were unable even to keep a decent record of. Most important, the Russian advances in East Prussia scared the Germans into tampering with the so carefully prepared Schlieffen plan. The German High Command sent two army corps away from the western to the eastern front, too late to help out in the victory at Tannenberg, but in time to miss the crucial battle of the Marne, which they might well have enabled the Germans to win.

All popular legends notwithstanding, the Battle of the Marne was unquestionably the turning point of the war. The German defeat was due in part to some further miscalculations of their generals, but in particular to their reasonable belief that the French army was completely disorganized. All the more real glory, then, for the French soldiers who surprised the enemy by their verve after their long, confused, demoralizing retreat. And so all the more depressing was the reward they won. Both sides now settled down to the murderous stalemate of siege warfare, punctuated by campaigns to exchange muddy trenches, now and then by a grand offensive to move the trenches a few miles ahead. The slaughter at Verdun was the symbol of an insanity that lasted for four years, cost millions of lives, and destroyed the chance of an honorable peace. "The nations were caught in a trap," concluded Barbara Tuchman, "a trap made during the first thirty days of battle that failed to be decisive, a trap from which there was, and has been, no exit."

The "great" war was indeed novel even apart from the huge casualties. It was fought not only on land and sea but in the air, underseas, and underground. With the trench spade came such new weapons as poison gases, submarines, tanks, and airplanes. Machines now took over war too, at more expense of human values; gone for good were the traditional glamour of red trousers, battlelines of infantry shoulder to

shoulder, dashing cavalry charges, and all chance that the heroic deaths
of a few hundred men (as at Trafalgar) could save their country. But
the generals were slow in catching on to the revolution in warfare.
Commander in Chief Sir Douglas Haig, described by Lloyd George as
"brilliant to the top of his army boots," was only typical in his main
tactic, simply to throw in more men and ammunition. Hence the war
required a vast mobilization of industry, in effect an all-out national
effort. Never before had such power been organized, massed, and controlled, and finally remained beyond control, its long-range effects beyond calculation.

As a people's war, it was unprecedented as well in the mobilization
of propaganda. Foreign Offices published the pretty "Rainbow Series"
—the British Blue Book, the French Yellow Book, the Russian Orange
Book, the White and Red Books of Germany and Austria-Hungary—
featuring diplomatic documents to prove their innocence or the purity
of their motives. The blend of skillful deception and high-minded self-
deception by which each country sought to justify itself in the eyes of
world opinion was a tribute to the moral order that most Europeans still
believed in and sincerely hoped to preserve. It nevertheless amounted
to psychological warfare, designed both to win over neutrals and bolster
morale at home. Patriotism was maintained by press campaigns to whip
up hatred of the enemy. Among the lasting consequences of the war
was the cultivation of the art of propaganda, more systematic means
of hoodwinking people or preventing independent critical judgment.

In this warfare the British and French had distinctly the better of it.
Having violated the neutrality of little Belgium, the Germans proceeded to win a reputation for "frightfulness" by shooting Belgian
civilians who misbehaved, dropping some bombs on Liège from a zep-
pelin, and burning down the city of Louvain in reprisal for continued
civilian disobedience. Although such atrocities were piddling by the
standards to come, not to say much exaggerated in Allied propaganda,
many people still thought them shocking. At first, to be sure, moral
considerations had little to do with the extension of the war, which
left only six neutrals in Europe. Turkey, long wooed by Germany,
entered on its side because Russia had always been the main enemy;
ambitious Japan lined up with the Allies as a gesture, with eyes on
Shantung province in China; Slavic Bulgaria chose the Central Powers
out of bitter hatred of Serbia, Romania the Allies out of territorial
designs on Hungary; and Italy also had chiefly territory in mind when
it turned on its former allies, since what it wanted in Europe could

come only out of Austria. But the American entry into the war was a much more complex as well as momentous affair. Another historic turning point, this not only settled the outcome of the war but gave it a new meaning. As the one major combatant that had no territorial ambitions, America insisted that the issues at stake were freedom and justice—the only possible justification for so catastrophic a conflict.

Now, its entry was unquestionably influenced by material interests too. In the throes of another depression when the war broke out, the United States had soon begun prospering mightily on its trade with the Allies, in time lending them huge sums to pay for the goods they needed. In the postwar disillusionment Americans came to believe that they had been deluded into fighting by munitions makers and financiers, abetted by Allied propaganda; as Senator Gerald Nye put it, they had fought only "to save the skins of American bankers" who had staked two billions on the Allies. Actually, however, there is no clear evidence that decisions in Washington were determined by pressures from big bankers and their clients. Material interests showed up most plainly in the concern over the whole economy: war trade with the Allies had become such a booming business that halting it would have meant a severe depression, from which workers too would suffer. Yet even this concern was not clearly the main reason for the final decision to enter the war, least of all in the thought of its author, Woodrow Wilson. We cannot hope to understand this fateful event and its aftermath—including the aid that American disillusionment lent to the rise of Hitler— unless we credit the idealistic motives that were among its complex, confused causes. However naïve they may now seem, Americans by and large did believe that they were fighting a war to end all war and to make the world safe for democracy. The great majority of intellectuals shared this belief, even taking credit for leading the public to it. The pessimistic Henry Adams himself now rejoiced in a new hope, "the building up of the great community of Atlantic Powers."

From the outset of the war President Wilson, like most Americans, was pro-Ally despite the policy of neutrality he had at once proclaimed; and herewith began the confusion and uncertainty of his foreign policy. There is no question, I take it, that Wilson really meant the sonorous generalities he was addicted to, lofty principles that today may also seem naïve—yet perhaps not so naïve as the supposed realism of most of the world's statesmen. He long believed that America could best serve both its national interests and the interests of mankind by remaining neutral, or "too proud to fight," thus keeping itself "fit and free to do what is honest and disinterested and truly serviceable for the peace of the world." His rhetorical appeals to the cause of justice and humanity made sense for the same reason that they sounded futile: it was essential "to assert the principles of law in a world in which the principles of law have broken down." He was not foolish either in believing that the world had entered a new era that called for "a new and more wholesome diplomacy," in which nations would be held up to the code of honor demanded of individuals, since the tremendous power at their command had outmoded the traditional power politics. Nevertheless, Wilson's own thinking was hardly adjusted to the realities of the new era. Some antiquated ideas deepened the confusion of his foreign policy, above all his efforts to maintain "the laws of neutrality." He was soon at sea over the issue of submarine warfare—the first example of the novel problems created by "modern" warfare, and so worth recalling in some detail.[3]

When early in 1915 the Germans announced their intention of torpedoing enemy merchant ships in the waters about Great Britain and Ireland, and warned neutrals to keep their ships out of the danger zone, Wilson at once replied that if any American ships were attacked or American lives lost, the United States would consider the act an "indefensible violation of neutral rights." In the next two years only a few American ships were sunk and fewer than two hundred American lives lost, but Wilson continued to protest vigorously on high principle —"the freedom of the seas," in the name of international law. The immediate difficulty remained that the Germans had a strong case. They were retaliating against an illegal blockade by the British, who were also flagrantly violating neutral rights—as Wilson recognized by repeated protests, but without forcing the issue. Many of the ships they torpedoed (including the *Lusitania*) were carrying munitions from the United States, a "neutral" that was serving exclusively the Allies as a great base of supplies. Presently the English started arming their merchant ships, giving the Germans a better excuse for sinking them without warning. Although the American government refused to designate armed merchantmen as vessels of war, or to prohibit Americans from traveling on them, they were in effect auxiliary warships; and neutrals certainly had no clear right to safety as passengers on them.

Hence Wilson's appeal to the laws of neutrality and freedom of the

---

3 In what follows I am particularly indebted to Edward H. Buehrig's *Woodrow Wilson and the Balance of Power*, a most patient, judicious, dispassionate study of Wilson's foreign policy.

seas only called attention to the basic difficulty. There was no accepted international law about submarines, for the simple reason that these were a new kind of weapon. So were the sea mines planted by the British, who otherwise were favored by the traditional rules of naval warfare. Modern technology was already making it impossible to distinguish sharply between belligerent and neutral, soldier and civilian; just as it was sparing more and more fighters from even seeing the people they killed, anticipating the wholesale, impersonal slaughter by bombers. Submarine warfare still seemed barbarous, to Americans another proof of German frightfulness, especially when twelve hundred people went down with the *Lusitania*; and Wilson then linked freedom of the seas with the cause of civilization and humanity. Nevertheless, both sides felt free to disregard his laws of neutrality, which had become obsolete. In the Versailles treaty there would be no mention whatever of freedom of the seas.

Meanwhile Wilson's inconsistent diplomacy was further confused by the ingrown immaturity of American public opinion about foreign affairs. Most Americans wanted their government to take a firm line with Germany, compel it to submit to their lawful demands; but a still greater majority were as firmly opposed to entering the war and typically had only vague ideas, if any, about what to do if the Germans refused to submit. They felt freer to indulge in moral indignation because they took for granted that the war was none of their business, America should avoid foreign entanglements. (It had taken no part in the frantic diplomacy just before the war.) As relations worsened, Wilson took up the task of teaching the people the elementary facts of international life, trying to make them realize that the country could not possibly help being entangled in world affairs. In 1916 he proposed a league of nations to assure future peace. He remained vague, however, about practical policies meanwhile, for this was the year he came up for re-election and had to face the realities of partisan politics. Theodore Roosevelt, who initially endorsed the policy of neutrality, had soon attacked the administration for failing to protest against the invasion of Belgium, and the Republicans now countered Wilson's campaign slogan "he kept us out of war" by charging that he had not been tough enough in maintaining "our rights as neutrals." They almost won the election by implying that their man would be much better at securing both neutrality and our rights, or eating the cake and having it too. German military leaders discounted the dangers of American entry into the war because the nation was obviously unprepared to fight.

Wilson was still far ahead of public opinion when he launched his peace offensive following his re-election. Now that the war had settled down to an uncompromising, exhausting "total" war, he saw clearly the most serious danger—that the bitterness it was engendering would destroy hopes of a lasting peace. He accordingly tried to force negotiations for peace by calling on all the belligerents to state their war aims, and he followed up with an address to Congress in which he made his famous proposal of "peace without victory." That nothing came of all this may again be attributed to Wilson's trust in glittering generalities, backed only by uncertain pledges about the eagerness of the United States to cooperate in the great purpose of securing "peace and justice throughout the world." In suggesting a league of nations for this purpose, Foreign Secretary Grey of Britain had put the critical question: "How much are the United States prepared to do?" It was not at all certain that American public opinion would stand for doing much. But again Wilson's peace move was made to look foolish by the immediate response to it, which thoroughly justified his fears. By this time the British government was headed by Lloyd George, all afire for the knockout and dead set against a negotiated peace; France joined in a reply making clear that the Allies would be content with nothing short of victory. Germany, now practically ruled by its military, was no more willing to negotiate. Two weeks before Wilson announced his famous slogan the German High Command had settled on the effective reply it would announce on February 1, 1917: unrestricted submarine warfare on all shipping, including that of neutrals—a high or desperate gamble to starve England into submission.

Thereupon Wilson promptly broke off diplomatic relations with Germany. Within a few weeks attacks on American shipping eased the way to a declaration of war. The President had all along been coming around to the conviction of Secretary of State Lansing that the war was essentially a struggle between democracy and autocracy, and the Russian Revolution now helped out by doing away with the autocracy that had obscured the Allies' devotion to the cause of human freedom. Hence the keynote of his War Message: "The world must be made safe for democracy." By this time he had Congress and the people solidly enough behind him. When war was declared, patriotic fever was so intense that the few "willful" men who opposed the declaration were branded as virtual traitors.

As this suggested, however, the crusade for freedom was still clouded. Secretary Lansing noted sadly in his diary that even patriotic senators and congressmen seemed blind to the great issues, seeing only that our neutral rights had been violated. Except for these violations it was in fact very doubtful that Congress would have been won over, or public opinion either. Most Americans evidently felt like Theodore Roosevelt, who said that while fighting for humanity we were also fighting primarily for our own vital interests, to "make the world safe for America"; their patriotic fever did little to clarify their ideas about either democracy or the world. (Among its expressions were the banning of German music and the transformation of sauerkraut into "liberty cabbage.") Wilson himself tacitly acknowledged as much by setting up a propaganda agency, the Committee on Public Information, to sell his lofty conception of the war. On the eve of his War Message he had confided further misgivings to a journalist friend. He had no doubt, he told Frank Cobb, that America's entry into the war would assure that Germany would be beaten, badly beaten, but that was the trouble: the Allies would then defeat his purposes by dictating a victorious peace.

Needless to add, he was quite right on both counts. Because the Allies had long borne the brunt, which enabled them to claim most of the credit for the victory, they were in pretty bad shape; and if they might nevertheless have won the war by themselves, America unquestionably made the decisive contribution. The terrific strain of the long stalemate in slaughter appeared in a serious mutiny in the French army, the rapid decline of German morale toward the end, and then the frenzy of joy in the Allied countries upon the signing of the Armistice. No victory in the past had touched off such wild celebration. No conqueror had been cheered so ecstatically as Woodrow Wilson would be in the streets of Paris.

In spite of the painful letdown to come, I judge that it was better for the free world that Germany lost the war. Certainly its leaders had given no promise of wisdom or generosity, least of all when they dictated the treaties of Brest-Litovsk to the Russians and Bucharest to the Romanians; the extreme harshness of these treaties was forgotten when people began deploring the settlement of Versailles. As certainly the German military would have had much to say about the terms of a victorious peace, and they were not modest types. If France might not have been "annihilated" to the taste of General von Bernhardi, a triumphant Germany would obviously have dominated Europe and put an end to the naval supremacy of Britain. America would have had good reason to fear (as Theodore Roosevelt did) a possible alliance between Germany and Japan. How democracy would have fared is anybody's guess; one need not assume that the Germans would have tried to root it out, to the greater glory of the Kaiser; but at best it would have had to make do with the uncertain uses of adversity. For the rest, a German-dominated Europe might have preserved European hegemony a while longer, but for purposes not clearly lofty or enlightened.

Perhaps better might have been an outcome that Wilson hoped for. When he summoned his Cabinet to break off relations with Germany, Lansing argued that the future peace of the world could be assured only by an Allied victory, adding (to quote his journal) that all the great nations should have democratic institutions "because democracies were never aggressive or unjust"; whereupon the President shocked him by expressing some doubts about this, declaring that "probably greater justice would be done if the conflict ended in a draw." Naturally he could make no clarion calls for a mere draw when the nation entered the war—the national end had to be victory; but his hope remained peace without victory. Toward the end of the year the Bolsheviks embarrassed him by publishing the secret treaties of the Allies, with promises of territory and agreements on the punishment of Germany that exposed some sham in the lofty war aims they professed, suggesting that democracies could be aggressive or unjust. Since the British and French refused to join him in an appropriate answer, Wilson independently spelled out his own war aims in his celebrated "Fourteen Points," which included demands for open diplomacy and self-determination by all peoples as well as his cherished freedom of the seas. This program was the measure of the wisdom, sincerity, innocence, and confusion of his idealism; and the measure too of the high hopes, the partial achievements, and the basic failures of the peace he helped to make at Versailles.

As we review the depressing aftermath, however, including the grievances that by this measure the Germans made so much of, we should remember that the German imperial government never committed itself to anything like so generous a program for peace. When Wilson announced his Fourteen Points, it flatly rejected them.

3.   *The Treaty of Versailles*

When John Maynard Keynes protested against the crushing reparations that were being imposed on Germany, he wrote nobly: "Nations
are not authorized, by religion or by natural morals, to visit on the
children of their enemies the misdoings of parents or of rulers." Unhappily, nations are always bound to do something like this—and to
their own children too. No people can possibly escape the consequences
of the doings of its fathers and its rulers; it has to pay for their follies,
just as it enjoys all the good they may have done. Whatever God wills,
"natural morals" in political life dictate that all states must be held
responsible for their actions and contracts, and that no state is entitled
to repudiate its past, cancel all its debts, and offer its children a clean
slate. We, who are still saddled with the consequences of the Treaty
of Versailles, should remember that our fathers were worse off, charged
immediately with the terrific costs of the war. First and last we must
emphasize that the treaty satisfied nobody, settled nothing for good,
dismally failed to secure a just and lasting peace; but simply because
of the complexity and the gravity of the problems we inherited we
need to recall the plain reasons, soon obscured by the revulsions against
the treaty, why the peacemakers could not possibly have satisfied everybody, decently settled everything, and done perfect justice at once to
the Germans and the Allies.

In general, the scale of the attempted settlement at Versailles was as
unprecedented as that of the war itself. The largest peace conference
in history was attended by delegations from some thirty Allied countries, and though presently the major decisions were made by the Big
Four (Wilson, Lloyd George, Clemenceau, and Orlando of Italy), they
had to take into account the conflicting interests of all these countries,
all over the globe, which were alike preoccupied with what they hoped
to get out of the peace. They deliberated in an atmosphere of bitter
resentments, intensified by fears of the latent might of Germany, which
had almost won the war singlehanded. They might have done better
had they attempted only a preliminary settlement, waiting a few years
for tempers to cool before drawing up a final, comprehensive one, but
they were confronted by the urgent needs of a disordered world. The
new nations that had been immediately formed by subject peoples
of the Central Powers, such as the Poles and the Czechs, were already

fighting over their borders; a dozen little wars were going on. These were but one example of the social, political, and economic upheavals caused by the war, not by the men of Versailles, who would later be blamed for all the troubles. The extraordinarily difficult problems of the peacemakers were aggravated by the very idealism of many of the delegates, especially the younger ones, who had high hopes of founding a new order and writing an "Eternal Peace." They were quickly disillusioned; like Keynes, they sensed a "nightmare" of frivolous unreality and utter futility; so they helped to keep all wounds open, tempers frayed, feelings bitter. They were slow to realize at once the immediate and the ultimate difficulty, that there was as yet no real international community on which to base a new world order.

The first issue was the harsh punishment of Germany, which together with its allies was formally declared responsible for the war. With the return of Alsace-Lorraine to France and the handing over of part of upper Silesia to the new state of Poland, it lost altogether about a tenth of its territory in Europe; it lost as well all its colonies in Africa and the Pacific; it was required to abolish conscription, reduce its standing army to 100,000, reduce its navy correspondingly, and hand over its merchant fleet; it was to begin paying reparations for the loss and damage caused the Allies, the exact amount to be determined later; and to assure fulfillment of these and many other incidental terms, an Allied force was to occupy the left bank of the Rhine for fifteen years.[4]

But the Germans had further grievances. Contrary to usual custom (as at the Congress of Vienna in 1815), they were not allowed to participate in the conference; the peace was not negotiated but dictated. Until they ratified the treaty, eight months after the Armistice, the Allies maintained their blockade of Germany, already suffering from hunger. They felt more outraged because at the time of the Armistice, in accordance with Wilson's demands, they had got rid of the Kaiser and proclaimed a republic. Wilson had promised freedom, justice, and self-government for all peoples, including the Germans, whom he distinguished from their "military masters"; now their brand-new republic, a difficult enterprise at best, got off to an almost hopeless start because it was forced to sign the treaty and assume all the costs

---

[4] As an example of the thoroughness of the treaty, Article 246 called for the surrender to England of the skull of Sultan M'Kwada, which had been removed to Germany from German East Africa. The best that the Germans could manage to do about this demand was to give London a choice of three skulls, of men unknown.

of the "war guilt." Likewise Wilson had announced that there would
be "no annexations," whereas in the extensive annexations that followed several million Germans lost the right of self-determination.
Worst of all was the huge bill for reparations, running into many billions. The amount need not be specified because it was strictly nonsensical, far beyond not only any fair estimate of damages but the
capacity of Germany to pay; and though it was soon scaled down it
remained a hopelessly unrealistic, stupid mode of punishment.

Yet the Germans complained more bitterly than they had a clear
right to. From the beginning they were truculent enough to recall
their own grim record as treaty makers and the boasts of the Kaiser:
"I will dictate the peace terms at the point of my soldiers' bayonets."
They did not fare too badly in the redrawing of the map of Europe,
considering how mixed up peoples were in some regions; in their outrage over their compatriots who were put under Polish and Czech
rule, they ignored the claims and resentments of the many more millions of peoples who had been under German and Austrian rule. It is
harder to sympathize with their bitterness over the disarmament of
Germany, painful as was the blow to their national or military pride;
and at that they at once began circumventing the disarmament provisions, laying plans for another military machine. Even the staggering
reparations bill did not discourage such intentions, since they still had
the greatest industrial plant in Europe. When in 1923 the German
government announced its inability to pay any more, and took to
printing hundreds of billions of paper marks, the wild inflation that
wiped out the savings of the middle class also liquidated the national
debt. Thereafter Germany prospered, until the world depression, with
the help of American loans much greater than the reparations it paid;
it had no trouble building new factories—carefully designed for
speedy conversion to war production. Hitler then demonstrated that
its economy was far from ruin.

The Führer also gave away the basic case of the Germans. It had not
been simply their "military masters" that got them into the war, but
their whole proud tradition. An overwhelming majority of the German
people had acclaimed the declaration of war, the indifference to mere
scraps of paper, and the early victories of their great army. Although
many grew querulous under the strains of the long stalemate, popular
discontent produced little demand for any sacrifice of German imperial
ambitions until near the end of the war. Then a People's League for
Freedom and Fatherland, dedicated to liberal, humanitarian ideals,

was countered by a more popular league, a pure Fatherland party. Nor were the Germans clearly chastened by their defeat, resolved to amend their ways.[5] Their Weimar Republic was set up by a minority, who in elections thereafter never won a majority; Hitler's party was only one of a number of extremist parties founded as promptly to sabotage it. If the republic might have grown more popular except for the incubus of the Treaty of Versailles, most Germans blamed all their woes on this treaty—not on the war they had ardently supported. They complained much more than they rejoiced over their freedom from universal conscription and the burden of heavy armaments. In 1925, when the nation was prospering, its temper was revealed by its election as president of its great war-hero, Field Marshal von Hindenburg.

Meanwhile there was much to be said on behalf of the French, who in the liberal revulsion against Versailles were severely criticized for their intransigence. In their pride they had in 1870 at once settled down to paying off the huge indemnity imposed on them, not whining as the beaten Germans would. Now as victors they came out of the war more impoverished than Germany, having suffered not only proportionately heavier casualties but immense damage, some of it due to wanton destruction by the retreating German army. Above all, they had good reasons for their seemingly neurotic fear of Germany. Having almost defeated the whole world, it had come out of the war undamaged, its much superior industrial plant intact; despite the loss of some territory it still had a much larger population than France too; and from their own experience the French felt sure that their potentially far more powerful neighbor would sooner or later seek revenge. When Wilson and Lloyd George turned down their demand for a protective frontier on the Rhine, they settled uneasily for an Anglo-American guarantee of their defense, but they were then denied this security. The United States repudiated Wilson's guarantee when the Senate refused to ratify the treaty. Britain drew apart, growing more lenient toward the Germans and critical of the French; it felt pleasantly secure now that the German fleet had been destroyed. Quite possibly the anxious French might have found it wiser to be lenient, bank on the hope of a regenerate democratic Germany, and unquestionably they were foolish when they banked instead on the "Maginot men-

---

5 "I have never felt as I do in this hour of shame," said Max Weber, "that it is a gift from heaven to be a German." A member of the German delegation sent to Paris, he advised that the Treaty of Versailles be rejected. When it was signed he retired from political life, to brood more somberly over heaven's gift of civilization.

tality," fortified by characteristically shortsighted military leaders. In any case, Marshal Foch's comment on the Treaty of Versailles turned out to be the most prophetic, accurate to the very year: "This is not Peace. It is an Armistice for twenty years."

More troublesome issues were raised by the relative success of the men of Versailles in making good Wilson's promise of self-determination. This was not extended to colonial peoples, of course, and everywhere the principle was to some extent sacrificed because of the secret promises the Allies had made to the Japanese, Italians, Greeks, and others who had joined them; thus Italy was awarded some territory populated chiefly by Yugoslavs. In Europe the issues were further confused by not only the intermingling of peoples but the kind of historic "rights" claimed by the Poles: some of the land they demanded—and seized—had been Polish only in that its peasantry, of different stock, had been dominated by Polish landlords. Nevertheless, the great bulk of the subject peoples were liberated. Whereas Metternich in 1815 had restored the map of Europe with an eye only to the historic dynasties, it was now redrawn largely in terms of nationalities; many millions of people were either formed into new nations or united with kin peoples in existing nations. The trouble was that in their nationalistic fervor they at once began exercising their rights to self-determination in traditional ways dismaying to Wilsonian idealists. They added to the hostilities on the European scene by quarreling over disputed territory and erecting more tariff walls, while none except Czechoslovakia established a really democratic government. Necessarily small powers, they failed to strengthen themselves by pooling their resources or cementing friendships. All contained restive racial minorities that would make them easier prey for Hitler's Germany, then for the Soviet.

Hence statesmen of the old school could say "I told you so." In *The Gathering Storm,* Winston Churchill pictured the breakup of the Austro-Hungarian Empire as a "cardinal tragedy," pointing out that in gaining their independence all its subject peoples had brought on themselves the tortures of the damned. Yet the peacemakers surely cannot be blamed for granting this independence. They could not possibly have restored the Austro-Hungarian Empire, much less made it secure against the internal dissensions that had brought on the World War. All idealism aside, they could not ignore the demands of the aroused subject peoples, who had already declared and made good their independence anyway. The principle of self-determination was no visionary ideal of Woodrow Wilson but a hard reality of modern international life, the consequence of a century of agitation. However difficult the problems it creates, no liberal or democrat can ever simply deplore it either; like persons, whole peoples are entitled to some independence in pursuing their communal interests and choosing their wider loyalties. The irrepressible stirrings in central Europe fore-shadowed the stirrings all over the non-Western world today, when there is no blinking the fact that most of the new nations are hope-lessly unprepared to govern themselves well, and it is nevertheless no longer feasible to deny them independence.

So, too, both idealism and realism went into the establishment of the League of Nations, on which above all Wilson had set his heart. This was by no means the threat to American sovereignty that his enemies at home would charge, since it did not make arbitration com-pulsory. The realistic French were perhaps more visionary when they tried vainly to have it equipped with an effective army of its own and powers of inspection of all other military establishments, as insur-ance against German aggression, for none of the great powers—includ-ing France—were really prepared to submit to such controls in matters they considered vital to their national interests. So far from being a supergovernment, the League of Nations came down to a mere promise of respect for the territorial integrity of all its members, and of efforts to resolve peaceably all their disputes. The promise was backed im-mediately by active cooperation in related bodies, such as the Perman-ent Court of International Justice, the Health Organization, and the International Labor Office. The last-named in particular stated in its constitution the hope behind the great deal of cooperation that would in fact be achieved in humanitarian endeavors: "Permanent peace can be established only if it is based upon social justice."

The obvious difficulty remained that there was no such firm basis for a lasting peace. The League was doomed to be ineffectual because the nations were still little inclined to work for peace and social justice at any expense of their own interests, much more inclined to put their trust in the old policies of alliance and balance of power. The democ-racies especially had yet to realize what Norman Angell wrote during the war, that they could least afford a divisive nationalism, had more need of international unity than did autocratic nations. And their fail-ure brings up another fond illusion of Wilson's. Believing that the European governments did not truly represent their peoples, he was as convinced that his Fourteen Points represented the real wishes of the common people everywhere. En route to the peace conference, he remarked that unless it "was prepared to follow the opinions of mankind and to express the will of the people rather than that of their leaders at the Conference," disaster would soon come again; and to the end he went on appealing over the heads of the leaders to the people, who had given him so tumultuous a welcome when he landed in Europe. But in fact public opinion was again an excuse for the failure of the leaders.

The French were naturally embittered and vengeful, and their press early started ridiculing Wilson as a busybody and a dupe of the Germans. Lloyd George had to contend with a "Hang the Kaiser" campaign, a fierce hatred drummed up by the popular press; the powerful Northcliffe set his howlers on him at the least suggestion of moderation toward the Germans. Orlando broke down in tears when he was denied Fiume, which the Italian people were clamoring for (though the secret treaty with the Allies had not promised Italy this plum). All the European leaders insisted on fabulous reparations from Germany if only to soothe their taxpayers. Even so all the Big Four would shortly lose office because of popular discontent, which was not at all due to feeling that they had been too harsh on the Germans. And though Wilson himself paid too little heed to American public opinion, he also made some concessions to it, including an ominous one. The settlement at Versailles and the League to guarantee it was more fatally inadequate as a basis for world peace and order because Russia was not represented in either. Wilson and Lloyd George both wanted to include Russia, but Clemenceau would not stand for it, and they agreed to drop the issue because public opinion would not stand for it either—Americans in particular were already too frightened by the Bolsheviks.

Finally, however, the statesmen at Versailles must bear a primary responsibility for the failures, at least in so far as statesmen are to be judged as leaders. If Wilson was deluded about his popular support, he was the only leader who tried consistently to educate public opinion and hold to a long and large view of the world's needs. His colleagues made little effort to enlighten their people, or even to keep them decently informed about the aims and the problems of the Peace Conference. Otherwise the kindest thing to say about them is that they were shortsighted. Early in the war Ambassador Walter Page had informed Wilson that the world was no longer the same—"nothing is the same." The leaders of Europe at Versailles proved that he was both right and wrong. Preoccupied with the same old national interests, they failed to realize the revolutionary consequences of the war itself. A partial exception was the revolution in Russia, which they could not help being aware of; here their intervention, inspired both by fear and by ignorance of what was going on in the Soviet, accomplished nothing whatever beyond securing its hostility to the West. For the rest, they were unable to lay the foundations of a new order because they were unable to perceive the imperious necessities of a new era that had already dawned. Another conspicuous example was their failure to give anything like adequate thought to the economic problems of an interdependent world.

But this was due as well to downright irresponsibility or simple lack of courage, most apparent in the preposterous reparations bill they fastened on the Germans. The common people naturally could not be expected to know enough economics to understand why it was impossible for Germany to pay any such bill. The statesmen at Versailles must have known—they had economic advisers, among others Keynes. They should have known too that since the Germans would have to pay chiefly in services and goods (all the gold in the world would not have sufficed), the reparations were bound to disrupt both international trade and local industry. Granted that it would have been very hard to educate taxpayers while passion was running so strong, they offered no semblance of leadership as they gave in to the popular idea of squeezing the Germans "till the pips squeaked." As Winston Churchill wrote (much later), "No one in great authority had the wit, ascendancy, or detachment from public folly to declare these fundamental, brutal facts to the electorate." Instead Lloyd George wooed the voters by tacking on many more millions to the reparations bills to pay for the separation allowances and pensions of British soldiers; just as he had gloated over getting the best of Wilson when he went home with a pocketful of German colonies to show for the unsubstantial League of Nations that Wilson had put over.

Altogether, the American Colonel House pronounced perhaps the fairest verdict on the handiwork of the statesmen of Versailles. "How splendid it would have been," he wrote the day after the treaty was signed, "if we had blazed a new and better trail!" As it was, he noted the good excuses for their choice of the usual low road. History could offer them little guidance; the new conditions "could be met only by an idealistic and unselfish spirit," which was too much to expect at the time; and always they had to reckon with the people back home, who were in no mood to support such a spirit. Nevertheless House wished that they had taken the other way: "We would at least have gone in the right direction and if those who follow us had made it impossible to go the full length of the journey planned, the responsibility would have rested with them and not with us." He wrote this in his diary, however, in a tense suggesting that he had his eye on posterity, not the people back home. His chief, like the other leaders, was preparing to defend the old road they had taken. And so we are brought back to the failures of the democracies in particular.

Although the French always had the best excuse in their understandable fears of Germany, the generally sorry record of the Third Republic between the world wars was foreshadowed at Versailles. France still lacked a free press, as Wilson soon learned; the government instructed the press to feature news of opposition to him in America, together with articles proving that Germany was able to pay the costs of the war. When the voters turned on their great war leader Clemenceau because "the Tiger" had not been fierce enough, politicians returned to the ceaseless squabbles and intrigues that assured a rapid turnover of premiers, including such jackal types as Pierre Laval. Obsessed with military strength, France fell back on its army; only this too remained a source of dissension because of its antirepublican tradition. The most ardent nationalists in its ranks, as in the country at large, were likely to be hostile to democracy.

In Britain, by contrast, the follies of Versailles were officially recognized as early as 1922, when the government followed Keynes' suggestion by proposing that both war debts and reparations be canceled. Hatred of Germany rapidly subsided for mixed reasons, ranging from apathy or simple disillusionment with the war to high-minded pacifism and internationalism, and including enlightened self-interest: a revived Germany was good for world trade, on which Britain depended more than any other country. But the growing lenience reflected as well a muddled complacence typified by Stanley Baldwin, who rose as the brilliant, unscrupulous Lloyd George fell, became prime minister in 1923, and remained a leading figure in both Conservative and coalition governments until his retirement in 1937. A sedate, peace-loving businessman, he made some effort at a new world order, including support of self-government for India; he also maintained the peace by making no effort to stop Hitler in the early years when it would have been easy to do so, staying placid as Germany rearmed; in assuring Parliament that there was no basis for Churchill's prediction that within a few years Germany would have a much greater air force than Britain, he remarked, "I cannot look farther forward than the next two years";

and in his last public address before turning over the government to Neville Chamberlain, another prudent businessman, Baldwin summed up his political wisdom: "It seems to me that one of the reasons why our people are alive and flourishing, and have avoided many of the troubles that have fallen on less happy nations, is because we have never been guided by logic in anything we have done." His fortunate countrymen vindicated his judgment of them by rewarding him with the usual honors, elevating him to the peerage. Similar honors were belatedly conferred on Lloyd George, an open admirer of Hitler.

But most disgraceful by all odds was the immediate behavior of America. Wilson announced the signing of the Armistice in a simple message addressed to his fellow countrymen: "Everything for which America fought has been accomplished. It will now be our fortunate duty to assist by example, by sober, friendly counsel, and by material aid in the establishment of just democracy through the world." In the Congressional elections held a few days before, however, his country- men had already intimated that they were not in a mood to assume such a duty. The Republicans won a majority in both houses by calling for a smashing victory and a punitive peace, warning against the Fourteen Points; their campaign strategy had been mapped by Senator Henry Cabot Lodge and the dying Theodore Roosevelt, who defined the basic issue as Nationalism versus Internationalism.[6] While Wilson worked hard in Paris to win approval of his League of Nations, Lodge was as busy preparing the Senate to reject any settlement involving "en- tangling alliances" or commitments of America to help maintain peace in Europe. Public opinion, at first most vocal in supporting the League, was reverting to the traditional isolationism. When Wilson told the Senate that the League was "the only hope for mankind," Senator Warren G. Harding voiced a more popular sentiment: he complained that the President's address was "utterly lacking in ringing Ameri- canism." The Senate's refusal to ratify the treaty sealed the national resolve to stay young, unspoiled, ignorant, and blind to the inescap- able involvement of America in world affairs. If the nation was de- luded when it entered the war in the hope of ending war, it was more fatally deluded by the time it officially made peace, in 1921—the last nation to do so.

---

6 To Senator Beveridge Roosevelt wrote: "I am for saying with a bland smile whatever Nationalism demands"; the blandness was needed to counter charges that the Republicans were "merely Prussian militarists." Lodge he informed, needlessly, that Wilson was cowardly, unprincipled, hypocritical, pro-German—in a word, 100 per cent un-American.

There is no question that Wilson himself was much to blame for this outcome. His partisan call in 1918 for the election of a Democratic Congress was a worse blunder because he asserted that a Republican victory would be a repudiation of his leadership; so he went to Paris repudiated, and the leaders of the Allies had better excuse for disregarding his promises. He went without any clear program beyond his Fourteen Points, as bent on total peace as the Allies had been on total victory, impatient of their legitimate claims to power and security in a world still disordered. The many concessions he perforce had to make were mostly as indiscriminate as grudging. He gave in without a fight, for instance, to Japan's grab of Shantung province, which the Allies had promised it; whereupon China refused to sign the treaty— further weakening any chance of a lasting settlement or a world order. Having little interest in economics, he left the problem of reparations to Clemenceau and Lloyd George, and for the same reason did nothing either about world trade, though his Fourteen Points had included the lowering of trade barriers. When the peace conference had finished its work, he privately confessed his grievous disappointment, even remarking that if he were a German he would not sign the treaty; but publicly he at once began defending it as a just peace. He alienated liberals both at home and abroad by stubbornly refusing to admit its patent violations of his promises, and disheartened his supporters by as stubbornly refusing to accept reservations that might have got the treaty through the Senate. He succeeded only in confirming the petulance of Americans, who always tend to get indignant over compromises and half measures in international politics that they accept as routine in their irresponsible politics at home. At his most eloquent Wilson was guilty of what he himself once called "the foolishness of preaching," for he hardened the opposition by taking too high and mighty a line and denouncing disagreement as wickedness.

Still, there is by now little question either of the moral grandeur of Wilson. The only leading statesman at Paris who was disinterested and unselfish, seeking nothing for his own nation, devoted wholly to the cause of world peace, he was the only one whose failure may be called a great failure. The hardest-working of the statesmen too, he had more excuse since he was constantly assailed by national greed and hatred, constantly petitioned by little people—Armenians, Irish, Jews, Albanians, Lithuanians, and many others—who were seeking only favors; nothing but an extraordinarily astute diplomacy, backed by a united public opinion at home, could have achieved an approximation of the kind of peace treaty he battled for. He even had some excuse for his hope that in spite of everything it was a fairly just peace, if only because the treaty satisfied nobody; and there was always the League of Nations, a means of rectifying it. In any case, the best as well as the worst in Wilson came out in his battle at home. Arrogant, self-righteous, self-deceived, obsessed, warped, he was carried away by a passion that was nevertheless above selfish interests, partisan politics, and national prejudices, and his eloquence was more genuinely lofty than the rhetoric of his enemies.[7] And in his selfless dedication to his high cause, or his overweening pride, he courted the fate of high tragedy. Worn haggard by his long ordeal, he set out on his last tour of the country in defiance of his doctor's warning that it might cost him his life, insisting upon his duty to the soldiers he had promised a war to end wars; for several weeks he carried on through daily speeches, processions, and crowds of handshakers, defending the treaty and the League with unfailing eloquence, which his advisers warned him was pitched too high and was stirring up more resentment in his opponents; until the terrific strain was ended by the stroke that partially paralyzed him, left him enfeebled the rest of his days, with just enough physical and mental strength to insist on retaining his nominal leadership during the remaining year of his administration, and to the end of his life to maintain in defeat—bitterly, proudly—that what he had fought for was "for the benefit of this nation and of mankind."

Most important, Wilson was basically right: the League of Nations was indeed "the only hope of mankind." If it was a much frailer hope than he believed, there was no other way of assuring peace. He was a much better prophet too than the patriots and the practical men who ridiculed him as a visionary. "I can predict with absolute certainty," he asserted on his last tour, "that within another generation there will be another world war if the nations of the world do not concert the method by which to prevent it"; and he added that America would find itself fighting Germany again on the same battlegrounds, with the

---

[7] Senator Lodge's speeches, which were applauded as among the greatest orations ever delivered on the floor of the Senate, rose to such climaxes as this: "I can never be anything else but an American, and I must think of the United States first. . . . I have never had but one allegiance—I cannot divide it now. I have loved but one flag and I cannot share that devotion and give affection to the mongrel banner invented for a league." Even a sophomore not yet bright with semantics might have pointed out to the enthralled senators that this undivided patriot ostensibly owed an allegiance to God too, and that among his somewhat plainer allegiances were the Republican party, the state of Massachusetts, the privileged Senate, the high society of Boston, and on occasion its many Irish and Italian voters.

same allies. Now that that war has brought most Americans around to agreeing with his principles, they might hope that he was right in another of his fond beliefs. When General Smuts, a fellow idealist, remarked at Paris that the people had failed their prophets, Wilson answered that they were not ready, perhaps they were right in thinking that the time was not ripe; but even in the bitterness of his last days he never faltered in his faith that the time would come. Colonel House had comforted him by a statement of Gladstone's: "Men ought not to suffer from disenchantment; they ought to know that ideals in politics are never realized." At the end Wilson attacked the usual conclusion of the disenchanted. "The world is *run* by ideals," he insisted. "Only the fool thinks otherwise."

By this time the fools had taken over America, with the aid of shoddier ideals. The Republican bosses in the smoke-filled room had picked out Senator Harding to serve as their front in taking over the government. A folksy, small-town nonentity, comfortably ignorant of the world, always at home with platitudes, Harding was an ideal puppet; he demanded nothing of the people, assuring them that the present need was "not heroics but healing," promising a return to "normalcy," the good old days of business as usual; and the voters responded by giving him an overwhelming popular majority. By general consent the worst President the country has ever had, he was presumably just the kind of man it then deserved. In any case he inaugurated the most inglorious decade in the nation's history.

| # THE AFTERMATH
OF THE WAR

1. The Immediate Political Consequences

In retrospect, the most portentous political result of the World War
was of course the emergence of modern dictatorship and totalitarianism.
Lenin, for whom the war was a godsend, was able to make a revolution
and establish the Soviet in defiance of orthodox Marxist theory. In
Italy, disappointed over its relatively meager share in the booty of
victory, a more obscure agitator, Mussolini, was able to exploit popular
unrest and nationalistic fever, and with the aid of a compliant army
to stage the legendary march on Rome that put him in charge of the
government. At the time, however, these events were not clearly portentous. The widespread fear of the Bolshevik menace was played up
chiefly by conservatives afraid of revolutionaries at home, who were
not in fact powerful; it soon became apparent—to the dismay of Lenin
—that there was little danger of communism's sweeping Europe.
Otherwise statesmen might continue to fear Russia simply because of
its vast size, but they hardly anticipated that the Soviet would become
the dominant power in Europe; conservatives themselves fondly argued
that communism was contrary to human nature and could never really
work. There much much less evident reason to fear the windy Mussolini. Italy still lacked the potentials of a great power, he had behind
him no great mass movement, and before staging his march he had
dropped his revolutionary socialistic program. At worst fascism looked
like a local aberration, a nasty little farce played offstage.

Hence Europe settled down into a semblance of the old civil order.
Elsewhere the most conspicuous changes in government, as in the map,
were chiefly of a kind liberals could applaud. Kings were on their way

out. The most powerful monarchs—the Kaiser and the Czar—were gone for good, most of the remainder were little but figureheads, and the few who retained any considerable power were confined to the Balkans, where enlightened popular government could not be expected anyway. The worst offender was King Constantine of Greece, who started an ugly war with the Turks; but among its consequences was the elimination of the sultan. As the tradition of monarchy weakened, so did the power of the aristocratic class that had managed or mismanaged diplomacy before the war, and that in central and eastern Europe still enjoyed remnants of feudal privilege on large estates. With the exception of democratic Czechoslovakia the new nations got off to a generally disappointing start, but they at least set up some forms of constitutional government. And both Germany and Austria were now republics, the former with the most liberal constitution on the Continent. It still appeared that the future belonged to democracy.

The established democracies had come through the war with their liberties intact despite an unprecedented concentration of power in the heads of state—much more power than was actually exercised by the neurotic Kaiser—and the attendant strains of censorship and security regulations.[1] France remained potentially unstable as it returned to its traditional ways of rapid succession of ministries, fierce controversy between Right and Left, and periodic scandal, but it still adhered to democratic processes and carried on its tradition of intellectual freedom. Paris remained the European capital of the intelligentsia, the favorite haven of exiles. Britain continued to keep its head, and its faith in its people and free institutions, better than any other of the great powers. Soapbox orators in Hyde Park went on denouncing everything or calling for revolution, to hear-hears or heckling, while unarmed bobbies stood by unheeding. Everybody knew that there would always be an England, solid with Englishmen mostly complacent over their traditional ways and otherwise free to express their discontents.

Immediately America made the worst showing. The war was followed by the great Red scare, which aroused more hysteria here than in Europe even though the country had much less reason to fear communism. Violation of civil liberties was officially authorized by Attorney General A. Mitchell Palmer, who became the leading Red-hunter; in the most spectacular of his illegal raids, on New Year's

---

[1] The Kaiser's mental state was exemplified by an inspiration he had in the last month of the war: he dreamed of an alliance of Germany with England and Japan, which would then drive the Americans out of Europe.

Day of 1920, he found no bombs but made a haul of six thousand alleged Bolsheviks and three real pistols.[2] Although the scare began subsiding as Harding's "normalcy" came in view, it left an ugly legacy because it had stirred up all the traditional prejudices—against Negroes, Jews, Catholics, aliens, freethinkers, and other such "un-American" types. The Ku Klux Klan, which in 1920 had only a few hundred members, within a few years got more than four million (by sales methods very profitable to its Kleagles and Wizards), and it dominated politics in a number of states even above the Mason-Dixon line. Immigration acts not only drastically limited the admission of foreigners, ending the long history of America as a beacon and haven for the poor, but discriminated against the peoples of southern and eastern Europe; the Statue of Liberty now held up her torch only for "Nordic" types. Liberals continued to be fair game for professional patriots. Workers in particular suffered, since they had provided the chief excuse for the Red scare by a wave of strikes for higher wages to offset the postwar inflation. Labor unionism was identified as bolshevism, the open shop as the bulwark of Americanism; the beating up of labor organizers was recognized as a civic duty of sheriffs.

This was an old story, however, not a new menace to American democracy. The Red scare and the revival of bigotry may be regarded as symptoms of "normalcy" in a land that had long been given to such nasty puerility. At the same time, as always, influential voices were raised against the hysteria. Among the respectable conservatives who united with liberals in opposing it was Charles Evans Hughes, due to be Harding's secretary of state: he braved the charge of being a "parlor pink" by protesting against the expulsion of Socialists from the New York State Assembly. Basically American democracy remained as noisy, vigorous, open, and liable to corruption and abuse as it had been for generations before the war. There was no immediate danger of its going either fascist or communist.

In other domestic respects the war led to positive, enduring gains in freedom for the many. Women, who had played so much more active a part in it than in any previous war, were rewarded with both more

---

2 "Palmer, do not let this country see red!" Wilson had warned him, but the sick President let him go on. His administration did little but drift in its last year because his intimates concealed from the country how feeble he was. On their behalf it might be said that a sick Wilson was perhaps a better leader than a healthy Thomas R. Marshall, the Vice-President, who in any case did not want to take over. Marshall was a product of the irresponsibility engrained in American political tradition, the habit of choosing mediocrities for Vice-President for vote-getting reasons.

political and social equality. The woman suffrage movement soon triumphed almost everywhere as popular sentiment swung heavily to their side. (In America Wilson proved that he was not wholly incapacitated by pleading for ratification of the new constitutional amendment.) Their suffrage had little appreciable effect on political life, to be sure, neither raising nor lowering its tone to any such extent as had been hoped or feared. In social life, where their increasing freedom made much more difference, this was likewise neither so elevating nor so corrupting as idealists and alarmists had predicted. All the possible consequences for better or worse were confused by the persistence of deeply engrained habits of thought and feeling; women still enjoyed nothing like equality of opportunity in the higher ranks of government, business, or the professions. But in view of universal, age-old tradition their emancipation remains among the most extraordinary achievements of our century.

The postwar unrest that frightened conservatives was due in part to some positive gains that had been made by workers too, and to prospects of further gains. Labor leaders had been included in the war administrations of not only Britain but the United States, where collective bargaining had even been encouraged in order to step up the war effort. Thereafter America fell behind again; the fierce opposition to labor unions continued throughout the era of normalcy, and by 1932 their membership had declined to fewer than three million. Nevertheless the legacy of Wilson's New Freedom remained alive enough to produce a New Deal, under which collective bargaining was at last recognized as a normal democratic process, not a mode of socialism. In England, meanwhile, the Labour party had taken over the government as early as 1924. Democratic socialist parties were growing more powerful on the Continent too; in western Europe they were respectable enough to be regarded as a loyal opposition and to form ministries without provoking class war or revolution. The most obvious reason why the workers of the Western world failed to unite was that they were being assured more voice in their government than they had had in the past, not to mention more freedom than workers in the Soviet enjoyed.

Similarly hatred was giving way to good will on the international scene. In 1925 Germany joined Britain, France, Belgium, and Mussolini's Italy in signing the Locarno Pact, which stirred much rejoicing by its mutual guarantees for keeping the peace. Within the next few years Germany was granted a permanent seat on the Council of the League of Nations, and it signed as well the Kellogg-Briand Pact, in which the nations of the world outlawed war. The United States was at least cooperating with the League in such efforts. Previously Secretary Hughes had boldly acknowledged that America was still part of a world it preferred to ignore: he took the lead in ending an incipient naval race by putting through the Washington Treaty, in which the United States, Britain, and Japan agreed on a 5:5:3 ratio in capital ships. The idealism of Wilson was far from dead. Among the millions who revered his memory was Herbert Hoover, head of the Commission of Relief that after the war had more effectively demonstrated American idealism by its voluntary task of bringing food to starving Europe. "Never was a nobler work of disinterested good will carried through with more tenacity and sincerity and skill," Keynes had written, "and with less thanks either asked or given." Now the "great humanitarian" was elected President.

Ten years after Versailles, in short, the men who drew up the treaty appeared to have been vindicated. In this year the Allies agreed to evacuate the Rhineland, well ahead of schedule. The League of Nations was growing more popular for its diplomatic as well as humanitarian activities. A prospering Europe was more tranquil than it had been for years before the war. No statesman worried about the rantings of one Adolf Hitler, leader of an insignificant party. Few people outside of Germany had heard of his preposterous book *Mein Kampf*.

At this very time, however, Winston Churchill published *The Aftermath*, in which he pointed to dreadful possibilities such as mankind had never before been faced with. In the last year of the war the Allies had been planning a terrific assault on Germany, involving thousands of bombers and "poison gases of incredible malignancy"; and though the Germans had surrendered in time to be spared these horrors, it was certain that war offices everywhere had preserved such knowledge, were busy exploring still more terrible means of destruction. It was as certain that nations believing their existence to be at stake would employ such means. "Death stands at attention," Churchill concluded, "obedient, expectant, ready to serve, ready to shear away the peoples *en masse;* ready, if called on, to pulverize, without hope of repair, what is left of civilisation. He awaits only the word of command." And the word might be given more readily than Churchill then anticipated, in a Europe that looked tranquil but was in fact less stable and unified than it had been before the war, and was still smoldering with the hatreds due to the war.

Mussolini, who had by now consolidated his control of Italy, kept shouting his militaristic credo: "I consider the Italian nation in a permanent state of war." He could shout more safely because Britain and France, still the major powers in Europe, had drawn apart. The League of Nations that Britain depended on instead had been put to no severe test, and was less likely to withstand such a test since it lacked any assurance of American support. Efforts to give it teeth had failed; the Canadian representative instrumental in defeating the principal effort had explained fatuously that commitments were not only dangerous but unnecessary: "We live in a fireproof house, far from inflammable materials." Americans had been pleased to sign the Kellogg-Briand Pact because it was only a pious gesture, providing no sanctions against violators. International good will, never so strong as the forces of nationalism, had flourished on the deceptive appearances of prosperity. When these appearances vanished in the economic crash of 1929, the old forces took over the scene, only in a more malignant guise. Within a few years Mussolini could boast that fascism was not merely an Italian but a "world phenomenon." Hitler had won Germany with his version of it. Other versions, or indigenous equivalents, were sprouting all over the civilized world—Austria, Poland, Greece, Spain, Romania, Japan, Argentina. A few more years and Americans themselves were making a best seller of a sad book suggesting that fascism was "the wave of the future."

Although the hollowness of Mussolini's pretensions was quickly exposed by the ignominious record of his army in the Second World War, the defeat of Hitler exacted a cost that more than justified the worst fears about modern total war. The ending of his bid for the domination of Europe, or possibly the world, was then followed at once by the as ruthless, massive bid of Stalin, who more explicitly sought to win the whole world in the name of revolutionary Marxism. The rise of totalitarianism, the most significant political development of our century, therefore calls for a separate chapter. But first we need to consider the economic, social, and cultural matrix of its growth, and also of the successful resistance to it.

2. *The Economic Developments*

Among the unprecedented results of the great war was an Economic and Social History of it, sponsored by the Carnegie Endowment for International Peace, which ran to some hundred and fifty volumes.

The world's rulers, however, could hardly be expected to digest this history, and the statesmen at Versailles had already decided on their basic policy—a return to business as usual by prewar standards. Having agreed on an utterly unrealistic reparations bill, they ignored the problem trumpeted by Keynes, the need of restoring the political economy of Europe on a sound basis as an integrated whole. Except for the maintenance of the international fetish of the gold standard, prewar policy meant economic nationalism. Prosperous industrial countries, such as Britain and Holland, might subscribe to the policy of free trade recommended by most economists; poorer countries understandably felt obliged to erect tariff walls to protect their infant industries; but all tended to take not only a selfish but a shortsighted view of their national interest. The rulers of America were only the most conspicuous offenders in their blindness to the commonplace that the world was growing more interdependent.

Until 1929 the old policies paid off fairly well. The United States, now become the greatest financial as well as industrial center, enjoyed its big boom; stricken Europe, for the first time a debtor instead of a creditor, nevertheless managed to raise its income above prewar levels. Then the commonplace was spelled out luridly by the great crash, followed by a prolonged world-wide depression in which countless millions of people lost their jobs and their life savings. Europe responded by a closer regulation of the flow of goods and money in the national interest. (The Scandinavian and Low Countries started to consider the different solution of a customs union but were discouraged by a warning from Britain, which would neither join the union nor tolerate any discrimination against its trade.) One consequence of the protective measures was a fatal blow to the prestige of the League of Nations: Japan retaliated against the many tariffs raised on its manufactures by seizing Manchuria, defying the League's request to remove its troops, and finally pulling out of the League. It could set this defiant example with more impunity because Europe long remained in bad economic shape. The world was more shocked when Britain went off the gold standard, while France recovered so slowly that ten years after the crash it was still producing less than it had in 1929. The conspicuous exception was Germany. Here the depression was so devastating that within a few years Hitler was able to raise the seats he held in the Reichstag from a mere 12 to 230; and once in power he solved Germany's unemployment problem by building up its army and war industry. The depression was among the plainest causes of World War II.

According to both Marxists and Fascists, the crash signaled the failure
of "capitalism," and many of its victims in the democracies came to
agree. Businessmen, on the other hand, generally blamed the prolonged depression on the war. As always, the issues were oversimplified
by the slogan thinkers on both sides. There was in fact no uniform
economic system in Europe, but varying degrees of private enterprise
and state control; only in America was *laissez faire* a rampant gospel.
And America aggravated the issues by its usual inconsistencies. Having repudiated any responsibilities to Europe, it demanded that the
Allies repay with interest their war debts (as President Coolidge put
it, "They hired the money, didn't they?"), while its bankers made
good money by floating huge loans to enable Germany to go on paying
reparations. At the same time it erected tariff walls to protect its
rugged businessmen against the competition of foreign goods—the only
means by which its former allies could possibly repay the money they
had hired. Under President Hoover tariffs were raised to a new high
by the Smoot-Hawley bill, against the virtually unanimous protest of
economists; one described the bill as a declaration of economic war
against the whole civilized world. In 1931 Hoover finally proposed an
international moratorium in reparations and war debts, but it was too
late to stop the spreading panic, make amends for the economic folly
of the Treaty of Versailles.

Still, few businessmen (naturally excepting Germans) had protested
against this folly. Generally they supported the return to prewar policies, which favored their own immediate interests. One reason why
Wilson did nothing about world trade in Paris was that he usually accepted the advice of his businessmen counselors, who reflected the
eagerness of Americans to get rid of all political controls. In Europe
the regulations that kept the economy under some measure of state
control were designed chiefly to protect vested interests. Representatives of the business class who took over political leadership and
diplomacy from the aristocracy were typically as shortsighted as
Baldwin, Laval, and Chamberlain. One of the wisest of them, the German statesman Gustav Stresemann, pronounced the harshest judgment
on business leadership: "Europe's future depends on industrial reconstruction, but the reconstructing will have to be carried out by
politicians and not by leaders of industry." As we now know, "capitalism" was much more vigorous than its Marxist critics believed, and
more flexible than its disciples realized; it was due to become still
more imprecise a term for an economy growing more mixed, involving

more "socialism"; but in this era the system that earned its name by the great economic and political power wielded by private corporate interests also earned its widespread disrepute. Its shortcomings may be specified by the goals that Keynes proposed for the modern state—economic efficiency, social justice, and individual liberty.

If capitalism was not alone responsible for the crash, this emphasized an always serious limitation of its vaunted economic efficiency. The depression was only the worst of a long series. The champions of free private enterprise had long since come to regard the business cycle as "normal," without proposing to do much for the many victims of the periodic slumps; free enterprise as such offered no solution to the abiding problem of the jobless. Much private enterprise, moreover, was not in fact very enterprising. While businessmen engaged in international trade and finance were learning to take a longer view of the national economic interest, they were still outnumbered by those who demanded protection from foreign competition; especially in France and America, many manufacturers were thereby enabled to remain inefficient. Other big industrialists eliminated international competition by forming cartels, which not only guaranteed profits at some expense to consumers but might impede technological progress too. A cartel that controlled quinine, for instance, kept its price so high that most people in malaria-infested countries could not afford it, and it made no effort to find a synthetic substitute, later seeking only to get control of atabrine when this was developed by the incentive of government.

Hence capitalism was most obviously vulnerable to criticism on the grounds of social injustice. Although big businessmen in most of industrial Europe had learned to put up with labor unions and some measure of social insurance for workers, they were dedicated to maintaining what Keynes called an "arbitrary and inequitable distribution of wealth and income." Few were enlightened enough to realize that assuring workers a larger share of their handsome profits would provide a better market for business. Despite considerable mobility, inequality was as flagrant as ever and class struggle often bitter. As for individual liberty, business leaders remained devoted primarily to an economic freedom for those on top. On the Continent they hardly made a name for themselves as defenders of civil liberties and political freedom, since it soon became clear that would-be dictators were friendly enough to big business. In Germany industrialists gave Hitler the support he needed to come into power, so that he might break the power of labor. From Italy American businessmen brought back good reports of Mussolini: he was not only making the trains run on time but had put an end to strikes.

It was above all the United States, however, that forced the basic issues of capitalism. Here the business class enjoyed more freedom and encouragement than it did anywhere in Europe. Industry had come out of the war with not only high profits but such further advantages as modernized plants and confiscated German patents. Under Harding, Coolidge, and Hoover it got from the government almost everything it wanted, beginning with repeatedly reduced taxes and tax refunds of several billions. The government had reverted to the nineteenth-century credo summed up by Grover Cleveland: "While the people should cheerfully and patriotically support their government, its functions do not include the support of the people." Businessmen continued to overlook an apparent exception—the support they got from it. All industries were assisted by tariffs, public utilities by exclusive franchises, the new airlines by mail subsidies, the auto industry by huge outlays for new streets, highways, and bridges. The courts helped in holding down labor unions and supporting resistance to government regulation. Another boon was the studies in the art of propaganda made by Wilson's Committee on Public Information. "The war taught us the power of propaganda," wrote Roger Babson, the popular forecaster and salesman of business; and he boasted that business now knew how to sell anything to the American people: "We have the school, the pulpit, and the press." In later years Edward Bernays, prince of public relations men, would give a speech on "How American Business Can Sell the American Way of Life to the American People" (a rather curious reversal of the natural subject and object); but at this time the people were thoroughly sold. Businessmen enjoyed an unparalleled prestige, verging on the awe with which kings had once been regarded in Europe. Many Americans even wanted to make Henry Ford their President. Most accepted the popular Rotary image of the businessman as "a man of vision"—the up-to-date replacement of the poets, prophets, and idle dreamers of yore.

Public confidence was rewarded by the big boom, an expansion of industry that neared half of the world's total production. Private enterprise distinguished itself especially in the development of new industries, from chemical and electrical to airplane and radio. Corporations finally began to realize the practical value of scientific research, setting up laboratories that accelerated technological progress.

The whole economy was stimulated above all by the spectacular growth of the auto industry. Ford won his reputation as an industrial genius by leading the way to standardized mass production on the assembly line, and then selling at low prices for the sake of larger volume. If the automobile was a mixed blessing, it was certainly dear to the heart of Americans; by 1929 they owned well over twenty million cars. The industry was providing jobs for millions in not only auto plants but the oil, rubber, glass, steel, and other metal industries, in the many other factories turning out accessories, in the construction of highways and suburban homes, in filling stations, roadside restaurants, country clubs, etc. Henry Ford accentuated another major change when he followed the lead of General Motors, which had grown into a formidable rival by producing fancier new models at fancier prices; the country waited breathlessly while he shifted from the once beloved Model T to Model A. The automobile was replacing the house as the most favored status symbol. It marked the coming of the "affluent society," in which people would no longer be content with merely an ample provision of the necessities but would value ever more highly the possession of accessories like radios and electrical appliances, and would swell the business of the luxury trades. Businessmen also helped to create the new American dream by a phenomenal expansion of advertising and salesmanship, together with credits to encourage buying on the installment plan.

But these artificial stimulants suggested unhealthy aspects of the boom, shaky foundations of the national prosperity. Basically this was little different from former periods of prosperity, if anything spottier. Although the wages of workers in the larger industries rose, there was no steady, uniform increase in the wage level. Most Americans were still far from affluence and millions of them were quite poor. The 10 per cent at the top got much more than their proportionate share of the increased national income; the low-income groups were relatively worse off. Farmers in particular suffered from a depression throughout the period, during which their income fell almost 50 per cent. While business profits were being fattened by tariffs, President Coolidge twice vetoed farm relief legislation; the business community agreed that such relief was economically unsound and socially unjust or demoralizing. Among the many other examples of inequity in the American system was the booming steel industry, in which as late as 1923 workers were still putting in a twelve-hour day and a seven-day week. When they went on strike, the leaders of the industry, headed by Judge Gary (also a church leader), maintained that economic efficiency required such a workweek. They were wrong even by economic standards, since businessmen would eventually learn that more can be got out of workmen in shorter hours; but the significant point was that they ignored the question of equity, put aside all democratic or Christian sentiments.

As in the past, moreover, a great deal of the profitable enterprise was purely speculative, socially unproductive. Realtors made billions as city land doubled in value, while that of farm land fell off sharply; big banking houses made as much by selling "securities" unworthy of the name; financiers exploited the rich possibilities of the pyramiding of holding companies, which enabled Samuel Insull to build on paper his private empire of public utilities that would cost investors a billion. Such wizardry helped to bring on the climax of the boom—the fantastic bull market of 1928–29. The dizzy heights to which stock prices soared were more fantastic because by this time the economy was stagnant; the market for productive capital goods was shrinking. And it was not "America" that now went mad—the great majority of Americans owned no stocks and could not afford to gamble on them. The craze was centered in the business community.[3] Although some financial leaders expressed misgivings over the wildly soaring prices, the community at large cheered on the bulls; they were only proving that prosperity was here to stay, no man of vision would sell America short. A month before the crash the president of the New York Stock Exchange declared: "We are apparently finished and done with economic cycles as we have known them."

In short, "vision" was precisely what most American businessmen of the period lacked. As they went on radically transforming America by ever-bigger business, they remained basically reactionaries, whose notions of normalcy—"safe and sane" policies—harked back to the nineteenth-century world of their childhood. Together with their political representatives they were quite incapable of understanding Keynes' observation after the war, that what they considered business as usual was in a historical view "intensely unusual, unstable, complicated, unreliable, and temporary." The crash that vindicated this judgment also demonstrated how little they understood the industrial machine they

---

[3] I may say modestly that I suspected the absurdity of this boom in the summer of 1929 when I worked as a clerk in one of the largest banks in New York. My fellow clerks kept running in and out of the stock market, not to start making a fortune, but merely to win enough money for a weekend party. An elementary knowledge of economics was enough to make one doubt that this could go on indefinitely, even though popular economists of the day (such as Irving Fisher) stated otherwise.

were running, and how helpless they were when it broke down. They were further unfitted for social and political leadership in a revolutionary age because they had no long-range objectives beyond material prosperity, and were mostly blind or indifferent to the social evils to be expected from their raucous celebration of the profit motive as the key to the American way of life.[4]

At best, the vision of capitalistic America was expressed by President Hoover, who in his acceptance speech proclaimed that the day was in sight "when poverty will be banished from this nation." If not the loftiest aspiration imaginable, this was at least a quite honorable one, becoming to a people whom Santayana had described as "idealists working on matter." Hoover stipulated, however, that to realize it the nation had "to go forward with the policies of the last eight years," under Harding and Coolidge. These policies had involved no active effort to remove or relieve poverty, assume any responsibility for the many millions of underprivileged. Rather they had encouraged a positive irresponsibility in the business world by relieving it from regulation, packing federal commissions with its representatives. Businessmen were quick to forget the scandalous corruption under Harding, even to forgive the big executives who had done the bribing, because they accepted as normal much shady dealing for easy profit. More insidious was a quite respectable kind of dishonesty, tinged with cynicism, that was most apparent—or to most Americans not really apparent—in the growth of advertising. This became a billion-dollar business by mastering the art of exploiting the gullibility of consumers, cashing in especially on their pathetic fears of being unsuccessful, unglamorous, unpopular, or unlike the Joneses. Among the famous slogans of the boom era was the one coined for a toothpaste manufacturer about pyorrhea, "Four out of five have it"; and one reason why most Americans never learned that in fact only one out of twenty had it, or that the toothpaste was as useless for preventing it as was all the stuff they gargled to prevent the dread "halitosis," was that newspapers buried such news, out of deference to business. They would never learn either from radio, fast growing into another billion-dollar industry. In the infancy of

---

4 The industrial wizardry of Henry Ford made him the most conspicuous example of political and cultural illiteracy, typified by his well-known saying "history is bunk." For the man whom many Americans wanted as President it appeared that even American history was bunk when in a public trial he described Benedict Arnold as a writer and dated the American Revolution in 1812. An uglier symptom of his ignorance was the anti-Semitism he endorsed in his Dearborn journal, which accused the Jews of not only an international conspiracy but all the evils of American life, from short skirts to high rents.

radio, Hoover remarked that so powerful an instrument for public education and public good should of course not be turned over to private interests; but naturally it was. The policies he endorsed assumed that only private enterprise could be trusted to promote the public good, and that any government interference with it was un-American.

The business class was accordingly stunned when what it thought was the biggest boom in history ended, not surprisingly, in the biggest crash. What followed in America was the worst depression in the world. Within a few years up to fifteen million jobless people, many of them hungry, some even starving, in a land full of idle machinery and surplus food, always fond of superlatives, were magnifying the normal failure of capitalism: the paradox of not only crying need amidst abundance but need because of abundance, in a system that somehow could not get the idle men and machines together to produce the goods that everybody wanted, and now produced instead such spectacles as a crowd of men fighting over the garbage put out by a restaurant. Herbert Hoover later explained that "in the large sense" the Great Depression was due to the war, as in some sense it surely was. But it was surely due as well to the shortcomings of American business and the government that served its interests. It was worse in America because the boom had been more artificial, inflated by speculators, false prophets, and sellers of worthless securities, and by millions of installment buyers who in time were paying as much for interest as for their goods. As a result, the business lords were more thoroughly discredited than their peers abroad, exposed as bankrupt morally and intellectually too.

President Hoover, who became the chief goat, was of course not to blame for the crash. He had nevertheless earned the blame by his complacence, for in his election campaign he had boasted of the unparalleled prosperity of America, made it the main issue, and claimed for his party a patent on it. Following the crash he remained blind to its rotten foundations, trying to restore confidence by ritual incantations about how business was "fundamentally sound" and prosperity "just around the corner." As business got worse, the national response was "Oh, yeah?" When Hoover then worried and worked as had no other depression President, he himself complained that bankers were letting the country down by their "ultraconservative" timidity, and like the rest of the business world were running to Washington for help; but he gave them the help they clamored for. In his last year he got Congress to set up the Reconstruction Finance Corporation, which began lending billions, chiefly to big business. He did more than any peacetime President before him, indeed, to "put the government into business"—what he and his party would call "creeping socialism." But he was steadfast in his opposition to federal relief for the unemployed, vetoing all bills providing for it. This he called "playing politics at the expense of human misery"; such a "dole" would only demoralize jobless workers, sap the American character. Businessmen alone were able to accept government aid without fatal injury to their character.

When Franklin D. Roosevelt took over from Hoover he hardly had in mind a clearer program, much less a radical one. He too talked of the need of federal economy and a balanced budget; he declared that the economy was "mature," perhaps overbuilt, and had no thought of expanding it; or as radicals complained, he sought to "organize scarcity" instead of abundance. That he at once succeeded in restoring confidence was due chiefly to his own breezy assurance ("The only thing we have to fear is fear itself"), his call for "direct, vigorous action" by the government, and his willingness to experiment. He could get away with the "brain trust" he brought to Washington—the novel idea of consulting professors instead of businessmen—because the public had lost faith in the wisdom of business leaders, who had no positive program in any case. The New Deal that presently earned him such virulent hatred as a "traitor" to his class was a medley of *ad hoc* measures designed to relieve the victims of the depression, to correct some obvious abuses of money power on Wall Street, and in general to regulate private enterprise in order to preserve it, not destroy it. Some of Roosevelt's experiments were foolish, most had only a limited success. He early proved both his Americanism and his superficial knowledge of economics by torpedoing an international conference in London that was seeking to stabilize currencies.

Yet the New Deal deserved the name it would get as "the Permanent Revolution." Not only were billions spent in direct relief and public works programs but the right of the unemployed to relief was permanently established. Workers were given the right to bargain freely through unions of their own choice, with a national board empowered to protect them against unfair labor practices; the unions rapidly enrolled millions of members, and despite stubborn opposition established themselves as permanently in all the major industries. Among other key measures that have stood up to this day were reciprocal trade pacts, minimum wage laws, banking reforms, federal deposit insurance, the Securities Exchange Commission, the Rural Electrification Administration, the Federal Housing Administration, the Social Security Act, and TVA. All pointed to the basic achievement of Roosevelt's New Deal—the belated acceptance in America of collective responsibility for the shortcomings and the failures of capitalism. Henceforth the government would do more to regulate and protect the economy, forestall or cushion the periodic depressions. It would recognize the obligation of providing some measure of security and relief to the great majority who were no longer self-employed or self-sufficient, and always liable to loss of job through no fault of their own. Likewise it would provide more social services that private enterprise was unable or unwilling to undertake.

The "welfare state," born in depression, was also born of the immense collective wealth that capitalism had amassed. American capitalism was thus rescued from all danger of violent revolution, which in the depths of the depression was beginning to seem a real possibility. Communists made some converts, especially among intellectuals, but remained a very small minority party; confidence in Roosevelt prevented the many embittered Americans from becoming properly "alienated." Even so, however, America made a slower recovery from the depression than any European country: ten years after the crash there were still nine million unemployed. Conservatives could therefore argue that business would have done better had it been let alone (except for government aid), and had the government not squandered billions in relief. New Dealers could answer that they had averted the complete collapse of the economy that seemed imminent, and that they then had a worse breakdown to repair or a bigger mess to clean up. At least none of the European governments had trusted to *laissez faire* to bring about recovery by itself. Economists in all the democracies were being converted to the exciting new theory of Keynes, who had early applauded the "reasoned experiment" of Roosevelt, and was restoring to economics its old meaning of "political" economy. Also intent on preserving free private enterprise by more government enterprise to remedy its deficiencies, Keynes argued that when producer's goods expenditure, or investment, fell off, the government should take up the slack, and so meet an incipient depression by the unorthodox policy of deficit spending—spurning the fetish of balanced budgets. Only Americans would still be told by their conservative leaders that the supreme task confronting the nation was always to balance its budget.

At any rate, this issue was confused by the resistance Roosevelt soon met from the business community, discouraging a concerted national effort—not to mention the extraordinarily bitter hatred of "that man," which made supposedly well-educated Americans spread stories that he was a Communist, a drunkard, a maniac, and so on. (Mrs. Roosevelt was embraced in the hatred, so that not until years after her husband's death was she generally recognized as one of the saintliest if not greatest American women of her generation.) A conservative Supreme Court declared unconstitutional some of his measures, threatened others, and threw out even wages-and-hours legislation by states. An American Liberty League sprang up to combat the outrageous interference with business, especially the liberty granted labor unions. Henry Ford distinguished himself in the prolonged industrial strife; having organized the most efficient battalion of spies and hired thugs to combat labor organizers, his corporation was among the last to accept a union (in 1941). The press, business-owned, turned overwhelmingly against Roosevelt. By his sweeping victory in 1936 he aggravated hostilities, having criticized his opponents more harshly as "economic royalists." He then strengthened the opposition by his proposal to pack the Supreme Court, as many of his supporters too were shocked by its threat to an independent judiciary. In 1938 a conservative coalition of Republicans and Southern Democrats won the lasting control of Congress that all Presidents would have to contend with thereafter.

The basic issues of capitalism therefore remained confused when the problem of recovery was finally solved by the coming of World War II. Workers at least proved that they had not been demoralized by the "dole," grown content to live on relief, for they flocked to the factories as soon as jobs were available. The war effort called out an extraordinary increase in production, far surpassing the boom in the Coolidge era; within a few years America doubled its national output.[5] Businessmen hailed the "miracle" of war production as further proof of the value of free private enterprise, and certainly industrialists

[5] As an example of how startling this achievement was, Roosevelt was criticized when he called on the country, before Pearl Harbor, to produce 50,000 airplanes a year; Governor Thomas Dewey—a staunch enough champion of American business—charged that he was deluding the people by this impossible proposal. Come Pearl Harbor, Roosevelt responded by demanding 75,000 planes a year. And well before the war ended the nation was turning them out at a rate of over 100,000, including fleets of big bombers. Even this rate could have been vastly increased had not the military granted that they had enough planes except for the latest models; and when the military say they have enough of anything, one may be confident that they have at least three times as much as they are likely to need.

proved their resourcefulness, managerial skill, and capacity for immense organization. The miracle was nevertheless achieved under elaborate government controls of the whole economy, the most extensive to date; the First World War had already demonstrated that no modern nation will trust to *laissez faire* during a national emergency. Confusion was deepened because the war accelerated the "organizational revolution," the growth of both bigger government and bigger business. Alarm over a "socialism" under which giant corporations were setting new records in profits obscured the plain reality that had been established by the New Deal, as in all the European democracies before it: a mixed economy, with varying combinations of private and government enterprise, degrees of freedom and regulation, measures of planning—differing in each country, but everywhere representing an effort at a rationally, democratically controlled economy. If nothing was settled to the satisfaction of either conservatives, liberals, or radicals, the nation was better set for an era of still more rapid change in which nothing could be settled simply or for good.

3.   *The Social and Cultural Consequences*

Dangerous as had been the economic crisis, one may now speak of a graver crisis of mind—the mind that had so astoundingly transformed the Western world, and that was therefore faced with the appallingly difficult problem of mastering its achievements. As the war ended, this crisis was most acutely felt and eloquently expressed by Paul Valéry. The shock of the war had made him realize as never before what it meant to be a European, how much mankind owed to a tiny minority in Europe, and how precarious its state was. "We later civilizations— we too now know that we are mortal," he mourned. Presently he wrote his classic epitome of the modern condition: "We hope vaguely, but dread precisely; our fears are infinitely clearer than our hopes." Valéry was speaking for intellectuals, of course, or more precisely for some European intellectuals. Few American ones felt such dread, while in Russia most were busy building up the Soviet, with high hopes. The Russians were demonstrating most plainly the power of the intelligentsia. They were also deepening the crisis, however, in ways that would more directly affect the common people everywhere—to whom they appealed, as Valéry did not. So first let us consider the popular state of mind.

Now, people in general did not come out of the war full of dread or sense of crisis. The most apparent mood after the initial rejoicing or mourning was what one would naturally expect—a letdown from the long strain. In some countries, notably Germany and Italy, many men indeed never did become really demobilized in fact or in spirit; the letdown was too much for Hitler's Brown Shirts and Mussolini's Black Shirts. But it was apparent in the many more men who were fearful of revolutionists. They belonged with the great majority who, like businessmen, wanted most of all to get back to life as usual; and while this might include more discontent than usual, in view of the sacrifices people had made, most were not in a revolutionary mood if only because it would have meant more strain. However vague their hopes for the world, their hopes for themselves were clear enough: their goal was a decent, comfortable living. It could therefore be labeled bourgeois or materialistic, and certainly their living values were not lofty, aristocratic, or heroic; both Communists and Fascists despised their type. The rest of us might say that their hopes and desires were not simply or necessarily mean.

Their unheroic spirit was more pardonable because of the postwar disillusionment, especially in the democracies. "All the great words were canceled out for that generation," wrote D. H. Lawrence, and some such feeling was widespread, even apart from the many shell-shocked veterans. There had been so much valor and sacrifice, suffering and slaughter—for what? Though one's country had been victorious, the alternative of defeat grew less meaningful, the reality of a world no better for the bloodbath was much more obvious; when the great words were sounded, a common response was best summed up in the popular American expression: So what? The disenchantment then took many forms. In some people it encouraged an ambition not merely selfish but unscrupulous and ruthless; in more it showed up as political apathy, verging on cynicism. Among the plainest symptoms was the popularity of debunking the national heroes and the ancestors. Among the by-products was the revolt against convention, social or moral, which in turn took on different meanings; it ranged from mere slackness or giddiness to a responsible aspiration to more personal freedom and fullness of life. At best, the disillusionment led to a revival of pacifism and internationalism, and so again to a genuine idealism; though again this might blind people to the realities of nationalistic politics, which were brewing another war. In schools everywhere history courses were glorifying the national heroism during the war, doing little to re-educate the youth.

As naturally the social consequences of the war differed in the various countries. France produced its share of earnest statesmen, but more than its share of irresponsible, corrupt politicians, who undermined the faith of its people in their government; the Stavisky scandal, for example, set off a wave of popular cynicism. After 1930 fervor was largely confined to the Left and the Right, and only split the country more deeply. The outbreaks in 1936, when the socialist León Blum became premier, sealed the division; he aroused such hatred as to spread the saying "Better Hitler than Blum." Most Frenchmen were no longer in a mood to fight and die for *la patrie,* or for anything beyond their class interests, when they found themselves in a war again. The nation was mortally sick some years before the Third Republic collapsed under another defeat by the Germans, more humiliating than the defeat in 1870 out of which it was born.

By contrast, the English might be softened or confused by their disenchantment, but were never seriously corrupted, demoralized, or divided by it. Their major domestic crisis was the general strike of 1926, which quickly failed because public opinion clearly disapproved of it as too revolutionary. To the crash of 1929 the people then responded by giving an overwhelming majority to a Coalition government that offered them only a drastic austerity program, an economic version of the later call for blood, sweat, toil, and tears. Mussolini and Hitler thought their temper was degenerate because of what Winston Churchill called the "ever-shameful" resolution passed by the Oxford Union in 1933, "That this House will in no circumstances fight for its King and Country." Their failure either to call a halt to the dictators or to start rearming soon enough—a failure supported by a majority alike in the Conservative, Liberal, and Labour parties—was actually due to the usual muddle of motives, including apathy, complacence, pacifism, and feelings of guilt over the Treaty of Versailles. They were more directly responsible than the French for the shame of Munich, the most shocking exposure of the apparent degeneracy of the democracies, the spiritual rot of Western civilization. But at Dunkirk and the ensuing Battle of Britain they gave much clearer proof that they had been neither enervated nor demoralized.

It was again in relatively unscathed America, however, that the letdown after the war was most pronounced. Here we can hardly speak of any bitter disillusionment, except in the minority who remained devoted to the ideals of Woodrow Wilson. Having voted for the return of "normalcy," most Americans put away thought about all serious issues, national or international, and settled down to the pursuit of happiness. They were little shocked by the exposure of the scandalous corruption that helped to drive Harding to his timely death. As Will Rogers remarked, they were not merely satisfied—they just didn't give a damn. Hence some may still feel nostalgic as they read the lively account of the fabulous twenties in Frederick Lewis Allen's *Only Yesterday*. Although the license and lunacy of this era are still with us, they were then purer and more exuberant, not yet jaded or routine. Fad ran riot in marathon dancers and flagpole sitters. The gaudy additions to popular culture—radio, tabloids, true-confession magazines, movie magazines, beauticians—still had the thrill of novelty, the new shrines of Hollywood and Miami their pristine glamour. Bathing beauties and sports heroes performed in a more dazzling limelight; murder trials were played up into bigger and more lasting sensations. The national circus was a continuous performance, staged with more ballyhoo and in many more rings than P. T. Barnum had dreamed of. And so on *ad nauseam*, in a people whom it was getting harder to nauseate.

Beneath all the self-indulgence were some changes of lasting significance. One was documented by Leo Lowenthal in a study of the ever-popular biographies of successful men in the big magazines. Before the war these biographies were mostly of leaders in business, government, the professions, and even literature and the arts, and they served as educational models, however trite: the great man succeeded by dint of character, enterprise, and responsible, creative effort. After the war the still more popular biographies, narrated with ever more meaningless superlatives, were mostly of leaders in the entertainment world, "idols of consumption" rather than production. Though the celebrity usually came up "the hard way," he was a "born" actor or what-not who did not develop but got the breaks, met the right people, and succeeded especially because of his "personality"; and though the stress was on his private life, he usually had no more vital human relationships than creative passion, interest in any serious issues, or pride of individuality—he was just sociable, cooperative, and well adjusted. The new style of success story paralleled the change in the world of big business, the rise of the "organization man." This was a smooth type, not the rugged, ambitious, self-reliant individualist of business folklore; the Horatio Alger hero was passé. As for "spiritual values," business was cementing its alliance with religion. In *The Man Nobody Knows*, for two years the best-selling nonfiction book, Bruce Barton edified Americans by the fiction that Jesus was a great executive, "the founder of modern business," whose parables were "the most powerful advertisements of all time," and who "would be a national advertiser today"—just like the author himself, except for the possibly regrettable difference that Barton would never be crucified.

A somewhat anomalous resurgence of Fundamentalism contributed to a unique fiasco of patriotic idealism—the National Prohibition Amendment. Fundamentalist sects had done much to put this through during the war, when Americans were disposed to let nothing interfere with the war effort, and following the Armistice state legislatures quickly finished the job of ratifying it. Now at last, said the Methodist Board of Temperance, Prohibition, and Public Morals, "mankind shall be truly free." But almost as quickly the nation's mood changed. Like the League of Nations, what Hoover would call the "noble" experiment of prohibition was a casualty of the return to normalcy: Americans went on drinking, soon more heartily because it had become smart to do so, and Congress refused ever to appropriate anything like the money needed to enforce the new law. Within a year or so national prohibition was on its way to a state much worse than a farce. Gangsters began flourishing on bootlegging, and gangster war over a business soaring into many millions carried on the frontier tradition of violence. Chicago became famous the world over as the capital of organized, unpunished murder, but other big cities soon disputed its claims to notoriety. Gangsters then expanded into the still bigger business of racketeering of all kinds. Out of the noble experiment came the most powerful, prosperous underworld of the democracies, which still makes America pre-eminent for organized crime and corruption.[6]

An incidental aid to criminals was the motorization of America, helpful for quick getaways. The profound effects of the automobile on American life were more ambiguous and of much more import to Europe, which would eventually have its millions of cars. Everywhere the automobile transformed not only the landscape but the life of its owners. Like the movie and the radio, it brought the great world to Main Street, and with more variety and change brought more standard-

[6] In piety I add a tribute to another casualty of this experiment—the "Happy Warrior" Al Smith, who heartened many of us by his refreshingly outspoken campaign for the Presidency in 1928. Coolidge prosperity and his Catholicism doubtless assured his defeat, but the drys helped: while Hoover hedged enough to retain the support of damp Republicans, Smith was frankly wet, refusing to dignify the national hypocrisy. Embittered by his defeat, and then by the easy victory of Roosevelt, he was among the tragic victims of the inglorious twenties.

ization. It led millions of Americans to move to the suburbs, where they could have a home of their own, and where they would be subjected to stronger pressures to conformism. In suburbia they would be more likely to join a church for social reasons, and also less likely to attend church regularly, as they took off for Sunday drives or picnics. In cities the automobile began producing a congestion that made a mockery of modern progress, trucks in downtown districts moving more slowly than horses had. It gave Americans both status and a sense of power, while it killed more of them than the World War had. It was the perfect symbol of the era: a restless people forever on the move, with no clear idea where they were going or why.

Among the many other uses of the automobile was a means of escape for the young from home and chaperon. The postwar mood had generated the notorious revolt of the younger generation, whose notions of "true" freedom were rather different from that of the Methodist Board. The "flapper" entered the scene, in short skirts and bobbed hair; smoking, drinking, and petting replaced parlor games. Many alarmed parents were themselves soon infected by the spreading popularity of "modern" ideas. In upper circles the most popular insignia of sophistication was sexual freedom, which owed as well to the influence of Freud. The chief taboo was on taboos, or "inhibitions"; the fashionable convention was freedom from conventions, which were now given the bad names of Victorian and Puritan. Women in particular grew more independent in dress, manners, and morals. While the business world offered them many more jobs, and household duties were eased by modern appliances and service industries, Hollywood provided models of glamour, the cosmetics industry a choice of thousands of perfumes, face creams, and lipsticks. The emancipated woman would have no more of the double standard. If she might be freer in talk than in behavior, the accepted ideal was not so much romantic love as frank, easy, full companionship.

Needless to add, the uses of this greater personal freedom gave some reason for the alarm over the state of American morals. Many people were plainly irresponsible; young and middle-aged alike were giving in to mere self-indulgence, seeking thrills rather than a fuller, richer self-fulfillment. Americans were not clearly recovering the frank, natural pleasure in sex, enjoyed by most past societies, that the Victorians had cast a pall on. Much more conspicuous was the growth of sexiness: an obsession with sex exploited by the mass media, commercialized as never before in history by advertisers, which might make prostitution seem relatively decent, and surely made it harder for Americans to be sexually healthy or really to enjoy the freedom they had won. Sophisticates debased the theories of Freud by much cocktail chatter about inhibitions that flouted the obvious necessity of inhibition for mature, intelligent, civilized behavior; many were prone to a compulsive kind of unconventionality. In general, the new freedoms were still too novel and self-conscious to be natural, easy, or gracious. The revolt against convention, always exciting at first, produced much confusion and conflict of values, since people could always change their minds more easily than their feelings, and old ways were discredited before new ones were mastered. A steep climb in the divorce rate was but one sign of a restless pursuit of happiness that was not clearly making Americans happier. Again women in particular forced the ultimate issue—freedom for what? They suffered most obviously from the confusion of old and new ways, in a society in which they still did not actually enjoy full equality, and themselves often did not wish to be treated as equals or mere comrades of men; and in so far as they had the opportunity and the incentive to be more than housewives and childbearers, they had to face the problem of how then to fulfill themselves. Hollywood was helping to make them known all over the world for their freedom and their discontent.

Still, they did in fact have more freedom and opportunity than women had ever had before, and they did not simply suffer thereby. The higher rate of divorce was an ambiguous symptom; it meant too that many people were no longer condemned to loveless marriages. Similarly the spreading knowledge of birth control that encouraged sexual adventure was more plainly a boon for women. The aspiration to be "modern" meant for many people not merely being smart and fashionable but a wholesome liberation from the rigid conventions and harsh judgments that had warped or impoverished many lives, especially in small towns. Among the many signs that Americans were growing more tolerant and more genuinely sophisticated was the Broadway theater, which in the twenties began rivaling the European theater in both serious drama and urbane entertainment. They were also providing a larger audience for the serious novelists, almost all of whom were severely critical of American life. As Coolidge prosperity got under way the businessman himself became known all over the land as Babbitt; the big boom fostered a boom in self-criticism too. Among the educated, who were rapidly increasing in number, the most influential writer was H. L. Mencken. Many who were young in the

twenties may testify how exhilarated they were by his lusty, slambang,
all-out offensives against all the shibboleths of the American Way, all
the accepted restrictions on personal liberty; though perhaps they did
not realize that his popularity belied his own thesis that America was
a cultural Sahara.

As always, we cannot be sure to what extent Americans were actually
emancipated, or total up either the profits or the costs of the obvious
changes. In most people the changes were probably superficial. The
trends to both self-indulgence and maturity were confused by the usual
welter of conflicting fashions—the success of religious revivalists, the
Ku Klux Klan, the American Legion, the Boston Watch and Ward
Society, and assorted groups bent on keeping America pure or purely
American. But at least it became clear that Americans had not been
fatally corrupted. The Great Depression was a terrible shock and then
a prolonged strain, to not only the many millions of unemployed but
the millions more who lost their savings, status, security; yet the people
weathered it without losing their morale or their basic hopefulness.
Naturally sobered by it, they became more socially conscious. Many
took to an anxious kind of self-criticism, much less exuberant than
Mencken's, but more thoughtful, discriminating, and possibly heartening; Mencken's popularity faded when his attacks on the New Deal
revealed more clearly that his ridicule of the "boobeoisie" sprang
from a Nietzschean contempt of the common man and essentially of
the democratic ideal. Sinclair Lewis sounded one keynote in his best
seller *It Can't Happen Here,* showing how fascism could happen.
Thomas Wolfe sounded another in *You Can't Go Home Again,* which
recorded his own experience of the horrors of the depression and the
falsity of the good old days that were gone for good; but in a sense he
had gone home again, to the epical promise of America and its habitual
devotion to the future tense, the optative mood. So he could conclude:
"I believe that we are lost here in America, but I believe we shall be
found."

There remained plenty of confusion and distraction, of course.
Other best sellers of the period included *Life Begins at Forty, Wake Up
and Live,* and *How to Win Friends and Influence People,* while up
to a hundred million Americans a week went to the movies, virtually
none of which gave the slightest idea of what the country had been
through and what it was now up against. Hollywood stamped more indelibly on the rest of the world a false impression of American life,
which its popularity nevertheless made a true reflection of American

mentality. As the clouds gathered over Europe, the threat of war revived isolationism, another illusion of normalcy. The people were
slower to respond to Roosevelt's efforts to alert them to the dangers
because the leading isolationists intensified the historic confusions of
Americanism; they ranged from progressives like Senators Borah and
Nye, who maintained the parochialism of the Populist tradition,
through the national hero Lindbergh to the "radio priest" Father
Coughlin, who exploited the ugly prejudices that Populists had also
been prone to, including anti-Semitism. When the nation was forcibly
involved in the war it was almost too late. But Pearl Harbor then
restored more than the economy; the confusions of the immense war
effort involved little question of the morale of the people.

Much deeper and more complicated, however, had been the effects of
the first war on the intelligentsia. These were naturally most pronounced in Europe, which had suffered most from the ordeal. In
France the Dadaists were quick to speak the last word in disillusionment—nihilism. "Art has no meaning!" they proclaimed; and with this
catcall they made a clean sweep of logic, morality, all universal principles. Although their flamboyant ventures in meaninglessness had only
a passing vogue, they announced a major theme of art and thought
between the wars. Almost all intellectuals felt that Europe was sick,
perhaps mortally. Many a work declared or illustrated the larger thesis
that made T. S. Eliot famous: modern Western civilization was a
"waste land."

But it was Paul Valéry, once more, who as a wholly dedicated disciple of mind most acutely and comprehensively stated the plight of the
European intellectual.[7] He was haunted by the decline of Europe, no
longer the dominant power in the world nor the master of its destiny.
He knew that a novel, more profound and essential kind of uncertainty had entered history because of science and technology; the
unprecedented interdependence of regions and events all over the world
made it impossible for statesmen to gamble safely any longer on "the
isolation of events," or to foresee "the effects of effects incalculable."
He was revolted by politics even apart from its common inanity,
for it was bound "to falsify all the values which it is the mind's
business to verify." Above all he feared for the freedom and
dignity of the mind, which had been so cruelly wounded by the

---

7 Always self-conscious, he knew that his worshipful idea of intellect—not "soul"—as the
supreme value could be called a Baconian idol. "I agree," he wrote, but he added, "I have
not found a better idol."

catastrophe of the war: "it doubts itself profoundly." As for the immediate future, Valéry saw modern man "staggering between two abysses," the constant dangers of both excessive order and disorder. Again and again he said, "We are backing into the future."

Although he also attacked history as written because it continued to justify anything or everything, while teaching nothing, the most famous historians of the era were confirming his own worst fears. Shortly after the war Bury published *The Idea of Progress,* in which he still called progress "the animating and controlling idea of Western civilization"; but already Spengler had published *The Decline of the West.* His outline of history, with its cyclical theory proving that this decline was inevitable and unstoppable, had much more influence on the mind of Europe. Arnold Toynbee then launched his *Study of History,* in which he disavowed the strict determinism of Spengler but as remorselessly insisted on much the same invariable cycles of growth, decline, and death; the early volumes declared his belief that Western civilization had broken down, that there was little hope for its recovery except through prayer, and indeed that it was hardly worth saving. Freud took as long and gloomy a view in *Civilization and Its Discontents.* While he saw a ray of hope in the unceasing efforts of the Ego, his readers were generally more impressed by his much greater emphasis on the inescapable discontents, and on the endless struggle with the dark powers of Id that were obviously threatening Europe. Similarly religious thought took a somber turn, marked by the popularity of Karl Barth's "theology of crisis" and the discovery of Kierkegaard, the father of *Angst.*

No more faith in Europe was expressed by most of the writers who between the wars emerged as the greatest of the moderns—Proust, Gide, Joyce, Yeats, Eliot, Lawrence, Kafka, and the like. D. H. Lawrence most passionately attacked modern civilization and all its works, in his extreme revulsion laying himself open to charges of sympathy with fascism.[8] So did Yeats and Eliot; and though none were actually Fascists, they were not democrats either. Few of the greater writers supported the liberal cause or any popular cause. They tended rather —like Valéry himself as a poet—to pursue the way of the nineteenth-

---

8 He could write such cruel passages as this:
    The tree of humanity needs pruning, badly,
    it needs thoroughly pruning, not as in the late war, blasting
    with unintelligent and evil destruction
    but pruning, severely, intelligently and ruthlessly pruning.

century Symbolists, turning inward, exploring their own immediate consciousness, communicating unique personal sensations. In this way they could render what Henry James called "the atmosphere of the mind," illumine the inner world of the individual, and extend the borders of consciousness, as Proust did most thoroughly and Joyce most ingeniously. ("Sink deep or touch not the Cartesian spring," wrote Joyce in *Finnegans Wake*.) Their way nevertheless suggested a withdrawal from the public world, when not a negation of its major concerns. It was always liable to the dangers that Edmund Wilson remarked in Symbolism: "cultivating one's private fantasies, encouraging one's private manias, ultimately preferring one's absurdest chimeras to the most astonishing realities, ultimately mistaking one's chimeras for reality." Thus Yeats ended in his Occult Vision, conjuring up a fantastic system of Masks, Demons, Wills, Bodies of Fate, etc. The most eminent writers were rarely eminent for either good sense or good humor.

They therefore tended, however unintentionally, to support the spreading irrationalism that more seriously threatened the freedom and dignity of the mind. One offshoot of Dada was surrealism, nurtured by a self-conscious worship of the unconscious. "May not one succeed," wrote Dali, "in systematizing confusion and so assist the total discrediting of the world of reality?" The answer, of course, was Yes. Hitler had already made the question academic, though he despised the surrealists—he needed no assistance from scatterbrained intellectuals.[9] Other writers lent more sober support to the fashion of celebrating the powers of Id, following Jung's view of them as a source of wisdom and high inspiration. Herbert Read was pleased to picture artists "dipping into a cauldron of timeless and intensely vital entities," though he was vague about the nature of these piping-hot essences. Myth now came fully into its own, but still without any clear criteria for distinguishing its timeless truth from the barbarism of Hitler's mythology. Nietzsche reached the height of his popularity, for reasons having much to do with the revolt against science and more broadly with the vehement thesis of D. H. Lawrence—that modern man was suffering from too much intellect. It often appeared that the European mind, whose plight so distressed Valéry, was not so much doubting itself as proudly scorning its rational uses.

---

9 In fairness it should be noted that other surrealists had also discredited Dali. Followers of André Breton charged him with some "cosmopolitan tendencies," which presumably obstructed the task of systematizing confusion or bringing the unconscious into its own.

For a time surrealism seemed more significant because it represented a historically novel alliance between the avant-gardes in art and politics, especially revolutionary Marxism. This was a doomed alliance, since Russian Communists soon made it clear that they had no more use for surrealists than Hitler did: "socialist realism" was at the opposite pole from such anarchism. It was nevertheless a logical alliance in that both parties were so radically opposed to traditional norms of reason-ableness, in their ostensible cause of liberating mankind. At any rate, it pointed to another conspicuous response of the European intel-ligentsia to the crisis of mind. They took to ideology, "the opium of the intellectuals."

They were drawn to communism by diverse motives. Sorel (now an old man) suggested one when he hailed Lenin and Mussolini as heroes of his cult of violence and myth: violence still had an evident appeal just because of the war. A quite different motive was guilt over the "treason" that Benda charged intellectuals with: the great majority had betrayed the cause of truth and justice by endorsing the official propa-ganda of their nation. But most were converted for more obvious reasons. Like Silone, they were appalled by the absurd, monstrous in-equity of capitalistic society, especially during the depression, and the indifference of its defenders to the rising evil of fascism. Like Arthur Koestler, many came from bourgeois families whose savings had been wiped out by the failures of capitalism, which confirmed their feeling that their society was rotten at its core, democracy a mere sham. Koestler stated most explicitly the deepest appeal of communism to the mind that doubted itself. It offered a total solution, a complete system of thought together with a program for action; and it represented "true faith," which to him had to be "radical, uncompromising, pure"— as it was in both Lenin and St. Paul. By contrast, parliamentary govern-ment offered the wounded mind only more compromises, at best a hope of gradual reform; or when it achieved a remarkable measure of effi-cient socialism, as in Sweden, this still seemed bourgeois, ideologically tame. American democracy in particular had little appeal for Con-tinental intellectuals, even aside from its depressing performance after the war; for it rested on a few simple ideas, unworthy of the name of ideology, and what was called Americanism was hardly suited for export.

But "opium" is not quite the word for the effects of the popular ideologies, which were seldom sedative. The revolutionary isms in both art and thought entailed a good deal of intellectual violence. At worst

they amounted to a degradation of mind, apparent in the verbal violence of Communists that debased language too; their spokesmen typically denied their opponents the dignity of being honestly mistaken,
calling other intellectuals lackeys, vile hypocrites, mad dogs, etc.
Koestler would learn that the man of "true faith" may be not only a
fanatic but a profoundly unscrupulous man. At best, the doctrinaires
conditioned the mind to crude, automatic responses, unfitted it for
sensitive, resourceful, responsible dealings with the obvious complexities and uncertainties of a revolutionary age. When disillusioned,
they were still likely to support authoritarianism, or else to be demoralized. Thus some ex-Communists sought refuge in the Roman Church,
others turned Fascist, while those who returned to the support of
democracy often felt guilty and unhappy; the best they might say for it
was that "We are defending a half-truth against a total lie"—a statement itself only partly true. Meanwhile intellectuals on the Right
contributed their share to the violent simplicities that ruled out
reasonable, civil discourse.

We may accordingly feel unhappier as we recall the challenge of
H. G. Wells: "From now on history is a race between education and
catastrophe." Much of the art and thought between the wars constituted
a pretty dubious education. It tended to deprive Europe of the tragic
dignity of history, to inculcate instead a brutal sense of catastrophe
or a paralyzing sense of futility. When catastrophe came again, Wells
himself—the most ardent apostle of education—gave up. In his last
testament, *Mind at the End of its Tether*, he concluded: "There
is no way out or round or through. . . . It is the end." Yet the race
is still on, the end is not actually in sight, mind remains as active as
ever; and its cause—the cause to which intellectuals are willy-nilly
committed—had by no means simply suffered from their activities
before the catastrophe. Valéry, who had never been so confident as
Wells about the "progress" of Western man, lived just long enough to
see France liberated, and to leave a different testament: "May there
never come into your mind these cruel words: What was the use?"
Although writers had often used such cruel words about the First
World War, very few had recommended the perennial wisdom of
quiescence or nonattachment—the best wisdom for any really hopeless situation.

In general, the intelligentsia had continued to maintain the mind's
freedom if only by their continual disagreement. Thereby they had
demonstrated, too, the exceptional freedom of thought, speech, and

press still permitted in the democracies, for it did not take great courage to express radical opinions; there was still no easier way to fame than by shocking the bourgeois. Above all, they proved the singular vitality of the European mind. The great writers who had a low opinion of modern civilization and its prospects won their fame by the exceptional originality and often the magnitude of their works; the generation between the wars stirred up more ferment and produced more works of genius than had the generation before the war.[10] Despair was never so apparent as the continued quest for salvation or certainty, however feverish. Among the common themes of intellectuals was the spiritual pilgrimage—to Moscow, to Rome, to the East. Even those, like the Dadaists, who proclaimed the meaninglessness of art, philosophy, or any universal cause characteristically did so in *manifestoes*. They were out to make converts, "emancipate" men from bondage to mere logic or common sense.

All along, moreover, there were of course many defenders of the liberal faith and the basic values of Western civilization. They included some of the most distinguished intellectuals of the period— Bernard Shaw, Bertrand Russell, Thomas Mann, Ortega y Gasset, Berdyaev, Meinecke, Croce, and Einstein, to name a diverse few. They were truer to the Western spirit in that they were always critical of their society, unreserved only in their devotion to freedom of inquiry, criticism, and dissent. Ortega, for instance, was best known for *The Revolt of the Masses,* a restatement of the perennial alarm of European aristocrats and conservatives, which was more pertinent and acute because the masses he feared were no longer merely the "lower" class but were to be found in all ranks of society. But for this reason the liberal ideal was all the more precious to Ortega:

> Liberalism—it is well to recall this today—is the supreme form of generosity; it is the right which the majority concedes to minorities and hence it is the noblest cry that has ever resounded in this planet. It announces the determination to share existence with the enemy; more than that, with an enemy which is weak. It was incredible that the human species should have arrived at so noble an attitude, so paradoxical, so refined, so acrobatic, so anti-natural. Hence it is not to be wondered

---

10 Among the striking examples of apparent anomaly was Vienna: once the capital of operetta and the waltz, it now emerged as a major intellectual center. As Austria declined and its empire collapsed, it produced such widely known men as Mahler, von Hofmannsthal, Rilke, Schnitzler, Freud, Husserl, Max Reinhardt, Kafka, and Wittgenstein.

at that this same humanity should soon appear anxious to get rid of it.

As a class the intelligentsia were not at all anxious to get rid of it. Most of them did not subscribe to communism, or to any ism that would suppress all other isms. As the catastrophe approached, many were still confused or divided in their loyalties, the more so because Communists had taken the lead in opposing Hitler; but at least very few intellectuals outside of Germany supported Hitlerism. Within Germany Heidegger and Jung were the only distinguished ones to compromise with the regime.

For the long run, simple reaffirmations of the liberal faith, such as Benda's, were less wholesome than the fuller recognition of ambiguity, complexity, difficulty, and necessary uncertainty. Influential writers "discredited" the world of conventional reality much more effectively than did the surrealists, but without merely debunking it or substituting a nightmarish dream world. In *Man's Fate* and *Man's Hope* André Malraux did communism the rare service of preserving the tragic sense of human conflict. Pirandello dramatized the problem of illusion, the impossibility of distinguishing it with assurance from psychological reality; in his poignant but unsentimental awareness of how all of us perforce live on some illusion, and some of us try to live without it, men might be more compassionate and humane. In *Ideology and Utopia* Karl Mannheim attempted a comparable analysis of social reality. He dwelt on the illusions in all ideologies, the pluralism and relativism that doomed hopes of utter objectivity and certainty; but his aim was to preserve rationality, restore a common understanding, make possible more real objectivity and freedom from bias, and at the same time preserve some aspiration to utopia, without which "man would lose his will to shape history and therewith his ability to understand it." Others sought to maintain sanity by the new discipline of semantics, harking back to Bentham, but now become a more systematic effort to expose the linguistic sources of illusion.

In lieu of calling the roll, however, it may do to consider two representative, highly self-conscious "educationalists"—Thomas Mann, the most influential novelist in central Europe during this period, and André Gide, the most eminent of French literary intellectuals. Both addressed the basic problem forced by the dissolution of the old order and the old certainties: the necessity of living dangerously, in a full consciousness of an always problematical, ambiguous reality; and the need of living humanely and responsibly as well. Both exemplified the possibility of maintaining human dignity and personal integrity on these difficult terms.

Mann most explicitly took up this task of education in *The Magic Mountain,* a vast philosophical novel directly inspired by a guilty conscience owing to his fervent patriotism during the war. Steeped in Goethe, Schopenhauer, Nietzsche, and Wagner, he attempted among other things to reconcile the best in German tradition with the broader humanistic tradition of the West, but he also "took stock" of all the first and last questions of life and death. Steeped in Freud too, he took full stock especially of the powers of the irrational and the unconscious, and stressed the ambivalence of all the issues of body, mind, and soul, the "sacred, impure mysteries" of life, from love and disease to art and religion; in the "hopeful-hopeless" effort of conscious life to understand itself, everything is necessarily "two-faced" and "equivocal," including psychoanalysis itself. As an omniscient author, freely commenting from beginning to end, Mann was consistently playful, ironic, noncommittal; the end is a question mark. Yet by this very attitude he was committed to the humanistic values of breadth, tolerance, liberality, and catholicity. The entire adventure of his hero on the "magic" mountain was motivated by both piety and rationality, in a spirit of pride and humility somewhere "between recklessness and reason." At the spiritual climax Mann dared, for the one and only time, a whole sentence in italics: *"For the sake of goodness and love, man shall let death have no sovereignty over his thoughts."* The question at the end of the novel signifies neither defeatism nor mere skepticism, but restates this faith as a hope. The question could be asked again after Hitler dashed the hope by reviving the worst in German tradition, for he did not kill the faith.

The education offered by Gide was immediately much more equivocal. His early prewar novels seemed steeped in decadence, coolly exploiting deliberate immoralism, exhibiting the "rotten elegance" dear to the aesthetes of the time, and with it an apparent nihilism that later endeared him to the surrealists. In his major novel, *The Counterfeiters,* written after the war, he dwelt on not only the incongruities that make human conduct unpredictable and intractable but much perverted, vicious, monstrous behavior. Given his romantic concept of the artist as by nature a rebel, and his personal problem as a homosexual, he had every reason to feel alienated, and may have seemed so when he went off to the Congo. Nevertheless Gide was not another Rimbaud. He had a Calvinistic conscience that kept him in a state of tension, obsessed with incongruity and ambiguity, but nonetheless resolved to live a moral life. It made him the first major writer frankly to confess his homosexuality in an autobiography, after wrestling with it for many years had convinced him that it was the law of his nature. It gave him a high seriousness beyond a devotion to art for art's sake, or for his own sake. If he was a questionable guide in the art of living dangerously, he was no cynic or immoralist but an apostle of personal freedom, attacking moral conventions only when they prevented the individual from realizing his own distinctive strength and virtue. Under high tension he himself kept a level head. His contemporaries should not have been so startled when he announced his conversion to communism, but neither should Soviet critics have welcomed him so rhapsodically (one called him "the glory of our epoch"); a trip to the Soviet soon convinced Gide that it was nothing like the promised land of freedom, least of all for intellectuals. He remained critical of all other modern gods too, expressing his gratitude to Freud, for example, for having helped to remove some taboos, but deploring the absurdities sanctioned by "that imbecile of genius." An ultrasophisticated Puritan, he too could venture italics in his credo as an intellectual upholding the conscience of his society: "The world will be saved, if it can be, only by the *unsubmissive*."

Meanwhile the hopes, doubts, and fears of literary men had little effect on science, the dominant intellectual enterprise of the modern world. Astronomers, theoretical physicists, and philosophers of science were spreading the news about the mysterious universe, and the necessary uncertainty of our knowledge of it, that led Spengler and others to conclude rashly that science had reached a dead end, in keeping with the decline of the West; but the well-informed knew better. They could rejoice that natural scientists were now thinking more scientifically about science itself, and so were also thinking more freely and profitably, no longer hampered by arbitrary "necessities of thought." Otherwise scientists in all fields went on with their work quite confidently, mostly untroubled by doubts about their faith in the value of truth-seeking. Few were given either to despair about the prospects of modern civilization; the steady progress of science disposed them to regard all problems as challenges or opportunities. For intellectual purposes, the chief problem remained the widening gulf between general knowledge and the frontiers of science, and the tendencies of specialists to wall off their domains for the sake of efficiency or purity. Thus the logical positivism of Carnap and his followers, due to become the dominant school in philosophy, was producing much acute analysis, but it was also discrediting ethics as well as metaphysics, confining philosophy to the logic of science and withdrawing it from the arena of vital problems. Theoretical physicists, naturally remote from the public arena, felt differently when they mastered nuclear power and produced the atom bomb. Then they would at once sound the alarm and call for social action to control this terrific power, but still imply the characteristic confidence of scientists that man could meet the challenge.

Such basic confidence was as characteristic, lastly, of most American writers and thinkers between the wars. Although they were immediately as disenchanted as Europeans, and went in for as varied, confused modes of revolt, they were less apt than Continental intellectuals at either logical or ideological rigor on the one hand, profound irony and conscious ambiguity on the other. F. Scott Fitzgerald and Ernest Hemingway won their popularity as spokesmen of the "lost generation," which helped them to discover their talent but made it harder for them to mature; in the end they were "lost" as youthful romantics with a limited stock in trade, not as writers oppressed by the deep confusions of the postwar world, or by a loss of faith in man or mind. Other young writers who went to Paris and got excited by Dada, surrealism, Gertrude Stein, or simple bohemianism settled down when they came home and made do with more conventional criticism of the American way of life. The debunking realism in fiction, biography, and history barely ruffled the basic faith in American democracy; writers chiefly reflected this faith, criticizing society in terms of its ideals of human dignity and personal freedom, and implying that its ills were remediable. Few literary rebels were either political radicals or gloomy prophets. Most were popular enough to feel that they were in the main current of a stirring renaissance, if also to forget that many ordinary Americans agreed with them; soon little magazines were burgeoning all over the country, as were little theaters. Despite the incessant criticism and complaint, *The Education of Henry Adams* stood out as an exception for its pessimism, which in other writers was seldom philosophical, more a matter of mood. And when the excitement subsided in the dark days of the depression, writers kept their American form. Those who were converted to communism (notably Theodore Dreiser) were typically shallow or half-baked Marxists, poor at ideology, tender-minded, and hardly revolutionary types. Others went home again, sometimes to a quite conventional faith in America. Van Wyck Brooks exemplified a common way of coming of age, in his early works complaining of the immaturity of American culture, showing how Mark Twain had fallen victim to the genteel tradition, and then settling down to a too mellow history of New England, in literary criticism to too wholesale an insistence that writers be wholesome and affirmative.

As for thinkers, their main tendency was indicated by the continued popularity of the word "new," which had given birth to the *New Republic* under Wilson's New Freedom. Immediately after the war James Harvey Robinson sounded the call to arms in *The Mind in the Making*: the primary task was "the liberation of intelligence" from the reigning conservatism. He had high hopes of the "new history," devoted explicitly to the aim of explaining the present and offering a guide to the future. (At the time he was teaching at the New School for Social Research, which was acquiring its great prestige as a center of liberal studies.) John Dewey had already responded with *Reconstruction in Philosophy*, as confident a call for a new philosophy. While he became widely recognized as the leading American philosopher, the torch of the liberated intelligence was carried by such other esteemed thinkers as Charles Beard, Lewis Mumford, Carl Becker, Vernon Parrington, and Oliver Wendell Holmes, and it flared even in Washington when Roosevelt called in his "Brain Trust" for his New Deal. This period was in fact the heyday of liberalism in the intellectual history of America. The cause was supported as well by most of the leading social scientists, no less when they tabooed value judgments. Anthropologists, for example, were doing most to propagate the doctrine of the relativity of values, like Ruth Benedict insisting that we had no right to pass judgments on other cultures, all were "equally" valid; yet they also insisted that the doctrine of relativity was no reason for despair, as so many people thought, but properly should promote the values of sympathy, tolerance, and good will. In other words, they were committed to liberal, democratic values.

Now, time has been unkind to this whole generation. The reaction that has largely discredited its work set in in the late thirties. The "new critics," proclaiming that literature should be studied exclusively as an aesthetic text, dismissed most of its leading lights as crude artists, most shallow when optimistic; they suggested that about the only claim to dignity of modern civilization was the great European writers who had exposed it as a waste land, and perhaps the occasion and incentive it offered for the new criticism. (William Faulkner was among the few American contemporaries deemed worthy of this criticism.) Reinhold

Niebuhr led the revival of Original Sin; although himself a political liberal, he asserted that the cardinal sin of Robinson, Dewey, and the rest was the inveterate sin of pride, which blinded them to the ineradicable evil in man. Walter Lippmann anticipated the "new conservatism" to come. And however finicky or cranky the new fashions, the generation between the wars was indeed wide open to criticism. It had not responded to the crisis of mind by a really searching reappraisal of either America or Western civilization, or of the means and ends of the liberated intelligence.

By Continental standards, almost all the better known creative writers—Dreiser, Lewis, Anderson, O'Neill, Sandburg, Dos Passos, Wolfe, Hemingway, *et al.*—were hardly intellectuals, and could look woefully unsubtle and unsophisticated when set beside the great European writers. With their obviously limited powers of thought they had as limited a capacity for social analysis and criticism. Like Mencken, they had too easy a time attacking Puritanism and Babbittry, and while feeling bold or sometimes alienated, they failed to realize that their large audience was in fact too easy to impress. In particular most of them showed little capacity for growth, beyond a tendency to grow more conventional. Liberal intellectuals were in general no more distinguished for subtlety, acuteness, intensity, or profundity. However specific as critics of their society, they still tended to be fuzzy as social and political philosophers, and to ground their thought on too easy or cloudy a faith. They might have sharpened and toughened their minds by closer attention to such thinkers as Nietzsche, Weber, Pareto, Freud, and Spengler. Dewey, the bellwether, remained vague in his demand for continuous social experiment, to be guided and controlled by the "scientific" method of intelligence, in a studied avoidance of fixed principles; for he offered no scientific or any other definite standard for judging the results of such experiments, as in the New Deal. His condemnation of the Soviet, the boldest experiment of the time, indicated that he did after all have some fixed principles or absolute standards, but it also called attention to both the limitations and the possible abuses of his method of intelligence, the subordination of values to technique. As Randolph Bourne began to realize when his mentor Dewey supported the First World War, a philosophy of "adaptation" or "adjustment" that may do for a prosperous society at peace, with a fund of good will, may not meet the demands of a time of crisis merely because it seeks only to "meet" situations, and makes no provision for transcendence.

Yet the shortcomings of the liberal intellectuals of the period were due in part to their distinctive virtues. While independent and bold enough in criticizing their society or defending unpopular causes, they were more generous and humane than most intellectuals on the Continent, and more temperate, because less rigorous in their logic or their ideology. They maintained a rare attitude by their more consistent demand for both personal freedom and social responsibility, which Marxists could call inconsistent only because of their absurdly simplified concept of the bourgeois. In part because of their limitations, they did more to help their countrymen to keep their heads during the depression and the darker days ahead, and to remain united in their too simple faith and hope. Similarly the creative writers did more to help America come of age because they were not acute intellectuals. They stirred up more excitement and enthusiasm for literature, especially among the young, than would the very literary or academic "new critics"; they spread a livelier, more effectual awareness of the limitations of American culture than would the many fastidious, querulous, or ostentatiously alienated critics of our day. They brought American literature to maturity in another important respect, by bringing it into the mainstream of European literature. If sometimes still inclined to feel inferior to Europeans, for the most part they wrote freely and naturally, no less when under European influence, and felt little compulsion either to assert their Americanism or to apologize for it; while despite their limitations they won increasing attention abroad, more respect than they would later get at home. So too with American scientists and scholars, painters and composers. In all fields of culture, the period between the wars was uncommonly vigorous and expansive, on the whole the most fruitful in the nation's history.

Since it is now fashionable to look down on most of its leading writers and thinkers, we should remember that they made it easier for the coming generation to expose their limitations, flaunt its superior subtlety and sophistication. We might deplore the ungraciousness of modern America, which always tends first to overrate its lions, then to underrate or ridicule them, still worse simply to ignore them as unworthy of serious attention—to outgrow them without thanks. We might even look back wistfully to a period when readers were often exhilarated, critics were more eager to praise and encourage writers than to dissect or demolish them. In any case we should recognize that these writers and thinkers were by no means uniformly shallow, fuzzy, naïve, or tender-minded. When most confident, they never assured the country that progress was easy or certain; typically they gave a grim enough account of its shortcomings, in literature often with a vividness or an elemental power that might compensate for their own shortcomings in fine artistry. Neither were they uniformly deficient in irony. Carl Becker, for example, had ample sense of incongruity and ambiguity, as well as of impending catastrophe; in the late thirties he came pretty close to despair; and it was only after a full look at the worst that he affirmed that the "glittering generalities" on which the nation had been founded still did glitter. If the generation that entered World War II had too high hopes of winning the "four freedoms," it was at least somewhat more clear-eyed than the generation that entered the first war, and had a more sober idea of what it was fighting for and fighting against.

| *THE RISE OF*
TOTALITARIANISM

1. The Historic Sources

At the beginning of the preceding chapter we left a world alarmed over
the Bolsheviks in Russia and the revolutionaries at home, but frightened chiefly for reasons involving little passion for democracy, and
not really frightened enough. Few men in the democracies foresaw the
spread of totalitarianism, still less of a naked, brutal tyranny. They
could hardly be expected to, indeed, inasmuch as the Communists
themselves—the specialists in revolution and in prophecy—failed to
anticipate the rise of fascism. Although the whole movement now looks
like a natural, predictable consequence of the World War, it was no
more clearly inevitable than was the triumph of the Bolsheviks in
Russia. Despite its common appearances of tyranny, it was by no means
a uniform movement either, nor so simple as it still appears in popular
accounts of it. Dictators were a familiar enough breed, and their rise
was soon explained as the long-feared "revolt of the masses," but these
dictatorships were quite novel affairs: blends of nationalism and socialism, fired by fanaticism, which drew support from all classes, including
many men pleased to think that they were revolting against the masses.
Similarly they were supported by so many conflicting tendencies—irrationalism, scientism, authoritarianism, collectivism, elitism, primitivism—that thinkers may trace totalitarianism to whatever is their
favorite abomination. Its spiritual fathers appear to be as diverse a lot,
for it is described as a legitimate or a bastard offspring of not only
Marx but Rousseau, Hegel, Comte, Nietzsche, Pareto, and others.

By now, however, we have enough perspective to get our bearings on
the movement as a whole. In common usage, sanctioned by the diction-

ary, a "totalitarian" state is one completely controlled by a single party that outlaws all others. I should add that it has everywhere involved dictatorship, rule by the leader of the single party, and that its "total" control has embraced more interests—economic, social, cultural—than despotic monarchs tried to control in the past. Most students of it add that it is a product of "revolutionary mass movements," an assumption I shall presently qualify, but it is peculiarly modern in that the dictators have typically sought and won mass support. They have been able to exercise much more power over not only the bodies but the minds of people than despots ever could in the past because they could mobilize the immense technological resources developed over the past century. By the same token, they were able to seize and retain power because their creeds and policies were not simply novel, nor so revolutionary as they professed or even believed. Totalitarianism has deep roots in Western tradition. Its elements are as old and universal as civilization, but their combination is another distinctively Western phenomenon.

For a quick review, our story begins in ancient Egypt. This developed a highly organized, planned economy, controlled by a bureaucracy under the absolute sovereignty of Pharaoh, in theory the owner and manager of the whole country. Almost all the great states thereafter were ruled by monarchs whose power was restricted by custom, prudence, and slow communications, but in theory was absolute. For some centuries Europe too had known absolute monarchy, which in Russia persisted into this century. Hobbes had suitably described the nation-state as Leviathan, and conferred on it virtually unlimited power. The rights of rulers to intrude on every realm of social activity, from dress through commerce to religion, had been supported by the inveterate confusion of society with the state, from Plato on; Burke and Hegel alike had declared that men owed to the state not only their well-being but their virtue and culture. The practice of walling off some social or private domains, legally debarring the state from interfering with them, is a recent tradition, and in most European countries it was still a weak, uncertain one.

In medieval Europe totalitarianism was anticipated more distinctively by the recurrent millenarian movements. Down into the Protestant Reformation prophets stirred up the poor by visions of a heaven on earth, the promise of a total solution here and now. They were more prophetic than they knew because the way to their Millennium typically led through violence and bloodshed; first the righteous had to destroy Antichrist, exterminate the hordes of the Devil—an archenemy such as both communism and nazism would flourish on. Hitler even resuscitated the favorite victims of the millenarians, the Jews. Behind such errant movements lay the militancy to which Christian idealism was always prone. Soldiers of the Cross, Inquisitors, Luther and Calvin, Puritan saints—all were dedicated authoritarians, uncompromising in their war on error or evil and their demand for total faith and obedience. The medieval Papacy had asserted the absolute sovereignty of the Church, in temporal as well as spiritual matters, and denied autonomy to profane interests. Calvin had set up at Geneva his theocracy, a Christian totalitarian state, and Cromwell had ruled England as a God-fearing dictator.

Hence the Jacobins in the French Revolution were not being simply godless when they translated the Millennium into a secular Utopia, and sought to assure the "reign of virtue" in Rousseau's ideal republic by instituting the Reign of Terror.[1] Although their regime lasted only a year or so, Robespierre's legacy was preserved immediately by "Gracchus" Babeuf and his disciple Philippe Buonarroti—"terribles simplificateurs" who founded an undying tradition that came down through Marx. Their pure ideal was communistic equality and fraternity to be achieved under an omnicompetent State, a Grand National Community owning and managing the entire society. As Buonarroti saw it, the French Revolution had failed because the democrats had tolerated "diversity of views" and not invested a man like Robespierre with absolute powers; so he decided that only a revolutionary dictatorship could lead the masses to the promised land they wanted, but were still too confused or corrupt to enter by themselves. As for Marx, he was vaguer about his ideal Communist society, leaving no blueprints for it or for "the dictatorship of the proletariat" that would lead the way to it; but otherwise he was of course much more systematic. He called in all history to back up his messianic promises; he gave philosophical, "scientific" authority to the myth of revolution as the guaranteed way to universal peace and brotherhood; and he compensated for the God he removed by bequeathing a more substantial, visible Devil to keep the faithful united and enflamed—capitalism. Christ and Antichrist, the elect and the damned, were now rebaptized as the proletariat and the bourgeois.

Other ingredients in the brews of totalitarianism were prepared by

---

[1] On these sources of totalitarian idealism see *Freedom in the Western World*, pp. 82, 157–158, 160, 345–346, and 389–392.

thinkers mostly quite unlike Marx. Out of Romanticism came the organic theories of society and history, reactions against an atomic individualism that could and did lead to the opposite extreme of a complete subordination of the individual. With them came nationalism and racism, proposed both as fundamental historic realities and as ideals. Hegel added his celebration of the hero and the state, and his definition of true freedom as complete obedience to the state. In the name of science Comte contributed his vision of an ideal totalitarian state managed efficiently by expert positivists, for the benefit of all but without heed to the opinions or desires of the incompetent many. Nietzsche more positively scorned the many in glorifying the will to power and the superman who exercised it without scruple, while on high moral grounds he scorned as well the appeal to reason and science, or what Fascists would call "barren intellectualism." Pareto buttressed the cult of irrationalism by his demonstration of the primacy of non-logical behavior, Sorel amplified it by his cults of violence and the myth. Primitivists celebrated the natural instinctive life or the voice of the blood (affinities that would induce Knut Hamsun to collaborate with the Nazis). Social thinkers who had not the least desire for dictatorship helped to propagate ideas useful to dictators, as in studies of the herd instinct, mob psychology, and charisma. Hitler in particular often sounded like an up-to-date social psychologist, and was certainly a much better one than Marx.

Such potentialities of totalitarianism could hardly have been realized, however, except for the Industrial Revolution. While incidentally stimulating the growing obsession with power in both rulers and thinkers, this directly built up the necessary social machinery: the immense organization in both government and industry, together with the means of rapid transportation and instant communication, that made possible effective control of the whole society. It made totalitarianism attractive as a logical response to modern technology, a means of giving the fullest possible scope to management and the technical ideal of efficiency, regardless of human cost. It spawned the mass media, which developed the arts of exploiting vulgar hopes and fears, swaying and manipulating people. It created the masses that in Europe kept pressing against the old social order, in particular the new urban masses: men drilled in the routines of factory and office, inured to regimentation, yet emotionally unstable, lacking a genuine culture of their own, more rootless, restless, and godless than the traditional peasant masses, and though less ignorant, lacking the understanding they had much greater need of. While Marx was pleased to see in them a proletariat growing class-conscious, regimented for their manifest destiny of rebelling and establishing a classless society, they were in fact growing more addicted to another secular religion, the opium of tribal nationalism. Many of them would take to fascism, a semi- or pseudo socialism given an advantage by its label of "national." Out of them came Mussolini and Hitler, who had another possible advantage in that—unlike Marx and Lenin—they were actual proletarians, not bourgeois intellectuals.

But totalitarianism still might not have triumphed in Europe had it not been for the World War. This most obviously gave Lenin his opportunity. The German General Staff provided the train that moved him from his exile in Switzerland to the Finland station in St. Petersburg (Leningrad), in the hope that he might stir up trouble and take Russia out of the war; and he obliged by making the Bolshevik Revolution, with the help of war-weary peasant-soldiers, which under normal circumstances his small minority party would have had little if any chance of carrying through. The Bolsheviks then aided potential dictators elsewhere by enabling them to exploit the Communist peril, while setting them an example of violence in both language and deed. Violence was still in the air in postwar Europe. It seemed quite legitimate to the many men who exchanged their uniforms for brown or black shirts, and many more men who were sick of it were therefore indisposed to combat it, or liable to succumb to it in the confusion, unrest, and disenchantment of the letdown. The fledgling popular governments on the Continent were mostly weak and not very popular; their political parties were only beginning to learn the habits of a "loyal opposition." When the depression struck, the established democracies too were discredited in the eyes of many of its victims. Totalitarianism battened on the conspicuous failures of capitalistic democracy.

The war had also provided some useful texts for the dictators. For the first time in history, whole societies had been mobilized, converted into war machines; Germany in particular had almost defeated the world by its efficient organization and control of its economy, the nearest approach to national socialism. With this lesson the dictators learned the power of propaganda, which had likewise been employed more systematically than ever before. But on both counts their chief advantage remained the widespread feelings of frustration, insecurity, and impotence. Typically they proclaimed that they were leading "movements," not parties; no mere party would do for the many demoralized

people who had lost confidence in both their government and themselves, and so felt a need for movement—the more movement the better.
Although the rise of the dictators is commonly attributed to the spread
of irreligion and the breakdown of all authority, they appealed above
all to the type of the "true believer," the "authoritarian personality,"
by their demands for unconditional loyalty. They were not merely the
strong men that people have always tended to idolize, but were prophets,
messiahs. Least of all were the Fascist dictators utilitarians or avowed
materialists. They proclaimed themselves crusaders for "spiritual"
values, in the name of which they professed to despise mere utility, and
except for their military purposes they were in fact indifferent to the
material well-being that the democracies made so much of. They
exemplified the requirements Pascal laid down for any effective religion,
that it must be "contrary to nature, to common sense, and to pleasure."
They promised only "spiritual freedom"—a kind especially attractive
to the many people who were seeking an "escape from freedom," or
from its personal responsibilities, Mussolini declared that men were
weary of liberty; what they really wanted was "Order, Hierarchy, Discipline." Hitler most plainly echoed the thesis of Dostoyevsky's Grand
Inquisitor: "Providence has ordained that I should be the greatest
liberator of humanity. I am freeing men from the demands of a freedom
and personal independence which only a few can sustain."

Yet totalitarianism was not strictly a great mass movement. In all
countries it was the work of an organized minority, comparable to the
Jacobins in France; in none were the dictators elected by a popular
majority. Although they won massive popular support, taking great
pains to do so, they never trusted their popularity enough to permit
free elections, but felt obliged to terrorize the opposition. Nowhere
did they succeed in countries with an established democratic tradition,
where "the masses" had a real say in their government.[2] Popular
generalizations about totalitarianism need to be further qualified be-

2 In *Liberty or Equality, the Challenge of Our Time* (1952), Erik von Kuehnelt-Leddihn
cited with much relish the dire prophecies of nineteenth-century thinkers about the
most terrible despotism that would result from the rise of the masses. "It should be self-
evident," he declared, "that the principle of majority rule is a decisive step in the
direction of totalitarianism"; and as a Catholic monarchist he sought to make this more
evident by offering some thirty arguments on behalf of monarchy as a bulwark of true
liberty, and by demonstrating that historic Christianity was far from egalitarian. He
ignored the fact that dictatorship had triumphed in czarist Russia and Catholic Italy,
Spain, and Portugal, and had been opposed most vigorously in countries where the
principle of majority rule was firmly established. His book is worth mentioning because
it was praised by some of the "new" conservatives in America, not to mention those who
now insist that the United States is a republic, not really a democracy.

cause it assumed different forms in different countries, depending on
national traditions and the personal preferences of the dictators. In
Russia the Bolsheviks never talked of relieving men of the burden of
freedom, for a sufficiently obvious reason: the Russian masses had never
had to shoulder any such burden. The leaders of communism, the most
enduring form of totalitarianism, would feel much more secure if their
subjects had a real inclination to escape from freedom.

First, however, we must consider the varieties of fascism. It was this
that brought on World War II, the most direct and fearsome challenge
to the democracies. Although the war ended it as a world movement,
and should have discredited it once and for all, it is still live enough to
be something of a menace, conceivably to generate similar "movements"
in unsettled countries. In any case, its defeat made possible the spread
of communism: the most potent form of totalitarianism in both theory
and practice.

2. *The Varieties of Fascism*

For all the legendary fanfare, the beginnings of fascism in Italy were
almost as inglorious as its end. In forming his party the year after the
war Mussolini soon dropped his youthful proclivity to revolutionary
syndicalism, which won him fewer than 5,000 votes in a parliamentary
election in Milan, and by 1921 he was allying himself with landowners,
industrialists, and churchmen, who were frightened by the popular
unrest. He boasted that he had no program, only "men and will
power"—Italy already had too many programs. The famous March
on Rome in 1922 required little will power and less courage. Having
toughened themselves by raiding the headquarters of labor unions,
with the complicity of the army and the police, his Black Shirts made
the symbolic gestures of revolution by seizing railroad stations, gas
works, newspaper offices, etc., while the army stayed in its barracks; a
decree of martial law that frightened them off the streets of Rome was
immediately revoked by the weak-kneed King Victor Emmanuel, upon
the advice of military leaders; and it was the publication of this thrilling
news that started them riding to Rome, without opposition, from all
over Italy. Mussolini himself had gone to Milan, where Switzerland was
handy in case any serious trouble did start. He then marched to Rome
at the king's invitation, in a sleeping car.

Victor Emmanuel had also been persuaded to invite him to form a new cabinet, though his followers made up less than a tenth of the Italian parliament. Having as yet no program except the will to power, and little mass support, Mussolini settled for a coalition cabinet that preserved the forms of constitutional government. The "revolution" that a few regiments could have halted began to look more like an honest-to-God revolution two years later, when the socialist deputy Matteotti was murdered to prevent his exposure of corruption in the regime. Mussolini then emerged as Il Duce of a one-party state, in which all other parties were outlawed, civil liberties suppressed, and parliamentary forms reduced to rubber stamps of his decrees. Democracy was formally repudiated, together with the whole liberal creed; it became the main enemy. Other official devils included both communism and capitalism.

The version of totalitarianism that Mussolini proceeded to set up, the much-touted "corporate state," was more original in appearance than in actuality. Harking back to his early syndicalism, it divided up the economy into syndicates of workers, employers, and professionals that were in theory autonomous, in fact under state control; their representatives in parliament were likewise controlled by the Fascist party, under the dictatorship of Mussolini. Although this system could therefore be described as socialism, it was quite different from popular socialism, whose followers had been the first victims of his black-shirted thugs. It was not designed to protect workers or give them a larger share of the national income; in return for the nominal right to participate in the government, they were denied the right to strike and had to put in longer working days. Industrialists fared much better under the corporate state, with which they made a secret bargain in 1925. Big landowners did not suffer from it either: millions of poor peasants continued to work the land for them.

The political theory of Mussolini's Fascism (always capitalized by him) was more reactionary. Giovanni Gentile, the philosopher who responded when he felt the need of dignifying his state by a formal ideology, was a Hegelian who had come under Nietzsche's influence, and the Duce himself added ideas drawn from Machiavelli, Sorel, and Pareto. In the *Enciclopedia Italiana* (1932) he described this mixture as "a system of thought," but emphasized that it could be understood only if seen as "a whole way of conceiving life, a spiritualized way." The "keystone" was the concept of the state as "an absolute." "Nothing human or spiritual exists, much less has value, outside the State"; in a nutshell,

"All for the State, nothing outside the State, nothing against the State." Mussolini accordingly called this all-embracing state "totalitarian," a term apparently originated by his party. It required the complete subordination of the individual and the denial of civil liberties, since the only "real" liberty was that of the state, which constituted "the true reality of the individual." Fascism preserved his essential liberties, Mussolini added, limiting only "useless or harmful" ones; but "it cannot be the individual who decides in this matter." Because there are always some misguided persons, fascism "does not exclude necessary educational severities"—i.e., the imprisonment or execution of opponents of the regime. Unlike the nineteenth century of "liberal individualism," ours was to be a century of "collectivism." A political scientist (Corrado Gini) who contributed a "scientific basis of Fascism" explained that it differed from communism in viewing society as "a true and distinct organism," maintaining the concept of "organic unity."

Discipline and obedience were more essential because the end of the Fascist state was not the welfare or mere happiness of its people, as ordinary socialism had made out. "We have created our myth," Mussolini proclaimed at the outset (echoing Sorel): "our myth is the greatness of the nation!" This greatness could be proved, as always, only by "military glories and armed power." Hence fascism rejected all utilitarian doctrines infected by "a prejudice in favor of peace," or of concord. "War alone brings up to their highest tension all human energies and puts the stamp of nobility upon the peoples who have the courage to meet it. . . . Fascism carries over this anti-pacifist spirit even into the lives of individuals." Mussolini's increasing confidence that he was riding the wave of the future then involved him in some apparent inconsistency. He boasted that "the idea, doctrine, and spirit of Fascism are universal"—it was "an army on the march." Nevertheless he did not really believe that such belligerent nationalism was the moral prerogative of all other peoples; the Italian people had a superior destiny ("salvation can come only from the truth of Rome"), and in a Fascist Europe they would presumably clash with other armies on the march. But at least Mussolini was unequivocal in his scorn of internationalism and pacifism, any ideals that limited the freedom of the state.

He was basically consistent too in his scorn of democracy or any equation of the nation with the will of the majority. Although he kept flattering the Italian people, he made plain enough his contempt for "the masses"; perhaps the chief tribute he paid them was his policy of terrorism, which implied that many of them were not really docile. The Fascist state had to be ruled by the superior few, types like Nietzsche's supermen. This elite was not elected, of course, nor was it selected by any rational method; in effect it was self-appointed, having proved its superiority by seizing power. Once in power, Mussolini could add that fascism was "the purest form of democracy" because "the conscience and the will of a few, even of One" in time activated the conscience and the will of all. Meanwhile the leaders were not responsible to the people; instead the people were responsible to them, and the primary rule of their conscience was obedience. The One made all the key decisions without consulting their wishes. Italy was plastered with signs reading: "Mussolini is always right."

The huge mobs who cheered his frequent orations were evidently inclined to agree. There is some question whether Mussolini won the wholehearted support of the majority, but no question that he stirred mass enthusiasm and won over most Italians who had any political interests.[3] He was in any case an ultramodern type of dictator, unlike the Latin-American ones: he was not content with the support of the army, the wealthy, and the Church, but wooed the common people. If he gave them no more bread, he did give them more and bigger circuses, and then some. He exploited to the hilt the religion of nationalism, particularly the ancient cult of the Roman Empire; the glorious mission of Italy was to restore this empire. He dazzled the people by not only displays of military might but the prestige he won in Europe, whose leading statesmen were courting him throughout the ·thirties. His one military triumph, the expensive, not too impressive conquest of Ethiopia, at least sufficed to strengthen the popular illusion that he had made Italy a great power. The Hoare-Laval plan that tried to avert the war by appeasing him had suggested as much, whereupon Mussolini proved it by rejecting the plan and then successfully defying the League of Nations.

More dismaying than his success in Italy was the considerable respect and even admiration he won in the democracies. In fairness to the many men—including Winston Churchill—who were favorably impressed by him, one should first note that they had some excuse for not seeing through the flamboyant, dangerous nonsense that went with his corporate state. Until Hitler rose, he seemed the most dynamic leader in

---

[3] One may suppose that the many poor peasants, typically silent, were on the whole chiefly resigned to their invariable lot. Carlos Levi gives a vivid impression of their fatalism in *Christ Stopped at Eboli*.

Europe, and at first he collaborated with Britain and France against Hitler. His dictatorship was not so naked and ruthless a despotism as Hitler's, nor did he exploit such ugly sentiments as anti-Semitism, if only because there were few Jews in Italy; not until 1938 did he parrot the attacks on "Jewish capitalism." Catholics everywhere were disposed to respect him because he had come to such good terms with the Church in Italy that Pius XI hailed him as "a man sent by Divine Providence." His corporate state made good enough sense in its ideal theory, and in practice it seemed to be providing more competent government than had the feeble administration before him; the doctored statistics he published were quite impressive. Above all, Mussolini was not merely parading the old Roman virtues and the values of community but denouncing the actual corruptions of the democracies—the selfish individualism, the gross materialism, the flabby complacence, the paltry ideals of "happiness" conceived only as ease and comfort. Instead of appealing to economic motives, as American politicians habitually did, he called for courage, nobility, and self-sacrifice. It was symptomatic of the sickness of the free societies that so many men were taken in by Mussolini's ostentation of "spiritual" values, his tawdry brand of "holiness and heroism"; but some whom he impressed (like Churchill) were not themselves sick or demoralized.

Still, they were taken in, by a pretty crude, vulgar ostentation. It had been backed by little evidence of statesmanship, much more open contempt for civilized ideals of freedom, justice, and peace. If there was some excuse too for the ignominious failure of Mussolini, in that Italy was too poor a country to rank with the world powers, he was responsible for the delusions of glory and grandeur, and for the rottenness of both the material and the spiritual foundations he boasted of. His tardy entrance into the World War—an act thoroughly unheroic and unholy, but necessary to the maintenance of his prestige—at once gave away the whole sordid show. His Fascist state was proved to be inefficient and corrupt; his armies made a dismal showing on all fronts. The lively Italian people had lapped up his rhetoric, which came out of a long operatic tradition and a particular fondness for make-believe, but they now suggested that the power of mass propaganda has been somewhat overrated: they obviously had little fervor for the cause of fascism, and no heart for the war that was to prove the greatness of Italy. The "scientific" apologist for fascism had himself acknowledged a possible uncertainty in the system, "the lack of an objective standard" for determining either the interests of the nation or the superiority of the elite who had come into power by force or maybe chance. Mussolini and his henchmen were in fact far from supermen by Nietzsche's standards. One may see poetic justice in the violent end of Il Duce, a bloated corpse hung upside down from a lamppost in Milan.[4]

Other regimes that he helped to inspire had no more staying power. Some of the varieties of fascism were popular movements, as in Hungary, Romania, and later Argentina, where Perón expressed his admiration of the corporate state. Others were authoritarian Rightist regimes imposed by rulers, as in Poland, Yugoslavia, and Greece. These were not revolutions, involved little or no socialism, and picked up chiefly the tricks of exploiting nationalism; thus in Greece General Metaxas proudly inaugurated the "Third Hellenic Civilization," with an appropriate Spartan salute. In the democracies Fascist parties made little headway. They were strongest in France, but here their ideology or program was confused by the various extremists on the Right, including monarchists. In England Fascist sympathies were more apparent in some high social circles than among the common people; Sir Oswald Moseley won only a tiny following by his appeal to vulgar sentiment. ("I have had enough of the people who think. I am going to get the people who feel.") In the United States avowed Fascists, such as Lawrence Dennis, were respectable enough to become naval officers (since even during the war security agents were concerned chiefly with spotting Reds or pinkoes), but the Silver Shirts and others were lost in the crowd of hyphenated Italians and Germans, extreme conservatives, demagogues, and superpatriots, who were mostly incapable of thinking out an ideology or understanding anything so abstract as a "corporate state." Huey Long, dictator of Louisiana, observed that if or when fascism came to America, it would be called something else.

One Fascist regime that survived the World War, that of General Franco, most clearly belies the popular generalizations about totalitarianism and mass movements. Franco won the Spanish Civil War with the direct aid of Mussolini and Hitler and the indirect aid of the

---

[4] I am perhaps unfair to Mussolini, since I was revolted by him from the beginning and never saw in him the qualities of greatness that Churchill and others saw; even in my youth he struck me as a nasty fraud. I should therefore add that he may well have believed in the "holiness and heroism" of his creed, as Hitler did in his racial myth. But if mature reconsideration has been prejudiced by hindsight, the ignominious collapse of his regime under the test of war—the test he always glorified —leaves no doubt of the hollowness of his pretensions. Dispassionate studies of him (such as Ivone Kirkpatrick's) picture a hesitant adventurer who grew bold only because of the stupidity or cowardice of the opposition both at home and abroad, and who as a statesman was remarkably ignorant of the ways of other nations.

Communists, who confused the issues and split the Republicans. He was supported by a distinctively Fascist "movement," the Falangists, who dreamed of restoring the great Spanish Empire, but his basic support came from the wealthy, the landed aristocracy, the army, and the Church, which assured him the sympathy of the bulk of the peasantry. Upon winning the war, he replaced the Spanish Republic with a military dictatorship that had a veneer of syndicalism but at bottom was profoundly conservative, even literally reactionary. Its counter-revolutionary banner proclaimed a devotion to the family, the Church, and the principle of authority. It was in keeping with the absolutism of Spanish tradition—as Hugh Thomas has remarked, the most absolutist of European absolutisms, which helps to explain why anarchism too became a much greater force in Spain than in any other country, making some two million ardent converts.[5] Franco's regime might have survived even without the two billions of aid it would get from the United States, but in any case it remains, like the dictatorship of Salazár in Portugal, a local affair that has little connection with the mass movements in the modern world, or any possibly universal drift to totalitarianism.

Hitler's national socialism, however, was much more significant on this count too. It may be called the quintessence of fascism. To Mussolini's basic tenets—collectivism, elitism, militarism, nationalism, etc.—it logically added the dynamic illogic of racism. It was more thoroughly totalitarian in both its organization of the state and its control of society and culture, and it more completely made over the citizen into the worker and soldier, ready for total war. Hitler fully exploited the possibilities of mass propaganda, the deliberate appeal to unreason, in order to strengthen at once a Machiavellian policy and a sacred cause. He was unquestionably the genius of fascism, a much greater charismatic leader than Mussolini, whose rant was always likely to suggest a tin-hat dictator in an *opéra bouffe*. His success, backed by the might of Germany, made nazism the predominant form of fascism and left its mark on all other forms, as in the anti-Semitism taken over by Mussolini. But mainly he bids us pause for the obvious reasons, beginning with his direct responsibility for another catastrophic war.

5 All parties, Thomas adds, have inclined to the spirit of Narváez, a nineteenth-century general who on his deathbed, when asked whether he forgave his enemies, replied: "My enemies? I have none. I have had them all shot." No less distinctive was the slogan of the Spanish Foreign Legion: "Down with intelligence; long live death!" The intellectual awakening of Spain after its humiliating defeat by the United States produced a more active struggle between liberals and traditionalists, but the odds were still against intelligence.

Much more of the immense evil he wrought lives after him. We have to live with the unforgettable thought of what had once seemed unthinkable: that such a psychopath could become the ruler of a great modern nation, famous for its many learned men and its respect for learning, and that in a supposedly civilized age he could carry out such policies as the extermination of six million Jews—a deliberate, cold-blooded, systematic kind of barbarism much more monstrous than the simple atrocities of the past.

Although many Germans were inspired by Mussolini's success, and perhaps influenced by the grandiose theories that evolved with his corporate state, nazism was essentially an indigenous movement that got under way earlier. The Weimar Republic was weakened immediately by not only the obligation of signing the Treaty of Versailles but the myth of "the stab in the back": the bloodless revolution that set up the Republic was made out to be the cause of the defeat of the great German army, instead of the result that it plainly was. Among the many who wholeheartedly embraced this myth was Corporal Adolf Hitler, still in uniform. By 1920 he was the leader of the National Socialist German Workers party, whose name summed up the main elements of its appeal. A few years later he staged his legendary Putsch in Munich, with the aid of General von Ludendorff, in which the police killed a couple dozen of his followers. (They were careful not to aim at Ludendorff.) He then made good use of a prison sentence, reduced by lenient authorities from four years to thirteen months: he outlined his whole program in *Mein Kampf*, including key chapters on tactics. He accordingly had an advantage over Mussolini in that he had a definite program all worked out years before he became Führer. But he had other, far greater advantages, even apart from a much richer nation with a much greater industrial plant and a proved genius for efficient organization.

Hitler's gospel was more deeply rooted in an older, stronger tradition. His promise of a Reich that would reign for a thousand years (which incidentally could be traced to the dream proclaimed by the Anabaptists in Münster in 1535) drew on the militarism on which Prussia grew up, the nationalism flourishing ever since the Romantic movement, and the imperialism inspired by the triumphs of Bismarck. He did not have to glorify "the state"; his people had known a powerful state for generations. Long trained in habits of obedience, they were much more disciplined than were the poor Italians, whose peasants were submissive out of fatalistic resignation rather than training or fervent loyalty to the state; Madame de Staël had noted a century before how "vigorously submissive" the Germans were. Still more distinctively German were the traditional sentiments about "the folk," reinforced by the myths about blood and the habitual appeal to sentiment rather than reason. The related tradition of anti-Semitism gave Hitler a handier Devil and enabled him to keep his followers feeling at once superior and properly tense with hatred. Similarly he could better exploit the fear of communism, which was a more actual threat at home, and could stir up more hatred because Germany also had a tradition of prejudice against the Slavs. Above all, however, he was aided by exceptional circumstances. Brooding ever since Versailles over their grievances real and imaginary, the Germans had much more to brood over when the great depression struck; though it relieved them of the burden of reparations, it left some six million unemployed. Then Hitler offered them everything: devils and scapegoats, promises of revenge and atonement, messianic dreams of grandeur. He rose to power with more popular support than any other dictator, on what looked like an irresistible mass movement. It could be said that he did not impose himself on the masses, but democratically represented them, fulfilled their deepest longings.

Yet Hitler's triumph was not in fact clearly due to irresistible popular demand. His party never won a majority in free elections, getting at most some 40 per cent of the votes, and in 1932 even falling off somewhat; he himself ran six million votes behind von Hindenburg in the presidential election. Though he grew much more popular as Führer, to the end he felt the need of not only incessant propaganda but more terrorism than Mussolini and other dictators employed, putting many more people in concentration camps. Furthermore, "the masses" he represented were not the bogey of tradition. Unlike the Communists, he appealed to all classes, but especially to the middle class and the peasantry, who were hostile to the workers and fearful of communism. His supporters included many quite respectable people, propertied, educated, and godly. He rose to power, indeed, by toning down his early anticapitalist slogans and forming an alliance with the German elite. Big businessmen, impressed by his attacks on labor unions, not only helped to finance his campaigns but got him the support of the conservative press; Hugenberg, the overlord of this press, swung to his side the German National People's party (a typical misnomer for a party whose leaders were bent on sabotaging the Weimar Republic). With this Hitler got the indispensable support of the Reichswehr, the power behind the president and all cabinets. Although many army men had misgivings because of his wild revolutionary talk, as many had been attracted to him from the beginning; and now the General Staff was won over by his promises, in the illusion that it would remain the real power in the land. Hence President von Hindenburg, at first scornful of the noisy upstart, was induced to appoint him chancellor. When the senile marshal died a year later (1934), Hitler was able to abolish the presidency and get himself named *Reichsführer,* become a full-fledged dictator of a one-party state.

As chancellor he had promptly expressed his contempt for such dupes as Hugenberg, dismissing the other political parties on the Right as well as the Left. Thereby he indicated that his triumph had been aided by some luck and more stupidity, of both conservatives and Communists; the latter had characteristically kept battling with democratic socialists instead of uniting with them to combat a common enemy unforeseen in their ideology. Although Hitler was more cautious in his dealings with the big industrialists and the generals, whose help he badly needed in the job of rearming Germany, in time he laid down the law to them too. This emphasized that his government was a simple dictatorship, but it raised more complicated issues. First of all, in what respects was his nazism "revolutionary"?

Raymond Aron has reported how French intellectuals at the time heatedly debated whether the noble name of revolution could be given to so vulgar, prosaic an affair. Some pointed out that Hitler had come into power by legal processes; others decided that his movement was at most counterrevolutionary. So it appeared to most liberals as well as Communists everywhere. Like Mussolini, Hitler was violently opposed to popular socialism. His national socialism was a Prussian kind, not at all dedicated to the cause of the workers; it took away their right to strike or to form unions of their own; and his whole program to reduce unemployment was designed and carried through as a rearmament program, inspired by no such ideal as the worker's right to a job. In his first year as *Reichsführer* he staged the bloodbath that purged his party of the radicals who still talked of revolutionary socialism, having some thousands of them shot without a trial. In deference to big business he dropped his idea of nationalizing the banks, left industry in private hands. His military collectivism set no new goals for the German nation.

Nevertheless, his regime was revolutionary enough by ordinary historical standards. In his first year Hitler set about giving the nation a new constitution while eliminating all opposition; Germany had never known absolute dictatorship before. By modern standards his regime grew more revolutionary as it settled down. It introduced a considerable measure of socialism, extending planning throughout the economy, controlling wages, prices, and savings; businessmen themselves were forced to invest their surplus earnings in government securities. Hitler's propaganda featured violent attacks on not only democracy but capitalism, "Wall Street," international bankers—the powers of gold said to be conspiring against the common people of the world. Public life and culture were more systematically regulated to suit his totalitarian purposes. While ringing in "Providence" and the "Lord God" for reasons of propaganda, Hitler started "Germanizing" Christianity, jailing independent pastors. Education was put under strict control from top to bottom. History was rewritten to prove that the Nordic peoples had performed the greatest feats, so long as they kept their race pure, and that the Germans specifically had led the way to Western civilization, only to have their glorious achievements persistently undone by Latins, Slavs, and in particular Jews, the prime authors of the Weimar Republic. The people, especially the young, were edified by endless harangues, spectacles, national festivals, parades—above all parades. They were kept forever on the march, in what seemed to Hermann Rauschning a pure waste of time and energy, until he realized its psychological value: "Marching diverts men's thoughts. Marching kills thought. Marching makes an end of individuality."

Or call Hitler's regime counterrevolutionary, it still brought radical changes, and at its most reactionary was far from being a mere return to the past. It not only rejected in theory all liberal ideals of the rights of the individual, but did away in practice with the civil liberties that Germans had long enjoyed. It as flatly repudiated Christian ethics, humanitarian ideals, and civilized standards of justice. Hans Frank, head of the Academy of German Law, announced the official maxim of Nazi justice: "Right is whatever profits the German nation: wrong is whatever harms it." Likewise Hitler most explicitly rejected the claims of reason and science, in a land that had prided itself on its tradition of high learning and academic freedom. Alfred Rosenberg, his official philosopher, produced a Bible suitably entitled *The Myth of the Twentieth Century,* exalting his racial myth, rejecting even Hegel—he was too rational and not imperialistic enough. *Mein Kampf* had drawn on a crude social Darwinism as a more congenial interpretation of world history as the world's tribunal: "It has always sacrificed truth and justice to might and vitality, and doomed those peoples to death who considered truth more important than deeds, and justice more essential than might." In general, nazism severed the religious and rational connections of German nationalism with other romantic varieties. To some Germans of the old school, such as Karl Barth, it was so radical a break with the past that it looked as much like anarchy as tyranny.

By the same token it brings up the most disturbing issue—Hitler's success. Up to a point this is easy to understand, and not simply frightening. Immediately it was due in part to his taking care of the jobless, and then to the economic success of his national socialism, prepared for in the World War. Always he made the most of German tradition. While openly expressing a contempt for the masses that justified his new elite and his dictatorship, he tempered it by the flattery of his cults of the folk, the Nordics, the Reich, the collective might and glory, which made the masses feel superior—no true German was a mass-man after all. In so doing Hitler was not merely exploiting a demoralized people, eager to escape from freedom, but was restoring their morale by restoring their sense of personal responsibility, their pride in a tradition that called for discipline, self-sacrifice, and devotion to a higher good, or freedom from the self-indulgence and slothful ease to which so many free men in the democracies were addicted. It was this ambiguity that deeply troubled Friedrich Meinecke, who spent some thirty years in a painful reappraisal of his beloved Germany, and after Hitler's fall summed up his anguish and his faith in a last testament.[6] Prussian tradition produced not only Hitler but the officers who conspired against him, and who might remind us that the "authoritarian personality" is not necessarily neurotic. It also produced many simple men devoted to an ideal of simple fidelity, beautifully exemplified by Joachim in Mann's *The Magic Mountain.*

Nevertheless, as Meinecke sadly recognized, Prussian tradition had created a powerful officer class unlike that of other countries, more arrogant, unconditionally devoted to the military profession and the sovereign ideal of military efficiency. The many simple soldiers like Joachim would dutifully, automatically fight and die for any ruler, however brutal. The tradition had generated as well the dangerous trend pointed out by Grillparzer: "Humanity—Nationality—Bestiality." In making the most of the allied tradition of racism Hitler found

6 See *The German Catastrophe* (1950). An early phase of Meinecke's soul-searching was his classic study *Machiavellianism,* published shortly after World War I, in which he expressed his growing misgivings about Frederick the Great, Hegel, Bismarck, and others in the German pantheon.

willing agents for policies that were more frightful than simple bestiality, and that he himself liked to call "fanatic." His extermination of the Jews was more shocking because it was utterly senseless, utterly lacking in the pragmatic or "scientific" motives by which the rise of totalitarianism is often explained. A sensible tyrant would have used the Jews as slave-workers, especially during the desperate war effort. As it was, Hitler expended an immense amount of time, energy, manpower, and materials, with Prussian efficiency, in rounding up the Jews all over his domains, transporting them on his overburdened railroads, and finishing them off in his scientifically equipped slaughterhouses. No doubt he would have been able to invent some other devils to keep him going, but meanwhile he was eliminating the most serviceable one, the only one that gave his racism any international appeal.

In thus carrying to demonic extremes the nationalism that over the past century had become the most vital ideal for most people, Hitler may recall the perennial ambiguities of Western idealism, in its addiction to violence and ruthlessness. But his success in Germany had been made easier by something quite different in the democracies. They were suffering from both moral and intellectual confusion, immediately from too little effective idealism. Although his persecution of the Jews aroused much indignation, this was seldom expressed in high places, in either church or state; most of the spiritual and political leaders of Europe did not publicly declare a sense of outrage, or call on people to combat the evil, until their own church or nation was attacked by Hitler. When he settled down to his systematic extermination of the Jews, his victims were denied even the consolations of martyrdom, the feeling that they were dying for a cause that other nations were defending; so now they are even reproached for having gone dumbly to their death, like sheep, while so few men in high places were raising a finger to help them. And down through Munich the democracies had seemed most craven in their failure to halt Hitler's aggressions, the folly of their efforts to appease the author of *Mein Kampf*. Everywhere he would find quislings to aid him. The one exception in the countries he overran was Poland, but the refusal of the Poles to cooperate with their conquerors owed to their traditional nationalism, not to democratic or humanitarian fervor; for they had put up with a semi-Fascist government and had long been notorious for their anti-Semitism—or rather not really notorious, in a Europe not much concerned about this revival of medieval tradition.

We can never be certain that nazism was only a temporary, local aberration. It still has numerous supporters in Germany and Austria. Under severe stress, something like it might burst out again. Conceivably it might happen here too: America has millions of racists, bigots, fanatics, extremists of the Right, with millionaires to finance them and retired generals to lead them. Meanwhile the barbarism of our time is more appalling because so many people are not really appalled by it.

Yet we may be heartened by the obvious afterthought—that Hitler too failed. He made few converts in the free societies, arousing instead a mounting revulsion; and it is still almost unthinkable that even the Fascist types in them would ever call for the extermination of despised minorities. The collaboration of quislings in the countries he overran was more than offset by the underground resistance, which carried on in spite of the prospect of not merely death but torture. In Germany itself many of the people he deluded were only half converted, and many others were not converted at all. The failure of most of these to start or join a movement of resistance was pardonable, aside from the terrible power at the disposal of modern dictators: they would have courted more than personal martyrdom, since among the refinements of his efficient tyranny was the policy of punishing the families of his victims too. At any rate, he certainly did not succeed in killing the rival German tradition stemming from the Enlightenment, the source of Meinecke's faith and hope for the future. And if its strength is still uncertain, Hitler helped to discredit his own cause by leaving little but ruins, and no grounds for a myth about another stab in the back. While dying in a more Wagnerian style than Mussolini in his subterranean shelter in flaming Berlin, he more plainly betrayed his alleged devotion to the Reich. He is reported to have told his intimates that if he were denied victory, he would "take care that the German people do not survive this disgrace"; and in his last days he at least showed no concern for their welfare, attempted no provision for their future. His Götterdämmerung, appropriately staged underground, symbolized the death of the old gods without implying any promise of new ones.

Hitler's Machiavellian tactics had often involved an apparent cynicism that raised some question about the sincerity of his fanaticism. The grand mission of the Nordics had not deterred him from making an alliance with Japan, for example, handing over Asia to the "yellow race." But most suggestive was his cynical pact with Stalin. Although *Mein Kampf* had announced his intention of making Russia a German colony, the pact made some sense beyond the immediate advantage it gave him. Despite the ritual invective the two dictators had been exchanging for years, they were akin in their barbarity, their scorn of democracy, and their addiction to violent nonsense; so Meinecke surmised that in launching his last great offensive against the West, instead of strengthening his defenses against the oncoming Russian armies, Hitler was betraying a perhaps unconscious preference for having Russians instead of British and Americans take Berlin. At any rate, his attack on Russia had underscored the basic reason why his national socialism had no future. It had nothing to offer the world, especially Europe, except German domination. If Nazis in other countries did succeed in taking over the government, they could hope for nothing better than to be puppets of Hitler, ruling by sufferance like the inglorious men of Vichy. Mussolini himself was unhappy in his gamble on a German victory, knowing that whatever spoils he won would be crumbs from Hitler's table, and that his "Roman Empire" would perforce play second fiddle to the German Reich. Communism, however, had a future because it could appeal to all peoples. As the First World War made possible its triumph in Russia, with the help of the German General Staff, so the second war enabled it to become a world power. Stalin turned out to be the only real winner of the war Hitler started.

3. *The Rise of Communism*

While the Soviet under Stalin became the most literally, thoroughly totalitarian state in the world, it continued to differ from the varieties of fascism in its basic theory or ideology. Communism owes to Marx, of course, the universal appeal that Mussolini and Hitler could never hope for. Whereas they exalted the nation and the state, through which little people might feel big, it directly exalted the little people themselves. It promised the complete realization of the liberal ideals scorned by the Fascist dictators: the long-suffering workers would lead the world to the classless society in which all men would at last enjoy perfect freedom and justice. To their contempt of the masses and exaltation of a self-appointed elite it opposed a principle of complete equality, social and economic as well as political. It appealed to the intelligentsia too by rejecting their irrationalism and contempt of the intellectual per se, attacking him only in so far as he was a slave to bourgeois ideology. Its myths—of the Revolution, the party, the classless utopia—were never advanced as myths, but always as irrefutable deductions from rational premises. It offered a supposedly scientific version of the Christian millennium, in which modern technology would assure universal peace and plenty. Communism was accordingly a synthesis of the highest earthly hopes of Western man, the ultimate in his faith in progress. Meanwhile it could justify a totalitarian state, or the appearances of tyranny, by its guarantee of a total solution of all political and philosophical problems. The appearances were waved away in the *School History* that Stalin commandeered for the Russian youth: "The Soviet Government gave the Russian people complete liberation—such a liberation as has been conferred on no other nation in the world." After the war his henchmen would confer a similar blessing on other peoples of eastern Europe, and promise it to all the nations of the world.

By now the Soviet has confessed that Stalin's dictatorship entailed some brutal tyranny. It remains, however, the dictatorial, totalitarian state he made it, still denying its people the basic liberties enjoyed by Western peoples. From its birth it had been marked by evident tyranny. Although this too owed something to Marx, and more to Lenin, a primary source was suggested by a well-known saying of Marx: "The tradition of all the dead generations weighs like an Alp upon the brain of the living." Stalin had only accentuated the despotic tradition of Russia, lit up the Alp. It is now time to review the early history of Russia, a country in "Europe" but with a tradition essentially different from that of Western Europe, going back to the Byzantine Empire.[7]

The hordes of Mongols, or Tatars, who swept over Europe in the thirteenth century did their worst in Russia. Here they not only destroyed the brilliant kingdom of Kiev but settled down, to rule the land for more than two centuries. When the feudal lords of Moscow finally threw off their dominion, western Europe was undergoing its Renaissance and Reformation; the rulers of Russia got busy instead in consolidating another Oriental sacred monarchy, imposing serfdom on a peasantry that had been mostly free. The keynote of the new state was sounded by a monk, Filofei, inspired by the fall of Constantinople to the Turks. "Take note, O religious and gracious Czar," he wrote Ivan the Great, Grand Duke of Moscow, "that all Christian kingdoms are merged into thine alone, that two Romes have fallen, but the third stands; and there shall be no fourth." Ivan the Terrible, the first real czar of the new nation (1547–1584), completed the work of uniting Holy Russia. Most Western historians have accordingly dwelt on its

---

7 On the origins of the geographical fiction of Europe, see *Freedom in the Ancient World*, p. 145 and Index.

indebtedness to Byzantium, through the Russian Orthodox Church. (Among other things the Church invented a suitable lineage for Ivan the Great, starting with the Emperor Augustus, Caesar-Czar of the first Rome.) Lately some historians have argued that more important were its Tatar or its native sources in Muscovy. We need not worry over this debate, for all agree on the outcome—an absolute autocracy, sanctified by the Church. Ivan the Terrible also completed the job of subduing the aristocracy (the boyars) and eliminating personal rights, giving Russians a kind of equality in servitude. "The rulers of Russia," he declared, "have not been accountable to anyone." With this despotism he bequeathed a tradition of terrorism through his dreaded security police. The Church that supported the holy czars remained ultraconservative and obscurantist, dominating the whole culture, but inspiring only religious art and architecture; it did its best to discourage new learning and independent thought.[8] While it neglected to apply Christian principles to social and political life, it lent an aura of sanctity to Moscow, the Third Rome, which Sorel would hail as "the Rome of the proletariat."

The epoch-making reign of Peter the Great (1682–1725), who set Russia on a new course by his prodigious effort to Westernize it, has come to seem more momentous in the light of recent history. Russia was the first great society to respond to the challenge of surging Europe, whose impact it felt through the aggressions of the Poles and the Swedes; so it inaugurated the drama that in this century has convulsed the whole non-Western world. Glorified by Stalin as the first Bolshevik, Peter concentrated his terrific energy on introducing Western technology, an idea other societies would catch on to belatedly. Having gone to Europe incognito to learn for himself, he imported many technicians to help him create a modern professional army, a state industry to equip it, a bureaucracy to maintain it, and state schools to train men for all these new purposes. He built himself a new capital at St. Petersburg, on Baltic marshlands that had belonged to the Swedes, so as to have "a window on the West." He tried to Westernize the mentality of his people too by many cultural reforms, from printing translations of heretical foreign books to putting a tax on beards (shaving was another Orthodox heresy). He even tried to help the serfs, decreeing that killing them was

---

[8] An example of the backwardness of Russian culture is a fresco in one of the Kremlin cathedrals, picturing a whale swallowing Jonah and then disgorging him—crowned with a halo. It has a charming primitive quality, reminiscent of early medieval art; but it dates from the seventeenth century. The Kremlin itself evidenced this backwardness, for the czars called in Italian architects to build it.

equal to any other homicide, and that they should not be sold singly, like cattle, but only as whole families. A revolutionary working almost singlehanded, Peter the Great succeeded in making Russia a major power that Europe had to reckon with ever after.

By the same token, however, he left it a despotic state. He was able to accomplish so much because he was an absolute autocrat, bound neither by law nor by custom, and could be utterly ruthless in disposing of any opposition, even to murdering his son with his own hands. (Among his other barbarities was the murder of his wife's lover, whose bottled head he then compelled her to keep in her room.) His primary object in modernizing his state was always to build up its military power, not to promote the well-being of his people. His incredible energy enabled him to find time for incessant wars, mostly of his own making, all very costly. Inevitably the costs were paid for by the common people, if anything only alienating the great majority from the state; his remote new capital further isolated the government from the ruled. On the small educated upper class he had more effect, but this tended to isolate them from the common people, and to leave many in a no man's land between the old and the new ways. Russia would thereafter be a problem for thoughtful Russians—as other non-Western countries would be for their intelligentsia.

After a generation of confusion, Catherine the Great restored firm autocratic government by dint of arranging for the murder of her weak husband. The liberal tendencies that won her fame as one of the "enlightened despots" of the eighteenth century did not induce her to do anything for the serfs, whose worsening lot caused some uprisings; and these, together with her fright over the French Revolution, put a stop to her departures from tradition. Her son proscribed the dangerous words "citizen" and "society." In the Metternich era Alexander I, who had likewise begun as a sentimental liberal, ended as a thoroughgoing pious reactionary. The reign of Nicholas I (1825–1855) cemented the reputation of Russia in Europe for backwardness and despotism. The czars were in fact the most autocratic rulers in Europe, past or present; their power, unlimited in theory, was not effectively limited either by a tradition of *noblesse oblige* or customary equity. Nicholas I could reverse the policy of Peter the Great by doing his utmost to preserve Holy Russia from contamination by Western ideas, or any new ideas. His censors cut out such phrases as "the forces of nature" and "the majesty of nature" because they might imply some slur on the power and majesty of the czar.

The one practical check on the reactionary tendencies of the czars was the exposure of the actual weakness of their state. The Crimean War gave shameful proof that despite its immensity Russia did not have the military power that Peter the Great tried to assure it. Following this fiasco, Alexander II put through the first major social reform in Russian history—the emancipation of the serfs. Only it too exposed the basic weakness of the social and political structure. The good intentions of the czar were largely nullified by the dodges of the landowners, abetted by the conservatism of the bureaucracy and the Church, and the ignorance and confusion of the serfs; the radicalism it encouraged soon provoked the usual reaction by the government. Nor were the serfs helped much by their most earnest supporters, the intelligentsia. The activity of this class was by far the most significant development in nineteenth-century Russia, but it was still more ambiguous than the extraordinary achievement of Peter the Great.

Born in his era and encouraged by the cultivated Catherine the Great, the intelligentsia came into their own in the nineteenth century. Beginning with Pushkin, they produced perhaps the greatest literature of the century, and certainly one of the most sudden, brilliant flowerings in the history of culture. At the same time, however, they were the chief victims of the legacy of Peter the Great. They gave Europe the term "intelligentsia," connoting a painfully self-conscious, alienated class; more than in any other country they were outsiders, cut off from both the court and the common people, in Dostoyevsky's words "the great wanderers of the Russian land," always brooding over their spiritual plight. Nevertheless—or therefore—they had the most acute sense of social responsibility. As M. Katkov said, "Having ideas in one's head that can never be applied is a torture, a terrible torture." They turned to literature with more intensity because of the censorship of the czars, which kept on guard against political tracts but was typically as incompetent as despotic; a censor who asked a writer to explain what he meant by "the movement of minds" was apt to be too stupid to perceive such movement in poetry or fiction.

The whole challenge to the intelligentsia was summed up by Chaadayev in his immensely influential "Philosophical Letter Written to a Lady," dated from "Necropolis," his name for Moscow. The only one of his essays published in his lifetime, this got by the authorities in 1836, and though they were soon awakened by the sensation it made, dismissing the censor who had passed it, exiling the editor who published it, and declaring Chaadayev insane, the damage had been done.

As Alexander Herzen wrote, the essay was "a shot that rang out in the dark night; it forced all to awaken." Chaadayev's insanity was simple sorrow over the cultural barrenness of Russia, expressed without reserve.

Alone of all the peoples in the world, we have not given anything to the world, and we have not learned anything from the world. We have not added a single idea to the pool of human ideas. We have contributed nothing to the progress of the human spirit, we have disfigured it. From the first moment of our social existence we have not created anything for the common good of man. Not a single useful thought has grown in the sterile soil of our fatherland; no great truth has been brought forth in our midst.

As a result, Russians still had to learn the most elementary ideas, beginning with "duty, justice, law, and order." Yet Chaadayev did not despair—any more than would the many famous wanderers after him. Rather, he concluded not only that Russia should complete the work of Peter the Great, take her place in intellectual as well as political Europe, but that she had an exceptional advantage in her very backwardness or lack of a past: she was free to choose the best from Western tradition and avoid the errors of Europe. In his "Apology of a Madman" he asserted his faith that Russia had been appointed to a lofty, unique mission: "to resolve most of the social problems, to perfect most of the ideas that have come up in the old societies, and to decide most of the weighty questions concerning the human race."

Following Chaadayev's lead, many of the intelligentsia became ardent Westernizers, much more hostile than he was to the czarist regime. As a group, however, they remained uncertain just what to choose from the West, the more liable to confusion and conflict because Europe was now in an intellectual turmoil. Some, like Turgenev and Herzen, were liberals, devoted to the ideals of the Enlightenment and especially the cause of personal freedom. Others were radicals, who tended increasingly to become professional revolutionaries—wholly dedicated types that would abound in Russia as nowhere else. These were most embarrassed by a novel problem unknown to European radicals: how to get in touch with the common people whose cause they were devoted to. Early converts to Marxism looked particularly futile because Russia had neither bourgeois capitalists nor proletarians to speak of. In the last decades of the century the Narodniks, or Populists, accordingly led a movement back to the peasants, trying to live and work with them;

but they got nowhere. To the "dark folk" intellectuals were as alien as government officials, and their only response was to hand many of the Narodniks over to the authorities; they continued to revere the czar himself, their "Dear Father." (In Turgenev's *Virgin Soil* an old serf had this to say about the new emancipation: "To be sure, folks would forever be talking some such idle nonsense; like enough there was freedom among the Turks; but he, thank God, had escaped all that.") The Narodniks were then attacked by the Marxists, who began acquiring prestige in the late eighties when Russia began developing modern industry and with it a proletariat; like Marx, they maintained that the peasants were not a revolutionary class. For them the problem remained that the peasants were nevertheless a huge majority in a country that was far from being capitalistic, and so by definition was not ripe for revolution. Very few Russian intellectuals welcomed an alternative suggested by Belinsky, an ardent liberal who trusted to the growth of a middle class.

But Chaadayev was perhaps most influential in the opposition he stirred. Throughout the century the Westernizers were opposed by followers of the Slavophiles, apostles of nationalism and later of pan-Slavism. Among their leading spokesmen was Danilevsky, who in *Russia and Europe* argued fervently that Slav civilization was incompatible with Western civilization, far superior to it, and bound to conquer it. He anticipated the radically different meanings that Communists would give to common European words, asserting that from an "objective, factual viewpoint" the Russians were the chief guardians of religious truth, that no other people was "so capable of enduring such a large share of freedom," and that their nation was the embodiment of "true democracy." Although as champions of the Russian people the Slavophiles included some revolutionaries, they mostly tended to be religious and political reactionaries, inasmuch as the national tradition they glorified was perforce symbolized by the czar and the Orthodox Church. They were also somewhat confused by their idealism. Since Europe was plutocratic and imperialistic, it followed that Russia was devoted to universal brotherhood and peace; its sacred cause, Danilevsky concluded, was "in truth the universal and pan-human cause"; and his disciple Dostoyevsky wrote most ecstatically about "our great ideal—the reuniting of all mankind." But Holy Russia had to conquer Constantinople, of course; Danilevsky talked much of its inevitable war with the decadent West; and as an exalted jingo Dostoyevsky not only called repeatedly for war on the Turks but attacked Jews, Poles, Germans, and other Europeans who were not ripe for reunion. While the Slavophiles came out of Western Romanticism, they demonstrated that Chaadayev was imprecise: Russia did have a past and a strong tradition—one that was both militaristic and despotic.

At first glance, they were not only ineffectual but silly. Thus they hailed the Crimean War as the beginning of the crusade of Russia against the unholy West, and most of them failed to learn the elementary lesson it taught; they continued to make a virtue of the backwardness of Russia. The Slavophiles were hopelessly unrealistic in their pride, since czarist Russia could grow strong only by learning much more from the despised West. As idealists they were as hopelessly sentimental, for they were idealizing about the least holy tradition in Europe. Dostoyevsky, the greatest genius among them, was in this respect the most egregious offender against both common sense and simple humanity. In deploring the oppression of the masses in materialistic Europe, he ignored the much plainer oppression of the Russian masses; or still worse, he idealized the misery of the peasants, making out that their long acceptance of grinding oppression was proof of their spirituality, even their "craving for suffering, perpetual and unquenchable suffering."

Yet in a deep sense almost all of the leading intellectuals were Slavophiles, convinced that Russia was at least potentially much superior to the West. Chaadayev himself was pleased to think that his countrymen might become "the true divine people of modern times." The revolutionaries were naturally hostile to capitalistic Europe; some began building on the hope that Russia might escape the evil capitalistic stage, leap straight to socialism—a possibility they got Marx interested in. Liberals too were repelled by the faithless skepticism and materialism of Europe, and took to similar hopes. Herzen, their most famous exile, invested his faith in the natural simplicity of the Russian peasant, in particular the *mir*, the simple village community that contained the seeds of socialism, Christian brotherhood, or whatever ideal. (The Slavophiles had got this notion of the *mir* from a German scholar, and characteristically failed to realize that it was not a distinctive Russian institution, or product of the Russian folk soul, but was much like the ancient peasant village all over the world.) Hence moderates, reactionaries, and radicals were alike under the skin in their aversion to the bourgeois West and their dreams of a unique destiny of Russia. Lacking a critical, skeptical tradition, lacking as well popular support and political experience, while living on ideas alone, most of them were addicted to messianic visions. The more hopeless the present seemed, the more perfect the future had to be. As Nicholas Berdyaev concluded, the entire history of the Russian intelligentsia was a preparation for communism.

"With us," Chaadayev had noted, "new ideas sweep away the old because they do not spring out of them"; but in this deeper sense they did spring out of them. As the old ideas were absolutist, so the new ones tended to an inverted absolutism, likewise compounded of dogma and myth. Herzen pointed out that the Russian government had good reason to fear communism in spite of its apparently negligible following: "Communism is the Russian autocracy turned upside down." Most other intellectuals, especially the greater ones, were akin in their tendency to extremism, their contempt of the Western habit of compromise and contentment with mere reform. It was not enough "to resolve most of the social problems"—they had to solve all of them, at once and for good. Thus for Bakunin nothing would do except anarchism, a clean sweep of the whole political system, and as a pure idealist he finally resorted to the strategy of pure terrorism or atrocity; whereas for Tolstoy the only answer was an utterly Christian anarchism, an absolute pacifism—no use of force whatever was permissible. When nihilism became the rage among the young, Dostoyevsky confessed, "We are all nihilists." Because of this totalitarian mentality it was liberal ideas, Berdyaev remarked, that seemed utopian in Russia. Such ideas were always alive, as evidenced by the continued popularity of such writers as Turgenev; but like Turgenev the liberal was apt to feel most ineffectual, harassed by scorn from both Right and Left.

Except for the Marxists, accordingly, most of the intelligentsia were not excited or deeply gratified by the surprising progress in Westernization that Russia started making toward the end of the century, with the aid of foreign capital. Railways were flung across the whole continent, the production of minerals was rapidly increased, and by the time of the World War the industrial plant was big enough to employ three million workers. Though Russia still lagged far behind the great powers, its rate of industrial expansion in this period was higher than that of Western Europe or even the United States. The fiasco of the war with Japan then spurred extensive social and political reforms as well. For the first time in Russian history a parliament was set up, the Duma, and political parties were legalized; the people got some glimmering of decisions by a majority—what a Slavophile had called "the expression of a clumsy material superiority" instead of "a high moral unity." The censorship was relaxed, freedom of inquiry was permitted, and personal rights were protected against the arbitrary interference that had been sanctioned by tradition. Provincial self-government helped to promote public education and hygiene. An agrarian reform began emancipating the peasantry from the great feudal estates at a rate that in a generation would have amounted to a revolution, while workers were aided by social security laws. Standards of living were rising faster than they ever would under Stalin.

Nevertheless, the czarist regime remained basically incompetent and corrupt, as the World War soon made all too plain. To some of the intelligentsia, therefore, the great event of the period was the abortive revolution of 1905.[9] While this was due directly to the humiliating defeat by Japan—and at that the government had little trouble putting down the workers—their uprising was a mighty inspiration to Lenin, a still-obscure professional revolutionary who led a tiny faction he had named Bolsheviks ("majority-ites"). "The proletariat of the entire world," he wrote, "now looks with feverish expectation upon the Russian proletariat." In fact this uprising made little impression on the workers of Europe, who knew nothing about the Bolsheviks, but it confirmed the mystical faith of Lenin in revolution, or what he called "the art of uprising," as taught by Marx. In exile he continued to battle the great majority of socialists who were willing to forgo the revolution and accept democratic reforms.

The Russian proletariat then vindicated his faith by touching off the famous "February Revolution" in 1917. (It actually occurred in what the rest of Europe called March, for czarist Russia was backward in its calendar too.) Even so the Bolsheviks were caught quite unawares by it, for good reason. This was an impromptu affair, not led by masters of the art of uprising, and by Marxist standards was hardly a proper revolution at all. It began with spontaneous strikes and demonstrations in Petrograd, which quickly spread for lack of effective opposition; there was no real class war, no organized overthrow of the government, because no real support for the government. Within a few days the rotten czarist regime simply collapsed—as almost anybody might have predicted, except perhaps a doctrinaire Marxist. Only a thousand or so

---

9 Another event of some consequence in this fateful year was the publication of the *Protocols of the Elders of Zion* by Nilus, a holy man out of medieval tradition, who foretold herein the imminent coming of Antichrist. Too ignorant to realize that his Protocols had been forged by the czar's secret police, he could not have foretold the lasting use that would be made of them by anti-Semites all over the Western world.

people were killed in the confusion of the riots that started the great Russian Revolution. Thereupon the Bolsheviks supported the coalition government, headed by liberal democrats, which replaced the vanished government of the czar. From afar Woodrow Wilson rejoiced, explaining to Congress that those who knew Russia best knew that it had always been "democratic at heart" and that now it could add all its "naïve majesty and might" to the war for freedom, justice, and peace.

Actually the earnest effort of the coalition government to carry on the war destroyed whatever chance of success it might have had; the country no longer had either the economic means or the heart for a war that had proved so disastrous. But a sufficient reason for the government's failure was the irreconcilable divisions among its supporters. The intelligentsia were still split by their traditional animosities and engrained aversion to compromise; the liberal democrats, violently attacked by both conservatives and radicals, were still remote from the peasants and the workers. When Lenin was spirited in by the German military, he at once proclaimed his opposition to both the democracy and the war, pulled the Bolsheviks out of the government, and demanded that they stop cooperating with any other party; the founder of a collectivistic state would have no truck with cooperation. He began planning underground an orthodox revolution in the name of the proletariat, though it was to be led properly by his party of intellectuals, none of whose principal leaders was a workingman. In October (really November) he persuaded his fellow Bolsheviks to make this revolution. Initially it turned out to be an easy victory, as the unpopular coalition government quickly collapsed. The "ten days that shook the world" involved little more fighting and bloodshed than had the first revolution.

According to Trotsky's *History of the Russian Revolution,* the success of the Bolsheviks was due to an inevitable mass movement: they had only decided rather tardily to "fall in step and march out at the head of the masses," lead them where they had already resolved to go. Unquestionably the Bolsheviks did have much popular support, in particular from the soviets, or workers' councils, and the war-weary peasant soldiers. Like other dictatorships, however, they nevertheless represented only a minority. Although they had attacked the government for postponing elections to the Constituent Assembly, Lenin promptly and permanently dissolved this national parliament when at last it did meet: the voters had failed to give his party a majority. It was obviously the Bolsheviks who were deciding where the masses wanted to go. The peasant soldiers, for example, were not Marxists but simply wanted to go home, if possible get more land for themselves. Presently Lenin went the way of the other dictators to come by outlawing other political parties, including leftists who had supported the October Revolution. For he, more than anybody else, had been responsible for this revolution. Trotsky's own history shows very plainly that he made all the crucial decisions, and that he always had a hard time making his revolutionary comrades accept them. On the very eve he had to exhort the Central Committee of his party, explain that "the success of the Russian and world revolution depends upon a two or three days' struggle"—not, after all, upon an irresistible mass movement. Even then some Bolsheviks were unconvinced, for good reasons that Trotsky slurs over: Lenin was defying orthodox Marxist theory, which called for revolution in the most advanced industrial country. Long before this he had reversed Marx's position that there could be no revolutionary theory without a revolutionary movement.

Since Marx and Engels had provided no blueprints for "the dictatorship of the proletariat" they predicted, Lenin had from the outset concentrated on the problem of how to seize and hold power, and he early arrived at his solution, which Bakunin had previously suggested. It was organization—the key to modern society foreseen by Saint-Simon. The revolution had to be made by a "socialist vanguard," a small, tightly disciplined party of professional revolutionaries under a strong, ruthless leader. To this end Lenin worked throughout his long years in exile, insisting on iron discipline, rejecting all compromise, repeatedly splitting his tiny party by expelling dissenters. Always he worked in the name of Marx, and essentially in his spirit, never questioning his basic formulas; yet he drastically revised them to suit his single, lifelong purpose—the revolution. As fiercely dogmatic and intolerant of dissent, he differed from Marx chiefly in being more pragmatic, specifically in adapting the formulas to the peculiar needs of Russia: a "backward" country, like many in Europe and all in the non-Western world, but a type the master had neglected to ponder when he called on the workers of the world to unite. Thus Marx had said, "The emancipation of the working class is the work of the working class itself"; but no class can overthrow or set up a government without leaders and some sort of organization, and the small, untrained working class of Russia in particular was obviously incapable of carrying through a revolution all by itself. As a vast peasant country, Russia likewise called for revision of Marx's idea that the peasantry was a petty-bourgeois class, else Lenin could never hope to get away with his revolution; so he vindicated the Narodniks whom the Marxists had attacked by re-christening it as a revolutionary class and promising it land. Then it had still plainer need of leadership.

Now, Lenin's revolutionary elite was quite different in theory from the Fascist elite. He never argued for indefinite rule by the superior few or expressed contempt for "the masses"; he always assumed that his party was completely dedicated to the interests of the workers, as he himself was; and he justified its dictatorship as only a necessary means to the classless society, a transition to a perfect democracy. It was this democratic idealism that most clearly inspired his followers in Russia and won communism its many supporters in the rest of Europe; few foresaw the possibilities of tyranny. It appealed still more to the high-minded (like Silone in Italy) because it demanded personal sacrifice, without promise of material reward or prestige—the kind of sacrifice exemplified by the whole life of Lenin himself, much of it spent in exile without immediate prospect of success. There is no question, I take it, that he was quite sincere, even in his preposterously utopian promise that the whole state would eventually "wither away."

Yet there is no question either that meanwhile his Bolshevik dictator-ship was not of or by the proletariat, still less the common people as a whole. The Russian Revolution was not actually a proletarian revolu-tion, the Soviet was in no sense created by the soviets. Although almost all European Marxists had assumed, as Marx and Engels had, that the dictatorship of the working class would be absolutely democratic, Lenin had on principle rejected democratic methods. It was the very business of the "socialist vanguard" to make and enforce the key decisions that the workers were not yet up to; he explicitly denounced as "demo-cratic superstition" the supposed "right of the working class to self-determination," and in 1918 he added, "All phrases about equal rights are nonsense." Once in power he likewise denied civil liberties on prin-ciple, calling them merely "formal": his revolutionary theory required the suppression of all opposition. And though Lenin was by no means so neurotic as many professional revolutionaries, his temperament re-inforced the illiberality that prepared for the worse tyranny to come. He found intolerable if not incomprehensible the idea of a loyal opposi-tion, habitually assuming that contrary views were not merely false but treasonous. If only because he took such radical liberties with the Marxist creed, he could never tolerate any criticism of its basic tenets; it was the gospel he needed to justify his opportunism in practice; so in an essentially religious spirit he furiously attacked any deviation

THE RISE OF COMMUNISM

429

from dialectical materialism as heresy, an invitation to "fideism"—
his word for religion. More specifically, he prepared the way for Stalin
by the great powers he himself exercised, under no constitutional
limits. In 1918 he insisted on the necessity of "individual rule, the
recognition of the dictatorial powers of one man." If this theory was
hardly revolutionary in view of the long tradition of autocracy in
Russia, and the novelty of the recent dabblings in constitutional government and party politics, it was for the same reason more liable to
abuse. In his lifelong concentration on the issue of political power,
Lenin never got down to the most elementary problem—the truism
that power may corrupt and absolute power corrupt absolutely.

All such possible abuses were facilitated by his success. The October
Revolution became the model for Communists everywhere as the only
way to come into power, thus authorizing a method of conspiracy and
violence that would naturally make tyrannical their exercise of power.
The Third International at once began meeting in Moscow, the Third
Rome, where Lenin laid down the party line to delegates from other
countries, none of which yet had a Bolshevik party. The immediate
result was a permanent split in the labor movement, since in Europe
and America this was overwhelmingly committed to democratic methods; the Bolsheviks succeeded in wrecking especially strong movements
in Germany and Italy, easing the way for Mussolini and Hitler. But
thereupon the faithful began attacking most fiercely the many more
socialists who remained content with peaceful, democratic means of
furthering the cause of the workers. While always insisting on their
dedication to this cause, Communists invested the Party with a
Hegelian aura of sanctity and an infallibility suited to its historic mission; its cause became more important than any gains made by the
workers, while its failures were blamed on other leaders of the workers
—in some way they always "betrayed" the cause.[10] The interests of the
Soviet became primary because in theory it represented the world
proletariat, even though there was no such thing. The word from
Moscow was all the more authoritative because Lenin had mistakenly

---

[10] Among the distinguished opponents of Lenin's dictatorial policy was the much-
maligned Rosa Luxemburg, an ardent but civilized leftist who actually believed in the
proletariat. Years earlier she had criticized his theory and pointed out the dangers of his
bureaucracy. "Mistakes committed by a really revolutionary working-class movement,"
she wrote, "are historically infinitely more fertile and valuable than the infallibility of the
very best 'central committee.'" Unfortunately for her, there really was no such movement
in Europe. Her fate was atrocious murder by German troops, following what she knew was
a premature uprising. This whole story is very well told in Franz Borkenau's *World Communism* (1939).

assumed that the Russian Revolution would set off a world revolution, and could not succeed otherwise. ("It is absolutely true," he said in 1918, "that without a German revolution we will perish.") When it grew apparent that the ten days had not shaken sufficiently the workers of the world, and the Soviet would have to get along on its own, the crisis was met by conjuring up the villain of Western imperialism: the frightened capitalists of Europe and America were conspiring to destroy the Soviet.

The Allies had done much to make this myth plausible. Absorbed in their all-out war against Germany, they had immediately condemned the Bolsheviks for pulling Russia out of it and had refused to recognize the Soviet. Since they had no official representatives in the country, their ignorance of what was going on encouraged the stupid policy of military intervention, and then led to the incredible confusion and blunder of their intervention in Siberia. Many conservatives, some in high places (again including Winston Churchill), were actually bent on overthrowing the Bolshevik government. The Allies looked worse when its publication of their secret treaties exposed the hypocrisy of their avowed war aims, but their press compensated by spreading anti-Bolshevik propaganda based on more ignorance when not pure fake— for instance, the wild story that the Bolsheviks were nationalizing women. And though the expeditionary forces sent in by the Allies were too feeble to cause much trouble, the millions in aid lent to the White generals by Britain prolonged the civil wars that convulsed Russia for two years. These cost not only millions of lives but untold hunger and terror to millions of others. Quite possibly the Bolsheviks would not have managed to survive except for the popular support they won through resentment of Allied interference. Britain, France, and America helped to assure the success of the revolution that the Germans had enabled Lenin to start, and helped still more to seal the traditional hostility to the West.

Nevertheless, the Bolsheviks' theory remained substantially a myth. From the beginning they ignored the natural concern of the Allies with the World War, initiating their consistent policy of refusing ever to admit any honorable motives in their opponents, and they soon began playing up the fiction that the main concern of the Allies was to undo the Russian Revolution. The Allied intervention was more stupid because it was not in fact organized, directed by any clear or consistent policy, least of all by a concerted plot of "capitalists." America, the great land of capitalism, most obviously belied the supposed conspiracy.

Its expeditionary force in Siberia was much too small anyhow to over-throw the Soviet government, but it was always bewildered, unsure just what it was supposed to be doing there; while Americans at home were making it ever clearer that they wanted nothing to do with any kind of world mission. It was only the Bolsheviks who were dedicated to such a mission. From the outset their main concern, openly proclaimed, was not world peace but world revolution, which Lenin had said was necessary for their own preservation. A Comintern resolution in 1922 stated formally the theme endlessly embroidered by their leaders: "We are the deadly enemies of bourgeois society. Every honest Communist will fight against bourgeois society to his last breath, in word and in deed and if necessary with arms in hand." It was to promote this war to the death that Lenin propagated the myth of a bourgeois West similarly united by ideology, organized and regimented by a capitalist high command.

His own belief in this foolish idea was not surprising. It jibed with the delusions about the West nurtured by Russian tradition, with the wishful thinking natural to professional revolutionaries, and specifi-cally with the paranoidal concept of reality behind the stereotypes that passed for Marxist realism. Again, however, Lenin's basic inflexi-bility was tempered in practice by his pragmatism. As the devastating civil wars were followed by the worst famine in Russian history, which took more millions of lives, he began trying to restore normal com-mercial and diplomatic relations with an imperialist West he was not at all prepared to fight. (Trotsky had indulged a premature vision in an article about how, after winning the civil war, his Red army would conquer Europe and take on America.) At home a new crisis had been forced by the revolt of workers and sailors in Petrograd, the birthplace of the revolution, demanding the restoration of power to the soviets. While the bloody suppression of the revolt exposed the fic-tion that the Bolshevik dictatorship was of the proletariat, Lenin knew that most peasants were discontented too; he had succeeded in making the peasantry more revolutionary than it was in any other European country. "The most pressing and topical question for politics today," he had written in 1917, "is the transformation of all citizens into work-ers and employers of one big 'syndicate,' namely, the state as a whole." Now he retained for the state control of all major industries but granted a measure of free enterprise to millions of peasants and little businessmen. Thereby he set off more sharply the new phase of totali-tarianism that began with Stalin.

In view of the acknowledged tyranny of Stalin, I should first stress that he inherited from Lenin all the essentials of his totalitarian state. Lenin had already reversed Marx's dictum that economics determines politics, establishing the power of the state to determine the economy; his "new" policy was merely a policy and involved no concession of the right of the state to whatever control the leaders decided was necessary—a right they still take for granted today. Similarly he had established the one-party system, the basic principle of totalitarianism, which Mussolini and Hitler would adopt and the successors of Stalin no more question. It was unhampered by any formal principle of the rights of the individual, or in practice by good humor or habits of tolerance; among the most striking characteristics of a party devoted to collectivism was the lack of simple kindliness, any live feeling of the brotherhood of man outside the circle of right-thinking "comrades." Even Stalin's purges were only a ruthless extension of the policy of periodic purges that the Comintern had at once made a requirement for Communist parties elsewhere; they were necessary if only because the repeated failures of the infallible Communists had to be due to the work of "traitors," or scapegoats. As for Stalin's innovations in both foreign and domestic policy, he was no more opportunistic than Lenin and their common Bible provided no clear criteria for judgment. Marx and Engels had never considered the possibility of a workers' state surrounded by capitalistic ones, with no immediate prospect of a world revolution, and historical materialism offered no basis for scientific prediction or determination of policy; the dictum, for example, that "the superstructure must conform to the economic basis" left open the question just how it must conform, or what beliefs were appropriate to the new situation. And for the most questionable of Stalin's purposes Lenin had bequeathed a particular boon. With the basic revolutionary myths he had blown up that of capitalist-imperialism as the archenemy, constantly bent on destroying the Soviet, and so justifying any sacrifice demanded of the people—a Devil that Stalin would revive as soon as the Second World War was over.

Hence one of his significant innovations was not at first recognized, even when he got himself canonized in 1929 on his fiftieth birthday. Lenin had ruled as a dictator by virtue of his personal authority, the immense respect he inspired, not by the absolute power of his office. He habitually tried to win over by persuasion other members of the Central Committee who disagreed with him on policy, never threatening them with death, demanding only that they abide by the decisions

finally agreed on by the Committee; while he had some expelled from
the party, his trustiest weapon was the threat to resign as leader. When
Stalin succeeded to Lenin's office, however, he set out to eliminate all
opposition, beginning with Trotsky, and to get complete control of
the party, through control of the secret police. Quite consciously he
took for his model Ivan the Terrible, an absolute autocrat. In the
thirties he went Ivan more than one better by the purges in which he
exterminated all the surviving comrades of Lenin, as well as the bulk
of the officials on the upper levels and countless others on lower levels
—together almost a whole generation of erstwhile revolutionaries. In
effect, Stalin killed the Bolshevik party. None of its nominal survivors
could be independent of him, dared to oppose his decisions. Since his
victims ran into the millions, it is generally agreed that he grew patho-
logical in his fears and furies, but his crimes may obscure the significant point. Not many men in the West fully realized, and no loyal
Communists abroad or at home openly admitted if they did realize,
that he had silenced the party and substituted one-man rule. Lenin's
dictatorship had made it hard to draw such nice distinctions. Though
his one-party system did not call for autocracy, it could not prevent
it either; it provided no legal way of criticizing, much less opposing,
even so murderous a despot as Stalin. Lenin himself had silenced public
opposition, calling it treason, and had scorned such "bourgeois" principles as freedom of the press.[11]

While denouncing Stalin's crimes, the leaders of the Soviet today
continue to praise him for his "positive" contribution—the establishment of a totalitarian economy. The key measures in securing this kind
of state capitalism were the collectivization of the farms, designed to
assure complete control of agriculture, and the famous Five-Year
Plans to industrialize Russia. By Western standards the enforced collectivization was also extraordinarily brutal, claiming more millions
of victims in the imprisonment, execution, or starvation of dispossessed
peasants; but Stalin's heirs have not yet criticized his methods in putting through a measure they still approve. One reason is that they are
still meeting stubborn opposition from the peasants, who gave Stalin

---

11 As Stalin's first victim, Trotsky later speculated that it was "rather tempting to draw
the inference that future Stalinism was already rooted in Bolshevik centralism," but
he did not give in to this temptation. If he had won his struggle with Stalin, he would
most likely never have been so barbarous, but no more democratic either; he had fully
supported the dictatorship imposed by Lenin. In his last years in Mexico he was still
excommunicating heretics from his splinter sect, upholding a utopian revolutionary
dictatorship that had never been.

(he admitted to Churchill) more trouble than any other group. Another reason is that they are especially proud of his feat of industrializing Russia, which was achieved by methods less brutal but no less
coercive. This remains the chief argument for the superiority of communism as an economic system.

Indisputably Stalin did succeed in making Russia a major industrial
power. Leaders in the non-Western countries now trying to modernize
their economy may be awed by statistics showing that by 1938 the
prewar production of coal, iron, oil, etc., had been tripled or quadrupled, but Westerners too might be impressed by this demonstration
of the possibilities of large-scale, long-range planning. A mighty enterprise in any view, it was more impressive by contrast with the lack
of enterprise in predepression Europe and the long failure of the
United States to recover from the depression. As worshipers of efficiency, Americans in particular might consider other clear advantages
of the Communist system. It eliminated a great deal of strictly unproductive business, as in advertising and speculation; a great deal of
waste through needless competition, for instance, of transportation
systems, or through needless multiplication of products different only
in their fancy packaging; and all kinds of extravagant when not para-
sitic activities, from those of featherbedders in labor unions through
real estate agents and brokers to the corporation lawyers, tax specialists, and public relations counselors who serve big business. It cut
down as well on some human costs of *laissez faire,* doing away with
the cycle of boom and crash, and above all the problem of unemployment. Liberals might add that the Soviet under Stalin made real advances toward such ideals as equality of opportunity, especially for
women, and the extension of education, sanitation, and medical care,
especially among the illiterate, disease-ridden peoples of central Asia.
A visitor to Samarkand, Tashkent, and Alma-Ata may appreciate a
radical transformation that could scarcely have been achieved by private enterprise.

Yet Stalin's system was basically not very original, and his apparent
success calls for drastic qualification. Like industrialism itself, socialism
was of course a Western import, and both had got well started in the
state industry of the czars. Lenin had borrowed his blueprints for a
planned economy from bourgeois writers, notably Walther Rathenau,
who organized the German economy in the World War, and he had
stressed the need of introducing "the latest progressive measures of
capitalism," such as the Taylor system in America. In carrying through

his Five-Year Plans, Stalin frankly repudiated the Communist ideal of "to each according to his needs," condemning as petty-bourgeois the principle of economic equality, depending instead on the bourgeois profit motive; the increasing inequality in income between managers and unskilled laborers led to about as wide a spread or gulf as in capitalistic countries. He built the biggest bureaucracy to date, more subservient and highly centralized than others, but as hierarchical, impersonal, and remote from the lowly workers, if anything more exclusively devoted to the end of bureaucratic efficiency rather than public welfare; at best it had a stranger look in a state that was supposed to wither away. (Lenin himself expressed misgivings about this "bureaucratic utopia" shortly before he died: "I greatly doubt whether one can say that Communists are running that heavy thing. If I must tell the truth, then it is not they who are running it, but it runs them.") It also involved, of course, considerable bungling. As for the undeniable expansion of industry, this was little greater than might have been achieved had the prewar rate continued, and it was much less impressive than that achieved by Japan in the nineteenth century, with nothing like the natural resources of Russia.

Most pertinent is the question how the Russian workers fared. Although statistics about the standard of living are uncertain, it is clear that real wages rose much less than did the national income, or than they had in expanding capitalistic countries. The Russian masses were little if any better off than they had been before the first war, since Stalin sacrificed consumer goods to heavy industry. In the light of economic history, his unique achievement was to industrialize Russia without appreciably raising the living standards of its masses.

We are accordingly brought to something uglier than myth in the one-party state that was the most original contribution of communism to political history. The word from Moscow was always that Western countries were capitalistic, even when under socialist governments, and that their workers were *ipso facto* exploited and oppressed, no matter how demonstrable the improvement in their condition. On the other hand, the Soviet always remained the great champion of the nonexistent world proletariat; so by what Raymond Aron has called "the irrefutable logic of schizophrenia," it followed that Russian workers were "free." In fact they were denied the right to strike that workers enjoyed in all the democracies, and had much less voice in their government; their unions soon lost their autonomy, all effective means of protecting their own interests, any real function beyond working out the higher production rates and sanctioning the other demands made by the government.[12] The Russian peasants, not to mention the millions of people in Siberian prison camps, made it still clearer that the most powerful state in Western history was violating the ordinary rights of citizens more deliberately, systematically, and thoroughly than any other modern state, even Hitler's Germany. While the word went out that Western democracy was a sham, Stalin's "dictatorship of the proletariat" was about the most blatant sham in history. Since as revolutionaries Communists were especially self-conscious in their political thought, some must have grown cynical, many more in the Soviet were simply cowed; but in so far as their leaders and their propagandists abroad were sincere (as I assume most of them were) they represented the ultimate in the "false consciousness" that for Marx was the essential meaning of ideology.

In another respect Stalin reversed Marx more thoroughly than Lenin had by decreeing that the state not only determine the material conditions of life but manage culture, the whole ideological "superstructure." Thereby he avenged Hegel for having been set on his head, but he completely deprived the intelligentsia of the freedom they had won toward the end of the czarist regime, and brought them under official suspicion again. He set the tone of Soviet culture by describing writers as "engineers of the human mind" and putting them under a suitable bureaucracy, authorized to make them toe the party line. A pall now settled on literature and the arts, in which much lively work had been done in the early fervent years following the Revolution. The "socialist realism" that was prescribed was an unoriginal technique whose chief merit was the obviousness that made it useful for crude propaganda purposes, and by the same token assured an ineffable monotony. In literature it meant a Moscow-Hollywood kind of realism, all wholesome moral and happy ending, decked out with clichés, which suffered still more by contrast with the great literature produced under the czars; the culture manufactured for the Russian masses was if anything more depressing than the mass culture of America. Soviet architecture and painting were most conspicuously unrevolutionary, least suggestive of a great or new style. Architecture stood out for a preten-

---

12 When recently touring the Soviet I was proudly shown a textile factory in which workers were handling more than twice as many looms per capita than any American union would consent to. Add the quotas and the piece rates assigned by government officials, this showpiece might be called a sweatshop.

tiousness reminiscent of the nineteenth century, a "reactionary" style that might seem strange were it not that bad taste is natural to a class coming up in the world. The animus against modern art that Stalin shared with Hitler was perhaps a tribute to its freedom, or to the power of the Western influences they feared, but it also reflected their bourgeois tastes (which Khrushchev continued to rejoice in). As bourgeois were the puritanical tendencies that suppressed the freedom in sexual life and marriage granted in the early years. The ideal Soviet man represented in fiction and poster art was much like a good Victorian —industrious, thrifty, orderly, faithful, punctual in duty; only he was much less concerned with romantic love, family piety, personal sentiment, or any such pettiness of private life.

Science fared somewhat better, in a state that made a fetish of it in keeping with its Marxist philosophy, but it suffered for the same reason. Philosophers of science were saddled with Lenin's *Materialism and Empirio-criticism*, a ferocious attack on the "reactionary idealists" who were trying to adapt dialectical materialism to the revolution in modern physics, in which he betrayed at once the essential poverty of his thought, his barbarous manners in controversy, his ignorance of physics, and his essentially unscientific spirit. (As he understood this revolution, "Physics is giving birth to dialectical materialism.") Physicists could nevertheless carry on with distinction because of their obvious usefulness to the state, though also because no physicist can possibly operate anyway on the basis of dialectical materialism. Biologists had a harder time. Russia had been leading the world in genetics until Stalin followed Lysenko in not only rejecting the general agreement of biologists that acquired characteristics cannot be inherited, but requiring scientists to come out with the proper findings; eminent geneticists disappeared during the purges. The most eminent Pavlov had no trouble, since the possibly heretical idea that Soviet man was a creature of conditioned reflexes was offset by the uses of behaviorism for reconditioning, but his fame exposed the simple dishonesty of many intellectuals. "It was only under the Soviet Government that Pavlov, as member of the Academy of Science, could develop his talents," wrote the servile authors of the official *School History;* whereas in fact he had won his Nobel Prize in 1904. As for social scientists, they were bound to be doctrinaire when not servile; the possible value of their researches in expanding the insights of Marx was always limited by the impossibility of any basic criticism of his premises. For the same

reason the Soviet produced almost no distinguished work in philosophy, law, or any of the humanities, which chiefly reflected the squalor
of its intellectual life.[13]

In general, the Soviet under Stalin most clearly refuted the common
charge in the West that it was a product of the unbridled rationalism
and unholy faith in science stemming from the Age of Enlightenment;
for it flatly rejected the ideals of the Enlightenment, in particular freedom of inquiry, criticism, and dissent, and it denied the rights of the
scientific spirit on behalf of a pseudo-scientific philosophy that had
become a Russian religion. Both the managed culture and the police
state of Stalin harked back to the much older tradition of absolutism in
Russia, or in Europe down to the Enlightenment; his ruling ideal of
complete unity and conformity was essentially medieval. The most
modern ingredient he added was an intenser nationalism, which owed
much to the Slavophiles and brought communism closer to fascism.
Whereas Lenin had been a sincere internationalist who repeatedly
denounced all forms of chauvinism and imperialism, including the
Russian drive to Constantinople, Stalin now led a campaign to glorify
the Russian past, adorn his state with a full-blown national myth. His
motive in betraying Marxism was possibly to revive a patriotism that
was flagging because of the burdens he was laying on the people, or
more likely to strengthen the tradition of reverence for the *Autokrator*.
In any case, his policy gave away his pretense of a dictatorship of the
proletariat: it was basically a reversion to an Asiatic type of state.[14]

Thus the early Bolsheviks had made it a point to speak always of
the Soviet instead of "Russia," but in the thirties leaders turned to

13 The main exception was the Hungarian George Lukacz, a somewhat heterodox
thinker who lived some years in the Soviet as an exile, and is by common consent
the most acute literary critic and Marxist theoretician in the Communist world. His
emphasis on the concept of "alienation" made him suspect to the authorities because
it led him to emphasize implicitly as well the values of self-determination, and it could
have disagreeable implications for Soviet man. He expressed nothing but admiration for
Stalin, however, even after the purges, and he appeared willing to accept the party line as
the ultimate criterion of truth. Later he redeemed himself by participating in the
Hungarian Revolution.

14 I should now qualify the popular explanation (which I repeated in an earlier work)
that Stalin was himself an Asiatic. As a Georgian from the Caucasus he may be called
a man from the East, but the Georgians are an unusually lively, independent people, who
gave the Soviet much trouble in the early years. A visitor to their ancient capital of
Tbilisi (Tiflis) may be impressed by how much more European it seems than Moscow.
Among other things, it has many more cafés, full of vivacious people, and seems unashamed
of its reputation as the only Russian city in which men make passes at unaccompanied
women. Stalin was "Asiatic," I should say, mainly in that he was not so well educated as
Lenin and other of the old Bolsheviks, and therefore not so steeped in Western, cosmopolitan thought.

"Russian patriotism." Similarly early historians had dutifully turned out pure, if crude Marxist versions of Russian history, which disposed unkindly of its "feudal" czarist phase; now they were denounced as "vulgar determinists" who had maligned this unique history. Whereas Lenin had admired only Peter the Great, Stalin had the much more barbarous Ivan the Terrible made over into as great a national hero, whose calculated terrorism had merely upheld "with blood and iron" his statesmanship in creating a "mighty state." Czars victorious in battle became progenitors of the invincible Red army, to which Stalin restored the ancient titles and gold-braided uniforms, while he himself blossomed out as Marshal and Generalissimo. Even the defeats in the World War were explained away as stabs in the back: the czarina and her ministers had betrayed military secrets to the Germans. Hence Stalin was given an illustrious lineage—Ivan, Peter, Marx, Lenin— that to Westerners might make him look like a mongrel or bastard, but at home proved that he was both invincible and infallible. He took particular pains to have official revolutionary history rewritten too, since he had unfortunately played an obscure, minor role in the Revolution. By a thorough suppression of inconvenient evidence, it was made out that Lenin's right-hand man had been not Trotsky, the organizer of the Red army, but always Stalin. His victims in the purges included some scholars who had "falsified" the Revolution by recording the facts.

If this bizarre extension of socialist realism suggests that Stalin had as low an opinion of the mentality of Soviet man as Hitler had of the masses, it helps one to make sense of his devious, fateful foreign policy. To begin with, the Communist International had a long, dreary record of failure, redeemed by not one great success or the winning of one dependable ally. Moscow had given it a hopeless task, inasmuch as the labor movement in Europe was obstinately devoted to democracy; hence the Communist parties became "classless" in an ironic sense, appealing more to intellectuals than to workers. But the incantations about the world revolution were not allowed to interfere with Stalin's only apparent long-range plan, which was to make the Soviet stronger at any cost, except of his own power. He had no serious worries abroad until the rise of Hitler. Although slow to realize the danger, he finally grew alarmed, and in 1934 did an about-face. The Soviet then joined the League of Nations, which had been officially described as an "international organization of the capitalists for the systematic exploitation of all the working peoples of the earth"; Communists everywhere were ordered to cooperate with democrats, even with socialists, in a Popular Front against Hitler; and Stalin assured an American journalist that the idea of world revolution was a "tragicomical misunderstanding." The good will that this new policy built up for the Soviet survived other abrupt shifts, such as the withdrawal of the aid Stalin at first gave to the Spanish Republicans, while he could always count on the support of a hard core of intellectual schizophrenics or flunkies in the Communist parties. His chief embarrassment remained his obsession first and last with his personal power, which made him a slave to suspicion and fear. Thus he seriously weakened the military power of the Soviet—the chief excuse for the sacrifices he demanded of his people—by slaughtering thousands of top officers of the Red army during the Great Purge. After the cleansing his first major move was to begin sounding out the possibilities of his most startling reversal of policy, the pact with Hitler.

This was not pure cynicism. Stalin had good reason to mistrust the leaders of Britain and France, who had not invited him to Munich, and whose belated, not too earnest efforts to form an alliance with him against Hitler were distracted by the refusal of the Poles to allow Russian armies to pass through their country. Always he had put the interests of the Soviet ahead of any international cause. Communist parties abroad, long trained to do likewise, could be trusted to consider the pact no mere betrayal of their cause but a necessary shift of tactics; it was little more radical, after all, than the shift in joining the imperialist League of Nations or cooperating with the heretical socialists. Though many intellectuals were disillusioned, the parties everywhere did accept the new line, perhaps with some relief in being able to attack again the "real" enemy—the capitalist-imperialists. (In the United States the *Daily Worker* was caught completely off guard, the day after the pact not even printing the news that made headlines all over the world; but it needed no instructions to begin rehearsing the old clichés a day later.) What might look like a surrender of intellectual integrity was simple fidelity in men who had identified communism with the rule of the party. At any rate, it now seems clear that Stalin was basically consistent. Apart from his possibly unconscious sympathy with Hitler as a fellow dictator and German disciple of Ivan the Terrible, he had much more reason to fear the influences of democracy at home than any possible appeal of nazism. It is now known that he was not only surprised when Hitler cynically violated the pact, but panicked by his invasion of Russia.

The war then complicated judgment of Stalin's handiwork. American military experts unanimously predicted that the Soviet would be crushed within a matter of months, even weeks; whereas its armies recovered from their shattering defeats, held at Moscow, Leningrad, and Stalingrad, and thereafter made a far better showing than the Russians had in the First World War. Although in time they received a great deal of American aid, their recovery testified to the measure of Stalin's success in making the Soviet an industrial power. In particular it forced pertinent questions about the common people. Granted the notoriously bad record of military experts in this century, they were not unreasonable in assuming that the Red army and the common people had been demoralized by Stalin's wholesale purges; and many of the lesser nationalities, notably the Ukrainians, in fact deserted or welcomed the Germans. But the people of Great Russia remained loyal. They proved themselves most heroically at Leningrad, where they withstood a 900-day siege, kept on the job producing munitions under constant bombardment, on starvation rations, despite a civilian toll estimated as high as 900,000 lives. An American might wonder: would New Yorkers be as steadfast under so terrible an ordeal? Would any affluent society?

To be sure, the most apparent explanation of the fortitude of the Russians was simple patriotism. It was love not of the Soviet but of Russia: of the land itself; of its culture as represented especially by its great writers, whose works were sold by the millions under Stalin; and still of its Orthodox Church, to which he had prudently made some concessions. Nevertheless, there remained mixed attitudes, impossible to gauge with any assurance in a country that has never gone in for public-opinion polls, but evident enough to speculate about. No doubt many Russians were still devout Communists, proud of their Revolution; this had unmistakably stirred a great deal of fervor that at least made people *feel* freer, and persisted in a sense of high purposefulness. Others, especially the intelligentsia, clung to the hope that in time they would enjoy more freedom; the uncertain liberal, democratic tradition was at least live enough to have called out the Soviet Constitution, which on paper guaranteed civil liberties. It appears that most Russians, however, were simply resigned to Stalin's tyranny, more or less unhappy about it, but not deeply, bitterly resentful. They submitted docilely if only because they had no real alternative, their system having ruled out the possibility of any resistance except by conspiracy, but partly too because their tradition disposed them to regard government as naturally alien. And to some extent all must have been affected by Stalin's incessant propaganda, in school, press, poster, and parade. It kept all the basic Marxist-Leninist dogma and myth in the realm of truism—commonplaces beyond criticism or doubt, as to most Russians they still appear to be. By the same token most seem to have grown bored by the fearfully monotonous repetition, day in and day out; but a ruthless despot might risk the apathy, even prefer it to revolutionary fervor.

Hence Stalin's legacy to the Soviet was thoroughly confused. Among his involuntary bequests were a hatred of his secret police and a yearning for elementary legality and security that led to a more liberal regime. Another was the loss of the popularity he had won during the war, since upon victory he continued to demand sacrifices instead of rewarding the people by a program to improve their living standards.[15] On all counts he was roundly condemned for his "cult of personality," which was indeed disgraceful for a Marxist. Still, his disgrace only intensified the cult of Lenin, who now did double-duty in a more benign role as Dear Papa. Stalin's heirs retained his totalitarian state with absolute power centered in Moscow. Their more liberal policies were designed to secure, not diminish this power; their fears for their own security brought about the purge of Beria, head of the secret police. As Stalin's victory over Trotsky in his struggle for complete personal control had always been disguised as the "correct" interpretation of the scriptures of Marx and Lenin, so power politics within the Soviet is still conducted in terms of orthodoxy versus heresy; the "thaw" has not yet reached the party line and the habitual double-talk it requires. The now popular theme of "peaceful coexistence"— a phrase used by Stalin in the twenties—is still coupled with the hoary clichés about the Western imperialists, none of whom any longer has a colonial empire, while it suggests no more respect for the basic principles of international law, nor any sign of bad conscience over all the crimes committed at home and abroad in the course of Stalin's aggressions. The government-controlled press is described as a "people's press," the freest, most truthful and democratic in the world because (in Khrushchev's words) it is the most "ideologically upright," or in other words, is entirely free to twist all news and suppress embarrassing truths, as it did under Stalin.

---

[15] Robert C. Tucker, then attached to the American Embassy, has reported that in the four days of official mourning after Stalin's death he observed only one person weeping in the streets—a young girl. The people of Moscow had been much more obviously saddened by the news of Roosevelt's death.

So we may wonder again about the Russian people. On the face of it, the tyranny of Stalin did not kill either their desire for personal freedom or their faith in communism. Under leaders who are giving more attention to their well-being, they seem basically content, convinced of the superiority of their system; their complaints are always directed at the "bureaucrats," not the system itself. Simply because they are much better off, however, they evidently have no more revolutionary fervor than before. Neither does the vast bureaucracy to which Stalin gave responsibility without independent authority, but which nevertheless constitutes a privileged class, tends to generate its own means and ends, and is naturally more devoted to the cause of technology than of revolutionary Marxism. The leaders might worry because both workers and bureaucrats now look more and more like bourgeois—as all but Marxists might have predicted. Meanwhile they have plenty else to worry about in the problems bequeathed by Stalin, such as a backward agriculture, an unbalanced economy, and an immense shortage in housing. They might be grateful for the mentality he helped to form by schooling the people in falsehood, keeping them ignorant of the Western world, and treating them like not very bright children. Thus the Lenin Museum in Moscow, full of pictures of the Revolution, must have been plastered with pictures of Stalin only a few years ago; but today (1965) it has not a single picture of either Trotsky or Stalin. Evidently the leaders trust their children not to ask obvious, awkward questions.

Their official historians also have retained the lessons they learned under Stalin. Having had to rewrite history again after his death, and still again after the fall of Khrushchev, they can expect to be kept busy on the job indefinitely; but their notion of "objectivity" or ideological uprightness makes it an easy job. Even so, a bourgeois historian may not envy them.

Chapter Eight	*THE IMPACT ON THE NON-WESTERN WORLD*

1. The Resurgence of the East

When Europe let Lenin down by failing to stage a revolution for him, he found ample compensation by looking in another direction—"the revolutionary and nationalist East," especially China and India. This offered a more exciting prospect because it contained most of the world's people, and he was not at all troubled because very few of them were proletarians: its peasant masses could more readily follow the example of Russia, or his own example of a pure Marxist orthodoxy that never required consistency. Observing that this great mass of people "has been drawn into the struggle for emancipation with extraordinary rapidity," he was happy to add that "there cannot be the slightest shadow of doubt what the final outcome of the world struggle will be." Actually, of course, there was considerable doubt. Until the next world war the Communists got nowhere in any of the Near or Far Eastern countries except China, and here a promising revolutionary movement was wrecked by Stalin, who dictated a policy that enabled Chiang Kai-shek to massacre the Communists. But at least Lenin had recognized an extraordinary stir that was bound to have revolutionary consequences. While Europe still had an immense superiority in material power, it was fast losing the authority that in the long run could alone maintain its dominion. The Soviet had anticipated the breakdown of the old world order by its withdrawal from the European community.

The stir had been apparent, indeed, long before the World War. In the middle of the nineteenth century China had a great peasant rebellion, India staged a mutiny against the British, and Japan made an astonishing break with its past, to begin rising as a modern nation. Early in our century Young Turkish, Young Arab, Young Indian, and Young Chinese movements agitated for innovation and reform. Already revolutions were breaking out—in Persia (1906), in Ottoman Turkey (1908), and in China (1911). Lenin had taken a lively interest in the Persian revolution because it was directly inspired by the revolution in Russia the year before. But this pointed to a much more momentous event, for the East a historic turning point—the victory of Japan over Russia. All Asia, even to remote villages, was stirred by the demonstration that a native people could soundly whip a great European power. An Indian told how it affected the youth especially: "We felt an immense elation, a sort of reassurance in the face of Europeans, and an immense sense of gratitude and hero worship for the Japanese." An Englishman reported that even villages all over Africa were excited by the news, though most Africans had not the faintest idea where Japan was, knowing only that its people were not white or Christian.

For such reasons, however, the World War had a profounder effect on the East, indicated immediately by a surge of nationalism and a clamor for independence. It had irreparably damaged the moral authority of Europeans, eroded their claims to civilized superiority; they themselves had charged one another with crimes against humanity, calling their enemies barbarians. The war had also shown that the proud Europeans needed the help of Asians and Africans. China had been pressured into declaring war against Germany; Britain had depended heavily on Indian troops, and had promised the Arabs freedom in return for their help in fighting the Turks; France had drawn more than half a million soldiers from its colonies and protectorates. While the Chinese and the Arabs were therefore more embittered by the shabby treatment they got in the postwar settlement, all non-Western peoples had been given a lesson in the uses of violence, and impressed by the revelation of the inner weakness of Europe, the corruption, the hypocrisy—the worst qualities of the imperial powers. "I realized more and more," wrote Nehru, "how the very basis and foundation of our acquisitive society . . . was violence." Others rejoiced in the news about the decline of Europe publicized by Spengler and the like; "history" was now on their side. Europeans themselves were much less confident in their dealings with their subject peoples. Although still disposed to arrogance or lordly condescension, they were for the first time on the defensive. Their statesmen were under increasing criticism at home too by socialists, conscious-stricken intellectuals, and liberals sympathetic to the demands of Eastern peoples for independence.

Hence the old theme of East and West became more pertinent, and no longer in Kipling's simple terms that "never the twain shall meet." Arnold Toynbee and others spread an awareness that the twain had been meeting and mingling for well over two thousand years. They complicated the ancient Greek idea of a conflict between "Europe" and "Asia," beginning with the Trojan War. Such a conflict may be seen in the attack of the Persian Empire on Greece, the retaliation of Alexander the Great in overthrowing this empire, and the consolidation of the Near East under the Romans, who then continued to war with Parthians and Sassanians; but meanwhile Greek culture had spread over the East, Greeks and Romans came under Oriental influences, and the Roman Empire ended as something like an Oriental sacred monarchy, surviving only in the Byzantine Empire. In this perspective Westerners might learn more humility, for the upshot of the drama was the conquest of the Greco-Roman world by Oriental religions and finally the military triumph of the East, sealed by the fall of Constantinople to the Turks.[1]

Yet the resurgence of the East in our century is by no means a repetition of the old story. In this historical perspective one may see more clearly how radically different a drama it is, how unprecedented are the problems it raises, and how much harder these are to deal with.[2] In the first place, the Eastern societies have been much more

---

[1] For an outline of this theme, see *Freedom in the Ancient World*, indexed as East vs. West.

[2] The old theme is still popular, however. In *East and West*, for example, C. Northcote Parkinson recently offered a fashionably "realistic" version of it: he depicts a great power struggle of East and West over the past three thousand years, a "piston movement" in which the ascendancy of the one inevitably generated a resistance and finally a successful rebellion in the other, and so he concludes that the East is bound to triumph again. Elsewhere I have commented that in order to keep his pistons going steadily, he grossly oversimplifies and distorts history. Toynbee's better-known version of the theme is distorted by his fondness for neat analogies and religious morals. Thus he wrote that Greco-Roman culture "spread as widely in the Old World as our Western culture has spread in its day," and its impact "gave the world as sharp a shock"; but in fact it spread thinly over only a corner of India, never reaching China, not to mention the whole African continent except the northern coast, and the peasant masses of Asia were hardly shocked by it, if touched at all. Although Toynbee suggests the religious analogy as only a possibility, I can see no prospects whatever of Oriental religions conquering the West again, and should remark that among the radically different possibilities is the triumph of China, fired by its Western secular religion of communism. Meanwhile Toynbee's scheme for the past—discrete civilizations swinging through the same invariable cycles of growth, breakdown, and disintegration—makes it harder for him to size up the plainest reality of the present, that Western civilization has spread over the entire world and messed up the cycles of all other surviving civilizations. In fairness I should add that although he takes a God's-eye view of history, God himself might be embarrassed by the confusions of modern history.

deeply affected by the West than the ancient ones were. Their revolt
against it has been as much more conscious, enflamed by more resentment and more resolution. Their thought and feeling have been both
cause and effect of a novel, intense nationalism, conscious ideals of
self-determination that they owe to the West. Their struggles have
been complicated because they are relatively much more "backward"
countries, far behind the West in technology; all have accordingly
taken to Western science and technology, set the unprecedented goal
of "modernizing" themselves. On all counts, their intelligentsia have
played a much more active, influential role than they ever did—or
could—in the ancient world, often providing the political leadership
once monopolized by kings. They have been most sensitive to the
profound disruption of their culture, as old ways were discredited
before new ones were learned, and therefore have been liable to ambivalent when not inconsistent attitudes: eager to introduce advanced
Western ideas and methods, yet in their resentment of the Western
intruders inclined to assert the superiority of their own tradition, like
the Slavophiles in Russia. Adjustment has been more difficult because
the West itself was in the throes of revolutionary change. And with the
World War came another novel complication, the beginning of a conflict within the West over the soul of the awakened East. Disillusioned
with Britain and America after Versailles, Sun Yat-sen turned from
democracy to communism as the great hope for China. While elsewhere communism itself made little headway, it provided a revolutionary example for the nationalistic movements, giving them lessons in
the techniques of propaganda, conspiracy, and terrorism.

The one basic similarity between the old and the new story is a further source of confusion. Strictly, there never was an "East," or until
lately an "Asia" in any meaningful historical sense. Ancient Babylonia,
Persia, India, and China were very different societies; China was indeed
more like Rome than India. The "East" that surged back against the
West was the Arabia of Mohammed, who knew little if anything about
the much greater societies of India and China. Only in this century
arose a common consciousness of Asia, as the Japanese triumph over
Russia inspired the slogan "Asia for the Asiatics"; but Japan launched
its imperial career by aggressions against its fellow Asiatics in Korea
and China. Today the common consciousness has created nothing like
a uniform East; its countries are no more culturally akin than politically united. Hence the new story is not at all the same story everywhere.
The common problems facing the Asiatic peoples have evoked differ-

ent responses, in keeping with their different cultural traditions. Much has depended too on the caliber of their leaders, an unpredictable factor that became more obviously important than in the past. Between the wars the movement toward national independence already looked inevitable, and the farsighted could see that it was due to become irresistible; but the specific direction it took and the political form it assumed were largely decided by new leaders. On the face of it, such men as Atatürk, Gandhi, and Mao Tse-tung made a considerable difference.

Now that the resurgence of the non-Western world has swelled into a mighty tide, I should emphasize that all the revolutions I have so far dealt with directly affected only a small fraction of mankind. There had been two distinct worlds. Although the non-Western one had known some of the material benefits of modern technology, and more of the costs, essentially it had gone on living torpidly in its ancient ways, which left the bulk of its people resigned to poverty, illiteracy, and endemic disease. By the time of the World War the two worlds were still distinct, but with a permanent difference: the other one was seething both with hatred and with new hopes. While Westerners continued to talk of the "timeless, unchanging East," it was on the move under their eyes. It had more ardor for change than America or western Europe; however misguided, its leaders had more vision and more fervor. It was posing a confused but imperious challenge to the West— political, intellectual, spiritual. Colonial powers were responding to the challenge by stubbornly defending their imperial interests, making some concessions, but refusing to grant their subjects independence, doing little to prepare them for self-government, doing more to intensify their sense of being exploited and oppressed. They jailed "natives" for proclaiming Western ideals of freedom and justice.

But thereby they pointed to deeper, more novel paradoxes. Asiatic peoples were claiming a sympathy that conquered peoples had never expected in the past. They owed to the West the principles of their revolt, their political vocabulary, the new goals they were setting themselves, and the essential means to these ends. European rule had created an unprecedented popular demand for independence, and not at all because it was harsh; it was in fact generally less oppressive than these peoples had known under their native rulers. Among the main forces on their side, moreover, was public opinion in the Western democracies. Britain and France, the leading colonial powers, at least acknowledged in theory a responsibility to their subjects, and more and more of their people were sympathetic to the demands of these subjects, just as they had become to the cause of the poor at home. The conscience of the democracies had been quickened by the World War. The condemnation of the Japanese and Italian aggressions on Manchuria and Ethiopia, for example, laid them open to charges of hypocrisy, since Japan and Italy were only doing what Britain and France had done in the preceding century, trying to take their place in the imperial sun; yet the condemnation was not simply hypocritical—it reflected a real change in attitude. It anticipated the contemporary paradox, that the worst problems for the erstwhile imperial powers developed precisely as they grew less arrogant and selfish, and also still more powerful than the colonial peoples to whom they were giving in.

Between the wars there was no more conspicuous example of the debt to the West than Gandhi, who after many years in London and South Africa returned to India in 1914 to lead the movement for independence, became the best known of such leaders all over the world, and made India the bellwether of the rebellious colonial peoples. The Hindu spirituality for which he was famous was coupled with a Western kind of idealism that made him a crusader on behalf of the Indian masses, long ignored by the Brahmans. A type that Hinduism had not produced before British rule, he was the more inspiring because of the long centuries of stagnation in India, which—as in other Asiatic countries—had only confirmed the arrogant complacence of its upper class. His crusade exemplified a simple contribution of the West perhaps more important than the novel ideals of freedom and social justice: a realization of opportunity, a spirit of hope instead of resignation, a feeling that reform was not only desirable but possible. And his assassination by a Hindu fanatic was a reminder that the famed spirituality of India had always been shot through with gross idolatry and superstition. In the land of sacred cows, as everywhere in Asia, the revolt of the masses could look like a revolt against civilization. A Europe that had plunged the entire world into war might not be clearly entitled to consider itself a superior civilization, nor after Versailles clearly fit to assume the leadership of the world; but certainly no Asiatic country was yet fit to take its place. It still had much more to teach about government as well as technology—an elementary truth that all the non-Western peoples would acknowledge by doing little but imitate it when they won their independence, introducing no original forms or theories of government.

Still, this only emphasized the greater responsibilities of the West, and some further paradoxes. It was producing by far the most systematic, comprehensive study of history, society, and culture that man had ever made; yet except for some scholars it had shown little respect for the ancient cultures of the East, less understanding of the disruptions it had caused. Everywhere Europeans remained outsiders, aliens, aloof from the "natives," no less when they came to settle permanently; they did not mingle freely with them as the ancient Romans had mingled with their civilized subjects. Always assuming the inferiority of the natives, they were usually most impressed by traits or habits encouraged by the stigma imposed on them by this name; when not simply "unmanly," Orientals were wily, untruthful, untrustworthy, irresponsible. At best, administrators endeavored to bring their subjects the blessings of Western civilization, but with too little thought of the tensions between new ways and the old values they were discrediting. In their condescension they could not be expected to care enough about their subjects to ponder the difficulties in making good Europeans of men who had to live and work in societies with a very different tradition—and always under alien rule. With the awakening of the East the need of sympathetic understanding grew at once more urgent and more difficult. Its peoples were unlikely to be sweetly reasonable in pressing their natural desires for independence, born of justified resentment. It was easy to see that most of them were not prepared for self-government by Western standards, as easy to forget that their rulers had done too little to prepare them—but above all to forget that they had particular need of independence for the sake of simple self-respect, since they had been treated as inferiors. They were inclined to be more belligerent because they had been forced to recognize that in some respects they were actually inferior, and because they were still not self-reliant or self-sufficient enough. At any rate, their ambitions were staggering. As they aspired to freedom, popular government, and modernization, they were trying to do in a generation what it had taken Europe centuries to achieve, with a great deal of violence that is deplored when non-European peoples indulge in it.

Especially difficult issues were raised by their desire to modernize themselves. Here one may first ask a legitimate question: *Why* modernize? The "progress" of the West had culminated in the worst catastrophe in history, and the non-Western peoples would have to pay a heavy cost for trying to catch up with it—not only material but human costs, in the disintegration of their traditional cultures. Nevertheless the question is academic. The whole world has already answered it: all the countries now politely called "underdeveloped" want to modernize, for reasons quite obvious to all but some intellectuals. Apart from the needs of self-respect and self-defense, they want the elementary goods of material well-being. The costs only force the question of alternatives that it is too easy for disillusioned Westerners to forget. Are men really better for living in poverty and illiteracy? Worrying over getting enough to eat? Calling in saints or magicians instead of doctors? Believing in demons and witches? Is a society really healthier when it rests on the manual labor of masses of such men instead of the "inhuman" machine? The most common charge against the West the world over remains its "materialism," also for obvious reasons; yet the wretched masses of the world have never disdained the goods of material well-being, which they always sought through prayer or magic. Only moderniza- tion through Western science and technology can improve their earthly lot, or simply reduce the chances of starvation in countries where Mal- thusian theory still does apply.

Once non-Western peoples were independent, modernizing was im- mediately an economic or technological problem. Basically, however, it was a political problem. Private enterprise alone could not modern- ize their economy, since typically they lacked adequate resources of private capital and large-scale enterprise, and they were naturally wary of the alternative of foreign investment, which might mean only more exploitation or leave them at the mercy of foreigners again. The state had to supervise the whole job, itself directly undertake much of the enterprise. Their leaders then had a wide choice in Western political models and ideologies, all the varieties of republicanism, statism, socialism, fascism, communism; and their selection was likely to dismay supporters of democracy. For "freedom" could not mean to Asiatic peoples what it meant to Westerners, who over the centuries had built up a tradition of freedom under law, often fought for their rights, and grown accustomed to personal freedom. It meant national independ- ence, of course, but this was no guarantee of political freedom for the masses. Except perhaps in India, freedom could hardly mean democ- racy as we know it, given peoples largely uneducated, unaccustomed to participating in their government, lacking a tradition of political rights. Whatever it meant in the way of personal freedom would depend on their leaders, ultimately on their cultural tradition. And this brings up the more troublesome question of the cultural, psychological effects of modernizing. It meant in general an expansion of knowledge and power, an awakening to new hopes and opportunities, in which many people might enjoy more effective freedom and fullness of life, most might at least feel freer because their country was independent or the goal was in sight. It also required new attitudes toward work, income, family relationships, daily routines—personal adjustments that were always more or less difficult, unsettling, possibly painful; and many people might feel less free as they were coaxed or coerced out of the ways of their ancestors, and too often were disappointed in their hopes. Everywhere modernization became the order of the day, often celebrated as the main task of mankind; but on all counts it was by no means simply an exhilarating task or necessarily a rewarding one.

Although Americans tended to sympathize with colonial peoples seeking independence, because of their own War of Independence, between the world wars they were little concerned about the problems of the non-Western world. They were due to inherit the headaches, however, and their exceptional experience in a favored land made it especially hard for them to understand these problems. They were more inclined to be self-righteous because they identified imperialism with the possession of overseas colonies, forgetting that they had initially slaughtered or driven out Indians, instead of ruling over them, and that they had then built a kind of continental empire by seizing adjacent land from Mexico. Already fearful of revolutionaries, they would be dismayed by the elementary discovery that non-Western peoples were not so content with the *status quo*, and that their revolutions were quite different from the respectable American Revolution; abroad the most popular books on this subject were by Marxists. Worse, it would appear that American capitalistic democracy—the whole American way of life—was not for export, except in Hollywood versions that served merely to entertain; few political or intellectual leaders would display a proper horror of socialism or respect for an acquisitive society. Even American efficiency would fail to dazzle all Asiatics, and technical know-how somehow not always work in their alien cultures. Most of the slogans that stirred loud cheers in America would leave many Easterners cold.

Hence America best exemplifies the final challenge to the West, the need of better self-understanding. In reviewing the different responses of Eastern societies to its impact, we have to consider their different cultural traditions, and these throw light on both the values and the defects of Western civilization, in particular its distinctive tradition of freedom. The great societies of the East have little to teach us, I assume, about government or political freedom. They have much to offer on the life of the spirit, the art of living, or the uses and abuses of freedom. They suggest other possible conceptions of human dignity and modes of self-realization, through such ideals as harmony, propriety, and spiritual or psychological freedom. It is now time, at any rate, to consider the thought and experience of more than half of mankind, which has so far been largely ignored in this history.

2. *Japan*

The first Asiatic country to rise to the challenge of the triumphant West, Japan was by all odds the most successful. Its success was more amazing because for two and a half centuries it had been ruled by an ultraconservative feudal shogunate, behind a puppet emperor, which had tried to keep it an absolutely closed society by rigorously excluding foreigners and alien influences. When in 1853 Admiral Perry broke in, Japan was still far from ready to welcome such influences. But once it took the plunge it did a complete reversal: under the imperial restoration that ended the shogunate (1867) it immediately started going the whole way to Westernization, scorning the gradualism of conservative wisdom. The great emperor to be known as Meiji ("Enlightened Government") promised the establishment of deliberative assemblies, preparing for the written constitution and parliamentary government to come. Education was made compulsory, technical schools and colleges were set up. As quickly the country began to industrialize, building railways and factories, and to develop modern systems of trade, banking, and communications to go with its industry. As systematically it set about improving agriculture, bringing medicine and law up to date, introducing the latest techniques in every sphere of public life. By the end of the century—within a single generation—Japan had made itself a great modern nation, with an army and navy to match. Even before its crushing defeat of Russia on land and sea, Great Britain recognized its status as a world power by making an alliance with it —the first Asiatic country to be so honored by a European power. Altogether, Japan in this one generation far surpassed the achievements of mighty Russia in two centuries since Peter the Great, and its feat has not yet been equaled by any other of the non-Western countries that are trying to modernize themselves, despite the advantages of its example and of much financial aid from Western countries.

The immediate reason for the success of the Japanese was their willingness to learn in every sphere. "Knowledge," the Emperor Meiji proclaimed at the outset, "shall be sought for throughout the world." The government imported all sorts of technicians and advisers from Europe and America, while sending many students abroad to study Western methods and ways of life. Quite deliberately it picked out foreign models, looking to France for its new law code, to Germany for its medicine and the organization of its army, to Britain for its merchant marine, navy, banking system, etc. But its diligence brings up another consideration that may at once hearten and dishearten other countries eager to modernize: Japan owed its success most obviously to the high caliber of the leaders who acted through the young emperor. There was nothing inevitable about the initial decision they made or their subsequent achievement; no historical materialist or determinist could have predicted with assurance the new Japan. History offers no more striking example, indeed, of the power of men to determine their destiny by conscious thought and will—not only to make but to make over their history.

If in a longer retrospect historians do make out some deep, involuntary cause, the primary fact remains that the revolutionary political, economic, and social changes in Japan were deliberately planned and vigorously carried through from on top, not in any such haphazard way as the Industrial Revolution came about in Britain, nor in response to popular demand either. While little businessmen were permitted free enterprise, and in time a few powerful firms took charge of the major industries, the government played a much more direct part in planning, financing, directing, and controlling the industrialization than did European states of the period. Only so could this have been achieved so swiftly. And so it must be throughout the non-Western world (however disagreeable to American congressmen) if the economy is to be modernized at all rapidly or thoroughly: it has to be done largely from on top, by measures that may be called socialistic, in countries lacking not only adequate private capital but a tradition of large-scale capitalistic enterprise. In other ways too the state must play a much larger role than it once did, providing for education, sanitation, and various public services. Leaders elsewhere (and American congressmen) might therefore take note that the Japanese government never set communism or totalitarianism as its goal.

As unmistakably, however, the success of Japan's leaders owed much to the qualities of its people, who rose so promptly to the new opportunities; so we are brought to the cultural tradition of Japan. In general, the Japanese had been given to borrowing ever since the beginning of their history as a civilized people in the fifth century A.D.—much later than the settled society of China. They owed to China the essentials of their civilization, and thereafter most of their serious thought and high learning; never so brilliant or original as the Chinese, they remained basically more adaptable, less set in ways that were not wholly their own. A particular key to their culture was their early adoption of Buddhism. Introduced by the ruling class for its own aristocratic purposes, this rapidly grew popular, the more so because it was a tolerant religion that made no effort to suppress the primitive native religion of Shinto, which remained useful for domestic piety. A boon for civilizing purposes, Buddhism put a permanent stamp on Japanese culture, especially the fine arts; yet it never dominated society as religion did in most of Asia. Unlike Mohammedanism, for instance, it left the people free to embark on new adventures, offering no serious opposition when they took to Westernization.[3]

A more positive aid to the new leaders of Japan was its exceptionally thorough devotion to the principle of hierarchy. Although they felt impelled to abolish feudalism, they were themselves a product of a system that was more like the feudal system of medieval Europe than was aristocracy in any other great society. As in Europe, but with much longer and greater success, it resisted the growth of absolute monarchy, which prevailed in all other Asiatic countries. Always jealous of their independence, the feudal lords were able to reduce the emperor to a mere puppet about the time when the Russian czars were reducing their boyars to servitude. The virtues they prized—valor, loyalty, honor—were those dear to medieval knights, but earned them more respect from townsmen because the principles of duty and obedience to superiors dominated the whole society. The common people achieved self-respect through the proper fulfillment of their obligations, and habitually put duties above rights. Hence they did not have to

---

[3] In the medieval period it did become a nuisance when its monks were corrupted by their immense wealth: grown ignorant, greedy, and debauched, they defied the authorities and turned their monasteries into forts. But the soldier-monks were more a nuisance than a serious menace, and there was no national uproar when the shogun Nobunaga slaughtered them by the thousands. Meanwhile other forms of this hospitable religion had grown popular, in particular "Pure Land" Buddhism, which still has more worshipers than any other sect. By the infinite compassion of the Buddha Amida, this promised Paradise on very easy spiritual terms, merely by calling his name; and while it was therefore unlikely to inspire great works, it left the Japanese still freer for whatever works they had a mind and a will to.

be coerced when a small group of leaders decided to Westernize the country. They were not merely passive either, for their principle of hierarchy was compatible with a lively self-respect; it emphasized obligation to inferiors as well as superiors, a respect for the rights that all classes were guaranteed in return for their duties. Except for one feudal rebellion, the revolutionary change-over was remarkably peaceful; and the leader of this rebellion characteristically believed that he was being loyal to the emperor, fighting only his "evil counselors."

By the same token the Japanese did not, of course, simply shed their traditional culture and become out-and-out Westerners. While they soon took to Western clothes, sports, amusements, and arts, they retained their old customs in family life, their tea ceremonies and gardens, and their traditional code of values. Naturally they suffered somewhat from the strains of the new ways and conflicts with the old ways, tensions that we must consider presently, but on the whole the revolutionary changes were also remarkable for their relatively low cost in psychological instability or insecurity. Their intellectuals in particular suffered and quarreled much less than the Russian intelligentsia. In this respect their new leaders helped by introducing a conservative principle, if a dubious one for the long run. So far from repudiating the past, they popularized their program and succeeded in doing away with feudalism by a deliberate reversion to an older past. The Imperial Rescript of reform they issued called for not only modernization but "the Great Way of obedience to the Gods." They dusted off the venerable native religion of Shinto, officially made it over into a state religion, and thereby transferred the primary loyalty of every Japanese from his lord to the state. They intensified patriotism by reviving the archaic idea that the emperor not merely ruled by divine right but was himself literally divine. The educated, modernized Japanese, respectful of science and technology, nevertheless gloried in the belief that the head of their nation was a "manifest god."

In other words, incongruity and ambiguity—the polite terms for contradictions that may verge on absurdity—are no monopoly of Western civilization. Known at once for their docility and aggressiveness, sensitivity and ferocity, adaptability and hidebound conservatism, the Japanese had all the defects of their virtues; and eventually they paid a heavy price for their success. The obvious example was the imperialistic career they early embarked on, which in our time led to the worst disaster in their entire history. Among the primary objectives of the new leaders in industrializing the country was to build up its military power, among their early measures was military conscription. This objective may be considered a natural consequence of Westernization, since a great nation by modern standards had to be a great military power; it was even a necessity if Japan was to maintain control of its destiny, given the example of what the European powers were doing to China; and when it began its own aggressions on Korea and China it was only following the example of Western imperialism. Its militarism also entailed some departure from tradition, notably in conscription: this meant that peasants were accorded the privilege of fighting that had been reserved for the samurai or warrior class. Yet militarism was plainly rooted in the feudal tradition of Japan, the long celebration of the warrior virtues. The Japanese learned from the West only better techniques of war—they were no peace-loving people corrupted by the West.

Similarly with the nationalism deliberately played up by the government. Up to the point of simple patriotism this was another clear necessity for modernizing, as both a powerful stimulus and a means to the necessary cooperation. Nevertheless it involved the abiding dangers that beset all countries on the way to modernization. The primary aim is likely to be the power and prestige of the state, not the welfare of the people, still less their personal freedom; the means to building up the nation's pride may become ends in themselves. Despite its phenomenal success in Westernizing, moreover, Japan exemplified a further menace to peaceful progress. Its people were not simply happy, after all, in letting in foreigners and going to school under them. Although eager to learn, respectful of their teachers, and proud of emulating them, they tended to resent them too, and were hypersensitive about any suggestion of their inferiority. Antiforeign sentiment, always latent, could become virulent under strain, as it did in the thirties. Everywhere in the non-Western world modernization may similarly bring a better understanding and appreciation of the West, but is as likely to breed hatred of it and intensify conflicts with it. In Japan the danger was aggravated by another relic of feudal tradition —the habit of political assassination. Many Japanese statesmen fell victim to this, and they were mostly moderate men, their assassins fanatical nationalists. Such fanaticism became common among the military, who were not kept under firm civilian control.

Neither, finally, was the government. Given the long feudal tradition of Japan, the most remarkable political decision of the leaders was no doubt the measure of popular government they introduced, again not immediately in response to strong public demand; but in any case democracy was severely limited and converts to Western liberal ideals were a small minority. Ministers were formally held responsible to the emperor alone, not to the popularly elected legislature, which had no independent rights except an uncertain control over expenditures. The Constitution made the emperor completely immune to criticism by declaring him "sacred and inviolable," and in theory gave him almost absolute power. In practice the country was ruled by an oligarchy, just as it had been in the feudal past; this continued to dominate Japanese politics when universal male suffrage was finally granted in 1925. The chief threat to its power came from the ministers of war and navy, who had to be military men; they could always embarrass the government by resigning if they or their services did not approve of its policies, and in the critical thirties they came to dictate foreign policy. They could always exploit popular discontent too, or divert it into nationalistic fervor. Tenant farmers paid proportionately two or three times more in taxes than merchants and manufacturers did, and the oligarchy favored the interests of landlords.

Here too the key was the basic principle of hierarchy—the antithesis of Western ideals of freedom and equality. At its best, it deserved the praise of Herbert Spencer, one of the European advisers consulted by the new leaders, who told them that it was an ideal basis for the Japanese state, and gave it an advantage over the individualistic nations. The traditional ideals of loyalty and selfless obligation survived the modernization of Japan. General Nogi, hero of the war with Russia, gave a touching example when the Emperor Meiji died in 1912: ceremoniously he followed his divine master into the hereafter by performing hara-kiri. But this duty as he saw it was hardly a rational concept, and it exemplified as well the arbitrariness of the traditional system of obligations. Japanese feudalism differed significantly from medieval feudalism in the relation of vassal and lord: whereas in Europe this was a contractual relation, entailing a recognition of specified rights of the vassal, in Japan the vassal owed absolute, unconditioned loyalty to his lord, upon whom he had no claims at all, and who had the right to control his personal life. In practice there were similar anomalies, since the chivalrous warrior-lords felt free to assassinate the sacred emperor and were accustomed to treating peasants brutally; but again their callousness differed from that of medieval knights. It was not tempered by any religious ideal of brotherhood or the sanctity of the person, nor by the universal principle of "human-heartedness" or natural sympathy that Confucius made basic. Neither was the whole system based on rational, philosophical principles of justice. The elaborate code of duties governing Japanese life was purely formal. Every man had to learn his precise place in the system, his social distance from others (indicated by the varieties of "you" in his language), and a specific set of obligations. The Japanese ethic was accordingly free from absolutism, in a way pliable, and it was softened by the habitual politeness that carefully veiled the exercise of authority and the need of submission; yet it remained essentially arbitrary, in its way absolutely categorical in its demands, and the more narrow and rigid because it discouraged independent thought, any ideal of having a mind and a life of one's own. Known for their love of beauty, the Japanese were not distinguished by the much rarer love of truth that the Greeks had coupled with it.

As might be expected, they paid a considerable price for the hierarchical system that gave their lives order, propriety, and dignity, and that enabled their leaders to lead them into a new kind of promised land. The very young and the aged enjoyed unusual freedom, but with the approach of adulthood the Japanese had to shoulder an ever-increasing burden of formal obligations, and to be forever alert in keeping in their proper place, forever bowing. Although neither Buddhism nor Shinto saddled them with a doctrine of Original Sin or a predisposition to feelings of guilt, they were always exposed to possibilities of shame or "loss of face." Their ethical vocabulary and their folklore betray some resentment of the incessant obligations, and a nostalgia for the mythical or vanished days when they did not "know shame." And the strains were naturally intensified by the problems of personal adjustment that came with modernization. As many people rose in the world, some were dizzied by the discovery of the simple personal freedoms enjoyed in the West. Many others grew more aware of social injustices by Western standards. Tensions were not relieved by any burst of creativity in literature or the arts; culturally this whole period was undistinguished—as it would be over most of the non-Western world. Activity was most vigorous in business, but at some cost to a people that had prided itself on exalting spiritual above material values. Whereas the merchant had ranked at the bottom of the social scale, an economic oligarchy now took its place at the top of the political hierarchy; the alliance between big business and the main political parties was cemented by a deal of corruption, routine in America but shocking by traditional Japanese standards. All such problems were aggravated by a familiar by-product of success in modernizing, a rapid increase in population. In the first generation this went up about 50 per cent, and by 1925 it had doubled; Japan then had to support sixty million people on its small islands.

The World War was immediately no critical turning point for the nation, only confirming its status as a world power. Although its army had nothing to do but take a German stronghold in China, its navy lent valuable aid to the Allies. Most of all it profited from a big boom in industry, which put it among the great industrial nations (if at the cost of the emergence of another Western type—the profiteer). In the decade following the war liberal, democratic tendencies grew stronger than ever before; upon the introduction of universal suffrage, the first proletarians were elected to the Diet. The naval agreement with Britain and America also appeared to promise that Japan would take its place among the great democracies. But then the World War did bring about a fateful turn by its aftermath—the world depression. This gave Japan an excuse for its invasion of Manchuria in 1931. Thereafter the military won increasing control of the government, democratic tendencies were smothered by a Japanese version of fascism, and patriots helped out by assassinating more statesmen than usual. A logical alliance with the Fascist powers of Germany and Italy prepared the way for Pearl Harbor.

Admittedly the Japanese had good excuse for their disastrous venture in imperialism. They had first tried to take care of their fast-growing population by economic rather than territorial expansion, only to raise alarm in the West over the flood of cheap Japanese goods. They were especially hard hit when their customers met the depression by raising tariffs. Among the worst offenders was America, which for a long time had been giving offense in other ways. Ever since the presidency of Theodore Roosevelt many Americans, grown big-navy minded with their own ventures in imperialism, had pointed to Japan as the potential enemy in the Pacific and talked freely of the "yellow peril." In those days Californians had insulted the nation by demanding the exclusion of Japanese immigrants and segregating their school children. Although Japan then made and lived up to an agreement to restrict immigration voluntarily, it was humiliated again in 1924: the American Congress carefully discriminated against its people in passing a new immigration law, excluding them from the quotas allowed European countries. Previously the Peace Conference of Versailles had rejected its demand for a declaration of racial equality. If it imitated the worst of the West, it had hardly been treated to the best of it in foreign relations.

At any rate, its imperialism brought out the worst in the Japanese too. The reputation they won for cruelty was due in part to a spirituality that scorned the needs of the body while professing no respect for the person. Even aside from their atrocities they were not welcomed in China or other Asiatic countries they invaded, which had once thrilled to their slogan of "Asia for the Asiatics." They not only came as conquerors but in another respect seemed peculiarly insensitive. It appears that their leaders were shocked by the discovery that their rule was not welcomed, for in their devotion to the principle of hierarchy they believed that a lowly status was quite all right so long as it was a definite status. Their national ideal of everybody in his place, doing his duty punctiliously, was reasonable enough—except that to other peoples the place and duties they prescribed still seemed arbitrary. At its best, the traditional Japanese way of life was surely an honorable way, from which Americans could learn much in grace and refinement as well as discipline; but I see no reason to believe that it was clearly superior to the ways of the free societies of the West, or better suited to the needs of One World. A chastened Japan, under an emperor who has renounced his divinity, appears to be more attracted by Western ideals of freedom and justice.

3. *The Middle East*

As the term "Middle East" was not coined until our century (by the American Admiral Mahan), so the people from Egypt to India had only begun to talk of the "West" in our sense. This term had long meant to them North Africa and Spain—outposts of their own civilization of Islam. Europe they knew as the land of peoples they had called Franks and despised as barbarians. Down to the nineteenth century they continued to take for granted their superiority over these infidels, being disturbed only by Russian aggressions on the Ottoman Empire. The first great shock came in 1798, when a Frankish general, Bonaparte, invaded and easily conquered Egypt. Then one of their greater historians noted the "most portentous" event of this extraordinary year —"the cessation of the Pilgrimage" from Egypt to Mecca. Islam, for centuries complacent in torpor, had still worse shocks coming. It was shaken to both its spiritual and its political foundations as it began to realize that it was not self-sufficient, and that Europe had grown far more powerful. Moslems found more meaningful an old saying: "This world is the prison of the believers and the paradise of the unbelievers."

One common response of their intellectuals was summed up by the Egyptian Lutfi al-Sayyid: "The wave of civilization has come to us with all its virtues and vices, and we must accept it without resisting it." In trying to make the best of it, he added, Egypt had to assimilate not only the science and technology but the philosophical ideas that had made possible the progress of the West—just as the old Arabs had learned from the Greeks. Earlier a young Turkish diplomat had drawn a more specific moral when he contemplated a statue of freedom at the entrance of the Great Exhibition of 1878 in Paris:

> Oh worthy visitors! When you look upon this fascinating display of human progress, do not forget that all these achievements are the work of freedom. It is under the protection of freedom that peoples and nations attain happiness. Without freedom, there can be no security; without security, no endeavor; without endeavor, no prosperity; without prosperity, no happiness.

A much more popular response, however, was a violent revulsion against the West, which would produce more hatred of it in the Middle East than any other region. Islam reasserted, often fanatically, the superiority of its whole way of life, based on the one true faith. Mohammed had given all the answers men needed.

Both of these opposed ways still have many adherents and remain forces to be reckoned with, possible bets for the future; but neither has so far dominated Islam. The immediate future belonged rather to different movements somewhere between the extremes. Early in the nineteenth century military men took the lead in efforts to modernize, first of all the army; they could not for a moment deny the superiority of the West in technology. They took some interest in political reform too, but not primarily because of ideals of freedom; for their military purposes they wanted to strengthen governments that had been notoriously incompetent and corrupt. Out of this movement came the Young Turks, whose Society for Union and Progress in 1908 forced the despotic Sultan Abdul-Hamid to proclaim a republican Constitution. Although they inspired much talk about freedom, as well as fury over their ways as "Devils" aping the West, they soon revealed a limited conception of freedom: their way of achieving Union and Progress was the old way of muzzling or murdering their opponents. They were more stylish when they waved a new banner, Pan-Turkism, appealing to another movement that had been growing strong—nationalism. This was quite alien to Islam, whose people had had local or tribal loyalties but otherwise thought of themselves first as Moslems. (Arabic had no word for Arabia, nor Turkish for Turkey.) Beginning as simple patriotism, it developed into a nationalism much like that of Russia and central Europe—romantic, chauvinistic, mostly indifferent to the cause of personal freedom. It may be considered a still more unfortunate consequence of Western intrusion because most of Islam lacked clearly defined national states with national traditions, which in Europe could excuse it; only in relatively compact, homogeneous Egypt did such new slogans as "Egypt for the Egyptians" (coined by a Christian journalist) make good sense. Nevertheless, nationalism could arouse great efforts. It helped to inspire the most astounding response of the Middle East to the World War—the revolution of Mustafa Kemal that gave him the name Atatürk, "Father Turk."

When the victorious Allies began to fulfill their secret treaties by carving up Turkey, and a Greek army invaded it with their compliance, Atatürk defied the sultan too by organizing resistance in central Anatolia and setting up a new government. Although the Ottoman Empire had lost up to a quarter of its population in the World War, through starvation and disease as well as casualties in battle, he succeeded in driving out the Greeks after an exceptionally heroic, atrocious war, and then largely dictated new peace terms to the Allies. Undismayed by the loss of Ottoman provinces in the Middle East, he proceeded at once to tackle the terrific job of modernizing the impoverished remnant of the empire in Turkey proper. As one of the Young Turks, the hero of Gallipoli had learned his lesson from their otherwise dismal record in both the Balkan War and the World War: it was not enough to modernize technology and reform the government—the whole society had to be made over, and with it the mentality of the people. His model was the West, "the family of civilized nations" that he declared was the only real civilization. In his endeavor to Westernize Turkey he then went much faster and farther even than the Japanese had.

Thus he did away with the 600-year-old sultanate, in its stead establishing a republic. With it and the caliphate he scrapped the Sacred Law of Islam, substituting the Swiss civil code. While beginning to modernize the economy, he forced Turks to learn how to manage the commerce and industry that had been left to Greeks and Armenians. He started a system of public schools to provide a purely secular education. He replaced the Arabic by the Latin script, changed the alphabet, and began purging the Turkish language of many Arabic and Persian words. Likewise he replaced the Islamic by the Gregorian calendar and made Sunday the day of rest. He put his people into Western clothes, requiring men to wear hats instead of fezzes. He conferred complete equality upon women, including the rights to vote and to divorce; long degraded as women had been in no other civilization, they soon had proportionately more representatives in the Grand National Assembly than American women have in Congress today. And so it went—on every social front, all within half a generation. But the essential difference between Atatürk's program and that of Japan was his attack on the traditional religion. Most of his reforms were designed to weaken the authority of Islam, completely separate it from the state, and remove its influence from all other spheres of social life. Thus his new Turkish language with its Latin script at once cut all school children off from the Moslem classics, while it made illiterate all educated Moslems who wanted to read the newspapers or hold any position in public life.

Atatürk did not succeed, of course, in shaking off the hold of Islam on the Turks. It remained strong, especially on the peasants, by far the largest part of the population; and in recent years the government has been making concessions to it, such as religious instruction in the public schools. At the same time Atatürk's efforts to modernize his country fell far short of the Japanese success. Today, more than a generation after his revolution, Turkey is still a poor country, with relatively little industry, a backward economy, a shaky government, masses of illiterate peasants, and much less drive than Japan. The reasons for his relative failure are quite clear and still pertinent; they bear directly on the efforts being made by the rest of Islam, which also remains far behind Japan. But they call first for a tribute to the measure of success of his extraordinary enterprise, which most vividly illustrates the basic dilemmas confronting the non-Western world, as well as the truism that no revolutionary can ever foretell the ultimate results of his work.[4]

---

[4] I have presented a much fuller account of modern Turkey in Chapt. 10 of *The Loom of History* (1958). This was based on my experiences in the country after World War II, when its problems were complicated by the need for maintaining a large army in self-

"If in the last few years we have been able to save ourselves," Atatürk told his fellow Turks, "it has been because of the change in our mentality. We can never stop again. We're going on, whatever happens; we can't go back. We must go on; we have no choice." At least the Turks are still going on, if in ways confused and uncertain. Most educated ones are still facing West; almost none dream of going back to the Ottoman regime. In public life Atatürk ended this regime once and for all, made it virtually impossible to go back. He remains the father of modern Turkey, revered as its greatest hero, because he had indeed aroused the people, given them a new self-respect, and filled many of the young in particular with something of his terrific determination. He achieved substantial progress toward modernization, reducing illiteracy and disease, making a start in land reform, leaving the people on the whole better off than the common people were in all other Islamic countries, less at the mercy of a very wealthy few or a corrupt government. To carry on his endeavor he left a larger middle class, and a broader and more active elite. Most of his major reforms have endured, including such remarkable ones as the emancipation of women and equal suffrage. In view of his legacy from the Ottoman Empire, his failures are much less surprising than his lasting achievements.

This legacy was even more of an incubus than he realized. To begin with, Atatürk took over a country as backward as any nominally civilized country in the world. The great bulk of its people were illiterate peasants, farming by the most primitive methods. It had no good roads, no industry to speak of, no native tradition of enterprise; its business was run largely by foreigners and racial minorities, who likewise largely monopolized what little modern technology it had mastered for all but military purposes. For ambitious Turks the chief field of opportunity outside the army and the church had been the government, a bureaucracy with a long tradition of corruption and fantastic inefficiency. In all spheres independence of spirit was discouraged, as were private associations for independent purposes. Authoritarianism was the key to the Ottoman mentality that Atatürk was resolved to Westernize, and that he said had changed, though he knew it had not in most of the peasantry. It indeed served his purposes by the

---

defense against the Soviet; but the main issues of the new Turkey were clearly defined before 1938, the year Atatürk died. Here I wish to repeat my tribute to the ordinary people, who in their still "underdeveloped" country may appear backward, and whose admirable qualities may have little bearing on my present concern—except that these may suffer from modernization. A traveler will meet no more honest, obliging, and hospitable a person than the "terrible Turk" in the countryside.

habit of obedience; foreigners had often observed that most Turks regarded an act of government as much like an act of God, expecting both to be arbitrary. Nevertheless this mentality always menaced the enterprising, experimental spirit called for by his program; and it soon carried over into his own enterprises. In government, which he tried to build all over again, he ended with a bureaucracy as cumbersome, wasteful, and fearful of individual initiative. In education the ideal remained perfect learning by rote, without question or discussion; independent thinking was frowned on in universities too, and rarely indulged anyhow by students who had never been encouraged to think for themselves. In science and technology the best students could carry out instructions faithfully, but few were capable of research on their own. Untrained in habits of self-reliance, the builders of the new Turkey exhibited little creativity alike in government, business, and culture.

More ambiguous were the consequences of the nationalism that Aataürk took pains to foster. The patriotism inspired by his heroic defense of the country was no doubt absolutely essential to the success of his revolutionary program, and it brought out the best in his people. He both simplified and purified his cause by renouncing not only Pan-Islam but Pan-Turkism, any allegiance to the related peoples in central Asia. Sticking to the slogan "Turkey for the Turks," he shifted the capital from cosmopolitan Istanbul to Ankara in the heart of Anatolia, where he appealed especially to the peasants, the forgotten men of the Ottoman Empire and the last of its subjects to be emancipated. City people had not even called themselves "Turks," which was commonly a term of contempt applied to Anatolian peasants; now Atatürk described them as "the masters of the country," honoring the fortitude and loyalty that had enabled him to save it. In renouncing Pan-Turkism, moreover, he explicitly renounced all design of territorial expansion or aggression against other countries. The nationalism he proclaimed was in the liberal tradition of the West, compatible with the ideal of international order and peace, for which he himself worked in his foreign policy, and which emphasized his own rare qualities as a military hero who put away his uniform, gave up all thought of winning more military glory. Similarly the pride in the Turkish past that he tried to build up could ideally preserve the best of its tradition, and hence enrich both the national life and the world commonwealth of culture. "Turkism" meant that the country could take a dignified place in "the family of civilized nations."

Yet it also tended to cloud and finally to defeat Atatürk's purposes. Under his guidance scholars began creating a mythical past, including such delusions of grandeur as that the Turks were the parents of the whole family, the very authors of civilization. (The Sumerians were made out to be a Turkish people.) National pride was inflated by the usual distractions from concern with the public welfare; agriculture— the livelihood of "the masters" of the country—was neglected while money went into fancy industrial enterprises, such as a useless airplane wing factory, and much pretentious building in Ankara. Turkism then led to a glorification of the Ottoman past, the very tradition Atatürk was trying to repudiate.[5] It heightened sensitivity to any criticism of Turkish methods, stiffened resistance to the advice from Western experts that the Turks sought and needed, and so helped to keep the economy backward. Worse, it discouraged healthy self-criticism, which was more necessary because the state was trying to do so much more for the people. As "Turk-disparagement" became a punishable offense, so the government silenced its critics, calling them traitors.

Hence it called attention to the oppressive tendencies of Atatürk's rule, and another of the dilemmas confronting almost all non-Western countries. The "Republic" he set up was a one-party state, and he, its "President," soon became in fact a dictator. Temperamentally an Oriental autocrat, who had been elected by a small majority of the Grand National Assembly, he took no chances with either a liberal or a reactionary opposition; within two years of the founding of the Republic he ruthlessly suppressed all political opposition, hanging a number of eminent men. The trouble remains that dictatorship too was no doubt necessary to his success. Certainly he could never have established at once a full democracy in a country 90 per cent illiterate, with almost no experience in popular government, nor could pure parliamentary government have devised and carried through so radical a program as his; he had to force his measures through the Assembly. And however cynical in his methods, he was unquestionably patriotic, wholly devoted to the best interests of his people as he saw them. No demagogue or mere power-seeker would ever have worked so hard at so unglamorous a task, for such thoroughgoing reform.

The issue was complicated because Atatürk apparently set a Western type of state as his goal for the long run. Unlike Mussolini and Hitler

---

5 An incidental consequence is the proud display of the treasures of the sultans in Istanbul. For barbaric splendor, waste, and folly, these are rivaled only by the treasures of the czars in the Kremlin, likewise amassed at the expense of an impoverished peasantry.

(whom he privately criticized), he did not celebrate either dictatorship or elitism on principle, but constantly took pains to explain and defend his measures to the people, without demagoguery. After the early hangings he no longer resorted to terrorism or any systematic oppression. When the ambiguity of his position led a journalist to ask him whether he was a dictator, he answered, "If I were, you would not be allowed to ask me that question." He could write: "I have always been wholeheartedly in favor of the system of free discussion of national affairs, and the seeking of the nation's best interests by the efforts of all men and parties of good will." His party as he left it, at any rate, before many years permitted the formation of a rival Democratic party, and then even permitted it to win a free, honest election by secret ballot. Within a generation the Turkey he created had achieved a remarkable measure of democracy, considerably more than Japan had in its first generation. But then the deeper trouble appeared. Once in power, the Democrats in turn grew oppressive and began muzzling criticism of their policies, which were less disinterested than Atatürk's: their opponents ostensibly lacked "good will." (One of their newspapers attacked a rival editor for telling an American reporter that Turkey did not enjoy complete freedom of press, adding indignantly that if his paper repeated such slanderous remarks it should be suppressed for good.) Even enlightened, benevolent dictatorship provides a clouded atmosphere in which to develop democratic habits, engrain the indispensable idea of a loyal opposition.

The principle of "statism" that Atatürk had written into the Turkish Constitution was less bothersome. The crisis of the world depression convinced him that the state had to take charge of the economy, own or control basic industries and mines as well as railroads and public utilities, and a Five-Year Plan then dramatized the measure of socialism practically unavoidable in underdeveloped countries seeking to modernize rapidly. This policy stirred relatively little opposition, since Turkey had no big capitalistic enterprise of its own; if the government did an inefficient job, there were few if any businessmen prepared to do a better one. Neither was there wide indignation when the Democrats later turned over some state industries to private enterprise, now grown more experienced, and so gave Turkey a kind of mixed economy more like that of European democracies. Atatürk had never proposed to collectivize the economy, do away with private enterprise, or interfere at all with agriculture. Although he got indispensable aid from Lenin during his war with the Greeks, and signed a treaty of friendship with the Soviet, communism was no more his ideal than fascism. Turkish delegates returning from an early congress of the Comintern, who were stoned by villagers en route, were arrested and thrown into the sea by the government.[6] Communists remained a negligible influence in Turkey, useful to the authorities as a brand-name for any critics of the government, long before Russia under Stalin resumed its traditional role as the main enemy. The Turkish peasant soldiers were always ready to fight it, but not because of any passion for either statism or democracy.

They were still mostly loyal Moslems, however, and they bring up the final issue of Atatürk's efforts. In no other Moslem country has an important liberation movement cut itself loose from Islam, or any political leader dared to disavow it openly, no matter how secular his primary concerns. Atatürk, long an agnostic, considered it simply a superstition; but in any case he had obviously good cause for his attack on it. Religious leaders were generally hostile to his program of Westernization, and not because of fervor for religious or any other kind of freedom; they represented the ultra-conservative, authoritarian tendencies that had dominated Islam throughout the centuries of its torpor; and these tendencies were a more serious obstacle because Islam was no mere religion but a whole way of life, unlike Christianity dominating law, education, culture—all other major interests except business and war. The religious revival in recent years, and the concessions to it by which the Democrats sought popularity, have in general vindicated Atatürk's policy; for what came out of the revival was mainly the old-time religion and with it considerable fanaticism, promoting hatred of the West. But the question remains whether Atatürk might not have done better by seeking some compromise, recognizing the spiritual force that Islam plainly was, and looking into its possible uses for his own purposes. This is a question of much wider import, involving the whole Moslem world—some 300,000,000 people. And though as usual it cannot be answered positively, we may now better size up the alternatives pursued by the rest of the Moslem countries, all of which have become independent since Atatürk's death and are trying to modernize on an Islamic basis.

First it should be noted that the Turks had an advantage shared

---

6 *Izvestia* had characteristically hailed the Turkish revolution as "the first Soviet revolution in Asia." Lenin soon knew better, but as a pragmatist he continued to support Atatürk, whose alliance was useful to him. As always, orthodoxy required neither logical consistency nor steady idealism.

only by the Persians. The Ottoman Empire was propped up by Europe during its long decay, protected by Britain especially against possible conquest by the Russians; it remained independent and its homeland was never invaded until the World War, whereupon Atatürk drove out the Greeks. Hence the Turks could always feel that they were by nature a ruling race, and Atatürk could tell them that throughout their history they had been "a byword for freedom and independence." By contrast, the Árab countries were obviously dominated by Europe, no less because they had not been conquered in battle—they were too feeble to resist. Thus when Egypt was occupied by a British force in 1882, ostensibly for a limited time and purpose, the British stayed on and took charge of the country. Western domination was more disruptive in the Middle East just because it was not pure colonialism. Policy was less clear and consistent than it was with subject peoples in crown colonies, rule was less stable and responsible; the limited or nominal autonomy granted native rulers tended to make them as irresponsible.

Resentment was then enflamed by the World War, during which Britain and America held out promises of self-determination. The excitement in Egypt won it a grant of independence in 1922, though with reservations that were not withdrawn until years later; Britain made too plain its reluctance to give up its control of the country. Together with France it intensified Arab nationalism by protectorates over Syria, Lebanon, Palestine, and Iraq, formerly under Ottoman rule. The Arabs had felt enough resentment of the Turks to join the British in fighting them, but they felt far more under infidel masters who had gone back on their promise of freedom. They were inclined to sympathy with Hitler's Germany, as later they would be with the Soviet, simply because it was an enemy of the West. And though most of them were neither outright Fascists nor Communists, they were not repelled either by the tyranny of totalitarianism; for the independence they clamored for had little connection with the ideals of political freedom that had spread in Islam during the nineteenth century.

These ideals could be based, as they still are by liberal Moslems, on principles of liberty and equality stated explicitly in the Koran. The main reason for their spread, however, was Western influence. Thus in 1861 the Bey of Tunis proclaimed the first constitution in the history of Islam, providing for the first experiment in parliamentary government. When the British occupied Egypt they supported similar experiments that had started some years earlier, and helped the Egyptians to establish a constitutional government with a measure of political freedom. Likewise they and the French established such governments in their protectorates after the World War. In the period between the world wars constitutions and parliaments became the vogue all over the Middle East, and Islam appeared to be headed for democracy. Yet almost all these constitutions were scrapped when its nations won their independence, and the whole effort at democratic government collapsed —nowhere more completely than in Egypt, which had had the longest experience with parliaments. Although the failure of the movement toward political freedom was briefly disguised when most of the newly independent countries called themselves "republics," this meant only that they had dethroned their kings. The kings deserved their fate, none more so than the fatuous, corrupt, obscene Faruk of Egypt; but a republic in Islam had no necessary connection whatever with democracy. The successors of the monarchs were dictators. The struggles that went on were between small minorities, factions headed by rival candidates for dictatorship.

The revulsion against democracy was not at all surprising, nor simply deplorable. The parliamentary governments had been imposed by Europeans or a few Westernizers, with the active support only of some intellectuals and aspiring politicians. The common people were wholly unprepared to take a live, much less intelligent interest in them; they comprised the usual mass of illiterate peasants, a negligible working class deserving the name *lumpen-proletariat,* and a small middle class, whose businessmen were mostly of alien extraction and had no tradition of political responsibility. The rising nationalism, focused on the cause of independence from foreign rule, only obscured both democratic ideals and the immediate actuality of peoples not at all ready for self-government. Similarly the growing hatred of the West blinded Arabs to the freedoms they enjoyed under European rule, and to the necessary conditions for maintaining such freedoms on their own. The real grievances from which the hatred sprang were beyond the comprehension of most men, for they had not been brutally exploited —merely humiliated and left stranded by an indirect, absent-minded kind of imperialism that assumed too little serious responsibility for good government. The hatred accordingly grew more irrational, as America would discover: Arabs would be no less hostile to it, though it had never ruled them, while much more friendly to the Soviet, though it ruled over Moslem peoples in central Asia. The archenemy of "imperialism" could distract attention from tyranny or misrule at home.

Wanting above all to be strong, the Arab countries were likely to get oppressive government, which was as likely to become weak government.

But the most uniform, deep-seated reason for the collapse of the movement toward democracy was the legacy of Islam. Granted the democratic principles stated in the Koran, Islam in its prime had never realized these principles in political life nor made a serious effort to realize them. Instead of constitutions, parliaments, or any kind of representative government, it produced only autocracy, while teaching that obedience to caliph or sultan was a religious duty too. "Freedom" became a purely legal concept, distinguishing the free man from the slave; it gave him no political rights. As its brilliant period faded, Islam settled down into the rigid authoritarianism that governed both its political and its intellectual life thereafter.[7] During the centuries of stagnation the Arab world became inured to the root evils summed up by Edward Atiyah, a champion of the Arabs: "the poverty and ignorance of the vast majority . . . the little-cared-for health and well-being of the masses . . . the selfishness and cynicism of the big merchants and land-owners . . . the inefficiency and corruption of the governments that grew out of, and reflected, this unhealthy state of society." Add that the many religious fundamentalists in Islam are still hostile to efforts at popular enlightenment and social reform, and this is pretty much the state of modern Persia too, which had preserved its independence. It retained the liberal constitution that came out of the revolution in 1906, and under a vigorous shah in the twenties made a start at modernizing, but observance of the constitution was largely nominal, the social structure remained rotten, and only in recent years has the government made a serious effort to emancipate the peasants from the big landowners. (As I write, a reform premier has been assassinated by a Moslem fanatic.) Like the Arab countries, Iran has made less progress toward modernization than Turkey has, despite the advantage of its oil. The chief exception is little Lebanon, which is also the only other country to retain its constitution; but it is only half Moslem.

A striking contrast was offered by another people in the Middle East who became fervent nationalists—the Jews. In the nineteenth century they started coming to Palestine from central or eastern Europe, under the pressure of anti-Semitism; Zionism was the Jewish response.

[7] For a fuller account of the history of Islam in this context, see *Freedom in the Western World*, Chap. 1.

Following the World War many more came because Britain, given Palestine as a mandate, promised them a "homeland." Still more sought refuge when Hitler began his persecution, but were denied entrance; Britain, wooing Arab support, restricted immigration and in 1939 prohibited it. And though by that time there were only about half a million Jews in Palestine, the lines of the future battle were already drawn. Resembling Arab nationalism in its close connection with religion, Zionism differed in its aspiration to not only independence but political freedom, the establishment of a democratic state. While the Jews had more reason to resent the West, they had assimilated much more of its culture and took naturally to its political ways. A strong labor movement, for instance, was fought by the Arabs under the leadership of the Mufti of Jerusalem. (He was supported by the Comintern, which as usual subordinated the interests of labor to Soviet foreign policy.) The Jews further exasperated Moslems by modernizing much more rapidly. Hatred of them reached its present peak of ferocity when they won their independence from Britain and clinched it by defeating the Arab countries in war. A shocking demonstration of the backwardness of these far more populous countries, it was more humiliating because Israel was a "Western" country.

It accordingly spotlighted the crux of the matter, the common observation that the essential conflict between Islamic countries and the West is not political but cultural—a conflict between civilizations. Islam has been profoundly, permanently affected by the impact of the West; yet it has retained its identity and its vitality as an autonomous culture more successfully than have the ancient civilizations of India and China. It is still inclined to be most defiant because it did not give in on fundamentals, as Atatürk did. Presumably it will go on trying to modernize, but until it has made considerably more progress it will most likely continue to feel more resentful than grateful to the West for all that it has borrowed in culture and technology, a tacit admission of the superiority of the West. It might recover its poise through more creativity in culture, which has been generally barren of great or original work in this century. Its political experiments, like that of Turkey, may well become more liberal as its people become literate and capable of self-government. "Arab socialism" as defined by President Nasser, for example, is on paper essentially democratic, only using other than constitutional or parliamentary means to the end of "social justice and equity for the oppressed class," finally "economic liberty and social equality" for all.

Meanwhile these slogans have a distinctly Western ring, inasmuch as they hardly resounded through Arab history; and they raise the question of what an autonomous Islam has to offer in return to the West and the rest of mankind today, beyond the principles it shares with Judaism and Christianity, and the great works of its brilliant period that have entered the common heritage. Its most apparent advantage over Christianity is an explicit ideal of racial equality that has traditionally been maintained in practice. Arnold Toynbee, a specialist in these spiritual matters, adds that it may help to cure the world's ills by its traditionally strong feeling of unity and the brotherhood of Man. This is questionable, however, even apart from the fervid nationalism in Islam today. The brotherhood was always confined to Moslems— the rest of mankind were infidels, eligible for holy war. Although Islam in its prime was much more tolerant than Christendom, it grew more exclusive during its decline, and it has not kept pace with the liberal movements in Christianity in this century. Most of its religious leaders are still conservatives, many of them reactionaries; very few of its liberals dare to say openly what I assume many of them believe, that Mohammed was a fallible man and the Koran was his word, not literally dictated by the Angel Gabriel. The limited freedom of its intellectuals makes it harder for them to be effectual. So far the very strength of its tradition, I should say, precludes Islam from breaking any new paths for mankind or suggesting better alternatives to the ways of the West. At best it may bring a tradition of discipline to the support of these ways.[8]

4. India

"If I were to ask myself," wrote Max Müller, an early student of Sanskrit, "from what literature we here in Europe—we who have been nurtured almost exclusively on the thoughts of the Greeks and the Romans, and of one Semitic race, the Jewish—may draw that corrective which is most wanted in order to make our inner life more perfect, more comprehensive, more universal, in fact, more truly human a life,

[8] Toynbee has remarked another possible contribution in Mohammed's prohibition of liquor. Most men, however, stubbornly refuse to consider prohibition a mode of "true freedom," and want to go on drinking as the human race has done throughout its recorded history. A great many Moslems also feel free to drink, with a preference for hard liquor, since the literal-minded Prophet banned only wine.

not for this life alone but a transfigured and eternal life, again I should point to India." The experience of India has come to seem still more pertinent in an "Age of Anxiety." It has had a far longer history than either Islam or Europe, maintaining the self-sufficient culture that was approaching a golden age when the Roman Empire was collapsing. Centuries before Christ it gave birth to two of the world's major religions, which stamped it as the most spiritual of the great societies. Although Hinduism and Buddhism resembled early Christianity as otherworldly salvation religions, they differed from it in fundamental respects and nurtured ways of life as fundamentally different from Western ways, above all the American way; it is especially to India that disillusioned Westerners from Schopenhauer on have looked for a truer wisdom and piety, or peace of mind. At the same time, India under British rule had an intimate association with the West that until the World War was friendlier and more fruitful than the experience of other colonial peoples, and for which its intelligentsia were more grateful, especially after it won its independence. It became the great hope of the West in Asia as the most democratic of the newly independent nations, not to mention the most populous democracy in the world. As Arnold Toynbee sees it, "our Western iron has probably entered deeper into India's soul" than any other. Others may see considerably more of this iron in the soul of modern China—both Red and Nationalist—and regard the experience of India as a unique effort to unite a venerable Eastern tradition with the liberal tradition of the West.[9]

In either view no society presents more striking incongruities. A land swarming with diverse peoples, speaking at least a dozen languages, India was never a nation through its long history until Britain made it one. It was held together by its religion, which stressed the oneness of man with Brahma, and by its fantastic caste system, which most rigidly separated people and condemned millions of them to the status of untouchables, the most degraded status known to history. Another name for its prolonged cultural self-sufficiency was parochialism, although no religion was more catholic and hospitable than Hinduism, and among

---

[9] I should acknowledge that in the eyes of orthodox Hindus I am completely unqualified to do justice to their tradition. One who reviewed my *Freedom in the Ancient World* described me as a pure materialist, "totally lacking in any spiritual understanding," who defines freedom as the American way of life and considers our "civilization of gadgets and tranquilizers" the summit of man's achievement. Although I must believe that this misrepresents my position, I have made a point of going to Indian sources for judgments of their tradition. My criticisms of it are substantially those of Nehru, who was perhaps not spiritual enough by traditional standards, but was not a pure materialist either, much less a devotee of the American way of life.

its consequences was about the longest period of stagnation in the history of civilization. The spirituality for which it became famous was similarly the most ambivalent in religious history. Hinduism was hospitable to all kinds of primitive superstition, which came down to a gross materialism; it reigned over a land teeming with holy men, fortune-tellers, and temple prostitutes, pervaded by the odor of sanctity and of indiscriminate defecation; it enabled men to achieve the ultimate in spiritual self-reliance, and in callous indifference to the misery of fellow men; and so on—down to the saintliness of Ramakrishna and Gandhi, and the sulky arrogance of Krishna Menon. At both its best and its worst, it appeared more completely opposed to Western tradition than any other civilized tradition, yet has been accommodated to it: partly because Hinduism had a genius for assimilation, partly because through the British its devotees became more conscious of both the best and the worst.

The political history of India before the British arrived may be dismissed briefly here. The early civilization in the Indus Valley survived in some cultural motifs but not in political tradition; it was entirely forgotten until excavated by Europeans in this century. The Aryans who came in about 1500 B.C., inaugurating a long series of foreign invasions, left their mark chiefly on religion and the caste system, which apparently evolved from their efforts to maintain their superiority over the native population. (Herodotus knew that a fair race in India ruled over dark aboriginals.) The rise of the first considerable empire, the Mauryan in North India, was stimulated by the invasion of Alexander the Great but Persians seem to have had more influence on it; in any case, it settled down as a typical Oriental sacred monarchy. Its glory was the Buddhist Emperor Asoka, grandson of the founder, who is still revered in India because after conquest he renounced war and tried to make amends for the misery he had caused; but while this made him unique among the great monarchs of recorded history, it unfortunately did not establish a new tradition or avert the usual fate of empire—the Mauryan regime began disintegrating after his death. In the fourth century A.D. a greater empire arose under the Hindu Guptas, holding up until the seventh century, and in culture stimulating the most creative period in Indian history. This golden age contributed no new political institutions to speak of, however, and the Gupta Empire was the last native one of consequence. In the centuries of confusion that followed, Hinduism was consolidated, the Brahmans established themselves as the leading caste, and society grew more conspicuously conservative, passive, and indrawn.

A commission of Indian scholars that in recent years scoured their political history for traditions serviceable for the new purposes of their democracy could find only the self-sufficient village, often autonomous, which they realized was not very different from the timeless village all over the non-Western world. What political thought had been recorded was fragmentary and perfunctory, little concerned with basic principles and less with such notions as the rights of subjects.

The Turkish invaders who planted Islam in India turned out to be something of a godsend even though they came with fire and sword. Firmly established from the twelfth century on, they restored order to North India and protected it against devastation by the Mongols. In the sixteenth century the Turkish conqueror Babur founded the brilliant Mogul Empire, which made India known to Europe as the land of the Great Mogul. The reign of the greatest of its emperors, Akbar (1556–1605), introduced an era of peace and prosperity such as the country had not known for a thousand years. An agnostic philosopher-king, he sought to unify the empire by treating Hindus as equals. But except for this tolerance, reminiscent of Asoka, Akbar introduced no novel political ideas or institutions. He founded a cult that gave him an aura of sanctity, like other Oriental monarchs; he did nothing for the peasants, who as usual paid the costs of the splendor of the empire. A century after his death the familiar decline set in, during which peasants suffered still more from tax collectors and Hindus grew resentful of their Moslem rulers, though without growing any more vigorous or creative. A land that had not yet become a nation was more deeply split than in the past, since Hinduism had been unable to assimilate the Moslems as it had previous invaders. The British, who had not come as conquerors, gradually took charge of the country through their East India Company, and in the process learned that the land of the Great Mogul was not the "real" India. This belonged to Hinduism —the heart, mind, and soul of its civilization.

At first glance, Hinduism is another swarm—an astonishing medley of ritual and belief, sect and school, with hordes of gods between man and Brahma: altogether most abundantly, extravagantly fulfilling St. Paul's aspiration to be "all things to all men," including even agnostics. Nevertheless Brahma, or the World Soul, provided a basic unity. The countless deities were ranged under the great gods Vishnu and Shiva, who were manifestations of Brahma. This was a pantheistic God, immanent in the human soul, that all men could therefore know directly, and trained mystics knew only somewhat more perfectly. The idea of incarnation that served as a bridge to monism was amplified by the common belief in reincarnation or transmigration, with the related ethical doctrine of karma—that a man's deeds in this lifetime determine his status in his next incarnation. Likewise the essential mysticism underlying all the varieties of Hinduism led to a general agreement that the highest goods were won by detachment from the temporal sensory world, in the holiest men by a renunciation of worldly goods and a liberation from consciousness of self. However diverse their practice and belief, accordingly, all Hindus *felt* akin. And always their feeling of unity was reinforced in daily life by their common acceptance of the Hindu institution of caste. Although its origins are obscure, it was clearly established by 500 B.C., and ever after to this century it worked powerfully to maintain obedience and order.

The caste system survived the attack on the Brahmans by Buddha, an apparent atheist, who with Confucius, Zoroaster, and Isaiah made the sixth century B.C. the most remarkable period in the history of religion. Although he might have seemed a dangerous enemy to Hinduism, he and his followers never disrupted India as Protestantism did Europe. He offered only another way of salvation that all men could attain through the familiar means of meditation, nonattachment, and renunciation, and Buddhism as popularized by his followers looked more like just another Hindu sect. He himself was brought into the ubiquitous company of savior gods. In Mahayana Buddhism (the "Great Vehicle") Hindu exuberance produced a host of saviors, bodhisattvas who by following the master's way had gone up through enough reincarnations to demonstrate that any man could become a Buddha. As the first great missionary religion Buddhism was further transformed when it spread over China, Japan, and Southeast Asia, sometimes surrendering even its founder's basic doctrine of renunciation, until it resembled Hinduism chiefly in its hospitality and tolerance of diversity. In India itself, strangely, it died out after more than a thousand years of vigorous life; but its disappearance seems less strange in view of the genius of Hinduism. While its popular forms absorbed much Hindu belief and practice, Hindu thought assimilated Buddha's lofty teaching about the necessity of enlightenment and spiritual discipline instead of ritual and priestcraft. The Upanishads, dating from about his period, likewise emphasized knowledge as the way to salvation.

Let us therefore consider at once what Hinduism has to offer the modern world, beginning with its advantages over both Christianity and Islam in serving the religious needs still felt by most men. It bases its claims not on a doubtful historical revelation but squarely on religious experience, the spiritual consciousness inherent in all men; it asserts in effect that God has always revealed himself to all men everywhere, as one would expect of a universal deity. It stresses the sense of oneness with God or cosmos that all men may feel in meditation or transport, when they get beyond their little selves, and that may give men a deeper sense of community, make more meaningful the One World in which they have now been brought together. At the same time it respects knowledge and the claims of reason, never having suffered from the conflict with reason and science that has plagued Christianity and Islam. Unlike them, it has never pretended to finality or totality; its holy men have always taken for granted that man is finite and fallible, that his many gods represent necessarily limited, partial visions of Brahma, and that any claims to a monopoly on divine truth are as blasphemous as irrational. Hinduism frankly declares itself to be what man's whole religious history has in fact been—a spiritual quest. It remains on principle an "open" religion, suited to an open society. In the words of Radhakrishnan, it offers "a spiritual home where we can live without surrendering the rights of reason or the needs of humanity," which are no longer compatible with a dogmatic supernaturalism. He sums up the reason for the appalling record of crime committed in the name of Christ and Allah, an idealism sacrilegious in its exclusiveness: "If we believe absurdities, we shall commit atrocities."

For the purposes of a free society, Hinduism accordingly has some comparable advantages. Tolerant on principle, it regards religious freedom as not merely an expedient concession but a necessity of the religious spirit itself. Although in this century it has bred unwonted fanaticism, because of conflict with Moslems in India, no Hindu thinker would ever say, as Karl Barth once did, that an effort to see or admit anything valuable in other religions was only "howling with the wolves" or giving in to their demons. Similarly Hinduism is free from the authoritarianism of Christianity and Islam, for it requires no strict faith in any set of dogmas, gives no church or priesthood exclusive control over the means to salvation. In particular it most emphatically asserts a principle of spiritual self-reliance. It declares that every man is not only free but able to achieve his immortal destiny here and now, and that he requires no uncertain gift of divine grace to do so; God is within him, never against him, never having cursed the race with original sin. Historically, Hinduism has most clearly demonstrated in practice as well as affirmed in theory the actual power of the human spirit, and has made most meaningful the concept of "spiritual freedom." Not only its holy men but many ordinary Hindus have attained a composure, an inner peace, a tranquil freedom from care and need that contrasted with the tyrannous desires and fears of most Westerners even before our age of anxiety.

In this view more can be said on behalf of the caste system, representing the most extraordinary effort in history to achieve a completely static, closed society. The original four castes—priests and scholars, rulers and warriors, artisans and merchants, and unskilled workers— made for an orderly provision of wisdom, power, skill, and labor resembling the estates in medieval Europe. As like everything else in swarming India the system proliferated into more than 3,000 castes and subcastes, it incidentally helped to assimilate invaders, who could be assigned new quarters in the commodious institution, but it also provided an efficient, harmonious division of labor to meet the demands of growing complexity and heterogeneity. Each caste had its own body of custom and law to order the life of its members. Since every man had a definite appointed place, all were protected against economic competition, class conflict, and arbitrary rule, and could feel secure. Hence an institution that might have been expected to discourage cooperative effort and weaken communal bonds actually maintained a strong sense of solidarity; it held India together for more than two thousand years in spite of all the foreign invasions, political confusions, and spells of anarchy—a feat unequaled by any Western society past or present. Possible resentments of a hierarchy in which status was determined arbitrarily, absolutely, by birth instead of merit were relieved by the principle of karma, which assured men a higher status in their next incarnation if they did their proper duty in this one.

Yet the caste system also represented the ultimate in segregation or *apartheid* (now deplored by Indians when practiced in Western countries), and it preserved not only glaring inequities but some monstrous iniquities. The lower caste of workers or slaves was early forbidden even to recite or listen to the Vedic texts, under penalty of torture. This taboo led to the pure abomination of the untouchables, who came to number about a seventh of the population—creatures excluded from temples, schools, public conveyances, and all decent company, since any association with them was considered more defiling than the company of animals. They recall other common practices, such as the burning of widows, that seemed more abominable in a society that made the life of the spirit its main business. And through the ages the Brahmans of India remained tranquil and composed in the face of appalling misery as well as apparent injustice. "No society," confessed Vivekananda, a modern holy man, "puts its foot on the neck of the wretched so mercilessly as does India." The common spectacle of people starving to death—even the starvation of sacred cows—did not disturb the transactions of its sages with the World Soul, which was evidently as indifferent to the sufferings of the human souls it dwelt in.

For the "knowledge" they prized was purely intuitive. Although the Brahmans distinguished the "higher" truth they possessed from the low superstitions they tolerated in the common people, it provided no rational criterion for making this essential distinction. It could not answer either the obvious questions about the relation of the World Soul to the natural, temporal world they regarded as unimportant if not unreal: how and why this world came to be, why it took such arduous effort by human souls to escape from the illusion of its reality, and why it contained so much apparent imperfection or ungodly evil. It was in no strict sense knowledge that led to belief in such basic doctrines as the transmigration of souls.[10] One reason why Hinduism was spared a conflict with science was that India produced little pure science and never cultivated the scientific spirit as the Greeks did. Today A. M. Ghose points out that there is no continuity between its ancient science and modern science; the Upanishads set its tradition by disparaging trust in the human senses and the intellect, positing spiritual truths that could be known only by unconsciousness of them, as achieved by yoga. But the main issue raised by Hinduism for a free society is its traditional lack of reverence for life, tendencies to nonattachment so pronounced that they amount to life-denial and may make its holiness seem essentially nonethical.

In answering this common charge, Radhakrishnan has no trouble finding a great deal of lofty ethical precept in the rich variety of Hindu and Buddhist scriptures. Many texts anticipated the teaching of Christ

---

10 This is in many ways, to be sure, a more attractive doctrine than Westerners may realize. It deepens the sense of oneness with all life. Together with a principle of spiritual continuity it asserts a kind of conservation of spiritual energy that would seem more logical than the endless creation of new souls, which are therefore not strictly immortal, lacking a pre-existence. It is ethically more reasonable and just than the Christian doctrine of an eternity of bliss or torment awarded for the deeds of a single lifetime, not to say less implausible than the doctrine of the resurrection of the flesh. It makes more sense of animal life, which in the Christian view is soulless and ethically pointless. But the critical objection remains that there is no evidence whatever to support the idea of transmigration, and that all our positive knowledge about life tends to discredit it.

in the Sermon on the Mount; India more than any other society, indeed, has preached the gospel of nonviolence, the Jains even extending it to all living creatures; and at the same time the most famous *Bhagavad-Gita* explicitly sanctions a life of action. Yet the dominant tendency in Hindu thought has clearly been life-negation. Even the *Gita* demands that men surrender all desire for the fruits of action, renounce the very point of it, while it justifies killing in war because death is unimportant. The plainest proof of this tendency remains the historic record of India. Always indifferent to the wretchedness of the masses and the injustices to the lower castes, its sages and holy men never led a movement for political freedom, social reform, or any human rights. India never wrote its history, or any history at all, because this perforce takes place in the temporal world, which by definition was unimportant if not illusory. Likewise it produced no tragedy, instead virtually tabooing it; tragedy takes too seriously the earthly sufferings of man and the apparent evils of life. And such attitudes are quite logical consequences of the essentially mystical, otherworldly spirituality of Hinduism. Westerners drawn to it have rejoiced, like Aldous Huxley, in its "holy indifference" to worldly causes. Radhakrishnan himself lends support to this kind of spirituality. While maintaining that true Hinduism is an affirmation of life, he also declares that like all true religion it calls first of all for renunciation of the world, and that good Hindus are naturally content to be "fit for heaven but of no earthly use."

For such reasons British rule made a very great difference. When early in the nineteenth century the British government took over sovereignty from the East India Company and made India a dominion, it introduced Western principles of political order. It set up a uniform law, based on the principle of equality before the law, that undermined the caste system, with its different laws for different castes. It further weakened caste regulations by bringing in modern technology and the beginnings of industrialization. It established a Western system of secular education, while Indian students began going to British universities. Many administrators and teachers shared Macaulay's vision of "a class of persons, Indian in blood and color, but English in taste, in opinion, in morals and intellect," who would finally be made fit for self-government. Many Hindus, naturally, did not take kindly to this process; they protested when their casteless rulers tried to suppress practices like the burning of widows, regarding this as a violation of their rights or restriction of their freedom. But some soon began changing their mind. Early in the century appeared Ram Mohan Roy—the first Hindu to break with caste and come out for social reforms, who would later be honored as "the Father of the present Indian renaissance." Many of the educated adopted English political ideas and ideals. While aroused from the torpor that had settled on India, they learned as well a new respect for the best in their cultural tradition, which was heightened by religious movements led by Ramakrishna, Vivekananda, and others. Intercourse among them was facilitated as English became the lingua franca in a land of many tongues. Nationalist sentiment spread more quickly because the English had not only unified the nation politically but greatly improved communication and transport. Railways helped to make possible the first annual meeting of the Indian National Congress in 1885—the first such representative assembly in the history of India.

The new nationalism was also nurtured, of course, by growing resentment of the English. Their rule had at first been irresponsible simply because it lacked any imperialistic plan or design. Clive of India, who defeated the French in the south and put down the princes in Bengal, was merely trying to protect the commercial interests of the East India Company; he assured the reign of simple greed and folly until Parliament took over control. Although the English were not yet hated, if only because they had restored order and there was no feasible native alternative to their rule, the familiar hostilities soon commenced. Conservative Hindus were outraged by the sacrilegious new ways imposed by their rulers; piety provoked the celebrated mutiny of the Indian army in 1857, which was easily put down but with a severity that left bitter resentment. At the same time the ostensibly progressive English allied themselves with the conservative landlords and archaic native princes in order to ease their rule or further their own interests. Except for some irrigation projects, they did nothing for the great mass of peasants. So far from rising, the standard of living declined considerably during the century. India was swept by a series of terrible famines that took many millions of lives; one in 1896 was the worst known in its history. And the human costs were still higher because of the usual profound disruptions—economic, cultural, and psychological—resulting from Western domination.

The Indian village world had for centuries been largely self-sufficient, importing and exporting little, operating on a small-scale subsistence basis. However well intentioned, the English disrupted it by introducing a capitalistic market economy. Since one of their main interests in

India was raw materials, peasants were turned to cash crops, such as cotton and jute, which exposed them to the vicissitudes of the world market and possible shortage of food. Another major interest, a market for British manufactured goods, especially textiles, ruined much cottage handicraft industry, leaving many unemployed artisans to swell the ranks of the wretchedly poor. Many of the educated also were left unemployed, psychologically when not economically. They were useful chiefly as clerks, higher positions being reserved for Englishmen; there were more college graduates than suitable opportunities in the civil service. Always they were treated as not only political but social inferiors, at best worthy of kindly condescension by rulers who remained aloof from them. Lord Curzon, for example, was fascinated by the impact of the West on the venerable East, and warned against the common assumption that what Europeans found strange was necessarily inferior; but he reserved for Europe the word "civilization." A government report in 1918 described Indians as "intellectually our children."

Now, the movement for independence still owed its means and ends to the work of the English in unifying and educating the nation. The early leaders of the Indian National Congress were mostly devoted to the liberal, democratic tradition of Bentham and Mill, which had also inspired such early administrators as Lord William Bentinck. ("I shall govern in name," he wrote Bentham, "but it will be you who will govern in fact.") Yet simply as moderate men Indian leaders grew more impatient when the government ignored their requests for representation in it. In 1906 the Congress finally demanded self-government, backing up its demand by calling for a boycott of English goods. With the stir of the World War a nationalism that had been largely confined to the intelligentsia, remote from the village world, swelled into a mass movement. The key figure was Gandhi, who from 1920 on was the recognized leader of the Congress. Symbolized by his loincloth and spinning wheel, he appealed directly to the villagers, while stirring the educated too by attacks on Western materialism. He thrilled all classes by departing from the method of windy speech and futile resolution, offering a program of action, through boycott and nonviolent civil disobedience, in which all could participate. One may doubt that the policy of nonviolence for which he became world famous would have worked under the rule of a Hitler or a Stalin, but it was effective with the English. (What could a locomotive engineer do when a crowd of Hindus lay down on the railroad track and refused to budge?) The

India Act of 1935, preparing the way for self-government, made it clear that the full independence of India was only a matter of time; and when this was granted, shortly after World War II, it signaled the end of colonialism for all the rest of the non-Western world.

It was already clear, too, that India would try to set up a democracy. Again the English had obviously prepared the way in spite of all exploitation; the liberal education they offered was more effective because it was empirical, less ideological than the French and less rhetorical than the American. In their Congresses Indians had acquired the habits of representative government with free, open discussion— an opportunity no other colonial people so fully enjoyed. Gandhi, who in the spirit of English law attacked the degradation of the untouchables, was especially devoted to the village masses, lacking any inclination to elitism. Nehru, his Western-educated lieutenant, was a convinced democrat, whose leanings to socialism were as free from any desire for a totalitarian state; he differed from Gandhi chiefly in his secularism, being much more critical of Hinduism. Fascist and Communist movements between the wars made little progress despite the growing hostility to Britain. Hence the only surprising thing about India's new government—to jump ahead of our story— was its boldness in breaking away from Hindu tradition. Within a few years after winning their independence Indians not only wrote the longest constitution in the world, guaranteeing all the basic civil liberties and establishing a parliamentary democracy with universal suffrage—they declared India a secular state, passed laws prohibiting all public forms of caste discrimination, and gave special privileges to the lowest castes in education.

Still more obvious beforehand were the very difficult problems that would confront the government, although these were not clear enough to most Indians. They had been assured by their embattled National Congress that with independence would come not only full freedom and justice but economic opportunity and rapid progress. What came first of all had been foreseen by Winston Churchill—the separation of Pakistan from India, initiated by riots and massacres, followed by mass migrations of homeless, starving people, which took about two million lives.

Hindus who had felt aggrieved under Moslem rule were matched by Moslems when the British finished the Mogul Empire: a ruling people then found themselves a minority, many of them at the untender mercy of high-caste Hindu landlords. A common desire for self-government might have united the two peoples, a prospect that seemed real when several Moslems were elected president of the annual Indian National Congress, but in this century bad feelings between them steadily worsened. The Hindu revival generated more hostility to Moslems, which was reciprocated by a Moslem League founded in 1906. Although Gandhi earnestly sought cooperation, it was doomed by the very nationalism he succeeded in inspiring; violence broke out at meetings of the Congress. By the time of World War II the leaders of the Moslems had decided that their interests would never be safe under a Hindu majority, but required an independent state. At this point there is only to add that the "Republic" of Pakistan faced much more uncertain prospects than Indian democracy. Moslems had been less inclined to enter the British civil service, they had a more authoritarian tradition, their League was committed to an Islamic state based on the Koran, and in general they were little more prepared for democratic government than were the Arab republics.

India's worst troubles were bound to be economic. In this regard Britain had failed to prepare it at all adequately for the task of modernization, which was the more urgent because of the extreme poverty of most of its people and the constant pressure of a growing population. It would face the task with little industry, little capital, a largely village economy that yielded little if any surplus, an illiteracy rate of about 70 per cent, a crying need of health and sanitation services, etc. Under these circumstances its response was predictable: enough state socialism, with five-year plans, to upset Americans, but with provision for the private enterprise long experienced under British rule. Communism had attracted few followers between the wars even though it initially had in Manabendra Roy an exceptionally capable leader, steeped in both Western and Hindu culture, whom Lenin considered his prize colonial revolutionist. (Later he was dropped from the Comintern because of his independent views.) Lenin's gospel would become more attractive, however, when India was on its own. Hopes of rapid progress impossible to realize except perhaps by very bold methods naturally produced potential converts in dissatisfied workers, rootless or frustrated intellectuals, and youthful idealists impatient of gradualism; while the leaders of the new India were still liable to suspicion of the "imperialistic" West, since many of them had spent some years in British jails.

A handicap peculiar to India was its caste system, embodying the grossest inequality in the modern world. So venerable an institution could never be legislated out of existence overnight. Many Brahmans would of course resent and resist the deprivation of their high privileges, especially because of their conviction of their spiritual superiority—beyond the ordinary aristocratic conceit that caused Nietzsche to rhapsodize over the whole system as an ideal way of producing supermen. Feelings about caste would remain strong throughout the society, no less because Hindus had learned to condemn Westerners for their treatment of Negroes. And caste loyalties were but one of the many narrow loyalties—ethnic, linguistic, tribal, religious—that were transcended when India was struggling for its independence, but were due to distract, confuse, and impede the national effort in a society only recently and partially united. "Freedom" in a liberated India would mean quite different things: for many in the middle and upper ranks primarily the right to preserve their property and their status; for many others the right to escape domination and enjoy social, legal equality; and for still others, in all ranks and regions, the right to maintain their traditional ways—their native language, diet and dress, family solidarity, treatment of their womenfolk, burial customs, religious practices, and so forth.

There remains the heritage of Hinduism: the tradition that was the chief unifying force in historic India, and that has been fundamentally inimical to Western ways. In this century modernists have been most active, but they have always been a minority. Traditionalists, still a power in the land, can appeal to both the natural conservatism of the peasantry and the nationalism that played up the superiority of the Indian way of life. Gandhi, the greatest champion of its spirituality, shocked his followers when he killed a dying calf to put it out of its agony; and a year after independence he was assassinated by a fanatical defender of the old ways. Nehru more clearly anticipated the difficulties he would meet in a priest-ridden land, observing that "the past is jealous of the future and holds us in a terrible grip." He was nevertheless revered by most Hindus, including many who had a higher regard for the values of the past. Even those who are wholly committed to the new ideals of freedom and equality may still assert, as some leading thinkers do, that time and history are unimportant, nonattachment or renunciation is the highest good. They accordingly suggest the possibility of an ideal synthesis of Hindu and Western ways, which as Radhakrishnan sees it might help to make our "brilliant and heroic" Western civilization the greatest in history by making it more tolerant and humane, less self-seeking. They also accentuate the ambiguities of India's spirituality and the immediate uncertainties of its prospects; for any effective political leader must take time and history quite seriously, as Nehru did, and can no longer afford to celebrate a "holy indifference" to suffering in the temporal world.

The traditionalists in India may still be right. I see no way, once more, of absolutely deciding between the active, affirmative ideals of the West and the perennial wisdom of nonattachment, or of absolutely demonstrating that the worldly freedoms achieved by the West are worth the costs in the kind of spiritual freedom known to India. I should also repeat that Americans in particular can learn much from its devotion to spiritual values: an inwardness to moderate their incessant busyness and concern with externals; a composure to lessen their need of togetherness, with a mildness to lessen their constant demand on others; a sense of oneness to enlarge their precious, too little selves; a sense of the eternal in the here and now, because of which the march of time is not so imperious or all-important; and always the elementary lessons in patience, in serenity, in a peace of mind secured without pills. Yet it is demonstrable, logically and empirically, that the time-tested Hindu way is a poor way to secure a free society, and with it the material well-being that men all over the non-Western world now aspire to. It remains possible for Westerners to reduce the costs of their active ideals and earthly freedom. The genius of Hinduism for assimilation, now being put to its severest test, may permit an agreement that the pride of self-assertion and effort to improve man's earthly lot is no more inhuman than the possible pride of "holy indifference." Those who agree might then endorse Paul Valéry's tribute to Western civilization for its "most intense power of radiation combined with an equally intense power of assimilation," because of its adventurousness, its thirst for knowledge, and its rare blend of ardor and disinterested curiosity, imagination and rigorous logic, self-confidence and capacity for self-criticism.

Many Westerners (notably Toynbee) can therefore agree with Radhakrishnan that history shows that "the world in the end belongs to the unworldly." Many others, however, can raise an eyebrow and point to China—a country that had maintained a mature civilization over a still longer period than had India, by a much more impressive political achievement, and that today is a much greater power in Asia. The history of China shows nothing of the sort.

5. *China*

"It is easy for China to acquire the civilization of the West," said a Chinese scholar quoted by Hu Shih in 1933, "but it is very difficult to master its barbarism. Yet I suppose we must first master this barbarism, before we can feel at home in this new civilization." If Red China now seems in a fair way to such mastery, it brings up the deeper reasons for the scholar's distress: that he spoke out of one of the most gracious civilized traditions, and that his statement was only partly true. Historic China had had long experience mastering barbarians, repelling some, assimilating others, always preserving its own tradition of high culture; but its very success made it harder for the Chinese to deal with the arrogant invaders from the West. For more than two thousand years they had maintained their kingdom. Through all the usual ups and downs—the fall of dynasties, civil wars, periods of anarchy—it had always righted itself on essentially the same basis, under a vigorous new dynasty; and over long periods it was the strongest, wealthiest, most civilized empire in the world. Although its people knew too little about the world to realize that their achievement in holding together so large a nation for so long a time was the most impressive achievement in political history, rivaled only by much smaller Egypt, they had every reason to believe, as they did down into the nineteenth century, that they were the most civilized people on earth. Hence they were more profoundly shocked and humiliated than any other Asiatic people by the intrusion of the West, the long series of blows to their pride that started suddenly, brutally, with the Opium War of 1839. The exposure of their weakness was only more mortifying because rivalry among the European powers forestalled any designs of making a colony of China; so they were left nominally independent, actually forced to make concessions to all comers, and exposed to aggression by the Japanese too.

From the beginning of their history as a mature civilization their experience was radically different from that of India. The Chinese were not at all an unworldly people. Their culture was basically secular, humanistic, and rational, not religious; the goods they sought were mundane goods, to be enjoyed here and now; their spiritual values were purely human values, such as beauty, grace, and wisdom, neither dedicated to the service of God nor derived from communion with a

World Soul. Hence Hu Shih could say easily what would be almost unthinkable for a good Hindu: "Today the most baseless and, moreover, the most poisonous legend is the deprecation of Western civilization as 'merely materialistic' and the honoring of Eastern civilization as 'spiritual.' " Yet Chinese civilization was radically different from the West too. On the one hand, it was even less religious. It had no belief in a personal Creator, no divinely inspired scriptures or commandments, no idea of original sin, no sharp dualism of body and soul, no priesthood with high privileges, no powerful church; its God was Heaven, an impersonal moral order that was to be respected, not loved or feared, and that authorized no idea of either personal salvation or damnation. On the other hand, the Chinese were more devoted than Westerners to spiritual ends. They did not worship mammon either; their most cherished goods were ethical, aesthetic, and intellectual; they never exalted business, ranking merchants at the very bottom of the social scale; and although an uncommonly practical, inventive people, they never developed anything comparable to modern science or modern technology. As a practical people they made it their primary business to order harmoniously the human world, neither to conquer nor to escape the physical world. It was for such reasons—not military might or imperial conquests—that over the many centuries the Chinese took for granted the superiority of their civilization, that they then had so hard a time adjusting themselves to the superior power of the West, floundering for a whole century before they took to communism as the way to restore their greatness—and that their experience, until lately neglected by students of government, is so helpful to better self-understanding by the West.

The soul of Chinese civilization was Confucianism. Coming out of the extraordinary ferment of the "Axial period," which was everywhere a time of troubles, Confucius differed from the other great religious pioneers in preaching a gospel that was primarily ethical, not supernatural, and so worldly and reasonable that some Christian thinkers deny it the name of religion, Christopher Dawson going so far as to say that it is "unintelligible to us by reason of its very rationality." The Chinese did not even make Confucius a god. Nevertheless they remained more loyal to him than other peoples did to their religious prophets, so much so that in A.D. 1800 he might have felt at home in China, whereas Jesus would long since have been a complete stranger in all the societies that worshiped him; Dawson admits that his teaching had a stronger hold on China than any "true" religion had on other societies (though he forgets this when he echoes the conventional refrain that men cannot live by merely rational or secular ideals). While it was supplemented by Taoism and Buddhism, which it tolerated, Confucianism remained the accepted basis of both culture and the state.[11] It gave China all the virtues of conservatism, lacking only a clear awareness of the defects of these virtues.

Confucius also differed from the other religious prophets of the sixth century B.C. in that he was no radical innovator, but in his own words "a transmitter, not a maker, believing in and loving the ancients." If he was more of a maker than he admitted, or perhaps realized, his primary aim was certainly conservative. It was not to extend freedom or promote growth but to secure social order, harmony, and stability. His genius lay in his blend of conservatism and liberality of spirit. Thus in spite of his stress on the duties rather than the rights of men he was still no strict authoritarian. While believing in Heaven, he never pretended to an intimacy with it. "Respect spiritual beings, but keep them at a distance," he advised; and as for obeying them, "We don't know yet how to serve men, how can we know about serving the spirits?" Neither did he spell out the dictates of Heaven in a set of commandments: "The superior man goes through his life without any one prescribed course of action or any taboo. He merely decides for the moment what is the right thing to do." For a guide Confucius offered his modest "silver" instead of golden rule: "Do not do unto others as you would not have them do unto you." Heaven obviously did not command men to love their neighbors as themselves, for it displayed no such love of man itself; it commanded only justice. In sum, the ideal man according to Confucius was no saint but a sage, and his wisdom lay in temperance, tolerance, reasonableness, graciousness, and tact. Would-be saints only exemplified the folly of trying to live "too high, high above the ordinary moral self."

The esence of this self, and the basis of the whole Confucian ethic, was *jen,* the natural sympathy, fellow feeling, or "human-heartedness"

11 Toynbee makes much more of Buddhism, a religion closer to his heart, which he sees as the mother of a later "Far Eastern" civilization that he distinguishes from an early "Sinic" one in China. I know of no other important historian, however, who denies the basic continuity of Chinese civilization or the continued dominance of Confucianism up to this century. Although Toynbee's split enables him to find two proper cycles in Cathay, it leads him to the as dubious conclusion that "the Far East has still less in common with the West than the Hindu world has in its cultural background." The always worldly Chinese perhaps did not deserve to endure so long, or swing through only one cycle; but their secular tradition makes it much easier to understand why they have adopted communism.

known to all men. Chinese culture was indelibly stamped by the efforts
of Confucius to cultivate *jen*, the natural means to social harmony. This
he did spell out in terms of duties—to the ancestors, the father, the
emperor, and so forth; filial piety was especially important, since the
family was the school for all civic virtues. A particular means was *li*,
the ritual and ceremony that engrained propriety, a sense of one's place
in the social order; among the ancient rites sanctioned by Confucius
was ancestor worship, which steadied men by a promise of a kind of
biological immortality. Another essential means was education, designed
to produce a harmonious soul. This typical concept of a "practical"
education, so alien to Americans, led Confucius to stress music and
poetry as basic subjects, not mere frills, but as a conservative he also
put great stock in learning, a knowledge of the classics of the ancestors.
In this view, his ideal man was a well-read, cultivated, refined gentleman—a type that was most highly honored in China until this century,
ranked far above military heroes. Likewise the classics that he complied
remained the basis of Chinese education and higher learning. Among
the consequences of his teaching that so radically distinguished Chinese
from Indian culture was the great importance attached to the study
and writing of history. Until modern times, no other people had so
complete a record of their past.

In view of both the strength and the tolerance of Confucianism,
rival religions could be readily accepted because not regarded as
actually rivals—a good Confucian might also be a Taoist or Buddhist.
Taoism, which likewise dated from the Axial period, was originally
akin to Indian mysticism, another means to a harmonious soul, but in
practice it was a form of primitivism, a more informal conception of
the "natural" life that accommodated the vagabond, individualistic impulses of the Chinese, and was confined to private life. As a popular religion it degenerated into primitive forms of magic. The popularity of
Buddhism was stranger, since its gospel of nonattachment would seem
alien to the Chinese spirit, but it entered China in the first century
or so of the Christian era, an especially troubled period, which made
attractive its promise of personal salvation. In time it was characteristically transformed into a more cheerful, affirmative religion, which
enabled the Chinese to become Buddhas by an easier discipline than
Indians had to undergo, while providing heavens for the common
people. Although it suffered some persecution when its monasteries
grew wealthy and attracted too many young men to suit the emperors,
they could tolerate it because its leaders had little ambition to make

it a state cult, and it remained popular as another easygoing religion
for private life.[12] Any possible question of the supremacy of Confucianism was settled by a Neo-Confucian revival in the eleventh
century that borrowed some popular ideas from its rivals. Thereafter
the only notable religious development was the coming of Jesuit missionaries in the seventeenth century. They were received with typical
hospitality and had considerable success in converting their hosts by
reciprocating, tolerating some unorthodox Chinese belief, until the
Pope ordered them to give up such heresy; whereupon the emperor,
enraged by the insult to Chinese tradition—the first experience of
Western arrogance—had them expelled.

As the state religion, Confucianism contributed all that was original
to a government that otherwise looked like a typical Oriental sacred
monarchy. China was a highly centralized state, ruled by an autocratic
emperor called the "Son of Heaven," through a vast bureaucracy that
was free to regulate all major activities, and that made a Chinese city,
in Max Weber's words, "a place with officials and without local autonomy." All orders came from on top, and there was no other center
of power—feudal, religious, commercial—strong or independent enough
to oppose the government. Nevertheless Confucian theory stressed the
duties rather than the rights of the emperor too. Although he ruled
by a "mandate from Heaven," he had no divine right to rule as he
pleased. The accepted ideal was benevolent, paternalistic rule by a
sage-king who did not separate the political from the ethical, as Western
monarchs did on Machiavellian principle, and who was always devoted
to the interests of the people. Mencius, the foremost disciple of Confucius, explicitly put the people first: "In a nation the people are the
most important, the state is next, and the ruler is the least important."
In theory they even had the right to judge the emperor, and if his rule
was unjust "to change the mandate"—the Chinese term for revolution.

Most original by far was the Chinese bureaucracy, which deserved
the kinder name "civil service," and in fact gave this idea to the West.
(When the British, only a century ago, adopted the civil service system
they are now so proud of, it was attacked as a subversive proposal to
"Chinesify" Britain.) It differed from other bureaucracies in that
officials were selected impersonally on the basis of merit alone, proved

12 Among its varieties was Chan Buddhism, which took on something of Taoism and
through Japan became known to the West as Zen. It was characteristic in its promise of
salvation here and now, by a sudden enlightenment. Its monks contributed most to what
little religious thought China produced after the Axial period.

by competitive examinations, instead of aristocratic birth or royal favor. The examinations were based on the Confucian classics, which it took candidates many years to master, and they tested as well a mastery of prose style and an ability to compose poetry on any prescribed theme. The bureaucrats were therefore scholars and literati—types that would be hooted at in America if they sought office. (They had never met a payroll.) The winners, who were a very small proportion of the applicants, became something like national heroes, the top class in the kingdom. Known to us as mandarins, they came mostly from wealthy families, because of the long preparation required, but anyone was eligible to apply and bright sons of poor families might make the grade; China had nothing like the rigid class distinctions of India, and more social mobility than other Asiatic societies. Once in office, the mandarins assumed heavy responsibilities, remained subject to regular test by efficiency ratings, and if not up to par might be not only dismissed but punished. This system, which grew up in the second century B.C., lasted until our century. As it came through the periodic collapses of dynasties, it appears to be the main reason for the most impressive achievement in political history.

The civil ideals that the Confucian-trained mandarins helped to preserve might shame Westerners. Except for a short-lived school of Legalists in the third century B.C., resembling modern fascists, the Chinese never glorified war and conquest, endorsed Machiavellianism, or exalted the Nietzschean type of superman. More broadly, Confucianism offers an ideal corrective to the inhuman tendencies alike in Western religion, philosophy, and science. While concentrating on a spirituality of this world, it is especially pertinent because of its crowning ideal of harmony: a social harmony based on an assumption of natural harmony between man, the universe, and Heaven, reflected in Chinese painting. The ruling thought of the oldest civilization on earth gives the clearest perspective on the deep splits in Western thought and life: the sharp separations of business, politics, and ethics; the many double standards in morality, one for each province as each sex; the radical dualisms of body and soul, mind and matter, natural and supernatural; the conflicts between religion and science, science and the humanities; the whole concept of life as endless struggle— all commonly regarded as natural or even necessary, as up to a point they may well be, yet not clearly essential expressions of human nature or the human condition, since wholeness and unity seemed as natural to the very human Chinese. Likewise the Confucian method of promoting harmony by cultivating natural sympathy, always keeping human relations primary, might moderate the excessive faith of Westerners in social machinery or organization. And now that many are reverting to the traditional pessimism about human nature they might consider the more cheerful Confucian view of the goodness in man, the essential perfectibility of a being who could be expected to learn and do his duties—a view shared by most Chinese thinkers of other schools, in keeping with their common assumption of the natural harmony between man and the cosmos.

The Legalists who thought otherwise may serve to belie the popular idea of "a cycle of Cathay," for they came out of a brilliant period of diversified philosophy. Chinese civilization was by no means so static, nor its history so monotonous, as Westerners assumed. Some of its emperors tried novel political experiments, such as price control and the idea of the ever-normal granary picked up by Henry Wallace in America; its great native dynasties—Han, Tang, Sung, Ming— were distinguished by brilliant cultural achievements in diverse styles; and the Mongol dynasty that so dazzled Marco Polo by its splendor, and that the Chinese regard as a vulgar materialistic interlude, at least demonstrated that they could match Westerners at their own game of wealth-getting. Early in the fifteenth century the Mings sent out fleets of more than two hundred ships to the Indian Ocean as far as Africa, establishing control over some key ports—expeditions much greater than Europeans would be up to a century later; but then an emperor changed world history by deliberately calling off the whole enterprise.

His policy was not clearly high-minded, however, apparently resulting from some court intrigue. It brings us back once more to the invariable incongruities, specifically to the essential conservatism of the Chinese state, which in view of its repeated breakdowns had an unhealthy aspect. We need not review here the rise and fall of its dynasties, nor the monotonous follies and crimes to be found in the annals of all states. The basic trouble from first to last was the weakness of the long-lived imperial institutions. Despite the theory that the people were "most important," the state was never, of course, a democratic one; there were no popular elections, representative assemblies, or political parties, and no constitutional guarantees of rights. In particular there were no institutional checks on the power of the emperor. China never worked up a formal system of law that limited the powers of government or defined the liberties of subjects. By way of institutions to offset the emperor it had only the bureaucracy, which was not under public control, and the mandarins had no legal right to oppose him, while as careerists most tended to court his favor. (One Son of Heaven boasted that "all the talents and heroes in the empire are in my bag.") The emperor was always suspicious of any appearance of organized opposition, for good reason: about the only practical way "to change the mandate" was assassination or revolution. This way brought in many a new ruler—but never a new political order or any lasting reforms.

Under this order the common people fared no better than they did in other sacred monarchies. The wealth and splendor, grace and refinement, were largely confined to the few. The peasant masses did the hard work, paid the taxes, bore the brunt of misrule, often rose up in desperation, more often died of hunger; in the nineteenth century they were as notoriously poor as the Indian masses. The common wretchedness bred as notorious contradictions. The reputedly practical, rational, skeptical Chinese, sometimes described as the first great people to have outgrown religion, indulged in an incredible riot of superstition, more primitive than the popular religion of any other civilized society, even India, because it was mostly pure magic. Similarly a people devoted to "human-heartedness," famous for their courtesy and refinement, were as famous for their callous indifference to suffering and their addiction to cruelty. And if such contradictions are commonplaces in history, the significant point remains that most good Confucianists, even the sages, were not deeply troubled by the wretchedness, superstition, and callousness, and that those who were troubled still accepted the political order that was at least partly responsible for them.

Although there was often tension because of the wide gap between political theory and practice, the accepted ideal and the often sordid reality, no important thinker ventured a fundamental criticism of the theory or the ideal. A characteristic response was *A Plan for the Prince* by Huang Tsung-hsi, one of the most liberal Confucianists, written after the fall of the Ming dynasty to the Manchus in the seventeenth century. Under the Mings despotism had reached a peak. Eunuchs— a popular feature of Oriental monarchies—had become more powerful than ever before, an especially vicious one presiding over the last years of the dynasty. Ministers, the only possible restraining influence within the government, were flogged at court, sometimes so brutally that they died. Huang therefore complained that officials were treated like mere servants, not given the status in the hierarchy that Mencius had said they should have, and he called for better laws. He also complained that state schools educated men only for state purposes, and that the government was hostile to private academies, where Neo-Confucianism was studied; he recommended a system of public education for broader purposes. Yet he still hoped for nothing better than a virtuous prince, or benevolent despot. He proposed no legal checks upon the powers of the emperor, never dreaming of anything like constitutional government. He did not call for academic freedom in the schools, having no more thought of a pluralistic society. He suggested no democratic ideals whatever—his book was not addressed to the people. For Huang, as for all good Confucianists, the solution was simply to put authority in the right hands; and after two thousand years of carefully recorded history he was still incapable of facing up to the elementary problem—how to put and keep it there, or what to do when authority got into the wrong hands. No Confucianist ever questioned the basic doctrines of the master or the authority of his classics, which the mandarins had to learn by heart in order to pass their examinations. The essential shortcomings of Chinese civilization were implicit in Confucianism itself.

The rationality of Confucius has commonly been somewhat over-rated. If his Heaven is "unintelligible" to Christians, one reason is that he neglected to explain just how he knew about it and its mandates. For his acceptance of prehistoric superstitions like ancestor worship, he offered only the authority of a largely mythical past. He did not rationalize either the laws he accepted, which amounted to sanctified custom. His followers accordingly neglected to work out a system of law or a legal philosophy. Similarly they failed to develop a logic, modes of critical analysis or systematic thought. Clinging to the essentially verbal knowledge embalmed in the Confucian classics, which they went on learning by heart, they built up no comprehensive, systematic body of natural knowledge.

Hence the failure of the practical, inventive Chinese to develop anything like modern science and technology. They early demonstrated their ability at great engineering projects, as in irrigation, and they passed on an amazing number of inventions—among others not only such well-known ones as the magnetic compass, gunpowder, porcelain, paper, and printing, but the wheelbarrow, the horse harness, the sailing carriage, the iron plowshare, the wagon-mill, the sternpost rudder, canal lock-gates, and the mastery of cast iron. With these skills they accumulated potentially scientific knowledge about the natural world. Yet astronomy in China never became a science, physics remained especially backward, and no great pioneer appeared in any science, while no important thinker extolled the possibilities of applied knowledge. One reason for the halt was the addiction of the Chinese to magic; thus astronomers served chiefly as interpreters of celestial portents, on the side making up calendars to demonstrate the magic powers of the reigning dynasty. A more important reason was the disdain of utilitarian interests by the Confucian literati, and in particular the traditional contempt of the merchant class, which accumulated wealth but never acquired the power or prestige it did in Europe. Such attitudes were fortified by the revulsion against the rule of the Mongols, whose nomadic tradition made them hospitable to traders; the culture exalted by the scholar-heroes then became pure sweetness and light, free from all vulgar utility. Many of us are now in a mood to respect the Chinese scale of values, to condone their use of gunpower chiefly to scare away demons, perhaps to condone even their failure to develop science. Still, the untold millions of peasants who died of starvation and plague, in spite of all the magic at their command, might have welcomed a superior technology. The sweetness and light brought no more humanity in social or political life. A respect for spiritual values does not require a scorn of material interests, which could also look vulgar in mandarins living in luxury.

Beneath such exaggerations or corruptions of the teaching of Confucius lay the neglected defects of its virtues. Many of us may also be in a mood to respect his stress on duties rather than rights, filial piety rather than self-assertion. In any case his way of assuring harmonious human relations found little room for personal independence. Confucianism never emancipated the individual as Western tradition did—for better or for worse—or gave him such confidence in his own powers. He was always subordinated, never really free to live a life of his own. Historically the Chinese misbehaved often enough, fell down on their duties or failed in respect for their superiors; but not many rebelled on high principle or dared publicly to defy tradition. The individual was not encouraged to think for himself either, make up his own mind on fundamental issues. For as a lover and teacher of humanistic wisdom Confucius was basically different from Socrates, the great teacher of the West. Though a seeker of the truth, he announced himself as a transmitter, not an inquirer; and though undogmatic in spirit, he mapped out the whole proper way of life, which was not the way of spiritual quest or ardent pursuit of truth. In its many times of trouble, and during a century of humiliation by the West, China might have done better had it had more independent thinkers, more inquirers with a scientific spirit. As it was, when its young students were finally aroused in this century, many unfortunately felt compelled to reject entirely the wisdom of Confucius.

The obvious reason why it took China so much longer than Japan to respond successfully to the challenge of the West remains the profound conservatism implicit in Confucianism, rigidified by two thousand years of tradition, during which controversies were always over the proper interpretation of the master's teaching, never over proposals for basic innovation or reform. The educated Chinese became more set in their ways than any other people since the ancient Egyptians. The "superior man" of Confucius was at best not an adventurous type, given to eager curiosity, flights of imagination, or indulgence of spontaneous impulse, but he tended to become—especially as a bureaucrat—complacent in a verbal, formal, ultimately sterile wisdom. In times of stress he also tended to a fatalistic passivity that was likewise implicit in the master's teaching. Despite his belief in human perfectibility Confucius had no idea of progress, of course—Heaven gave only hopes of stability and harmony; but he often remarked that Heaven brought misfortune too, though for reasons unclear or seemingly inconsistent with his belief in natural harmony; and the wise man resigned himself to whatever fate it decreed. Some historians were led to pessimistic theories of inevitable decline by the repeated failures. Otherwise Confucianists combated resignation chiefly by some effort to learn or forestall their fate through speculating in the popular forms of magic. The worldly Chinese were not much more disposed than the otherworldly Indians to vigorous, concerted, rational effort to mitigate the evils of their society or of the human condition.

Long before the shock of the Opium War there were clear signs of stagnation or worse in the Celestial Kingdom. The Manchu government had failed to meet an earlier challenge—a surprisingly rapid increase in population over a century or so. In 1800 the census takers counted about 300,000,000 Chinese, or some three times as many as the country had ever had before the Manchus, and its economy had not been developed correspondingly; uncounted millions of landless people were growing desperate again. In mid-century the Taiping Peasant Rebellion broke out, the worst in China's history and perhaps all history, lasting fifteen years; up to 30,000,000 people died before it was crushed, with the aid of Westerners. The mandarins and the gentry, lined up on the emperor's side, helped him to resist reform. When, after the humiliating defeat by Japan in 1895, a young emperor did launch a belated program of reform, he succeeded only in losing his "mandate"; a despotic court government returned to the ways of elaborate ceremony and fatuous incompetence. At the end of the century the fierce hatred of foreigners found vent in the Boxer Rebellion, backed by the popular faith in magic: the fanatical Boxer sects promised recruits invulnerability and freedom from all future misfortune through the spirits they invoked. But their hocus-pocus was no match for Western and Japanese troops, who put down the rebellion and rewarded themselves by looting Peking.

Hence intellectuals led the reform movement that finally succeeded, under the banner of a nationalism that recognized the need of learning from the West. In 1905 the civil service examinations were abolished, signaling the end of the Confucian order. By this time the lessons learned from the West were making revolutionaries of the reformers; as one intellectual later put it, "The strength and brilliance of Europe today . . . comes from the grace of revolution." In 1911 Sun Yat-sen led the revolution that overthrew the Manchus, with a grace aided by feeble resistance, and that ended the Celestial Kingdom too: the last emperor abdicated, acknowledging that Heaven now mandated a Republic. The republic that Sun tried to set up was on the Western democratic model, with a parliamentary government and a program of social reform to raise the standard of living. Although his government soon collapsed, since provincial warlords were the real power in the land, his young disciple Chiang Kai-shek eventually built up an army strong enough to deal with them. Meanwhile the World War had fueled both nationalistic and revolutionary ardor. The prestige of the West, lowered by the spectacle of the war, sank still more when the men of Versailles disregarded China and handed Shantung over to Japan. Students now began demonstrating against the "imperialists," organizing boycotts of British and Japanese goods—preparing the way for a professional revolution. By far the most important consequence of the war was the Chinese turn toward communism.

Already disenchanted by the behavior of the democracies at Versailles, Sun Yat-sen got from them none of the help he badly needed to build the new China; whenever their interests were involved, they usually backed instead the more powerful warlords. He got help only from the Soviet, which sent him advisers and generals. Lenin had been much interested in the Chinese Revolution, and though he mistakenly saw in it a prime symbol of "the heroic democracy of the popular masses," Chinese intellectuals were now ready to join the crusade against Western imperialism. With the help of his advisers, Sun reorganized his Kuomintang (National People's party) as a revolutionary party. He sought out the support of the Chinese Communist party, which Moscow had also helped to found in 1920. Whereas he had at first emphasized personal freedom, he now told his followers that for the sake of spiritual unity "the first thing is to sacrifice freedom, then the whole party will have freedom." Shortly before his death in 1925 he wrote his last testament, a letter to the leaders of the Soviet exalting "the heritage left by the immortal Lenin to the oppressed peoples of the world," and pledging the Kuomintang to support of this heritage. The spiritual father of the new China concluded: "Taking leave of you, dear comrades, I want to express the hope that the day will come when the U.S.S.R. will welcome a friend and ally in a mighty free China, and that in the great struggle for liberation of the oppressed peoples of the world both those allies will go forward to victory hand in hand." In deferring this hope, Chiang Kai-shek only prepared the way for Mao. Having received his military training in Moscow, he carried on for a while an uneasy alliance with the Communists, under the supervision of the deluded Stalin; but then he turned on them, in 1927 staged his frightful massacre in Canton, and wrecked the Communist labor movement. What eventually emerged from the blood-soaked ruins was a new party, rebuilt by intellectuals on a sounder peasant basis.

Knowing the aftermath, we may overlook the considerable progress the Chinese made between the world wars. The Kuomintang at least succeeded in unifying the country and setting up a national government, with a constitution promising full democracy in time, and it made a start toward modernizing its economy, law, and public education. Intellectuals were busy propagating Western science, philosophy, and political thought, chiefly of a liberal tendency; among their favorite thinkers was John Dewey. Westerners might have been more impressed by a "New Life Movement" that sought to preserve the best of Confucianism, or to achieve an ideal synthesis of its values and Western values; for liberals there could be no better synthesis. And the political failures of the Chinese were made more pardonable by the Japanese. Their invasion of Manchuria, followed by encroachments on North China, was obviously a prelude to further aggression. The Chinese had to concentrate on building up military strength for an almost certain war, which in 1937 the Japanese provoked.

Nevertheless, this was in other respects a period of deterioration. The very eminence of Chiang Kai-shek was a portent, for the leader of China was now a general—a type once ranked far below the scholar-gentleman. His Nationalist government, devoted primarily to material interests, accentuated a common story in the non-Western world—peoples losing hold of the best in their own tradition while adopting some of the most questionable ways of the West. Culturally, the whole period since the Opium War had been about the most barren in the history of China, and now the New Life Movement failed to stir the country; the effort to preserve the best in Confucianism steadily lost ground. But most portentous were the political failures of the Nationalists. No such idealist or visionary as Sun Yat-sen had been, Chiang made no earnest effort to extend the fuller democracy promised by the Constitution. He ruled virtually as a dictator, with a prudent eye to the interests of the wealthy and powerful, and a suspicious eye on liberal critics of his regime, as on students and professors. He carried through no program of fundamental social or agrarian reform. Instead his government became notoriously corrupt (though the American public was shielded from this disagreeable truth). It had little popular support because no appeal to either peasants or intellectuals except for its resistance to the Japanese, and such patriotic appeal was clouded by popular hatred of rule by generals. Hence it was not at all surprising that Chiang finally lost the civil war he had started against the Communists, in spite of a couple billion dollars of aid from America: his armies would fight them halfheartedly if at all, having little to fight for, and would help arm them by surrendered weapons. It was the Chinese themselves—not Russians or Americans—who decided their future; and none but Americans believe that they are now pining for the return of Chiang Kai-shek.

In 1937 the apparently shattered Communists had proved their courage, fervor, and resourcefulness by their "great march," through the whole of China to the northern province of Shensi, where the 20,000 who survived out of their army of 90,000 set about rebuilding the party. They had ample appeal. To the peasants, who had been little affected by Western ideas, they promised the only kind of freedom these knew or cared much about—freedom from want, or from oppression by landlords; they had a positive, if ruthless program for redistributing the land. To students and intellectuals, who under the Nationalists had enjoyed a limited, uncertain academic freedom, they offered something even more inspiring—a constructive faith with a program of action, a kind of spiritualized materialism promising that China at last had a real future. The proletariat on whom the Communists had originally banked were a small minority largely confined to the coastal cities, but still a potential help; the disillusionment occasioned by Stalin's blunder was offset by Chiang's ferocious treatment of their leaders, as well as by frightful exploitation by factory owners, who were mostly foreigners. The small middle class, less favorably disposed, was not strong enough to offer dangerous resistance. In all classes the Communists could exploit hatred of the Western imperialists, since the Russia that had joined in the grabbing had been repudiated by the Soviet. By contrast, America was losing much of the early appeal it had had for intellectuals. Although it had shown more sympathy for China than had any other of the great powers, it offered only abstract ideals of liberty, not very meaningful to the Chinese masses, coupled with a celebration of business that was no more attractive to intellectuals; and when at last if offered material aid too it backed Chiang and his fellow warlords, for reasons having more to do with American than Chinese interests.

The whole political tradition of historic China, moreover, was in fundamental respects suited to the purposes of the Communists, enabling them to make much harsher demands of the people than Europeans had of colonial peoples, and even so to seem less tyrannical. It was an authoritarian tradition, lacking the basic concept of freedom under law—an idea that would seem obviously attractive to common people everywhere, but is not at all easy to convey to most of them in the non-Western world. Mao would be only an up-to-date substitute for the autocratic emperor, his bureaucracy only a more elaborate version of the bureaucracy of yore; the rule had always been highly centralized government, by an elite not under public control. The avowed ideal of a classless society was especially attractive to a people with a strong social sense, whose accepted ideal had always been not individual freedom but social harmony. By the same token capitalism was less attractive than socialism, even apart from its association with Western imperialism; it glorified the long-despised type of the businessman, the wealthiest of whom were now commonly allied with the hated warlords, and its gospel of free enterprise looked more like another example of Christian hypocrisy than an expression of human rights. And communism met no such religious opposition in China as it did in India and Islam. As a secular religion of dedication, it served rather to fill the spiritual void left by the decay of Confucianism, while its disciples maintained the Confucian tradition of quarreling over only the proper interpretation of its scriptures.

Still, its gospel was fundamentally alien to the cultural tradition of China. This was not an absolutist tradition, but had fostered habits of tolerance, moderation, and compromise, in devotion to the art of living. It included no school of philosophical materialism, much less of economic determinism; in their abiding concern with the human, social order, the Chinese had not entertained such demeaning views of the human spirit, and had played down economic interests. They had not been given to militarism either, or glorification of the heroic virtues; they had never dreamed of regretting that they had only one life to give to their country. Above all, the Communists had to contend with the primacy of the family, the sovereign virtue of filial piety. The idea that a man's primary duty was to the state or the party was completely foreign to Chinese tradition, which in family life was still very much alive. Hence intellectuals, who provided the leadership of the movement, were due to become as suspect as they were to Communist parties in Europe. They were likely to be too independent, some because of the seductiveness of Western liberalism, others because of devotion to their native cultural tradition. The peasants too were a potential threat. The rapid modernization to which the Communists were dedicated would necessarily demand sacrifices by them, since the predominantly agricultural economy provided little surplus for extensive industrialization; and while tending to be especially loyal to the family and the ways of the ancestors, they were also less passive than most other peasants in Asia, having a tradition of rising up against oppression.

All in all, the Communists in China had evident advantages over their fellows in the rest of Asia, and over the democratic leaders of India; but they faced the same problem of forming a new mentality. On both counts they would pose an especially difficult challenge to conservative America, which preferred not to recognize the existence of a Red China, but still had to reckon somehow with the disagreeable fact that it contained 700,000,000 people.

6. Postscript: Latin America

Although Latin America owes its language, religion, and most of its culture to Europe, it is for my present purposes more akin to the non-Western world. Most of its countries are underdeveloped, full of illiterate peasants who are only beginning to live in the twentieth century. Their poverty is accentuated by the usual gulf between the very wealthy few and the wretched many. Even in such advanced countries as Argentina and Brazil government is unstable, still likely to revert to military dictatorship. In only a few countries are democratic processes firmly established. And all Latin America shares the most popular sentiment in the non-Western world, the resentment of colonialism. In this century its peoples too have awakened to new hopes and old grievances. They too have been stirred by a fervid nationalism, while they have grown more conscious of their common culture, pleased to look down on Yankee materialism. Long disregarded by the great powers except as a source of investment, or regarded chiefly as a scene of comic opera politics, Latin America is emerging as another force to be reckoned with.

Here the role of imperialist villain was played by the United States instead of Europe. It proclaimed the Monroe Doctrine without consulting its neighbors, primarily on behalf of its own interests. After its successful aggression on Mexico, it was too busy building up its continent to pay much attention to Latin America, but by the end of the nineteenth century it was free to expand its interests and flourish the big stick. By blatantly imperialistic means Theodore Roosevelt managed the separation of Panama from Colombia for the sake of the Canal, not the Panamanians. He followed up by announcing his Corollary to the Monroe Doctrine: as a civilized nation the United States would be forced, "however reluctantly," to exercise "an international police power" in cases of chronic wrongdoing or disorder in the Western Hemisphere. Reluctance was overcome when American businessmen began setting up shop in Latin America. "Dollar diplomacy" sent U.S. Marines into several Caribbean countries, where they stayed as long as twenty years. Woodrow Wilson confused the issues by declaring that the United States would not recognize governments that had come into power by unconstitutional means—a high moral line that if followed consistently would have meant disowning most countries in the Western Hemisphere, but in practice meant discrimination against governments the Big Brother did not like. The better feeling inaugurated by Franklin Roosevelt's Good Neighbor Policy had to contend with a deep suspicion and resentment, kept smoldering after the war by the policy of continuing to recognize or even support brutal, corrupt dictators. The increasing embarrassment of the United States over these dictators failed to overcome its fears of revolutionaries, who throve on their wrongdoings. A policy compounded of idealism, self-righteousness, self-interest, and jitteriness would make Fidel Castro popular all over Latin America.

Yet the grievances of Latin America were much less real or reasonable than those of the strictly non-Western world. Except for Mexico, it had suffered very little from Yankee or any other alien aggression. The United States could not possibly satisfy its awakened peoples by any consistent policy, for the very reason that they had long been independent. It had to recognize governments that had seized power illegally, since this was a common procedure, and no matter how dictatorial or unpopular they were it could do nothing about them except by intervention, which would lay it open to the charge of imperialism. It was in any case sure to be resented simply because it was so much more prosperous and powerful than the Latin-American countries, whose people did not really despise its material wealth. Prone to the usual ambivalent attitudes of admiration, awe, jealousy, and dislike, they were as inclined to blame it for their own shortcomings. Their poverty, illiteracy, and ill-health, their backward economies, their weak, irresponsible governments, their tradition of military dictatorship—the sources of the frustrations they tended to take out on the Colossus of the North were all results of their own doings, not of foreign exploitation. All were implicit in the culture they had inherited from Spain, and preserved in an independence that had not brought political freedom.

In the first centuries after Columbus the Spanish colonies were far wealthier than the American ones, and in their cities had more imposing cathedrals, universities, public buildings, and other appearances of a more advanced culture. This was a stagnant culture, however, dominated by Church and Crown, in which the Inquisition helped to insulate an ultratraditional society against the stirring changes that were coming over Europe. Like Spain itself, Latin America was by 1800 a backward region, whose people were not at all ready for self-government. The mass of nominally Christian natives remained serfs who were in but not of the society; they had no share in its wealth and little in its culture except Catholicism, which taught them only to serve the Church and obey the government it was allied with. Their offspring by Spanish sires formed a *mestizo* class that likewise remained poor relations and had no say whatever in the government. The masses accordingly had nothing to do with the wars of independence that started when Napoleon dethroned the king of Spain, and that by 1825 liberated all the colonies except Cuba and Puerto Rico. The revolutions were led chiefly by "creoles," Spaniards born in the colonies, who had been infected by the example of the United States and the ideals of the Enlightenment; but upon winning independence they attempted no social revolution, providing only new masters for the common people. Simón Bolívar, the greatest hero of the liberation, was also the most prophetic. A student of Spinoza, Locke, and Rousseau, he was sincerely devoted to republican ideals, but soon learned that his compatriots lacked the political virtues necessary to realize them; he decided that the first requisite of the new republics was a strong army and centralized government rather than a constitution, in Colombia assuming the powers of a dictator in order to suppress disorder; and at that he failed—disorder became the rule. "America is ungovernable," he wrote shortly before he died in 1830. "He who serves a revolution ploughs the sea."

In his disillusionment Bolívar left a more specific prophecy: "Many tyrants will arise upon my tomb." This was realized immediately by the rise of *caudillos,* leaders or generals who if not pure tyrants at least made government a matter of personal rule rather than of law. They introduced the Latin-American type of revolution, the *coup d'état:* one that had the virtue of taking only a few lives, but that usually involved no new principles, introducing only a new dictator. Liberal parties helped to keep alive republican ideals and preserve some measure of civil liberties, now and then introducing a brief period of freedom or anarchy, and swelling the steady stream of new constitutions. (Venezuela—the homeland of Bolívar—has run through twenty-four of them.) But arbitrary rule was eased by the typical constitution, which conferred dictatorial powers on the president in times of "emergency." Legislatures had little power and were not representative anyway, since few men had the privilege of voting; courts were still weaker, seldom daring to resist the will or whim of rulers. Whatever the regime, the main power in the land remained a small oligarchy. *Caudillos* could count on the support of wealthy landowners and leaders of the Church, the greatest landowner, neither of whom had any desire for democratic government, and they could feel secure so long as they had the support of the army, which in most countries remained the decisive political force. In time they sought as well the backing of foreign investors, who could enrich them and their friends.

The major changes in the nineteenth century were economic. About mid-century Argentina, Chile, and Brazil started to modernize, with the help of foreign immigrants and foreign capital, especially British capital. Argentina was further helped by the foreign invention of refrigerator ships, which enabled it to sell its beef to Britain; by the end of the century it had progressed enough to fancy itself as the Colossus of the South (and so to harbor more jealousy of the United States). Chile was thriving on its nitrates and copper, Brazil on its coffee and rubber, as presently Venezuela would on its oil. Latin America, which had at first enriched Europe by its gold and silver, had become a source of raw materials and a lucrative field for investment. At the same time its countries were growing more dependent on the world economy, and would suffer more from fluctuations in the market because they derived their income mainly from one or two exports. They were also beginning to resent the foreign investment to which they largely owed the progress they had made in modernizing; Americans, now entering the field that the British had dominated, would incur most of this resentment of foreign corporations. But in particular the economic development was weakening the traditional order. Whereas there had been a negligible middle class between the landed aristocracy and the peasant masses, there was now a growing wedge of industrialists, merchants, technicians, white-collar workers, and industrial workers. While these diverse middle groups had conflicting interests, they alike tended to jar the wealthy landowners and churchmen, bent on retaining political control. The newcomers were much more open to change than was the old ruling class, as much less docile than the peasants. They required more education and made for more social mobility, diverting ambitious men from the Church and the army, which had provided about the only opportunities for poor boys to rise in the world. The upshot was a growing pressure on the government, a swelling demand for political reform instead of merely another exchange of dictators.

Now, the political history of Latin America had not been uniformly whimsical or chaotic. A few countries had settled on constitutions that lasted into this century, a few had known fairly long periods of reputable government. Among them was Brazil, ruled for more than forty years by a strong emperor who permitted a sufficient measure of democracy to prepare for the republic that superseded the empire; under a new constitution the usual oligarchy dominated government but provided relatively liberal rule. Argentina adhered to a constitution it adopted in mid-century, after the overthrow of a dictator, and thereafter enjoyed stable government under an oligarchy that permitted opposition parties, including the first Socialist party formed in Latin America (1896). More remarkable had been the progress of especially turbulent Uruguay. In 1877 a liberal intellectual had persuaded a dictator to introduce universal free education, despite the powerful opposition of the Church, and early in this century another liberal reformer, Batlle, was twice elected president; he attacked the causes of revolution by assuring fairly honest elections, and started Uruguay on its way to becoming the first welfare state in the Western Hemisphere. But most significant for the current purposes of Latin America was the unique political history of Mexico, beginning with its war of independence in 1810.

Unlike all the others, this was started in a village and led by a *mestizo* priest, Hidalgo. His battle cry—the "grito de Dolores" now celebrated annually on Independence Day in Mexico—was a call to the Indians to recover the land the Spaniards had stolen from them three centuries before. It was the first cry for a social revolution in Latin America; and though Hidalgo was captured and executed in less than a year, he remained the great hero of the revolution. After winning its independence in 1821, Mexico long had its full share of *caudillos,* with revolts and counterrevolts that were alike unintelligible to the masses of poor Indians, but out of these masses came another national hero, Benito Juárez. The leader of the victorious war against the Emperor Maximilian sent in by Louis Napoleon, he too was remembered as much for his failures: as president he tried vainly to put into effect a liberal constitution and carry through land reforms. His most successful general, Porfirio Díaz, thereupon became a modern type of *caudillo,* maintaining a long dictatorship (1876–1911) with the support of businessmen as well as landowners and generals. He started the modernization of Mexico on a large scale by calling in British and American capitalists, turning over to them mines, public utilities, railroads, and oilfields, while also making huge grants of land to foreign investors or speculators. The economic progress accordingly left most Mexicans as poor as ever, the Indian peasants even worse off; while Diaz gave away about a fifth of the entire country to his henchmen and favored Americans, more than 90 per cent of the peasants owned no land at all. The uprising that finally finished him turned into a real revolution by European standards: a civil war that over some years took a quarter of a million lives, and that ended in the beginning of a social and political revolution.

In the civil war the Indians again found a leader in Zapata: he amplified the battle cry of Hidalgo, demanding the return of lands to the villages and the breaking up of the great haciendas, on which the peasants were virtually serfs. The new Mexican Constitution that was drawn up in 1917 then redeemed the failures of Hidalgo and Juárez by outlining a program of land reform, to be carried out by future congresses. It declared that the ownership of the land and all its mineral resources was vested in the nation, which had a right to restrict the uses of private property in the public interest. Other revolutionary provisions included a great deal of social and labor legislation, considerably more advanced than the United States would get around to until the New Deal. In all these respects—none suggested by the Russian Revolution, which broke out after it was signed—it gave leads followed by the later constitutions of most Latin-American countries, and by some in Africa and Asia too. Mexico had become more of a pioneer than the United States.

Its new Constitution was not at all popular with its upper class, naturally, and was little heeded by its early presidents, who ruled much like *caudillos*. They took some steps, however, to redistribute land to the villages and to protect labor by supporting unions. In 1929 President Calles finally enshrined the Revolution by forming the National Revolutionary party to carry out its program, and upon the conclusion of his term, five years later, he did still more for it by choosing as his successor Lázaro Cárdenas, a full-blooded Indian who was wholly devoted to its avowed ideals. Cárdenas proceeded to break up many more of the great estates, providing land for nearly a million peasants, and then setting up cooperatives to provide the village communities (*ejidos*) with seeds, machinery, and loans; his agrarian program was another model widely studied in the non-Western world. He gave more support as well to the Confederation of Labor, headed by a Marxist. He ended the much-resented domination of Mexican industry by foreigners, nationalizing the railways and expropriating the American and British oil companies when they defied his order to raise wages. All this did not make him popular in the United States (though the oil companies eventually accepted the compensation he offered), nor with the growing business class in Mexico; his successors in the presidency would be much more conservative. Nevertheless most Mexicans are pleased to believe that they are still carrying on their revolution, which has become almost as respectable as the American one.

Another reason for its unpopularity with many Americans was its attack on the Church, reflecting the anticlericalism that developed in Latin-American as other Catholic countries. Although simple parish priests might be sympathetic to popular causes, the hierarchy everywhere had consistently opposed movements at social and political reform, supporting the dictators who maintained their wealth and privilege. In Mexico, where they had opposed the liberal Constitution that Juárez tried to enforce, they remained mostly hostile to the ideals of the Revolution, and attacked in particular the article in the new Constitution that excluded the Church from public education. When President Calles decided to enforce this article, violence broke out; the priests went on a three-year strike, while *Cristeros* roamed the land as bandits, burning government schools, sometimes cutting off the nose and ears of teachers. The strike failed, however, if only because Indian piety was a thin Christian veneer over an ancient paganism: peasants worshiped chiefly their local saints, who did not require the services of priests, and they were little concerned about the sacraments, which many could not afford in any case.[13] Eventually a compromise led to an outcome similar to that of bitter conflicts elsewhere in Latin America: a chastened clergy, shorn of much of its wealth and privilege, has regained much of its prestige and grown more disposed to favor democracy. While Mexico has gone further than all but a few countries in separating church and state and limiting the number of priests, everywhere the state now controls public schools.

The Mexican Revolution also reflected the important role of the intelligentsia in Latin America. They were natural leaders because they came out of the ruling class, which until this century could alone afford a university education, and it was they—not peasants or workers—who stirred up most of the agitation for political reform. (Hidalgo and Juárez were both well-educated men, exceptional in that they were sons of poor families.) Mexican intellectuals, especially active before the Revolution, then led the campaign against the almost universal illiteracy in the villages. In higher education they supported a movement known as "University Reform" that had started in Argentina after the World War and spread to other countries: students protesting against a curriculum that had been primarily classical or theological, demanding the introduction of the natural and social sciences, and demanding as well complete autonomy for the universities. Upon the

---

13 In the town of Taxco, where I have spent much time, virtually all the innumerable fiestas are in honor either of saints or of the Virgin in her many manifestations. One in honor of "Padre Jesus" is as close as the townspeople get to the Trinity. Their simplicity is attractive in that they associate religion with gaiety as well as solace, and so can enjoy a kind of spiritual freedom. On the other hand, most of them long spurned medicine, instead burning candles to their patron saint, especially when they knew that their illness was due to the evil eye given them by some witch. Before the Revolution, a town of but a few thousand poor people supported a dozen churches.

success of the movement students remained much more deeply interested in politics than are students in the United States, and tended to be as much more radical. In Mexico they often upset their elders, though as yet there are no Daughters of the Mexican Revolution to be properly horrified by them.

There remains, finally, the question of the success of the Revolution, and its possible portent for the rest of Latin America. Today, half a century later, a foreign observer is likely to be impressed first by the backwardness of a country most of whose people are still very poor. Political corruption is routine; Mexicans take for granted that *políticos* will enrich themselves at the public expense, like the dictators of old. (Cárdenas was one of the few conspicuous exceptions.) Justice is uncertain with men having any money or political influence, even homicide often going unpunished. The government-managed railways, utilities, and oil industry are not notable for efficiency, but neither are many private businessmen; foreigners who have to do business in the country are endless in complaint, or else stoical in endurance. Many of the *ejidos* have done poorly, failing to produce enough to provide for their fast-growing population. Despite the constantly reiterated reverence for the Revolution, and the many "transcendental" speeches reported in the newspapers, there is little real fervor and reform is slow. And so on, through all the usual difficulties of overcoming a venerable heritage, trying to get a people to perform miracles instead of pray for them. Of wider import is a problem created by the very progress of Mexico. The more ambitious have been flocking to Mexico City from the countryside, swelling the population by millions, but swelling especially the slums—as in capitals all over Latin America and Africa. Modernization has not kept abreast of this mass movement, which is ominous because the poor are now more prone to resentment. Among the consequences in more Westernized Mexico City is the growth of juvenile delinquency, bands of youngsters cooperating in the robbery and assault that used to be individual or spontaneous.

Yet Mexico has made steady progress—economic, political, social —substantial enough to make it about the stablest and the freest country in Latin America. The foreign observer who keeps returning, perhaps with some dismay at the increasing blare of radio and TV, is struck by the many more schools, local hospitals, medical and social security centers, and similar signs of increasing attention to the public welfare. Perhaps as impressive as all the statistics is the cultural revival, notably in painting and architecture, testifying to the vitality of the country.

Most pertinent, however, is the development of the National Revolutionary party that has ruled ever since its founding, making Mexico in practice a one-party state. It chooses the president, giving the people no voice in his nomination, and until recent years the national elections it staged were farcical; everybody knew that the opposition party would lose, nobody could know what the actual vote had been, since both parties claimed not only victory but a majority running over 90 per cent. Nevertheless, the government party did permit an opposition and a free press to support it, and the defeated candidates (usually generals) did not stage the counterrevolution that many observers expected. By now the official party unquestionably has a solid popular majority behind it. It embraces a wide range of opinion, from conservative to radical, but so far it has succeeded in ironing out its differences, and it has selected responsible presidents. Since 1946 all the presidents have been civilians instead of generals, none has been dictatorial. Mexico remains basically a novel kind of democracy, not a totalitarian state.

Presumably democrats can hope for no better kind of government in the newly independent countries in the non-Western world, most of which are not ready for a responsible two-party system with a sober opposition. Unfortunately, the Mexican system is not clearly a serviceable model. It has no built-in safeguards to assure responsible government by the official party or the turning over of power to a more popular party; its success has been due directly to a moderation that cannot be expected of one-party government, and to loyalty to an exceptional tradition. Hence it has not served as a guide for the rest of Latin America, beyond some inspiration to the broad movement toward political and social reform that was already under way. Similar National Revolutionary parties in other countries have not yet won lasting control. Neither have other popular parties, such as Christian Democrats. A new type of dictator, like Perón in Argentine and Vargas in Brazil, has appealed to the middle classes and the workers, but has strengthened Fascist or Communist more than democratic tendencies. Communists have a considerable following in all countries, especially among students; they exploit not only the resentment of the United States but the continued opposition of the wealthy to social reform, and their common success in evading taxation in proportion to their wealth. The generals who are most active in putting down leftist efforts at control of government are as likely to overthrow a democratic regime. On the whole, the movement in Latin America has clearly been toward democracy, conservative parties are fighting a rearguard delaying action; but government remains unstable in all but a few countries, and in none more uncertain than in the greatest countries, Argentina and Brazil. Although the violent swings indicate a kind of independent spirit, another name for this is an incapacity for the compromise and give-and-take of democratic processes.

At best, Latin America does not bid fare to teach the world anything about government. Mexico, its most original experiment, has offered little new in political theory or social thought. Similarly the modernization that is heightening the prestige of Latin America has involved no important contributions to either technology or economic thought. Brazil, for a decade riding a spectacular boom, might well emerge in time as one of the leading powers of the world; but meanwhile the boom has created a wild inflation, aggravating its economic, social, and political problems, and its need of financial aid from the United States. So almost all the Latin-American countries, united in their complaint that the United States was indifferent to their needs until only a few years ago, thereby acknowledge their dependence on it for aid in achieving their common goals. Their already larger population, growing at a faster rate than in any other region of the world, is no simple promise of greatness either, but immediately another grave problem. Eager to raise their low standard of living, they are having a hard time simply to maintain it.

Possibly their chief promise lies in the signs of a cultural renaissance. Long derivative and chiefly Romantic, their literature is becoming a more genuine, realistic expression of their own culture. Their composers, using native materials, are becoming known the world over, as are some of their musical and dance forms. Brazilian architects have impressed the world by planning and building an entire new capital in a nowhere, with perhaps questionable wisdom and taste, but laudable daring and imaginativeness. Mexican architects and mural painters have been as boldly imaginative in designing their new National University. All such creativity gives more point to José Rodó's *Ariel* (1900), which remains apparently the most influentiaʼ book ever written by a Latin American. While calling for political cooperation with the United States, Rodó warned against imitation of its way of life, in particular its materialism. There has since been considerable imitation of its gadgetry, popular culture, commercialism, or as usual chiefly its dubious ways; yet Latin Americans still have something to offer in the way of impractical values, the ideal of a gracious, leisurely life.

Inasmuch as this brief survey has perforce been on a high level of abstraction, it might properly conclude on a simple human note. I have heard of an American who after long absence dropped in at the shop of a Mexican acquaintance, whereupon the latter at once closed up his shop to devote the day to his friend. Quite possibly he was glad for an excuse to quit work—one reason why the Mexicans have not performed miracles in modernization. He was nevertheless acting on the civil assumption that when business and sentiment don't mix, sentiment should come first.

	EPILOGUE:
Chapter Nine	WORLD WAR II
	AND ITS AFTERMATH

As I approach the end of this volume, I should say at once that in my view of modern history it cannot possibly have a satisfying ending—any neat summary, rounded conclusion, or confident forecast. It cannot even be brought up to date. As I write, we are pondering the significance of the changes in the Communist world in the past year or so, and while what I am writing is going through the press almost anything might happen, always including the possibility that history itself might be ended. The pace of change has accelerated enormously, producing much more startling developments in a single generation than past civilizations experienced in a thousand years. Readers weary of the revolutions brewed in every chapter of this book might consider what has happened in the twenty years since the end of World War II: the dawn of the Atomic Age, with the manufacture of enough weapons to blast the whole globe many times over (I forget the latest estimate); the emergence of the Soviet as a great world power and the spread of communism, dominating up to half of the world's population; the establishment of the United Nations, now including dozens of brand-new nations; the revolt of the non-Western world, almost all of which has won its independence; the conquest of space, with the fantastic project of landing men on the moon; the sensational breakthrough in genetics that makes conceivable the control of human heredity; the whole "knowledge explosion" in science, because of which it has been observed that 90 per cent of the scientists who ever lived are still alive; the "education explosion" in America that has landed millions of young people in college; the "population explosion" all over the world, especially in the poorest countries; in the West the rapid growth of the affluent society, an essentially new kind, in which mass production and mass consumption go far beyond the basic needs of man as ever conceived in the past; the dawn of automation, with computing machines to take over much of the brainwork too; the multiplication of wonder drugs, including some that could make over human personality; the development of electronics, television, supersonic planes, intercontinental missiles—and so on, and so on.

No historian can hope fully to comprehend all these happenings, still less to total up their consequences, actual and potential. This will be at once the sketchiest and the most congested of epilogues. My excuse for venturing some reflections on the staggering history of our day is that it naturally colors our thought about the whole history of freedom since 1800, and at the same time that so much thought about past and present remains stereotyped, irrelevant, or anachronistic. Some writers even worry over the "stagnation" of the Western world that in a generation has made such a history.

Contemplating the Second World War, one must again begin with the simple horror of it. It was more appalling because the rise of Hitler could so easily have been checked by the democracies; no war was less inevitable, until the disgrace at Munich. (And Americans should remember that they had the least right to reproach Britain and France for appeasing Hitler, since at the time they were still wedded to a policy of isolationism that was basically as selfish and irresponsible as deluded.) Otherwise the war differed from the first one in being infinitely more barbarous, entailing a wholesale slaughter of civilians, who made up almost half the casualties. Hiroshima was a logical, almost incidental culmination of the total warfare started by Hitler. However startling the atom bomb, the latest triumph of technology only boosted fractionally the toll of men, women, and children in the mass bombing of cities, a retaliation that had grown more indiscriminate and frightful with the use of phosphorus bombs, and might have appalled people more because of the military habit of bolstering civilian morale by making exaggerated claims. (In the period when Berlin was being bombed regularly, I stopped toting up the claims of the communiqués when it appeared that the city had been 140 per cent destroyed.) As it was, the worst horror was that most of us had ceased to be horrified by such warfare. Today we can bank only on prudence, not humanity, to prevent a still ghastlier nuclear war. For again the holocaust settled nothing. Within a year after the war Stalin announced that there could be no peace "under the present capitalist development of world econ-

omy"; so for the democracies communism replaced fascism as the threat
to world order and peace, and presently the Cold War was on.

But again it is too easy in retrospect to dwell on the folly of the
generation before us, and to deny the war any tragic dignity. The
British and French were not simply blind in their futile efforts to appease Hitler, having some excuse in their all too vivid realization of
the probable horror of another war. The British, at least, soon redeemed
themselves at Dunkirk and in the Battle of Britain. The many who
owed so much to the few airmen were no less a credit to their democracy
as they rose to the inspired leadership of Winston Churchill and stood
most firmly when they stood alone, in the face of the overwhelming
power Hitler had flaunted. By this time he had also made plain another
difference from the first war by his unprovoked invasions of Denmark,
Norway, Holland, and Belgium: democracy now *was* fighting for its
life. His extermination of the Jews then put at stake the cause of simple
humanity too. Needless to repeat, the ideal cause was never pure or
simple, always clouded as well as fired by patriotism, and still more by
the atrocious retaliation against his atrocities; but I see no reason whatever to believe that we would be breathing any more easily had Hitler
won the war.

As mixed were its actual consequences. Unforeseen by any of the
combatants, the aftermath of the war has been much more ambiguous
than the aftermath of the first war, giving as much more reason for
both pride and alarm, and therefore making as much more difficult a
cool, balanced judgment. Such judgment is most difficult, and most
necessary, as one reflects on the extraordinary history made by America
in its natural, becoming, yet strange and ironic role as leader of the
free world.

Whereas after the first war "internationalism" had been a smear
word, like Red, America now took the lead in setting up the United
Nations, which this time its Senate approved almost unanimously. Its
new policies grew much bolder when it assumed the defense of the
free world. The Marshall Plan to speed the recovery of western Europe,
by donations that soon ran into the billions, would most likely never
have got through Congress except for fear of the Soviet; but it was
nonetheless a historically unprecedented show of enlightened self-
interest. It led to as unprecedented treatment of the defeated enemies.
Instead of trying to collect reparations, America spent lavishly in helping Germany and Japan to recover from the devastation of the war, and
it went so far in forgiveness, or perhaps forgetfulness, as to insist that

the reunification of Germany was the primary condition of peace in Europe. Meanwhile President Truman's Point Four program inaugurated the policy of assisting underdeveloped countries that expanded into the annual programs of both military and economic aid. This whole singular effort, on which the nation has by now spent a hundred billion dollars, was from the outset violently attacked by the Soviet as "imperialism," but actually the one passion of Americans after the war was to bring the boys back home and get them out of uniform; and they have never been enthusiastic over their new mission, had any desire to conquer or rule the world.

All the same, the boys were sent to air bases the world over, to back up a policy that could look aggressive. The programs of international aid, always sure to stir up wrangling in Congress, were put through with a squalid emphasis on the purely selfish, non-Christian interests that it seemed could alone sufficiently impress the solons and their constituents. Even so the nation's leaders acted as if America were fit to lead the whole human race, and could and should lead it to democracy. Secretary of State Dulles, who typified most conspicuously the national self-righteousness, managed to antagonize both European allies and most of the non-Western world, the latter by his insistence that there could be no neutrals in this struggle between good and evil—all countries had to be either for us or against us. His one reservation was that they did not have to be for democracy, only against communism; in a spirit of expediency that to unsympathetic foreigners looked like hypocrisy, he supported General Franco and other dictators. And though by now foreign policy has grown somewhat humbler, it is still hobbled by the assumption that America has both the right and the power to impose its will on peoples whose will is unclear, not to say sometimes clearly contrary to the will of the American military and intelligence, who in Asia have displayed a particular aptitude for placing their bets on corrupt, undemocratic, unpopular regimes. As I write, the futility of the war in South Vietnam, for years concealed by false assurances of the military that it was being won, is being met by the kind of brinkmanship that Dulles prided himself on, while the Pentagon has demonstrated its own ability to antagonize both neutrals and allies by sanctioning the use of nauseous gases.

The exorbitant self-confidence suggested by American policy might still seem healthier were it not for a deeper motive—fear. Beginning as a clear enough necessity for containing the Soviet, the Cold War developed into a national obsession. It has not only dominated political life but tended to enslave it by as rigid, unrealistic a policy as the revolutionary dogma and myth of the Soviet. Both sides have been saddled with a preposterous arms race costing more hundreds of billions, while their store of nuclear weapons has long since made war obsolete. At home the obsessive fear of communism has given America the worst political record of the Western democracies. When exploited by Senator McCarthy, it erupted in an ugly hysteria that further discredited the nation's capacity for leading the free world, since Americans themselves evidently did not trust their free institutions or their fellow Americans. A compound of fear and self-righteousness, both intensified by resentment because America cannot always have its own way with either friends or enemies, continues to breed more hysteria and hatred than plague western Europe. Its radical Right has the largest, noisiest, maddest following.

Nevertheless, we still have reason to hope that the Cold War will remain a substitute instead of a preparation for a hideous total war. Simple prudence is buttressed by an achievement that fear has led Americans to underrate—their considerable success in strengthening the free world. The Marshall Plan helped the European democracies to demonstrate the prodigious capacity of the West for reconstruction as well as destruction; within five years they had raised their industrial output to an average well above the prewar level. Once on their feet, they continued to manifest much more energy and enterprise than they had after the first war, when they settled down to a more or less dispirited effort to restore the old political and economic order. Americans might accordingly rejoice more over the strength and self-confidence of western Europe instead of worrying over its failure to worry enough about the menace of communism. They might also temper their annoyance over the apparent ingratitude of independent neutrals they have aided. For the Soviet too is realizing that it cannot have everything its own way. Although both of the great powers are still half-hearted in their proposals for disarmament, and keep on making the obsolete ritual noises, they are acknowledging tacitly that they have to negotiate with a pluralistic world, which neither is nor wants to be split into two rival camps. The tardy changes in their policies are due to political developments more important than the Cold War that has so long dominated the international scene—unless their tardiness brings on an all-out war.

Beginning with the career of the United Nations, these developments were mostly as unintended and unforeseen, but no more simply ironical. Like the ill-fated League before it, the United Nations remains a loose federation lacking the powers of a world government that some idealists would like to give it, but that a discordant world is certainly not ready for. It has long disappointed those who hoped that it might secure the ideals stated in its Charter, which in the spirit of Western liberal tradition affirmed a faith "in the dignity and worth of the human person, in the equal rights of men and women and of nations large and small," and pledged cooperation to promote not only peace and justice but "social progress and better standards of life in larger freedom." Much more unexpected was the shift of authority to the General Assembly when the Security Council was paralyzed by the power of absolute veto granted its members; the erstwhile "town hall of the world" offers the incongruous spectacle of backward little countries having an equal vote with the Soviet and America. Of late the prospects of the United Nations have grown more uncertain. Nevertheless it has been stronger and more active than the League of Nations ever was, and today still enlists more vigorous support. It has promoted a great deal of cooperation through its subsidiaries, such as the International Bank and the World Health Organization, supplemented by the thousand international congresses that meet annually all over the world. Otherwise the structure of the United Nations is not so ramshackle or absurd as may at first appear. A loose federation of states—now well over a hundred of them—can at once bring together and keep apart diverse peoples unwilling to submit their destinies to the compulsions of a world government, but growing more accustomed to habits of negotiation. The equality accorded the little states in the General Assembly makes more sense in view of the theoretical equality evolved by the Western nation-states, however abused in practice, and it has helped to make the great powers more sensitive to world opinion.

Hence the United Nations contributed to another movement of immense consequence—the revolt of the non-Western world that has ended the European empires. Although the colonial powers managed to exclude from its Charter the objective of independence for subject peoples, they found the world too much for them; and Britain soon started a quiet retreat by granting India its independence. The militant resistance of the French in Indo-China and Algeria only made plainer that there was no stopping this mighty movement. (If obstinate holdouts like the South Africans may manage for a while to resist it, they already look archaic, and can preserve their dominion only by curtailing the freedom of their own people too.) But once independent, the new nations forced more difficult problems on the West. Almost invariably their people have got poorer government from their own rulers than

they had from the British and the French; they can nevertheless maintain rightly that self-government is essential to their self-respect, and
that their colonial masters had not prepared them for it; as they fall
down on their political job they are likely to grow more belligerent,
hostile to the West; and their grievances as poor, backward countries
(to use the rude words for "underdeveloped" and now the more
euphemistic "developing") are exasperated by not only the "revolution
of rising expectations" but the population explosion. The Western
powers cannot feel simply flattered by the exceptional patience, tact,
sympathy, and generosity that the new nations expect of them. Their
per capita income, already up to twenty times higher than that of non-
Western countries, is growing still higher by the year, steadily widening
the gulf between the haves and the many more have-nots, heightening
the explosive possibilities.

The problems faced by the new nations are most staggering in Africa,
whose independence is perhaps the least expected political consequence
of the war. The extreme example is the Congo: by Western standards
an impossible nation, utterly unprepared to govern itself, requiring
some kind of prop simply to maintain its absurd existence. Other peoples are likewise mostly primitive, their independence only somewhat
less premature. As one who assumes that even so they cannot be denied
this independence, for both practical and moral reasons, I should say
that the most their well-wishers can hope for is fairly stable, responsible
government that will permit enough open criticism and peaceful opposition to make possible the growth of a somewhat more informed
public opinion; and this cannot be assured by democratic constitutions,
but requires uncommonly enlightened leadership. As it is, the charismatic leader who has emerged everywhere may well be a vain, arrogant
man given to delusions of grandeur; so we have an Nkrumah strutting
on the world stage, as in Asia a Sukarno. The necessarily small party
that first comes into power is naturally inclined to be jealous of its
power and prestige, hostile to any opposition. Government tends to
be more concerned with national "greatness" than with the freedom
or welfare of the people, and may be more oppressive and corrupt because it must manage the modernizing it is bent on.

Under the circumstances, a number of the new nations have made a
surprisingly reputable showing.[1] Americans are prone to unreasonable

---

1 I should remark, with the usual apology, that except for North Africa I have ignored
the pre-colonial history of a whole continent in my three volumes. Only recently have
Westerners begun to learn about native kingdoms and Moslem states of considerable

expectations of them. Committed to a more naïve kind of economic determinism than the Communists, who put more trust in their ideology, they have counted on the material aid they gave, and have therefore been more dismayed when this failed to create a strong American party in Africa, whose leaders often take the Soviet side in the United Nations. Likewise they have exaggerated the dangers of a Communist victory there, which in any case would hardly menace the West. The Communists indeed have evident advantages in their harangues against colonialism, their appeal to the poor, their promises of more rapid modernization, their skill at fomenting and organizing discontent; yet Africans are no readier for the discipline and deliberate sacrifice demanded by communism than they are for the participation in government required by democracy. Leaders attracted to Moscow have been unwilling to become mere servants of it if only because of their pride in their new slogan of "Africa for the Africans." And so they point to another startling, unforeseen development—the end of the Russian empire too.

Now, the recent split in the Communist world is not actually surprising. Obsession with the Cold War had led Americans to believe that the enemy system was as "monolithic" as Stalin tried to make it, by a ruthlessness that gave away its contradictions and dissensions. The split had been foreshadowed by the early break with Yugoslavia, the one Nazi-occupied country that had liberated itself. In the satellite countries, where communism was imposed by force, the revolts of East Germans and Hungarians only dramatized its unpopularity, which was as evident in Poland. China, where it took a much stronger hold, exposed another source of trouble: it was almost sure to create some dissension by its very success, since its spread over countries with different traditions and problems would lead to different interpretations of its inconsistent scriptures. But the plainest reason for the split was nationalism—a sentiment still much stronger than any ideology. Exploited by the Communists themselves in countries they were trying to win, it weakened their chances of getting these countries to subordinate their national interests to Russian interests. Thus Fidel Castro, the

---

interest. The great bulk of the continent, however, played no part in world history except for the sordid, profitable traffic in slaves (in which, be it noted, native chieftains gladly cooperated with Europeans). My excuse for ignoring African history is the usual one: that to my knowledge it made no significant contributions to the history of freedom, and that African leaders today are not drawing on native tradition to attempt important experiments in government, education, or any major enterprise. As yet it has little to offer the rest of the world beyond its art, or the possibility of a cultural renaissance through cross-fertilization.

darling of Moscow in the Americas, is an ill-behaved offspring who embarrasses it by his pride in his Cuban brand of communism.

Needless to add, the changes in the Communist world have not been simply comforting. China is giving more serious trouble to both America and the Soviet by its adherence to the obsolete dogma of world revolution. The chances for world peace would scarcely be improved by a complete break between it and the Soviet, any more than by an open revolt of the satellite countries. The Russians themselves have not yet learned how to live with the tensions normal to the West. Disagreements within the Communist world remain dangerous because they are still handled in terms of heresy or treason; different versions of Marxism-Leninism cannot be accepted as equally legitimate or equally fallible. Hence when Khrushchev was deposed he had to be at once reviled, if only for the illogical reason that like Stalin he had made absurd the party's claim to infallibility. For the same reason one cannot bank confidently on the more liberal, relaxed policies he introduced, including the theme of "peaceful coexistence" with a West still labeled imperialistic. These policies too might have been anticipated, given the Soviet as Stalin left it: a country with a mighty army, in no real danger of attack, and full of insecure bureaucrats, restive intellectuals, and ill-housed, dissatisfied, or apathetic workers. For the long run I would hazard the guess that the trend in the Communist world will continue toward more liberal treatment of its people, perhaps less shouting at the democracies, and that the leaders of China too will cool off once their own revolution is over. But I should repeat that one cannot be certain what may happen the day after tomorrow, inasmuch as leaders in the "people's democracies" are still free to make sudden changes that do not have to be publicly debated, much less approved by the people.

Meanwhile a related change emphasizes why there is no foreseeable prospect of communism's winning the world. Only ten years ago Raymond Aron expressed a common worry: "Democracies foment discontent, totalitarian regimes organize enthusiasm." Communism is now generating considerably less mass enthusiasm, at home or abroad, except in fringe countries like Cuba where fervor is chiefly nationalistic. The "new" Soviet man appears to be more contented but therefore more bourgeois, less fit for either ideal or practical revolutionary purposes. In Europe the strongest Communist parties, the French and Italian, have not been setting the workers on fire; they continue to attract many voters chiefly because they have settled down as respectable political parties, muffling talk about revolution, any call to arms or to sacrifice by the workers. As for democracy, it still foments discontent and apparently arouses no more enthusiasm over most of the world, or much fervor in its own youth; yet it has gained appreciable ground. So far it has worked much better in the defeated countries— Japan, Italy, Austria, and especially West Germany—than it did after the first war. The established democracies have clearly grown stronger. Even the lack of fervor at home may be considered a sign of their success, which makes fervor unnecessary. Except for the hysteria in America, discontent has been healthy enough to permit a calmer look at their problems.

In Europe political thinkers have been worrying about the decline of parliaments, long considered the heart of democracy, which have everywhere been losing effective power to the executive and the administration. The weakening of parliamentary institutions may seem more alarming when one substitutes for administration the unkinder word "bureaucracy," or even when one dignifies its top members as "experts." In America thinkers have worried instead over the frequent deadlocks between the President and Congress, and especially over the archaic, often irresponsible and undemocratic procedures of a Congress jealous of its power; but here the immense military establishment gives pause. General Eisenhower (than whom no man has more awe of big business) himself expressed alarm over the "military-industrial complex" centered in the Pentagon, and others might add that life-or-death decisions affecting all of us are made by a very few men, on the basis of secret information not available to the rest of us. Everywhere the bureaucratic activities of government have greatly expanded. (As a Swiss playwright observed, "Creon's secretaries close out Antigone's case.") Democracy appears to be turning into a vast technocracy, under the rule of experts ever harder to keep under public control. The "science" of public administration, which has eclipsed the study of political philosophy, is devoted primarily to efficiency, not statesmanship. Experts as such are not qualified to speak authoritatively on the ends of government, the larger, moral considerations of the national interest.

Yet this whole trend is not simply dismaying. Bureaucracy, in any case indispensable in any large nation, is never the antithesis of democracy or necessarily a menace to it. There is not in fact a tight "power elite" or solid "Establishment" (the British word for it), but an assortment of officials with diverse, often conflicting interests, who

as often compete for power or public favor. The top officials must heed
the ruling party, which in turn must heed the voters; the most dictatorial leaders, such as Adenauer and de Gaulle, have to keep an eye
on both their followers and opposition parties, and face periodic tests
at the polls. Ultimately the voters do exercise some control over their
government: never enough to permit one to say that all major decisions clearly express "the will of the majority"—which on specific
issues may not be clear anyhow—but enough to have assured responsive, decently responsible government in all the democracies. All have
maintained the essential conditions of democracy: free elections, open
discussion and criticism, a climate of respect for rights, private associations to represent the different national interests, government sufficiently concerned with the public welfare, and a sufficiently responsible opposition.

Similarly one may discount somewhat the worries over the deficiencies of voters, made more glaring by the increasing complexity
and urgency of the issues confronting them. Admittedly the great
majority lack a clear understanding of these issues, but the best-educated
can never be wholly qualified—no man can be well enough informed
about all the issues. Let any reader but an economist ask himself: When
the government takes steps to allay fears of either inflation or deflation,
does he really know whether its measures are sound? And if not, does
he feel disqualified as a voter? All that is necessary is that together with
some interest in their government voters have some idea of how it
works, what it is up against, where it falls down, how they should
behave—and in particular some ability to size up the candidates for
making the decisions beyond their own capacities. Whether, in a future
that promises only indefinite crisis, public opinion will be informed
and enlightened enough to come up to even these modest standards is
uncertain; but at least the record of the democracies to date does not
warrant despair.

There remains the obvious reason why most voters have acquiesced in
the greatly expanded activities of their government—that this has not
been seeking to increase its powers at the expense of their liberties, but
seeking chiefly to promote their well-being. Much of the new activity
is intended to give them more security, more of the new "freedom
from want" included in the Four Freedoms proclaimed by Roosevelt
and Churchill. Everywhere it has produced the welfare state. If this
too has its bureaucratic shortcomings and dangers, it has nevertheless
helped to minimize popular discontent and prevent any serious threat
of revolution in the democracies. Together with a marked rise in

living standards, it emphasizes that democracy has been doing much better than communism at producing the goods this promises—a better life for workers. It brings up the remarkable economic and social consequences of the World War, which have also been quite different from the aftermath of the first war.

In America the aftermath has been a fantastic welter of contradictions, amid a constant din of obsolete economic thought. The nation again came out of the war richer, only this time much more so. Its great industrial plant was half again bigger; corporate profits had doubled even after heavy wartime taxes; in spite of the immense production of munitions, civilian production had been boosted too; and in spite of some sacrifices at home (the most dreadful of which were probably the halting of automobile production and the rationing of gasoline) Americans had enjoyed the highest standard of living in their history, incidentally eating more than ever before. Shortly after the war Congress passed the Maximum Employment Act, designed to maintain the wartime prosperity and avert the depressions hitherto considered normal. Nevertheless "planning" was still a horrid word, even though the prodigious feat of doubling the national production had been achieved under government control; the specter of "creeping socialism" began to haunt the business world. At the same time, business profits were climbing to new highs and corporations were growing into giants so rapidly as to warrant Adolf Berle's name of "galloping capitalism" for the American economy. Conservatives were reversing their historic role by forgetting about the fickleness or rapacity of the masses, worrying instead about the popular desire for security, which they considered fatal to the competitive enterprise that had made America great; while the giant corporations were giving business an unprecedented security, in part by eliminating competition in prices, and personal security became the main objective of their young "organization men," good Republicans almost to a man. The big labor unions, still reputed to be nests of radicals, were in fact growing more conservative as they prospered, losing their crusading spirit, and producing their own organization men. As socialism kept creeping in, the Socialist party faded out of the political scene. In government even the obsession with the Cold War could not get rid of the fetish of the balanced budget, which President Eisenhower repeated was the supreme task confronting the nation; his archaic Secretary of Defense (an ex-president of General Motors) played along by refusing to waste money on basic scientific research, thus helping the Soviet to get ahead on sputniks. More feverish expenditures then assured more unbalanced budgets, with more alarm

over the rise in the federal debt, but inasmuch as production had
expanded so greatly since Pearl Harbor the debt has actually declined
by 50 per cent in relation to the size of the economy—a simple fact it
is still impossible to drive into the head of many congressmen and
businessmen.

Europeans, however, this time learned the lessons of the war and of
the economic stagnation preceding it. While retaining free private
enterprise, their leaders recognized the need of more government planning to assist it in spurring economic growth, and they made the state
more directly responsible for the maintenance of prosperity. The measure of unabashed socialism accepted all over Europe was followed by
a spectacular boom, now dubbed a "miracle" because it was quite
unforeseen ten years ago. On the Continent the rate of economic growth
about doubled the American rate. As the United States floundered
through periodic recessions, soothingly called "rolling readjustments,"
and always had some millions of unemployed, Europe rolled steadily
ahead with almost all workers on the job. One lesson of the miracle was
that it could manage very well without its colonies, since at the time
it was losing these supposedly valuable possessions. (Portugal, the only
remaining colonial power, remained poor.) Some American leaders
began to realize another lesson, that none of the prospering countries
had worried about keeping its budget balanced.

Because of these changes, western Europe today is commonly described as a "postindustrial" or "postbourgeois" society, on its way to
becoming an "affluent" society like America, and so to refuting as
completely the predictions of Karl Marx. Before rejoicing, however,
democrats should note that there is still sharp class conflict. Workers
are far from enjoying equality of opportunity, especially in education,
or a proportionate share in the boom in consumers' goods. Similarly
most affluent America has only begun a piddling war on the poverty
of millions of its people—a common degradation more scandalous than
in any of the European democracies except Italy. This has exasperated
the ugliest problem of the day, the long overdue revolt of the Negro. It
will no longer do merely to give Negroes their civil rights, which they
already enjoy in the North: the most difficult task is economic—to give
them something like equality of opportunity.[2]

---

[2] This is also complicated by another problem peculiar to America, the issue of states'
rights played up by Barry Goldwater. Under pressure from the federal government, the
Southern states in ten years integrated only about one per cent of the Negroes in their
schools; so at this rate it would take them a thousand years to complete the job. If such

Nevertheless, our immediate concern here is not the persistence of the old themes, but a fundamental change. Socialists themselves acknowledged the change in their international congress of 1958, where Karl Marx was mentioned just once and nobody spoke of the class war. Although the talk about "the end of ideology" may be premature, total commitment has lost its vogue on the Continent. Above all in America affluence has become so widespread that most people can no longer realize the universal condition of past societies, in which scarcity or want was a perpetual problem. Only most do not realize their own condition either. Marxist sociologists might take most comfort, oddly, in affluent America, where Marxist politics has failed most conspicuously; for here cultural lag has enlivened a naïve economic determinism, while economic change has more plainly affected the social "superstructure," creating a wonderland made for Alice. A people dedicated to the production and consumption of strictly superfluous goods—a function they must keep performing faithfully to the end of their days (in a costly casket) in order to keep the economy healthy—neglect to ask the obvious questions about these goods: What are they good for? Are Americans happier for having them? Or really free in their choices?

The answers to such questions seem to me, as usual, not so simple or clear as one usually hears; but I judge that critics of the affluent society are saying what most needs to be said. A great many of the goods are of course trivial or absurd, such as food products whose chief merit, as advertised, is that they contain few calories or no food value to speak of. (And let us remember that America is the first society in history in which more people die from eating too much than too little.) The prevalence of such goods is a tribute to the efficiency of advertising, a ten-billion-dollar industry whose business is not merely to sell standard brands but to manufacture new wants. That it serves a real economic need, in fact is now indispensable, accentuates the curious tyranny of the American economy: the imperious necessity of increasing production can be met only by creating wants that people have no real need to satisfy. The success of the admen in their appointed mission raises further doubts about the freedom of the ardent consumers. "The standards we raise" (to adopt a phrase reminted by a defender of Madison Avenue) are pretty low standards of integrity, and reflect as low an opinion of the intelligence and maturity of the affluent public; countless Americans are unhappy because they have been sold on wants that

---

a pace might still be too fast for Goldwater (at least when the direction is not backwards) it would mean a pretty long strain for Southerners too.

men free in mind would recognize as trivial or superfluous. Advertising has also magnified a fundamental irrationality of the economy that the nation has just begun to face up to—the neglect of vital public services that only government could provide. Proposed increases in expenditures for such services were always attacked as reckless extravagance, while the obsession with the Cold War that curbed such extravagance never discouraged production to satisfy selfish, private wants—a manufacturer of eyewash was doing his bit to keep the economy expanding. With the rapid growth of both population and affluence, accordingly, came overcrowded schools and playgrounds, dirtier streets and parks, inadequate police forces, reduced postal service, and various civic shortages, including mental hospitals for the many who cracked up in the race for affluence. Only the exorbitant requirements of the automobile were heeded.

Lately production has been speeded up by another revolutionary development—automation. A logical outgrowth of the assembly line, this differs enough in degree of efficiency to make an essential difference in kind. Enthusiasts predict that before many years a few million men will be able to do the work now done by fifty million Americans. Meanwhile the workweek, which over a century has been reduced from seventy to forty hours, may drop to thirty or less. Automation offers so wonderful a prospect of leisure for the sons of Adam, indeed, that it may seem inhuman to dwell first on its costs, and to raise the old question: "Who is the potter, pray, and who the pot?" For whatever the human costs, I assume that the whole drive to technological efficiency makes the trend to automation irresistible. Millions of workers will therefore be left with useless skills, and society with the task of re-educating them, finding work for them or somehow taking care of them—a task that will require much smoother cooperation between government, management, and labor than they have yet achieved. Meanwhile, too, popular magazines are rhapsodizing over the "cultural explosion" due to the increasing wealth and leisure, but others less impressed by popular culture may wonder what in the world Americans will do with all their spare time. A common guess is that most of them will pursue happiness by spending more hours staring at TV, or else taking more often to their automobiles, swelling the congestion on the murderous highways, completing the ruin of the American city. A long-range guess is that automation will provide the machinery for running something like Aldous Huxley's Brave New World, while the mass media and the service industries collaborate in keeping its inhabitants distracted, joylessly happy, free from fear of anything except boredom. In any case, the extraordinary economic achievements of the postwar era make the issues of culture more important than ever.

Now, I see nothing predestined about the fate of the affluent society, no assurance that life in it will be either wonderful or empty. Neither is American experience necessarily the key to the future of a "new" Europe grown comparably affluent. As Europeans have managed their economy and government rather differently, so they have different cultural traditions. Still, they are being "Americanized" in various ways. They are developing a similar passion for the automobile, television, and other forms of mass culture, including American imports. (An incidental depressing example is beauty queen contests: Miss America, God help her, has mothered Miss World and Miss Universe.) More important, if less deliberate, they are setting themselves similar goals of material prosperity and individual happiness. Hence they too now force the question of the ends of affluence. West Germany, for instance, has staged by far the most impressive economic recovery; but what of a cultural, moral, spiritual recovery? Similarly with the nations that have joined it in a Common Market for economic purposes, and now aspire rather vaguely to political unity. What would be the purpose of a United States of Europe? Before the wars Europe prided itself less on its material wealth and power than on its intellectual, cultural leadership, which was in fact its principal claim to glory; and what are the ruling values of the "new" European man we hear so much about?

The answers European intellectuals give to such questions are usually dismal. West Germany in particular strikes most observers as ultrabourgeois—smug, crass, conformist. It is something, however, that the questions are being persistently asked, and not only by intellectuals. Americans too are not quite so complacent as they seem to Europeans. Some years ago a newspaper editor raised a question that was discussed all over the land: "What is wrong with us?"—and the papers were then filled with complaints about the want of a National Purpose. As one who is not sure that people ought to agree upon such a purpose, or to be filled with it (as Fascists and Communists have been), I am inclined to stress that critical thought, never more necessary than it is today, is in ample supply in the Western democracies. There has been ample creativity too in high culture since the war—certainly much more than in the Communist world, or as yet in the non-Western world. So far from being moribund, cultural activity has been so vigorous and varied that here I can barely touch on a few of the significant developments. Since all who run may read plenty of calculation about where we are going, together with exhortation about where we ought to go, I shall once more dwell on the usual ambiguities in our situation, at the risk of seeming to seek refuge in them.

The most breath-taking achievement of our time, the conquest of space that not long ago would have seemed incredible, is more fantastic because already it no longer seems fantastic. To most men it is only the latest thrill, the astronaut the latest fashion in sports heroes. Jaundiced critics of our civilization seem mostly to have forgotten the wonder of it, and catch their breath only to stress the folly—billions spent to explore outer space while on earth a billion men go hungry. Others may note that it is the last word in the ambivalent influences of modern science from the beginning: intoxicating men by an exalted idea of their capacities, freeing thought and imagination for new adventures, while humbling men by accentuating their failure to master the inner world, achieve anything like a comparable advance in wisdom or virtue.

Scientists themselves, many of whom were humbled or horrified by the atom bomb that came out of their fabulous successes, are likewise of two minds about the tremendous expansion of scientific research since the war. Most of this research is subsidized by government and industry, which are scarcely devoted to pure science. With increasing organization, scientists are no longer so free to work as they please; they are harried by scientific ignoramuses who set policy, and within their own ranks by a new type of bureaucrat, adept at public relations and infighting over authority. Many are troubled as well by the increasing specialization that separates them not only from the public but from their fellows. A zoologist may find it as hard to converse with a theoretical physicist as a poet does, and all may know no more than I do about the branch of modern mathematics called topology, concerning which a mathematician writes that he is most disturbed: "the algebraic topologist has almost ceased to communicate with the point-set topologist." On the whole, however, natural scientists appear to rejoice in their progress, and to remain more optimistic about the prospects of mankind than most other thinkers are. The organization of research has meant closer cooperation too, enabling them to feel more like teamworkers in an international enterprise than do other intellectuals. They can play a more active role in aid to the non-Western world by such undertakings as the improvement of agriculture, the reduction of endemic disease, and the development of new sources of energy. Confident of their proved methods, they can indulge in the generous hopes expressed by Nikolai Semenov, Soviet Nobel Prize physical chemist, who in an article on the World of the Future predicted the real possibility of satisfying "all the material and spiritual needs of every man on earth" on a very high level.

Unfortunately, this hope is bound to strike the rest of us as naïve. Scientists remain prone to an excessive faith in their methods, and to unrealistic notions about the spiritual needs of man. Most confident are the newly fledged behavioral scientists, who are now hatching so many followers that their spokesmen have labeled this "the Age of Behavioral Science." Too many of them are prone to a brash scientism, a positivistic know-how that discredits thought not certified by methodology and expertise while evading the fundamental problems. The vogue of such scientism helps to explain the astonishing uproar over C. P. Snow's lecture on the "two cultures," in which he said nothing really new or highly controversial. Jacques Barzun has since announced that Snow's thesis is only another misleading cliché because we have only one culture—a scientific culture; but his resentment of this alleged state made plainer the actual separation of the cultures. Although most specialists in the humanities admit the importance and value of science, and most scientists speak respectfully of the humanities, they otherwise do not speak the same language, mostly lack a mutual understanding. Barzun himself aggravated the difficulty by endorsing the popular literary clichés about science and technology: that they are simply false gods, a fatal blight on our culture and our living purposes, because of which modern man suffers from alienation, *Angst,* self-hatred—"all discontents and no civilization." If so, there is no hope for us at all, since we obviously will have to keep on living with science and technology; but as obviously they have not been a mere blight, and the deeper trouble remains that too few men trained in either culture are well equipped to realize their values for broad human purposes, or to deal with the problems they raise for a free society.

In short, contemporary culture is difficult to size up because it has been neither blighted nor blessed by worship of any one god, false or true, but is shot through with the usual cross-purposes. The first thing to note, I suppose, is that the most conspicuous trends have hardly been exhilarating. Aside from scientists, not many intellectuals (including historians) seem inspired by any vision or live hope of a better future; the idea of progress is if anything more disreputable than ever. Religious thinkers have developed the "theology of crisis," tending to a profound pessimism. In philosophy the analytics and the existentialists—the former the dominant school in Britain and America, the latter the vogue on the Continent—are unable to come to grips, but for opposite reasons have arrived at similar negations. Both reject the whole tradition of speculative philosophy and maintain a formal detachment from social, political, and ethical problems, the analytics holding that no statements about values or ends can be valid, the existentialists insisting on a personal commitment that every man must make for himself in the knowledge that it can have no objective grounds; so both seem barren to outsiders concerned about ordinary living purposes.[3] In literature no such geniuses loom on the horizon as emerged after the first war, and the fashions most talked about have been expressions of disenchantment or modes of blitzing modern civilization—the beatniks, the theater of the absurd, the theater of cruelty, the sadistic sex school, the nihilistic "new novel" with its blank personalities, etc. Painters have carried on in the established abstract mode with growing publicity but no richer promise; such new fashions as "drip" painting and "pop art" may also suggest how little fervor there seems to be for any ideal cause except complete freedom for the artist, however mindless. Architects, stimulated by a tremendous boom in building, have responded with a medley of imaginative and conventionally modern buildings, on the whole falling short of Le Corbusier's dream of a "magnificent play of masses . . . a grand decisive gesture." In America the most revolutionary development has been the too tardy, indecisive effort at "urban renewal"—a term reminding us of the civic poverty of the wealthiest cities in history.

At the same time, there has been plenty of reputable achievement in every field of culture, and no actual crisis in any. Although the

---

[3] Among existentialists Sartre is an exception in his commitment to Marxism, but this strikes me as even more arbitrary and illogical than was Heidegger's to nazism. It suggested an unquiet desperation when the Rosenbergs were executed as spies in America. Although Sartre had managed to stomach the crimes of Stalin, this legal execution aroused in him a "contempt and horror" that by a less articulate man might have been called unspeakable. "By killing the Rosenbergs," he told Americans, among many other things, "you have quite simply tried to put a stop to the progress of science by means of a human sacrifice." Inasmuch as a good existentialist would hardly be dedicated to the progress of science, one may suspect that some feeling of guilt helped to work up this lather.

I should add, however, that Sartre's effort to unite Marxism and existentialism has served the purposes of liberal Marxists in the satellite countries. Czech philosophers who agreed that the stunt was logically impossible have told me that they nevertheless welcomed it as a means of insinuating the importance of the individual, long neglected in the official ideology.

popular fashions have spread an impression of decadence, I see no reason to believe that the Western world is growing incapable of creating
great works. One cannot in any case call for simple affirmation, given
the plain reasons for disenchantment, but out of these some writers
have wrested a toughened faith—notably Camus, a culture hero of
his day. Intellectuals have kept busy at their typewriters if only because
many tend to regard every serious problem as a crisis. Popular "neo-
orthodox" theologians, such as Reinhold Niebuhr and Paul Tillich,
mostly support the liberal cause in both religion and politics, and
though there was never better reason to fear the literal end of man's
world, none have reverted to the otherworldly tradition of Christianity
or preached a gospel of quietism. Church leaders have been especially
vigorous, and in Rome astounding, as the Catholic Church seems
prepared to make concessions—even to endorsing freedom of conscience—that only a few years ago were almost unthinkable; evidently
there were much stronger liberal undercurrents in Catholicism than
appeared on the surface. In philosophy a revulsion has been setting
in against the negations of both the analytics and the existentialists,
now that their positive contributions have been widely accepted. I
think it safe to predict that philosophers will resume their unsatis-
factory but humanly necessary effort to give satisfying answers to all
important questions. As for abstract art, one who has no idea whether
its possibilities are nearing exhaustion, or whether painters are only
beginning to take full possession of this new spiritual home of man's
own, may still be confident that painting is not petering out; for the
most striking development is its unprecedented popularity, especially
in America.

Behind all such questions about the state of culture lie the problems
of education, still racing against catastrophe. In America the war—
another victory for catastrophe—led immediately to an immense expansion of higher education, beginning with the GI Bill, "federal aid"
that in normal times would never have been approved by Congress. The
returning veterans heralded the extraordinary situation today: millions of ordinary Americans going to college, with many more to come,
ever more going on to graduate study, and even so educators worrying
because many bright students do not reach college, others drop out.
In Europe the expansion of education has been much less rapid but
has involved a more radical change: all the democracies have set about
reforming their aristocratic secondary school system to provide more
opportunity for the poor. Similarly Europeans are showing more inter-

est in a practical kind of education for an industrial age, such as Americans have long favored. But this trend is meeting stubborn resistance, centered in the older universities. Educators wishing to introduce more social and applied science are opposed by conservatives bent on maintaining the tradition of a humanistic education suited to an elite class.[4]

Americans might be more concerned over the abundant evidence that their schools are on the whole doing a poor job in training students to think clearly, critically, independently about fundamental issues. In this country the race against catastrophe has called out chiefly a cry for more scientists and engineers; a broad liberal education is not generally considered a vital need. Most students prize a higher education primarily for the better income and social status it assures, only a small minority professing a devotion to intellectual interests. Once nearing their degree, most are quite contented with themselves and their prospects, little interested in social and political problems. Given the millions in college, this leaves a very considerable number of thoughtful, independent students, and lately more have been getting restive. But given the concentration on technical or vocational training, most graduates are cultural illiterates by European standards, and for that reason tend to be more self-satisfied. And today debate over the ends of mass education may be given an ironical twist. In an affluent society, with automation on the way, much "practical" training is becoming obsolete. For Americans in particular the most practical goal of education might be that stated by Aristotle—the wise use of leisure. As it is, the popular refrain "Every man to his own tastes" helps Americans to forget that some tastes may give deeper, richer, more lasting satisfactions than others, and that popular tastes may not be really their own.

We are accordingly brought back to the vexing problem of "mass culture," now represented especially by TV—the most wonderful development in the mass media since the war. I do not propose to rehearse the depressingly familiar complaints about TV and its commercials. I shall not dwell either on the tiresome rebuttal by the networks, that they are only giving the people the entertainment they want, and in

---

4 A recent editorial in the London *Times Literary Supplement* deplored the addiction of the new University of Sussex to courses in contemporary thought and a "passion for bridge subjects like sociology." An administrator of the university protested that actually it had no professor of sociology, but had merely invited an American professor for a semester; whereupon the editor answered that the defendant had "acknowledged that sociology is taught at Sussex." It appears that even in an Age of Behavioral Science there will always be an England.

between do offer some serious programs. The plainest truth remains that the content of most popular programs is dictated by the Madison Avenue men, and that it is a meager when not a meretricious content, frankly designed for masses, rarely expressing or evoking anything like mature thought or deep feeling. For a historian, however, there remains a more difficult question. Everybody assumes that the mass media have considerable influence in molding public taste, interest, and desire, and almost all critics agree that it has been a deplorable influence; but to what extent has it actually blighted culture? Has TV in fact been transforming people into masses, making them less capable of either responsible citizenship or personal fulfillment? Do Americans today have coarser tastes, duller sensibilities, feebler intelligence than their ancestors?

First of all I should stress again that we cannot give precise, positive answers to such questions. Certainly many writers have been oppressed by mass culture, the more because its merchandising methods have invaded the book world, the art world, higher education—all spheres of cultural as well as public life. (Thus universities now have public relations officers to help sell their wares, including the spectacles provided by their football players—"amateurs" recruited more zealously and paid more handsomely than students gifted with mere brains.) Nevertheless, it is not at all certain that high culture has been deteriorating as a consequence. I know of no really first-rate writer, thinker, or artist who has sold out to the mass market, and I am not aware either of any growing tendency of genius to die of neglect, or of oppressed intellectuals to relapse into silence. As for ordinary Americans, critics usually imply that they are getting slacker, coarser, and more irresponsible in the self-indulgence constantly encouraged by Madison Avenue; but I know of no evidence that clinches this assumption either. The common worries over moral corruption obscure the plainer truth that in their worship of success Americans have never been strict or squeamish about morals, and that corruption in both business and government was much more flagrant in the nineteenth century, or again in the twenties (the golden age of Barry Goldwater). In general, their uses of leisure, surely disappointing in view of their exceptional advantages in affluence and education, have not surely debased their taste. A historian may be less impressed by the shoddiness of most popular culture—an old story—than by the rise in the general level of interest and sophistication. Since the war an appreciation of classical music, the visual arts, and other reputable forms of culture has become more widely diffused than ever before—especially than in the America of Thomas Jefferson.

Since the complaints of our standardized mass culture have grown more standardized, I am disposed to dwell chiefly on both the simplicities and the ambiguities that are commonly overlooked. Intellectuals often seem dismayed by the normal condition of their existence as a class, that the great public does not share their interests and tastes. They will always be liable to unhappiness in a democracy, for even with better education one could never expect most people to prefer intellectual pursuits to simple entertainment, have fine taste in the arts, or demand nothing but the best; nor need one therefore despair of the prospects of either democracy or the human race, which has always had to get along on such conditions. Critics still talk, moreover, as if mass culture were homogeneous and uniformly oppressive, whereas it now embraces an exceptional diversity of interest and range in quality, works bad, mediocre, respectable, and sometimes even excellent, taken with varying degrees of seriousness, enjoyed on different levels of understanding, by a heterogeneous audience unpredictable enough to worry the smart producers. First and last we have to face the verdict of the admen, who are supposed to know the ordinary American best, and who operate successfully on the assumption that he is not a mature, rational, responsible person; yet they sometimes ruefully admit what their ceaseless enterprise implies, that they are less confident of their influence than their critics are. In any case the mass media they dominate have to compete with other influences, as of schools, churches, and the family—all of which must therefore share the blame for the shortcomings of democratic culture, but bring up further complications obscured by the standardized complaints. Immediately they suggest a closer look at the "mass society" from which mass culture springs.

As commonly defined by sociologists, the mass is made up of people "separate" and "anonymous," and has (in the words of Herbert Blumer) "no social organization, no body of custom and tradition, no established set of rules or rituals, no organized group of sentiments, no structure of status roles and no established leadership." Ernest van den Haag adds that the mass-men are separated from both one another and themselves by excessive communication; others have long been stressing the shattering of all primary ties to family, town, parish, etc. Mass society looks lonelier, more atomized, and more inhuman because it has long been contrasted with the "organic" society of the past, made up of genuine communities knit by a common faith and understanding, in which all men had a known status or identity. Yet "community" is not clearly the right word for past society regarded as a whole. The masses were sharply cut off from the upper class and its culture, did not participate in such major social activities as government, and contributed little but their manual labor, which gave them the status of menials. As Edward Shils points out, mass society is new precisely because these outsiders—always the great majority—have been incorporated *into* society. Having achieved the status of free men with more rights and opportunities, they may be considered less anonymous. They are not really "separate" either, since countless millions of them belong to one or more of the 200,000 private associations in America, and with their friends and neighbors they obviously do share in some "body of custom and tradition"—family, regional, ethnic, religious, vocational. The fantastic variety of both voluntary associations and subcultures may emphasize that this is not an "organic" society, never so tidy as the traditional aristocratic order; yet it has a common faith and common values, a consensus in the "Americanism" its critics often ridicule. As one looks around in the big cities, the concept of the "mass-man" is still broadly applicable, even necessary for describing the conditions of modern life; but if one tries to make it fit all the people one has met, one may realize that it is both as literally inhuman and strictly unscientific as the statistical abstraction of the "average man" with his $2\frac{1}{2}$ children.

If "atomistic" may go better with the idea of "mass," another word for our society is "individualistic." For the purposes of rounding out this history it is a more suitable word, for it brings us back to the individual: the person who has been slighted in social science, who is nevertheless most important to all of us because he is you and I, and who may be regarded as the chief glory of the Western world—a civilization that has in theory accorded him more dignity, in practice offered him more scope, opportunity, and incentive, and in law granted him more rights than has any other civilization. It also brings us back to the basic theme of ambiguity or paradox: the multitude of individuals who have been emancipated in modern society, given extraordinary opportunities to discover and fulfill themselves, and who at the same time, for much the same reason, have been subjected to massive pressures, and who may look and act less like individuals than the much less favored men of the past.

Most conspicuously, the major developments since the war have magnified the threats to individuality considered in previous chapters.

In the democracies the chief threats remain not political constraints on personal freedom, as in the Communist world, but social pressures against individuality, above all in America. Here the growth of affluence has strengthened the tendencies to conformism. By putting still more emphasis on the production and consumption of material goods as the primary business of Americans, and the essential means to keeping up with the Joneses, it has clouded still more the end of being or becoming a real person in one's own right. The immense economic expansion has meant still more organization or bureaucracy in all spheres of life, at some expense of the interests and needs of all the little individuals in or under the big organizations, now including the big universities. In big business, most concerned with "image" instead of social reality, the "organization man" has come into his own, preserving the image of rugged individualism chiefly by complaints about the "rat race." The big growth of little business, primarily in the service industries, has swelled the white-collar class, which is as little given to individualism. To all classes the mass media sell by both ad and entertainment chiefly the values of conformity, the need of thinking, feeling, wanting, enjoying what everybody else does, or of being "different" only in buying the latest model or fashion, being a little bolder in a self-indulgence that has as little to do with genuine individuality.

Again, however, one must ask the critical questions. Granted the constant pressures against the individual, all the compulsions of American life, are people simply giving in to them? Are they becoming more slavish, actually less free in mind and spirit than their fathers were? Or granted, too, the many individual exceptions to these broad generalizations about American life, are they fighting a losing battle? Is selfhood doomed by the nature of an affluent mass society? Once more I take it that we cannot answer these questions positively. But here I am most inclined to discount the alarm of the many who assume that the answers are clear.

The very worries over the tendencies to conformism bring up another significant difference between "mass" and "organic" society. Unthinking conformity to the traditional way of life was always the rule for the masses in past societies, and no writers were alarmed by it: they expected nothing better of ordinary men, while political and religious leaders wanted nothing better. In America the alarm is another old story, rehearsed at great length by de Tocqueville more than a century ago. Today it may obscure the plain necessity of a basic conformity for the "community" that thinkers wish to restore, and for the actual consensus that has kept the democracies stable. It does some injustice to the great many simple, decent, conventional people who have a limited capacity for independent thought, but who have their own dignity and integrity. Among the chief threats to a full human life, William James observed, is the tendency to generalize prematurely about the meaning of other people's experience. This tendency is no less dangerous because of the wealth of evidence compiled by social scientists, for they naturally seek uniformities, tend to slight the exceptions, and tell us little about the private life of the individual. Even in suburbia, where they report that the pressures to keep up appearances are strongest, people still do have some privacy, lead lives of their own, and all the togetherness cannot smother personal dream and drama, little of which gets into the record. Sticking to the record, one may find signs of resistance to the social pressures, as one might expect if only because of the cussedness of man, and still plainer signs of both a growing sophistication and a growing tolerance. Suburbanites in particular are much more self-aware than were the people of Middletown studied by the Lynds a generation ago. The widespread alarm has made best sellers of the books about the organization man, the status-seekers, the lonely crowd.

All the major developments in the democracies that threaten individuality have created opportunities for the person to resist the threats and go his own way, opportunities that most people realize to some extent much harder to size up. The big city, the home of the mass-man, is not a good community, and today it is especially cold, impersonal, formless, fragmented by multitudinousness; yet it embraces many subcommunities, it enables every type of person to find congenial company, it also affords more privacy or freedom from the judgment of neighbors, and always it offers a multitude of opportunities. Similarly the technology that continues to regiment, mechanize, and standardize modern life also continues to serve as the main hope of the poor, to free many men from a fixed status and lowly job, to provide a wealth of varied opportunity for talented persons, and to give all more leisure for their private pursuits. It recalls that our standardized mass society is in another aspect by all odds the most heterogeneous and fluid in history, intrinsically much more open than "organic" society.

This aspect is most pronounced in the life of young people, whose emancipation is as revolutionary as any social development in the modern world. In past societies most started working in early childhood, on farm or in shop as their father had, usually following the same occupation and living in the same region, with little if any thought of an independent career. In America today most enjoy a full childhood, their freedom from toil is prolonged into their late teens, their schooling enables them to strike out on their own, and the millions who go on to college have a remarkable range of choice in profession or career. The many more millions of underprivileged youths evoke much more social concern than poor children did in the past; "underprivileged" is a distinctively modern term, marking another difference between "mass" and "organic" society. Otherwise the main problem is the uses that young people make of their unprecedented freedom and opportunity, including their role as favored consumers for the vast entertainment industries; and this recalls all the familiar worries. Nevertheless a great many are more or less independent, and the rest are by no means 100 per cent conformists—if only because they cannot possibly be. However set on becoming "well adjusted," the privileged youth are forced to exercise the power of choice on which individuality depends: in deciding on a career, in selecting from the wealth of available material and cultural goods, and in making up their minds about some of the social, political, moral, and religious issues that are under constant debate. They are not actually settled in their living beliefs.

Hence they bring up a seeming contradiction that further complicates judgments about the state of the individual. With the endless complaints about the complacence, conformism, and togetherness of Americans, one also hears that as mass-men they are lonely, alienated, insecure, born to anxiety. As positive evidence we have statistics about the millions who crack up every year, the millions more who keep going on tranquilizers. Yet this evidence may be misleading. An immediate reason why America has about the highest recorded rate of mental illness in the world is that it treats many more cases than are reported in less affluent countries, just as it is the most medicated nation on earth. (The Soviet, for instance, publishes no comparable statistics because it regards mental illness as a bourgeois disease, and its appearance among Russians as due to organic rather than psychic causes.) Other reasons are that Americans are getting into the habit of seeking help early, many are openly indulging anxieties that less favored people keep to themselves, and fewer families take care of queer or distraught relatives who once lived upstairs. At that, one study of Massachusetts hospitals in the past century indicated that insanity was about as common then as it is today. It supported the belief of some psychologists that the rate of mental illness is practically uniform in all societies—a belief that may seem less startling if one recalls the brute anxieties from which the peasant masses suffered throughout history, but accepted as "normal," and which in the "organic" Middle Ages flared out in the manias that periodically swept the countryside. In this view one may worry more about the millions of neurotics in pampered America, or perhaps worry less; but either way one cannot be sure that Americans are suffering more from anxiety than are other peoples, or that either the strain of modern life or the emptiness of affluence is breaking down personality.

At the end, I find I can only repeat that all we have learned does not yield a clear idea of what is going on in the heads of hundreds of millions of "mass-men" in the Western world, much less support the many sweeping generalizations that imply they are all thinking and feeling alike. We cannot be any more certain about the prospects of the individual than about the future of our civilization, just because of the extraordinary, daily increasing gains in knowledge and power; no one can foretell what man will know and be able to do in another generation, or how big or little ordinary people will be feeling. Meanwhile the impossibility of confident prediction involves the reasons for hope as well as dread. Like Europe, America is still manifesting the exceptional energy and creativity fostered by the Western tradition of individualism. It is still a free, pluralistic society, in which people can and do speak out, and all the worry over conformism testifies that this tradition is very much alive. It is, above all, an open society: open politically because of its democratic processes; open intellectually because nothing—no faith whatever—is immune to inquiry and criticism; open spiritually because it is never resigned, always resolved to keep working for a better future (even if by futile efforts to restore a mythical past); open, like all modern societies, because of the very technology that is tending to regiment and standardize its life, since this also assures continuous change; and open, therefore (lest I sound too cheerful), to horrors as well as wonders such as men hardly dreamed of before our century. A sober conclusion is that every person had better keep his eyes and ears open, and his mind closed only on the essential principles of his freedom, dignity, and responsibility.

BIBLIOGRAPHY

This bibliography is a highly selective one from works I have drawn on. It is designed for the general reader, with an eye to the representation of different points of view, and also to books available in paperback editions.

GENERAL
Adams, Henry: *The Education of Henry Adams,* New York (Modern Library), 1931.
Ausubel, Herman (ed.): *The Making of Modern Europe,* Book Two: *Waterloo to the Atomic Age,* New York, 1951.
Berlin, Isaiah: *Two Concepts of Liberty,* Oxford, 1958.
Handlin, Oscar and Mary: *The Dimensions of Liberty,* Cambridge, 1961.
Hayes, Carlton J. H.: *A Generation of Materialism 1871-1900,* New York (Harper Torchbooks), 1963.
Hobsbawm, E. J.: *The Age of Revolution, Europe 1789-1848,* London, 1962.
Popper, K. R.: *The Open Society and Its Enemies,* Vol. 2, London, 1945.
Russell, Bertrand: *Freedom Versus Organization,* London, 1945.
Schumpeter, Joseph A.: *Capitalism, Socialism, and Democracy,* New York, 1950.
Shotwell, James T.: *The Long Road to Freedom,* New York, 1960.
Thomson, David: *Europe Since Napoleon,* New York, 1957.

THE INDUSTRIAL REVOLUTION (Chapter 2)
Ashton, T. S.: *The Industrial Revolution 1760-1830,* New York, 1947.
Beard, Miriam: *A History of Business,* Vol. 2, Ann Arbor, 1963.
Boulding, Kenneth E.: *The Organizational Revolution,* New York, 1949.
Cochran, Thomas C., and Miller, William: *The Age of Enterprise, A Social History of Industrial America,* New York (Harper Torchbooks), 1961.
Derry, T. K., and Williams, Trevor I.: *A Short History of Technology,* Oxford, 1960.
Grazia, Sebastian de: *Of Time, Work, and Leisure,* New York (Anchor Books), 1964.
Hayek, F. A. (ed.): *Capitalism and the Historians,* Chicago, 1954.
Heilbroner, Robert: *The Worldly Philosophers,* New York, 1953.
Hodgen, Margaret T.: *Change and History,* New York, 1952.
Juenger, Friedrich Georg: *The Failure of Technology,* Chicago (Gateway), 1956.
Mumford, Lewis: *The City in History,* New York, 1961.
Rostow, W. W.: *The Stages of Economic Growth,* Cambridge, 1960.
Sée, Henri: *Modern Capitalism: Its Origin and Evolution,* New York, 1928.
Singer, Charles, and others: *A History of Technology,* Vol. 4, Oxford, 1958.
Taylor, Philip A. M. (ed.): *The Industrial Revolution in Britain: Triumph or Disaster,* Boston, 1958.
Thompson, E. P.: *The Making of the English Working Class,* New York, 1964.

THE POLITICAL REVOLUTIONS (Chapter 3)
Berlin, Isaiah: *Karl Marx,* New York (Galaxy Books), 1959.

 545

BIBLIOGRAPHY

Halévy, Elie: *The Growth of Philosophic Radicalism,* London, 1928.
Hartz, Louis: *The Liberal Tradition in America,* New York, 1955.
Hofstader, Richard: *The American Political Tradition,* New York (Vintage Books), 1948.
——: *Social Darwinism in American Thought,* Boston, 1955.
Jenkins, Roy: *Asquith,* New York, 1964.
Kohn, Hans: *The Idea of Nationalism,* New York, 1944.
——: *The Mind of Germany,* New York, 1960.
Meinecke, Friedrich: *Machiavellism,* London, 1957.
Miller, William: *A History of the United States,* New York (Dell), 1958.
Mowry, George E.: *The Era of Theodore Roosevelt,* New York (Harper Torchbooks), 1962.
Namier, L. B.: *1848: The Revolution of the Intellectuals,* London, 1946.
Plamenatz, John: *Man and Society,* Vol. 2, London, 1963.
Postgate, R. W. (ed.): *Revolution from 1789 to 1906,* New York (Harper Torchbooks), 1962.
Robertson, Priscilla: *Revolutions of 1848,* New York (Harper Torchbooks), 1960.
Schlesinger, Arthur M., Jr.: *The Age of Jackson,* New York (Mentor, abridged), 1945.
Taylor, A. J. P.: *The Struggle for Mastery in Europe 1848-1918,* London, 1954.
Tocqueville, Alexis de: *Democracy in America,* 2 vols., New York (Vintage Books), 1945.
Trevelyan, G. M.: *History of England,* Vol. 3, *From Utrecht to Modern Times,* New York (Anchor Books), 1952.
Wolf, John B.: *France, 1815 to the Present,* New York, 1940.
Wolin, Sheldon S.: *Politics and Vision: Continuity and Innovation in Western Political Thought,* Boston, 1960.

REVOLUTIONS IN ART AND THOUGHT   (Chapters 1 and 4)
Aiken, Henry D. (ed.): *The Age of Ideology,* New York (Mentor), 1956.
Appleman, Philip, and others (ed.): *1859: Entering an Age of Crisis,* Bloomington, 1959.
Berlin, Isaiah: *The Hedgehog and the Fox,* New York (Mentor), 1957.
Brinton, Crane: *A History of Western Morals,* New York, 1959.
Burn, W. L.: *The Age of Equipoise,* London, 1964.
Butts, R. Freeman: *A Cultural History of Education,* New York, 1947.
Dewey, John: *Freedom and Culture,* New York, 1939.
Dilthey, Wilhelm: *Pattern and Meaning in History,* New York (Harper Torchbooks), 1962.
Eliade, Mircea: *The Sacred and the Profane,* New York, 1957.
Freud, Sigmund: *The Future of an Illusion,* New York (Anchor Books), 1957.
Haftmann, Werner: *Painting in the Twentieth Century,* Vol. 1, New York, 1960.
Hauser, Arnold: *The Social History of Art,* New York (Vintage Books), 1958.
Hofstader, Richard, and Metzger, Walter P.: *The Development of Academic Freedom in the United States,* New York, 1955.
Hoggart, Richard: *The Uses of Literacy,* Fair Lawn, 1957.
Howe, Irving: *Politics and the Novel,* New York (Meridian Books), 1957.
Hughes, H. Stuart: *Consciousness and Society,* New York (Vintage Books), 1961.
Josephson, Eric and Mary (ed.): *Man Alone: Alienation in Modern Society,* New York (Dell Laurel), 1962.
Kaufmann, Walter: *From Shakespeare to Existentialism,* New York (Anchor Books), 1960.

Kroeber, A. L., and Kluckhohn, Clyde: *Culture,* New York (Vintage Books), 1963.
Laqueur, Walter Z.: *Young Germany,* New York, 1962.
Latourette, Kenneth Scott: *The Nineteenth Century in Europe: The Protestant and Eastern Churches,* New York, 1959.
Leeuw, Gerardus van der: *Sacred and Profane Beauty: The Holy in Art,* New York, 1963.
Lerner, Daniel (ed.): *The Human Meaning of the Social Sciences,* New York (Meridian Books), 1959.
LeRoy, Gaylord C.: *Perplexed Prophets,* Philadelphia, 1953.
Levi, Albert William: *Philosophy and the Modern World,* Bloomington, 1959.
Lowenthal, Leo: *Literature, Popular Culture, and Society,* Englewood Cliffs (Spectrum Books), 1961.
Masur, Gerhard: *Prophets of Yesteryear,* New York, 1961.
McLuhan, Marshall: *The Gutenberg Galaxy,* Toronto, 1962.
Mead, George H.: *Movements of Thought in the Nineteenth Century,* Chicago, 1936.
Meyerhoff, Hans (ed.): *The Philosophy of History in our Time,* New York (Anchor Books), 1959.
Morgan, H. Wayne (ed.): *The Gilded Age: A Reappraisal,* Syracuse, 1963.
Muller, Herbert J.: *Religion and Freedom in the Modern World,* Chicago, 1963.
————: *Science and Criticism,* New Haven, 1943.
Ortega y Gasset, José: *The Revolt of the Masses,* New York, 1932.
Popper, Karl R.: *The Poverty of Historicism,* Boston, 1957.
Smith, Henry Nash: *Virgin Land: The American West as Symbol and Myth,* New York (Vintage Books), 1957.
Stern, Fritz (ed.): *The Varieties of History,* New York (Meridian Books), 1956.
Tillich, Paul: *The Protestant Era,* Chicago (Phoenix Books), 1957.
Trilling, Lionel: *The Liberal Imagination,* New York, 1950.
Whitehead, Alfred North: *Science and the Modern World,* New York (Mentor), 1948.
Williams, Raymond: *Culture & Society 1780-1950,* New York (Anchor Books), 1960.
Wilson, Edmund: *Axel's Castle,* New York, 1909.

THE WORLD WARS AND THEIR AFTERMATH   *(Chapters 5, 6 and 9)*
Allen, Frederick Lewis: *Only Yesterday,* New York (Bantam), 1957.
Aron, Raymond: *The Century of Total War,* New York, 1954.
————: *The Opium of the Intellectuals,* New York (Norton Library), 1962.
Barzun, Jacques: *Science: The Glorious Entertainment,* New York, 1964.
Bell, Daniel: *The End of Ideology,* New York (Collier Books), 1962.
Berelson, Bernard (ed.): *The Behavioral Sciences Today,* New York (Harper Torchbooks), 1964.
Berle, Adolf A., Jr.: *The Twentieth Century Capitalist Revolution,* New York, 1954.
Buehrig, Edward H.: *Woodrow Wilson and the Balance of Power,* Bloomington, 1955.
Carr, Edward Hallett: *The New Society,* Boston, 1951.
Churchill, Winston S.: *The Gathering Storm,* New York (Bantam), 1961.
————: *The Grand Alliance,* New York (Bantam), 1962.
Cochran, Thomas C.: *The American Business System: A Historical Perspective 1900-1955,* New York (Harper Torchbooks), 1962.
Frankel, Charles: *The Democratic Prospect,* New York, 1962.
Fromm, Erich: *Escape from Freedom,* New York, 1941.
Galbraith, John Kenneth: *The Affluent Society,* New York (Mentor), 1958.

Graubard, Stephen R. (ed.): *Daedalus* (Winter 1964): "A New Europe?"
Handlin, Oscar: *The American People in the Twentieth Century*, Boston, 1963.
Heilbroner, Robert L.: *The Future as History*, New York, 1959.
Hicks, John D.: *Republican Ascendancy 1921-33*, New York (Harper Torchbooks), 1963.
Hughes, H. Stuart: *Contemporary Europe: A History*, Englewood Cliffs, 1961.
Jaspers, Karl: *Man in the Modern Age*, New York (Anchor Books), 1951.
Kohn, Hans: *The Twentieth Century*, New York, 1949.
Leuchtenburg, William E.: *Franklin D. Roosevelt and the New Deal, 1931-1940*, New York, 1963.
Meinecke, Friedrich: *The German Catastrophe*, Boston, 1953.
Riesman, David: *Individualism Reconsidered*, Glencoe, 1954.
Snow, C. P.: *The Two Cultures: and a Second Look*, New York (Mentor), 1964.
Stillman, Edmund, and Pfaff, William: *The Politics of Hysteria*, New York, 1964.
Taylor, A. J. P.: *Illustrated History of the First World War*, New York, 1964.
Tuchman, Barbara W.: *The Guns of August*, New York, 1962.
Valéry, Paul: *History and Politics*, New York, 1962.
Walworth, Arthur: *Woodrow Wilson: World Prophet*, New York, 1958.
White, Morton (ed.): *The Age of Analysis*, New York (Mentor), 1955.
——: *Social Thought in America*, Boston, 1957.

TOTALITARIANISM   (Chapter 7)
Arendt, Hannah: *The Origins of Totalitarianism*, New York, 1951.
Berdyaev, Nicholas: *The Origins of Russian Communism*, New York, 1937.
Borkenau, Franz: *World Communism*, Ann Arbor (Paperback), 1962.
Cohen, Carl (ed.): *Communism Fascism Democracy: The Theoretical Foundations*, New York, 1962.
Crossman, Richard (ed.): *The God That Failed*, New York, 1949.
Grimes, Alan P., and Horwitz, Robert H.: *Modern Political Ideologies*, New York, 1959.
Kennan, George F.: *Russia and the West*, New York (Mentor), 1962.
Kohn, Hans (ed.): *The Mind of Modern Russia*, New York (Harper Torchbooks), 1962.
Lenin, V. I.: *Materialism and Empirio-Criticism*, Moscow, 1937.
——: *The State and Revolution*, London, 1933.
Pares, Bernard: *A History of Russia*, New York, 1930.
——: *Russia*, New York (Mentor), 1949.
Rostow, W. W.: *The Dynamics of Soviet Society*, New York (Mentor), 1954.
Talmon, J. L.: *The Origins of Totalitarian Democracy*, New York, 1960.
Trotsky, L.: *The History of the Russian Revolution*, 3 vols., New York, 1932.
Tucker, Robert C.: *The Soviet Political Mind*, New York (Praeger Paperbacks), 1963.

THE NON-WESTERN WORLD   (Chapter 8)
Alexander, Robert J.: *Today's Latin America*, New York (Anchor Books), 1962.
Aron, Raymond: *The Dawn of Universal History*, New York, 1961.
Bary, Wm. Theodore de (ed.): *Sources of Indian Tradition*, New York, 1958.
Benedict, Ruth: *The Chrysanthemum and the Sword*, Boston, 1946.
Dean, Vera Micheles: *The Nature of the Non-Western World*, New York (Mentor), 1957.
Fairbanks, John T. (ed.): *Chinese Thought and Institutions*, Chicago, 1957.
Garratt, G. T. (ed.): *The Legacy of India*, Oxford, 1937.

Kennedy, Malcolm: *A Short History of Japan*, New York (Mentor), 1964.

Kinross, Lord: *Atatürk*, New York, 1965.

Kohn, Hans: *The Age of Nationalism*, New York, 1962.

Lamb, Beatrice Pitney: *India: A World in Transition*, New York, 1963.

Latourette, K. S.: *The Chinese, Their History and Culture*, 2 vols., New York, 1934.

Lewis, Bernard: *The Middle East and the West*, Bloomington, 1964.

Matthew, Helen G. (ed.): *Asia in the Modern World*, New York (Mentor), 1963.

McNeill, William H.: *The Rise of the West, A History of the Human Community*, Chicago, 1963.

Nehru, Jawaharlal: *Nehru on World History* (condensed by Saul K. Padover from *Glimpses of World History*), New York, 1960.

Northrop, F. S. C.: *The Meeting of East and West*, New York, 1946.

Pendle, George: *A History of Latin America*, Baltimore (Penguin Books), 1963.

Plamenatz, John: *On Alien Rule and Self Government*, London, 1960.

Radhakrishnan, S.: *Eastern Religions and Western Thought*, Oxford, 1939.

Spear, Percival: *India: A Modern History*, Ann Arbor, 1961.

Storry, Richard: *A History of Modern Japan*, London (Penguin Books), 1960.

Toynbee, Arnold J.: *The World and the West*, New York, 1953.

Waley, Arthur: *Three Ways of Thought in Ancient China*, London, 1939.

Wright, Arthur F.: *Studies in Chinese Thought*, Chicago, 1953.

INDEX

Women, the emancipation of, 58-59, 76-77, 103, 117, 299, 300, 359-60, 379, 380, 434, 464
Wordsworth, William, 4, 7, 8, 10, 16, 23, 24, 25
World War I, 30, 75, 79, 140, 163, 169, 177, 181, 223, 228n., 281, 302, 305, 323, 325-357, 370, 375, 396, 400, 439, 445, 460, 484
World War II, 217, 362, 363, 373-74, 395, 406, 516-18, 527

Wren, Christopher, 282

Yeats, W. B., 258, 259, 267, 383
Yellow Press, 176-77, 180, 249, 307, 309, 319, 331
Yugoslavia, 79n., 150n., 328n., 348, 407, 523

Zapata, 509
Zola, Émile, 4, 11, 252, 255, 267

About the Author

HERBERT J. MULLER, who is Distinguished Service Professor at Indiana University where, since 1965, he has been Professor of English and Government, was born in New York State and attended Cornell University. He taught at Cornell as well as at Purdue, and spent two years as visiting professor at the University of Istanbul. Mr. Muller is perhaps best known for his book *The Uses of the Past*. Among his other works are *The Loom of History, Issues of Freedom*, and *Freedom in the Ancient World* and *Freedom in the Western World*.

COLOPHON BOOKS ON AMERICAN HISTORY

COLOPHON BOOKS ON EUROPEAN HISTORY